The Righteous Among the Nations

THE RIGHTEOUS AMONG THE NATIONS

Mordecai Paldiel

Foreword by Elie Wiesel

Preface by Avner Shalev

Introduction by Israel Gutman & Mordecai Paldiel

YAD VASHEM
Jerusalem

Collins

Production Manager:	Rachel Gilon
Indexer:	Fern Seckbach
Photo documentation:	Tirza Oren-Feuchtwanger
Typeset and design:	Judith Sternberg
Produced by:	The Jerusalem Publishing House
	39 Tchernichovski Street, Jerusalem, Israel

HarperCollins books may be purchased for educational, business, or sales promotional use.
For information please write: Special Markets Department, HarperCollins Publishers Inc.,
10 East 53rd Street, New York, NY 10022.

Library of Congress Cataloging in Publication data is available upon request.

ISBN: 978-0-06-115112-5
ISBN-10: 0-06-115112-2

02 03 04 05 06 /RRD 10 9 8 7 6 5 4 3 2 1

Table of Contents

Foreword

*T*his book should be read. It should be read to better understand the agony and loneliness of Jewish communities under Nazi rule in occupied Europe. Their sense of isolation, desertion, despair – all while doors were closed to them. During that time, in that place, every policeman was the executioner's probable puppet, every passerby his potential agent.

Yes, we know all that. Auschwitz and Babi Yar, Treblinka and Ponar, Majdanek and the ghettos: countless documents and testimonies, chronicles and accounts are available to whomever wishes to approach the abyss that is the universe of night.

But we are not familiar, or not familiar enough with another aspect that we find in this book, which conveys some sense of human warmth to the reader.

Here, through the stories of these courageous and selfless men and women, we encounter the dignity in humanity. It is the Righteous Among the Nations who risked their safety, their families' and their own lives to save Jews.

These stories should be read. They enable us to understand that it was indeed possible – more than we tend to believe – to lend a hand to the persecuted. And yes, it was possible to prevent the enemy from killing and death from running rampant. It was possible to disrupt what appeared to be an omnipotent reign of terror. All that was necessary was to will it. A gesture, a hint of compassion, a spark of humanity sufficed. The determination of an individual – be it educated Christian or simple peasant, young or old – to not be weak or indifferent was all that was needed so that for one moment, in some small way, the enemy would be defeated.

This raises the distressing and unavoidable question: why were there so few of these valorous and exemplary people – these humble and private heroes who wanted no recognition for their deeds?

Read this disturbing and gripping book.

It helps us renew our faith in mankind.

Elie Wiesel

Preface

After Germany invaded France in June 1940, the Emergency Rescue Committee, a private American relief organization, sent Varian Fry to France to aid anti-Nazi refugees. Fry was under constant surveillance and was more than once questioned and detained by the authorities. His efforts resulted in the rescue of some 2,000 persons, including such distinguished artists and intellectuals as Marc Chagall, Max Ernst, Franz Werfel, and Lion Feuchtwanger. His covert activities angered officials of both the U.S. State Department and Vichy France and in September 1941 he was expelled from France.

In the spring of 1943, nine Jews who had survived the liquidation of the Ghetto of Lomza in Poland came knocking on the door of Mieczyslaw and Helena Gosk in a remote village near the town of Zambrow. Although the Gosks, who had already helped Jews before, were warned that if they hid Jews on their farm they would be killed and their house burned down, they took the Jews in and sheltered them until July 1944, when the area was liberated.

Ostensibly, Varian Fry, the American journalist, and the Gosks, a peasant family from Poland, were ordinary people like millions of others. But during the Holocaust, when indifference to the plight of the Jews and hostility towards the persecuted victims was the norm, they were exceptional in their humane behavior and the answer they gave to the biblical question: "Am I my brother's keeper?"

Awareness of the importance of the actions of rescuers was expressed in the Israeli law that established Yad Vashem in 1953. Yad Vashem has been recognizing the "Righteous Among the Nations" – a new term in twentieth-century European history – since the 1960s. By 2006 the title had been awarded to more than 21,000 men and women.

The Righteous persons symbolize man's humanity and the essence of man's freedom to choose good in the face of evil. These people, who came from all walks of life, from all European countries and from other places in the world, deserve to serve as an exemplar and as an educational model. They teach us that in the face of brutality and murder, collaboration, silence and indifference, there were people – though only a very small minority – who took a moral stance and mustered extraordinary courage to uphold human values in an attempt to save human lives.

In recognizing the deeds of Varian Fry, the Gosk family, and the other resucers, we take cognizance of the good in people and express our trust in the human spirit. This spirit, which transcended any personal or material interest, was evident in the actions of these people in the face of the evil that inundated Europe. The values underpinning civilization stem from the belief that man was created in God's image. They are rooted in the Ten Commandments, particularly "Thou shalt not kill," and in the observance of the basic rights of personal freedom, the right to property, and equality. During World War II, these values collapsed, a tidal wave of antisemitism swept over all of Europe and collaboration with Nazi Germany became an everyday occurrence.

As human beings who believe in man's right to free choice, we have recorded in this book the acts of rescue of some of the Righteous Among the Nations. These are fascinating and wonderful stories about human beings and about their humanity; they demonstrate that there is no limit to human courage and goodness. According to Jewish tradition "Whosoever saves a single life saves an entire universe." The Righteous Among the Nations demonstrate to us that, however difficult and frightening, some freedom of choice existed even during the Holocaust, and that each and every one of us can make a difference.

Avner Shalev
Chairman, Yad Vashem Directorate

Two sides of the medal given to the Righteous Among the Nations

VIII

Introduction

*T*he war unleashed by Nazi Germany in the middle of the twentieth-century was unlike any violent struggle for power in the history of organized human society, in that it did not represent a quest for independence or living space. It was also not an armed conflict between powerful nations seeking to carve out spheres of influence or aiming at expansion. Behind the war stood a leader possessed by insane ideas about the primacy of race and the ambition to conquer Europe and the world. The war saw the mobilization of forces whose spiritual world had been poisoned by an ideology of evil and destruction and which had at its disposal the most advanced means to realize such destruction – the fruits of modern science. Right from the outset of the conflagration Nazi forces made no distinction between the armies facing them and the civilian population in cities, in villages, and on the run.

The British historian Ian Kershaw wrote a monumental biography of Adolf Hitler, a figure who does not cease to fascinate people in our time. Kershaw maintains that while most dictators are content with total control of their countries, Hitler did not see this as an end in itself. Control of the government had two ideological aims: the destruction of the Jews – seen as the sworn enemies of Germany – and through their destruction, hegemony over the entire European continent as a springboard for the conquest of the world. The Jews were mostly concentrated in big communities in Eastern Europe and small ones in the West and their participation in political life was minimal. Paradoxically, it was in Germany that the Jews of the generations preceding Hitler aspired to integrate into social and economic life by demonstrating loyalty to the country and its culture. It has been argued that the attitude of nations and governments to the Jews are the litmus test of their tolerance and humanity.

The destruction of European Jewry from the beginning of the war commenced with the repression and starvation of the Jews of Poland after its occupation. In the middle of 1941 this became a system of total and systematic extermination, planned and implemented by the Nazi police and army, by their helpers, and in concentration and death camps. This murder of millions of people, the Holocaust - was a crime without parallel in the European civilization.

It is hard to say whether the nations of Europe could have saved the Jews among them. The Nazi rulers in the occupied countries persecuted people who tried to hide and help the Jews who were fighting for their lives, and in a few countries executed them. Unfortunately, those fighting actively against the Nazis did little to help the Jews. National bodies in the occupied countries, other than Denmark, also did not do much to rescue Jews, nor did the underground organizations. In fact, in the Nazi satellite nations or those deeply infected by antisemitism there were many who took a direct or indirect part in the terrible crime.

Nonetheless there were people whose soul and conscience were dear to them and valued human life who could not reconcile themselves to the existing situation. They acted as individuals, and out of an inner need joined the rescue effort. They took in Jews to their homes and had to hide them from the prying eyes of neighbors and even relatives, they fed them out of their own meager rations, they risked their lives and the lives of their families and not a few of them paid for this with their lives. These people who swam against the current in those dark days were like sparks of light in a murky sea, seeing their mission as an overriding duty. They came from different countries and different social strata, from different walks of life, from among the educated and uneducated, and had different political views. There were those among them who had known and dealt with Jews and those who had not. Few were public fugures, politicians, or clergymen. Almost all were people whose conscience and commitment to justice and response to a child's suffering moved them to action.

From the outset, Yad Vashem in Jerusalem, which was founded around the time of the establishment of the State of Israel, saw it as a sacred duty to trace every rescuer, to memorialize his or her deeds, and to recognize such individuals as Righteous Among the Nations. These righteous people number over 21,000. Their stories have been told in the *Encyclopedia of the Righteous Among the Nations*, which is an epic and moving saga of human courage and decency, of people who not only saved the living and enabled them to recover and raise families but also reaffirmed our faith in humanity, of unarmed heroes giving hope for the future.

The present volume contains a selection of such stories from this roll of honor, prepared and written by Mordecai Paldiel, head of the Righteous Among the Nations Department at Yad Vashem.

Israel Gutman
Academic Advisor, Yad Vashem

◆　◆　◆

"*I* was only a vessel through which the Lord's purpose was fulfilled. I know that when I stand before God on Judgment Day I shall not be asked the question posed to Cain – where were you when your brother's blood was crying out to God?" These words were spoken by the Hungarian rescuer, Imre Báthory, during a ceremony in his honor, at Yad Vashem. During the Holocaust in Hungary, he had met his first Jewish ward on a train ride. "I think you're in need of help," Báthory told the frightened Martin Wiesel. He followed this up by sheltering four more Jews in his farmhouse.

Báthory's simple, yet profound words, at the ceremony, are to be contrasted with a different type of pronouncement, that of Dr. Ludwig Fischer, the SS military governor of occupied Warsaw. "A Jew who in the future illegally leaves the designated residential district [ghetto] will be punished by death. He who deliberately offers refuge to such Jews or who aids them in any other manner (i.e., offering a night's lodging or food or by taking them into vehicles of any kind, etc.) will also be subject to the same punishment... I draw the attention of the entire population of Warsaw district to the new statutory decision because it shall be henceforth applied with pitiless severity." Dr. Fischer was a university graduate, with a doctoral degree in law. Imre Báthory was a simple farmer, with no university degrees up his sleeve. The one had specialized in law, but missed the main point of the essence of human existence; the other had absorbed the biblical message of "you shall not stand [indifferently] beside the blood of your neighbor" (Leviticus 19:16).

The Holocaust is a horrific event of unimaginable proportion that still defies explanation. Many have tried to advance theories of what made so many university graduates orchestrate man's greatest slaughter of innocents in history, but the answers so far fall short of satisfactorily explaining this sordid phenomenon that will forever stain man's record. The Holocaust was a volcanic eruption of man's most destructive forces, and a warning sign for generations to come.

At the same time, another facet of human behavior came to light amidst this terrible hecatomb – a most elevated form of humanitarianism – the rescue of other persons threatened with destruction, at one's own risk, and for no other reason than to save innocent lives. These are the Gentile rescuers of Jews, honored by Yad Vashem under the program of Righteous Among the Nations.

We, therefore, have before us two extreme types of human behavior, separated by an unbridgeable chasm – the totally evil and the fully good. The Holocaust is, paradoxically, one of those defining events that bring out the worst in man – as well as the best. If civilization is to survive, the one is to be eliminated or curtailed and bound in chains; the other, encouraged and allowed to prosper and expand. A Dutch rescuer of Jews who was cautioned by her mother to think of her children, toward whom she had first responsibility, responded: "That's exactly why I'm doing it; giving our children the right model to follow."

When the Knesset, Israel's parliament, in 1953 legislated the creation of the Yad Vashem Holocaust Institute, it defined its functions to include "the Righteous Among the Nations who risked their lives to save Jews." Based on that stipulation, in 1962, Yad Vashem established a public commission, named the "Commission for the Designation of the Righteous," to be headed by a Supreme Court Judge. This public body has established certain criteria for the attribution of the Righteous title, including three principal conditions – one, already stated in the law, of "risk" to the life or safety of the rescuer when performing the rescue act; and in addition, that the rescue operation was not preconditioned upon the receipt of a substantial reward, and that each story be verified by the recipient party of the rescuer's benevolence, or bona fide archival material. So far, this honorific has been conferred on close to 22,000 men and women of all nationalities and ethnic backgrounds, and from all walks of life, and they represent close to 10,000 rescue stories, all of which have been accredited, and the rescuers honored with the title of "Righteous Among the Nations." In this book we selected 155 such illustrative stories.

Justice Robert Jackson's opening statement for the prosecution at the Nuremberg Trial of the top Nazi leadership, on November 21, 1945, stated: "The wrongs which we seek to condemn and punish have been so calculated, so malignant, and so devastating that civilization cannot tolerate their being ignored, because it cannot survive their being repeated." We cannot, indeed, afford a repetition of such a horrific event. The stories and deeds of the Righteous in this book – a small selection of a vaster literature accumulated at Yad Vashem – will hopefully help in guiding future generations to a different kind of behavior, in line with the biblical command, "You shall love your neighbor as yourself." People, like the knights of the spirit during man's darkest chapter portrayed in this book, can help us steer the right course, to offset challenges in the future to civilization's accumulated moral values.

Mordecai Paldiel
Director, Righteous Among the Nations department,
Yad Vashem

Certificate of honor to a non Jewish rescuer of Jews during the
Holocaust, recognized as a Righteous Among the Nations
and awarded by Yad Vashem

Abbeloos, Antoine & Flore (Devos)

BELGIUM

*M*ajlek Traksbetryger was beside himself. The landlord of the apartment just leased by Majlek Traksbetryger refused to let him in when he found out that he was Jewish. It was August 17, 1942, and Traksbetryger had secretly left his home in Brussels when he received an order to report for deportation, renting the other apartment in Genval, some six miles south of the city. He was now left out on the street with all his possessions in two vans. At this point, the van operator came to the rescue, inviting Traksbetryger and his family into his home. The man was Antoine Abbeloos. His was a spur-of-the-moment decision, made right out there on the sidewalk.

The 50-year-old Traksbetryger and his wife, Esther, along with their three children, were quickly moved to the second floor of the Abbeloos home, then still under construction, in the Anderlecht section of Brussels. There the Traksbetryger family lived in hiding for about a year, after which they were helped to move to several different locations for their continued safety, until the country's liberation in the fall of 1944. Their three children were sheltered at the home of Mrs. Abbeloos's mother. All survived, even Georgette, the 16-year-old daughter of Majlek and Esther Traksbetryger, who, disregarding her benefactors' instructions, slipped out one evening to go to the movies. She was recognized, arrested, and carted off to the Auschwitz concentration camp, which she luckily survived, and was reunited at the end of the war with the rest of her family, who had been saved by the Abbelooses.

Before the war, in the 1930s, Antoine Abbeloos had extended aid to refugees from Nazi Germany and Fascist Italy, and with his van had driven the length of France to the Spanish border to convey materials and goods for the International Brigade in their struggle against the Fascist armies in the Spanish Civil War. Then, on June 22, 1941, the day of the German invasion of Russia, he was arrested and held in confinement for five months at the Breendonck prison. Flore, his wife, was also arrested and interrogated by the Gestapo for ten days, then released for lack of evidence. This did not diminish the couple's resolve to continue helping people in distress, especially Jews on the run, despite the risk of a second arrest and more severe punishment.

Antoine and Flore reportedly kept their trucks on the move to help Jews hiding in various parts of the Brussels metropolitan area who needed to be quickly relocated for their safety. As for the Traksbetrygers (and possibly also for others), this help was extended without the expectation of payment. In fact, when Majlek Traksbetryger placed a substantial sum of money in the care of his protectors, Antoine Abbeloos insisted that this transaction be properly witnessed by a trustworthy attorney. At the end of the war, the whole sum was returned to Traksbetryger. Another gratis service was to move the Traksbetrygers' furniture, which had been stored with Abbeloos, back to their original apartment when the war was over.

Shortly after the war, on May 5, 1946, the Abbeloos couple was honored by the Belgian Jewish Association in the presence of Queen Mother Elisabeth. In 1975, Yad Vashem conferred the title of Righteous Among the Nations on Antoine Abbeloos and wife, Flore Devos.

Abegg, Elisabeth
GERMANY

A teacher by profession, and a member of the Quaker Church, Elisabeth Abegg was reportedly of Swiss ancestry. Raised in Strasbourg (part of Germany before World War I), she came under the influence of Dr. Albert Schweitzer and his universal and humanitarian teachings. For many years, she taught at the prestigious Luisen Girls' School in Berlin. After the Nazi assumption of power, in January 1933, the headmistress, Mrs. Behrens, was dismissed, and replaced by a Nazi headmaster. This was a bad omen for Jewish students, whose life became increasingly difficult. In one case, Gisela Heinrich was ordered expelled days before her final exams. Thanks to Elisabeth Abegg, she was allowed to take the exams, which she passed successfully. Then came the turn of Elisabeth Abegg, who made no secret of her outspoken anti-Nazi views. Very soon, some more incautious remarks of hers – all of which were dutifully reported to the headmaster – led to her removal from the Luisen school and her placement in another girls' school, with the proviso that she be forbidden to teach history. Here too she ran into "trouble" because of her outspoken opinions, such as in the following incident.

In one of the classes one girl had said to a Jewish girl: "All Jews are bad people." "Oh no," replied Elisabeth Abegg, "you cannot generalize; every one of you certainly knows one Jew who is not bad, and if you ask other people, they, too, know Jews that are not at all bad people." These words offended the girl's father, and led to the final banning of Elisabeth Abegg from all school teaching assignments. It was now 1940, and Elisabeth Abegg had, with the aid of her ailing sister Julie, already earlier created a circle around her known

Elisateth Abegg

as the *Soziale Arbeitsgemeinschaft* (SAG), to help Jewish students expelled from non-Jewish schools. The "Club girls" continued to meet secretly even after the SAG was disbanded by the Gestapo in autumn 1940. As recalled by Hildegard Arnold, born Knies, a former student of Abegg's, in spite of Gestapo interrogations and the tap on her telephone, she never hesitated to fill the time of her unwanted retirement by illegally helping her wards. She transformed her three-and-a-half room apartment in Tempelhof into a home for Jewish people who had gone underground. In this apartment she lived, in 1942, already at the age of 60, together with her bedridden 86-year-old mother and her sister Julie, who was over 60 years old and of delicate health but very courageous. In spite of being severely handicapped by a spinal disease, she sewed all day to help support Jewish refugees." Abegg's home became a shelter for the persecuted, for whom she arranged hiding places in a variety of locations, without consideration of the danger to herself and her immediate family. She nevertheless took precautions, in light of the fact that several Nazis, as well as a Nazi regional leader, lived in the same building as Abegg. The latter once reprimanded her for not displaying the Nazi flag on national occasions.

Meeting again her former Jewish student Gisela Heinrich, who after completing her high school studies was refused entry into university as well as jobs, Elisabeth Abegg put the girl's sewing skills to use and arranged orders from private customers. "I had to work behind a locked door which bore the sign No Admittance." Gisela recalls Abegg's motto: *Tue recht und scheue niemand* ("Be just and fear no one"). When Gisela was about to leave the country, Elisabeth came to ask her whether she could do anything for her. "Had I known how difficult it was going to be, I would not have asked her to look in on my mother and grandmother now and then. Elisabeth promised and regularly went to see my mother and my grandmother and brought them food and many other things. My grandmother was betrayed when she bought a newspaper in the street and was arrested on the spot and deported to Theresienstadt. My mother moved into another apartment and kept in touch with Elisabeth." When the Gestapo was about to arrest Gisela's mother, Elisabeth found a temporary hiding place at a former student's home and arranged false papers that enabled her to travel to friends of Elisabeth's in Alsace (at the time annexed to Germany), where she lived under an assumed name until the end of the war. In Gisela's words: "A sacrifice like this is so enormous that no words of gratitude would be sufficient to express its merit."

Yitzhak Schwersentz was a counselor for a group of Jewish youngsters when he first met Elisabeth Abegg in 1943. "There was something special about her. She welcomed me with an open heart and without any reservations. From that moment and until my escape to Switzerland in the spring of 1944, she stood by my side and helped with everything … Besides finding shelters, she made sure we had warm meals. I myself used to come to her about twice a week to have a warm meal, and I was not the only one …. In addition, she got us ration cards, without which we could not have gotten food. On top of all this, she made sure we got money, some of it from her own pocket. Her jewelry paid for my escape to Switzerland."

Following are some of the homages written and presented to Elisabeth Abegg by her former wards on the occasion of her 75th birthday in 1957, under the heading *Und ein Licht leuchtet in der Finsternis* ("And a Light Shone in the Darkness"). Liselotte ("Lilo") Pereles wrote:

When I first heard from a good friend, in the waiting room of the Lichterfelde subway station, the name Elisabeth Abegg, I had to memorize it without writing it down. On my first visit to you, I was charged with bringing you a young kindergarten teacher, Eva Fleischmann, and asking you for an illegal lodging.... You found a hiding place for Eva with the family of the gardener Linde in Hohenneuendorf. With your help, and increasing difficulties, Eva found other new hiding places. On the eve of the surrender, she was in East Prussia, to where she had traveled without documents... She was saved and emigrated in 1945.

At that time [of my first visit to you] I was living with my nine-year-old foster child, Susi Manasse, at Charlottenburg in two empty rooms in an overcrowded Jewish apartment; as in every other Jewish apartment, people were waiting anxiously, day and night, for the next ring of the doorbell, which could mean arrest by the Gestapo. One evening, when I returned from my work in the Jewish community, Susi told me that you had come to see us. It was in early January 1943 when you arrived at this Jewish apartment with the Jewish star on the front door, where already three couples had been arrested. The message for me was that the time had come, and that you were waiting for me. I was still reluctant and did not leave before February 1, 1943, although by that time most of the staff and all the children from the nursery had been taken away. Out of 140 children, today three are alive!

For a short time I had been in an assembly camp of the Gestapo in the Grosse Hamburger Strasse, from which, however, I had managed to escape. From Charlottenburg Station I called you and told you in code that I had "dived." You answered quietly and joyfully: "Greetings to my friend from Ferdinand." This was the code word that would open the door to my first illegal lodging. The address had once been given to me for emergencies.

During the first days of our life in hiding, when it was impossible for us to leave the apartment, you sent me food with one of your friends, who was hiding in your apartment for a short time ... Food, ration cards, and money came, and later on you came yourself. Always quiet and kind; always only caring for our well-being and safety; always without any fear for yourself ... Wandering from one place to another, I sometimes ended up in your house. At first only for short stays, until replaced by others, then for ever longer periods until the liberation. You and your sister Julie used to take your illegal guests with you into the air-raid shelter of the building which was full of active Nazis.

Do you remember how sometimes such an air raid could become a social gathering of all your hidden people?... In the empty next-door apartment, for which you had gotten the key ... you had housed one of your Jewish refugees.... You also had the keys of the apartment across the hall. Every Friday for two long years, during which millions of people were murdered in Europe, the Abegg sisters served lunch to many Jewish refugees. You prepared the whole meal. You had studied the science of cooking after having been banned from teaching history. On those Fridays, however, you not only nourished us physically. For two precious hours conversation and thought turned to the world of art and science and made us forget that we were no longer allowed to live a human life. In the course of time, you had to use ... your real profession of teacher, and thus you founded a small clandestine school for youngsters ...

It was far more dangerous to shelter "children on the run" than grown-ups! Children had to be taught how to lie, and to do that at an early age, when they were not quite able to differentiate between truth and falsehood. We were living in permanent uncertainty as to whether our children could answer dangerous questions and endanger all of us by their fear or hesitation. The children had to learn a new name and a false date of birth. They had to memorize the histories of diseases they never had … They had, like my foster child Susi Manasse, to change their religion when they changed their hiding places from a Protestant pastor's family to pious Catholic people in Alsace, and from there to socialists… Five-year-old Evi suddenly started reciting a Hebrew prayer in her Protestant kindergarten that she knew from her Jewish kindergarten. Immediately she had to be taken whisked away a different hiding place. You not only gave money for lodging and food for the children, you also acquired for my foster child a false vaccination certificate and a false certificate of baptism from the vicar.… You gathered around you more and more people in hiding, but the number of helpers you had was shrinking. Bombs destroyed houses, money and valuables were consumed, and the danger of being discovered was growing with the increasing number of air raids…

Many a day I met you dead tired. The thought of those protected by you didn't give you rest at night… There was especially the thought that one of them or even those unknown to you might be wandering through parks and forests, or using the subway as long as possible at night, or waiting for the morning locked in some toilet.… During this time of deepest depression and danger you kept for all of us the certain faith and confidence that in the end we would be rescued… On August 1, 1945, you and your dear sister Julie joined the Social Democratic Party of Germany in order to help strengthen the values of freedom and tolerance. I thank you with the words of Hoelderlin, to which so often you gave vital power, Und dann werdet Ihr sein wie die Träumenden ("Then you will feel as if in a dream").

As for Evi Goldstein, she recalled "Aunt Elisabeth's" help in 1943 to find a shelter for her with a poor family in East Prussia, with Elisabeth helping out with money and ration cards and Elisabeth's sister Julie providing clothes. "Even my mother didn't know the amount and who had contributed it." Also – after liberation Elisabeth Abegg took Evi to school, "as I was already ten years old and never had been at school and was hardly able to read and not at all to write."

Evi's mother, Herta Lang, born Goldstein, wrote of her fears for herself after the arrest of her husband. After wandering the streets and parks of Berlin for two full days and nights, not knowing where to turn next, she met Hildegard Knies, who took her to meet Elisabeth Abegg. "After having given my word of honor not to look at the name on the door, we went into an apartment where I found some other ladies." There, Herta was told to lie down and sleep. When she woke up, Elisabeth had already arranged clothing and money for her. "Just my size – shoes, stockings, a silk dress. I don't remember how much money she gave me." Eventually, Herta was able to join her daughter in East Prussia.

Hildegard ("Hilde") Arnold in her turn wrote of the group of friends who helped Abegg in her rescue operations. Such as Lydia Forsström, a former student of Elisabeth's, who "in her quiet way, without much ado, was always available, ready to offer every kind of help, such as collecting ration cards from the members of the Confessing Church or hiding people in her apartment." or the tailor Mrs. Dabbeck, who hid in her small two-room apartment at Winterfeldplatz, and later in Mulhouse, Alsace, sometimes up to five Jewish people. Also the *Baeckertante* ("bakery aunt") in Lindow, who had two Susis in her apartment, Susi Collm and Susi Manasse. Not to overlook the Linde family in Hohenneuendorf, who illegally employed a Jewish couple in hiding on their extensive property as assistant gardeners. and the list goes on. "All the time you were active in pulling the strings of this clandestine network … During all that time, I don't remember having seen you fainthearted or unsure of yourself, even during critical situations. We always found you on an even keel, cheerful and calm, just as you have remained until today. To conclude, I repeat the words you would speak in good or difficult times: "It is good to have each other."

Finally, Ludwig and Steffy Collm were referred to Elisabeth Abegg after running out of hiding places. "My heart pounding, as always during that period, I rang the bell. How relieved I was when a white-haired lady with a kindly expression opened the door and immediately asked me in. I did not need to say much about our distress. She knew everything." After a few days she found a place for the Collms with a family of workers near the Schlesischer train station, from where they moved on to other shelters. As for the couple's six-year-old daughter, Susanne, she moved in with Mrs. Becker in Lindow-Mark, where she met another hiding girl in hiding – Susanne Manasse.

No one knows for certain how many people owe their lives to Elisabeth Abegg – certainly dozens, perhaps more, many more. She was fortunate to be able to carry her humanitarian mission to a successful conclusion, without any harm to her person, in spite of all the attendant dangers.

In 1967, Yad Vashem recognized Elisabeth Abegg as Righteous Among the Nations.

Alice, Princess
GREECE

She was born at Windsor Castle, London, in 1885, as Princess Victoria Alice Elizabeth Julie Marie, the eldest child of German Prince Louis of Battenberg and Princess Victoria of Hesse, granddaughter of Queen Victoria. Her father anglicized the family name to Mountbatten in 1917. One of her brothers, Prince Louis, better known as Earl Mountbatten of Burma, was a naval commander during World War II and later viceroy of India. Princess Alice spent most of her girlhood in London. Deafness was diagnosed when she was a young child and by the age of eight she had become a fluent lip reader. In 1903 she married Prince Andrew, son of King George I of Greece, and four daughters were born to the couple in Greece, and an only son, Prince Philip, born in 1921, future Duke of Edinburgh and consort to Queen Elizabeth II of England. In 1928, while living in France, where she and her husband had been exiled by the Greek government after the debacle in the war with Turkey in 1922, Princess Alice entered the Greek Orthodox Church. In 1940, she returned to Athens alone, and during World War II she worked with the Swedish and Swiss Red Cross. Dur-

Prince Philip plants a tree in honor of his mother, Princess Alice

ing the war years, she lived in the palace of Prince George, brother of her husband, Andrew, in the Psychiko suburb of Athens.

Prince Andrew's father, King George I, had been well acquainted with the Jewish family of Haimaki Cohen – a former member of Parliament who had lived in Tricala, Thessaly, before settling in Thessaloniki (also known as Salonika) when it came under Greek rule. On several occasions, between 1907 and 1912, he had hosted King George I and the royal family in his Tricala home. With the German invasion of Greece, in April 1941, and their occupation of Thessaloniki, the Cohen family fled to Athens, then under Italian administration, which proved to be lenient toward the Jewish population. However, with the surrender of Italy to the Allies, in September 1943, the Germans occupied Athens, and the hunt for Jews began. With Haimaki Cohen gone (he had died in Athens in January 1943), the family, consisting of Rachel Cohen and her five children (daughter Tilde and sons Elie, Alfred, Jacques, and Michel) was at a loss what to do. The choice was either to join the partisans in the hills or flee to Egypt, via Turkey and Syria, to join up with the Greek government in exile in Cairo and other Greeks there, but the trip proved too hazardous, especially for Rachel and Tilde.

At first they found refuge on the farm of the Chrisaki sisters, outside Athens. However, after a stay of two or three weeks, they had to leave suddenly when it appeared that the secrecy surrounding their stay had been violated. At this point, Princess Alice, who years earlier had been a guest at the Cohen house in Tricala, learned from a friend of the Cohen family's distress. She then offered to shelter Rachel and her daughter, thus making it possible for the four brothers to proceed with their planned voyage across the sea. "It was for us a miracle," Jacques Cohen said. Rachel Cohen and daughter Tilde moved into the Princess' home on October 13, 1943. The third story of the building was placed at their disposal, including two bedrooms, a foyer and bath, with all the conveniences. Princess Alice made sure that the service personnel maintained the strictest discretion with regard to the stay of the two Jewish women at the Princess' residence. The story told to them made the two Cohens out to be a former governess of her children and her daughter who had come to stay there because they were being persecuted by the Germans, but without disclosing the Jewish identity of these guests. During their long stay, Princess Alice took a personal interest in their well-being, visiting them often in their quarters, and sitting with them for many hours. According to Jacques Cohen, "She often spoke about religion and felt very close to Judaism."

In the meantime, three of the brothers left Greece secretly in December 1943 and eventually reached Egypt, where they joined up with the newly formed Greek army. The fourth brother, Michel, after a short stay on Spetsai Island, returned to Athens, where he was hidden on a farm outside the city. He then joined his mother and sister at Princess Alice's residence. The Cohens stayed there for over a year, until December 15, 1944, several months after the country's liberation in October 1944. Afterwards, Princess Alice maintained contact with Rachel Cohen, visiting her often in her Athens home. "In conclusion," Jacques Cohen stated in his deposition, "I have to say that every member of our family cherishes eternal gratitude towards Princess Alice." Princess Alice eventually moved to Buckingham Palace, in London, to be close to her son and grandchildren. She died there in 1969, aged 84, and as requested by her, her coffin was eventually transferred to the Russian Orthodox church of Saint Mary Magdalene on the Mount of Olives in Jerusalem, in 1988, and placed close to the tomb of her mother's sister, Grand Duchess Elisabeth of Russia, who was assassinated in 1918 during the Bolshevik Revolution.

In 1993, Yad Vashem recognized Princess Alice as Righteous Among the Nations. A year later, on October 31, 1994, her son, Prince Philip, and daughter Princess Sophie, participated at a ceremony at Yad Vashem, in their mother's honor, on which occasion Prince Philip spoke the following words.

"My sister and I are deeply honored to have been invited to this moving ceremony at what must be the world's most poignant memorial. I have to say that we do not really deserve to be here, since the events that are being commemorated took place without our knowledge or involvement. We knew, of course, that our mother stayed in Athens after Greece had been overrun by the German army. We also knew that she had moved out of her modest flat to take care of a larger house belonging to her brother-in-law, Prince George. We did not know, and as far as we know, she never mentioned to anyone, that she had given refuge to the Cohen family at a time when all Jews in Athens were in great danger of being arrested and transported to the concentration camps. In retrospect, this reticence may seem strange, but I suspect that it never occurred to her that her action was in any way special. She would have considered it to be a perfectly natural human reaction to fellow beings in distress. You must also bear in mind that she had been well aware of the Nazi persecution of the Jews for many years.

Even I, at the age of twelve in the 1930s, had first-hand experience of the antisemitic frenzy that was gripping the members of the National Socialist Party in Germany in those days. I had just moved from a private school in England to attend the boarding school at Salem in the south of Germany belonging to one of my brothers-in-law. The founder of the school, Kurt Hahn, had already been driven out of Germany by Nazi persecution and this was well known throughout the school. It was the custom of the school to appoint a senior boy to look after the new arrivals. I was unaware of it at the time, but it so happened that our 'Helper,' as he was called, was of Jewish origin. One night he was overpowered in his bed and had all his hair cut off. You can imagine what an effect this had on us junior boys. Nothing could have given us a clearer indication of the meaning of persecution....

It is a small and insignificant incident, but it taught me a very important lesson about man's capacity for inhumanity, and I have never forgotten it. We may dislike individual people, we may disagree with their politics and opinions, but that should never allow us to condemn their whole community simply because of the race or religion of its members. This, it seems to me, is the essential message of this memorial. It is a message that all of us who were alive at the time of the Holocaust fully understand, but is only too apparent that this message needs to get through to present and future generations of all races and religions... The Holocaust was the most horrific event in all Jewish history and it will remain in the memory of all future generations. It is, therefore, a very generous gesture that also remembered here are the many millions of non-Jews, like my mother, who shared in your pain and anguish and did what they could in small ways to alleviate the horror."

Annoni, Fosco & Tina

ITALY

*K*lara Zilberman was desperate. It was the end of May 1943 and the Jewish ghetto in Lwów, Poland (today Lviv in Ukraine), was going up in flames as the Germans decided to liquidate the remnants of this once proud Jewish community. Klara had already lost her family – parents, three sisters, and three brothers to the Germans in earlier killing raids. Fleeing the ghetto, she desperately looked for a safe haven. She moved from place to place in the city, each time for just a one-night stay. "I had nowhere to go." She went to a former family maid and pleaded, "Andzia, dear, let me sleep over here only this night." "I cannot, my dear child," Andzia tearfully replied. "You see, I married an old railroad worker and he comes home late in the evening. Sometimes he is drunk and if he finds you here he may kill you and me, too. When he is drunk, he beats me and I am afraid of him." Andzia suggested a different place for Klara. That other woman agreed to let Klara stay over for one night, in return for a payment of 100 zloty.

Klara then recalled the Italian army base in the city where she had worked a year earlier with some other ghetto women, doing kitchen and cleaning work. The Italians were part of a military contingent from their home country, Fascist Italy, which was allied to Nazi Germany and had a sent an army to fight alongside the Germans in their war against the Soviet Union. In Lwów, the Italians kept a small supply base and military post, where Klara remembered a certain officer named Sabattini who had been kind to her and had on occasions sent her food packages in the ghetto and had even saved her from being taken to the notorious Janowska work camp on the city's outskirts. She had not heard from him for a

year, after the Italians had dismissed their Jewish workers. She now decided to look him up. Approaching the Italian base, she was told by a soldier on guard that Sabattini was not in. Another officer told Klara to leave the premises immediately.

Back on the street, Klara decided to look up a non-Jewish acquaintance named Olga. On the way, she was stopped by a Ukrainian policeman who began to question her. In total despair, she invited him to shoot her. Instead he fired a shot into the air and left. When she heard the shot, Klara believed it was meant for her. "For a moment, I was in state of shock. I didn't know if I was still alive or not. Perhaps I was only injured. I saw no blood and didn't feel any pain." She continued on to Olga's house; she was not in, but her mother invited Klara to stay the night, on straw in the attic, but only for that night.

Early next morning, Klara slipped out quietly. "I didn't know where to go. What should I do? I sat in the field under a tree thinking of my past. I had no future. I didn't know what I should do next." She began the day by wandering from house to house, begging for some milk. "Everybody looked at me as if I were condemned to death." She then decided on a last attempt to find the Italian officer at the base. If that were to prove futile, "I decided to throw myself under the wheels of the rushing cars to end everything. I could not bear suffering anymore."

Fosco Annoni and his sister Tina

Arriving at the Italian base, she again asked for Sabattini, and was told to return in the evening. She spent the day in a park, watching children play. Going back toward evening, she was surprised when a group of soldiers led her to the attic of the base building and told her to spend the night there.

The following morning the soldier she had run into the previous evening, named Giovanni, brought her food, bread and salami, which she had difficulty swallowing due to the combination of fear and not having eaten heavy food for quite a while. Giovanni then came back with some army friends and brought her an Italian army coat and a cap to wear. An army vehicle was waiting nearby, for they were going to take her to their camp, in a different place. There she was led to to a room that served for storage. They told her to sleep on the pile of uniforms. She stayed in that room for two weeks. Throughout the period the Italian soldiers fed her, even removing her chamber pot.

Fosco Annoni was one of the soldiers who looked after her needs, and later also arranged for her to be smuggled out of the camp aboard a train going back to Italy. In the meantime, the Germans decided on a close inspection of the Italian compound. When Klara learned of this, she panicked, but was told to keep herself locked in the room, and under no condition respond to the knocks on the door. The Germans came up to the room where Klara was staying, pounded on the door, and left after they were told by Italian soldiers that there was no one inside.

It was the summer of 1943, and the Italian contingent in Poland was being withdrawn to Italy to face a possible Allied invasion there. Annoni and his friends decided not to leave Klara to her fate but take her along with them. They dressed her up as a soldier and backed an army van up to the building where she was staying so that she could get into the back without setting foot outside. The van brought her to the train station, where she joined the other Italian soldiers on the train to Italy. Annoni and his friends kept a close watch on her in an isolated place on the train during the long ride to the Italian border. The trip lasted three days.

After passing through Vienna, the train crossed the Austrian-Italian border in the Udine section of northeast Italy. There the soldiers disembarked, but not before Annoni left Klara his address, where he lived with two sisters and an elderly brother, and instructions how to get there by herself as soon as she made her way out of the station. Before leaving, the soldiers also told Klara of another Jewish boy hidden on that military train.

As Klara stepped off the train, holding the suitcase given her by the soldiers so she would look like a regular traveler, she was nevertheless stopped and taken to a nearby police station. Before questioning her, the police asked her if she was hungry and then took her to a restaurant. The police were friendly and helpful. As Klara noted in her memoirs, "All the questioning was in a very friendly manner," in contrast to what she had known from police behavior in her home city. All they wanted to know was how she managed to get aboard an Italian military convoy. In her broken German, Klara explained that all her family had been killed by the Germans, that she had escaped and wandered into the Lwów train station and simply boarded a train. Not really understanding her, the police called in a priest who knew some German. At this point, not sure what they would do to her, she decided on a different story – that she had fallen in love with an Italian soldier and, yearning for him, she had decided to look him up in Italy. That ended the interrogation.

Klara was then taken to a hospital run by nuns, to check for possible infectious diseases. After a two-week quarantine period she was moved to a convent where she met some 30 Russian women, married to men in the army of the renegade Russian general Vlasov who had gone over to the German side.

As for Annoni, when he reached home on leave, he immediately sent his sister Tina to find Klara and get her. Traveling four hours on the train, she was finally able to locate Klara in the Udine area convent. The two managed to leave the convent and came to the train station for the trip to Annoni's home when they noticed people in a state of panic. It was September 9, 1943, and the German army had just invaded Italy after their former ally had surrendered to the Allies. Klara saw Italian soldiers buying civilian clothes to replace thir uniforms and avoid imprisonment by the Germans. Tina left to rush home, fearing for her brother's safety, and telling Klara to come a little later.

Klara decided not to return to the convent, and with her broken Italian managed to board a train heading for Bologna and Parma, and from there she proceeded by bus to the Annoni home. Meeting Tina's other sister, Lidia, and brother Vittorio, Klara found out that they already knew about her from Fosco. As for Fosco, she was told that the Germans had interned him. Klara stayed there for a while and then decided to visit Fosco in the company of his brother, Vittorio. Fosco told Klara not to leave the house and not to speak to anyone, but to stay indoors. Later, Fosco Annoni was able to escape and hide with friends. Occasionally the family would go out to the hills to meet him, and he also dropped in at home for brief visits.

As for Klara, Fosco's family contacted a local priest who arranged for Klara to be admitted into a nearby convent for her continued safety. Because of her accent, Klara was told to say that she was from the Bolzano region in northern Italy, a mixed Italian-German community, and introduce herself under a different name. Her work at the convent consisted mostly in peeling potatoes and grating cheese. On holidays, such as Christmas, and on other occasions, she spent time with the Annoni family, and they would also visit her on Sundays.

With the war over, in May 1945, Klara felt it was safe to return to the Annoni home. Her benefactors arranged a meeting with a rabbi who was looking for Jewish survivors, and one day a group of soldiers from the Jewish Palestine Brigade came to see her, and eventually took her along. She left for Palestine in 1946 and has lived in Israel since then.

There she met her brother Herman Zilberman, the only one of her family that had survived. She later also met the Jewish child who was on that same Italian military train with her; his name was Mark Herman, and he presently lived on a kibbutz. In 1947, Klara married to Shraga Rosenfeld and gave birth to two children. After her husband's death in 1987, she decided to look up her benefactor's family, with whom she had had no contact since the end of the war. Klara's work at Ben-Gurion Airport translating Polish and Italian into Hebrew, and her travels overseas, facilitated her search. She learned that Fosco Annoni had already died, and also his sister Lidia, but Tina was still alive, though very ill.

Through a fortuitous set of circumstances, a 19-year-old Jewish girl, in 1943, alone in a hostile world in a Nazi-occupied city, found succor and was helped to survive by an Italian soldier and his men fighting in an army that was allied to Nazi Germany but who felt that a Jewish woman had the same right to live as anyone else. They acted on that principle, and in violation of military regulations they took her along on a military train to safety — a timely rescue from the hellish city where she found herself trapped and doomed.

In 1993 Fosco and his sister Tina Annoni were recognized as Righteous Among the Nations.

Anonymous Rescuer
MOLDOVA

*F*ollowing is a letter dated November 1989, by Hanna Deutsch-Harash, born in Belts, Bessarabia, and currently residing in Israel. Bessarabia was incorporated at different times within Romania and the Soviet Union; since 1991, it forms the independent republic of Moldova

"Dear Sir, I saw the TV program "This Is Your Life" on Ephraim Kishon [the noted Israeli satirist, during which a Hungarian man was introduced who had saved Kishon during the war], and said to myself that this Gentile was lucky; for he lived to be acknowledged for his deeds [the man was honored by Yad Vashem as Righteous Among the Nations]. I too have a Gentile, but his fate is not known. And that is why my conscience gives me no rest. Here's the story.

On the first day of the war between Germany and Russia, my eldest uncle gathered up his widowed sister and her 35-year-old son, his second sister with her husband (who were about 60 years of age), his brother, his wife, and her paralyzed mother with their 12-year-old daughter ... We proceeded on our journey in a carriage drawn by two horses and arrived at a village where we found lodging with a farmer's family in return for payment. There we naively waited for the war to end. After one or two nights, very late at night, the farmer awakened us with shouting and insisted we leave his house with all our belongings,

Statue dedicated to the anonymous rescuers whose names and heroic actions are not known or told. Sculpted by Shlomo Selinger

for the Germans were 15 kilometers from the village, and he was told that they were killing anyone who was sheltering Jews or their property …

We fled for our lives towards the east, in the direction of the Dniester River, in order to cross into Russia proper. My parents and I went on foot. From all our belongings we took only those items that served as cushions for the elderly ones. We only stopped at night, for the competition between our horses and the German tanks was "a bit unfair." … On the third night, totally exhausted (our horses as well), we stopped at a farmer's house in a big village. We had barely helped the older people out of the carriage and entered the house, when we saw facing us three or four tall, sturdily built men. They stood next to the door, examining us with "murder in their eyes," and asked about our belongings and our money. Then they left.

The men in our group interpreted this visit as a rehearsal for robbery and murder, and it was immediately decided to leave and continue on our way. We stepped out only to discover the whole village assembled in front of the house. We asked them politely to help us move eastwards, but they refused, egged on by the men who had examined us on our arrival. Whenever someone said he would help us for money, the tall men shut him up. They evidently expected the planned robbery to net a tidier sum. Our pleading grew more urgent, but no one moved a muscle. They all stood there like a wall, motionless and in total silence. Suddenly, a youngish-looking man (about 20-30 years old) stepped forward from the group to the right and said: "I will take you." This caused a stir, with people muttering that he'd better forget about it. They also let him know what he could expect from them later on. But he stood his ground. They continued insisting that he take back his offer of help, when he suddenly shouted at them: "You want to kill them, I will not allow it!"… They screamed at him: "The Germans will kill you if you help them escape." But he remained adamant.

A woman, with an infant in her arms came running up to him from the left and begged him: "If you don't have pity on me, if you don't care about yourself, protect the child; don't leave us by ourselves. They will kill them, and we have no bread to eat. If they tell the Germans, they will kill you. What do you care about the Jews?" Without answering his wife, and without embracing the infant, the man loaded our family and our belongings onto two wagons and we left.

I remember that night as if it was yesterday: a full moon, clear skies, a warm and beautiful night. The man took us through secondary roads, between fields with corn as high as a horse with a rider … He took us out of the danger zone, bid us farewell, and left. When my uncle and father wished to pay this honest and dear man, he categorically refused. I remember when we were sitting in his wagon, my father asked him what he planned to do when he returned to the village, with the farmers so hostile to him. He replied: "If they kill me, let them kill me. I have done my duty. I could not be a party to murder."

Perhaps there is a way to immortalize the deed of this anonymous great man? You will probably ask, why did I not awaken earlier to tell about him? Well, my father died in 1954, and my mother did not remember the name of the village. My other relatives who were present during the episode, and were even older than us, remained in the Soviet Union. In their formal letters, they did not respond to any of our inquiries, and now when correspondence is possible, they are no longer alive. That's it. I would be prepared to go in search of the village, but I have no idea where the place is, and Bessarabia [today Moldova] is too big … I should be happy if something could be done."

At Yad Vashem, the monument to the Unknown Righteous, standing at the entrance of the Avenue of the Righteous Among the Nations, is dedicated to the many unknown gentile rescuers of Jews during the Holocaust. The monument by the French sculptor Shlomo Seligman is made of reddish granite stone, and appears in the form of rising flames – the inferno of the Holocaust. The flames turn into the faces of two persons. The one to the right hides his face with his hand: he, like many other bystanders, does not wish to get involved. To his left is the Unknown Righteous who gazes straight ahead without any reservations, as he conceals a Jewish woman and her child.

Antal, János
HUNGARY

János Antal (courtesy of Library and Archives Canada/Istavàn Anhalt fonds)

*I*stván Anhalt's unit, in one of the Jewish-composed labor battalions in the Hungarian army, was on retreat from the city of Sátoraljaujhely in eastern Hungary toward the Austrian border, and earmarked to be handed over to the Germans. It was November 29, 1944, when Istvan's unit suddenly came upon a long column of Budapest Jews (women, children, and old men) similarly on a forced march – for them, the infamous Death March ordered by SS colonel Adolf Eichmann and the pro-Nazi Arrow Cross regime in Hungary. "I recognized a few familiar faces in that crowd and was filled with fear of seeing, perhaps, a member of my own family among them, but fortunately this was not the case. My first thought was: I have to try to get to Budapest to be close to my family, now in danger of their lives, even more so than was my case."

István decided to leave his unit and escape, but how? Quite by accident, he learned of a Catholic institution near the barn where his unit was put up for the night. When it became dark, István quietly slipped away and walked over to what turned out to be the Esztergom center of a Salesian monastery. When he rang the bell, a monk opened the small window in the gate and asked the purpose of his visit. István asked: "Is there in the house a Father who is responsible for music in the service?" "Yes, there is," came the answer. "May I speak with him?" Another monk came up to the gate, and

István addressed him "Father, I am a musician and haven't had the opportunity in months to play my instrument, the piano. Is there a piano in the house? Could I play it for a short while?" The monks were dumbfounded by this strange request, but they decided to allow him in, and directed István to a room with a piano in it. With a monk watching him closely, István played some piano pieces, which he had picked up previously as a student at the Budapest Academy of Music. Then, after a few minutes of playing, István stopped and told the monk his true identity, and that his life was in danger. "I wanted to avoid going to Austria and asked him if he could help me get to Budapest." Visibly taken aback by István's story, the monk took István to the head of the monastery, who after asking him a few questions agreed to help him get to Budapest that same night. He also gave István identity papers, issued in someone else's name, which stated that he was a member of a paramilitary organization. István was taken by a monk to the nearby railroad station. The monk bought him a ticket and stayed with him until the train arrived to make sure of his safety. To help pass the time István asked him to relate the history of the Salesian Order. "I don't remember anything of what he said," István related. "My thoughts must have been on the others matters."

Arriving in Budapest late that evening, he noticed the nearly deserted streets – a dangerous situation. "It was clear that I should not attempt to go to our home on the Pest side (the train terminal was on the Buda side), as our apartment was in a house located in the so-called International Ghetto (it was a Swedish-designated house on Pozsonyi street)." Instead he headed for nearby Rózsadomb, a hilly residential area of Buda, towards the home of Professor Jenö de Kerpely, whom István knew from his music studies. De Kerpely was one of Hungary's most distinguished cellists, a professor at the Academy of Music. Not wishing to jeopardize his hosts' safety in a city teeming with Arrow Cross gangs, after a night's stay there István decided to move on. But where? He thought of stretching his luck with what he termed the "Salesian connection." A quick check in the telephone directory told him that not far away from the De Kerpely home, in the Óbuda section, there was another Salesian house (St. Aloysius House of the Salesian Fathers).

Arriving there at nightfall, István found the place crowded and in turmoil, with excited Jewish-looking people, adults, women, old men, and numerous children of various ages filling the corridors. Men in priestly garb dashed to and fro trying to create some order. Finally, a priest told István that it was not safe for him stay there, but he suggested another Salesian branch – in fact the central house of the Order, in Rákospalota, or Ujpest, a suburb on the Pest side of the capital. He was taken there by a young seminarian wearing a cassock. There István was introduced to the Provincial Father, the head of the entire Order in the country, János Antal. In late 1944 Father János Antal was the Provincial (highest-ranking official) in the Salesian Order of St. John Bosco, in Hungary as well as specifically its three locations in the Budapest area: Esztergom, Óbuda, and Rákospalota (or Ujpest). When the door opened, István saw a small man in priestly vestments staring at him. The man told him to wait a minute as he had a visitor with him. "He smiled at me and his voice was calm, and bespoke of kindness and understanding. I immediately felt that I would not have to explain or plead too much with this man." A little later, after listening to István's story, Antal told him to try on a priest's garment – a cassock. It proved too big for him. Antal burst out laughing. "I took it off my visitor who just left. You see, I am too short and my cassock would not do for you. Tomorrow we shall adjust its length to fit you." Antal then led István to a secluded room for the night's stay.

Next morning Antal gave him a set of identity papers issued in a seminarian's name, a certain István Zserdény who was in Russian-occupied territory. Then Antal suddenly noticed the signet ring on István's finger, a present from his father. "You cannot wear this," he told me. "Only bishops can wear rings. Give it to me and I shall safeguard it for you while the war lasts." Indeed, the ring was returned to him after the war. "Upon leaving his room I felt secure for the first time in two years, since entering labor service. I now could do what I wanted, or what I felt I had to do." The next day, when István's cassock was adjusted for size, István affixed a photo of himself to the identity card and purchased a wide-brimmed abbot's hat of black felt. "When I looked in the mirror I noted with some satisfaction that I 'looked the part.'" In his priestly garb, István visited his family and some friends in the underground, for whom he became a sort of courier. Evenings he spent in the Salesian center in Rákospalota.

Then, suddenly tragedy struck the center, when on the night of December 14, 1944, the Arrow Cross staged a raid on this house and discovered about 40 Jews hidden in the basement, as well as an illegal printing press. Father Antál was led away together with all the Jews. Istvan luckily escaped arrest, after showing his papers, which proved to be in good order. He was now asked by Father Lászlo Adám, who as the administrative head of the house was in charge in Antál's absence, to deliver an urgent letter to the Vatican Nunciature in the Buda section of the city, where István was heading (to return to the De Kerpely home), and alert them to the arrest of Antál. Istvan carried out this mission, and as he learned later, the Nunciature's intervention led to the freeing of Antál as well as of Father Adám, who was also charged with personal responsibility for sheltering the large group of Jews. The unfortunate Jews were led away and shot by the Arrow Cross men.

In 1948 Mrs. Pal Biró, one of the Jews arrested on the night of December 14/15 who was beaten and tortured but luckily survived, related of Father Antal that she had witnessed his torture at the hands of the Arrow Cross. "They attacked him with the usual brutality, without regard for his priestly dignity, and asked him if he knew the consequences of his acts of hiding Jews?… A bullet in the head!… Is he aware of this? Upon which, with his body erect, he replied: 'I would do the same, even after this; I would provide help to my fellow human beings in need, and under persecution, and if the consequence of this would be death, I put my life in the care of the Lord.'" Mrs. Biró heard herself murmuring a silent prayer for the Provincial Father's life. "The good Lord heard my prayer, and the Provincial Father survived despite the severe torture and suffering that ensued. I shall never forget those sad thirty minutes." Mrs. Biró may not have known that Antal's life was also saved by the quick intervention of the Vatican nuncio in Budapet, Monsignor Angelo Rotta.

After the war, István Anhalt maintained contact with János Antal until István's departure from Budapest in January 1946. From Paris, in 1946–49, where he again took up again his music studies, István corresponded with his rescuer. Father Antal eventually also left Hungary and moved to the Torino (Italy) central house of the Salesian Order. From there, on behalf of the Order, he visited numerous countries, and continued to correspond with Anhalt. Moving to Canada, Anhalt taught music at the School of Music, Queen's University, in Kingston, Ontario. In 1975, he dedicated to Antal's memory an opera, entitled *La Tourangelle.*

In 1992, Yad Vashem recognized Father János Antal as Righteous Among the Nations.

Babilinska, Gertruda

POLAND

Gertruda Babilinska, a teacher by profession, was born in 1902 in a village outside Gdansk (formerly Danzig), Poland, a city and region with a large German population that was then part of Germany. For many years she worked as a domestic for the Stolowitzky family in Warsaw, where Michael was born in 1936. In September 1939, at the age of three, he fled with his mother to Vilna, and Gertruda accompanied them there. Soon afterwards, the mother came down with a terminal illness and, near to death, she made Gertruda promise that she would continue to care for her son throughout the war years and then take him to a relative in Palestine. Michael's father was stranded in Paris and communications with him were broken.

Representing Michael as her son, Gertruda had to get through the dangerous period for Jews in Vilna when the city came under German control. To earn a living, she used her familiarity with the German language to work as a translator into German of requests to the authorities in exchange for food (eggs, chickens, etc). Gertruda reportedly also managed to help some of her Jewish acquaintances in the Vilna ghetto with food and provisions. Fearing for Michael's safety, she asked the help of a local priest, disclosing his true origin. The priest agreed to protect Michael by accepting him as a choirboy in a Catholic church, for which Michael had to undergo baptism. Afterwards, during masses on Sundays, he often sprinkled "holy water" on German officers who attended services.

After the war, Gertruda first returned to her home, where her family tried to persuade her to remain there with Michael. But she said that she had made a vow to the boy's mother, and she had decided to keep it – that is, to take Michael to Palestine. In 1947, after a stay in a displaced persons camp in Germany, the two boarded the illegal *Exodus* ship with other Holocaust survivors. With Britain then ruling Palestine under a mandate and enforcing a stringent immigration policy, the British navy intercepted the boat on the high seas

Gertruda Babilinska with Michael Stolowitzky

and had all the passengers sent back to Germany. In the words of Bracha Chabas, the author of a book on the Exodus, *The Boat that Won*, a witness described Gertruda as "a quiet and intelligent woman who never complained about anything that happened to us … She cared for the 11-year-old boy with devotion and love. Emissaries from Palestine urged her to allow them to take the boy with them, but she refused. 'I took an oath and I must fully keep it, even if takes years.'" When the boat was returned to Lübeck, she had only one request – to take a short leave from the camp in order to take part in a prayer service in memory of her Polish husband, who had fallen in the war.

In 1948, Gertruda and Michael finally reached Palestine on another illegal ship. In Israel, to support herself, she did various menial household chores, while Michael was sent for his education to a children's boarding school in Ben Shemen. Gertruda was years later admitted to a nursing home in Nahariya, where she died in 1995 and was laid to rest in the special section of Righteous Among the Nations in the Tel Aviv-Kiryat Shaul cemetery. Inspired by Babilinska's story, Barbara Streisand produced a special television documentary on Gertruda's rescue of Michael. Eventually moving to the United States and going into the travel business, Michael Stolowitzky does not miss any opportunity to talk about his dear "Mamusha," and has recently written a book about her. In 1973, Yad Vashem recognized Gertruda Babilinska as Righteous Among the Nations.

Báthory, Imre

HUNGARY

On May 4, 1944, several months after the German invasion of Hungary, and the beginning of the deportation of the Jews in that country, twenty-four-year-old Martin Wiesel (born 1920) was riding a train from Szatmárnémeti (today Satu Mare, in Romania) to Budapest. He had run away from that city after he learned that the Jews there had been ordered to enter a ghetto two days later, in preparation for their deportation to concentration camps in Poland. Wiesel felt that he stood a better chance of survival in the large metropolitan city of Budapest, with the help of friends, and of his brother Saul. On the train, suddenly Hungarian gendarmes stepped into Martin's coach to check the passengers' credentials. Jews were by then forbidden to ride the trains. To Martin's luck, as the gendarmes advanced toward him, the alarm sounded – it was an approaching air raid. The train screeched to a halt; all jumped out and ran for cover in a nearby ditch. With the alarm over, Martin Wiesel, as did the other passengers, boarded the train; this time he chose another seat for himself. He sat down and contemplated the rolling fields and the peaceful scenery outside.

About an hour later, a middle-aged person came over and sat down opposite him. He smiled toward Martin and struck up a conversation. He then whispered to Martin, "I know that you are a Jew in trouble, don't worry, I'll help you." Martin, fearing a trap from a provocateur out to catch a Jew on the run, felt uncomfortable and declined the man's offer. But the man opposite him persisted. Martin looked into the stranger's eyes, and decided the man could be trusted. When the gendarmes resumed their tour of inspection, the man presented his documents and then said, that the young person opposite him was his son, and he had forgotten his papers at home. The gendarmes bowed, saluted, and left. Martin Wiesel had been saved from arrest. The man introduced himself as Imre Báthory, and stated he was a farmer from Csepel, a town north of Budapest.

As Báthory later told Martin Wiesel, he had earlier seen the young man sitting in the same coach visibly alarmed by the approaching gendarmes, and correctly guessed that he was a Jew. After the air alarm, Báthory decided he had to help the man, and went over to sit across him. The two continued to converse in a friendly manner, while the train sped towards Budapest. Báthory then asked Wiesel to come with him to his home in Csepel, some five kilometers from Budapest, and Martin agreed. The two got off at a Budapest suburban station and headed to Báthory's home. It was nine in the morning.

Upon arrival there, Báthory told Wiesel that due to the increased bombings of the factories in the vicinity, he had sent his wife and three children elsewhere, and he had remained alone in his home. Báthory told Wiesel, "Hard times are coming and you can stay with me, but on one condition. I know you are Jewish and only you and me are to know it. You are lucky, since you resemble my wife, so you will be introduced as my brother-in-law," and so it was. At Báthory's house, Martin helped out with farm work.

Later, Báthory also hid Martin's brother, Saul, who had fled to him after a daring escape from Nazi imprisonment in Budapest. Despite the personal risk involved in hiding Jews, Báthory provided the brothers with food and all their other needs until the liberation of the area on January 15, 1945. In the beginning of November 1944, with power in Hungary in the hands of the intensely antisemitic Arrow Cross movement, Martin smuggled his friends, a married couple named Alexander and Bella Fuchs, out of the endangered ghetto in Budapest, and brought them to Báthory's house. Báthory took them in without hesitation and told his neighbors that the two new arrivals were family members whose home had been destroyed during an air bombardment. In December 1944, when Bella Fuchs was accidentally wounded by a German stray bullet, Báthory hitched his horse-drawn wagon and took her to a German doctor, telling him that she was a relative, and the doctor removed the bullet.

Báthory's charges learned that their benefactor was a believing evangelical Christian, belonging to the Pentecostal church, and he stated to them that this was the reason why he was taking risks to himself to help out Jews on the run. He later added, "I prayed that God would save me and in so doing save the people in my home. I never thought of sending them away. With God's help, we all survived."

Martin Wiesel remembered his benefactor as a man who did not particularly care for money. "He was selling in the open market, and I was his help. He gave me food, the best he had, and accommodation." Since food began to be increasingly scarce, Báthory allowed Wiesel to work in the Manfred Weiss ammunition factory, to help out with extra income. Eventually Martin's uncle joined him. There were now five people hiding in Báthory's home, while his own family was away in the countryside. They all survived.

Years after the war, asked what had lead him to save persons, strangers to him, and thereby jeopardize his own life, Imre Báthory thought for a moment, then gave the following answer: "I was only a vessel through which the Lord's purpose was fulfilled. I know that when I stand before God on Judgment Day. I shall not be asked the question posed to Cain – where were you when your brother's blood was crying out to God?" By these profound words and his saving act, the farmer Imre Báthory encapsulated the important biblical message of the sanctity of human life.

Recognized in 1986 (3531)

Battel, Albert
GERMANY

*I*t was an event unheard off in the annals of the Third Reich. A German military officer had dared to raise his weapon against the SS to prevent them from carrying out a fateful deportation action against Jews. This occurred on the morning of July 27, 1942, in the city of Przemyśl (pronounced Pshemyshl), in German-occupied Poland. A detachment of SS and police had made preparations to cross the bridge over the river San to the side where the ghetto was located and to round up Jews for deportation to the Bełżec extermination camp. As they approached the bridge, they were stopped by a detachment of the Wehrmacht, the German army, whose commander on site told the advancing units that he had orders to block the entry of the SS and police into the ghetto. He warned them that these orders originated with the city's military commander, Major Max Liedtke, and his deputy, Captain Albert Battel, and also included an order to open fire against the advancing SS and police units should they try to force their way across the bridge. Especially humiliating to the SS was the sight of Polish civilians and even some Jews on the way to the work detail watching the German officer in charge brandishing his revolver and forcing the SS and Gestapo to withdraw – an unseemly sight! What was it that caused this altercation between the two branches of the German security establishment in Poland which nearly led to something almost unheard – the German military opening fire on the SS in order to prevent them from deporting the Jews in the Przemyśl ghetto?

In his report of the incident, Bentin, the regional head of the Gestapo, pointed an accusing finger at First Lieutenant Albert Battel. Battel was a 51-year-old reserve officer and lawyer from Breslau (today Wroclaw, Poland), a decorated soldier in World War I and presently the adjutant to the German military commander of Przemyśl, Major Max Liedtke. Bentin wrote that on Wednesday, July 22, 1942, SS regional chief Fellenz had chaired a meeting with the Przemyśl German civilian chief (*Kreishauptmann*) to discuss the planned deportation of Jews. Subsequently, appropriate plans were made in the following days, including the listing of the thousands of Jews slated for deportation. On the morning of July 26, Major Liedtke rang up Bentin on the phone and complained that he had learned (probably from Battel) that about 95% of his special team of Jewish workers was included on the list. Bentin's response was that the deportation would go through as planned. Liedtke reiterated his need for the Jewish labor force for army-related details. Bentin would not budge, but hinted that on the following day – the day of the *Aktion* itself, Monday, July 27 – perhaps a compromise might be reached with the SS officers in charge of the operation concerning the army's labor force requirements. Later that same morning, Lieutenant Battel appeared at Bentin's office, and reported that his superior, Liedtke, had forwarded a complaint to military headquarters and that the Wehrmacht would not be able to do its job properly if the Jewish laborers were removed. Battel told the surprised Gestapo chief that until a decision was received from military headquarters he had ordered the closing of the San bridge to all civilian traffic, including the police (i.e., Gestapo).

Bentin went on to detail a meeting held several weeks before, on July 4, at Liedtke's office, during which the question of the Jewish Wehrmacht laborers was also discussed. At this meeting, Battel had stated that he intended to issue a red card to every Jewish laborer employed by the Wehrmacht to safeguard them from deportation, as unfortunately had happened with the 1,000 workers already taken away. Bentin agreed to this arrangement but added, significantly: "I was sure that the Wehrmacht would not give up a single Jew or Jewess working as Wehrmacht laborers, whereas I, according to orders and also on my own would try to resettle as many Jews as possible." "Resettle" was the standard Nazi euphemism for deportation to the death camps. Following this, on July 26, Battel had 60 to 100 Jews with their wives and children moved from the ghetto and lodged in locations controlled by the military. Continuing his report, Bentin complained about the blocking of SS and police vehicles on the San River bridge. "A police vehicle that tried to cross the bridge in spite of its being closed was even threatened by a machine gun." This went so far that that even wives of German officials were prevented from going to their regular lunchtime haunts. The bridge was reopened at about 13:45 hours, and that same evening SS–*Hauptscharfuehrer* Fellenz arrived to investigate the situation. In summary, Bentin complained that "it should be mentioned that the closing of the bridge stirred up great excitement among the populace, who were surprised to see the Germans facing off against each other on the issue of protecting the Jews."

SS chief Fellenz also submitted a report on the events of July 27, 1942. He stated that at a meeting on July 2, in the presence of all the respective German civilian and police agencies (including the *Kreishauptmann, Stadtkommissar,* officers of the *Ordnungspolizei, Sicherheitspolizei*), the appropriate measures were decided on for the planned Action against the ghetto Jews. "I especially pointed out the new order of the Higher SS and Police Chief East, SS-*Obergruppenfuehrer* and Police General Krueger, according to which the age limit of the Jewish laborers is fixed at between 16 and 35." In other words, persons below and above this age would be automatically eligible for deportation, with the exception of a small contingent of especially skilled Jews, who would be retained for the time being. "I also indicated that women … who are being used for simple cleaning and gardening work are in no case to be allowed to stay. They can be replaced by the wives of those Jews with a residence permit." This arrangement, according to Fellenz, should satisfy the requirements of the Wehrmacht.

Fellenz was therefore quite surprised when Bentin informed him of the closing of the San bridge, and also that Battel had appeared at the Gestapo office and asserted that the San bridge would be closed to all civilian traffic including the police, until a decision was received from military headquarters, to which the matter had been referred. Arriving on the spot, Fellenz stated that he first tried "a diplomatic solution," by telling Major Liedtke that the concerns of the Wehrmacht with regard to its labor requirements would be considered. "On the other hand," he told Liedtke, "I don't understand that even today the Wehrmacht is keeping a large number of so-called house-and-court Jews, used for cleaning the rooms or shining the boots of officers." Fellenz assured Liedtke that in the future all Jewish laborers aged 16 to 35 employed by the Wehrmacht could remain without regard to their skills; but at the same time all Jewish laborers above 35 were to be "resettled." Fellenz also told Liedtke in private that his closing of the bridge was not justified or authorized, even by military headquarters, and he reminded Liedtke that the deportation of the Jews was a police Action and does not at all

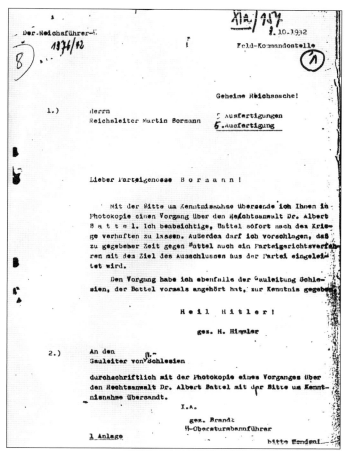

Heinrich Himmler's letter to Martin Bormann to have Albert Battel arrested right after the war

concern the Wehrmacht. "At the same time I asked him not to interfere with the *Aktion* any further, as otherwise countermeasures would have to be initiated," including the bringing in of SS reinforcements. Major Liedtke replied that he represented solely the interests of the Wehrmacht and that according to operating regulations, in cases of differences between the Wehrmacht and the civilian authorities, the Wehrmacht was to have the final say. Liedtke, according to Fellenz, was not able to accept the fact that recently, as a consequence of the absence of the Jews, a hospital train with wounded soldiers could not be removed. "I replied to Major Liedtke that in other areas the Wehrmacht may be privileged, but not so when it concerns police actions." As to the wounded soldiers, had Liedtke previously indicated that he needed more workers, the SS would have seen to it. Alternatively, the guards and sentries posted on the bridge to stop vehicles could have been deployed for the purpose of helping the wounded soldiers, hence the claims advanced by Liedtke and Battel were unjustified. In closing, Fellenz was satisfied to report that in spite of the obstacles created by these two officers, during the *Aktion* of July 27 a total of 3,850 Jews had been "resettled." A few Jews, trying to flee or resist, were shot. All the Gestapo and SS personnel "acted decisively and harshly," and "in an exemplary way."

An additional Gestapo report remarked that local military headquarters, to where the 80 to 90 Jewish workers and their families were moved, "resembled a Jewish assembly camp." When this Gestapo officer asked Liedtke the reason for the blocking of the bridge, he was told that it was done "because of the Jewish *Aktion* and that … the bridge would be closed until I stopped my measures against the Jews … He also told me that the measures of the police were sabotaging the work of the Wehrmacht." When the Gestapo officer assured Liedtke that the *Aktion* was not intended to include Jews working for the Wehrmacht, both men decided to look up Battel to clarify this point. Meeting Battel on the bridge, "from the following discussion, I could see that Lieutenant Battel was the soul of the whole enterprise." Whereas, according to the Gestapo officer, Major Liedtke was prepared to reopen the bridge, "it is to be remarked that on both banks of the San hundreds of people had gathered to watch this strange spectacle of the Wehrmacht fighting with the police." Later, SS-Major Schweder had come on horseback to the bridge together with an officer in his company, and he, too, was warned by the sergeant on duty that he was ordered to shoot if Schweder tried to cross the bridge. "As I learned from some officers of the local Gestapo, as well as from the city head, Lieutenant Battel is known to be a friend of the Jews. My own observations confirm this fact."

Battel's humanitarian action was also confirmed by Samuel Igel, one of Battel's lucky beneficiaries. He worked in the Wehrmacht's munitions and clothing section, where he reported that some 500 Jewish workers were employed. He described how on July 25, 1942, Battel was shocked to learn that the Gestapo had canceled the Wehrmacht's special red-colored work passes. At first he thought this was the result of a misunderstanding. When this was confirmed to him, he immediately alerted Major Liedtke and then phoned Gestapo chief Bentin. When Bentin refused to postpone the planned action, Battel received permission from Liedtke to close all approaches to the ghetto. Battel also commissioned army trucks to move some 90 Jewish workers with their families out of the ghetto and into the Wehrmacht security zone, where they remained for about a week and were fed by the army canteen.

The Gestapo investigation also uncovered that Battel had a prewar record of being a *Judenfreund,* a friend and protector of the Jews, and this despite his card-carrying membership in the Nazi Party. The investigation revealed that in 1933 Battel helped the Jewish Heims family emigrate from Germany. Moreover, in 1936, Battel was fined for having extended a loan to a Jewish lawyer, which he then helped the man pay off by employing him in his own law office. Also damaging to Battel's reputation, in SS eyes, was his "cordial" shaking of hands with Dr. Duldig, the head of the *Judenrat* (Jewish Council) of the Przemyśl ghetto.

As a result of Battel's acts, he was transferred to the Russian front. In 1944, he was discharged from the army due to his heart condition and returned to his law practice in Breslau, only to be drafted again in the last weeks of the war in the hastily established *Volkssturm,* the People's Army. Released from Russian captivity in 1946, and with his city of Breslau renamed Wroclaw and annexed to Poland, Battel moved to West Germany. He died in 1952, at the age of 61.

Unbeknownst to Battel, the SS and Gestapo reports of the incident reached the highest level of the SS hierarchy, SS-Chief Heinrich Himmler himself, and probably also landed on Hitler's desk, or at least reached his chief adjutant, Martin Bormann. Documents discovered after the war revealed the following letter addressed by Himmler to Borman, dated October

7, 1942, and classified State Secret. It said: "Dear Party Member Bormann! Requesting you to take notice that I am sending you a photocopy of a file concerning lawyer Dr. Albert Battel. I intend to have Battel arrested immediately after the war. Besides, I suggest initiating against Battel, at a proper time, steps for his exclusion from the party." Fortunately for Battel, the war ended in Nazi Germany's defeat.

Michael Gilad, a member of the Yad Vashem Commission for the Righteous, remembered well the July 26, 1942, incident on the San bridge. "The day was my 16th birthday, and although I never saw Battel we Jews knew that we had a protector in him. A few of the people he took out of the ghetto survived the war and are in Israel now." Battel's action represents the only case known thus far of a German army officer placing troops at a strategic point in order to prevent the SS and Gestapo from carrying out a deportation raid on a Jewish ghetto during the Holocaust.

In 1981, Yad Vashem awarded the late Albert Battel the title of Righteous Among the Nations.

Beccari, Arrigo
Moreali, Giuseppe
Italy

*A*rrigo Beccari was a priest and teacher at the Catholic seminary in the village of Nonantola, near Modena, Italy. In July 1942, a group of 50 Jewish children arrived there, originally from Germany, Austria, and Poland, having fled from the war zone in Dalmatia, Yugoslavia, caught between Italian troops and local partisans. The group was lead by Josef ("Yoshke") Itai. With the help of Delasem, the officially recognized Jewish emigration and welfare agency, the children were housed in an abandoned mansion known as Villa Emma. Eventually the number of Jewish children arriving there from Yugoslavia rose to 100.

Soon, Josef Itai befriended Father Arrigo Beccari, and the two frequently had conversations late at night on religious and social issues; on Marxism and faith; on man and evil; and on hope; and Itai was impressed with Beccari's tolerant views in general and especially toward

Arrigo Beccari (left) and Giuseppe Moreali (right)

Jews. Nonantola seemed a safe place to sit out the war, but when Italy surrendered to the Allies on September 8, 1943, and the Germans overran the parts of the country not yet in Allied hands, a reign of terror began for the Jews. In order to keep the children at the Villa Emma from falling into German hands, Beccari persuaded the hesitant seminary rector to allow a group of children to be hidden there. The seminary rector, Ottaviano Pellati, reportedly exclaimed, "For a thousand years a woman's feet have not trodden in this house, but let it be so in the name of the Lord." Beccari also arranged for other children to be housed

Villa Emma, Nonantola

with friendly villagers. Food supplies and other provisions from the Jewish Delasem organization were stored in the seminary's attic. Part of these provisions was also sent to Florence, upon the request of Cardinal Della Costa, for help to Jews in hiding there. When the Germans came in search of the children at the seminary, Pellati assured them that no children were to be found there.

As the Nazis and their local collaborators stepped up the search of Jews, it became urgent for the children to be moved somewhere else. At first, it was planned to try to sneak them through the German lines to the Allied forces in the south of the country, and Beccari arranged for Itai to be dressed in a priest's habit, so as to accompany the children – supposedly Italian war orphans – heading for an orphanage in the south of the country. This plan, however, proved too risky and was dropped. It was then decided to take the whole group north toward and across the Swiss border. With the help of Dr. Giuseppe Moreali, the village's physician, all the children and those responsible for them, about 120 people, were provided with forged documents identifying them as Italians, and from Larino, a town in southern Italy already in Allied hands, with himself signing the documents as the town's supposed mayor. Then they boarded a train for the Swiss frontier, a ride fraught with terrible but unavoidable risks, for most of them could hardly speak Italian, and their papers may not have saved them during a police check. Luckily, no mishaps occurred during the long train ride, and on Yom Kippur eve, 1943, the group waded through a shallow river and passed safely into Switzerland.

The Gestapo, discovering the loss of the children, and incensed at Beccari for his help to partisan fighters, imprisoned him in Bologna. Despite the torture inflicted on him over the next few months, he held his ground, refusing to disclose the names of the persons who had helped him or to reveal the whereabouts of other Jews in hiding. His religious superiors interceded on his behalf and he was released. Years later he wrote: "It would be difficult for me to erase the memory of the terror and suffering of those days or of my joy at doing the small good which was my duty and which had to be done."

In 1964, Father Arrigo Beccari and Dr. Giuseppe Moreali were awarded the title of Righteous Among the Nations by Yad Vashem. The following year both planted a tree in their name in the Avenue of the Righteous at Yad Vashem.

Beitz, Berthold & Else

GERMANY

*B*oryslaw (today Borislav in Ukraine) was an insignificant village until the discovery of oil in the 18th century. Since 1772 part of the Austrian-Hungarian empire, after World War I it reverted back to Poland, where it became the most important oil-producing center in the country (supplying 75% of the country's oil). The city attracted thousands of workers – chemical engineers, laboratory workers, mechanics, and administrative workers needed by the burgeoning local oil industry. By the time of the German invasion, the Jewish population there had risen to between 15,000 and 17,000 out of a mixed Polish-Ukrainian population of 50,000.

On July 1, 1941, Boryslaw fell to the invading Germans; this was followed with a pogrom by local Ukrainians and the murder of some 200 Jews. Killings, or as euphemistically termed by the Germans, *Aktions*, followed one another in quick succession – on each occasion claiming the lives of thousands of Jews, who after being assembled either in the local Colosseum cinema or the municipal slaughterhouse were then either massacred in nearby forests (such as on November 28, 1941) or deported to the Bełżec extermination camp (such as in summer 1942 and afterwards). The only Jews spared were the 1,500 workers of the city's important oil facility and their families, who were kept in a special camp commanded by SS-officer Fritz Georg Hildebrand. The company was managed by a German civilian named Berthold Beitz.

Born in 1913, Beitz had worked before coming to Boryslaw for the Royal Dutch Shell Oil Company, where he gained experience in the oil industry. Arriving with his wife, Else, and the couple's two daughters, Beitz was appointed business manager of the important Beskiden Oil Company, renamed as *Karpathenölgesellschaft* (Carpathian Oil Company) under German control. Understandably, the extraction and refining of oil was an absolute necessity for the German war industry, and it was Berthold Beitz's job, as manager of the firm, to run the company as efficiently as possible under war conditions. Beginning in February 1942, Beitz began to employ Jewish labor, first in an administrative capacity, such as

Berthold and Else Beitz with their daughter Barbara, 1942, in Boryslaw (Jewish photographer: Holzmann)

for internal auditing in the bookkeeping department. As time went by, Beitz hired more Jewish clerks, and then did something quite unusual in terms of the proper functioning of the oil facility – he began to add to his work force many other Jews who had no professional background for this type of operation, such as merchants, tailors, shoemakers, hairdressers, housewives, laundresses, and unskilled laborers who knew nothing of the rudiments of the oil industry. Quite obviously, the intent was to save them from Nazi extermination.

In order to protect his Jewish workers from the sporadic anti-Jewish German actions, Beitz had these workers housed with their families in segregated labor camps, with the workers having a special badge sewn on their outer clothes – the letter R for *Rüstungsarbeiter* (armaments worker) – and a life-saving work permit with Beitz's signature. As reported by Beitz's non-Jewish secretary, Evelyn Hajdu, to be in possession of a work permit with Beitz's signature meant to remain alive. Beitz's total work force, which included the workers' families, eventually rose as high as 1,500 men and women, kept in a special camp under the surveillance of SS commander Fritz Hildebrand. This was the man that Beitz had to be on good terms with, which included bribery in order to make sure that no harm would come to the Jewish population in the special camp.

Beitz's humanitarian behavior manifested itself during the Nazi-staged *Aktions* of 1942 and 1943, which also affected even his workers and their families. He was given the special privilege of releasing any Jews rounded up that he claimed were essential for his oil extracting and refining operations. Paradoxically, many of the released were anything but experienced professional oil workers; most were merchants, hardly indispensable for the strenuous work on the oilrigs. In addition, on several occasions, he sheltered in his home Jews who were on the run, thus exposing himself and his wife, Else, to severe punishment in the event of disclosure.

As reported by Blima Hamerman, during the summer *Aktion* of 1942, Beitz saved her son-in-law, Moshe Bergman – an unskilled worker. This happened when Beitz, who did not know Bergman, noticed him at the railroad station with other Jews who had been rounded up. Beitz walked up to him, took him by the arm, and told the Gestapo officers who were guarding the Jews that the man worked for him and he needed him – thus saving his life. In addition, Dr. Jechezkiel (Henryk) Kudisch reported that he initially worked as a doctor in the Jewish Council's Health Center ("Specifically, I wrote out death certificates for the dead, the number of which was growing from day to day due to pogroms, starvation, typhoid fever …"). Then, in August 1942 during the roundup of 6,000 Jews at the railroad station, "I found myself among those who were segregated by Mr. Beitz, who … singled out from the transport some 1,200–1,500 Jews." Kudisch said he saw how Beitz pulled out hundreds of Jews, who were then employed in the oil industry ("including myself"). These people were immediately sent to the labor camp, where they were provided with conditions for minimal subsistence, with a salary paid to some. Kudisch also heard rumors that during one of these *Aktions*, Mrs. Else Beitz sheltered a group of Jews in her home, also providing them with food.

Mina Horowitz related that she had been taken with her child to the assembly point in the Colosseum cinema ("one of the greatest and most bloody actions in our city aimed mainly at women and children") before being led to execution. After losing her daughter, she sat in a stupor awaiting her fate, when suddenly she heard a cry: " 'Beitz has come, Beitz has come!' and my name immediately afterwards. I did not react, but people started pushing me forward so that I faced Mr. Beitz and the head of the Boryslaw Gestapo, Wippert." When asked where her child was, she grabbed a boy standing beside her and pushed him forward, saying he was hers. "It occurred to me in a flash that I might save another Jewish child in place of mine." At this point Beitz told her: "Mrs. Horowitz, you are free, stay right there in the corner and the child stays here." However, she refused to leave the boy behind. When Beitz questioned her, she replied: "I came back to get my child." He asked: "Is this really your child?" to which she answered with a determined "Yes." Beitz told her to take the child and stand aside and wait for him. In the meantime he continued to pull out more people who were directed to the oil workers' camp. Mrs. Horowitz continues: "I learned in the office that Mr. Beitz knew that my child was two years old and was a girl, and I had chosen a nine-year-old boy called Duno Schapira. On the same day I gave the child back to his father." As for herself, she was taken to the oil workers' camp, where she remained until the end.

Berthold Beitz's humanitarian disposition was shared by his wife, Else. As told by the then 14-year-old Arthur Birman, in the summer 1942 he was told to go to Beitz's home outside the camp to do some minor repair work in the bathroom. Arriving there, he was first invited to have breakfast at the table at which Beitz's wife and two daughters were seated. "I was a bit embarrassed to sit at the same table with them, and seeing all the gourmet food, like white bread, honey, cold cuts, on the table I thanked her for the invitation and asked whether instead of eating there I could take something for my mother." Mrs. Beitz, however, insisted that Arthur sit at the table with them and share their breakfast. She then packed a loaf of bread, honey, and some cold cuts and told him, "This is for your mother. You are a fine boy because you care for your mother." As he left, Arthur bowed to Beitz, to which he responded "*Grüss Gott!*" ("Good-bye!" also literally "Greet God!" i.e., not me). A year later, during the *Aktion* of August 1943, Beitz grabbed Arthur at the assembly point, telling the Gestapo that he needed the boy for work in the oil company, and had him join the others. "When I was walking to the other side I told him with an imploring look that my mother was also there, at the railroad store. He told me to indicate where she was standing and he also saved my mother, ordering her to walk to where the soil experts were standing. I must note that my mother had no profession and was not employed anywhere at that time. I must stress that when he saved me and my mother Beitz did it completely disinterestedly, not even knowing us."

Equally if not more impressive is the story told by Bezalel (Salek) Linhard, also 14 years old in 1942. His father, a furrier, had been commissioned by Beitz to sew him a coat. Beitz persuaded Bezalel's father to be paid in food to ease the starved condition of his family. The food consisted of generous amounts of flour, sugar, and other foodstuffs. Bezalel accompanied his father to Beitz's house, where they spent a few weeks, eating with them and sometimes even staying there overnight. "For the night I had my bed made up with a sheet and clean cover as if for a dear guest." During the August 1942 *Aktion*, Bezalel went to look for his father, who had been seized, and was himself caught and locked up in a warehouse crowded with other Jews, and there he met his father. Upon orders from Beitz, Bezalel's father was released. As for Bezalel, Beitz insisted that he too be released, and the SS relented. Beitz then took Bezalel and his father to an out-of-the-way courtyard where he fed them; he then had them taken to his house in a horse-drawn carriage, where the two stayed for three nights – until the *Aktion* was over.

During the same *Aktion*, Beitz went up to Samuel Wegner at the railroad loading point. "He didn't know me personally and when he saw me he asked where I worked. I told him that I worked as a gardener, and he told me to walk to the side where the oil experts selected by him stood. I wish to note that when he saved me at that time Beitz did it disinterestedly without knowing me." In Bezalel Linhard's words, "I wish to underline that Beitz did not receive a dime for saving me and my father ... When Beitz came back home [from work], he liked to sit with my father and talk with him freely and cordially *[in herzlichem Ton]* about many things, politics not excluded. For my part I can also declare with a clear conscience that of all the people I have ever met Beitz was one of the most irreproachable.... I never heard about Beitz requesting any payment for saving Jews."

In addition, as attested by Edmund Nowak, Beitz allowed groups of Jews to hide in the attic in one of his office buildings during Nazi roundups of Jews, with Beitz bringing them food there. Also, Beitz, who was in close contact with the higher SS and Gestapo echelons, took advantage of this to alert Jews to coming *Aktions* – operations that were usually kept secret even from lower-rank Nazi officials until the last minute. In the words of Edmund Nowak, "At all times Beitz warned the Jews about the beginning of the *Aktions*, ... which wouldn't have gone unpunished had the Gestapo known about it."

In March 1944, in the wake of Germany's deteriorating military situation, Beitz was relieved of his post in Boryslaw and inducted in the German army. Before leaving, he urged his Jewish workers to seek hiding places for themselves with local non-Jews since he could no longer protect them, as he had done in the preceding two years. With the approach of the Red Army in summer 1944, some of his workers were deported to the Plaszów camp, where the inmates, scarred by the brutal conditions of the camp, were surprised at how good the new arrivals looked. When the Russians liberated Boryslaw on August 6, 1944, only about 200 Jews were to be found who had survived by hiding in the city and environs – many of them former wards of Beitz. Many years after the war, Berthold Beitz rose to one of the leading industrial positions in postwar Germany – the director-general of the Krupp Corporation in Essen.

Immediately after the war, and in the following years, Berthold Beitz received many expressions of thanks and appreciation from his former Jewish wards. Josef Hirsch thanked Beitz for giving "us hope of a change for the better," and instilling "in us renewed courage to face life ... I will never forget his noble way of acting and wish with all my heart that God will reward him and his family for this by way of a kind fate." Leon Morski underlined that Beitz's charitable deeds "were the work of a master of the art of living"; of "never doing anything but good and showing an understanding of other people's misfortunes." Such as Henryk Engelberg who wrote, "We will never forget that you, on your own initiative, brought my daughter out of the sealed freight car – the destination of which we were already aware of at that time – from the same train that took my wife and my son, at the time 15 years of age, to a terrible death." Michael Halski added, "You were ready to help and you did help. Not in one single case but as a rule. You searched for opportunities to help and you gave help wherever you could, exposing yourself to grave dangers in doing so ... Your heroism went beyond the bounds of heroism." Jan Jaworski, who wrote to Beitz in the economically difficult year of 1947, emphasized "that If God forbid, you are in need of anything, we are at your disposal at all times. Approximately 60-70% of the former employees from the naphtha [oil] excavation area are here." Explaining his motives in helping, Berthold Beitz stated that it was not due to any particular anti-Nazi feelings, although he had never belonged to the Nazi Party, but in response to the atrocities he was witnessing in Boryslaw. "When you see a woman with her child in her arms being shot, and you yourself have a child, then your response is bound to be completely different." Earlier, during the war years, as he witnessed the Nazi atrocities, he confided to a German colleague, "Who is going to pay for this? The German people are going to pay for it."

Berthold Beitz was awarded the title of Righteous Among the Nations in 1973, followed by his wife, Else, also honored with the title in 2006.

Benoît, Pierre-Marie
FRANCE

*H*e was a Catholic monk, but he is better known as "Father of the Jews." How so? Born Pierre Péteul in 1895, in Bourg d'Iré (Marne-et-Loire), France, to a family of flour millers, in 1913 he decided to enter the Capuchin-Franciscan Order. The following year came the war, and the newly religious-named Benoît served in the French army, where he was wounded. After the war he took up theological studies, earning a doctorate in theology, and he taught at the Capuchin College in Rome. With Italy's entry into World War II, in June 1940, he was sent back to France and took up residence at the Capuchin convent in Marseilles, at 51 Croix-de-Regnier Street. This eventually became a beehive of activity to help Jews in flight to acquire lodgings, identity papers, and baptismal certificates, as well as aid, with the cooperation of other clandestine organizations, in facilitating flights to Switzerland or Spain. Benoît's rescue activity may have been prompted, or further promoted, by the visit of Fernande Leboucher, a young woman who came to seek his help in mid-1942 to free her Polish-Jewish husband, Ludwik Nadelman, arrested and imprisoned in Rivesaltes, near Marseilles. He promised to help. As he told her: "The law under which Ludwik is imprisoned is an immoral one, and one is not allowed merely to ignore such laws but should actively resist them. There is no doubt in my mind that this is such a law, and such a time."

"What could one do to help them?" Benoît wrote in his memoirs. "Provide them with identity cards under different names ... hide them temporarily when they were being looked for, and for this purpose have on hand rooms ... while they waited to escape to Spain or Switzerland." Such an operation entailed contacts with Jewish and Christian religious organizations and institutions and clandestine escape networks. Benoît was aware that the French police was keeping tabs on his activities. "But I had devoted friends among the police themselves who helped me evade danger." Despite all the precautions, incidents could not be avoided, such as when one of Benoît's wards was arrested while trying to cross into

Spain and was forced to admit that he received his false identity card from Benoît. People continued to flock to Benoît's center seeking aid. "I was visited every hour day and night. People escaping the internment camps or, for example, the Hotel du Brebant at Marseilles (center for selection for internment or deportation) came directly to me." The bishop of Marseilles appointed Benoît to visit the camps of Les Milles, near Aix-en-Provence, and Hotel Bompart (internment center for women), and "this enabled me to transmit all kinds of secret messages."

After the German occupation of the Vichy zone, in November 1942, which included Marseilles, Benoît traveled regularly to Nice, then under Italian occupation, to meet clandestine operatives, both Jewish (such as Joseph Bass) and non-Jewish (such as the Jesuit Father Brémont), and coordinate aid to fleeing Jews trying to reach the Italian zone and find accommodations there. Every Sunday evening, accompanied by Joseph Bass, Benoît took the train to Nice and Cannes where he stayed until Thursday, working closely with Jewish organizations. The Italian Jewish banker Angelo Donati, who also served as an intermediary between the Jewish committee and the Italian authorities, introduced Benoît to Guido Lospinoso, the recently appointed Italian commissioner for Jewish affairs. "He wanted to know, for example, if the God of the Jews was the same as the God of the Christians, and why I, as a Catholic, was involved with them. I did not have much difficulty explaining and justifying myself, and he then declared that he would be favorably

Father Pierre-Marie Benoît in 1984

disposed toward the Jews." He also approved Benoît's request to be allowed to continue his rescue activity on behalf of the Jews.

In summer 1943, fearing a German takeover of the Italian zone, Donati suggested to Benoît a plan to remove the more than 30,000 Jews there to Italy proper. After receiving the blessings for this audacious plan of the still-functioning Jewish leadership in southern France, including Rabbis Schwarz, Kaplan, Berman, and Salzer, as well as the lay leaders Raoul Lambert and Edmond Fleg, Benoît took the opportunity of his being called back to Rome by his superiors to promote the Vatican backing for this grandiose rescue plan. In an audience with Pope Pius XII, on July 16, 1943, Benoît requested the Vatican's intercession with the Italian government to facilitate the transfer plan. In addition, he asked for the Vatican's help in obtaining news of French Jews deported to Germany and improvement of conditions for Jews in French detention camps, as well as intervention with Spain to allow the repatriation of Jews claiming Spanish ancestry. During this unusual audience between the head of the Catholic church and a Capuchin monk, and after listening to details of the Vichy roundup of Jews in France, the pope commented: "One would not have believed this coming from France." It is not known the full extent of the Vatican's action on these requests, other than Cardinal Maglione's letter to Benoît, of September 9, 1943, in which he wrote of the willingness of Spain to be of help to Jews claiming Spanish nationality, but on condition of the preliminary verification of their status by Spanish diplomats in France. Unfortunately, by the time this letter was written, communications between Italy and France had been severed due to the German takeover of the Italian zone in France as well as of Italy itself, and Benoît found himself unable to do anything further in this regard.

Benoît had also asked the pontiff for the Vatican's support of his large-scale evacuation plan of Jews from the diminishing Italian zone in France to Italy proper. In the meantime, with the overthrow of Mussolini, on July 25, 1943, the transfer plan was amended to move the Jews by ship to North African havens. The new Italian government of Marshal Badoglio was prepared to provide four ships (*Duilio, Giulio Cesare, Saturnia, Vulcania*) to make three voyages from Nice to North African ports with 2,500 persons on board on each crossing, thus allowing 30,000 Jews to escape. The U.S.-based Joint Distribution Committee was prepared to underwrite the cost of this large-scale operation. Benoît also received support for this undertaking from Francis Osborne and Myron Taylor, the British and American diplomatic representatives to the Vatican. Angelo Donati arrived in Rome to coordinate plans with various Italian ministries. Eighty trucks were assigned to take the first batch of Jews on boats in Nice, escorted by the Italian police. Then, suddenly, Italy's premature announcement of its surrender to the Allies on September 8, 1943, and the immediate German occupation of Italy and its zone in France, led to the scuttling of what could have been one of the largest rescue operations during the Holocaust. "In sum," Benoît wrote after the war, "a beautiful project which resulted in disaster for lack of time to carry it out."

This failure of the evacuation did not dim Benoît's determination to help Jews escape the Nazi dragnet. In Rome, Benoît now went under the name of Padre Benedetto and worked closely with Delasem (*Delegazione per l'Assistenza dei Emigranti Ebrei)*, becoming a member of its executive board. Delasem had been originally created to facilitate Jewish emigration and was presently occupied with helping Jews in hiding. During the tragic "Black Saturday" of October 16, 1944, when the Germans staged a large-scale roundup of Roman Jews, the Delasem office was closed and its main archives were moved to Benoît's Capuchin convent at 159 Via Sicilia. There the Delasem committee continued to meet secretly. A back door leading to Via Boncompagnie was to be used for emergency flights. The Delasem executive committee was now headed by Benoît and included Settimio Sorani and his secretary Giuseppe Levi on behalf of Delasem and Aron Kastersztein and Stephane Schwamm on behalf of refugees from France. "I was the only one with sufficient freedom to appear everywhere, at the police, embassies, and various agencies." Hundreds of desperate people turned up every day at the door of the Capuchin convent. "Some who did not know my name asked at the gate for 'The Father of the Jews.' " This presented a risk, so several other locations were designated for aid.

Benoît's network dealt mainly with obtaining various kinds of forged documents, additional food, and ration cards; and billeting Jews with families (many of whom had fled to Italy from other regions) throughout the city, armed with false papers. Together with his Jewish aides, Stefan Schwamm and Aron Kastersztein, both recent arrivals in Italy from France, Benoît solicited the aid of the Swiss, Romanian, and Hungarian legations, the last two countries allied to Nazi Germany, in obtaining various documents, including "letters of protection." Money was received from Delasem funds, the Joint, and Genoa-based Cardinal Pietro Boetto. When a law went into effect under which persons who had arrived after December 6, 1943 would have to leave Rome, Benoît sought out Mr. Chauvet at the Swiss legation, who issued letters of protection for persons at risk of being expelled. Another tactic was to falsify hotel registers to show that people had stayed there before the December 6 cutoff date. "The most difficult part was to obtain fiscal stamps. We replaced them with postal stamps … that we bought from philatelists. However, we needed a lot of them, so we made use of canceled stamps that we doctored as well as possible. It was crazy, but it worked." Other than Chauvet, at the Swiss legation, the Romanian ambassador, Crigorcea, and the Hungarian consul, Szasz, also helped out.

For additional ration cards, Benoît had Schwamm (then going under the alias Bernard Lioré) use the manual copier in the basement of the convent to print out 500 copies of certificates of a fictitious Refugees Assistance Committee (in formation). The word "formation" was necessary for such a committee was not yet registered. Benoît added his signature as president and this was notarized by a helpful cleric at the Vicariat office. At the Food Service for Foreigners office, the Vicariat seal proved efficacious and Benoît received over 1,300 ration cards. As the number of people seeking aid increased, it was decided to disperse them in other places in northern Italy with the assistance of religious institutions there. When Benoît was informed that all French persons, about 400, were to be repatriated to France, the Hungarian consul Szasz agreed to Benoît's request to issue identity cards stating that these people were Hungarian nationals. Benoît then returned to the Swiss legation the letters of protection issued earlier to these people, now Hungarian nationals, but not before removing their photos. "One could continue to 'manufacture Hungarians' at full speed." It is estimated that as many as 4,000 Jews benefited from Benoît's aid.

Benoît had been warned that the Gestapo head in the city, Kappler, wanted him arrested, and a confidant in Kappler's office warned Benoît to go into hiding. Benoît wrote: "I always remained at my place. Why did they never come to get get me? I still ask myself this question … We often received anonymous threatening letters." One day, such a letter included the demand of a ransom payment of 20,000 liras; if not, the letter writer threatened to denounce Benoît to the German police. The Committee met, and it was decided that a friendly police officer, named De Marco, would meet this strange person at a predetermined place as if to pay him. He was to be followed from a safe distance by his companions. It turned out that the culprit was a woman who wanted to extract money from Benoît's organization. She was sent off with a warning not to try this again for her own safety. On another occasion, two Gestapo men appeared at the Capuchin College, masquerading as Jewish refugees and speaking a broken Yiddish, ostensibly seeking help. Benoît was tipped off, scaled the walls, and escaped, but not before instructing a monk to answer the door and telling him what to say. The Roman police were also hepful, especially De Fiore, who headed the Foreigners Sections. "Without the goodwill and aid of the central *Questura* we would certainly not have been able to go on," Benoît stated. The Roman police were fully aware of Benoît's clandestine activities. "It is not that they did not bother us, they were actually our accomplices." One example cited by Benoît is the case of a foreign Jew who arrived at the *Questura* armed with a Spanish passport and was told, "Go to Via Sicilia 159 and look up Father M. Benoît. Over there, they'll arrange everything."

In early April 1944, Benoît and Schwamm traveled north to discuss plans to smuggle people across the Swiss border. Stopping in Florence, Schwamm, armed with a false letter of reference from the International Red Cross under his borrowed name of Bernard Lioré, was given a room by the German military command in a first-class hotel that also served the German military command. Both continued to Milan, where Schwamm was arrested, while Benoît managed to flee and hide in a Capuchin monastery. Secretly making his way to Genoa, he was helped by Cardinal Boetto and his secretary, Monsignor Repetto, and made his way back to Rome. There he learned that Aron Kastersztein had also been arrested. Benoît's Committee then held its meeting at the International Red Cross office. With the Germans in earnest search for Benoît, he went into hiding for barely a month, for on June 4, 1944, American troops liberated Rome.

Immediately afterwards, the Jewish community feted Benoît in the city's main synagogue. Invited to respond to the hallelujahs bestowed on him, Benoît spoke at length, concluding by saying, "I end my speech by recalling Moses' great command of love of God and one's fellow man, and I state emotionally 'I love the Jews with all my heart.'" As he left the synagogue, the congregants lined up to press his hands. On December 31, 1944, in an additional ceremony, Benoît and his fellow clerical helpers were again honored by the Jewish community. A Jewish speaker praised him with the following words: "Who among us can forget this noble person who came to save us … We are sure and convinced that a place is reserved for them [Benoît and his helpers] among the righteous in the eternal life … My friends, let us rise! Let us face the Superior [of the convent], Father Benoît, and all his Brothers! They are the personification of goodness, of love, and of humanity. Let us salute them."

In October 1945, the Jewish Labor Committee, in New York, asked Benoît to represent it in Rome for the distribution of money and packages to refugee Jews. Benoît consented, adding in his response, "I consider it a religious obligation and an honor to be able to work for the always persecuted Jewish people." Two years later, Benoît addressed a special appeal to the Jewish Labor Committee. Reminding it of his past work for Jews, he went on to state that he had recently been greatly troubled. "I am not content. I am not content, because a heavy burden is pressing on my soul." It had to do with the situation of his wartime Jewish collaborator, Schwamm, and his wife. "At the moment they both face infirmity, before reaching their forties…. I appeal to you and to your brethren to save these two heroes, for the sake of Israel and of humanity … Send me money. Much money." Allowing himself some effrontery, Benoît asked, "How much is a Jewish life worth? Israel owes five thousand lives to one *am-haaretz* [non-observant Jew] and one *Goyke* [Schwamm's wife was non-Jewish] … If the people of Israel really want me to be their ambassador, I now ask them for a vote of confidence. This vote of confidence will be expressed in the answer they make to this appeal, most likely the only time that I will get to address a request to my Jewish friends." An immediate initial sum of $1,000 was sent to Benoît.

Earlier, on July 8, 1945, Benoît had spoken before a Jewish audience on the significance of the Jewish people for Christians.

"We speak of the friendship between Jews and Christians. Who are the Jews? Who are the Christians? … The Jews are the descendants of the great and holy patriarchs Abraham, Isaac and Jacob. The Jews are the people chosen by God to preserve the true primitive religion of

Adam and Eve in the midst of the idolatry of the other nations, and to prepare the coming of the Messiah. The Jews are the followers of Moses, their immortal teacher and lawgiver and the disciples of the sublime and courageous prophets of God. The Jews are, by the will of God, the legitimate inhabitants of Palestine, which they conquered and in which they remained for more than twenty centuries until the destruction of Jerusalem, after which they dispersed throughout the world in which they live, always faithful to the holy covenant of God, putting at the disposal of every nation their intelligence and their activity, though subject to inexpressible suffering and persecution. The importance of the Jewish people is not in their numbers but in their sublimely divine vocation… Geographically, ethnically and politically the Jews do not attract attention in any special manner and do not count among the more important nations of the world. But according to the religious divisions of humanity, the Jews, by the will of God, hold first place among the races of the earth, so that from this aspect humanity is divided into Jews and non-Jews; the Jews chosen by God to preserve and to give back to the world the true religion, and the non-Jews or Gentiles ('goyim' in Hebrew) fallen in the worship of false gods awaiting liberation by Israel. Who are Christians? Differing from the Jews, Christians do not belong to any determined human family: they can derive from the Jewish population – in fact the Founder and the first apostles are Jews as well – as from any other people, because they are a purely spiritual society. The Christians believe that their founder, Jesus Christ still lives. Who is Jesus Christ? Christians believe in the only God of Abraham, Isaac and Jacob, but in God in three divine and distinct persons – the Father, the Son and the Holy Ghost. According to the Christians Jesus Christ is the Son of God made Man, the revealer, the redeemer, the sanctifier of all men … Christians feel that they are the spiritual children of the great patriarch Abraham … [Antisemitism] is a movement of antipathy, a movement in which we Christians can have no part … In common with the Jews Christians hold the sublime doctrine of Moses, that all men are created in the likeness of God, sons of God, therefore brothers, and called upon to show this brotherhood by observing the Mosaic laws. The best moralists recognize this. This Decalogue is an unchangeable and universal code, which can be likened to nothing else in any civilization either old or new. After more than thirty centuries the Decalogue remains the indispensable basis of human progress and of lasting pace, and your synagogues, as sanctuaries of the Holy Covenant of God, remain and prove perpetually this fact to the whole world … Christians reciting the Psalms of the Bible, which are the highest form of prayer that man has ever offered to his Creator, are in a continuous unity of prayer with the Jews. It is not without a special design of Providence that the Catholic Church has retained as Her official prayers the same prayers as those of the Jews … Hearing and singing this hymn, the non-Jewish Christians, having come from the Gentiles where they were submerged in the shadow of death, in the worship of false gods, recognize that they owe the true faith to the Jewish people by the mercy of God … In this continuous dialogue of prayer with the Jews and not only with deceased Jews who existed in pre-Christian times, but also with the Jews now living, Christians aspire to live with them a common faith and a common sharing of the gifts of divine mercy. For this reason Christians feel united to the Jewish people in a bond of special affection and they love them, not only because they must love all men without distinction, but also because of a special predilection, by duty of a particular spiritual relationship, like older brothers, in the faith of the God of Abraham, of Isaac, and of Jacob … The Jewish-Christian friendship must be understood. It could not aspire to the fusion of two unreconcilable religions. The contrast remains essential … It is a mystery of Divine Providence that allows for particular ends we cannot understand, the differences of mind and human will. But as a mystery and like all mysteries it is the object of our admiration and, understood in this sense, can never give rise to hate and aversion but on the contrary, show respect of conscience to the highest degree … Jews and Christians must convert themselves to God, each in the intimacy of his own conscience, becoming friends of God and friends among themselves, each with mutual respect of conscience. In this way, too, Hebrew-Christian friendship excludes that unintelligent proselytism which wishes to impose, at all costs, an unfelt Christian faith upon his Jewish brother, and it prefers to confide to God the care of illuminating hearts and directing them in his ways."

In 1966, Yad Vashem awarded Father Pierre-Marie Benoît the title of Righteous Among the Nations. In 1978, he wrote to Yad Vashem:

"What I did for the Jewish people, what I did to merit being called 'Father of the Jews' is but an infinitesimal contributon of what should have been done to prevent this most heinous and satanic slaughter of some six million Jews, which will undoubtedly remain mankind's foulest disgrace – a shame affecting all those who paricipated or allowed it to happen … It is by divine providence that the Jewish people wishes to live and fulfill its divine goals – first, for its own good, then for the good of all humanity … Long live the State of Israel. May the God of Abraham, Isaac, and Jacob be of help to it."

In 1984, the French government conferred the *Légion d'Honneur* on Benoît. At his request, the French chief rabbi and former wartime clandestine associate Jacob Kaplan placed on his shoulders the honorific accolade.

Bertrand, Paulette
Bertrand, René & Gaby
France

*I*t was midday, March 20, 1944, and the Mizrahi family had gathered for lunch in their home in Marseilles, France, when the bell rang at the downstairs door. Mrs. Estelle Mizrahi descended the steps to open it and was confronted by three men in civilian clothes. One of them shot out, "Algazy?" Mrs. Mizrahi responded: "She is not here," thinking of her mother, who lived elsewhere. The man continued: "Menasse?" Again the response: "He's not here," *thinking of her brother-in-law living at a different address. Then came the question: "Miz-rahi?" and she answered, "Yes, it's here." At this, the man blurted out: "German police!" and the three rushed up the stairway. They were actually French policemen who had been tipped off about this Jewish family and had come to arrest them and turn them over to the Germans.*

Mordehay (Marcel) and Estrella (Estelle) Mizrahi had arrived in France from Turkey many years before. Turkey's neutrality in the war probably was one of the things that had saved the Mizrahis from harm by the Germans. In 1944, as Turkey edged closer to the Allied camp, the Germans decided to strike at Turkish Jews in occupied France. Dashing into the Mizrahi apartment, the policemen immediately arrested all those present, including Mrs. Mizrahi's husband, Marcel, his mother, and the two sons, Robert, aged 13, and Victor, aged 8. It had been previously agreed by the Mizrahi family, and those knowing of their whereabouts, that the front door would only be opened after three consecutive rings of the doorbell. The policemen had done just that, probably tipped off by an informer.

In the meantime, in the downstairs apartment, 22-year-old Paulette Bertrand happened to be visiting her parents during the lunch break and the noise and commotion upstairs had attracted her attention. She instinctively realized what was happening: the people upstairs were about to be taken away and deported to an unknown destination. Not losing any time, Paulette acted quickly and decided to save at least the two Mizrahi boys. Running upstairs, she shouted to Robert and Victor: "Children, don't you know that Mother doesn't want you to be here?" and immediately told them to return to their presumptive house downstairs. The three policemen did not interfere. Once downstairs, she had them flee through a window in her parents' groundfloor apartment and told them to head for her married brother's

Gaby and René Bertrand

house. When they were out of sight, Paulette hurried to the Menasse couple to break the bad news that their in-laws had been arrested and urge them to immediately vacate their home, for the police would surely be on their way there. The whole dramatic episode had lasted a bare 20 minutes.

In the meantime, from the Bertrand home, the two boys watched helplessly as their parents passed by in a German vehicle. They were never to see them again. Two days later, Robert and Victor Mizrahi were secretly whisked out of Marseilles to the small town of Aurillac, where arrangements were made for the two brothers to be taken in by two local families. The two boys' parents were deported to the concentration camps and did not survive. Their two sons, Victor and Robert, escaped a similar fate – thanks to the spur-of-the-moment act of Paulette Bertrand, who just happened to be visiting her parents, the downstairs neighbors of the Mizrahi family.

In 1997, Yad Vashem conferred upon Paulette Bertrand, as well as her brother René Bertrand and his wife, Gaby, the title of Righteous Among the Nations.

Bielecki, Jerzy
POLAND

*I*t was the most daring escape from Auschwitz camp – in broad daylight! The story begins in May 1940, when 18-year-old Jerzy Bielecki was arrested in the village of Michałowice near Kraków with several of his companions as they made plans to flee occupied Poland by crossing into Slovakia. They had hoped to reach France (still unoccupied then) to join up with a new Polish army being organized there to continue the struggle against Germany. Taken to Nowy Sącz, Bielecki underwent several interrogations accompanied by beatings with a whip and repeated blows to the jaw. When an SS man hit him over the head with a gun, Bielecki lost consciousness for a while. Forced to sign a confession, without having a chance to read the contents, he and his arrested companions were taken to Tarnow and then, after several days there, by train to Auschwitz. "I still didn't have any idea where I was." The men were ordered off the train under another hail of blows. Germans ran around beating the prisoners with truncheons and whips while cursing them. "Polish swine!" they shouted, "you haven't come to a holiday camp!" Then the camp commander addressed them, repeating that this was not a holiday camp but a concentration camp. If anyone wanted a free ride out, he could walk over to the high-voltage barbed wire fence. After the speech, the camp drill began: first pushups, then running around the square, followed by a combination of running, crawling, and rolling on the ground. When night fell, Jerzy Bielecki fell down on his plank bed, exhausted.

The next morning, the men were moved to a former Polish military barracks, with three or four to a room. Reveille was at 4.30 a.m., followed by physical exercises and the morning roll call. The German-appointed "block leader" (*Blockführer*) was a former criminal. After a sip of black coffee came a series of tortuous physical exercises – running around the barracks, with repeated falls to the ground, crawling, getting up, and duck-style walking. Those who couldn't keep up were taken aside and kicked and beaten by *kapos* (group leaders, also prisoners). After a noon roll call, the "sports" events resumed: running in the dust and a froglike version of deep-knee bends. Since the men were by then physically exhausted, the kapos started beating them on their backs, forcing them to sing ("I was once in Auschwitz camp, Holla-Ho. So many months, days and years, Holla-Ho. But I happily think, I happily think, with delight and joy, with delight and joy, of my relatives far away"). This routine was followed in the coming days. After two weeks, the prisoners were moved to a new place – 40 people to a room and straw mattresses to sleep on. Work meant carrying rocks from the nearby Sola River, a tributary of the Vistula, breaking them up with hammers into gravel, which they spread beside the barbed wire fence.

Once Bielecki tried to escape the "sporting" routine of running around buildings by running out of the group and joining the stone workers. As he turned a corner he ran straight into an SS man. Jerzy was hit with a blow to the jaw which knocked him him onto a pile of stones. "I wanted to get up, but he's kicking me, and I fall back on the stones. Now the kapo comes towards me with a stick, kicks me and hits me … My cheek has a hole right through it, I lost two teeth from the kicking. Blood running down my cheek and neck, I'm covered in blood. That's how they did me over." At the so-called camp dispensary, one of the prisoners pinned together parts of Jerzy's face with the help of some instrument. "I wore it for few days, then took it off."

Bielecki was then assigned to a detail digging ditches for a new road in the camp. From September 1941, the prisoners were allowed to write one or two letters a month to relatives, as well as to receive mail from them, including food packages, with the exception of liquor and medicines. Some of the parcels were stolen by prison guards. In the meantime, the camp was expanding, with thousands more arriving. In 1943, Bielecki was tattooed, with an instrument that looked like a pen, with a needle sticking out at the end and inking coming out when the needle was pressed into the skin. Bielecki recalled that before the gas chambers were built, they used to kill people in ditches. When the ditch was full, they dropped calcium chloride on top of the victims and poured water over it. This created gas and the people suffocated. Afterwards they filled up the ditch with earth. Later, the order came to remove all the corpses and burn them. "It was hell for the prisoners who had to do it. Dante's Inferno is nothing compared to those decomposed corpses. The prisoners had to pile up the remains and burn them with gasoline."

The first experimental gas chamber was in a former peasant's home. Before that, in August and September 1941, after the German attack on the Soviet Union, some of the Russian prisoners of war as well as sick people from the camp hospital were shot in Block 11. Then the basement windows were sealed with sandbags and others were gassed there. The affiliated camp, Birkenau, was built during this time. to accommodate the large influx of Russian POWs. The Germans were especially cruel to the Russian POWs – worse than to the Poles. Later, the gas chambers were built. The Birkenau gas chambers had "changing" rooms: a big room to undress in, another for taking a "bath" – men, women, and children all together.

After the doors were sealed, the light would go out and Zyklon B pesticide pellets would be dropped through vents in the ceiling. After 20 minutes to half an hour the doors were opened, the bodies removed, and the chamber ventilated. The corpses were taken to an upper story and thrown into cremation ovens. The ashes were then collected and dumped into the nearby Soła River. Trains carrying thousands of Jews arrived from everywhere in Europe. Some transports went straight to the gas chambers. Others went through a selection process. Generall, healthy people of a younger age could survive the selection. Four crematoriums operated full time in Birkenau; a fifth was located in the main Auschwitz camp.

In August 1943, Bielecki was assigned work in a unit (called "kommando") repairing agricultural equipment and also bicycles. Then, in return for a favor to an SS man (exchanging his broken bike for a new one instead of fixing it), Jerzy got an easier assignment – assistant to the bookkeeper, Janek, located in a block that also stored grain collected by prisoners from the surrounding fields. Jerzy's and Janek's job was to weigh the grain, sort it, and get it into large sacks. Most were shipped to Germany; some to the camp bakery. Three SS men were assigned as supervisors. There, one day, a group of Jewish women, with scarves on their head, blue skirts, and gray aprons walked in. One tall black-haired girl smiled at Jerzy as she passed him, and evidently he was immediately smitten. He later went to see the women's work place on the second floor, where they repaired flour sacks. Janek introduced Jerzy to the smiling girl. "This is Jurek (Jerzy), and this is Cyla Cybulska from Lomza." The two shook hands. The other women noticed how Jerzy stared at her for some time. The two took a liking to each other and decided to meet again secretly.

Jerzy Bielecki (courtesy of the Jewish Foundation for the Righteous, New York)

"I was very attracted to her and I wanted to see her as often as possible. The best time was the lunch break. We fed the girls with whatever we had in the kitchen: oats, potatoes, etc.... Cyla and I used to meet in a little corridor which was the way up to the storage loft. Sometimes we closed the door so as not to be seen by Cyla's girlfriends. We talked during those lunch breaks. We told each other about our lives, our short twenty-three-year-old lives. Sometimes we walked all the way to the door of the loft to have some privacy. There Cyla cried and there as well we kissed each other. Cyla knew already that her parents, sister, and two brothers were dead ... There isn't too much to say, I think we fell deeply in love ... In these conditions

it was a gift from heaven for me, the fact that I could fall in love with a girl, that I could experience this feeling in the camp. For me, Cyla was a hope, that with luck we would survive together, and would never part. It was clear to me that one day she would be my wife. The meetings were the flame of hope in my life in the camp."

Of course, things like that were strictly forbidden. Consorting with a woman, a prisoner, might be dealt with by 25 truncheon blows, or endless beatings that could result in death. "It was strictly forbidden, but life is life, feelings are feelings, love is love, and we took a risk for this love." One day, a weeping Cyla told Jerzy that her school friend had been shot for smuggling potatoes out of the kitchen. This drove Cyla into a deep depression, and the feeling that she would not survive the camp. Jerzy consoled her; "Don't worry, Cyla, I will get you out of here." Of course, she didn't take him at his word, since escape from Auschwitz was impossible. But as for Jerzy, gradually he became obsessed with the idea of escape, since if Cyla stayed in the camp she would surely die there. But how to escape? One night Jerzy had a nightmare in which he saw Cyla being led to the gas chamber. "I was standing on the other side of the fence. I could see her walking naked, with other girls. I was screaming, 'Cyla ! Cyla!' She couldn't hear me. I woke up terrified. The dream convinced me that we had to escape." As for himself, after four years in that dreadful camp, Jerzy believed he would somehow survive even if they liquidated the camp. "My body after a couple of years was very tough. By then, I hadn't caught any diseases for a long time. I was 24, a well-built young man. But now mere survival was no longer so important. The moment had come when Cyla's life was more important to me than my own … If it hadn't been for Cyla, I would never have tried to escape from Auschwitz." He then confided to Cyla his decision. They talked about their future. "I planned to finish technical school and Cyla was going to raise the children. How were we going to raise them? In such a way as to be both Catholics and Jewish." Cyla spoke about her hard-working father, and her brothers, one of whom had had an affair with a maid who worked for the family. Jerzy told her about his life and friends – Edek, arrested with him, who had died in the camp. He didn't tell her exactly about the escape plan – only that they would survive by escaping. "I didn't mention the plan for safety's sake. If the information got out we could all be hanged." Even the disclosure of a plan to escape meant the death penalty.

The plan was for Jerzy's friend Tadek (Tadeusz Srogi), who was responsible for the SS clothing store, to secretly get an SS uniform – trousers and jacket. Jerzy would then use it to walk out of the camp together with Cyla, as a captive on the way to further interrogation at another place. When Jerzy first asked Tadek for an SS uniform, the latter was more than shocked – he was terrified – and asked for time to think about it, since if discovered he could pay with his life. At first, Tadek listened to Jerzy's detailed plan of escape, and then several weeks passed. Jerzy assured the hesitant Tadek that he had contacts outside the camp who would help him once he fled, which was far from the truth. When Tadek agreed it was on condition that he be included together with his girlfriend, Regina. At this point, when Jerzy's *kapo* (prisoner group leader, himself a prisoner) was caught drunk and was dismissed, the SS appointed Jerzy as a temporary kapo replacement. He now had more freedom of movement. Tadek then decided to smuggle out the SS uniform in two stages: the trousers under his belt, and the larger, heavier jacket in a garbage container. The uniform was hidden between the sloping roof and one of the ceiling boards in the grain warehouse. This was the first step. During the next four weeks Tadek delivered a holster and the insignia of an *SS-Rotterführer*. The idea behind the lower rank was that the other SS officers would not necessarily have to know him if they crossed one another's paths. Tadek was also able to get a camp entrance and exit pass from one of the uniforms left by an SS officer. When that officer realized he had left the pass in his uniform pocket, he hurried back to Tadek's warehouse. But it could not be found among the pile of SS jackets there. The SS officer had the feeling that Tadek had stolen the pass, but he could not prove it. Passes were of several colors: white, green, blue, and yellow. For security reasons, the colors were changed every few days. Using the stolen pass as a model, Jerzy was able through his contacts at the local printing shop to have fake passes printed – seven or eight passes on differently colored paper. Jerzy also received a knapsack from Tadek and a pair of boots for Cyla, smuggled out of the camp shoemaking shop in exchange for cigarettes. Jerzy's knowledge of German was fairly good, having studied the language for six years in elementary and high school. Besides, Jerzy thought to himself, many of the SS guards originated from different countries – Lithuania, Latvia, Romania, even Denmark. They didn't speak perfect German themselves; some hardly spoke any. "And if I had to face a German, I could be a *Volksdeutsch* [ethnic German] from one of those countries."

The decision was to make the escape on a Friday. Tadek had by this time taken fright and backed out. The Thursday before the SS had changed the color of the passes to brick red. "Why on Friday? I thought: I was arrested on a Friday, I came to Auschwitz on a Friday. I wanted my luck to change this time. This time I wanted to leave the camp on Friday, July 21. On Thursday the 20th I told Cyla that the next day around 3 p.m. I would come to her work place (she was now in the knitting 'kommando') dressed as an SS man, and I would take her away for interrogation." That hour was a good time, since it was four hours before the last roll call, when Cyla's absence would be noted and the alarm sounded. "The night of the 20th to 21st of July was the longest night of my life. I didn't sleep at all. I reviewed all the possible scenarios of our escape. I prepared answers for guards, SS men, and gendarmes in case we met them on the road." It was to be his last night on this hell on earth. "My last night either way, no matter what."

The following morning, Jerzy appeared at work as scheduled. "Time was passing very slowly. Every minute was a century." At five to three, Jerzy told his German supervisor, Titze, that he had to step out for a while to get sausages – a practice he had begun these past weeks to get Titze used to the idea. Jerzy quickly ran to the grain store to get his SS uniform. He removed his striped jacket, pants, and shoes. "It has begun. There is no way back now." Dressed in an SS uniform, with the standard German army belt buckle insignia *Got mit uns* ("God is with us"), and sunglasses, and sweating profusely from tension and fear, Jerzy proceeded to Cyla's work place. As he passed prisoners clearing the road with spades and brooms, they interrupted their work and pulled their hats off, as required before an SS officer. When he entered Cyla's work place, the girls sitting behind the machines sped up their sewing. A *kapo* approached Jerzy and asked for instructions. Then an SS woman also appeared. Jerzy said that he was from the political department (i.e., Gestapo) and he had to take a certain woman for interrogation. Who is she, he was asked? Jerzy pulled out a slip of paper, where Cyla Cybulska's name appeared. The SS woman ordered the *kapo* to get her. When Cyla appeared, Jerzy asked her: Cyla Stawiska?" She nodded her head and lowered her eyes. Jerzy: "Number 29558?" She nodded her head. He told her to follow him. He shook hands with the SS woman and gave the Nazi salute. Outside, Cyla walked several meters ahead of Jerzy. Approaching the checkpoint tower of the camp exit in the direction of Budy, Jerzy recalled his tense mood: "I am so nervous … I am completely soaked with sweat. I am walking again. Forty, thirty, twenty-five meters to the post. I see the SS man coming down from his observation platform. Tall, no hat. He buttons his jacket on the way down. He tightens his belt, puts his hat on. Fifteen, ten, five meters. I say loudly: "Heil Hitler!" and then he takes the pass out of his pocket, and hands it to the guard. *"Oberscharführer*! *Eins; eins nach Budy und zurűck"* ("One guard, one prisoner, to Budy and back"). The guard inspects the pass. "Thousands of thoughts go through my mind. He looks at Cyla and at me, folds the pass, and hands it back to me." Jerzy says *Danke* ("Thanks") and orders Cyla to continue. "I'm convinced that he has noticed something wrong, but he also thinks that I have a gun, because I have the holster. He has let me go now, I think, but in a second he will pull his gun out and I will hear the scream: HALT! I wait for it. It's impossible to describe what I went through in those couple of minutes or few seconds." But nothing of the sort happened. A few dozen meters further, and the two were on their way from Auschwitz to Budy. Incredible! The two had walked out of Auschwitz, the most guarded Nazi concentration camps, in broad daylight, and through one of its guarded gates.

When he saw a stork fly by, Jerzy felt like shouting with happiness. The two turned off the road to a trail that led to some marshy ground, where they rested for a while among the reeds. "Thousands of butterflies were flying there." Jerzy said, "Cyla, Cyla we are free," and Cyla said, "Jurek, I can't believe it," and started to cry. The two moved on. After a while they reached the bank of the Soła River. At around eight in the evening, they heard the camp siren. "It had to be for us. It went on for a minute or so. It was the signal for all checkpoints to tighten controls and prepare for a chase … But in my mind this siren was the siren of freedom." The two continued, moving only at night, hiding during daylight hours in bushes, forests and corn fields, and avoiding being caught by German guards. From time to time, the two embraced each other. At times, Cyla felt she could not go on walking aimlessly, through the heat and sometimes drenching rain, but Jerzy urged her to keep going. "We escaped together and we'll go on together." Approaching an isolated house, Jerzy decides to try his luck. He will tell the people inside that he's an escaped forced laborer from a camp in Wrocław and is trying to get back to Cracow. He knocked on the door and heard a woman's voice – in German: "*Herman bist du da*? ("Herman, are you there?"). Jerzy and Cyla quickly ran away. In another near-fatal encounter, deep in the night, Jerzy and Cyla ran into a German patrol. With his SS uniform, it seemed at first fine, until upon further questioning by the patrol, suspicions arose about these two people. Jerzy and Cyla again fled for their lives, with bullets whistling past their ears. They managed to reach a nearby forest. Totally exhausted, they fell asleep.

It was the fifth day of their escape. Jerzy's plan was to go to his uncle's farm in the village of Muniakowice. Cyla worried about how they would react to her, as a Jewish girl. "I hadn't thought about that yet. We talked about religion again and our future. We always ended these discussions by agreeing that it was premature to worry about the future now. Soon we would be a married couple anyway. I was always a religious person. Going to church with my parents, serving as altar boy. My stay in the camp had shaken my faith. When I watched the macabre happenings there I thought about whether God existed. Because if he did, how could he let things like that happen? No punishment for murderers, but punishment for the suffering prisoners. Many times I felt a grudge against God. Why did he let us suffer? Why had he abandoned us? I knew that similar thoughts had shaken the faith of many prisoners. But some believed even more strongly because of what was happening. When they were dying of hunger, or disease, they commended their souls to God. I came to think that what is really important is to try to be a good human being. Religion itself didn't matter to me anymore."

On the seventh day of their escape, Jerzy decided to try his luck and approach a farmer out in the field. "Sir, I am in great need ... I am hiding here in your oats ... I am Polish and a Christian ... I ran away from a labor camp near Wrocław. I am trying to get to Kraków. Please, please, help me, sir." After staring at Jerzy for a while, then further reflecting, the man told Jerzy to stay hidden in the field until dark, then head for his cottage. Jerzy had some doubts. It sounded too easy. Maybe the man would report him to the police? Jerzy convinced myself that if he had reported him to the police, they would already have been there looking for him. After 10 p.m. he decided to head in the direction of the cottage. Jerzy parted from Cyla, telling her that if he did not return, she was to continue to a certain place in the Kraków area and ask for a certain Słomniki. Another alternative was to head to Muniakowice and look up his uncle, Jan Marusa. As it turned out, these emergency measures were not needed, as Jerzy was heartily welcomed in the farmer's cottage, where his wife prepared some food for him. Gaining their confidence, he then asked whether he could bring his "sister," waiting outside. They naturally agreed.

Jerzy asked for directions to get from this area of Polish, presently annexed to Germany, to the other part of occupied Poland, known as the *Generalgouvernement.* The border crossing point was near the next village of Bachowice. With the help of another Pole, Jerzy and Cyla made it safely toward Michałowice, near Kraków, "the very place where my adventure had started four years earlier," and continued toward Muniakowice, their destination, the home of uncle Jan Marusa. When Jerzy felt that his presence was making his uncle a bit nervous, he decided to head for his grandparents in Janikowice – two kilometers further on. When the villagers began to show too great an interest in the two guests, it was decided to move on. But at this point Jerzy's mother turned up with Jerzy's youngest brother, Karol. She was not too happy to see her son together with the Jewish Cyla, and one day she arranged for Cyla to be sent elsewhere. Jerzy was able to catch up with her, and they embraced. The two arrived at another uncle, Leon Banasiak, in the village of Przemeczany, and were welcomed by Aunt Kasia. People were beginning to talk. Afraid that news would eventually reach the Gestapo ("The birds on the roof are singing that you are Auschwitz escapees and that Cyla is Jewish," Leon told Jerzy), it was decided that Jerzy and Cyla, for the moment, should split up – Cyla going with a poor elderly farmer called Czernik to a nearby village. At the end of September 1944, Jerzy's mother arranged for Jerzy to be moved elsewhere, to Kozienice, near Igołomia, some 50 kilometers away. The two parted. Cyla had tears in her eyes, and the two swore fidelity to each other, and to meet immediately at the war's end. It was nearly 40 years before they would see each other again.

After the liberation by the advancing Russians Jerzy went to find Cyla. It was February 9, 1945, and the ground was covered with snow. He was told that Cyla had left four days earlier for Kielce to take a train. "Poor child, she waited for you for so long. Every day she went to the top of the hill and looked for you." Indeed, she had waited for Jerzy since January 12, when the Russians liberated her area before they occupied the area where Jerzy was staying. He had missed her, and with the war over, and no news of Cyla, Jerzy moved to Kraków and he completed his high school studies; then to the School of Technology, where he met Stenia, and they married in November 1946. He was then told that a postcard had arrived from Sweden with news that Cyla was there and seriously ill. A bit later, Jerzy was falsely informed that Cyla had died in a Stockholm hospital.

Cyla was indeed in Sweden, and very much alive, remaining there for five years. From there, she was herself also purposely misinformed, via mail from Poland – that Jerzy had not returned from his partisan unit, and was considered lost. Cyla married and moved to the United States with her husband. Some 35 years later she was told by her maidservant, a recently arrived Polish girl, that she had seen a story on Polish television of the escape from Auschwitz, of a man also very much alive, and of a girl named Cyla Cebulska. So Jerzy was alive and, as it turned out, was residing in Nowy Targ. She called him on the phone. "Jureczku, do you recognize my voice" – "Who is it? Who is it?" – "What do you mean who, your Cylutka." – "Are you alive?" – "Why should I be dead?" – "I heard you died in a hospital in Sweden." – "Who told you that?" – "Auntie Czernik." – "Impossible! And you didn't die in the forest?" – "Where did you get that idea?" – "Auntie Czernik ..." Everything became clear. Jerzy's relatives had concocted the whole story to separate the two, so that Jerzy, a Catholic, would not marry Cyla, a Jewess. Soon after, Cyla flew to Poland to meet Jerzy. It was 1983, 39 years after they had parted in tears, and both now had families of their own.

The Auschwitz museum preserves the frantic Gestapo report of the escape of Jerzy and Cyla, with urgent instructions to other Gestapo affiliates in Poland to apprehend the two – dead or alive. In 1985, Yad Vashem awarded Jerzy Bielecki the title of Righteous Among the Nations. In 1998, Bielecki was part of a delegation of 50 persons honored with the Righteous title who were invited to Israel to participate in the country's 50th anniversary celebrations.

Biliewicz, Piotr

BELARUS

*B*efore the war, Celia Cymer had befriended Piotr Biliewicz at the school they both attended. The Biliewicz family owned a large farm in Lapushino. Piotr Biliewicz, the youngest of four brothers, and his parents, Jan and Maria, ran the farm with the help of hired hands. During the German occupation of the area, the Jews were confined in the Sharkowszczyzna ghetto. In May 1942, a month before the ghetto's liquidation, Piotr made his way there and told the 17-year-old Celia of the fate that awaited the ghetto's inhabitants. Celia did not seem to take Piotr's words too seriously; or perhaps she did but would not act alone. In her words, "At the time my family was intact: mother, father, four sisters, and two brothers. Would I abandon them? No way. We would stick it out together." Then came "that cursed day," with the local militia participating in the carnage. "Bullets were flying everywhere; people were falling like flies; but we ran and ran, not knowing where to."

Running for her life in the nearby forest with her ten-year-old sister, Slava, Celia found herself huddling in the woods with many other Jews: men, women, and children. "Some were very badly wounded, some were dying, and many were already dead. And who should show up but Piotr, risking his life looking for us. He had been combing the woods for al-most a week, but he found us! We were scared, hun-gry, and cold. He dragged us to his farm, which was some distance away." Not wanting the two girls to be seen on the farm in broad daylight, Piotr hid them in the tall corn, then at night he smuggled them into the barn. There he prepared a dugout, and at night he would secretly bring them food.

Piotr Biliewicz (center) with Zalman and Slava Cymer at Yad Vashem

But the two sisters could not stay there for long. There was the serious problem of being discov-ered by some of the shep-herds in the employ of the Bieliewiczes who, in the words of the Cymer sisters, were making it a game to turn in Jews and collect considerable rewards from the Germans. Then there was the risk to the Biliewicz family, for those on whose property Jews were discovered were rewarded with torture and death. Some of the locals were on the lookout day and night for Jews on the run that they could turn the over to the Germans in return for a reward.

Celia and Slava decided to follow many other Jews who were heading for the nearby Glybokie ghetto after Jewish emissaries sent by the Germans into the woods promised that no harm would befall them. In Glybokie, they met their mother, two sisters, and other rela-tives. The ghetto was bursting at the seams. What Celia and Slava learned once inside the ghetto was that in order to make room for the new arrivals the Germans had exterminated about 2,000 people.

Again Piotr made his way into the ghetto. He put on two yellow stars, entered the ghetto as a Jew, took Celia to a wagon waiting outside, removed the yellow star, and, as retold by Celia, "off we went in the opposite direction as though we were gentiles. We had no papers, no identification of any kind. The road was swarming with SS. How we made it back to the farm only God knows. But by nighttime we were at his home." On the way to the farm, who should they run into but Celia's brother, Zalman. He was on his way to Glybokie after having spent some time in the woods. On the way there, as Zalman tells it, "I saw a wagon approaching, with the driver signaling to me from a distance with his hand on his mouth. As I got closer I could not believe my eyes. It was Piotr, the gentile who had lived in one of our rented rooms in Sharkowszyzna as a schoolboy, and he was now transporting Celia, with two Germans sitting behind. I could not utter a word, and I understood that Piotr was saving my sister Celia." It turned out that Piotr had not consulted his parents before bringing Celia to the farm.

In the meantime, back in Glybokie, Slava and her family decided to head for Postav, which was her mother's birthplace, and she had three brothers there. The German death machine struck at them there too, in December 1942. Again Slava was running for her life. As told by her, during the shooting, "my mother and I started running away from the ghetto into the fields. My mother was shot dead and I received several wounds and remained lying in the field besides my dead mother. I played dead when the local peasants collected the corpses on horse sleds and threw them into a prepared pit. The rest of my family in the ghetto perished. During the night I crawled out of the pit and ran into the forest, covered in bloody rags. It took me several nights of roaming through the forest to find the Biliewicz farm in Lapushino." When she knocked on the door in the dead of night, Piotr stepped out, "and seeing me looking like an animal, took me to the steam shed. Being full of wounds and boils, with frozen feet, he washed me, covered my body with lard and draped me in linens. Because of my inhuman looks, he did not show me for more than a week to my sister Celia hidden on their farm. Slowly and lovingly he nursed me so that he could move me to the dugout under the barn, where Celia was hiding." The dugout was narrow, cold, wet, and full of huge rats. But the two girls were alive. Every day, when Piotr appeared in the dugout with food, he would raise and clasp his hands, and say: "God, when will this end?"

By this time, the girls' two brothers had joined them – fleeing from the Germans and their relentless search for Jews. Previously they had stopped by on occasion to await the end of a German raid on Jews in the forest. Now they asked the girls to make room for them in the dugout. The two brothers squeezed into the narrow tunnel built for two slender girls. "It was torture." Once a day, Piotr used to smuggle in food for the girls, but it was never enough, as Piotr had to hide from his parents the presence of four instead of two fugitives. Some of the family members started cracking under the constant pressure. "Yet they baked bread day and night, because every night Jews invaded the farm in search of food; they never refused and never asked for anything in return."

By the summer of 1943, as the suspicions of neighbors and farmhands grew, brother Zalman took Slava with him to a group of Jews hiding in the forest. Later she was attached to a partisan unit where she stayed until the arrival of the Soviet Army. Celia had stayed behind, but not for long. For, in the summer of 1943, all of a sudden, hundreds of Germans descended on the farm, which they used as headquarters for a large-scale operation to flush out partisans in the forest. Celia recalled that "Piotr and I hid out in the fields, and when darkness fell we ran for our lives toward the woods and the partisans. We joined them and became soldiers." There too, Piotr was of help, volunteering for dangerous assignments, risking his life to get guns for the Jews so that they could join the fighting force. Celia remembered him as a person for whom others always came first. "He was a very kind, rare, selfless, modest individual who didn't like to be praised and coddled. Nor did he ever accept remuneration of any kind for his extraordinary help … He completely forgot fear and devoted his life to saving others." Many years after the war, Piotr Biliewicz helped the Cymer family erect a monument in memory of the Jewish victims of Sharkowsczyzna.

In 1998, Yad Vashem recognized Piotr Biliewicz as Righteous Among the Nations.

Bindel, Hélène & René & Jean Pava, Clotilde

FRANCE

*M*ichel Deutscher, a refugee from Germany, and his wife, Claire, had fled to France in July 1939 on the eve of World War II together their three-year-old son, Guy, and had settled in Paris. At the start of the war, Michel enlisted in the French army, was taken prisoner by the Germans, and spent five years in a prisoner-of-war camp. Returning to liberated France in April 1945, he learned how his wife and son had miraculously been saved by strangers.

Upon her husband's imprisonment, Claire had rented an apartment near her brother Simon Dankowitz, who had owned a metallurgical company with a non-Jewish partner. When the French government forced Jews to relinquish ownership of their businesses (under the so-called Aryanization program), Simon ostensibly sold his rights to his partner, Mr. Robert, in whom he had great confidence. Before Simon was arrested and deported, he had told Claire that in the event of danger she was to contact his former partner, who would surely help her. On the transport, on the way to Auschwitz in August 1942, Simon had managed to drop off a postal card reminding his sister about the man she was to contact.

In July 1942, Claire Deutscher and her son were arrested during the mass arrest of foreign Jews in the capital, but the two were released in consideration of her husband's service in the French army and his current imprisonment in Germany. But Claire feared another arrest, so in August 1942, soon after her brother's deportation, she went to see her brother's former associate in the company's office in Bousségui. In Guy's words, "We knew no one else in Paris or elsewhere who could help us." To her great chagrin, the man, evidently overcome with fear, declined to be of any assistance. At a loss what to do next, she got up to leave. Her six-year old son remembers what happened next. "This only possible recourse having been exhausted, my mother knew very well that sooner or later we were fated to be deported" (as Jews and on account of their non-French nationality). Leaving the director's office in tears, she was stopped by the latter's secretary, Madame Hélène Bindel. Through the half-open door, she had overheard the whole conversation. "She, whom we did not personally know, spontaneously offered us her help and immediately undertook to have us hidden."

Claire and Guy were first sheltered for a few days in Hélène's small two-room apartment, which she shared with her husband, René, and their grownup son Jean in the Ivry-sur-Seine suburb. After a further short stay, with René's mother, the two were moved to Hélène's aunt, Clotilde Pava, who lived in a sixth-floor garret apartment on Rue Lafayette, Paris. There, Claire remained secluded for two years. As for Guy, in October 1942 he was enrolled in a boarding school in Vincennes, a Paris suburb, under a false name, with René claiming to be the boy's uncle. The Bindels arranged for Claire and Guy to meet secretly on occasions. Guy: "I remember very clearly those stolen moments (so incautious …) when we met for a few hours 'among ourselves.'" In May 1944, the Bindel son, Jean, active in the resistance in Montreuil aux Lions (Aisne) had Claire and Guy brought to him, and after providing both with false identities arranged for them to be hidden in the village until the liberation of France.

When the liberated prisoner-of-war Michel Deutscher learned the story of his wife's and son's rescuers, he expressed his effusive thanks to the Bindels. Moreover, as he wrote in his deposition to Yad Vashem, "Even after the war, we remained so close to one another that it would be no exaggeration to say that Hélène and René Bindel served as the grandparents our children lost in the Holocaust. For my wife and myself, they had become much closer than family." In Guy's words, the Bindels "were the only ones who were connected with the before and after of the war; the only ones with whom we could talk about everything … When my sister Sylvie was born in December 1945, when it was clear that none of our loved ones would ever return, we and they [the Bindels] became members of a single family." Guy Deutscher eventually studied engineering and specialized in experimental physics.

In 1982, Yad Vashem recognized Hélène and René Bindel, and their son, Jean, as well as Clotilde Pava, as Righteous Among the Nations.

Blaauw, Cornelia

Netherlands

*I*n 1961, Ruth Klein, representing the Israeli Ministry of Welfare, attended an international welfare conference in Arnhem, Netherlands. There she met Cornelia Blaauw, who served as a child-care inspector for the Dutch Welfare and Justice Ministries in Arnhem, and heard from her of her rescue of Jewish children during the war years. Upon her return to Israel, Mrs. Klein passed the information on to former Dutch residents living in Israel, and some had heard, indeed, of Cornelia Blaauw's beneficial activity on behalf of Jewish children. In 1965, Nico Visjager, a boy saved by Cornelia Blaauw, visited Israel and stayed on a kibbutz for some time before returning to the Netherlands to continue his studies. The story began to unfold.

Aliza Heyman, formerly Els Ortt, related that during the German occupation of the Netherlands she worked for the Dutch underground and lived in Haarlem, where she became acquainted with Cornelia Blaauw, a child welfare worker in charge of a child care center. Cornelia shared an apartment with Jacoba van Tricht, and both occasionally sheltered Jews in their home, especially children brought to them by Dutch underground operatives, such as a boy named Robert and a girl named Vera.

At the end of May 1943, Heyman learned that a Jewish family in Amsterdam, named Visjager, had received an order to report for deportation and wished to save their six-week-old boy, Nico. Aliza Heyman notified Cornelia Blaauw, who immediately went to Amsterdam to take the child from the parents. As young people, the parents felt they would be strong enough to survive the rigors of hard labor somewhere in Eastern Eu-

Cornelia Blaauw

rope, never suspecting that their destination was the Sobibor death camp, where with the exception of about two dozen people, over 34,000 Dutch Jews were gassed within hours of their arrival, and their bodies burned. Cornelia Blaauw promised to return the baby boy immediately upon the parents return from the "labor camp," and took the child back with her to Haarlem to join the other Jewish children already under her care. In adding little Nico to her charges, she considered it as nothing else but a natural extension of her dedicated rescue activity.

In August 1943, Cornelia Blaauw and Jacoba van Tricht decided to go on vacation on a farm in the Friesland region, up north. After finding reliable addresses for their refugee children, including placing Nico in a day-care center whose director was well known and trusted by Cornelia, and who agreed not to have the child entered in the center's register, the two women departed. "How little did we realize even then how great the dangers were that threatened us from all sides," Jacoba recalled. "Fate, however, was against us." One evening, the police raided the day-care center, looking for hidden Jewish children. They soon discovered that one of the boys, Nico, was not registered and immediately suspected that the child was Jewish. The nursery director immediately telegrammed Cornelia Blaauw at her vacation spot, and Cornelia dropped everything and hurried back to Haarlem to save the boy.

Interrogated by the police, the 40-year-old Cornelia Blaauw hit upon a contrived story that she felt would save the boy from deportation. She claimed that the baby was hers alone, but born out of wedlock. To add a bit of spice to her story, she revealed that she had had an affair with a German officer, unacceptable behavior for a child care worker in Dutch society under occupation, and this man had in the meantime been transferred to the Russian front. In fact her sick leave at the time corresponded to the time of the baby's birth. Asked the name of the doctor who had helped with the birth, Cornelia replied that her flat mate Jacoba van Tricht, a maternity nurse, had managed it all alone, and this also explained the lack of a birth certificate. Being a single woman, she feared that the registration of the boy born illegally would cost her her job as head of a nursery, and that is the reason the child was not properly registered.

After a nerve-wracking 24-hour interrogation, she convinced her interrogators and the child was returned to her, but not before being rebuked by a public prosecutor for her "inexcusable" conduct and her lack of moral deportment. But at last she got the necessary birth certificate that gave the child an official status. That same evening Cornelia returned with little Nico to her farm vacation spot in Friesland, for a well-deserved rest, with the boy totally unaware how close he had been to being deported to a concentration camp.

After the war, the boy's parents having failed to return from the camps, relatives consented with the Jewish Supervision Board for Cornelia Blaauw to continue to raise the child. When Nico reached the age of understanding, she revealed to him his Jewish identity and the fate of his parents. He continued living with her, first in Haarlem, then in Arnhem. After returning from a long vacation in Israel, he decided to study psychology at the university.

In 1966, Yad Vashem conferred on Cornelia Blaauw the title of Righteous Among the Nations.

Boom ten, Cornelia ("Corrie")

NETHERLANDS

Born in Amsterdam in 1892, Corrie ten Boom moved with her family to Haarlem, where she trained as a watchmaker and worked in her father's watch repair shop. Deeply religious Christians, of the Calvinist church, who still viewed the Jews as the Chosen People – it is reported that her father Casper ten Boom, in response to his son's comment of a Jewish person who had opened a watch store near to his own, that this was unfair competition – "Never speak like this. You must know that he is a fellow colleague. He belongs to the Jewish people, and that is a great honor." Once, the ten Booms watched as Jews were being rounded up. At this, Casper intoned, "These poor people." Corrie thought he had in mind the Jews. But as Casper continued, it became clear that he meant the Germans. "I pity the poor Germans, Corrie. They have touched the apple of God's eye."

As her brother Willem wanted to become a religious minister – to help out her family, Cornelia devoted herself to the family's watchmaker trade. Deeply religious like her Calvinist family, she also earned a certificate as a Sunday school teacher. In 1923, she started the

Triangle Club for women, teaching crafts, studying the Bible, and putting on yearly performances in a concert hall. In 1940, the Germans disbanded the club. During the war years, Corrie and her family became deeply involved in various underground activities, including help to Jews on the run. The ten Boom house was known affectionately as "Beje," which were the initials of the street where the family lived – Barteljorisstrasse. A certain Sluring, known as Uncle Herman, whisked children out of the Jewish Orphanage in Amsterdam, and Corrie helped find hiding places for them with the help of other organizations and a special clandestine cell. In her own words, "the group consisted of 30 young men between 16 and 20 years old, 20 young women in the same age group, 20 older women and 10 older men. The youngest was a boy of 11 who, for example, went around to 'clients' with a bag with shoes to be repaired, and in that way secretly passed on food coupons. At one point we got together in our home and planned a raid on the distribution office… Later, we obtained coupons with the help of employees working in these distribution offices."

When the ten Booms witnessed the Germans ransacking the furrier's store and the home of Mr. Weil, a Jewish neighbor, they arranged for him to be sheltered elsewhere. Then came the turn of Harry de Vries, who had converted to Christianity and was married to Cato, a Christian by birth, and feared arrest. One day, Harry came rushing to the ten Booms with the story that he had been forewarned by a Dutch Nazi sympathizer (a member of the NSB) that trouble was in store for him. When de Vries protested that he was no longer Jewish but a converted Christian, the NSB man shot back, "Who cares? Any Jew can convert to avoid trouble." The ten Booms arranged for the man and his wife to be taken in by a friendly Dutch person who was already hiding over a dozen Jews. Later the hiding place was raided by the Gestapo, but Mrs. De Vries was released when she told them that she was not Jewish. She rushed to the ten Booms to ask for their help in getting her husband released, but this proved to be impossible. Then came Mrs. Kleermaker, whose clothing store had been closed by the Gestapo, and she was afraid to return to her home. Casper's response was: "In this household God's people are always welcome," and she was taken in. As it proved too dangerous to keep Jews in their home in this way, in the open, after providing them with stolen ration cards the three Jews were moved to different locations. Many other Jews passed through the ten Boom household for brief stays before being helped to move elsewhere.

Before deciding to turn their home into a refuge for Jews, the ten Booms at first consulted with a friendly clergyman who lived just outside Haarlem. They first asked him whether he was prepared to shelter a Jewish woman and her baby. "They will almost certainly be arrested otherwise," Corrie added. The pastor frowned and he began lecturing Corrie. "Miss ten Boom! I do hope you're not involved with any of this illegal concealment and undercover business. It's just not safe! Think of your father! And your sister [Betsie] – she's never been strong!" At this, Corrie ran upstairs to get the baby and showed it to the pastor. "No, definitely not," he said. "We could lose our lives for this Jewish child." Corrie's father, Casper, entered the room and took the baby in his arms. Turning to the reluctant pastor, he said, "You say we could lose our lives for this child. I would consider that the greatest honor that could come to my family." At this the pastor excused himself and left the ten Boom house. Later, Corrie learned that the Gestapo had raided the place where the mother and baby had been referred and both were arrested and taken away.

With the decision made to build a secret hiding place, the place chosen was Corrie's upstairs room, where part of the space was blocked off by a double brick wall, in front of which was placed a built-in bookcase. The entrance to the secret hideout was through a sliding panel beneath the bottom shelf, two feet high and two feet wide. Mr. Smit, the underground man, assured Cornelia, "The Gestapo could search for a year. They'll never find this one." A warning system was also improvised in the form of a triangular wooden sign advertising "Alpina Watches." When the sign was in place in the dining room window, it meant that it was safe to enter. In addition, an alarm was installed near the top of the stairs – loud enough to be heard everywhere in the house – with buzzers all over the house and in the downstairs watch repair shop.

A system of coded messages was also agreed upon. "We have a woman's watch here that needs repair. But I can't find a mainspring. Do you know who might have one?" (meaning: "We have a Jewish woman in need of a hiding place and we can't find one among our regular contacts"). "I have a watch here with a face that's causing difficulty. One of the numbers has worked loose and it's holding back the hand. Do you know anyone who does this kind of repair work?" ("We have a Jew here whose features are especially Semitic. Do you know anyone who would be willing to take an extra risk?). "I'm sorry, but the child's watch you left with us is not repairable. Do you have the receipt?" ("A Jewish child has died in one of our houses. We need a burial permit").

The first Jew admitted to the hiding place was Meijer Mossel, a cantor in an Amsterdam synagogue. When he first came into the ten Boom house and saw the elderly Casper, he exclaimed, "One of the Patriarchs!" Casper ten Boom corrected him, "But a brother of the Chosen People!" Mossel had been a cantor in an Amsterdam synagogue. His wife and children were already in hiding on a farm. Corrie decided to rename him Eusebius, probably after one of the Church Fathers, but Mossel did not particularly like this. Finally it was decided that his new name would be Eusie Smit. Another hidden Jew, the 76-year-old Mary Itallie, posed a special problem because of her asthmatic coughing, but she was taken in. There were others whose names Corrie did not know, for under the circumstances it was sometimes better not to know the names of the people with whom one was in contact. Shlomo Ganor, who passed through the ten Boom

Corrie ten Boom pointing to the hiding place in the room. (Courtesy of the Corrie ten Boom Foundation, Haarlem, the Netherlands)

household on his way to another hiding place in the Friesland region, reported seeing more than 10 Jews there. Some of the hidden Jews stayed for short periods of time, such as a Mrs. Israels, a certain De Costa, and an Ascher, before being moved elsewhere, where some were eventually caught and deported. There were also non-Jewish people who stayed for various periods of time; they were fleeing from forced labor in Germany.

In the secret hideout, people would sit on the floor, using cushions. There were four permanent "lodgers" and those who stayed in the ten Boom household for a while before moving on to other addresses. The daily routine included cultural evenings to lift the spirits of the fugitives. Corrie's sister Elisabeth (Betsie) was especially active on the cultural front, giving concerts in the evening (violin and piano). There were also readings, Hebrew lessons (by Mossel), and Italian (by Mary Itallie). On Christmas 1943, the ten Booms also decided to celebrate the Jewish Hannukkah festival. A candelabrum was somehow found and placed on the piano. Each night one more candle was lighted, with Mossel reading the story of the Maccabees. Then all would sing some melancholy song. "We were all very Jewish those evenings," Corrie remembered. Mossel liked to exercise his cantorial expertise, and at times quite loudly. As Corrie recalled, he had a beautiful voice, mixed with pathos, joy, and sadness, and Corrie had to counsel him to keep his voice down. One such evening, a neighbor came to complain, "Do you think your Jews could sing a little more softly? We can hear them right through the walls."

One day, while Corrie was playing the piano when there was a knock on the door. A Jewish man and his wife stood there, trembling with fear and begging to be let in. "I brought them into the room and served them hot coffee. The man spilled the coffee from his trembling hands as he could not hold the cup. His teeth were chattering in fear." The decision was to have them stay overnight. Other problems arose that needed immediate attention. A Jewish woman was about to give birth and arrangements had to be made for her admittance into a hospital. In a certain hiding place, a child had died of diphtheria and had to be secretly buried. "The number of people helped rose day by day. Over 80 "divers" (those going underground) spent some time at the "Beje" – mostly seven at a time. Twelve was the maximum of permanent people. The nucleus consisted of Mossel, Itallie, and several other Jews, followed by three non-Jews fleeing the Germans for various reasons.

When people had to be moved to different addresses, Corrie went first to make sure that the house included a special secret shelter for people to flee to during emergencies, and she and her family checked on how the fugitives were being treated in their new hiding places. To finance operations, sometimes the well-to-do among the Jews gave money. Contributions were also collected from trustworthy people and monies also came from the ten Booms own resources. "We put out a lot of money from our own pocket, our business at the time was successful; everyone wanted his watch fixed." Corrie added amusedly, "Money was not the important thing in that period. Instead of 'making money' we lived in order to 'save people.'"

One day, Corrie was summoned to the Dutch chief of police, who told her that he was aware of her clandestine work and that some in his police force were sympathetic to this, with the exception of one man who was also an agent for the Gestapo, so that the utmost caution was necessary. As for the man, it was decided to get rid of him – by execution. At this, Corrie recoiled. "I have always believed that it was my role to save life, not to destroy it … Let us pray together now that God will reach the heart of this man so that he does not continue to betray his countrymen." The police chief nodded his assent but was puzzled by Corrie's response. This episode proved that too many people in Haarlem knew what the ten Booms were up to, but they decided that in spite of these mounting risks they had no choice but to keep on doing their charitable work. Corrie consoled herself: "We could not run away from it. Perhaps only when human effort had done its best and failed would God's power alone be free to work."

Sure enough, the ten Boom rescue operation could not go on too long without being detected. With so many people coming in and out of the house, "sooner or later, in Corrie's words, "we were going to make a mistake." Once, during lunch, Corrie saw a man staring through the window at all the people who had sat down to eat. On another occasion, someone on a ladder, washing the windows – although no one had hired him – stood motionless staring in. The ten Booms began to go over what to do in case of a sudden police raid. Corrie failed the first test. When suddenly asked, "Where are you hiding your nine Jews?" Corrie responded, "We have only six Jews now." She was told, "The answer is, 'What Jews! We don't have Jews here.'" A few nights later, with Corrie in bed, her underground friends tried again. Bursting into her room, they shouted "The Jews you're hiding, where do they come from?" Corrie said: "I don't know. They just come to the door." Rolf, one of her associates, threw his hat down. "No, no, no!" he shouted. "What Jews! There are no Jews! Can't you learn?" Gradually, with repeated drills, Corrie caught on, learning to lie – something hard for her to do since it went against her religious beliefs. Then came news of the arrest of Corrie's sister, Arnolda ("Nollie") van Woerden, together with Annaliese, a Jewish woman in her house. The Jewish woman was taken to Jewish Theater in Amsterdam (which had been converted to a detention house for Jews on their way to concentration camps), but Corrie's underground friends were able to get her out. As for Nollie, she was also moved to Amsterdam and imprisoned there. Corrie went to twice to see a jail doctor to plead for the release of her sister, arguing that her continued detention would become a burden to the State, which would have to support her six children. Nollie was released after seven weeks.

Then came the raid on the morning of February 28, 1943, during the family's weekly Bible study and prayer meeting, as Corrie lay in bed with a bad cold and high fever. In her half-conscious state, she heard voices, "Hurry! Hurry!" Sitting up in her bed, she saw people running past her toward the hiding place. She thought, "But I hadn't planned a drill for today!" She quickly realized that this was the real thing. She sprang from her bed and quickly slid incriminating papers into the hiding place; then, she pushed the panel down. Suddenly another man appeared. He too squeezed himself into the secret annex. After sliding down the panel again and replacing the bookshelf, Corrie got back into bed just as a man appeared. "So you're the ring leader!," he shouted at her. "Tell me now, where are you hiding the Jews?" She denied everything. The man began to look through her papers; then told her to get dressed and hurry downstairs. A soldier was guarding the rest of the group, including those who had come to attend the weekly prayer and Bible session. Kapteyn, a Dutch policeman turned interrogator, pushed Corrie against the wall and shouted: "Where are the Jews?" "There aren't any Jews here," she replied. Kapteyn slapped her hard across the face. "Where do you hide the ration cards?" "I don't know what you're – ." Kapteyn hit her again and Corrie fell back against the clock on the wall. He slapped her repeatedly, causing her head to jerk back. "Where are the Jews?" Another blow. "Where is your secret room?" Blood came out of her mouth and she began to lose consciousness. She cried out, "Lord Jesus, protect me!" At this, Kapteyn warned her, "If you say that name again I'll kill you." She then noticed that the triangular sign on the window sill was in place – a signal that the coast was clear. "Our home had been turned into a trap," she thought, as more of her underground colleagues showed up, unaware of what was happening inside. Why was the sign not removed? As it happened, when the police burst in, Betsie had pushed the triangle away; so forcefully that it broke. A German then said: "This must be a sign, eh?" Betsie was so taken aback by this remark that she said, "Yes."' The German then fixed the triangle and put it back in the window, which made people think that the house was safe, and so they came trooping in, and were promptly arrested.

Betsie had also undergone brutal treatment at the hands of Kapteyn. After discovering the old radio beneath the stairs, Kapteyn then turned to 82-year-old Casper ten Boom: "Law-abiding citizens, are you? You! The old man there, I see you believe in the Bible. Tell me, what does it say in there about obeying the government?" Casper calmly responded: " 'Fear God and honor the Queen.' " Kapteyn sid: "It doesn't say that. The Bible doesn't say that." Casper said: "No. It says, 'Fear God, honor the King.' But in our case, that is the Queen." Kapteyn roared back, "It's not King or Queen! We're the legal government now, and you're all lawbreakers."

With the initial interrogation over, the whole ten Boom family was moved to the local jail, as well as the others, a total of 35 people who worked closely with the ten Boom network – but the secret hiding place was not discovered. Then came the turn of the Gestapo. First in line was Casper ten Boom. The Gestapo chief addressed him: "I'd like to send you home, old fellow. I'll take your word that you won't cause any more trouble. Casper said: "If I go home today, tomorrow I will open my door again to any man in need who knocks." The Gestapo man shouted back: "Get back in line. *Schnell!* [Fast!] This court will tolerate no more delays." Passing his son Willem, Casper asked him to read Psalm 91 ("…*My refuge and my fortress; my God, in whom I trust. For he will deliver you from the snare of the fowler and from the deadly pestilence … You will not fear the terror of the night, or the arrow that flies by day …*") The prisoners were then loaded onto a van and taken to a jail in Scheveningen. There Corrie, still suffering from severe influenza, continued her coughing. In the jail's dispensary, she was given some medicine. Corrie asked one of the nurses for a Bible, and surprisingly she was later secretly handed the Four Gospels of the New Testament. Still with fever, Corrie was sent to solitary confinement for no apparent reason. Alone in the tiny dark cell, Corrie befriended a small black ant who appeared frequently through a crack in the floor. Corrie scattered some crumbs from her daily bread ration, "and to my joy he popped out almost at once. He picked up a heroic piece, struggled down the hole with it and came back for more. It was the beginning of a relationship."

In May 1944, Corrie was brought in for a series of interrogations by a German – Lieutenant Rahms. He tried, in his friendly way, to extract information from her on her underground connections, but could not make any progress. Corrie insisted on talking of her church activities and her help to mentally retarded people. "What a waste of time and energy?" Rahms remarked. "If you want converts, surely one normal person is worth all the half-wits in the world!" Corrie took him up on this and quietly replied. "The truth, Sir, is that God's viewpoint is sometimes different from ours … In the Bible I learn that God values us not for our strength or our brains but simply because He has made us. Who knows, in His eyes a half-wit may be worth more than a watchmaker. Or – a lieutenant." At this, Rahms stood up, "That will be all for today," and had a guard take her back to her cell.

Some of the imprisoned people were eventually released, sooner than expected, including Corrie's brother Willem, Herman Sluring, Peter van Woerden and his wife, Nollie. But Corrie's father died on March 9, 1944, after ten days of imprisonment, having falling ill. Good news came from Nollie, in a coded message, "All the watches [i.e., hidden Jews] in your closet are safe." A few days after the German guards were removed from the ten Boom home, the hidden people were secretly moved to another safe location. To Corrie's great satisfaction, Nollie was also able to smuggle in a complete Bible for Corrie. In June 1944, Corrie and sister Betsie were moved to the Vught camp inside the Netherlands where Corrie was assigned to the Phillips electronic factory in the camp. Her job consisted of measuring small glass rods and arranging them in piles according to length. There, Corrie learned that the man who had betrayed them was Jan Vogel, who had occasionally visited the watchmaker's shop for watch repairs. It turned out he had been a Gestapo agent for a long time. "I could kill him," was Corrie's reaction to the news. Her sister Betsie, however, reacted differently; she prayed for him, and asked God to forgive the man, which also caused Corrie to recite a prayer for her betrayer, "Bless him now and his family," she implored God. In September 1944, Corrie and Betsie were deported to Germany, taken there in a train with 80 women packed in a cattle car. After a four-day journey, the train arrived at the Ravensbrück camp. As she was marched into that dreaded women's concentration camp, with the Bible hidden inside her dress, Corrie wondered whether it was to this world that God had spoken his biblical message.

Before settling down in the putrid barracks, the women had to spend several nights in the open, in drenching rain. This affected Betsie severely, causing her to suffer from agonizing intestinal cramps. Then the women were told to undress and pass before a dozen SS men into the shower room. Corrie was able to hide her Bible under a stack of old wooden benches crawling with cockroaches, then secretly retrieve it. The two sisters were consigned to Barrack 8 and had to find a place in a bed already occupied by three women. From their bunks they could hear the screams of women being beaten by SS women guards. In this godforsaken place, Betsie began to organize a Bible-reading group. As they were still under quarantine, from time to time they had to undergo medical examinations, undressing in front of a group of doctors. On their second week there, they were moved to permanent quarters in a large dormitory, Barrack 28, with no beds but tiers of flea-infested bunks, where they had to crawl over other women to get to their assigned places. Nine women shared each bunk. Names were forgotten. Corrie became Number 66729, Betsie – 66730. "We were 1,400 people in one barrack that was really suited for only 400 … Jews were not treated any worse than other prisoners, meaning that non-Jews too were treated very badly." From the camp, around 100 kilometers north of Berlin, the prisoners could see the red glow in the sky; the result of the incendiary bombing of Berlin by Allied planes. Through it all, Betsie's spirit was not dimmed. The Bible reading comforted her, as she read from the New Testament (I Thessalonians): "Comfort the frightened, help the weak, be patient with everyone. See that none of you repays evil for evil, but always seek to do good to one another and to all." Turning to Corrie she said, "That's it! That's His answer. 'Give thanks in all circumstances!' That's what we can do. We can start right now to thank God for every single thing about this new barracks!" Betsie added that the crowding in the barracks had a certain advantage. "Since we're packed so close, that many more will hear!" She then continued, "Thank You for the fleas and for–." This was too much even for the very religious Corrie. "Betsie, there's no way even God can make me grateful for a flea." To which Betsie responded, " 'Give thanks in *all* circumstances.' It doesn't say, 'in pleasant circumstances.' Fleas are part of this place where God has put us." Corrie kept silent, but felt that Betsie may have gone a bit too far.

The daily routine began with a long 4:30 a.m. roll call in the morning cold, followed by the daily ration of bread and coffee, and then women went to their assigned work place – Corrie, Betsie, and many others to the Siemens factory. There Corrie and Betsie were made to push a heavy handcart to a railroad siding where they unloaded large metal plates from a boxcar and wheeled them to a receiving gate at the factory. At night, back in the dormitory, Betsie and Corrie held their daily Bible readings, with some women translating the Dutch version into other languages. This was followed by religious prayers of the various denominations, Protestant Lutheran, Catholic, and Greek Orthodox. Betsie's physical condition continued to worsen as the women were shifted from the Siemens plant to leveling some rough ground. As Betsie could not keep up, a women guard hit her across the face with her leather crop. With the increasing winter cold and rains, in November Betsie began coughing up blood. As her fever rose, she was taken to the camp dispensary, then released after three days, and assigned to a knitting group. Soon the cold in the dormitory and outside began to affect Betsie's legs, until one day she could not move them. Taken to the dispensary again, she died a week before Christmas 1944, at the age of 59.

Then, unexpectedly, Corrie ten Boom was released, on December 28, 1944, a week after her sister's death. She referred to it as "a blunder of man and a miracle of God." It happened as follows. "When my name was called, I was sure I would be killed. I hoped that they would shoot me, because this was the best death: you do not see anything nor do you feel anything. When I heard I would be released I did not dare believe it." It turned out that back in the Netherlands, people in her close circle of Calvinist friends had been active on her behalf. Also two physicians had written letters to Ravensbrück camp to try to get the two sisters released on medical grounds. In addition, Corrie believes that her deep religiosity may have struck a chord in the heart of Lieutenant Rahms, and he also helped to get her released. But her release was postponed for a while. Due to her swollen legs, a doctor decided, "Edema," and she was sent for several days to recuperate. Then, outfitted with a new set of clothes and shoes and given travel vouchers, starting out on New Year's day 1945 she gradually made her way back to Groningen, and after a certain interlude to Haarlem, where she was warmly greeted by her family (brother Willem, sisters Nollie, and Toos) and friends. Corrie later learned that after she left, the Germans had started gassing prisoners in the camp; first, the sick; then those who could not walk well; finally the elderly, those over 50 – I would definitely have qualified in all three categories."

Back home, Corrie was told that all the hidden Jews were safe with the exception of Mary Itallie, who had been deported following her arrest in the street. At first, still dazed by what she had gone through, she had some difficulties readjusting to normal life. Thinking about Betsie's love for flowers, Corrie bought plants for every windowsill, but she forgot to water them and they died. Soon enough, she renewed her work with the underground and was sent to deliver a falsely written release paper for a colleague in jail. When she presented the false document to a policeman on duty, she was told to return the following day with the document, when the police chief will be present. Corrie started trembling and hurriedly left the place. "If I had ever needed proof that I had no boldness or cleverness of my own, I had it now. Whatever bravery or skill I had ever shown were gifts of God – sheer loans from Him of the talent needed to do a job. And it was clear, from the absence of such skills now, that this was no longer His work for me." With this thought in mind, her underground work was over.

After the war, Corrie ten Boom began to tell the story of her family's aid to Jews. She also wrote her autobiography. "This implied that I do not hate my enemies: in the war I refused, ten times, to kill someone when this was asked of me. I have a message for the world, because I know from personal experience, that if Jesus says to love our enemies, he gives us the love that he asks from us." She also participated in the creation of absorption homes in several places for returning concentration camps detainees and former underground workers. The home in Zonneduin, belonging to the ten Boom Foundation, continued for many years to serve those in need of rest and recuperation. She also exerted herself in countering the large-scale blight of antisemitism still current in Germany. "After I had fought Hitler's German antisemitism for one and a half years [starting at the end of 1942], it was now necessary to fight the antisemitism that rose in postwar Germany. I worked a lot in that country in order to spread the Word." She traveled much, preaching her message of fundamentalist Christianity and love of the Jewish people. In 1975, a movie called *The Hiding Place* retold the fascinating story of her family's rescue activity. In 1977, Corrie moved to California, where she died in 1983, on her 91st birthday.

In 1967, Yad Vashem recognized Cornelia ("Corrie") ten Boom as Righteous Among the Nations.

Boonstra, Dirk

NETHERLANDS

*I*n 1988, Professor Louis de Jong, the leading Dutch historian of the German occupation of the Netherlands in World War II, wrote to Yad Vashem about a unique group of Dutch policemen led by Dirk Boonstra who refused an order to arrest Jews for deportation. The story began on a Tuesday morning, March 9, 1943, when Boonstra, the commander of the Grijpskerk police station, received a telephone call from Grootegast police headquarters ordering him to arrest the Jews who still lived in the municipality and bring them to the main railroad station in Groningen. This occurred at a time when most Dutch Jews had already been deported to the concentration camps and gassed. According to the police report, Boonstra flatly refused to carry out the assignment. He then asked constable Jan Deddens, who also served at the post, if he was willing to carry out the arrest, without telling him of his own refusal, "Because he did not want to influence Deddens' decision." Deddens replied that he had already decided the previous year that he would not obey such orders and therefore he was not going to obey them now. Boonstsra and Deddens then decided to look up constable Willem Vlijm, also from the Grijpskerk station, to find out what his position was. It turned out that Vlijm was of the same opinion – that they should refuse to carry out the order. In order to get around it without bringing things to a head, Boonstra decided to stall for time. He reported to brigade headquarters in Grootegast that most of the Jews earmarked for arrest were sick. He was told to get a written confirmation from a physician and to send it to police headquarters in Groningen. This Boonstra did, producing a medical report signed by a certain Dr. Staal and having Deddens deliver it.

Two days later, on March 11, 1943, Boonstra was summoned by the district commander, Lieutenant Rauwerda, who ordered him point blank to arrest the Jews. Boonstra again refused. He also refused to pass on the order to Deddens and Vlijm. Rauwerda then informed Boonstra that he was under arrest and was to return to his house and remain there. This was followed by an announcement that an ambulance was on the way and that Deddens and Vlijm were to carry out the arrest and transportation of the "sick" Jews. The two policemen declared that they would refuse to do this. Around noon, a message arrived that all the policemen involved were to report to the Grootegast station as soon as possible. It turned out that following Boonstra's initial refusal, Lieutenant Rauwerda had gotten in touch with Sergeant-Major De Wit, another unit commander, and ordered him to assign other personnel from the unit to arrest the Jews in Grijpskerk. De Witt's reply was: "It shall be done, Lieutenant." He then passed on the order to Sergeants Roelof Mulder, Theodorus Buunk, and Geert Holvast from the Grootegast station, but these three also refused. De Witt passed on the same order by telephone to several other policemen – including Tonis Bulthuis and Tjerk van der Hauw – but they too refused to comply. As for Jan Elzinga, when he heard about the order, he decided to go into hiding. De Wit had no other choice but to inform Rauwerda that his whole unit had refused to carry out the order. Lieutenant Rauwerda then decided to assemble the recalcitrant policemen and warn them of the severe consequences of their act.

Rauwerda's words failed to budge the policemen – they stuck to their refusal when each in turn was asked for his answer. Rauwerda thereupon ordered them into a police van and they were taken to a nearby police barracks, where they were told to await the arrival of the regional commander De Boer. After a long wait, the man arrived and after haranguing them about the dire consequences of their defiance, threatened them with imprisonment in concentration camps. The policemen still refused to budge and were now told to place themselves under house arrest and await further orders.

That evening they all received messages ordering them to report to the Helpman barracks the next morning, where they would have the opportunity to explain their position in the presence of German police officers. They were also told that if they still stood by their refusal, they would be sent to a concentration camp. The following morning, all the men, including Elzinga, reported as ordered. One by one, they were called into De Boer's office, and stood by their refusal, in the presence of two German police officers. They were then told to go upstairs and hand in their weapons. They were then taken to Vught, a dreaded concentration camp on Dutch soil. Arriving there in the evening, they were registered and given prisoner's garb.

The police report relates what befell these defiant policemen. Buunk, Vlijm, Van de Hauw, Bulthuis, and Elzinga were released after two months' imprisonment. Holvast and Deddens were held as prisoners-of-war until the end of the war. Berga was taken to Germany for forced labor. Mulder and Boonstra were confined to Dachau concentration camp. In September 1944, Mulder was released; Boonstra died in Dachau. In De Jong's estimation this incident, which was widely reported in the Dutch underground press, influenced the attitude of many Dutch persons to the idea of helping Jews.

In 1988, Yad Vashem awarded the title of Righteous Among the Nations to Dirk Boonstra and his fellow courageous policemen: Jan Deddens, Klaas Berga, Tonis Builthuis, Theodorus Buunk, Jan Elzinga, Tjerk van der Hauw, Geert Holvast, Roelof Mulder, and Willem Vlijm.

Borkowska, Anna
LITHUANIA

*I*n 1984, the Israeli poet Abba Kovner was told that the Polish nun who had helped him and his beleaguered comrades during the early phase of the Holocaust in Lithuania, and who was believed no longer to be among the living, a woman to whom he had dedicated a poem entitled "My Little Sister" – was indeed alive and living in Warsaw. That year, he wrote to Yad Vashem asking that this 85-year-old woman be awarded the Righteous title. "In my name, and in the name of the Vilna fighters, I ask you to please award the title of Righteous Among the Nations to Anna Borkowska, who is to be counted among the courageous woman of World War II." He then hastened to her side in a tiny, nondescript Warsaw apartment and presented her with the Yad Vashem medal of Righteous Among the Nations. She wondered, "Why do I deserve this honor?" To which Abba Kovner replied: "You are Anna of the Angels."

The story unfolds in Kolonia Wilenska, on the road between Vilna (today, Vilnius) and Vileika, previously within the Polish borders, where Sister Anna Borkowska (born Bertranda Siestrzewitowska) served as Mother Superior in a convent consisting of a small group of nine Dominican Sisters. She was then about 40 years old and had studied earlier at the university in Kraków and was active in socialist academic circles. She then left everything and decided to become a nun. After the horrible Ponary massacres of Jews in the summer months of 1941, Anna Borkowska consented to allow 17 members of an illegal Jewish pioneering group to hide in the convent for brief periods of time. The idea came to her from a fellow lay companion, Irena Adamowicz, who told her about this group of Zionist pioneers and their ideas. As Borkowska recalled, Irena "read letters from Palestine to me from her friends. A new world opened up before my eyes – a world marked by steadfast efforts of a group of people to establish a just and true mutual relationship … My sympathy was on their side." This was still before the war. Anna then visited this group on their "kibbutz" on Mickiewicz Street. "That was my first meeting with them. We looked at each other searchingly. Then three members of the *Shomer* (pioneers) visited us in Kolonia Wilenska. I had some very vague notions about Marxism and since the discussion revolved around this we could not understand each other very well. Some time was needed to adapt my ideology at the time to this completely new concept that life presented to me." Then came the German occupation, and soon thereafter the convent of nine nuns was bristling with activity, for the youthful Jewish men and women were plotting, behind the secure walls of the Dominican convent, an eventual uprising in the Vilna ghetto.

"They called me *Ima* (mother)," Anna Borkowska fondly recalled. "I felt as if I were indeed their mother. I was pleased with the arrival of each new member, and was sorry that I could not shelter more of them." Recalling those who passed through the convent walls, Anna mentioned Arieh Wilner: "I gave him the name 'Jurek'" – the code name under which he was to be known for his exploits in Warsaw, where he was eventually to perish during the Warsaw Ghetto uprising of April 1943. As a member of the Zionist socialist movement *Hashomer Hatzair* (Young Guard), he held to Marxist views. "Two different world met," she stated. "Nevertheless we found points of contact, or rather bridges, since each of us wished to be able to look into the other's soul. We had respect for one another's convictions; we shared our intellectual achievements, not without some degree of influence on one other. In our discussions we tried to escape from the monstrous reality into the world of ideas. In spirit 'Jurek' was the closest to me. He went to Warsaw, to do some important and difficult work; he suffered greatly and died a heroic death. I tried to find his final resting place in the ruins of the ghetto. Those who survived and even more those who died will remain forever in my memory. Among the whole ocean of small and gray events in life those moments when one was gambling for high stakes were the most beautiful and valuable. Such moments occur only once in a lifetime."

Then there was Abba Kovner, the moving spirit of the Vilna underground – "my right hand." Kovner presided over the secret conclaves in the convent where plans were hatched for an uprising in the Vilna ghetto. Until those plans could mature, Kovner and his 16 colleagues worked side by side with the convent nuns performing laborious work in the fields. "He put on an apron, tied a kerchief around his head and went with us to do field work. From afar he looked like a woman with a pale ascetic face." The others, too, to conceal their presence from the eyes of suspecting neighboring peasants, ever watchful of the unusual comings and goings of the convent, dressed in nuns' habits and were thus able to cultivate the nearby fields.

Continuing her recollections of some of the people sheltered by her, Sister Borkowska mentioned Tauba, "who loved life so much, gentle, pleasant," and later died during an attack on a German convoy. Also Margalit, who did work in the kitchen while shedding tears for her lost child; Mrs. K., who was torn by terrible doubts: could God be good if he permitted such monstrous things to occur? She was to die during the Warsaw Ghetto uprising in April 1943; Michas, Abba Kovner's brother, who had remained hidden for many weeks in an attic without light and air, and was pale "as a holy wafer." While in the convent, he helped during the harvest and got tanned. He, too, did not survive the Holocaust. A former Jewish resident of the convent called it "the only spark of light that shined in the general darkness; the only place where one found brotherhood and human compassion. The Mother Superior had become elevated in the hearts of those who stood in her presence to the symbolic image of the ideal person."

In the convent cells, Abba Kovner issued his famous clarion call of rebellion, the first of its kind in Nazi-occupied Europe, which opened with the ringing words: "Let us not be led like sheep to the slaughter!" This manifesto, secretly printed in the convent and distributed inside the ghetto on January 1, 1942, served as an inspiration to many ghetto and partisan fighters. When the time came for Abba Kovner and his comrades to return to the ghetto, telling Sister Borkowska, "If we are to die, let us die the death of free people, with arms in our hands," she rushed to join them. "I want to go with you to the ghetto," she pleaded with Abba; "to fight and fall alongside you. Your war is a holy war. Even though of Marxist orientation and denying religion, you are a noble people for there is religion in your heart. A great God – now you are closer to Him than I." Kovner told her she could be of greater help by smuggling in weapons. Indeed, she did just that. As told by noted Yiddish poet Abraham Sutzkever, "The first four grenades... were the gift of the Mother Superior, who instructed Abba Kovner in their proper use ... She later supplied other weapons." After a while, according to Suzkever, she returned to the ghetto gate and asked to be let in. She wore a yellow star and showed the police a counterfeit pass, but the policeman at the gate suspected her of not being Jewish and turned her down. After this incident, Sister Borkowka agreed to serve as a messenger between the ghetto partisans and the illegal organization of the Poles. However, this proved unsuccessful, as that particular Polish clandestine organization refused to supply weapons to the Jewish underground.

As suspicions mounted concerning the activities of the convent, the Germans had Anna Borkowska arrested in September 1943, the convent closed, and the Sisters dispersed. One nun was dispatched to a labor camp. Surviving the Holocaust as a fighting partisan and moving to Israel, Abba Kovner sought to reestablish contact with her after the war, but was misinformed that she had passed away. As for Sister Borkowska, she reportedly asked to be released from her monastic vows and was granted a dispensation, while at the same time remaining a deeply religious person. Now, having found her again, and himself fighting an illness to which he would succumb only a few years later, Kovner had fulfilled a longstanding wish, to see Anna Borkowska once more, and perhaps bid her a final farewell.

During the ceremony in Warsaw in her honor, on July 11, 1984, after receiving the honors associated with the Righteous title, awarded by Yad Vashem, the 85-year-old Anna Borkowska turned to Kovner and said: "Isn't it right, my dear, that you were always a believing person?" "Yes," Kovner replied, somewhat ambiguously. Addressing the audience, Kovner then said, "During the days when the angels hid their faces from us, this woman was for us Anna of the Angels. Not of angels that we invent in our hearts, but of angels that create our lives forever."

Thus, in 1984, Yad Vashem awarded the Righteous title to Anna Borkowska. Two years later, Abba Kovner planted a tree in Anna Borkowska's name in the Avenue of the Righteous at Yad Vashem.

British Prisoners of War: Wells, Stan; Hammond, George; Noble, Tommy; Edwards, Alan; Letchford, Roger

ENGLAND

*T*he story is as told by Sarah Rigler, born 1928 in Lithuania, to Samuel-Leib and Gita Matuson. Three years earlier, during a short stay in Palestine, Sarah's sister Hannah had been born in Tel Aviv. The family then moved back to Lithuania. When the Germans entered Lithuania in June 1941, they arrested Sarah's father together with a group of other Jews, and they were never seen again. The rest of the family was forced into the Siauliai (also known as Shavli) ghetto. Then, with the approach of the Soviet army, the survivors of the ghetto were taken by cattle car to Stutthof on the Baltic coast. It was December 1944, with the inmates in rags unsuited to the cold winter and given little food. After a three-week stay there, and with the Russians dangerously closing in, the surviving inmates began a tortuous Death March towards Germany. They were scantily dressed, with wooden clogs on their feet, and marching in sub-zero temperature. In Sarah's words, "We were about 1,200 women when we started in late November and were about 300 in January 1945. We walked the whole day, clubbed by the German guards who were watching us, and led into barns for the night.... During the whole two months we were only fed a few times.… We were very hungry and all we could talk and dream about was bread."

The British prisoners of war with Sarah Rigler (second from right), during the tree planting at Yad Vashem

The column of marching women, whose numbers kept diminishing as many fell from exhaustion and extreme cold, reached Gross Golemkau, a town not far from Danzig (today Gdansk). "We had not eaten in weeks, the snow underfoot was dirty but that was our only water; we were not human beings anymore. We were so hungry that we even ate food prepared for pigs – potato peels and manure." At this point, Sarah asked her mother to give her the diamond ring that she had managed to hide with her, to try somehow to exchange it for bread. "How that feat was to be accomplished, I didn't think. To be really *hungry* is a state that only other survivors can understand and feel; normal everyday people cannot fathom it. My eternal dream and vision was to have a piece of bread and a sliced cold potato on top as a special treat, and I'd never ask for anything more. I didn't think how I'd get back, all I was thinking about was bread. I took the ring, my mother wished me luck, and we parted. That was the last time I saw my mother and sister alive. My mother's hands were frozen stiff, and she couldn't use them. My sister suffered in silence." Hannah was wearing a very thin coat, bare feet in clogs with a thin blanket to keep out the bitter cold. Quietly slipping out of the line of marchers, Sarah ran past the guards and into a barn with a few horses, and waited. A young boy came in and Sarah immediately asked him in German for a piece of bread in return for the ring. He said he would soon be back, and returned with the police. "I was taken to a police station, where I was asked was I doing there. I said I wanted bread. They started chasing me back and yelling at me that I was dirtying their *Judenrein* ("Jewish-cleansed") town. She was pushed back into the line of marchers. Sarah tried again; this time the guards fired shots in her direction. "I ran as fast as possible with my frozen feet! I ran through the whole town. My only thought was that I didn't want my mother to see me killed, because she was right there. The streets were lined with bystanders watching the people dragging their bodies along the road. I pushed my way through them and ran into a barn and lay down in a trough and waited for my executioners." Sarah was 16 years old at the time.

After a while someone came into the barn to feed the cows. "I spoke to him in German, assuming that he was Polish too [and understood German], and told him to kill me or to help me." It turned out that the man was a British POW, named Stan Wells. He looked at Sarah, saw the situation, left the farmhouse and returned with some bread. Not knowing what to do with her, Stan talked to a Russian girl, a prisoner in a Russian camp, asking her whether her people could hide Sarah for a few weeks. When she left, Stan tried to tell Sarah that the barn belonged to a certain Mrs. Hoffman, whose husband had died in the war, and she was a dedicated Nazi. Since she didn't trust the British POW to feed the cows properly, she came every night to check for herself if the cows had food. She indeed appeared around midnight, and saw Sarah's clogs, but for some mysterious reason she did not investigate further and left the barn.

When Stan and the Russian girl returned the following morning, he told Sarah that the Russians didn't want to hide a fleeing Jewish girl, but that his ten British POW companions, who were being held in a converted barn, might be willing to do so. But first, he had to discuss it with them. At the time, they had been moved from a prisoner-of-war camp to a farm near Gross Golemkau, where about a dozen of them would be locked up overnight in an old farmyard; in the morning they would be unlocked and walk a few kilometers to the farm to work. At it turned out, these men agreed to hide Sarah in the hayloft of their barn – next to the chimney, to provide warmth for her. That night someone came to fetch her

– it was William Fisher. "I was so frightened, I didn't know who this man was and I thought he might be drunk." Instead he brought her a full-length military coat, to disguise her, and walked with her through the town. "Luckily we weren't stopped – the guards must have thought I looked like a prisoner of war." He took her to his companions' barn, known as Stalag 20b, and placed her upstairs in the hayloft. Some of the men returned from work that night; one of them, Bert Hambling, who acted as a medic, brought along some ointment for Sarah's bleeding, frostbitten feet.

The following is from the diary of British POW William Fisher:

"26th January: 1945. God punish Germany … I have seen today the filthiest, foulest and most cruel sight of my life … At 9 a.m. this morning a column straggled down the road towards Danzig – a column far beyond the words of which I am capable to describe. I was struck dumb with a miserable rage, a blind coldness which nearly resulted in my being shot … They came straggling through the bitter cold, about 300 of them, limping, dragging footsteps, slipping and failing, to rise and stagger under the blows of the guards – SS swine. Crying loudly for bread, screaming for food, 300 matted haired, filthy objects that had once been – Jewesses! A rush into a nearby house for bread resulted in one being clubbed down with a rifle butt, but even as she fell in a desperate movement she shoved the bread she'd got into her blouse… 27th January, temp 15 below … Stan comes to me after dinner and tells me a Jewess has got away and he has her hiding in cows crib. I suggest moving her to loft over camp. Plenty straw and the chimney from our fire will keep her warm. I arrange to take her to the camp. Wait till nearly dusk and go to Stan's farm, he hands over girl. I tell her to walk 5 paces near on other side of road and speak to no one. She is crippled, too frightened to understand me, grabs my arm. I am a bit windy as the Gerries [Germans] will stop us as it is definite 'crime' for prisoner to speak or walk with women. Have luck … Hot water soap towel-old clothes, slacks food rushed up to her… Take all clothing off kid, give her parafin for lice in her hair and bid her goodbye. She grabs my hand and kisses it, and tries to thank me, calls me 'Herr.' I say roughly, drop it we are comrades, only doing what we can… January 27th. Everyone brings in food for our escapee! … Hundred weight peas, ducks, hens, best part of a pig. Bread by loaves, and believe me she's ate 3 loaves today and 5 bowls of soup – somewhere around 22 lbs. of food. She's ill now – sick diarrhea. Suggest only milk for a few days. 26th: … She is sixteen years of age. Comes from Lithuania. Been in various concentration camps – last being Stutthof… Been on the march for days… Today I could go no further. I said: 'Mother I am going to run away.' My mother said: 'Child if you must, then do so; God watch over you'… I know God helped me, for shortly after Stan came to me and said to me: 'Don't move, I am English, don't be afraid.' English! I knew I was saved!… We had a good look at her. Her eyes are large as it usual with starvation, sunken cheeks, no breasts. Hair has not been cut, body badly marked with sores caused by scratching lice bites. Head still a bit matted and lice still obviously in… Feet blue and raw with frostbite, the right heel is eaten away by frost and constant rubbing of badly fitting clog. We have stolen clothing and a pair of shoes off the refugee wagons to replace hers which is marked with the Jewish star in red hue. She sat till twelve making a new hat from material and sewing and talking. She will keep harping on her mother and sister and the concentration camp, but we forbid her to mention them …"

Stan Wells recalled that when he found her in a cow crib, "she was very thin and looked like a bundle of rags." Alan Edwards was surprised that "it was only when we got our bundle there that we found that we had rescued a girl." George Hammond, another British POW, remembered working in the village, and when he and his companions returned to the camp, they were told that they had someone in the cupboard. "There in the cupboard was what I thought was a bundle of rags, in it was a girl who didn't even look like a human being. She was so thin … She told us that her name was Sarah. We decided to keep her for as long as possible; every night we would visit her with food. We found her a pair of shoes and a sweater to put over her ripped dress." Sarah recalled being bathed by George Hammond, who also brought her paraffin for the lice in her hair. "He tried to make me comfortable." The rest of the British POW's contributed food, which was brought to her every day by Alan Edwards. "I was terribly hungry. They then bathed me. All I had was a dress with a very big red Jewish star on the back of it, a thin coat and a blanket. I was very sick – I had diarrhea. I was with them for three weeks and they nursed me back to health." Alan Edwards stole a coat, shoes, stockings and sweater to cover Sarah's camp dress which had a very large Star of David on the back. Tommy Noble, Roger Letchford, Bill Scrutton, Jack Buckley, and Bill Keable used to alternate in bringing food every morning and evening when they came back from work. "They took turns assisting me with personal hygiene."

When they learned that they would soon be moved out, they assured Sarah that they would think of something to save her. "They were all in this together." Alan Edwards told her that they had arranged for a Polish man to pick her up and keep her, until the arrival of the Russian. But the man never showed up. Stan Wells, the man who found Sarah, made his escape when the men were evacuated and headed for the woods, where he hid for three weeks until the Russians arrived. Sarah was finally liberated too.

After the war, Sarah found out that her mother and sister did not survive; the mother dying of starvation in one of the camps, and "Hannale" succumbing one day after the liberation. Sarah poignantly added: "Before the war, my first name was Sarah, but I assumed my sister's name Hannah to keep her name alive." Sarah also tried to relocate her helpers. But because she did not have the men's service numbers, nor their full names, the British War Records Centre found it difficult to help. The only full name she knew was Alan Edwards. Through an English friend, she wrote to every Edwards in the telephone directory, but with no luck. Eventually, the War Records Office managed to trace the right Alan Edwards. She eventually met George Hammond again in 1962. That year he spotted an article in a newspaper about Sarah, who had spent 20 years trying to track them down. He replied and a reunion was finally arranged in London in 1972. Alan Edwards, had met Sarah earlier, in 1966, for about an hour at Heathrow airport, when she and her husband were on their way to Jerusalem, and Stan Wells, who had escaped to the woods to await liberation, met Sarah in 1972. Sarah had moved to the United States and was married to New York State Court Judge William Rigler; her name now being Hannah Sarah Rigler. In 1986 she was director of food and services for the elderly and homeless on the city's Board of Education.

Writing to Yad Vashem, Sarah Rigler explained, "Forty-three years later, living in America with a loving family and secure, how can I explain to you the fear and loneliness I felt at that time... The men took an extraordinary risk, as a unit. Had I been discovered, I would certainly have been shot together with the ten prisoners of war, all of whom had families and homes in England. I had nobody and no one would have known had I been killed. I would just have been another one of the six million but they had much more to risk and it was close to going home. They could touch freedom. I owe them my life, ten British prisoners of war who jeopardized their own meager existence to save one Jewish life. They nursed me back to health. After four weeks they were moved out, but before they left they tried to help me by giving me some advice and addresses." Asked why he and his fellow companions risked their lives to save her, Alan Edwards said: "It was just one of those things. What else could we do? We couldn't turn her back to the Germans. They'd have probably killed her like they did all the others. We didn't think about it being dangerous – you don't in wartime. Anything you can do against the enemy you just do." George Hammond added to this: "We think of her as our little sister."

In 1988, Yad Vashem awarded the title of Righteous Among the Nations to Stan Wells, George Hammond, Tommy Noble, Alan Edwards, and Roger Letchford. The following year, Wells, Hammond, Noble, and Edwards visited Israel and planted a tree in the Avenue of the Righteous at Yad Vashem.

Bružková-Diskantová, Věra
CZECH REPUBLIC

On April 23, 2002, Shmuel (Arnost) Rosenzweig wrote a letter from Copenhagen, Denmark, to Yad Vashem. Born in 1937, in Kežmarok, Slovakia, in late 1944 he was deported with his family to the Nazi concentration camp of Ravensbrück, inside Germany. There his father and elder brother were separated from the rest of the family and sent elsewhere, and all traces of them were lost. Left behind were Arnost, his sister, and their mother. Soon afterwards, Arnost fell ill with typhus and was placed in the camp's dispensary. In the meantime, his mother and sister were transported to Bergen-Belsen camp. Back in Ravensbrück, a certain Czech woman prisoner noticed the sick boy and decided to smuggle him into the non-Jewish compound, where she hid him and cared for him until he got well – in fact until the camp's liberation in April 1945. Afterwards, the strange woman took the boy back with her to Prague, where he stayed with her for three months.

In the meantime, she listed the boy with the Red Cross, as well as having his name announced on the radio, in the hope that someone from his family would show up. Indeed, an uncle, named Chaim Miller came to get the boy. Soon afterwards the boy's mother also presented herself, and after thanking the Czech woman rescuer of her son, took him with her to Israel. Arnost did not remember his savior's name, and his mother had already passed away. The only memento he had were two photos of himself with this Czech woman, taken in Prague after the war. In Arnost's words, "After having looked in vain for my rescuer for years I got in touch with Mr. Milan Grus, the editor of the partisan paper, *Národní Os-*

vobození, in Prague, who published my story with the photos. Ten days ago I received an answer. They had found the Czech woman. I went to Prague to meet her. Her name is Věra Bružková-Diskantová. I met her at the hospital where she lives. She suffers from Parkinson's disease. After 57 years we met again."

It was a moving reunion. Věra gave him photos of him that she had kept all those years, and also showed him two letters written by him and his mother from Israel. In the undated letter of his mother, Rozaliá Rosenzweig, she wrote, "I should be happy if you could arrange to come. Arnoš would be very happy to see you – since his second mother will arrive ... All the time he tells me what he experienced in Prague. Next time I will take a photo of him and send it to you." There was also a letter from "Arnoš" to "Dear Verushka. I also send you warm greetings, and I am happy that you will come to us ... I kiss your hands." This was probably the last communication between both sides for many decades.

In his letter to Yad Vashem, Shmuel-Arnost Rosenzweig emphasized, "I have been looking for my rescuer for years but without a name it seemed impossible. I am so happy now that we have met and hope that she may live to receive the honor that she has so very much deserved. Vera told me that I was always a good child and that I never cried, but now I do." Since meeting her, Arnost has flown every weekend from Denmark to visit her, the 87- year-old woman who saved his life in a Nazi concentration camp.

In 2003, Yad Vashem recognized Věra Bružková-Diskantová as Righteous Among the Nations. On September 4, 2003, the Israeli ambassador in Prague, Arthur Avnon, hosted a ceremony in his home, where in the presence of Shmuel-Arnost Rosenzweig and his family the ambassador handed Mrs. Bružková-Diskantová a medal and certificate of honor in her name. The event was widely covered by the Czech media. At Yad Vashem, her name proudly adorns the honor wall in the Garden of the Righteous together with other rescuers of Jews from the Czech Republic.

Bunel, Lucien (Father Jacques)
France

*B*orn in 1900 into a working-class family in Barentine near Routen, the fourth of eight children, Lucien Bunel entered the priesthood in 1925 and a little later entered the Carmelite order and assumed the name of *Jacques de Jesus*. In 1935 he was assigned by the Provincial of the Carmelite Order the task of opening a private religious school in Avon (Seine-et-Marne), the Petit Collège des Carmes, designed for children of middle-class, well-to-do and aristocratic families. With the start of the war, the school closed its doors, as the teaching staff, including Father Jacques, were drafted into the army. Taken prisoner in June 1940, he was released in December of that year and the following year reopened his private school.

He also decided to hire as a mathematics teacher the Jewish natural sciences professor Lucien Weil, fired from his teaching position in accordance with the anti-Jewish French Vichy laws. Before the war, Weil had been a well-known botanist and had studied various forest growths, such as edible mushrooms, and had published numerous articles on the subject. In addition, the Jewish Maurice Bas was hired as a household domestic. To cap it all, he admitted in 1942 three Jewish boys into his Catholic school, under assumed names: Hans Michel (alias Jean Bonnet), born in 1930 in Germany, Maurice Schlosser (alias Sabatier), and Jacques Halpern (alias Dupré).

On January 13, 1944, suspecting that someone might turn him in, Father Jacques wrote in a letter: "It is very likely that very soon serious things will happen to me. If I am shot, rejoice, for I will have fulfilled my ideal – giving my life for all those who suffer." Indeed, two days later, on January 15, 1944, after the presence of the Jews was betrayed to the Germans, the Gestapo raided the establishment. Maurice Bas was able to hide in a closet and was not discovered. As for Lucien Weil, he was arrested in his home in Fontainebleau with his mother and his sister and deported to Auschwitz, where they were sent to the gas chambers. The three Jewish boys were also arrested and deported to Auschwitz, from where they did not return.

As for Father Jacques, he was led away by the Gestapo. Before that all the pupils were assembled in the courtyard, where a Gestapo agent berated them: "Three Jewish pupils were arrested in this school. Are there any more Jews among you?" The boys answered in one voice, "No." Suddenly, one pupil cried out, "They are our friends like the others." The German

Lucien Bunel (Father Jacques)

shot back, "You are not friends with a Negro; you are not friends with a Jew." Father Jacques was led away, dressed in his cassock with his brown beret and holding a suitcase – he passed the pupils lined up in the schoolyard by the Gestapo; he stopped for a moment, looked at them seriously, and with a smile called out, *Au revoir les enfants. A bientot!* ("Goodbye children; see you soon").

Jailed in Fontainebleau, he underwent interrogations for several days. Gestapo officer Korf asked him why he had disobeyed the laws against sheltering Jews. Father Jacques said: "I do not know them. I know of only one law, that of the gospels and of love. You may shoot me if you wish. I am not afraid of dying; on the contrary, it would be for me the greatest joy. Instead of killing fathers of families, and turning their wives into widows and their children into orphans, take me instead and shoot me." Korf reportedly burst out: "This is a man. What a man! He only has one fault: that of not being a Nazi." Father Jacques was then moved to a camp in Compiegne, and from there, on March 29, 1944, he was deported to Germany, and eventually to the Mauthausen concentration camp in Austria. Moved from there to the Gusen camp, he was assigned to hard labor. Grievously weakened, he managed to hold on until the liberation of Gusen, on April 25, 1945, but was by then totally exhausted. He was taken to a hospital in Linz, where he died on June 2, 1945. His body was then returned to Avon.

In the burial ceremony, France's chief rabbi Jacob Kaplan bewailed the brave man: "Through Father Jacques' behavior, we celebrate and glorify the deeds of many priests and heads of Catholic institutions, of the many Sisters of Charity and Mother Superiors, who did not hesitate, in spite of all the risks to themselves, to extend shelter to persecuted Jews … Thus, we have seen [during the Holocaust] the deepest form of a horrible cruelty, and at the same time of a love of the most elevated degree of nobility and beauty." Father Jacques' humanitarian endeavor was also featured in a 1980s movie by Louis Malle, one of the former students of the Carmelite school, entitled *Au Revoir les Enfants* – Father Jacques' parting words to his children as he was led away by the Gestapo. In 1935, Father Jacques had written: "The true life; the life that is worth living and which leaves a profound joy, is a life of giving oneself, where one cultivates a clean and animated soul – in constant friendship with God." In a 1988 ceremony by former pupils of the Avon school, a sign was unveiled on the door of the school's entrance, which reads:

> *"In remembrance of the arrest of Father Jacques by the Nazis on January 15, 1944, and of the three Jewish pupils of the Petit College, arrested together with him, and who died in the gas chambers in Auschwitz on February 6, 1944. Hans-Helmut Michel (Jean Bonnet), 13 years old; Maurice Schlosser (Maurice Sabatier), 15 years old; Jacques-France Halpern (Jacques Dupré), 17 years old."*

In 1985, Yad Vashem awarded the title of Righteous Among the Nations posthumously to Father Jacques (Lucien Bunel).

Burlingis, Wiktoria & Pawel
Drzewecka, Aleksandra
Lithuania & Poland

A baby girl was born to David and Lea Gitelman in the Vilna ghetto on January 7, 1942. It was the worst possible time to bring a Jewish child into the word, but Lea's pregnancy had begun six months before the sudden German invasion of Lithuania, then part of the Soviet Union, in June 1941. The child was aptly named Getele – that is, "of the ghetto." After slaughtering 35,000 Jews in Vilna (today, Vilnius), the Germans herded the remaining

38,000 into a ghetto and continued to systematically reduce their number by further killing raids, with 20,000 remaining by the end of the year. During one of these raids, Getele was given sleeping pills, and so was able to join a dozen other people who cooped up in a secret hideout on the roof of one of the ghetto buildings.

In 1943, rumors were rampant that the ghetto would soon be liquidated, except for a few hundred able to work as mechanics in a German army garage located outside the ghetto perimeter. David Gitelman, a construction engineer who before the war had worked in that capacity for the municipality, was added to this group to supervise the sanitation conditions of the living quarters of these fortunate workers. The Germans agreed to allow David, as well as the other workers, to have his wife Lea, daughter Getele, and David's parents join him in the new place. It was just in time, for a week afterwards, on September 5, 1943, the Vilna ghetto was liquidated, and its inhabitants either killed or shipped off to forced labor camps.

During one of David's work-related sorties outside the work area perimeter, he met Wiktoria, a Polish woman married to the Lithuanian Pawel Burlingis, and she promised to save little Getele should it become absolutely necessary. In the meantime, the Germans began to liquidate the garage workers and their families. The Gitelmans were able to survive by hiding in a specially prepared underground hiding place. Two-year-old Getele was drugged to sleep during the tense hours of the Nazi killing raid above ground. Her parents then decided the time had come to place her in the safe hands of Wiktoria Burlingis, who had a girl of her own, as previously agreed. Getele was again put to sleep, placed in a sack and carried outside the work area. Her mother, Lea, decided to stay a few days with the child at the Burlingis home. On one occasion during this early period, Getele began to sing the Yiddish song, "I am Queen Esther," evidently to please guests who had suddenly arrived at the Burlingis house. She had learned the song several weeks earlier, during a Purim celebration organized for the children in the labor camp. Lea, who overheard this from a safe and unseen distance, was terrified at the thought that one of the guests would betray her child to the authorities. Wiktoria calmed her, assuring her that a solution would be found by having the little girl moved elsewhere. A very concerned Lea rejoined her husband.

Then Lea was informed that Getele had fallen very ill and needed immediate medical care. A Jewish doctor in the work place gave Lea the address of a non-Jewish doctor in Vilna who could be trusted, and Lea passed on this information to Wiktoria, with a request to inform her whether the child had recovered or not. The secret signal was for Wiktoria to move the curtain on her outside window, which faced the work place of the Gitelmans. If the child was healthy, the curtain would remain drawn. If the child had succumbed – the curtain would be raised. Happily for everyone, Getele recovered from her malady.

Some time afterwards, David Gitelman secretly visited Getele, who in the meantime had been moved to another location. Wiktoria had arranged for the child to be brought back to her place in time for her father's visit. An elderly woman appeared pushing Getele in a carriage. It was later learned that this was a Polish Catholic nun named Aleksandra Drzewecka. Getele looked at David, and recognized him as her father, but now spoke only Polish – her Yiddish was gone, or purposely stored away in her mind. Who knows the mind of a two-year-old child who had already undergone several traumatic experiences to stay alive? When David handed her a biscuit, Getele thanked him as "my daddy" in Polish.

As the Russians neared Vilna, in the summer of 1944, David and Lea, who were among the few remaining people at the German work place, were able to escape, while under fire, and stealthily made their way to Wiktoria's home, where they met David's parents, who had also made their escape. From there, Lea headed for Drzewecka's home to get Getele and bring her to the Burlingis home. After the war, it was learned that Sister Drzewecka had also sheltered an additional Jewish child – a boy, and according to another account a few more children. She then relocated to Warsaw, and the Gitelmans, established in Israel, provided her with money, medicine, and other necessities. The Gitelmans desperately tried to reestablish contact with the Burlingises, but to no avail, as they probably had relocated too. As for Getele, under her new Hebrew name of Rina (i.e., music, song) – she is the happily married mother of three.

Of the original tens of thousands of Jews in Vilna, only an estimated few hundred survived by remaining in hiding in the city. The Gitelmans, including little Getele, were among the fortunate few – thanks to the family's non-Jewish rescuers. In 1992, at the request of Lea Gitelman (her husband, David, having by then passed away), Yad Vashem conferred the title of Righteous Among the Nations on Wiktoria and Pawel Burlingis, as well as on Aleksandra Drzewecka.

Burzminski-Podgórska, Stefania
Podgórska, Helena
POLAND

*I*n 1942, sixteen-year-old Stefania Podgórska, together with her younger sister, Helena, began to shelter in Przemyśl (pronounced, Pshemyshl), in a small rented apartment – for what would be two full years – at first 7, then 10, and finally 13 Jewish survivors. Before the war, Stefania had worked part-time in the grocery of one of the survivors. Her father had died before the war, and her mother and younger brother were taken by the Germans for work on farms in Germany. As told by Dr. Josef Burzminski (previous name Max Diamant), one of the survivors and future husband of Stefania – before the war she had worked half a day in his parents' grocery store and half a day in their home, helping out his mother. When the Germans ordered all Jews to move to the ghetto, Stefania remained in one room of the Diamant's old apartment and helped by smuggling food and medicine to the Diamant family inside the ghetto. In June 1942, Max lost his brother Isidore with 1,000 other young boys from the ghetto – taken and murdered by the Germans in the Janowski camp in Lwów (today, Lviv). In August 1942 came the turn of Max's parents – taken away in cattle cars and shot somewhere. "We never saw them again." In a third action, on November 18, 1942,

Max himself was taken together with his elder brother, Dr. Chaim Diamant, and cousins – snatched from their hiding place inside the ghetto. Max related what then ensued.

"They beat us very badly (we were about 50 people) with sticks and packed us into cattle cars like sardines. Many people suffocated and died. I had a pair of flat pliers in my pocket and luckily I was near a narrow window with barbed wire. I was working on the wires with my pliers and before we reached the small town Zurawica … I jumped out the window to commit suicide. When I hit the ground, I was unconscious for a while, but I quickly came to. I waited until dark, hidden in the forest, then I went back to our old apartment where I found Stefania. Quickly and quietly along with her sister she helped me, washing my injured legs and hands, and crying the whole time. I hid there for a few weeks, under the bed."

Max returned to the ghetto but kept in touch with Stefania and sought her help to find an apartment where a large bunker could be built to accommodate seven people. Stefania, indeed, found such a place, at the edge of the city of Przemyśl, to where she moved with her younger sister, Helena. The seven people chosen included: Max, his brother Henryk and wife Danuta, Wilhelm Schillinger with daughter Krystyna, and Leon Hirsch with son Sionek. A few weeks after Stefania moved into the apartment, Max Diamant and Sionek Hirsch slipped out of the ghetto to the new apartment and began silently to prepare a bunker under the wooden floor. "We dug with only rudimentary tools and the soil we disposed in a nearby forest. Eventually we found out that this would not work because there were a lot of very nosy neighbors who came to visit Stefie almost daily and they would certainly suspect something." So the group decided

Stefania Burzminski-Podgórska with her husband Josef Burzminski, one of the persons saved by her

instead to try the attic; the hiding place was behind a false wall at one end of the attic, separated with planks of wood from destroyed homes brought by Stefania. To inquisitive neighbors she explained that the wood was to be used as firewood in the winter. The boards were quickly cut down to size. "In order to mask the sound of hammering, Stefania told the neighbors that she needed a line to hang her laundry in the attic. This way she would also have an excuse to go to the attic frequently without arousing suspicion." When everything was ready, the seven people secretly sneaked out of the ghetto, and over a period of several weeks came one by one and into the hiding place. Then, before the final liquidation of the ghetto, some more people joined them; Mrs. Zimmermann came along with her two children, Janek and Cesia, and during the liquidation phase three more people arrived – Monek Hirsch, his wife, and cousin Janek Dorlich. There were now 13 people cooped up in the hiding place in the attic of Stefania's apartment. Stefania, Danuta, and Mrs. Hirsch started knitting sweaters, gloves, and hats from old army sweaters and socks bought on the market. Stefania washed and dyed them and then sold them to the neighbors, who resold them on the market, thus bringing in much needed money on top of her regular factory wages. "She was constantly knitting, sitting by the open window so the neighbors would see her and not suspect anything." Her eight-year-old sister, Helena, helped her with the knitting. This went on for a full two years, until the city's liberation in summer of 1944.

Knowing that an oversight could lead to disaster, the fugitives thought of all contingencies. Pepper and paprika, for instance, were placed on the floor so that if the Germans came with dogs they would find it hard, if not impossible, to detect the presence of people. Also, next door lived a woman whose brother was in the SS. To use the outhouse, he had to pass directly under the place where the Jews were hiding. When he came, someone would give a signal and they would all freeze. For two years they spoke in whispers, and ate mostly bread and onions, and drank plain water. One particularly tense moment was when Germans officers, who had transformed a nearby school into a military hospital, arrived one day and told Stefania that she had two hours to vacate her apartment. At this juncture, Max begged Stefania and Helen to leave and save their lives. "We would stay and fight to the end because we expected to be killed. She said no, she would stay and die with us." When the Germans reappeared with two nurses, they accepted Stefania's suggestion that she and her sister give one of the apartment's two rooms to the nurses and keep the other room for themselves. This went on for six months. "We stayed there, hiding up in the attic, with the German nurses and their visiting German soldiers."

In the liberation, when two Russian soldiers appeared and asked for vodka, Stefania obligingly gave them some. Then one of them said he was a Russian Jew. At this, the door to the attic burst open and everyone cried and hugged each other. "We couldn't walk," Josef recalled. "Nobody would walk after the war," after being cooped up for two years in a sitting position. But the worst was finally over. After the war, Max Diamant, under his new name of Josef Burzminski, married Stefania, and in 1957 both moved to Israel, where Josef practiced dentistry. In 1961, he was a witness at the Eichmann trial in Jerusalem. He then moved to the United States and settled in Brookline, Massachusetts.

In 1979, Yad Vashem recognized Stefania Burzminski-Podgórska and her sister Helena Podgórska as Righteous Among the Nations. In her response to Yad Vashem, Stefania wrote, "I didn't expect such an honor and reward, because helping other people in need, or in some disaster, is a human obligation, and that was how I felt. I was prepared for seven people, then came six more. I gave them a shelter and protected them. My sister and I were standing beside them to protect them, even to die with them, if such a situation would have come. We wouldn't betray them." She also stated that after the war she didn't sleep for a few years, because of the "ferocious, ugly pictures in my head" of that period. Now, her being honored has brought back these memories, "and I don't sleep again even though I've been in this country for 20 years. You can't imagine what it was like."

Celis, Hubert & Louis & Joseph

Belgium

*H*ubert Celis was a parson in the small parish of Halmaal, near St. Trond-Sint Truiden, of the Liege diocese. In September 1942, he was one of the clerics invited by Monsignor Louis-Joseph Kerkhofs, Bishop of Liege, to a meeting at the Dean of Hasselt, to discuss the persecution of the Jews. Kerkhofs asked his clerics to involve themselves in helping Jews. While he did not want to impose this on anyone, because of the attendant risks for those involved, he wanted his priests to know how proud he would be of those prepared to risk their lives to save others. Father Celis could not imagine that he would face this moral challenge on the same day. For, upon returning to his presbytery,

"On the same day – for the first time in my life – a Jewish woman came to see me, accompanied by one of my parishioners. She was the mother of the Rotenberg children, and had arrived with her family in my parish after leaving Brussels, where life for Jews had become more and more unbearable. Mrs. Rotenberg wept profusely as she explained that she was about to be arrested and wanted to be reunited with her children after the war – hoping she would survive. It is then that I gave her my word of honor, and promised her to save her children, and give my life, if necessary, in that endeavor. Thank God, I remained true to my promise, and when I now see the children's happiness and their respective families, I give thanks to God for having given me the necessary strength."

The Celis family: the father Joseph (center) flanked by Hubert (left) and Louis (right) (courtesy of Regina Wolbrom-Rotenberg)

In keeping with his promise, Celis placed the two girls, 16-year-old Regine and two-year-old Sonia, with his father, Joseph, at St. Trond and the two boys, 13-year-old Wolfgang and nine-year-old Sigmund, with his brother, Father Louis Celis, a priest in Gotem, near Halmaal. The parents were hidden elsewhere. Wolfgang Rotenberg related that while the boys were in hiding, Louis Celis took great care that they should keep up their Jewish religious practices. Noting that they were not donning their phylacteries on Saturdays, Celis questioned his ecclesiastical superiors and was then satisfied that this practice was not required on the Sabbath. When Louis Celis learned that his name figured on the German black list, he immediately placed the two brothers elsewhere, first with Maria Louise Tabruyn; then with Baron and Baroness Tornaco, in Voort. When things had calmed down, the boys came back to Louis Celis.

As Mrs. Rotenberg had correctly feared, on October 29, 1942, she and her husband were betrayed to the authorities by an unknown informer and were arrested. Before that Father Hubert Celis had frequently met with the Rotenberg parents. In his words, "the father Rotenberg was a pious person who had only one wish: to follow God's commandments; his wife was a tender mother, the symbol of honesty and goodness, and very religious. Hence, I am certain that these two good and faithful people, who had no evil in them, went straight up to heaven." It was now left to the two priest brothers to continue caring for the Rotenberg children. But not before Hubert Celis had talked himself out of serious trouble.

For on that same day, he was arrested for the first time and accused of helping the underground and downed Allied pilots, as well as of having a hand in hiding the Rotenberg children. While they were reading out the charges, Celis decided that he had better confess to the last one, to keep the police from searching his family's premises, while fully denying the others. The police then asked him to disclose the children's whereabouts. He refused. The situation turned ugly, as they began to threaten to have Celis shot. To all this, Celis replied calmly: "I am in your hands; I know I will be shot but I will never speak. A priest is not a traitor." When the interrogator mentioned that he too was a Catholic, Father Celis decided to berate him for his un-Catholic behavior.

> *"You are a Catholic, and have forgotten that the Virgin was a Jewess, that Christ was Jewish, that He commanded us to love and help one another ... That He told us: 'I have given you an example so that you should do as I have done'... You are a Catholic, and you do not understand what a priest is! You do not understand that a priest does not betray!"*

The officer began to mumble, apologizing by saying that he had received orders to carry out the interrogation, and if he did not do so he would himself be punished. To this Celis replied that as a cleric he too was accountable for his behavior, and he therefore would not talk. This impressed the interrogator, for Celis was freed with a warning not to provoke the authorities a second time. Celis hastened to disperse the Rotenberg children, who were secretly moved to other places. On May 3, 1944, Regine in turn was denounced by an informer and arrested in the home of the 80-year-old Joseph Celis. That same day, Hubert Celis was again arrested, and again was able to talk himself out of trouble and was released. Regine was sent to the Auschwitz extermination camp, which she luckily survived, returning to Belgium and her siblings in 1945.

In his postwar account, Father Hubert Celis had this to say about his obligation toward the Rotenberg children.

"I consider myself as having only done my duty. We are after all, irrespective of our religion or our religious and political opinions, the children of the Good God, hence brothers who should help one another! This is precisely what Christ wanted to tell us when he asked us to help our fellow men. I never thought of trying to convert the Rotenberg children to the Catholic faith. I always respected their religious beliefs: (1) because I did not want to take advantage of their unhappy situation to influence their minds; (2) because Mrs. Rotenberg had placed her full trust in me, and I had given her my word of honor as a priest. I had no right to betray this trust, but had the duty to remain faithful to the word given, so as to be able to restore these children to their parents or their family, in the same way they had confided them to me; (3) because I foresaw that the children would, after the war, be returned to their family and to a Jewish environment. So I preferred a good Jew to a bad Christian."

The Rotenberg children eventually settled in the United States. The ties between the rescued family and the Celis brothers remained close in the ensuing years. In 1947, Father Hubert Celis led Regina to the canopy when she married Isaac Wolbrom. In 1965, he was present at their son's Bar Mitzvah celebration in a New York synagogue. Senator Robert F. Kennedy sent a congratulatory letter to the President of Congregation Tifereth Israel in New York, where the ceremony was taking place. "His acts of heroism and selflessness during the Second World War will never be forgotten. You are expressing the gratitude of all of us to a man who has put love of his fellow men ahead of his own safety. With all best wishes." On that occasion, Regina stated, "My children have no grandparents. I think it is only fitting that Father Hubert should be on hand for my son's Bar Mitzvah because he was the last to see my parents."

Earlier, in a 1949 letter to an Israeli, Father Louis Celis played down his deeds during the war: "And so, my very dear Mr. Rabinowitz, you insist on considering me a saint because I was unfortunately able to save only a few Jewish lives. But was this not an urgent and serious obligation of every person, Jew, Christian, or atheist, still worthy to be considered human? The only profound regret that I must always bear with me is for my not having been able to provide for the welfare of all Jews in distress in Belgium and elsewhere, without any distinction whatsoever, and not having been able to hide them and thus fully remove them from this bloody persecution which, let's admit it, will forever remain an irremovable stain for the whole of Europe. And to think that these abominable crimes were perpetrated in a century considered the century of civilization and high culture. What an irony!"

His brother Hubert Celis, reminiscing about his former charitable deeds, noted: "I have never been the recipient of so much gratitude as from these children, who gave to us so much more than we gave them. These four children are ongoing proof of how much they merited this aid." Finally, Regina Wolbrom: "He kept us alive. We can never do enough for him."

In 1980, Yad Vashem conferred the Righteous title on Fathers Hubert and Louis Celis and their father Joseph.

Chotel, Marie & Briard, Henri

FRANCE

*M*arie Chotel was born in 1883 in Lorraine province, France, to a young unwed mother. With a minimal education, she worked mostly as a domestic, then as a waitress, a seamstress, and a concierge. Married twice, she eventually met her true love as a nurse in World War I caring for wounded soldiers, one of whom was Henri Briard. Moving to Paris in 1919, she lived in a common-law marriage with Briard, whom she eventually married in 1957. They could not marry before this, as he was legally married to a woman who had been committed to an insane asylum and therefore could not divorce her. Henri's children from his first wife moved in with him and Marie, but then left and had little contact with them.

In 1934, Marie and Henri became acquainted with the Melszpajz couple. As paradoxically told by their daughter, Odette, "Madame Marie came into my life before I did." This happened when George (born Icek) Melszpajz and wife Bertha (Bronka), recent immigrants from Poland, moved into the building on 90 rue d'Angouleme, where Marie worked as a concierge. At the time, Bertha was pregnant with Odette and was looking for a more comfortable apartment. Answering a newspaper ad, Bertha showed up, knowing that no children were accepted there. So Bertha tried to hide her pregnancy. When Marie saw that Bertha liked the apartment, she said, "Don't worry. You don't have to hold in your stomach. I won't say anything to the landlord. You need the apartment." The Melszpajzes moved in, and Odette was born that November. Her mother, Bertha, related that Marie did not have children of her own, so "she began to treat

Marie Chotel and Henri Briard (from Odette Meyers, *Doors to Madame Marie*, University of Washington Press, 1997)

us like her own children. When my daughter was born, she called herself her godmother and gave her a blanket to which she sewed religious medals (she was a devout Catholic); and when my husband left for the army, she did the same for him. It was a form of protection." Marie kept herself busy with sewing for customers in the neighborhood, and little Odette would lend a helping hand, such as by picking up needles from the floor with a magnet. Then came the war, and George Melszpajz was taken into the French army. In 1940, when he fell into German captivity, Marie sent him food packages. Bertha, alone with a child, joined the resistance, and Marie agreed to serve as a messenger. Her apartment became a place where personal mail and messages could be deposited and forwarded elsewhere. Then near-tragedy struck.

On July 16, 1942, there took place the infamous raid on the city's Jews by the French police, known as the Vel d'Hiv, after the Winter Sports Stadium (Vélodrome d'Hiver) where some 13,000 Jews (men, pregnant women, the old, and the young) were rounded up before being deported to the death camps. Very early that morning, when Marie heard a commotion in the street as French gendarmes began to block off streets where many Jews lived, in Odette's words she went upstairs, pulled mother and daughter of out their beds, rushed them downstairs, and hid them in the broom closet of her minuscule apartment. It was just in the nick of time. They could hear the French gendarmes talking to Marie, telling her that they had come "to rid France of Jewish vermin." To which Marie, playing along, replied: "It's about time! We've let those Jews take over our jobs, our houses, our money, everything! We've been pushed around too long!" The gendarmes could not be more pleased with the concierge's words, while Odette and her mother stood frozen in the closet a few feet away. Marie then opened a bottle of Alsatian wine, one of the best she said, to toast the gendarmes and their work. In the closet, in Odette's words, "our bodies stiffen, our breath is muted; we become ears, nothing but ears." Suddenly one of the gendarmes put down his glass and asked, "Where are your Jews?" At that moment, eight-year-old Odette recalled, "I think my heart sank into my stomach." Not losing her composure, Marie assured them that they had left. "I'm glad they're gone! Good riddance! I hope they don't come back. Let's have a drink to that, shouldn't we?" One gendarme voice was heard admonishing Marie: "You know, Madame, what will happen if we find you've lied about your Jews?" They then asked to see the vacated apartment. To which Marie assured them that the place was terribly ill-kept, filthy and smelly, and not worth an inspection. Convinced, and for whatever other reasons, the gendarmes had had enough and left.

Bertha Melszpajz could not thank Marie Chotel enough for saving them from arrest, and said to her, "The Pope has not objected to the [French] anti-Jewish laws, or to Vichy's antisemitic propaganda. It's like a mandate to Catholics not to intervene in whatever happens to Jews. How then do you reconcile what you did to save us with your own Catholic faith." Marie's response was as simple as it was profound. "Don't worry. Popes and governments come and go; only God is eternal. This is between me and God. If he thinks I've done wrong, He will let me know."

Later when Henri Briard, affectionately known as Monsieur Henri, returned from work (he was a carpenter), he and Marie decided there was not a minute to lose to find an another place for Odette, far from Paris, and this was quickly arranged. Henri and Odette began walking in the direction of the subway station. "There were German soldiers everywhere… He held my hand. I was trembling. My hand was shaking." Briard "told me to look at my shoes and not to answer if anyone called my name." At the train station, a strange woman appeared and took over, accompanying Odette and several other children to the village of Chavagnes-en-Paillers, in Vendée province, southwest of Paris, and to the home of Marie Raffin. There, the children were to be passed off as Catholics from the big city, sent to the country for fresh air and healthy food. Their parents paid for room and board.

Madame Raffin carefully instructed the newly arrived on their new identity and the appropriate behavior. "First: never, never say that you are Jewish, no matter what happens." Then, they had to learn some Catholic religious customs, such as the sign of the cross, the Lord's Prayer and the Hail Mary; also, how to kneel and greet clerics in the village. Odette at first found these requirements bewildering, but was comforted with the thought that "the peasants in that village affectionately called the Virgin Mary, 'Madame Marie.' It was then that I knew that I would be safe. I figured, 'If they have one – a Madame Marie – here, then I'm OK.'… This way, whenever I would pray to the Virgin Mary, my own Madame Marie would slip into the statue, and both would help me"; sort of a double protection in her mind. Odette's education continued at the local school, directed by teachers of the Ursuline Order. Odette's mother remained another eight months in Paris before leaving to hide in the village of La Basse Clavelière, near St. Fulgent, where Odette eventually joined her, and both appeared under the borrowed names of Marie and Odette Petit. From there, Bertha sent Marie Chotel as a holiday gift a goose with lots of fats, for her own use. Later, Bertha found out that Marie had cooked it, packed it up in tin containers, with the meat parts completely covered with the fat. She then sent it to George Melszpajz in the prisoner-of-war camp.

Back in La Basse Clavelière, Odette frustratingly kept encountering the traditional anti-semitism preached by the church. In one such incident, during a mass dutifully attended by Odette, she had to listen to the priest's sermon on the "evils" of Jews, where he asserted that they acted on behalf of Satan and used various ploys to divert Christians from the right path, such as the ridiculous claim that Jews in the garment industry were making the skintight women's clothing to lead men astray. The priest also gave some guidance to the faithful on how to recognize a Jew, especially, as he pointed out, in these days when many had fled the big cities and were passing as non-Jews in the countryside. The priest suggested the following: "If a Jew, even one mistaken for a Christian, so much as crosses the threshold of your house, someone in your family will soon die. Then you will know for sure that you had been dealing with a Jew." Sure enough, someone soon died in the village: a young man belonging to the family of the landlord who had rented the house to Odette's mother suddenly died from an illness. A group of children ganged up on Odette, accusing her of being responsible for the death, on top of having crucified Jesus. Odette shouted back: "Me? I didn't kill Jesus! I'm only nine and I'm not Jewish. I'm a Christian! A Christian!" This did not help, for the children threw her into a pond, then beat her when she came out, warning her that they would report her to the Gestapo. When she got home, Bertha went to seek the help of the mayor of St. Fulgent, who was also active in the Resistance. He reassured the people in La Basse Clavelière that Bertha and Odette were true Catholics, a fact he said he had known for a long time. Things quieted down again in the village.

In the meantime, in the absence of the Melszpajz family, some people took an interest in the vacant apartment. Marie Chotel discouraged them, describing the apartment as small and ugly and saying that it belonged to a prisoner of war who might come back at any time. She thus saved the apartment for the eventual return of its prewar tenants, and in the meantime used it as a refuge for other people of illegal status. Returning to Paris after the liberation, Odette was greatly relieved to see "Madame Marie and Monsieur Henri."

Bertha described Marie as a person with "a lot of folk wisdom, the ability to judge right from wrong at all times." Her daughter Odette remembered Marie Chotel's description of her philosophy of life. "The heart is like an apartment, and if it's messy and there is nothing to offer, no food or drink to offer guests, nobody will want to come in. But if it's clean and dusted every day, and if it's pretty and there are flowers and food and drink for guests, people will want come in and they will want to stay for dinner. If it's extra nice, God himself comes in and does something to make it even nicer." To this Odette added her own thoughts. People like Marie, who are not so literate and lack a formal education, had to do their own thinking at all times, she concluded. "They didn't follow what was 'taught' them; they figured out everything for themselves. They had to think through everything." People like Chotel do more of their own thinking and make their own decisions, because they are more removed from those in society who shape everyone the same way. "I think Madame Marie thought with her heart, that was the important thing … Her principles came from making decisions according to her heart, her conscience, her own mind … She saved not only my life – my physical life – but my spirit also." Typical of Marie's thinking was her forgiveness of a young woman, one of the residents of the house, whose wartime lover was a German officer. After the liberation, Marie arranged for her to leave the area before local people had time to seek revenge by humiliating her in public. In Marie's estimation, "It's not fair: those who did the most harm will surely get away, especially if they have money on their side. It's the little people they'll pick on, as usual. She was just young and poor … She just enjoyed going to the opera in a fancy dress, escorted by a soldier in uniform."

In 1949, the Melszpajzes left France for the United States, where they Americanized their name to Miller. In 1978, when Odette (whose married name was Meyers) submitted her testimony, she lived in California, was an assistant professor of French and French Literature, married, and the mother of two children. In 1985, Yad Vashem recognized Marie Chotel and Henri Briard as Righteous Among the Nations.

In 1997, Odette Meyers' war reminiscences appeared, in a book called *Doors to Madame Marie*, which ends with the following encouraging words.

"As always when I am given to doubt, Madame Marie appears to me … I feel that if we petition her politely, she'll put her signature on our passports and let us in through the doors of the new apartment house of the next century, telling us how to be good tenants: 'Just be courteous, considerate, helpful, and enjoy yourselves! And don't forget to keep your own apartments tidy … and keep a vase of flowers on your tables.'"

Chrysostomos, Demetriou
Karrer, Lucas
GREECE

*A*lready in the first millennium B.C.E., the famous Greek poet Homer mentioned in his *Iliad* and *Odyssey* the island of Zakynthos off the western coast of the Greek peninsula, saying that it had received its name from the son of King Dardanos of Troy, who was called Zakynthos. It is also mentioned that the Greek hero Ulysses (Odysseus) of Ithaca conquered the island. Over the centuries Greek-speaking Zakynthos, part of the Ionian Islands, passed through many hands. During the early phases of World War II, it was held by Italy. The Jewish community on the island numbered some 275 souls.

On September 9, 1943, the day after Italy surrendered to the Allies, the Germans landed on Zakynthos, also known as Zante, and remained there for a full year, until September 12, 1944. Soon after the German takeover, a saga involving the local bishop of the Greek Orthodox Church began that compares favorably with Ulysses' courageous defiance of the gods that wished to do him harm. The new gods were the Nazi rulers of the island who demanded, initially, from Mayor Lucas Karrer a list of the Jews on the island. There are several versions of what then occurred.

After leaving the German commander's office, the mayor reportedly consulted with Metropolitan Chrysostomos, and the two decided to try to persuade the German commander to forgo the roundup of the island's Jews. They took along an expensive gold ring as a gift for the man in return for his favorable consideration. It worked, and the deportation plan was shelved and for the time being forgotten.

After this incident, some time later, a new officer appeared on the scene – Alfred Lütt – who was not well disposed to any further postponements. In fact, he called Mayor Karrer to his office and gave him a 24-hour ultimatum to deliver the list of the Jews or face death. The

Metropolitan Chrysostomos

mayor first alerted his men to take the Jews to the hills or hide them with their Christian friends in the countryside. That same evening the mayor escaped on a fishing boat to another island, and the list of the island's Jews was not to be found. The Jews remained hidden until the German departure on September 12, 1944.

Another version has it that the mayor together with Metropolitan Chrysostomos returned for a face-to-face confrontation with the German commander. Chrysostomos, who had studied in Germany and was conversant in German, pleaded with Major Lütt: "The Jews of Zakynthos are Greeks, peace-loving and industrious. They are pureblooded Zakynthians and totally harmless. I beg of you to rescind the criminal order." When the commander refused to relent, the bishop pulled out a sheet and said: "Here, take the list of the Jews on Zakynthos." He had scribbled on the paper his own name. He added: "I am at your mercy, you can arrest me, not them. If this does not satisfy you, then know that I will march together with the Jews straight into the gas chambers." The German commander was taken aback at the Metropolitan's words and stopped the meeting. He too gave up on the idea, at least for the time being.

In yet another version, in the confrontation with the German commander, Metropolitan Chrysostomos was accompanied by Dr. Dimiotrios Katevatis. Perhaps this took place at a second meeting between the cleric and the military man – the first one in attendance with Mayor Karrer. This was also a highly charged meeting. When Katevatis returned home, he told his son Nicholas Katevatis what had taken place, and the son jotted down his father's words:

> *"Chrysostomos: Sir, I as the spiritual leader of the island, and together with Dr. Katevatis, who is a graduate of the Berlin University, we beg you not to deport Jews."*
>
> *Lütt: "We are not molesting in any way any Christian or Greek. The order of deportation is a matter of general policy and I must obey. After all, when the war is over, they will return.*
>
> *Dr. Katevatis: I disagree with you, Major. Judaism is a faith, a religion, and not merely a citizenship. These people had lived for centuries here. They are Greek nationals. Furthermore they are Greek soldiers who fought and shed their blood for this country. May I remind you that according to the armistice no Greek soldiers will be taken prisoner. So far there has been no trouble on this island."*

Katevatis then went on to warn the German commander of the presence of an underground on the island, numbering some 800 armed men in the hills, and continued, "I must warn you about the dire consequences of deporting the Jews."

The younger Katevatis questioned his father on the wisdom of addressing a German officer in this insolent way, thereby placing at risk Katevatis' own family. To this, his father replied, "Do you know that unlike others, no Jews committed murder, no stabbing, no beating. There is no Jewish criminal in the jail on the island. They are extremely good people, and I am happy that I protected them. That's all, I do not permit any more argument on this matter."

Whatever the correct historical version, all confirm that an ill-tempered and unpleasant meeting took place with the German commander that was fraught with danger for those on the Greek side of the clash. Furthermore, the Germans, with their hands full fighting guerillas on the Greek mainland, evidently did not feel that they had sufficient manpower to take on the Greek partisans on Zakynthos while at the same time also trying to flush out the 275 Jews hiding throughout the island. Time passed, and with the worsening military situation the Germans withdrew from Zakynthos on September 12, 1944.

The result was that Zakynthos became the only Jewish community in Greece where no deportation of Jews took place, and much of this credit goes to two principal heroes, Metropolitan Chrysostomos and Mayor Lucas Karreri. The Jewish population numbered 275 at the start of the German occupation, and other than those who died of natural causes, this community survived fully intact during the German occupation – hidden either in island's villages or in mountain retreats. In the words Nicholas Katevatis, "The story sounds like fiction, but it is true history."

In 1978 Metropolitan Demetriou Chrysostomos and Mayor Lucas Karreri were recognized as Righteous Among the Nations.

Csizmadia-Kovacs, Mária & Malvina & Olga & Irén

HUNGARY

*M*ária Csizmadia-Kovacs, an ethnic Hungarian, had lived on the Czech side of the border before she was widowed. She then moved to nearby Sátoraljaujhely, in northern Hungary, together with her three daughters, Irén, Olga, and Malvina. There Mária worked as a seamstress and Olga, the eldest daughter, helped out by working in a Jewish-owned store. Several months after the German occupation of Hungary, on March 19, 1944, a ghetto was created in Sátoraljaujhely. The Csizmadia girls helped by sneaking in food to the Jews inside the ghetto, whose inhabitants were soon deported to Auschwitz. At about the same time, in May 1944, a contingent of over 200 Jewish laborers, conscripted into special Hungarian hard labor units known as labor battalions, arrived in the city and were encamped in a school next to the Csizmadia home, separated from them by a fence. When Malvina took out the garbage, depositing it near the garden fence, she would strike up conversations with the men on the other side. They asked her for food, which they would pay for and which Malvina gladly provided, rushing off to a nearby store to get it. At a later point, some of the men were invited into the Csizmadia home to freshen up as well as listen to news on the radio and the men's relatives were also permitted to visit them in the Csizmadia home as well as send packages to them there.

Malvina was the middle sister. When her family had lived in a small village, near the city

Malvina Csizmadia receiving the Righteous Among the Nations award at Yad Vashem from Justice Moshe Landau, Chairman, Commission for the Designation of the Righteous

of Kosice, then inside Czechoslovakia, her father had been a butcher and also owned vineyards. At the age of three, she fell and broke several vertebras, which left her bedridden for a long time. Poor medical treatment led to the deformation of her back and a protruding hunchback. She managed to cope with this impediment and went to elementary school and then commercial school.

When on October 25, 1944, ten days after the installation of the intensely pro-Nazi Arrow Cross in power, the labor battalion unit (number 107/11) received orders to leave the place and head toward the German border, where they feared they would be turned over to the Germans. At this point, many decided to escape and head in the direction of the front, hopefully to link up with the advancing Russian army. The Csizmadia women helped several dozen men of the labor battalion escape, hiding them with their relatives in three separate villages.

Karol Fiszer had earlier escaped and hid in a washerwoman's home together with three other men. As the place proved unsafe, they managed to contact Olga, who arranged for the men to meet her near the railroad where Olga's cousin worked. Providing the men with railroad workers uniforms, she then led them to her cousin's home, where they hid in the attic for about eight weeks. The Csizmadia family also hid some Jews in the basement of their own home, as well as delivering food to Jews in various other hiding places, such as abandoned houses, basements, and attics. They neither asked for, nor received, compensation for their deeds.

All together, the Csizmadias managed to save at least 29 Jews, caring for them until the area's liberation on December 7, 1944. They also helped other men of the labor battalion to find safe shelters – and cared for them for as long as ten weeks in hay lofts and potato cellars. One of the men, László Surányi, related that after walking with others for about eight kilometers in order to reach the advancing Russians, he had to cross a certain guarded bridge, and it was Malvina who kept the guards busy with small talk to distract their attention while the men crossed beneath them. The men continued on a road filled with terrible sights – bodies of labor battalion men shot and left hanging from trees, carcasses of dead horses, etc.

After the liberation on December 6, 1944, Karol Fiszer suddenly fell seriously ill and Olga was told by a doctor that Karol's life was in danger and desperately needed penicillin. Olga was given an address where to get it. She traveled for three days in cargo trains with fighting still raging in nearby Miskolc, and was able to obtain the much-needed penicillin and take it back to where Karol lay sick. The two were already romantically involved, and after Karol's recovery they decided to marry. However, sensitive to her Christian upbringing, Olga first asked permission from an evangelical pastor, then went to see a rabbi. "I told the rabbi that I did not wish to bring bastards into the world; they should have a father. I took lessons in Judaism and was converted in March 1946 and then was married in the rabbinate." In 1949, the couple headed for Israel with their two children.

Olga's sister Irén, was also romantically involved with a former labor battalion man, László Surányi, and they too married and moved to Israel. Many years later, recalling that sad period and Malvina's role in his and the others' rescue, he wrote: "Words on paper cannot express everything that one might say about this poor physically handicapped woman. Even these few words quickly put into writing I cannot inscribe without shedding a tear, for until today I dare not remember everything."

Yad Vashem honored the three Csizmadia daughters and their mother with the Righteous title: Malvina Csizmadia in 1965, Olga Fischer in 1987, and Irén Surányi with Mária Csizmadia in 1995.

Damaskinos (Papandreou, Dimitrios)
GREECE

*O*n April 6, 1941, Nazi Germany invaded Greece and quickly conquered the country. Thessaloniki (also known as Salonika) contained the largest Jewish population, some 56,000 of the country's 77,000 Jews. While Athens and the major part of the country were turned over to Germany's ally, Fascist Italy, Thessaloniki remained in German hands. There, the Jewish population was subjected to increased restrictions and maltreatment, culminating on March 15, 1943, with the start of the systematic deportation of the entire Jewish population to the death camp of Auschwitz in the space of a few months.

At this point, Metropolitan Damaskinos, head of the Greek Orthodox Church, decided to let his voice be heard against the liquidation of the Jewish community. Born in 1890 as Dimitrios Papandreou, he was ordained a priest in the Greek Orthodox Church in 1917, later assuming the name of Damaskinos. After filling several clerical positions, he was appointed, on June 2, 1941, Metropolitan (or Archbishop) of Athens and thus head of the Greek Orthodox Church of Greece. When the news first reached Athens about the deportations in Thessaloniki, Damaskinos received a Jewish delegation that pleaded with him to intervene. He reportedly was moved to tears, and he immediately summoned an urgent meeting of all the leaders of prominent associations and organizations in Athens and dramatically reported to them on the tragedy that had befallen the Jews in Thessaloniki. At his initiative, on March 23, 1943, a protest was delivered to Constantin Logothetopoulos, head of the puppet government in Athens, signed by 29 prominent figures, leaders of organizations representing the gamut of the spiritual and professional leadership of Greece. The following day, a similar petition was forwarded to the German diplomatic representative in Athens, Gunther von Altenburg. Both petitions called for the cancellation of the deportations.

Metropolitan Damaskinos delivering a speech in Athens, shortly after the end of Word War II (courtesy of the Photographic Archive of the Jewish Museum of Greece)

In the letter to Prime Minister Logothetopoulos, of March 23, 1943, Damaskinos began by mentioning the "surprise and distress" of the Greek people at the deportation of Jews to Poland currently taking place in Thessaloniki. Damaskinos went on to remind the Prime Minister that according to the terms of the armistice, all Greek citizens were to receive the same treatment by the occupation authorities regardless of race and religion. He then continued by lauding the contribution of the Jews to the welfare of the Greek nation. "The Greek Jews have not only proved themselves valuable factors in the country's economic performance, but have generally shown themselves to be law-abiding and fully cognizant of their obligations as Greeks. They have thus shared in the common sacrifices for the Greek homeland and have been in the forefront of the battles which the Greek nation has fought in defense of its inalienable historical rights." Damaskinos characterized the Jewish population as "the children of our common Mother Greece" and as "indissolubly united and equal members of the body of the nation, regardless of any religious or denominational difference." The head of the Greek Orthodox Church then reminded the Prime Minister that the Christian religion "recognizes no discrimination, superiority or inferiority based upon race or religion," and therefore, "any inclination toward discrimination deriving from racial or religious difference must be condemned."

As a sop to the collaborationist Prime Minister, Damaskinos injected a few words pleasing to his ears. Perhaps, the prelate stated, a "profound opposition" does exist between Germany and its Jewish population, and perhaps as well, world Jewry in "this or that activity" has overstepped certain bounds. Be that as it may, "what is of interest to us today and disturbs us deeply is the fate of our 60,000 [actually over 70,000] Jewish fellow-citizens, whose nobility of feelings and humanitarian disposition, whose progressive ideas and economic activity, and, most important of all, whose unimpeachable patriotism we have come to know during a long co-existence in slavery and in freedom." If, as the Germans claimed, the Jews represented a security threat, why deport them outside Greece, Damaskinos asked? Why not confine under surveillance the able-bodied among them (excluding, of course, old men and children) in a certain area of Greek territory "against the hypothetical danger," and thus prevent their deportation.

The Jews, Damaskinos reminded the Prime Minister, "are among the most peaceable, the most law-abiding, and the most productive elements in the country." If, however, against all hopes, the Jews are to be deported, the Greek government should not be at all involved in this sordid affair, "leaving to the foreigners the entire responsibility of the manifest injustice being committed." Then came a warning. "No one, we believe, is entitled to forget that all the acts of this difficult period, even those which lie beyond our wishes and power, will one day be investigated by the nation for the due judgment of history. And in the moment of judgment, the moral responsibility which our rulers have shouldered, even for the acts of the occupying powers, will weigh heavily on the conscience of the nation if they omitted to express, by noble-minded and courageous gestures, the entirely reasonable indignation and unanimous protest of the nation against actions which grievously affect its unity and honor, such as the deportation of Greek Jews now beginning."

Not content with this letter to the Greek Prime Minister, who lacked the authority to stop the deportations, on the following day, as mentioned, Damaskinos drafted an equally strong letter to Gunther von Altenburg, the German ambassador, stationed in Athens – also countersigned by an eminent array of the country's cultural, educational, professional, and economic organizations.

The letter of March 24, 1943, went straight to the point. It began by stating that the undersigned had no intention to interfere in any way with the administration of the German occupation of the country, with the exception of one issue "which in recent days has held the entire society of Greece in a state of concern and emotion, being certain that you will examine it in a spirit of profound good will and even more profound understanding. The issue in question is that of the expulsion from Thessaloniki of the community of Jews of Greek nationality who, for a very long time, entirely and lawfully integrated into the institutions of this country, not only never gave occasion for complaint on the part of any Greeks but, on the contrary, always set an example of serious and cooperative solidarity with them and, at moments of crisis, proved themselves to be capable of self-denial and self-sacrifice in their country's cause." Damaskinos went on to remind the German diplomat that throughout the entire length of Greek history "our relations with the Jewish community have always been harmonious and smooth – from the depths of antiquity through the time of Alexander the Great and his heirs, down all the years of tolerant Greek Orthodoxy and through our recent life as a nation." The expulsion of the Jewish community from Greece should be suspended, at least on a temporary basis, until the whole question of the Jewish presence in Greece can be studied "in the light of special and thorough research" – that is, practically speaking, for an indefinite period of time.

Damaskinos reminded Von Altenburg that one of the Greek conditions for laying down their arms during the German invasion was to have the rights of the Greek population respected without any regard to religious or racial divisions. As stated by General Tsolakoglou, the first German puppet Prime Minister, "the Jewish question does not exist in Greece nor will it ever be raised." Presently, the Greek people "feel pain when it sees its very brothers, snatched away from the altars of their homes, which over so many years they had inhabited with boundless trust and a spirit of irreproachable solidarity towards us." The signatories therefore beg the German diplomat for the suspension of the deportations, "and we assure you that the entire Greek people will be in a position to appreciate in due manner the magnificent gesture you will have made."

The following impressive educational, cultural, professional, and economic organizations added their signatures to that of Metropolitan Damaskinos, on behalf of the Greek Orthodox Church: Academy of Athens, University of Athens, National Metsovian Polytechnic, École Supérieure of Economic and Political Sciences, Journalists Union, Association of Greek Writers, Greek Actors, Greek Authors, Technical Chamber of Greece, Union of Greek Industrialists, Athens Professional Chamber, Athens Chamber of Commerce and Industry, Athens Chamber of Craft Industry, Piraeus Commercial Chamber, Social Security Foundation, Athens Bar Association, Association of Notaries Public of Athens and the Aegean, Union of Greek Theatre and Music Critics, Panhellenic Pharmacists Association, Panhellenic Dentists Association, Medical Association of Attica and Boeotia, First Aid Shelters, Union of Greek Chemists, Piraeus Medical Association, Athens Pharmacists Association, Dental Association of Athens, Pharmacists Association of Athens, Piraeus Pharmacists Association, and Kallithea Medical Association.

These appeals proved unavailing, and the 56,000-strong Jewish community of Thessaloniki, in existence for over 2,000 years, was decimated. In September 1943, the Germans took over the previously Italian-controlled regions of Greece and began to plan to deportation of the Jews from there, beginning with Athens. Chief Rabbi Eliahou Barzilai was summoned to Gestapo headquarters and told to submit a list of his flock within two days. Instead, with the help of the Greek underground, he was spirited out of the city and into the mountainous region controlled by it. At this juncture, Damaskinos went to see Von Altenburg but was rebuffed by the German diplomat who told him to stop interfering with German policy with regard to the Jews, since the orders had originated in Berlin and affected all Greek Jews. Returning from this meeting, Damaskinos urged a Jewish delegation to be ready for difficult times, assuring them of his commitment to their cause. He reportedly told them: "*We are all the children of the same Father, for God created us in his own image, and we are obligated to extend our help to fellow men and not allow Satan to rule over us.*"

Damaskinos then met with Panos Haldezos of the Athens municipality and told him: "I have made my cross, have spoken with God, and decided to save as many Jewish souls as I can. Even if I were to endanger myself, I will baptize Jews, and you will issue municipal documents, so that they obtain identity cards as Christian Greeks." He then also enlisted the cooperation of Angelos Evert, head of the Athens police, in the effort to save Jews from the liquidation. At Evert's orders, the police issued thousands of false identity cards to protect all those in hiding and help others escape. It is also reported that through his secretary, Jean Georgakis, Damaskinos urged all priests to extend aid to the Jews and to open convents to all those wishing to hide there. It is told that when the German commander threatened him with execution, Damaskinos responded: "According to the tradition of the Greek Orthodox Church, our prelates are hung and not shot. Please respect our tradition." All told, close to 10,000 Jews survived on Greek soil, many of them thanks to the aid solicited by the Greek Orthodox Church, under the imprint of its head, Metropolitan Damaskinos.

In October 1944, the Germans retreated from Greece, and in December of that year Damaskinos was appointed Regent until the establishment of a duly constituted government. A year later, in October 1945, Damaskinos served for several weeks as Prime Minister. He died in 1949.

In 1969, Yad Vashem bestowed upon the late Metropolitan Damaskinos the title of Righteous Among the Nations.

Deffaugt, Jean
FRANCE

*D*uring the war years, Jean Deffaugt was the mayor of Annemasse, a large town of some 8,000 inhabitants abutting the Swiss border – and the closest to the Swiss city of Geneva, on the other side. The terrain was flat, and consequently Annemasse became a popular transit and meeting point for clandestine organizations and people on their way to the Swiss border. Deffaugt had been appointed mayor by the Vichy government and had high regard for Marshal Philippe Pétain, the Vichy head of state who followed a policy of collaboration with

Nazi Germany after France's defeat in the war. Deffaugt's loyalty, as he openly confessed after the war, stemmed from Pétain's heroic role in World War I – a war in which Deffaugt took part as a soldier. "I kept the photo of the *Maréchal* in my office, despite the pointed remarks by my associates, who did not understand or did not want to understand," Deffaugt said candidly after the war. "My conscience is clear. I served neither Marshal Pétain nor General De Gaulle but first and foremost my country." At the same time, paradoxically, Deffaugt also created close links with the underground, where he was known under the code name "Charras."

His loyalty to Pétain did not diminish his concern for the fugitives, many of them Jews, passing through his city on their way to the Swiss border. He had a sympathetic ear for their plight and offered the city's assistance as much as was possible. During the Italian phase of the city's occupation, this did not present too great a problem, but when the Germans took over direct control in September 1943, Deffaugt had to operate more circumspectly.

He made it a habit to visit people caught by the Germans trying to cross the border and other prisoners who had run afoul of the Nazis. These were incarcerated in an annex of the Pax hotel, turned into a

Jean Deffaugt, in front of the Annemasse City Hall upon the Liberation, together with Jewish children he had rescued

prison. Some of the arrested people were subjected to brutal interrogations by the Gestapo, who were anxious to discover the names of the organizers of the clandestine crossings of the French-Swiss border. The Gestapo jail register speaks abundantly of the makeup of the "criminals" assembled there, for example,

> *Folio 642:32, children aged 3½–18, caught trying to flee to Switzerland – sent to Drancy [assembly point outside Paris for deportation to concentration camps]. Folio 127, Mila Racine, arrested October 21, 1943 – sent to Drancy.*

Mila's brother, Emmanuel Racine, was an important figure in the French-Jewish resistance in the area. Mila was arrested in the nearby town of Annecy leading a group of children toward the Swiss border. Before being sent to Drancy, she left the following verses etched on her cell door. "For a friend who passes and one day occupies this cell, remember: always keep your faith and smile, whatever happens." She was conveyed to the Ravensbrück women's concentration camp in Germany, where she perished.

When visiting the prisoners at the Pax hotel jail, at times on a daily basis, Deffaugt did not arrive with empty hands but brought along food, medicaments, and blankets, which he personally delivered to the prisoners. He also went to great lengths to try to free prisoners – Jews arrested for being Jewish, or for attempting to flee to Switzerland, as well as non-Jewish prisoners fleeing conscription for forced labor in Germany.

After the war, Deffaugt related how in one case he tried to help a certain Jewish family incarcerated in Hotel Pax. Marcel Lyon had been imprisoned there in November 1943 with his wife and daughter Josette. When Deffaugt visited them to see how they were bearing up in jail, he brought along a fancy cake. This led one of the German guards to sarcastically exclaim that Pax was no longer a jail but a resort. Mr. Lyon asked Deffaugt to at least help liberate his wife and daughter by writing to a certain address in Corrèze province to people who would supply false baptismal certificates for them. Deffaugt obliged and with the false documents he persuaded the head of the prison to free the two women. "I might describe all the drama, the anguish, and the crying – all the scenes that I witnessed when the husband parted from his wife and daughter." Deffaugt was determined to liberate the husband as well. Learning that the prison warden was an avid stamp collector, Deffaugt bought him off with a supply of stamps. In return, Marcel Lyon was reregistered, no longer as a Jew but as someone chosen for forced labor in Germany. Then, when Marcel was to be sent away, Deffaugt contacted a friend in Annecy, where the train was to make a stop, and asked him to get on the train and find him. The next stop being the city of Lyon, Marcel was able to jump off. He survived. In 1947, Josette married, and the Deffaugts were invited to the wedding. The whole family had been saved thanks to Deffaugt's courageous intervention.

The incident that remained most vivid in Deffaugt's memory was a mixture of joy and sadness – joy at having successfully negotiated the liberation and the life of 28 Jewish children; sadness at the price paid, the tragic end of the children's group leader – Anne-Marie (better known as Marianne) Cohn. She was arrested on May 31, 1944, as she led the group of 28 Jewish children toward the Swiss border. The children had been carefully rehearsed to identify themselves under their false names if stopped. Once across the border, they were to quickly remove from the linings of their clothes their authentic documents, bearing their real names, and show them to the Swiss guards. But they had all been arrested and incarcerated in the Hotel Pax prison.

When he learned of the children's arrest, Deffaugt visited them, bringing food, bandaging their wounds, and raising their spirits. He then decided to intervene with the Gestapo to at least get the younger children in the group released in his custody. The Gestapo agreed to have 17 children, aged four to eleven, released to Deffaugt. He had them divided among trustworthy people and sheltered in several locations, including a summer resort and a hospital.

There remained imprisoned five boys and six girls, over the age of 11, together with their guide, Marianne Cohn. They could be seen walking together in the street every day en route to the various tasks their jailers had assigned to them, such as kitchen details for German officers at their headquarters in the Hotel de France. As time passed, a plan was hatched for Marianne's escape. In a secret meeting on a train making the Annecy–Aix-les-Bains run, Deffaugt met with Emmanuel Racine and planned her rescue. The plan called for a car with its engine running to be parked on a street corner, and when Marianne passed by with the children on their day's work detail to snatch her and speed away.

But it did not work out that way. In Deffaugt's words, "When I told Marianne about the plan ... she almost immediately rejected it." She was assigned a mission, she exclaimed to Deffaugt, the care and safety of these children. She could not entertain the thought of the Germans wreaking revenge on them for her escape. Her mind was made up. She would not abandon them. Her duty was to carry out her mission to the end. "Alas," Deffaugt wrote after the war, "you did not suspect, dear little Marianne, that at this precise moment you were so close to death." Defiant as ever, she told her interrogators, "I have saved more than two hundred children, and if I am set free I will continue to do so."

On the night of July 7, 1944, she and four French underground men were dragged by the pro-Nazi and intensely antisemitic French Milice from their prison cells to a nearby forest and shot. After the liberation, a month later, her body was found in a terrible state. Evidently she had been tortured before being shot. She was not yet reached her 20th birthday. In her cell, she had written the following defiant poem:

Tomorrow I will betray, not today.
Tear out my nails today, I will not betray.
You don't know how long I can hold out, but I know.
You are five rough hands with rings.
You have hobnailed boots on your feet ...
Today, I have nothing to say.
Tomorrow I will betray.

That same month, Gestapo chief Meyer told Deffaugt that he had to make room at the Pax hotel for military purposes. The invasion by the Allies in Normandy had turned France into a battleground. Due to the shortage of available transportation, there was no alternative but to make the 11 imprisoned children "disappear." "Alas, I did not need to think much," Deffaugt later wrote, "and guessed immediately what these words meant. During an emotional discussion with him, I tried to find in him a little remaining humanity, and I succeeded in getting the conditional liberation of these children." This was in the form of a statement signed by Deffaugt, as follows, "I acknowledge having taken charge today of eleven young Jews, that I undertake to return at the first request." A similar verbal guarantee had been given by Deffaugt for the previous 17 children freed from jail. Deffaugt quickly placed the additional 11 children in good hands, as the signs of liberation grew clearer each day.

On August 18, 1944, Annemasse was liberated by U.S. forces. The 28 children were saved, and subsequently turned over to Jewish organizations. Before that, Deffaugt had them brought for a photo session on the steps of the Annemasse municipality, where he was shown shaking hands with Emmanuel Racine.

"As a believing Christian, I always undertook to help and protect all those stricken by calamity, without distinction," Deffaugt said of himself after the war, his motto having been, "Justice, love, happiness, and righteousness." On his many speaking engagements, he repeatedly returned to the tragic image of Marianne Cohn, whom he described as "beautiful, whose mischievous eyes expressed faith, courage, and determination."

As to his initiation into rescue activities, he said, "It is only the first step that counts. Afterwards I produced dozens and dozens of false identities." Still, it was not without serious risk. As he later reminisced, "I do not believe those who say they never knew fear. I was afraid, I admit. I never mounted the Gestapo stairway without making the sign of the cross or murmuring a prayer." He added that he told an underground contact that if were ever seen being taken away by the Gestapo, the resistance should try to shoot him. He feared he would not able to withstand the brutal interrogation and would betray his resistance comrades under torture.

In 1965, Yad Vashem declared Jean Deffaugt a Righteous Among the Nations. In June 1972, two years after his death, a monument was erected in the center of Annemasse in his honor, and the square was renamed Jean Deffaugt. The inscription mentioned his courageous work during the occupation on behalf of the many prisoners of the Germans and included among the honors bestowed on him: "Medal of the Righteous, by Israel."

Douwes, Arnold
NETHERLANDS

Arnold Douwes, born in 1906, was the son of a Protestant minister, and a rebel at heart. Early in his life, he had emigrated from Holland to the United States, where he was incensed by the discrimination against the black American population. He was deported from the U.S. after he was arrested and charged with being a communist and committing the "crime" of forcing the management of a restaurant in Chicago to serve a black man. His case reached the Supreme Court, where he actually won, but by that time he was already back in Holland and totally absorbed in the fight against the racist Nazi ideology. Throughout the German occupation of the Netherlands, Douwes devoted his life to the rescue of Jews and others whose lives were at risk. He was among the first people to actively resist the Nazis, initially by publishing illegal newsletters and sabotaging German targets. He was also instrumental in forging identity cards, acquiring food coupons from the distribution offices, and securing the financial wherewithal for keeping fugitives alive in various hiding places.

Before long, Douwes found himself on the Germans' wanted list and so he went into hiding. In May 1941, he found shelter with Johannes Post and his wife on their farm in Nieuwlande, a small village in Drenthe province. Over time, Johannes and Douwes became close friends and worked together in the re-

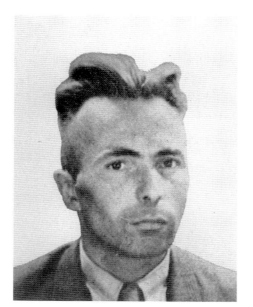

Arnold Douwes, from a photograph on a German "Wanted" poster of May 21, 1942

sistance. After being in Nieuwlande for a while, Douwes realized that it was an exceptional place for hiding Jews because of its geographical location and because the residents were especially cooperative. The village became a base of operations from where Douwes arranged hiding places for Jews. When Johannes Post became a national leader of the armed resistance, Douwes replaced him in his former job of rescuing Jews from Amsterdam.

Douwes often spent hours convincing the host families to welcome the guests. He would promise them support with provisions and food coupons, as well as money. His connections with the LO, major Dutch resistance group, enabled him to pay a monthly annuity for many of the Jews in hiding. His methods were not always tactful. He would often ask for a place for one fugitive, yet bring two. He sometimes requested shelter for a small child, but would bring an older one. Douwes often got carried away with emotion and it was not uncommon for him to resort to shouts and insults. His confrontational methods, which reflected the extreme urgency of the situation and the danger posed to both fugitives and hosts, earned him widespread criticism. He was accused of bringing too many Jews to Nieuwlande, of being reckless and irresponsible, of placing everyone at risk. However, Douwes persisted with his efforts and remarked in his diary that his method "worked." Dozens of people were often crammed in a back room waiting anxiously for a place to hide. The work did take a considerable emotional toll. Douwes was the "father" of his "onderduikers" and they were totally dependent on him. Despite the attendant emotions, and although his methods were tactless, Douwes carried out his task with care and concern. He helped ensure that fugitives without enough clothing were provided for. He ensured that correspondence was kept up between dispersed families. He assisted in the relocation of anyone who was unhappy in his shelter. Throughout this entire period, Douwes kept a coded diary. Despite it being essential that his actions remain undisclosed, he updated the diary, which he kept hidden in the ground, every few weeks. Arnold Douwes explained further how it worked:

"The technique used was to beg people in Amsterdam to hand over their children and explain to them that there were excellent hiding places for them, when in truth, there were none! The plan was to find an immediate suitable place for someone who had just arrived. One had to improvise, and places were indeed found. Hence, the importance of the temporary hiding places… Our work was not easy. First, there was the problem of locating places. The victims themselves presented the greatest difficulty. One had to invest great effort in order to persuade them. Many of them did not recognize the danger they were in… I did not realize this. As for me, already in 1941, when I saw a man by the name of Sam Jacobs arrested by the German police, I understand what was in store for them. Sam was the only Jew in our village. His daughter now [1977] lives in Beersheba. Unbelievable how so many people were so naïve… As for the children's parents, lies were used. " In order to separate parents from their children, one had to lie. To persuade the children, we told them stories of green fields and more such fictions … When we told people 'one week' it really meant 'until the liberation.' When we said 'two days,' it meant 'two years.' … Above all, the fear of betrayal … The mutual trust [between me and Nico] was so strong that when I was caught and thrown in jail for two months, Nico, who was then in hiding in the house of the Nieuwboer women [a teacher and her sister] was one hundred percent sure that I would not reveal his hiding place."

Mrs. H. Strauchler-Alter wrote that she fled with her son Joseph from her hiding place in Limburg province to Drenthe in the northeast. "Douwes waited for us at the station of the village of Nieuw Amsterdam and took us further, providing money, ration cards and places to hide whenever possible and so saved our lives."

Lou Gans added his own account how he was helped. In the autumn of 1943, as an 18-year-old youth, he was alone in Amsterdam, as his parents and other family members had already been deported. "I myself often had narrow escapes, I sometimes slept in parks and playgrounds, sometimes in my parents' house, where now and then I was able to hide fellow Jews, also hunted by the Germans, for a few nights." Lacking ration cards, Gans kept himself alive by often stealing food from the shops. After eight months of life under such harrowing conditions, he ran into a colleague of his father's, a man named Piet van den Akker, who urged him to go into hiding. "I told him that I had no money and therefore it was impossible to hide myself." Van den Akker assured him he would find a way to bring Lou Gans to the north of the country. With the man's sister, Nel Van den Akker, he traveled north to Hoogeveen, where she turned him over to Douwes. Nel served as a secret courier, who brought over weapons and various false papers, but her principal assignment was moving people, especially children, to hiding places. In Douwes' words, she was at times insolent and discourteous, "but she was and remains a remarkable personality."

Douwes took Gans to the mailman, Jan Dekker, in Nieuwlande village. When it became dangerous to stay there because of the appearance of the Germans, who searched each house, Douwes took Gans into the nearby woods, where the two dug a pit, and with blankets provided by Douwes, as well as food, Gans spent several weeks there, until it was safe to return to Dekker's home. Some months later, Douwes reappeared with his Jewish helper, Max ("Nico") Leons, and the two took Gans to another place; the farmer Hendrik Kikkert and his wife, Griet, who were already sheltering a Jewish child. Douwes describes them as "modest farmers and wonderful people." Some time later, Douwes returned and took Gans to another safe house – the Ottens': Jan, his wife, Seine, and their nine-year-old boy. The Ottens were school teachers and were already hiding two Jewish women, one of whom, Jet Reichenberger, married Douwes after the war, as well as close to a dozen other Jews cared for by the Seines in their various hiding places. Douwes used the Ottens' place as a transit point for the many Jewish fugitives whom he moved to different locations. There were two hiding places in the Ottens' home, one in the attic, the other under the basement. Douwes related that he once arrived there in the middle of the night, straight from Amsterdam, with six Jewish children. Seine served them all coffee and sandwiches, and then put them to sleep. On top of his school activities, Jan Otten, dressed in a German uniform, raided the local distribution offices for food coupons to keep his sheltered Jews supplied with food.

Eventually, someone betrayed the Ottens to the Germans and the Gestapo raided their home, but the Ottens has been pre-warned and managed to flee in time. When the Gestapo burst into their home, looking in vain for the Ottens as well as the hidden Jews, Lou Gans and Douwes – who happened to be there – and a Jewish fugitive (Isidor J. Davids) were hiding in a shaft under the house where they also kept weapons, printing equipment (for manufacturing false papers and fliers), and a carrier pigeon dropped by an Allied plane. The Gestapo did not find them during their three-hour search of the house and immediate vicinity.

From there, Gans was taken to the Simon Dijk family. Simon, a house painter, with wife and four children, was already sheltering four Jewish and four non-Jewish people in his home (including two escaped Russian prisoners of war). Now were added Douwes, Gans, and Davids, for a total of 11 people in hiding with the Dijks. Their daughter Frauke would often go out into the fields with two buckets full of food for the Jews hiding in the open – understandably, a very risky undertaking for this woman, in the event of her apprehension. After Gans and Davids had been moved to another location, Douwes, who stayed behind, was eventually arrested in the Dijk home. As for Gans, he moved to the home of the village baker, Engel Bolwijn, where he met other Jews in hiding, such as Miriam Whartman. Whenever danger threatened Gans' stay there, he would go into the fields, and the family's eldest daughter of 18 would bring him food secretly, every day, until the danger had passed. Miriam felt a bit uncomfortable there due to the constant readings from the New Testament, and the requirement to attend church (twice on Sundays), and asked Douwes to move her elsewhere. Gans described Douwes as,

"One of the few. You met him. Look in his eyes; look at his tight-lipped face. Then you will understand that no brute in the whole world could resist his will … I am very happy that I once met this remarkable man, who not only saved my life, but also enriched it…. Did he save 50 Jews, 100, 200, or 500? Heaven knows! He himself could hardly say, because there were so many Jews he helped!"

In this household, Lou Gans was visited by Nel van den Akker, the woman who had originally taken him from Amsterdam by train to the region and had arrived to see how some of her Jewish wards, especially the children, were faring. The danger of betrayal to the Germans had increased considerably after it was learned that a local inhabitant had gone over to the Nazi side and was informing on people suspected of harboring Jews. On hearing this, Nel van den Akker wanted to whisk him off to another place, and for this operation she told Lou Gans to disguise himself as a woman. "So I did, and together we went by bicycle to Amsterdam, where we arrived after some days," and to Nel's house. There he ran into other persons in hiding – Jews as well as non-Jews, and there he stayed through the terrible "hunger winter" of 1944–45, with Nel keeping her wards alive by scrounging food from various places (many people lay in the streets starved to death), until the country's liberation in May 1945. She later married one of her wards, Ernst Asscher. "The nightmare was over. I lost many relatives, but I found people who had the courage and the right human feeling to protect those who were hunted by the murderers."

Isidor J. Davids relates that he arrived at end 1942 in Hoogeveen with the help of the underground. He went to Johannes Post, who took him to the leading underground man in the region, Albert Nijwening, a 26-year-old baker, married to Jacoba and father of a little boy. The couple also kept with them for a long period, in fact until the war's end, a Jewish child named Salomon ("Sally") Appel and treated him like their own. The fact that he supplied bread to the whole village made it possible for him to locate suitable homes for Jews. During the war, many people passed through his home for short stays until moved elsewhere. When Davids arrived there, where he stayed for two weeks, he met other Jews in transit at Nijwening's home. After two weeks, Nijwening took Davids to Nieuwlande, where he found him various hiding places for the next two years. In addition, Nijwening joined raids at places where food ration cards were kept and distributed them among the persons who were hiding Jews. On top of these activities, Nijwening was also deeply in-volved in various clandestine activities for the Dutch resistance (the LO and LKP organiza-tions). Davids reckons that between 200 to 250 Jews passed through the Nijwening home at one time or another. He had a brother, Jan Nijwening, living in Nieuwlande, who also helped. According to Douwes, Davids, under his code name of "Peter," also helped forge various documents and send secret messages to London. Together with Gans (code name "Hermann") he once secretly printed a flier countermanding a previous German order for the billeting of troops in the village. The printing machine was located in the basement of a church, without the pastor's knowledge.

Another story is that of David Kool, born 1921. For a time he was protected from depor-tation because he worked for the *Joodse Raad* (German-controlled Jewish Council). But in summer 1943, even this protection seemed no longer certain. A friend told him to head by train for Zwolle, in Drente province, then enter a certain restaurant where a man would be waiting for him. This turned out to be the farmer Roffel, from Nieuwlande. After a cup of coffee both proceeded, again by train, to Hoogeveen, where they switched to bicycles for the last leg to Nieuwlande. There, Roffel dropped Kool off at the Simon Ryk household. Later, in September, or October, 1943 Douwes appeared and took Kool to a certain Mrs. Mulder, then to Fennigje Seinen-Mekkes, where he met other Jews in hiding. The German police (the notorious *Grüne Polizei*) raided the Seinen home on August 16, 1944, and arrested the son Seine Seinen, and jailed him in Amersfoort camp, from which he made his escape. In the meantime, David Kool was moved to several others locations. Arrested while out in the field, on December 31, 1944, Kool was moved to Westerbork camp, where due to the end of deportations to the concentration camps of Sobibor (already destroyed) and Auschwitz (no longer reachable due to the deteriorating conditions on the German side), where he was kept until liberated by Canadian troops, on April 12, 1945.

In yet another story – Joseph Roet (then 17), brother Roet (11) and another brother were fetched by Douwes together probably with Piet van der Akker in Amsterdam, in 1943. Dou-wes accompanied the two by train to Zwolle and arranged a night's sleepover. The following morning, the party headed for Dedenswaart. There, Joseph stayed with his brother. When Joseph came down with a serious skin infection and the local doctor could not treat him, Douwes came quickly, accompanied by his Jewish colleague, Max Leons, and they traveled by bicycle to the train station and from there to Zwolle, and to the care of a trustworthy doctor; then to Dedenswaart, to the care of a dependable nurse, where Joseph stayed until the war's end. Through Douwes, he received letters from his parents, hidden in Limburg province."

Haim Roet, born in 1932, related that "In October 1943, a woman came to fetch me and my two brothers, and took us to the train station. After a night's stay with a local Nieuw-lande farmer, Douwes arrived with Leons and took us on a bike for a ride of 30–35 kilome-ters on side roads, in order to avoid German patrols, to Nieuw Amsterdam, and dropped us off at the Antony and Aleida Deesker home. While there, Douwes and Leons brought Haim letters from his parents and also brought a Jewish woman for hiding there."

Douwes: "Once I brought a little Jewish girl to the home of Mrs. Jantina Zwiers. The child had black hair and was very beautiful. She was to be represented as a war orphan after the Rotterdam bombing and a cousin of the Zwiers, and to attend school with the Mrs. Zwi-ers' five children – all of them with blond hair. Every week we brought a Peroxide bottle and made her hair reddish. L.E. Anholt-Davidson said of Douwes, "He was a hero in the eyes of the Jews. Day and night he fought for us to save us from the hands of the Germans. When I sometimes asked him: 'Douwes, what would we have done without you,' he answered, 'That's nothing. No, I meant it's important, for God sent you to us.'"

On October 19, 1944, the Gestapo finally caught up with him. He was arrested and incarcerated in the Assen prison, where he was tried and sentenced to death. On December 11, 1944, only a few hours before his execution, the armed resistance succeeded in freeing him and some other underground activists. Once free, Douwes was obliged to go into hiding. By this time, the hiding places provided by the resistance had become unsafe and Douwes was compelled to relocate regularly from one address to another. In April 1945 he crossed

the line to freedom in Coevorden, a nearby village that had already been liberated. After the war, Douwes married Jet Reichenberger, one of the women helped by him. The couple moved to South Africa and a few years later they moved to Israel with their three daughters. In Israel, Douwes resumed the practice of his actual profession, as a landscape architect. After 30 years, he returned to Holland.

On March 23, 1965, Yad Vashem recognized Arnold Douwes as Righteous Among the Nations. Douwes was not happy that only he was honored, and insisted for many years that the inhabitants of Nieuwlande who helped him in the giant rescue operation also be awarded the honorific Righteous title since, as he repeatedly stated, he could not have done his work without the help of the townspeople, including his closest aide, the Jewish Max Leons, known by his code name as Nico, who passed as a church seminarian. To hide his identity Leons went to church every Sunday. Since he did not know the religious chants, he practiced moving his lips by watching the others. This way he managed to fool everyone and, according to Douwes, even Johannes Post, "but

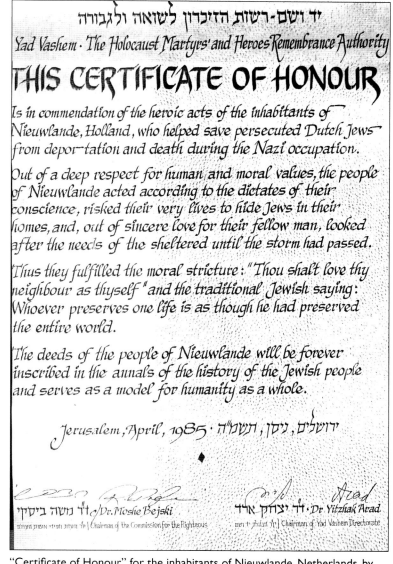

"Certificate of Honour" for the inhabitants of Nieuwlande, Netherlands, by Yad Vashem

not me, your obedient servant" (in a 1977 letter to Yad Vashem). At first, Douwes and Post did not fully trust Leons, but this suspicion was short-lived and the two became close collaborators in the giant rescue operation to get as many Jews as possible removed from the clutches of the Nazis. Douwes mentioned 270 names of village rescuers, and was willing to provide a list. Over the years, the list underwent several changes, down to 170, and then up some more, to 202 names, including some husband and wife teams.

We mention here a few of Douwes' other Nieuwlande rescuer colleagues, as per his postwar summarized list:

Jans Keimpena: seven Jews hid in his home and managed to escape minutes before the arrival of the Gestapo.

Willem Marissen: the temple's sexton, he hid Jews in the basement.

Klaas Nienhuis: at first refused to accept Jews, out of fear. He was then persuaded to take in Jews.

Johannes Norder was a carpenter and helped build hiding places. Hid the Hertz family in his home. At night his daughter secretly brought food in a bucket to people hiding in the nearby forest.

Frederik Eppinga and wife: at first they refused, but then admitted a Jewish boy who stayed with them until the war's end.

Dr. Hendrik Brouwer: treated sick Jews in hiding, and also hid some in his home. One day, an Allied pilot whose plane had been shot down knocked on his door. Brouwer took him in and fed him, then reported him to the Germans. His explanation: the pilot's presence endangered the Jews with him. Underground people were very angry with the doctor. He explained that the pilot would be taken to a prisoner-of-war camp; but the Jews, if caught, would meet a more terrible fate.

F. Dekker van Dyk: a 16–17-year-old girl who distributed food to hiding places in the forest. Her parents' house was used as a transit point.

Hendrik Winkel: During a search of his home a German opened the wall closet and found a Jew. In an attempt to save himself, he gave the German a gold watch. The German closed the closet door and said to the soldier with him: no one here. (Douwes: "This also happened. It's a pity we didn't have enough gold watches. Perhaps we could have saved more people").

Jan Douwes: a Protestant minister. Close to death, he asked that his body be incinerated, as a sign of identification with the six million Jews.

Johannes Wildschut: a Catholic, active in break-ins at offices to steal documents; arrested and imprisoned. Johannes Post failed in his attempt to free him and both were killed during the rescue operation.

Karolina Nonnekens: Nico Leon's parents were hidden there and others too. After being betrayed the men had to flee, through the roof of the church.

Hendrik Zylstra: a teacher who hid Jews in his home. Sat in jail together Douwes, and was freed with him.

These persons, as well as the others mentioned in this article, are among the 202 Nieuwlande residents also honored with the Righteous title.

Dragan, Stepan & Olga
UKRAINE

*I*t all began with a cup of sugar. Stepan Dragan had taken a chance in sneaking into the Zbarazh ghetto, where the Germans had confined the town's Jews, and was asking passers-by where he could get some sugar. His two-year-old son Wladek was very ill, and Stepan was told to get sugar as part of the medication. He was told that this hard-to-find item could perhaps be gotten inside the ghetto. He ran into Jacob Lachman, who invited him to his small ghetto living space, and gave him the much-needed sugar. "How much do I owe you," Stepan asked? "Don't mention it," Jacob answered. "We are living in difficult times. Today, I help you; tomorrow, maybe I will need your help." A friendship was born between the two, and from that moment Stepan Dragan took a personal interest in Jacob Lachman and his family. On his return trips to the ghetto, he would say, "Lachman, I have to save you."

These were indeed hard times for the Jews in Zbarazh. There were 5,000 Jews in the city when the Germans marched in, in June 1941. The following month, a pogrom took the lives of the first batch of victims. In September 1941, Jewish intellectuals were targeted, including the city's rabbi, Shperber and his son, lawyers and doctors – a total of 70 persons murdered in the nearby forest. In the spring of 1942, it was the turn of 600 sick and aged persons, who were marched out and shot. August 31, 1942, saw hundreds deported to Bełżec (pronounced Belzhets) extermination camp, followed by another 1,000 in October and 1,000 more in November. On April 7, 1943, hundreds more were shot outside the city. June 8, 1943 was the official end of the ghetto, with the removal and murder of the last Jews. When the Russians liberated the city, there were only 60 Jewish survivors – nine of them kept alive by Stepan Dragan and his wife Olga.

There were a total of six *Aktions*, the German euphemism for killing raids. After each such action, Stepan would show up and repeat his pledge to save the Lachmans. After the fifth action, March 1943, he was ready to act. He had by then moved out of town to a suburb called Przegródek. Jacob and Sabina Lachman stole out of the ghetto with Sabina's two sisters, Mina and Zhenia. In Sabina's words, "We left after midnight during a terrible snow storm. When we arrived at Stepan's place, he stood at the door, shaking and trembling from worry." It turned out that the shelter prepared for them (the "cage" in Sabina's words) was too small – on top of not being totally secure. With the help of some other of Lachman family members (who returned to the ghetto after the work was done), at night they started digging a bunker under the house, leading from beneath the stove. The soil was spread in the attic and not outdoors, so as not to arouse suspicions among neighbors. The bunker was two-and-half meters long, one meter high, and two meters wide. There was no room for beds – only sheets and blankets on the bare ground. To allow for more air, a tunnel was dug, 7–8 meters long, leading to an exit blocked by a crate of potatoes. Sometimes at night, the Dragans allowed some of the fugitives to sleep upstairs.

Eventually, two more people joined the fugitives, Sabina's brother Izak Pollak, who had escaped from hard labor in a stone quarry near Ternopol and later had jumped from a train taking him to the Bełżec extermination camp, and also a family friend – Malka Tenenbaum. Pollak remembers how he saved himself during the "intellectual" action. Caught on the street, he was asked his profession. "I answered, carpenter. That saved me." Malka Tenenbaum (born 1924) had lost her father in the third action, October 1942. In the fourth action, several weeks later, mother Esther, sister Rózia, brothers Eliezer and Abraham and Malka were sent to Bełżec. In Malka's wagon, the people were able to make a small opening and through it Malka jumped from the moving train. "I was urged to do this by my family so as to continue to live and be able to save my father, who was in a death camp. But it was too late for him … He was already no more among the living." Before the sixth and final action, Dragan suddenly appeared and took Malka to his house and into the bunker.

Malka related one incident that almost spelled doom for everyone. One day, during a heavy snowstorm, Stepan decided to go into town to take care of some affairs. He had left the entrance to the bunker open, figuring that no visitors would come on such a wintry day. Suddenly city inspectors came to search for hidden and unreported dairy animals. Olga was alone. Malka immediately ran into a storeroom and hid behind the door. Olga followed the inspectors around everywhere, maintaining her composure and praying to herself they would not notice the entrance to the bunker. They also did not enter the room where Malka stood behind the door, "holding my breath and waiting for the worst – the loss of our lives."

On the eve of the Zbarazh ghetto's liquidation, in March 1943, Stepan Dragan went to get Jacob Lachman's sister, Lea Chajkin, and her little girl, Zilla. As for Lea's husband, Samuel, he had fled from a labor camp in nearby Ternopol, to which he had been sent earlier, and found his way to an abandoned building near Stepan's house. He spent three days in the attic of the building before approaching Stepan – in the middle of the day – and begging him for bread and water. Stepan recognized him, but told him to leave and slammed the door, so that the neighbors who were watching would be reassured about Stepan's attitude to Jews. That night, Stepan opened the bunker door totally distraught. "Can you forgive me, Jacob, for chasing away your brother-in-law? If you agree to admit them, I'll go get him." And so he did.

It had all begun with Stepan Dragan's commitment to helping Jacob Lachman and his immediate family. This had now grown to Lachman's expanded family – to nine persons huddled in the constricting hole in the ground. Feeding these nine people was not a simple matter for the Dragans. Olga was most helpful; from the beginning until the end, she cared for her charges with great dedication, preparing their meals and removing their bodily wastes. Jacob Lachman had brought along some money, which helped cover part of the added expenses.

Liberation came on March 5, 1944. Some of the hidden persons had been in the underground hole for a year; others, for nine months. Mina Freund, one of the earlier arrivals had been sick most of the time. In her words, she had become immobilized and turned into a "vegetable." "We were afraid that our rescuers would not be able to manage the difficult task of feeding nine people. It was not at all simple." All nine fugitives survived, together with their rescuers.

After the death of her husband, Olga remarried and moved to Nottingham, England, where the local Jewish Welfare Board supported Olga's children and grandchildren (some living in Poland). She died in 1997 and her body was flown back to the Ukraine for burial.

In 1989, Yad Vashem conferred on Stepan and Olga Dragan the title of Righteous Among the Nations.

Duckwitz, Georg Ferdinand
GERMANY

Germany invaded Denmark without warning on April 9, 1940, and the occupation there lasted until literally the end of the war – May 8, 1945. For reasons only partly explained, Hitler surprisingly decided to treat Denmark with silk gloves; to make it a "model" protectorate. The Danish government and king were left in place, the parliament continued to function with as little German interference as possible, and Denmark was allowed to keep its small army and navy. A German ambassador sat in Copenhagen, in recognition of the country's sovereignty. Part of this strategy was based on cool calculation – partly to show the world that Germany knew how to treat a conquered country beneficently, but also out of a more important consideration – to maintain the flow of Danish agricultural products to Germany in significant quantities to help feed the German population under wartime conditions. The price paid for this concession was that Germany would not interfere with the country's nearly 8,000 Jews, who continued to enjoy the freedoms held under the law in spite of calls by the local Danish Nazi party to impose

Georg Ferdinand Duckwitz lighting the eternal flame in the Hall of Remembrance, Yad Vashem

measures similar to those in other countries in the German sphere of influence. The Danish government had stated in no uncertain terms that it considered the Jewish issue one of the fundamental tests of German non-interference in Danish affairs. When King Christian X learned of the attempt to torch the Copenhagen synagogue by a local Nazi, in December 1941, he sent a warm message to Rabbi Marcus Melchior, in which he expressed his "deep sorrow" at this incident, adding his "happiness" that the damage caused was light. He ended with: "I wish you and your community a happy new year. Yours, Christian."

This tranquil state of affairs began to unravel in the summer of 1943, as the Germans declared a state of emergency in response to continuing acts of sabotage by the Danish resistance, an act which led to the resignation of the Danish government. The king declared himself a prisoner of war, and the Danish navy scuttled its boats in the port of Copenhagen to avoid their seizure. Under the screen of the state of emergency, the Nazi leadership decided that the time had come to deal with the Jewish population in one giant swoop. SS general Dr. Werner Best, who had earlier been appointed as the virtual man in charge in Denmark, in a message to Berlin on September 8, 1943, suggested that the time was ripe to round up and deport the small Jewish population in the country. At this point, another German stationed in Denmark entered the picture, trying to get the deportation plan scuttled. He was Georg Ferdinand Duckwitz, the maritime attaché at the German embassy in Copenhagen.

The scion of a commercial family in Bremen, Duckwitz had years before the war served in Denmark as the director of a coffee firm. As befell others, he was at first captivated by the mesmerizing appeal of the Nazis, and he joined their party in 1932 but soon became disenchanged with Nazism. During the years leading to the war, he worked for the Hamburg-America shipping line, and this brought him back to Copenhagen in November 1939. His extensive knowledge of Danish affairs, including its language, led to his appointment as a maritime expert in the German embassy, with the task of coordinating commercial shipping ties between Denmark and Germany. When Best appeared on the scene in 1942, he consulted often with Duckwitz on matters affecting German rule in Denmark. At first, Best seemed opposed to any action against the country's Jews. Duckwitz was, therefore, surprised that it was precisely he who provoked the action against the Danish Jews. What then took place is mainly culled from Duckwitz's postwar account of the train of events during the critical days of September 1943.

On September 11, Duckwitz learned from Best of the telegram he had sent to Berlin three days earlier. When the two met that evening, "I immediately noticed that only now did he realize the effect that his ill-considered, or too considered, step would have. He declared that his telegram was only of academic interest. No untoward consequences would follow," for the Nazi leadership would certainly not wish to further aggravate the tense situation already prevailing in the country. In Duckwitz's estimation, Best did not realize that he had set in motion a train of events which he could no longer control. At any rate, no longer sure of himself, Best gave Duckwitz a free hand to do whatever was necessary to derail the planned deportation of the Jews, by stopping the cable from reaching Hitler's desk at his advance military headquarters in Eastern Prussia. Duckwitz decided to fly immediately to Berlin. Arriving there on September 13, he soon learned that Foreign Minister Joachim von Ribbentrop had already forwarded Best's message to Hitler's headquarters, and Duckwitz was told that the Fuehrer had already confirmed the deportation of the Jews. "I had arrived too late." In the Third Reich, a decision by the Fuehrer was like something out of the Gospels, Duckwitz later wrote. "The highest authority had spoken. Its words were law."

At this point, Duckwitz could have raised his hands in despair and dropped the whole matter, which in any case was not of his making. Instead, he decided to take matters into his own hands, perhaps with the tacit consent of Best. At any rate, on September 22 he flew to Sweden, where he secretly met with President Per Albin Hannson, who asked Sweden's ambassador in Berlin to verify Duckwitz's alarming account with the German Foreign Ministry. The response received was a denial that any deportation action was planned – clearly a lie. The Swedish president assured Duckwitz that should the action against the Danish Jews indeed take place, Sweden would in principle be ready to admit them. Returning to Copenhagen on September 25, Duckwitz learned that the raid on the country's Jews was scheduled for the evening of October 2. Reporting to Best on his mission, he heard him say that he could no longer prevent the action from taking place and that the only way out, as put by Best, was "if I could, within a matter of days, build a bridge over the Oeresund [separating Denmark from Sweden] so that all these people could save themselves in Sweden." To which Duckwitz replied: "Be assured that the bridge will be built." Best did not respond to this, but Duckwitz felt that he had been given the green light to go ahead with whatever plans he had in mind. If the plan should fail, Best would probably place the entire blame on the shoulders of Duckwitz.

Earlier, during the tense period of August 1943, Duckwitz had made contact with Danish underground circles, notably with Hans Hedtoft-Hansen, and in a secret meeting on September 28 Duckwitz told them that the raid on the country's Jews would be launched on either Friday afternoon, October 1, or the evening of October 2 – that is, possibly within 72 hours. As related by Hedtoft-Hansen after the war, in the course of the autumn of 1943, rumor had been rampant to the effect that the Germans now intended to carry out the deportation of the Danish Jews in the same way as in other countries. Then on September 28, Duckwitz came to see him with bad news.

> *"Now the disaster is about to occur, he said. The whole thing is planned in full detail. Ships are going to anchor in the roadstead of Copenhagen, your poor Jewish fellow countrymen who are found by the Gestapo will be forcibly transported to the ships and deported to an unknown fate. He was white with indignation and shame. I frankly admit that – although, during those years, I was accustomed to get many surprising messages from this very man – I became speechless with rage and concern... This was a bit too Satanic. I just managed to say: Thank you for the news, and Duckwitz disappeared. As far as he was concerned, he did what was humanly possible in order to save those human lives that could be saved at all. My friends [Vilhelm Buhl, H.C. Hansen and Herman Dedichen] and myself divided the tasks between us."*

On Friday morning, October 1, Duckwitz notified the Swedish diplomat in Copenhagen, Erik Nils Ekblad, that one could expect that the action would start that same evening; that around 9 p.m. Copenhagen would be closed and and telephone connections cut off. At this point, the roundup of Jews would begin. Several boats were already docked at the Copenhagen harbor to take the Jews to concentration camps. After passing on the information to the Swedish envoy, Gustav Von Dardel, Ekblad with the help of Duckwitz made his way back to Sweden to alert the Swedish government to be ready to admit the fleeing Jews.

Duckwitz's last desperate hope was that the *Wehrmacht* (German army) would act discreetly and not place all of its forces at the command of the Gestapo, but instead allow the Jews to slip out of the country in the direction of Sweden. In a secret discussion between Duckwitz and Cammann, the German commander of seaborne patrol ships and a former colleague at the Hamburg-America Line, the latter promised not to have his boats seaworthy during the critical days of the Jews' escape to Sweden across the narrow channel separating Denmark from Sweden. Indeed, very few of the German navy patrols were at sea during the following days. According to Duckwitz, Cammann was later reprimanded for his inaction by the top regional commander of the German navy.

After the crucial meeting with Duckwitz on September 28, Hedtoft decided to alert the Jewish community. "I myself first went to the villa of the president of the Jewish community, barrister before the Supreme Court Carl Bernhard Henriques at Charlottenlund. I shall never forget this meeting with the leader of the Danish Jews ... I asked to speak alone with Henriques, and when we were left alone I said in my agitated and unhappy state, 'Henriques, a great disaster is going to happen now. The feared action against the Jews in Denmark is about to begin. It is going to happen in this way that, in the night between October 1 and 2, the Gestapo is going to round up all Jews in their homes and then to transport them to ships in the port. You must immediately do everything in order to warn every single Jew in the city. Obviously, we are ready to help you with everything.' Today I may reveal that Henriques's reaction was different from what I had expected. What he said was: 'You are lying,' and it took some time before I was able to persuade him that he must believe me. 'I do not understand how it can be true,' he kept repeating in despair. 'I have just been in the Foreign Ministry with Permanent Undersecretary Svenningsen and he calmed me and said that it is his belief that nothing is going to happen.' I answered that Svenningsen's statements were made in good faith; he could only repeat what the Germans were saying."

The Germans launched the deportation action in the evening hours of October 1, 1943, as previously indicated by Duckwitz. Close to 500 Jews (many of them elderly persons) were caught, and sent to Theresienstadt camp on the boats docked in the Copenhagen harbor. There they were visited by Danish and Swedish Red Cross representatives to make sure that their treatment was somewhat better than that of the other unfortunate Jews in that camp. During their one-and-a-half year internment they kept receiving the parcels that were sent to them through government agencies in Denmark. In 1944, a mission visited them on behalf of King Christian X to see how they were faring.

As for the overwhelming majority of Danish Jews, some 7,200 were secretly ferried by the Danish Resistance across the Sound to Sweden during the months of October–November 1943, where they were freely admitted and remained until the war's end. On October 3, 1943, Dr. Best proudly informed Hitler: "My Fuehrer, Denmark is free of Jews (*judenfrei*)." Of course, this was only a half-truth, for most Jews were still on Danish soil, only in hiding and awaiting their secret crossing into Sweden. But, for outward appearance, there were no more Jews to be seen in public – at least until the war's end. The overwhelming majority of an entire Jewish community had been saved in time, initially, largely through the intervention of the German diplomat Duckwitz.

As for Duckwitz's motives in this large-scale rescue effort, he said after the war, "Everyone is obliged to imagine himself in another person's position in a given situation. I do not think that my life is more important than the lives of 7,000 Jews." All this, he added, was not without risk to himself. Kannstein, the civil director general at German general headquarters, cautioned Duckwitz that he had been singled out by the Gestapo, who were waiting for the opportune moment to move him out of Copenhagen. In the words of historian Leni Yahil, "There is no doubt about Duckwitz's great role in the Danish people's undertaking to save the Jews. His early warning on the deportation about to take place made it possible for Danish people and organizations to warn the Jews in time. We have no knowledge of any other highly placed German official who was involved in such a rescue misson, with risk to himself." After the war, Duckwitz returned to Copenhagen as a Foreign Ministry commercial attaché. His new diplomatic career took him then to Helsinki, Finland; ambassador to Denmark; head of the East European Department in the German Foreign Office; and ambassador to India.

In 1971, Yad Vashem bestowed on Georg Ferdinand Duckwitz the prestigious title of Righteous Among the Nations.

Dzhyvulski, Vasili & Marina
UKRAINE

One day, in the summer of 1942, 18-year-old Michael Ehrlich, who was hiding in the forest to avoid capture by the Germans, had wandered up to a farmhouse and decided to have a closer look at the place from the safety of some bushes. Suddenly, he saw a man come directly toward him.

"I started to run away. He called to me, 'Don't be afraid, I want to help you.' I overcame my fear for the moment and went towards him. As I came close to him he recognized me because he had been a guest in my parents home many times. I explained to him that I was hungry, as I had not eaten in two days. He convinced me to go to his house which was very close to the woods where I had been hiding … In a few moments he came back with food for me. He then told me that I should come to him every night and knock on the window. Every night I went to his house and knocked on the window as he had told me to do. When I did this he would open the door, bring me into his home, and feed me. This all had to be done very quietly and under cover of darkness so that his neighbors would not observe our activities."

The man's name was Vasili Dzhyvulski. He and his wife and four children (another lived elsewhere) resided in an isolated hamlet near the village of Rublin in the Ternopol region, today in Ukraine. The family belonged to the Ukrainian Baptist community which, in sharp contrast to other Ukrainians, saw it a religious duty to help save Jews, considered God's Chosen People.

Before the war, Vasili had worked as a night watchman for the Ehrlich family, who were cattle dealers in Potok Zloty, the nearest town in the region. Now, whenever Michael Ehrlich dropped into the house, the other members of the family would keep watch behind the windows to see that no one was approaching. These were dangerous times for Jews and their rescuers. The Germans made it clear that anyone found with a Jew in his home would be shot and his house burned.

A year earlier, when the Germans entered Potok Zloty in July 1941, together with local Ukrainians they immediately began murdering Jews, who numbered then less than a thousand, and looting their property. Young able-bodies Jews were conscripted for hard labor in labor camps. That summer, Michael Ehrlich witnessed a horrific sight. Some of the Jews driven from the Carpatho-Russia area, annexed to Hungary, into the German-controlled Poland arrived in Potok Zloty, where they were forced by the Ukrainian police toward the Dniester River and shot near the river bank.

At this point, Ehrlich decided not wait further but to find a hiding place for himself in the nearby woods. His father had controlled many acres of land in the forest, a region where very few people lived, and for Michael Ehrlich this was the start of a Robinson Crusoe-type saga.

It was early spring 1942 when he took a shovel and a saw and went into the forest. He carefully chose spots that were near streams so that he would have a source of fresh drinking water, and also close to places where he would be able to scavenge fruit and vegetables from nearby orchards and gardens at night. His diet consisted mainly of raw potatoes, raw corn, and raw mushrooms. "Whatever a cow or horse would eat in the fields, I ate to fill my stomach and stay alive. In the fall I used to fill up my bunkers with all kinds of food: apples, potatoes, and corn.... I ate everything raw because I was afraid to make a fire that might be seen." Michael built a series of such bunkers. "All my bunkers, or perhaps I should call them foxholes, were built on a riverbank. I arranged to enter from the water; no footprints would show." At night, to keep himself warm, he wrapped himself in heavy rags and old coats.

The locations chosen were isolated spots, places where he would not be afraid to close his eyes at night. The area between the village of Rublin and the hamlet of Kotasivka was inhabited mostly by Baptist farmers who were known for their friendly attitude toward Jews, and some of them had done work on the land owned by Michael's father, Joseph Ehrlich. Michael felt he could count on them in times of distress. During the initial period of his forest days, Michael would return home to Potok Zloty to pass the night. One evening, while still asleep at home, he was awakened by a knock on his window. One of the Ukrainian police who was friendly with Michael's father called out, 'Misha [diminutive for Michael], run." It was a warning of another roundup of Jews. "I quickly dressed and ran into the woods."

Sometime later, after his friendly encounter with Vasili Dzhyvulski, Michael asked him for permission to use his stable as a hideout and build a bunker there, to which Dzhyvulski gave his consent. For more than two months, at night, Michael dug behind the wall of the stable, placing the dirt into bags and dumping it in the nearby stream so as not to leave any traces of freshly dug earth on his benefactor's land and thereby arouse suspicion of something unusual taking place inside the household. Dzhyvulski helped out by providing the necessary tools and preparing wooden beams to support the ceiling. He also helped dig and remove the dirt.

After two months the completely camouflaged bunker was ready to be used. The entrance to the bunker was underneath the cow stalls. "When he fed the cows, he would put food for me in the bucket with the cow fodder, and slip it through the hidden entrance in the floor."

In the summer of 1942, the Germans emptied Potok Zloty of its Jews, who were taken to nearby Buczacz, where the killing of Jews went on without respite. At this point, Michael asked Dzhyvulski whether he could bring over some of his family to hide in the bunker. The answer again was yes. Michael walked close to 40 kilometers to Buczacz at night to find his family and succeeded in being reunited with his brother Israel, Israel's wife, Ita, and their 18-month-old daughter Tzipora. With the parents' permission, Michael brought the young child to Vasili Dzhyvulski, who decided to keep her with them and present her as the baby of their daughter Hanka, who lived elsewhere. They renamed her Marusia.

In Buczacz, Michael's mother was down with typhus and could not be moved. She was killed by the Germans, together with Michael's brother Israel (the father of Tzipora-Marusia), and his sister Zosia. Michael's father was somewhere else with a friendly Ukrainian. Israel's wife, Ita, had already gone to stay at the Dzhyvulski farm, taking along her brother Getzel Strauber and wife Malka (Michael's sister) and their daughter Genia-Tova. Also added were Zosia Petrover with husband, Shaya, and their two children. Then the Kuppermans, friends of the Ehrlichs, joined them in their lair – Avraham, wife Fruma, and their two children. Kupperman brought along some money to help the Dzhyvulskis defray the additional expenses for food and other necessities. This made a total of 13 people hiding in the bunker, including Michael Ehrlich but without little Marusia, who stayed indoors in the Dzhyvulski home. They stayed there for close to two years, until the area's liberation in July 1944.

To return to the bunker, it was built, as mentioned, under a cow stall in a barn extending into the side of a hill. The entrance was through a two-foot-wide trap door covered with dirt to hide it and located under a feed trough that could be slid sideways to allow people to enter or leave. There was no light other than what penetrated through a narrow opening under the feed trough. The cramped bunker consisted of two sections. In the larger one, shelves were built into the wall to serve as beds, three in each niche and made out of sawed logs. The other, smaller section served for personal hygiene. There was a pot and each person had to walk backward into the room; then bend over in order to use it.

Vasili Dzhyvulski fed his charges with whatever his family could spare. Every evening he would bring them soup prepared by his wife, Marina, 100 grams of bread, and some water. Marina would go to distant places to do her shopping so as not to be noticed. Vasili also took upon himself the unpleasant task of removing the buckets of waste and disposing of them. Cleanliness was also a major problem, specifically fighting off mice and lice. Periodically the hidden people were taken out one or two at a time to wash or bathe in a tub. They had arrived with only one set of clothing on them and this was washed from time to time. During such times, the people covered themselves with a blanket until their garments were dry and returned to them.

With so many people seeking protection in the cramped bunker, Michael thought it best not to remain there. He preferred his "foxholes" in the forest and was confident that he could survive there alone, next to the clean waters of the stream and the fresh forest air, only dropping in at the Dzhyvulski farm once or twice a week to bring along additional food gathered in the forest and other locations. At harvest time, Michael would gather potatoes, cucumbers, apples, pears, and ears of corn and bring them to Dzhyvulski, where Marina cooked the food for the hidden persons.

In October 1942, during one of his forays in Buczacz to find out how his father was faring in the vicinity, Michael Ehrlich ran out of luck. He was seized and taken to Fedor Hill – the killing site for the town's Jews. On top of the hill, Michael and other Jews were led to a mass grave with planks of wood laid across it and told to stand on them. The SS then opened fire and the people began falling into the grave.

"Realizing what was happening, I jumped quickly into the grave. I pretended to be dead in order to save myself. Other people fell on top of me and hid me from view. I was lying between corpses; I was shivering and saying to myself, 'Oh God, I don't want to die. Don't let me die.' It is difficult to describe the terror of lying between the dead bodies and listening to the screams and shouts of those wounded and dying around me. It seemed to go on forever and ever. Today I can still hear those screams. Late that night I crawled out from underneath the dead. I was covered completely with blood. I had to step over the dead bodies in order to escape from that grave."

Finally Michael made it back to the Dzhyvulski farm, where Vasili undressed him, washed his clothes, gave him a bath and some old clothes. Michael then returned to his riverside hiding places, with occasional visits to the Dzhyvulski family and the people in hiding there. While walking through the forest, his fears of detection were never at rest. Once he thought he saw someone following him. "I ran into the bushes and listened, certain that someone was near but I saw no one. I soon discovered that the sound I heard was the beating of my heart. This shows the sad state I was in. I can laugh about it now but at that time the terror was very real." He also occasionally visited his father and his brother Zalman and wife Sarah, who had fled back to Rublin and were hidden by a man named Rublenik. Michael would bring them bread and sugar that he would get from Vasili Dzhyvulski. Unfortunately, his father did not survive. During the initial German retreat from the area, in March 1944, Joseph Ehrlich left his hiding place, not suspecting that the Germans would temporarily recapture the Buczacz area. He was caught and killed.

In Michael Ehrlich's words, referring to his rescuers, the Dzhyvulskis, "It was impossible to repay this most wonderful human being and his family for saving our lives. We had nothing tangible that we could give them. Their philosophy was that they and we, all together, would live or die. We live because of him, and our lives are richer and fuller for having known these beautiful human beings." Fourteen people owe their life to this brave Ukrainian Baptist and his family. It had all started with a chance encounter between Michael Ehrlich and Vasili Dzhyvulski in the depths of a Ukrainian forest.

In 1974 Yad Vashem recognized Vasili and Marina Dzhyvulski as Righteous Among the Nations.

Fajo, Erzsebet
Hungary

*T*he story is as told by Zsuzsanna Abonyi. She was born in 1931, in Subotica, Yugoslavia. That same year her family (including Zsuzsanna's two-year older brother, Ivan) moved to Hungary, where her parents purchased a pharmacy in the small town of Békéscsaba. That same year, too, Erzsebet Fajo ("Erzsi") was taken into the Abonyi household, as a 13-year-old nursemaid. Erzsi came from a poor family in Békéscsaba, and as happened in many parts of Europe among poor people, she was urged at a young age to drop out of school and support herself. Soon afterwards, Laszlo Abonyi was forced to sell his pharmacy as a result of the increasingly anti-Jewish economic measures taken by the Hungarian government, which had allied itself with Nazi Germany. The Abonyis relocated to Budapest, taking Erzsi along. It was September 1941, and Erzsi continued to live with the Abonyis until the German occupation on March 19, 1944. During this time, she worked in a bicycle shop that Laszlo Abonyi had bought with what he got from the sale of the pharmacy (which he had sold at a fraction of its market value).

After the German occupation, Laszlo Abonyi decided that it was best for all concerned if Erzsi lived apart from the family, and she moved in with a friend. "But," in Zsuzsanna's words, "she visited us every day, vowing again and again that she would not let us be killed; that she would, no matter what it took, rescue us." In the following months, as the Holocaust engulfed hundreds of thousands of Jews in the Hungarian provinces – but not yet in Budapest – Laszlo learned to his chagrin that his brother, conscripted into a Hungarian labor battalion, had disappeared on the Russian front. Laszlo was so depressed that when his daughter Zsuzsanna proposed that the whole family commit suicide, he did not voice any objection. Erzsi, however, did, and she began to talk incessantly about her rescue operation, instilling hope in the Abonyis. First, she decided to save the Abonyi's household goods from being impounded by the Germans, including the family's clothing and linen. These were packed into 15 crates and with Erzsi's help moved to an uncle of the Abonyis who was married to a Christian and thereby temporarily safe from persecution. As for the family's money and jewelry, Erzsi herself took charge of them. As she moved their belongings out of the Abonyi home, she had to pass the the apartment of the caretaker, a person not to be trusted as she was pro-Nazi, as were many people on that street who might have found it odd to see

Erzsebet Fajo

a person carrying boxes during the daytime. Yet Erzsi was able to outsmart the neighbors and bribe the caretaker, thereby strengthening the resolve of the Abonyis to make the effort to be saved, a hope that helped the father, Laszlo, to overcome his deep depression.

On April 5, 1944, when the decree on wearing the yellow star came into effect, Erzsi insisted on accompanying the Abonyis whenever they stepped out. She also got food and other necessities for them, including books, games, and toys, and spent much time with them to raise their spirits. When, on July 1, 1944, rumors spread that it was the turn of the Budapest Jews to be deported, Erzsi decided to move back in with her employers, determined to be deported with them. The Abonyi parents insisted that she leave and thereby save herself, but she cried: "I don't want to live without you! If I cannot share life with you, I will share death!" As it turned out, on July 7, 1944, literally at the last moment, the Hungarian government, bending to foreign pressure, called a halt to further deportations. The Budapest Jews were saved – for the moment. In the following months, Erzsi visited the Abonyis every day, bringing along food and other necessities. She also kept their spirits up with whatever good news was to be had, promising them that she would not let them be seized by the Germans, "that she would save us, live or die with us!"

As the Russian army crossed into Hungary, the general feeling was that the war would soon be over. However, on October 15, 1944, the pro-Nazi Arrow Cross movement seized power with the help of the Germans and immediately instituted a reign of terror against the more than 200,000 Jews in Budapest. Laszlo Abonyi was apprehended and taken to a camp near Budapest, but was saved by Erzsi, who managed to get him a letter of protection from the Red Cross. In addition, Erzsi visited the other members of the Abonyi family, bringing along canned goods to get them through the expected siege of Budapest by the advancing Russians. In the meantime, Laszlo Abonyi escaped and returned to his family. Then the Arrow Cross, known for their random shooting of Jews, began to evacuate Jews from the street where the Abonyis lived. As told by Zsuzanna:

"I still don't know how it happened but Erzsi appeared, fighting her way through throngs of people, getting to us and managing somehow to drag us away from the house. It was November 17, 1944. The streets were replete with check posts, guards, soldiers, Nazis, Germans demanding that people show their identification papers. If Jews were caught, they were either marched to Jewish groups rounded up in the Jewish houses, or, in many cases, shot on sight. Running with us from house to house, she found a deserted pharmacy whose owner allowed us to spend the night there. During the course of the next day, she managed to get a 'letter of protection,' this time from the Vatican legation. While she stood in line there, however, Germans came and shot into the crowds, killing and wounding many people; in addition many were arrested. Erzsi stood in line; she wouldn't budge. And the Germans never got to her. With the letter in hand, she took us to a so-called Vatican House … In spite of the mortal danger she was in, here too she visited us every day, bringing whatever she could."

The danger was not over for the Abonyis, and Erzsi moved back with them, to be there to ward off further threats to her prewar employers. On December 3, 1944, Zsuzsanna and Ivan were taken to the Jewish ghetto. At that point, Erzsi was able to acquire for Laszlo a Swedish letter of protection and have him moved to a Swedish protected house. As for his wife, Margit, Erzsi had her taken to her cousin's home. Erzsi then headed for the ghetto to find out how the two children, Zsuzsanna and Ivan, were faring. Running from house to house, she located them, and with false papers in her hand got them out and through all the posts guarding the ghetto. As is well known, during this period the Hungarian Arrow Cross gangs ran amok in the streets of Budapest, beating, plundering, and killing thousands of people publicly, without anyone stopping them. During the terrible and chaotic month of December, Erzsi took Zsuzsanna to five different hiding places, four of which she had to leave quickly to save herself. As further told by Zsuzsanna, in her litany of flight and rescue, with the help of Erzsi:

"I was in a Red Cross Children's Home (suddenly closed down), then in a convent (with false papers, but becoming suspect when I started to talk about my experiences in the ghetto), in a Swedish House (closed), in an apartment house on the riverside (a place where I was left by myself for days; its owner left for Germany after having accepted a diamond bracelet from Erzsi). On December 23, she came to get me and take me to the Red Cross Hospital where my parents hid. Making the right connections, she obtained the appropriate papers for me. During this time period (December 5-23), she moved my parents twice and my brother three times … As Budapest was under a total siege, shelled and bombed for 24 hours a day, without public transportation, she usually came on foot, in snow or freezing rain, running from house to house, seeking protection from the incessant bombardment. On December 23, she took Ivan to live with her in our former apartment and me to the hospital in Kisfaludy Street. Ivan, however, was recognized by the caretaker on January 2, 1945, so that Erzsi felt she had to take him away from there immediately. Getting papers for him, she took Ivan to the same hospital where I and our parents hid. On this day, Budapest was under its most severe bombardment. Ivan and Erzsi ran, crawled, and groped their way there, starting out at 8.00 in the morning and arriving at 8:00 at night. Had they been caught… they would have been shot, both of them, on sight … She stayed there with us at the Red Cross Hospital; for the first time in months the family was together … Next day she went home. On January 17 we were liberated. Since we were very sick, it took us a whole day to get home. When we arrived, she was waiting for us outside. Although our apartment was not destroyed, we cried in Erzsi's arms for months, and I am still crying ever since that time."

Great were the losses sustained by the family – Margit's four sisters and one brother and Laszlo's brother and sister – all lost in the Holocaust. But the four Abonyis, the parents and two children, were saved thanks to the efforts of their former housemaid Erzsi. "Driven by the desire to save us, Erzsi defied the Germans. She saved us from death, saved my brother and me from becoming orphans and my parents from the worst anguish that can befall people, from losing their children. It was her strength and heroism that gave us life, allowed us to grow up, and eventually to have children on our own."

Adopting Erzsi after the war, the Abonyi parents looked after her in whatever way the could: they sent her to school and divided their estate among the two children and Erzsi. She was able to get a good job at a pharmacological firm after she graduated with a diploma as a lab technician, where she worked until her retirement, in 1982. She lived close to Ivan Abonyi's family and helped raise his daughter. Zsuzsanna, who moved to the United States, visited her often. "She truly is our sister, as she has always been throughout the time we have known her, a sister who gave us life when we were sentenced to death, a sister who waged war against the whole world and managed to save us from destruction."

In 1986, Erzsebet Fajo was awarded the title of Righteous Among the Nations.

Foley, Francis
ENGLAND

*I*f Francis ("Frank") Foley had been told in 1919, when he arrived in Berlin at the end of World War I, that he would one day be involved in saving the Jews of the country from a rapacious regime, he would have dismissed this prophecy as the rantings of a madman. For in 1919, Germany was considered a haven for Jews from other countries. Foley had just ended his service as a lieutenant in the British army and was sent to Germany as an intelligence officer on behalf of the British MI6 section. His job was to spy on the activities of communist-led organizations (such as Rosa Luxembourg and her Spartacist movement), which were particularly strong and active at the time in Germany. As a cover, his official position was Chief Passport Control Officer for the British embassy, with wide latitude to decide on the admission of foreigners everywhere within the vast British Empire of the time. The Nazi Party had not yet been born. Foley was to remain on this job until the start of World War II, but in the 1930s his attention shifted to the Nazi Party, which came to power in 1933 and began the systematic persecution of the country's Jews. While still preoccupied with his intelligence work, Foley gradually shifted to helping Jews leave the country to various destinations within the British Empire – a need which assumed urgency after the Nazis staged the pogrom of November 9, 1938, the notorious *Kristallnacht* (Night of Broken Glass). In that endeavor, Foley was not beyond stretching to the limit British immigration laws and regulations, twisting them in such way as to ostensibly justify the granting of visas to Jews desperate to leave Nazi Germany.

The following stories exemplify some of the unorthodox methods employed by Foley to get around Britain's strict regulations. For entry into Palestine, then under a British mandate, immigrants were required to arrive with a £1,000 in hand so as to qualify for a "capitalist" visa and therefore not be a burden

Francis Foley (from Michael Smith, *Foley: The Spy Who Saved 10,000 Jews*)

on the country's economy. This was then a sizable sum, the equivalent of £40,000 today and unavailable to many Jews whose assets had been frozen by the Nazi government. Elisheva Lernau (born in 1913 as Elsbeth Kahn) had only £10 with her, although her father, attorney Berthold Kahn had opened a bank account in the amount of 20,000 marks, money blocked for many years by Nazi regulations. She was referred to Foley, who was impressed that the balance of £990 would be available to her the minute she landed in Haifa, and on that supposition issued her a "capitalist" visa for Palestine in 1935. "Next month, I landed in Haifa with 10 marks." In her words, "I am convinced that without the 'unlawful' help of Captain Foley I would not have reached Palestine in time … I have always been deeply grateful to this unknown man."

Similarly in the case of Wolfgang Meyer-Michael, Foley suggested finding the money through someone who would vouchsafe it. "Just get a promise; you don't have to use it," Foley told the surprised Meyer-Michael. The latter looked up a cousin in the Netherlands, and together they drew up two documents. In the one, the cousin promised to lend Meyer-Michael the £1,000 when needed; in the other, Meyer-Michael declared the first letter was invalid and promised not to make use of it. The result? Foley gave Meyer-Michael a visa for Palestine. In his words, "It is thanks to Mr. Foley that I am alive today." Heinz Romberg, another man who left Germany in time on the strength of a "capitalist" visa without having the necessary funds, wrote to Yad Vashem that Foley enriched my life with a wife, three children, eight grandchildren, and five great-grandchildren (so far)." Others were helped to leave the country by Foley through various stratagems, such as Ida Weisz, who as a last resort traveled from Vienna to the British Passport Office in Berlin in 1939. "Mr. Foley let me stay at his house for a few days and then he came home late one night with the necessary exit visas and papers. I left for Belgium and then on to England on the early train the next morning. The last time I saw Mr. Foley was at the station."

Gunter Powitzer's story is quite extraordinary. He had been jailed for maintaining illicit relations with a non-Jewish woman – a violation of the 1935 Nuremberg laws – that produced a son, Zeev (his current Hebrew name). Gunter was arrested and jailed for 21 months; then deported to the Sachsenhausen concentration camp. When Foley heard of his case, he went to see the commander of the camp with a British visa for the unfortunate prisoner. Allowed to speak to Gunter, he told the surprised prisoner, "Tomorrow you will be freed and papers are waiting for you in the consulate for travel to Palestine." Gunter asked: "And what about the child?" Foley reassured him that the child would be included in the visa. On February 1, 1939, a car was waiting for Gunter Powitzer when he was freed from Sachsenhausen camp. After 12 days, he and his son left Germany for Italy, then on to Palestine.

Another extraordinary story is that of a 20-year-old woman, known by her initials as H.H. She had been imprisoned because of her membership in the outlawed Communist Party. While in jail she gave birth to a child, and the father had already left for Rhodesia (then a British colony). He now wished her to join him, but British immigration laws forbade granting visas to communists. The Gestapo had released her on condition that she leave the country within two weeks. When Foley learned of her predicament, he told Hubert Pollack, the Jewish emigration activist who had brought the matter to his attention, "She has spent two years in prison; she was therefore eighteen when she was sentenced. How do you say in German 'youthful fervor?' At least, this is my impression. Or do you think that in Rhodesia the young lady will become an active communist?" Pollack: "Hardly so." Foley: "Then please send her to me." Pollack: "Is the child also to be entered in the passport?" Foley: "Yes." Miss H.H. left for Rhodesia with her child, in time.

Benno Cohn, head of the Zionist Federation in Germany, testified at the Eichmann trial in 1960 that after *Kristallnacht* he succeeded in getting many Jews to leave Germany for Palestine. "That was thanks to a man who is to my mind to be counted among the Righteous Gentiles … He helped many people of all categories ['capitalists,' students, etc.] … One may say that he saved thousands of Jews from death." On August 24, 1939, days before start of the of the war, Foley left a message for Hanan Baram, an active Zionist operative in Berlin, to quickly pick up 80 immigration certificates for England before the closure of the British consulate at 4 o'clock in the afternoon of the following day (August 25). A week later England was at war with Germany, and Foley's diplomatic (and intelligence) career in Germany was at an end. In 1958, Francis Foley passed away at the age of 73.

On July 10, 1959, during the consecration of a forest outside Jerusalem in Foley's memory, Benno Cohn praised the late diplomat. He recalled the period in Germany when a visa meant the difference between life and death for Jews. "During those days, Captain Foley's great humanity became obvious. Day and night he was at the disposal of those seeking help. He generously distributed every kind of visa, thus helping the liberation of many thousands from the camps." As to the man's motives – "the basic factor was – he was a *Mensch* (decent person). It was really a rare experience to meet a person like him behind a desk in a German [-located] office … He often told us that, as a Christian, he wanted to prove how little the Christians then governing Germany had to do with real Christianity … He hated the Nazis and, as he told me once in a conversation, considered them as the realm of Satan on earth … Today, on the first anniversary of his death, we look back to his deeds and recall the fact that in those gloomy days he gave back to some of us the belief in mankind."

In 1999, Yad Vashem awarded the late Francis Foley the title of Righteous Among the Nations.

Fort, Alban & Germaine

FRANCE

*I*t was a couple of months before Julien Engel's 11th birthday and the fifth birthday of his brother, Georges. Up to that moment, life in Cannes for the two brothers had been peaceful. The city and surrounding area had been placed under Italian administration since November 1942, when the Germans had swept into Vichy France. Mussolini's Italy was allied to Hitler's Germany, and part of the deal was a division of the spoils, with Germany getting the lion's share. Fascist Italy, while imposing civic restrictions on the Jews, felt that this was as far as it would go – no physical abuse, let alone liquidation of Jews in death camps. Then, faced with the invasion of its homeland, Italy capitulated to the Allies on September 8, 1943. Forewarned of this eventuality, the Germans immediately swept into the Italian zone in France and the chase was on after Jews who had fled to the Italian zone to avoid arrest.

The Engel parents, David Mordka and Rose, were born in Poland and educated in Germany, where they married and David established a successful furniture business in Dortmund. After Hitler's rise to power in 1933, the family fled to Belgium, and Julien was born on September 6, 1933 – two weeks after their arrival in Antwerp. A new life of comfort and contentment began for the Engels, and another son, Georges, was added to the family, on November 5, 1938. With the onset of the German invasion of Belgium, on May 10, 1940, the family fled to France and made its way to Nice in the summer months of 1940. By then France had surrendered. The Engels decided to head to the Mediterranean resort city of Cannes, which was part of the so-called Free Zone or non-German occupied part of France. Being out of direct German control was one reason for choosing the place. There was an additional factor. Rose Engel had cousins in nearby Nice, two sisters who had lived there for many years. They were naturalized as French citizens and well established, and could therefore be of help to the fleeing Engel family.

Life under the Vichy regime was at first tolerable for the Jewish population in the Cannes/Nice area. Julien attended primary school. "My very worst memory of this period [1941] is of having my stamp album stolen from my classroom desk." However, the situation changed for the worse in the summer months of 1942 as the French responded to the German demands to hand over Jews for deportation by first arresting foreign-born Jews, such as the Engels. It was time to flee again. So, in September-October 1942, the Engel family headed toward Annemasse, on the Swiss border, which they hoped to cross with the help of a French guide. However, they had bad luck and were apprehended by French border guards and jailed in Annemasse, and then handcuffed and dispatched to Rivesaltes, one of the French detention camps for foreign Jews – a place from which people were deported to concentration camps elsewhere. In Rivesaltes, Julien and Georges were separated from their parents, and two weeks later they were released together with a group of other children – probably due to the intervention of one of the foreign humanitarian agencies still allowed to operate in Vichy France. It was just in time, for on November 11, 1942, the Germans moved in and occupied the Vichy zone, and the foreign agencies were told to pack up and leave.

At first placed in a children's home in Toulouse, the Engel brothers were soon released to the care of their mother's cousins, in the early weeks of 1943. Julien wrote:

"We returned to Nice very uncertain of what the future would hold. As a Jewish refugee, I could not envisage resuming my schooling in the public system. By now the situation for Jews of French nationality had become as precarious as that of their 'irregular' brethren. They were all equally the object of the same hunt, picked up in street roundups during the day and from their dwellings in the middle of the night. For us developments were not long in coming. In late April or early May, the two sisters were arrested in a street roundup while they were out shopping in the center of Nice. Fortunately, they were in the company of a Gentile friend, who was left free. She hastened back to the house to warn us. Georges and I

instantly made for the house of a neighbor, whose garden adjoined our own. A Frenchman (whose name regrettably I do not recall), with family attachments to Sweden, he served as the Swedish honorary consul in Nice. Long before, he had offered our cousins his help and protection, and we had been briefed about what to do in the event of need. Thus, over the garden wall we went, without a moment's hesitation, leaving everything behind. Within a few hours the police raided the cousins' house and put it under seal. The sisters were never heard from again. Little detail remains in my mind of the anxious days that followed. Clearly, it was not prudent to stay very long in the consul's house. After putting us up for a day or two, he arranged to have us taken in hand by the Catholic authorities in Nice. The archdiocese operated an underground rescue network to spirit Jews out of Nice and place them in safe havens in the rural back country. It is through the auspices of the Nice archdiocese, sometime in early May 1943, that Georges and I were presented to and warmly welcomed by Alban and Germaine Fort at the Rayon de Soleil of Cannes. We were to remain at the Rayon for three full years, virtually up to the eve of our departure for America."

The Rayon de Soleil was a family-style, privately supported home for homeless children, a chain of some eight such homes founded in France during the interwar years by dedicated people concerned about the condition of orphaned or parentless children, as well as children who were taken from their parents by the courts because of the situation at home. In the Rayon de Soleil homes, these children received more attentive and dedicated treatment then in the state-operated child welfare homes. There the child was made to feel he was a member of a community bound by mutual affection and common purpose. In the mid-1930s Alban and Germaine Fort, then a newly married couple who had been active in the French scouting movement, opened a Rayon home in Cannes. During the Engel brothers' stay there, the home numbered between 40 and 60 children, about a quarter of whom were infants abandoned by their mothers and available for adoption. Jewish children, fleeing arrest and deportation, had also been admitted, for stays of various periods, until moved to other secure places. A few were there when Julien and Georges Engel arrived and left in subsequent months, as did others who arrived afterwards. As for the rest, half or more of the Gentile children remained legal wards of Alban and Germaine Fort, who would be their parents until they came of age and left to find their way in society. Since arrival and departures occurred with some frequency, the comings and goings of Jewish children, who numbered up to eight at any one time, was not out of character with the pattern of life at the Rayon. Julien estimates that, when he and his brother Georges were there, some ten to fifteen Jewish children came to the Rayon for varying periods, and he remembers two names: Serge Cymerman (whose name was changed to Castel) and Anne Zimmer. Records at the Rayon de Soleil mention 33 Jewish children who passed through during the war years in addition to several adult Jews who were sheltered there for some time.

During the war years, the Rayon was housed in the hills directly above Cannes, in the Villa Clémentine, an estate with ample, park-like grounds, elaborate facilities, and rich decor. As an isolated children's home, it provided a fairly good cover for hiding young Jews. In the words of Julien Engel, "We did take some precautions. Our false identity cards carried our family name slightly altered. The addition of an E to the German-sounding Engel (thus Engele) gave it a French or Italian intonation. Our very French first names happily required no tampering." The children had little reason to venture into town, and in fact seldom did, as schooling through the primary grades was provided at the Rayon itself, mostly by outside teachers. Excursions, always in large groups, generally headed toward the hills overlooking Cannes and to nearby villages in the interior. "Though we were no more than two or three miles from the center of Cannes, the physical isolation of the Villa Clémentine, its relative self-sufficiency, and particularly the inner-directed ambiance created by Alban and Germaine Fort, enabled us all to lead almost a life apart, buffered from the brutal realities of the world outside." At the same time, it should be mentioned that the Rayon was well known in Cannes; it drew substantial financial support from prominent people as well as a subsidy from the municipality and occasionally received visitors, including one time, disconcertingly, a group of German officers.

After the liberation of France in the late summer of 1944 (Cannes was liberated on August 24, 1944), Julien continued his education in local schools before heading for Paris under the auspices of the Jewish OSE welfare organization in 1946, and arriving in the United States in 1948 to join his mother's family there. "I have no doubt, however, had we not been given the opportunity to start anew with family in America, Alban and Germaine Fort would have wanted us to continue our lives with them, and we for our part would not have sought to do otherwise." From his new home in America, Julien kept in close touch with his benefactors, including numerous visits. In his testimony of 1986, Julien Engel emphasized,

> "I have always felt immense gratitude and affection for the Forts. Their extraordinary courage, generosity, and strength of character have left an indelible mark on me. Were it not been for the tragic circumstances that brought me to the Rayon, I would be unreservedly thankful for the opportunity I was given to spend an important part of my young life with them at the Rayon. Paradoxically, these were happy years for us, at a time when so many others in Europe lived in sorrow and suffering."

In 1985, Yad Vashem conferred the title of Righteous Among the Nations upon the late Alban Fort as well as his still living wife, Germaine.

Frolova, Elena
BELARUS

*I*n Borisov, to the east of Minsk, in Belarus, Elena Frolova bid farewell to her son, a fighter pilot in the Russian air force as he took to the skies in defense of his country at the start of the war with Germany in June 1941. Alone with her husband, Ivan, who worked for the railroad, Elena worried about her son's safety and fervently hoped that he would return safe and sound from the war. As a deeply religious woman, the idea came to her that if she rescued a helpless child, preferably a Jewish one, then her son stood a better chance of returning home safely, with the help of divine grace.

Having made up her mind, she journeyed to Minsk, 65 kilometers to the west of Borisov, and visited an orphanage, where she was shown a two-year-old girl named Galina who had been placed there by a certain Hasia Rubenchik – probably her mother – from the Minsk ghetto in order to save her. Elena Frolova took an immediate liking to the forlorn girl, who was not in the best of health, and took her home with her. She nursed the child back to health and gave her much love.

Borisov was not an ideal place to be for persons wishing to rescue Jews. The 7,000 Jews locked in the local ghetto by the Germans had all been brutally murdered in October 1941 near the local airfield, and two years later their bodies were exhumed and burned. Danger to Frolova lurked from neighbors who suspected that the child was Jewish; some even threatened to denounce her to the authorities. Moreover, the Gestapo had arrested Helena's husband, Ivan, on suspicion of sabotage. After undergoing a brutal interrogation, accompanied by torture, he was sent home, where he died shortly afterwards.

Elena Frolova with Galina Rubenchik

Due to the increased danger, Helena Frolova left Borisov, taking along Galina, and headed for the Grodno region, where she stayed with relatives. There she formally adopted Galina, and the child grew up not doubting that Frolova was her natural mother. For her part, Helena developed a strong maternal attachment to Galina, which lasted for years.

In 1944, Helena Frolova returned to liberated Borisov and was happy that her prayers had been answered, as her son returned home from the war safely. Despite her dire economic situation and poor health, she refused to turn over the child to an orphanage, as her son entreated her. After her son left, as he was stationed in Austria in the Soviet occupation zone, Helena, in 1951, in a state of deep depression, tragically committed suicide, willing half her house and possessions to Galina. To all intents and purposes, Elena had taken to the grave the truth about Galina's true origins.

That remained the case until 1993, when a certain Peotr Rubenchik, living in Minsk, wrote to Yad Vashem the astounding account of how, after many years, he had discovered that his long-forgotten sister Galina was indeed alive and living in Borisov, not far from where her natural mother had resided, in Minsk. This is the story as told by Peotr.

Born in 1937 to a family of four children, he numbered among his siblings Boris, born in 1930, Misha, born 1936, and sister Galina, born in 1941. His father worked in a leather factory and his mother, Hasia, in a general goods store. When war broke out, Peotr and brother Misha happened to be in a children's summer camp that was quickly evacuated to the east in advance of the invading Germans. Peotr's father was drafted into the army, whereas his mother with her other two children, Boris and Galina, were trapped inside Minsk and confined in the ghetto.

When the killings of Jews started, Hasia and her sister persuaded a policeman to allow Galina to be taken to a Russian orphanage so as to save her life. It was learned later that this policeman was shot by the Germans for his link to the underground. Little Boris fell victim to the Germans together with his grandfather and 30 relatives. In the winter of 1943, Hasia and her brother David were among a group of 16 people who managed to flee the ghetto and join the Shkalov partisan unit, where the two fought the Germans from forest lairs. David tragically fell during one of these actions. Hasia's twin brother, Israel, had earlier been hanged in the ghetto on the charge of sabotage in the firm where he worked.

With the liberation of Belarus in the summer of 1944, Hasia began to search frantically for her children. She was able to locate Peotr and Misha in the interior of Russia and bring them back to Minsk. However, all searches for Galina were in vain, as the documents in the orphanage were either lost or in a state of disarray. According to one of the nurses there, the Nazis often visited the orphanage and took away children whom they suspected of being Jewish, and Galina may have been one of these victims. Hasia's husband came back from the army, and together with his wife visited all the orphanages in Belarus, but Galina was not to be found.

They returned to the Minsk orphanage where Galina had been placed, and another nurse told them that, in fear of the Germans, many children had been turned over for adoption. In Peotr's words, "For all these years, it remained an open wound for us, but we could do nothing." In 1954, when orphans were brought to Minsk from Korea, Hasia wanted to adopt one of the Korean girls in remembrance of Galina, but her request was declined due to the family's poor economic situation – all living in one room.

Nothing much happened until the summer of 1964, when a cousin of Hasia named Avraham Kreyndel, who had once lived in Borisov, attended a friend's wedding and noticed there a young woman who sat with her husband opposite him. He was stunned by the resemblance between the young woman and Peotr. During a pause in the dancing, he went over to her and discreetly asked her about her background. She told him she was an orphan who during the war was taken from Minsk for adoption by Elena Frolova. Her foster mother had told her that she had a large family in Minsk.

When Kreyndel passed the astounding news to Hasia and her husband, they immediately went to Borisov to meet this strange Galina. Hasia said she would recognize her daughter by her birthmark between her belly and thigh. When they met, Hasia and Galina went into a separate room, and indeed the mark was there. "It is difficult to describe what came over us," Hasia's son Peotr wrote in his letter to Yad Vahem; "how many tears were spilled. Even strangers, neighbors that came to congratulate us, could not withhold tears from so much joy."

Galina told Hasia that when Elena's son had returned from the war and married, he had tried to persuade his mother to give up the child. He told her, "You did an act of goodness; you saved a Jewish child. Now the government should care for her." Elena stood by her determination to hold on to Galina. After Elena's death, her son sold the house and all its contents and divided the proceeds equally between himself and Galina (hers placed in her name in a bank). Galina was returned to an orphanage. After finishing her studies, she married Mihail Fradkin and bore two children; and the family later moved to Israel.

Galina had rediscovered her roots and her true mother and family. As for Yad Vashem, another name was added to the honorific Righteous Among the Nations – the tragic Elena Frolova, recognized in 1996.

Fry, Varian
United States

*O*n September 7, 1941, soon after his expulsion from France, Varian Fry wrote to his wife, Eileen, in the United States from his hotel in Barcelona, Spain, of the transformation he had undergone as a result of his rescue operation in France:

> *"I have just reached the end of the most intense twelve months I have ever lived through ... I still don't quite know what happened to me ... I do not think that I shall ever be quite the same person I was when I kissed you goodbye at the airport and went down the gangplank to the waiting [Pan American] Clipper. For the experiences of ten, fifteen and even twenty years have been pressed into one ... I have developed, or discovered within me powers of resourcefulness, of imagination and courage which I never before knew I possessed."*

Fry was referring to the unusual rescue operation that he headed soon after France's fall to Germany in the summer of 1940. When it was learned that under the armistice agreement between victor and vanquished, France was obliged "to surrender on demand all persons under German jurisdiction named by the German government," including thousands of Jewish intellectuals on the Gestapo wanted list, an Emergency Rescue Committee was launched by a group of concerned persons, during a hastily organized luncheon at the Commodore Hotel in Manhattan. The aim was to spirit out from recently fallen France intellectuals and renowned people in the fields of the humanities – mostly Jews – who because of their past activities and anti-Nazi pronouncements stood in danger of being turned over to the Germans. Thanks to the intercession of Eleanor Roosevelt, wife of the American President, the State Department allowed for a limited number of 200 people to be admitted to the United States, and Varian Fry was then chosen to head the rescue operation.

A Harvard graduate and a freelance journalist, he had no previous practical experience in clandestine work. Later, in France, Fry told Mary Jayne Gold, one of his rescue aides, what prompted him to accept the assignment, a mission that he was warned by friends not to take on because of the dangers involved. In 1935, when as a journalist he visited Nazi Germany, he witnessed several Nazi Storm Troopers driving a knife through the hand of a Jewish man in a Berlin coffee shop. The mental image of that hand nailed to the table beside the beer mug had something to do with his decision to go.

His letter of assignment afforded him "reasonable latitude" and mandated him to use his personal judgment to explore rescue possibilities for the individuals on his list in order to get them either to Lisbon or Casablanca. In Marseilles, he was to examine the availability of small coastal boats capable of reaching North Africa for the temporary refuge of his wards. Bearing in mind that much of the shipping in Marseilles was in the hands of underworld figures, he was to use discretionary judgment in negotiating with them. He was scheduled to leave in mid-August 1940 for a month's stay in Europe with the possibility of an extension, but not beyond October 31, 1940.

Varian Fry, 1942 (Chambon Foundation, Los Angeles)

"I had never done underground work before and I did not know a single person on the list," Fry wrote later. "Armed with $3,000 in cash [which was taped to his leg] and the conviction that every Jew in France ... was in danger of his life, I arrived in Marseilles on August 15, 1940." However, once there, "I was at a complete loss about how to begin, and where. My job was to save certain refugees. But how was I to do it? How was I to get in touch with them: What could I do for them when I found them?"

He took a small back room at the Splendide hotel, and began writing letters to all those on his list whose addresses were known. There was soon a stampede of people to his hotel room, and letters began arriving from many parts of Vichy France (the unoccupied part of the country). By the end of his second week, the lines outside his door were so long that Fry decided to move to a nearby office, named *Centre Americain de Secours.* Realizing that the job was beyond the strength of one person, he organized a staff of trustworthy people to help him in what he realized would be a vast rescue operation – way beyond the 200 people on his list. This staff interviewed between 60 and 70 refugees a day.

With so many people looking for a chance to flee the country, Fry was faced with a serious problem. "We had no way of knowing who was really in danger and who wasn't. We had to guess, and the only safe way to guess was to give each refugee the full benefit of the doubt. Otherwise we might refuse help to someone who was really in danger and learn later that he had been dragged away to Dachau or Buchenwald because we had turned him away." For fear of entrapment, Fry's organization stuck to one fixed rule: no help extended to people without references.

Some of the fleeing refugees had been active anti-Nazis and as such were subject to extradition to Germany, with Jews more than well represented on this list – quite over 50 percent. Some people were smuggled out of the country by Fry's group in the guise of demobilized French soldiers, on troopships sailing from Marseilles to North African ports, then still under French control. In the frantic search for visas, even distant countries such as Siam (Thailand) and China were approached for entry visas. The Chinese obliged but not exactly as Fry had hoped. The Chinese visa read: "This person shall not, under any circumstances, be allowed to enter China." But French border guards hardly read Chinese, and it looked to them like a legally approved visa to China and the holder of this document was allowed exit from the country.

Some of the people on Fry's list were reluctant to leave France, such as artist Marc Chagall. Fleeing from Paris, under direct German rule, he had settled in Gordes, northwest of Marseilles, and was completely absorbed in his painting, inspired by the pastoral setting outside his home, including grazing cows. In Fry's words:

> "I spent a weekend there, telling him of his danger and assuring him that there were cows in the United States – yes, and goats, too. Finally, he consented to go. But when he came down to Marseilles to get his papers prepared for the trip, he was arrested in the first of a series of Vichy police roundups to separate Jewish from non-Jewish foreigners ... I called a high Marseilles police official I knew and threatened to telephone the press corps at Vichy to make sure he and his superior received world publicity and lifelong disgrace if they did not release Chagall immediately. Half an hour later Chagall was back at his hotel; we rushed him and his family out of France."

When Fry met Austrian expatriate Willi Spira (alias Bill Freier), he asked him: "Why do you believe that the Nazis will arrest you?" "I think I am on their blacklist." Why so, Fry asked. "I was a cartoonist in Vienna until the *Anschluss* [Austria's annexation to Nazi Germany], and later in Paris too. Nearly all my political cartoons were directed against Hitler and his fascist regime. If possible, please help me and my fiancée escape to the United States." Spira's name was not on Fry's original list of 200 people, so he made sketches of Fry and his staff to give Fry an idea of his talent. "I will think it over," Fry told him; "I hope I can do something for you. Come again in two or three days!" When Spira came to see him, Fry smiled. "We can use your talent. If you agree, you will forge rubber stamps for us and for your endangered fellow refugees. They need passports and identity cards ... We know somebody who will show you all the tricks to become a perfect forger. Immediately, in return, I will cable New York to get you and your fiancée a visa to the States." Bill Spira forged false passports for author Franz Werfel and his wife Alma Mahler, among others, that helped them get out of France.

Back in the United, the Emergency Rescue Committee in New York responded to Fry's appeals by expanding the original list of 200 names approved by them, but this proved insufficient to cover the thousands of cases being handled by Fry's operation. For additional funds for his rescue operation, while on a short visit to Spain Fry negotiated a deal with the British ambassador there: in return for $10,000 from the British, Fry would also try to spirit out stranded British soldiers, mostly by sea, to whom Fry was allowed to attach his own refugees. In Fry's words, "I had come to think of illegal emigration as the normal, if not the only way to go."

The escape routes included various mountain passes: from Banyuls, France, to Port Bou, Spain, or from other departure points in Toulouse and Pau, across the formidable Pyrenees Mountains, or by boat to distant French colonies. They may be enumerated as follows. Route A – from Marseilles to Lisbon, via the Cerbere railroad station, or from the town of Banyuls, or the surrounding hills, into Port Bou, Spain; Route B – for refugees in the greatest danger of arrest – over the hills to various locations in Spain; Route C – refugees with high-quality forged papers and real exit visas – from Marseilles to Pau, then by rail to Saragossa, Madrid, and Lisbon; Route D –refugees with authentic Cuban visas on questionable passports, who avoided Lisbon and went directly from Spain to Cuba; Routes E and F – to North African ports by boat; Route G – from Marseilles directly to Martinique by boat.

Some of the well-known people helped included famed sculptor Jacques Lipchitz, pianist Erich Itor-Hahn, political scientist Hannah Arendt, novelist Hans Habe, and physiologist Otto Meyerhof. As for the noted German-Jewish author Lion Feuchtwanger and his wife, Marta – Fry turned them over to a Unitarian-sponsored rescue committee, headed in France by Martha and Waitstill Sharp, who spirited them out of the country all the way to Portugal and from there by boat the United States. According to Fry's count, by May 1941 the office had handled more than 15,000 cases, of which 1,800 fell within the scope of Fry's direct work, representing some 4,000 people, of which 1,000 had been spirited out of the country. Writing to his wife, Fry noted: "If I leave, I abandon those human beings, many of whom I have come to know and to like very much, and most of whom have come to depend on me."

Learning of the wide scope of Fry's unorthodox methods, the French protested to the American consul in Marseilles. U.S. diplomats in France (the United States and Vichy France maintained diplomatic relations until late 1942), adhering to the restrictive U.S. immigration policy, informed the French police that it had a free hand "to get rid" of Fry. The local French police chief added his recommendation that Fry be expelled from the country, and the French police several times raided Fry's offices in search of incriminating documents. Fry was then summoned to the chief of police of the Marseilles region, who warned him to leave the country or face harsh consequences. "Why all this," Fry asked? "Because you are defending too many Jews and anti-Nazis," the police chief

Planting a tree at Yad Vashem in honor of Varian Fry; the son of Varian Fry shaking hands with Warren Christopher

blandly replied. Finally, in August 1941, Fry was arrested, given an hour to pack, and accompanied to the Spanish border. He was told that his expulsion had been ordered by the Ministry of the Interior, "with the approval of the American embassy," and the decision could not be reversed. In an ironic twist, in 1967, months before Varian Fry's death, the French government, recanting its wartime behavior, awarded him the prestigious *Chevalier* of the *Légion d'Honneur*.

As for Fry's own country, the United States, it took it much longer to make amends for its harassment of the man (whose passport was taken away from him by the Marseilles Consulate). During his stay in France, to overcome the ongoing pressure by U.S. diplomats, Fry had appealed directly to Cordell Hull, the U.S. Secretary of State. In a telegram dated November 10, 1940, Fry called the Secretary's attention to the plight of the refugees. "Thousands find themselves in prisons and concentration camps of Europe without hope of release because they have no government to represent them ... Cannot U.S. and other nations of Western Hemisphere take immediate steps, such as creation new Nansen Passports [formerly used to help stateless Russian refugees] and extension of at least limited diplomatic protection to holders of them?" Writing again to Hull, on November 18, Fry asked, "Is this not an occasion for the United States and the other nations of the Western Hemisphere to take extraordinary measures? Cannot the Government of the United States intervene in behalf at least of those upon whom it has seen fit to confer its visas, so that they may be released from the concentration camps, be granted French exit visas and Spanish and Portuguese transit visas, and then be able to proceed on their way to Liberty?" No answer was received to these two appeals. When diplomatic prodding failed to move Fry to leave France, his passport was confiscated in January 1941. A secretary at the U.S. embassy in Vichy told him: "My instructions are to renew it only for immediate return to the United States, and then only for a period of two weeks. So I'm afraid I'll have to keep it here until you're ready to go." From that moment, until his forced departure seven months later, Fry was without a passport.

After his forced return to the United States, Fry lashed out against the State Department's immigration policy. In an article in *The New Republic* on December 21, 1942, entitled "The Massacre of the Jews," he wrote: "There are some things so horrible that decent men and women find them impossible to believe, so monstrous that the civilized world recoils incredulous before them. The recent reports of the systematic extermination of the Jews in Nazi Europe are of this order." Fry then surveyed the liquidation of the Jews in each country, and appealed to President Roosevelt and Prime Minister Churchill, writing:

"A joint declaration, couched in the most solemn terms ... of the retribution to come might be of some avail. Tribunals should be set up now to begin to amass the facts ... The Christian churches might also help, at least in countries like France, Holland, Belgium, Norway; the Pope by threatening with excommunication all Catholics who in any way participate in these frightful crimes; the Protestant leaders by exhorting their fellow communicants to resist to the utmost the Nazis' fiendish designs ... We should broadcast the news of them day and night to every country of Europe, in every European language ... Finally, and it is a little thing, but at the same time a big thing; we can offer asylum now, without delay or red tape, to those few fortunate enough to escape from the Aryan paradise.... There have

been bureaucratic delays in visa procedure which have literally condemned to death many stalwart democrats."

Put under surveillance by the FBI as a subversive on the orders of J. Edgar Hoover, Fry was neglected by former friends and colleagues until his premature death at the age of 59. He was neither honored by his own country nor by the Jewish community. Only France belatedly honored him 26 years after expelling him from the country. When he died in 1967, he was a Latin teacher at a boys' high school.

Learning of his death, Jacques Lipchitz wrote to Fry's wife: "In some way I owe him my life. I did not want to go away from France. It was his severe and clairvoyant letters which helped me finally to do so … I mourn with you this wondrous man ... and I will cherish his memory to the end of my life."

Miriam Davenport-Ebel, one of Fry's close associates in Marseilles, explained the tragic impasse Fry found himself in: "Needless to say he soon had to choose between saving people's lives and saving that job! He lost his job." Davenport then went on to describe the climate then in the United States: "Anti-war, anti-Allied sentiment was rife. In truth, many influential men and women still considered Hitler our last bastion against Communism ... The Neutrality Act, still on the books, was enthusiastically enforced by the State Department ... Not many cared what was happening to the Jews."

Returning to Varian's letter to wife, Eileen, from the Hotel Espana in Barcelona, on September 7, 1941, he wrote,

"I have lived far more intensely in this last year, far more objectively, actively, really, if you like, than I ever have before, and that experience has changed me profoundly … Sometimes I feel as if I lived a whole life (and one to which I have no right) since I first walked down the monumental stairway of the Gare St. Charles at Marseilles and timidly took a small back room at the Hotel Splendide. Since that day I have had adventure ... of which I never dreamed. I have learned to live with people, and to work with them … And I have fought a fight, against enormous odds, of which, in spite of the final defeat, I think I can always be proud."

Dr. Albert O. Hirschman, another of Varian Fry's close aides in Marseilles, wrote: "The Fry story almost brings to mind the successful fight of David against Goliath, or the Greek myth that pits crafty Ulysses against the huge Cyclops." Precise figures are hard to get, but it is estimated that Varian Fry and his team were responsible for saving one or two thousand lives – a majority of them Jews on the run from the Nazis and their collaborators.

When Yad Vashem learned of the man's rescue record, supplemented by documents released by the newly established U.S. Holocaust Memorial Museum in Washington, D.C., in 1994, he was posthumously awarded the Righteous title and a tree-planting ceremony in his honor took place in February 1996. The ceremony was attended by the then U.S. Secretary of State Warren Christopher, who took the occasion to apologize on behalf of the State Department for the abusive treatment of Varian Fry during 1940–41 and emphasized the pride the United States felt that a man of such caliber was now honored as a great humanitarian under the Yad Vashem program of Righteous Among the Nations.

Gallay, Simon
Mopty, Pierre
Simond, Albert

FRANCE

*L*eaving the village of Varces, near Grenoble in southern France, Shlomo and Hinde Wajsfeld and their children headed north on the advice of an unknown person, for the purpose of trying to cross into Switzerland. It was early September 1943 and the Italians were hastily withdrawing their troops to Italy from the area in France they had administered, in the wake of the Allied invasion of the Italian mainland. It was feared that the Germans would soon sweep in and take over, placing the thousands of Jews who had sought refuge in the Italian zone in danger. Shlomo and Hinde had been told to look up a certain priest, codenamed Mr. "Lebain," in Evian-les-Bains, the resort town on the shores of Lake Leman separating France from Switzerland. This man, they had been assured, would help them make the risky border crossing. To travel by train in those days one needed a permit. The Wajsfelds had received such a document from the prefecture in Grenoble upon presenting a doctor's referral to Evian for a medical checkup. As she looked less Jewish than her husband and was more conversant with the French language, Mrs. Wajsfeld decided to check out the lead herself, leaving her husband and the younger children behind to be on the safe side.

Mordecai Paldiel with his rescuer Simon Gallay (right)

The Wajsfelds had fled from Belgium upon the German invasion of the country in May 1940 and had wandered from place to place in France – St. Gaudens, Toulouse, Marseilles, Grenoble, and the village of Varces – always a step ahead of the Germans. Presently, the whole of France, including the until-recently secure Italian zone, was coming under direct German control, and with it the danger for Jews wishing to avoid deportation to the concentration camps.

Arriving in Evian, Hinde Wajsfeld approached the church to which she had been referred. In her words, she knocked at the door.

A woman, possibly a nun, came out and led the anxious Jewish woman into a room and told her to wait. A little while later, a man appeared, a priest. He struck her as handsome, tall with blond hair, blue eyes, and most important, a kindly and trustworthy face. He was accompanied by another priest, a bit older. She was led into a beautiful room and the two clerics asked the tense woman what she wanted.

> *"I began to weep and told them my whole story, that I was temporarily here with three children: Annie, Mordecai, and Leah [aged, respectively 7, 6, and 4], and the others were with Papa behind in Varces.... I was then taken with the children to a nursing home, where the nuns gave us something to drink and a room with mattresses on the floor for us to rest. The priest, 'Mr. Lebain,' told us to wait until the time was ripe to smuggle us over. He would then tell me when to bring the rest of the family. A couple of days later, he came over and said, 'Now it's time.' I was crying and wanted to give 'Mr. Lebain' my wedding ring for his good deed, but he said to me, 'My dear lady, keep the ring, jut remember me.' I remember him to this day — his lovely and friendly face."*

In a coded telegram, Hinde Wajsfeld sent a message to her husband to come with the other three children (Frieda, aged 3, and the nine-month-old twins, Mania and Simon), as well as with her elderly mother, Yocheved Kanner. The family rented a room near the train station and stayed there for around a week. Then Father "Lebain" told them to head for Thonon-les-Bains and from there by bus for a certain village (which the Wajsfelds remember as "Vardigue"), where they were to get off and head for the nearest bistro, where one or several passeurs (professional border crossers) would be waiting for them. On the way there, two German soldiers (probably from an advance contingent to replace the retreating Italians) got on the bus and, with the bus filled to capacity and no sitting room, the two soldiers stood astride the Wajsfelds, who could follow their conversation (German has a familiar ring to Yiddish-speaking people). It went as follows, as one of them looked at the bearded Shlomo Wajsfeld: "Look here, isn't that a Jew?' The other replied: "Why, no! Look at his wife; she's not Jewish. Don't be silly." The two Wajsfelds trembled with fear, but the soldiers got off at the next stop. At the bistro, two passeurs met them, and led them through the fields. It was a clear night, and the moon was shining bright. After crossing into Switzerland, the two men told the Wajsfelds to sit on a ridge until they were picked up by Swiss border guards, who would soon be passing by on

Police photo of Mordecai Paldiel (Wajsfeld) after his crossing into Switzerland

their patrol. The passage took place on September 8, 1943. It was just in time, for on that day Italy formally surrendered to the Allies and the Germans immediately swept into the areas of France held by the Italians until then. Once inside Switzerland, the adult Wajsfelds and the younger children were separated from the two older children. Annie and Mordecai (Paldiel – the writer of these lines!), were placed in a children's home in Bex-les-Bains supervised by the Jewish community and the others in various refugee camps. While Jewish refugees (those that were admitted) were not enthusiastically welcomed by the Swiss, at least they were safe from harm, and their lives were no longer in danger.

In 1984, the cleric who aided the Wajsfelds was finally rediscovered and identified as Father Simon Gallay. The mystery of the man's name was resolved by the Catholic scholar Professor Eva Fleischner, who met and interviewed the cleric. In an October 1985 letter to Paldiel, she explained. "There is absolutely no question but that he is the one your mother remembers…. He clearly remembers your mother's offering him her ring." As she further explained, the man known as "Lebain" was actually Gallay's colleague – Abbé Albert Simond – and he was actually called "Mr. Plebain," from the Latin "plebs," "people," "man of the people," apparently a title sometimes given a rural pastor – misheard by the Wajsfelds as "Lebain." Simond was probably the older man who handed them over to Gallay. Fleischner: "Everything fits; there were only these two priests in Evian during the war … I believe I can say, mission accomplished … I am glad I could do this for you – you can put aside all doubt." Responding to a letter by Dr. Paldiel, Father Gallay wrote.

"Yes, it is I who took care of you at Evian and arranged your passage to Switzerland. I helped many Jews cross into Switzerland, but I was not alone in doing it. The passeurs were Yves Roussey, shot by the Germans, Jacques Moulard – deported for one year; he now lives in Evian. I was encouraged in this work by Mr. l'Abbé Albert Simond (deceased), Abbé Camille Folliet (deceased), Abbé Jean Rosay, deported to Germany. He did not return. I must point out those who worked with me, for I would not have been able to do much all by myself. Thank you for writing to me. If you need more information, ask me. Sincerely yours. Gallay."

Furthermore, Mrs. Wajsfeld positively identified a wartime photo of Simon Gallay as the man whom she met in the Evian church. As further confirmed by Sister Aline (Josephine Tremblet), Gallay was the one who was directly involved in organizing the passage into Switzerland. "He exhausted himself on account of this, and often worked away at night to arrange a passage – to the point of falling asleep the next morning in church." Gallay was the principal organizer of these rescue operations, and Simond covered for him. A third cleric, Abbé Pierre Mopty often came to help out. He had a canoe which he often used to take people across the lake, himself rowing. He risked arrest, either by the Italians, the Germans, or the French police.

Ruth Lambert, in a postwar statement, further described some of Mopty's courageous exploits. She stated that in 1943 she happened to be in the Rivesaltes detention camp (near Perpignan) as part of the joint effort of Jewish (Andrée Salomon) and non-Jewish people (Father Albert Gross) to exert pressure on the French authorities to release Jewish detainees brought there from another camp, so as to save them from deportation. One evening, as they sat on the floor of their assigned hut, there was a knock on the door and a young priest with a black umbrella and a big smile entered. "Bonjour, I am Abbé Mopty. I am here to save Jews …" The volunteer workers were stunned. Abbé Gross got up and responded, "Bonjour, I am from Lausanne." "And I am from Evian," Mopty replied. He then explained that he was asked by a priest in Lyon to take three people across to Switzerland who were being sought by the Gestapo because they were Jews. But before he could act, the three (father, mother, and son) had been picked up and were now interned in Rivesaltes. This was during

Christmas time 1943. So he came, quite simply, "to get them out of here." He organized a taxi; then arranged for them to be hidden behind the altar of a church in Perpignan; finally, he took the three to Evian. On a certain evening, Mopty and his three charges showed up at the Evian harbor. Mopty got a rowboat and all four left for Ouchy, on the Swiss side, where Abbé Gross was waiting for them. Mopty returned alone that same evening to Evian and put the rowboat back. It belonged to the police chief! No one had noticed that it was missing. Mopty often told Lambert that "wanting what God wants is the only science which gives me relaxation," a reference to his university studies during this period.

Gallay once gave Mopty 300,000 francs to turn over to a passeur in Douvaine for the purpose of smuggling Jews over the border. Gallay also mentioned Father Jean Rosay in Douvaine, who also helped take people across the border. He was eventually apprehended and sent to a concentration camp, where he perished. Father Camille Folliet was also involved in this type of clandestine work. In Gallay's words, "One day he phoned me from Annemasse: 'There are two packages [i.e., Jews] to pick up at the train station – take care of it.' Folliet later left to serve as a chaplain on the Italian front in southern France, where he was wounded and died. Gallay had to be careful of Gestapo agents provocateurs. He remembers the case of a beautiful woman who ostensibly came for help to cross into Switzerland. "I suspected a trap and acted as though I didn't know what she was talking about. I am sure to this day that she was sent by the Gestapo."

Born in 1913, the tenth of thirteen children, Simon Gallay was ordained in 1937 and served both during and after the war in various posts in Evian-les-Bains and other nearby localities, finally retiring in 1982. In his letters to Paldiel, he spoke of his philosophy of life. "I always try to take an interest in people's lives … I love every human being. I don't have enemies. Those who are angry at me and consider me their enemy are wasting their time. I love them and am always ready to be of assistance to them." During the war years, some people said: "One must follow the Maréchal [Petain] with closed eyes," to which Gallay responded, "We will follow the Maréchal, if we so wish, with open eyes." Many fleeing Jews came to seek help. Gallay never went himself on the crossings. "I did not have the time and I did not know the region well." Besides, as vicar in Evian he was occupied with church duties: catechisms, the choir, confessions, gatherings, etc. He used three professional passeurs – the brothers Yves and Raymond Roussey and Jacques Moulard. The Roussey brothers were arrested and shot by their German captors in prison in reprisal for an attack by the resistance on a German convoy. Jacques Moulard was arrested and deported to Germany and was lucky to survive. Other collaborators of Gallay who were arrested included Dr. Bernex and Gabriel Blanc, who returned from deportation ("a living corpse"). As for the Wajsfeld family, "They came to me one evening: father, mother, and six children. The mother offered me her wedding ring so that we would take them into consideration." Gallay declined. "There was among them a five-year-old boy [Mordecai!]. I think he carried in his arms a smaller child. We acted."

In 1989, Yad Vashem conferred the title of Righteous Among the Nations upon Father Simon Gallay, Father Pierre Mopty, and Father Albert Simond. A ceremony in Gallay's honor was held in Annecy on May 6, 1990, in the presence of the town mayor, the prefect, a representative of the local Jewish community, and a delegate of the local bishop – as well as Dr. Mordecai Paldiel, who flew over from Israel for this purpose and who also planted a tree in the Avenue of the Righteous at Yad Vashem in the name of his and his family's rescuer.

Geulen-Herscovici, Andrée

BELGIUM

Born in 1921 in Brussels, Andreé Geulen sat together with Jewish pupils at school but was oblivious to their presence. Even at home, although Catholic by birth, Andrée does not remember any discussions about Jews, and was surprised to learn that the family doctor was Jewish. Then, "When I asked my father why we were no longer seeing the doctor, he answered that he was hiding him – hiding his doctor! I was surprised. Only then did I discover that the doctor was Jewish." In 1941, with Belgium already under German occupation, Andrée qualified as a teacher. One day she was stunned to see five or six students in her class appear with the obligatory yellow star on their clothes. "That was the first time that I came face to face with the persecution of Jews in Belgium. Up to then, I was not conscious of the anti-Jewish measures in Belgium." She told her non-Jewish pupils not to poke fun at the Jewish ones. To make sure there were no distinguishing outward signs among her pupils, she told them to come to class in aprons so that the yellow star would not be visible. At a later date, when Jewish children could no longer attend public schools, Andreé gave them private lessons at home. Then one day, "I did not see them again – they were picked up in a *razzia* [German roundup] and deported."

Andrée Geulen in 1944 (courtesy of Andrée Geulen-Herscovici)

At the time, Andrée also taught at the Gatti de Gamond boarding school in the Woluwé section of Brussels, where she discovered about a dozen Jewish pupils in hiding there. She and the principal of the school, Mrs. Odile Ovart, discussed how best to help them. The children had been brought there by Ida Sterno, a Jewish activist with the clandestine Jewish Defense Committee who also seconded in dispersing Jewish children in various institutions. When Sterno confided to Ovart that she needed a non-Jewish assistant to help out in her clandestine work, Ovart told her she had someone for her – Andrée Geulen. At their first meeting, Ida asked Andrée whether she was prepared for this type of work, including assuming a new name, which would be Claude Fournier. "I immediately agreed, for I wanted to do something. I was impatient; something had to be done, and here came the opportunity. I did not tell my parents of my decision." In the meantime, she was asked to stay in Ovart's boarding school, where she had her own quarters.

At the time Andrée did not know that Ida Sterno was Jewish. One evening, as she made her rounds of the bunks to make sure the children were tucked in, one boy pulled himself up to Andrée and said he wanted to tell her a secret, but she should not tell anyone. "I am in fact, Jewish, and my real name is so and so." Andrée thought to herself: "What kind of a world are we living when a child must hide his true name? It is a world turned upside down!"

In May 1943, tragedy struck when the Gestapo raided the premises deep in the night. Evidently, someone had betrayed them. Since it was the Pentecost holiday, all the non-Jewish children had been sent home, with only the Jewish children left there, but the Gestapo did not know this. For they ordered, "every Jew to the right, every non-Jew to the left." The older ones went to the right; the smaller ones to the left, since they had been taught not to mention anything Jewish, so they did not understand the Gestapo order. Not satisfied with this selection, the Gestapo took away all the children – a total of 14. They then interrogated Mrs. Ovart, and asked her, "Why?" She replied, "I am Belgian, not German, and do not check credentials." One Gestapo agent slapped her across the face. Andrée was then asked, "What are you doing here?" "I give lessons," was the reply. Gestapo: "Aren't you ashamed to teach Jews?" Geulen: "Aren't you ashamed to make war on Jewish children?" Gestapo: "If one does not want to suffer from bugs, one must squash them when they're small."

Odile Ovart and her husband, Remy, were arrested and dispatched to concentration camps, where they perished – Odile in Bergen-Belsen and Remy in Buchenwald. Their 22-year-old daughter, named Andrée, was also jailed for six months. As for Andrée Geulen, she was told to leave and not come back. She hurried to the homes of people who were sheltering Jewish children who were due to report for school in a few hours, to alert them to the danger, for several Gestapo agents had remained at the school to bag some more Jewish children. "I then remained alone on the street with only a basket and the clothes on me. I had left all my other belongings in the school." Andrée Geulen's clandestine life had just begun, but at first she did not know what to do next.

Passing the night at the home of the Ovart daughter's boyfriend, she then tried to contact Ida Sterno, but did not know her address, or even her underground name. She then somehow learned that her code name was Jeanne and she was hiding in a convent. She went there and spent the night with Ida, and there she "suddenly noticed the yellow star on her clothes. I was shocked. 'So you're also Jewish!' I had not known it until that very moment." Andrée then leased an apartment under her code name and the two women stayed there. Ida kept a notebook with a list of the children needing a hiding place, and addresses, and this notebook was hidden under the floor of the apartment, covered with a carpet.

It was the beginning of Andrée's intensive work for the Jewish underground, where she met other Jewish as well as non-Jewish operatives, such as Brigitte Moens, a Catholic, who looked for hiding places for children in convents and monasteries, or the Jewish Yvonne Jospa, who searched for shelters in official places, such as institutions for retarded children. Andrée admitted that in the case of Jospa she also did not recognize her as Jewish in the beginning. "In fact, I did not know how to distinguish between a Jew and non-Jew." Three times a week Andrée checked a post office box in an antique shop for messages about people needing to be hidden. Addresses were not written down but learned by heart, so that people would not walk around with incriminating information. "I was known for my good memory." Only in the hidden notebook, at home, were the addresses of the hidden children listed, as well as other vital information, such as illnesses and other data that the host families needed to know about the children in their care.

"I am not a believer, and I don't think much of priests and rabbis," Andrée acknowledged. "However, I will admit that the lower clergy helped us greatly, and without their assistance we would not have achieved much." Most of the boarding schools in Belgium were, in fact, under Catholic supervision. Ida and Andrée regularly went to pick up the children who needed to be placed.

"We told the parents to prepare a suitcase, and we shall return in a day or two ... I still weep when I think of the times when I had to snatch children from their parents, especially children aged 2 or 3, without being able to tell the parents where I was taking them. Surprisingly, the children willingly accompanied us. In some cases, the children told their parents not to weep. To the children we said that due to the shortages of food in the city and the threat of air raids, we were taking them to the countryside to enjoy fresh air, food and a good life. So they went willingly. The number of children that I thus accompanied alone I estimate at around 300."

Once in their new homes, the children understandably yearned for their parents, who were forbidden to visit them, to avoid entrapment. Many underwent severe mental torment as they grappled with their new identities side by side with their previous ones, as in the following touching story. A five-year-old boy, placed with a host family, stole and hid the decorative religious artifact of Mary with the little Jesus in their Bethlehem manger, which the family's eight-year-old girl had received as a gift for Christmas. Questioned about this, after a long silence the boy timidly admitted: "Little Jesus and the Holy Virgin are Jews; so I hid them. The Gestapo will not get them." Overcome with emotion, he then burst out in tears.

The system generally worked as follows. Andrée and Ida kept secret notebooks in addition to Ida's notebook in her apartment. In the first was listed the child's real name with a number, such as "10, Appelbaum, Annette;" in the second – the number without the name and the address of the child parents. In the third – the number with the child's new name; in the fourth – the various institutions with their code numbers, such as "400, Institut Réligieuse at Heverlée." All these notebooks were kept at one address (Rue de la Brasserie), but in different rooms – in cupboards of an empty rented apartment.

Then, in May 1944, Ida Sterno was arrested by the Gestapo, and somehow had Andrée's address on her. When Andrée got home, she saw that locks had been placed on the door to the apartment. A neighbor told her to leave immediately, for only seconds before the Gestapo had raided the house. One problem was how to get the notebook under the floorboards. Finally, a doctor working for the Jewish Defense Committee volunteered to slip into the apartment from the basement, and got the notebook as well as Andrée's clothing. She then moved from place to place, with the assistance of her Jewish colleagues, until the country's liberation in September 1944. During this period, with the Gestapo on her trail, Andrée continued her clandestine work of accompanying children. Surprisingly, under her assumed name, she was able to visit Ida Sterno in the Malines camp, with the Gestapo not aware that she was someone they were looking for. Ida luckily survived.

Andrée does not have an exact figure, but she is certain she cared for at least 300 Jewish children. After the war, she continued to care for the children, but in the opposite way: to get them back to their parents – those who survived. Then, with the assistance of the American-based Joint Distribution Committee, many children were turned over to various Jewish agencies. Andrée Geulen also made it a point to stay in touch with her former charges. One of her great satisfactions is running into a former child-ward in the street, hurrying to work or home to his family. In 1948, she married Charles Herscovici, who lost his parents in the Holocaust. "We have two daughters and five grandchildren ... My daughters consider themselves Jewish, although they're not believers."

During the period of her underground work, she told all sorts of stories to her parents, to which they responded, "Who knows what she is up to? ... When, after the war, they found out what I did, they all took pride in me. My father said: 'I always suspected you were doing something forbidden.'" Reflecting on her wartime activity, with all its attendant dangers, Andrée refuses to be seen as a hero.

> *"I deserve nothing for what I did. I am not a hero. It is true, that at the war's end I relished with satisfaction what I did. At the same time, I did not seek recognition and medals... Those who refused to help – I do not condemn them. There is fear. I do not say that what I did was the normal thing to do; perhaps it also has to do with my character – of fighting against injustice. At heart, I incline toward leftist ideas, although I am not and was never a communist... Already before then, I was different from others. I had taken an interest in the fate of refugees from the Spanish Civil War. I was by nature rebellious – against the established order. Already in 1939, I worked for the Red Cross, and I went to receive children who arrived on the Kindertransport from Vienna and was assigned to find locations for them."*

In 1989, Yad Vashem declared Andrée Geulen-Herscovici a Righteous Among the Nations. In 1992, in a ceremony in her honor at Yad Vashem, in the presence of many her former wards, she said, "How was it possible not to love you? In a certain way, you are my children, and I take pride in your scholarly and professional achievements, and am understanding with regard to your slight imperfections. This affection that I felt for you, I tried to express by speech, gesture, and touch. This message, young as you were, I am sure you felt deeply, because today you reciprocate it a hundredfold."

Gineste, Marie-Rose

France

*O*ne summer day, in August 1942, Marie-Rose Gineste, a Catholic lay social worker in Montauban, Tarn-et-Garonne department, southern France, received an urgent phone call from Bishop Pierre-Marie Théas. He asked her to come over for an assignment that he wished to burden her with. When she arrived at the Grand Séminaire for retired priests

Marie-Rose Gineste and her bicycle

of the diocese, Théas showed her the pastoral letter he had just written and asked her opinion. Would she be willing to take it back to work with her and have it stenciled and copied for distribution to all the diocese's parishes? She read her bishop's words, which were a stinging denunciation of the recent deportation of Jews carried out by the Vichy French government.

"I give voice to the outraged protest of Christian conscience, and I proclaim that all men, Aryans and non-Aryans, are brothers, because they were created by the same God; that all men, whatever their race or religion, have the right to be respected by individuals and by states. Hence, the recent antisemitic measures are an affront to human dignity and a violation of the most sacred rights of the individual and the family."

Gineste was moved by this strongly worded protest, a bit unusual for clerics in high position. In her words, "It was with great enthusiasm that I accepted this assignment." She then innocently asked the bishop by what means he planned to transmit the message to all the parishes, so as to be read from the pulpit on the following Sunday, just a few days off? By mail, he said. She responded that this was not a practical solution, for the authorities would probably open the letter and censor it. Then what do you suggest, the Catholic prelate asked? "I suggested that I go myself by bicycle to deliver the message to all the priests in the diocese's parishes."

Not losing precious time, she had the pastoral letter printed and copied, and the following morning she was off on her bicycle. It was a lengthy trek. Pedaling her bicycle, she stopped off first at Montauban, itself; then, Bressols, Labastide St. Pierre, Reynies, Villebrumier, Varennes, Orgueil, Nohic, Campsas, Canals, Pompignan, Grisolles, Aucamville, Savennes, Verdun sur-Garonne, Dieupentale, Bessens, Monbequi, Finhan ("where the good Curé Hebrard offered me a cool drink and some biscuits"), then Montbartier and the return trip to Montauban at sunset. It had been a long day, and Gineste was exhausted, having biked over 100 kilometers. She followed this up with similar trips the next three days. A colleague, upon her request, delivered the bishop's message to the parishes of Montech, Larrazet, Beaumont-de-Lomagne, Lavit, and environs. "Hence all the parishes of the Montauban diocese were in possession of the Protest Letter of Monsignor Théas that was read on Sunday, August 30, 1942, during all the Masses in all the churches of Tarn-et-Garonne (with the exception of one, that of the Ardus parish, where the priest was known as a collaborator)." Marie-Rose Gineste felt that avoiding this cleric was the prudent step to take, to avoid the possibility of his alerting the authorities and thus spoiling the plan to have the message read from the pulpit the following Sunday.

Historians of the Holocaust in France concur that Théas's pastoral letter, which followed that of Archbishop Jules-Géraud Saliège of nearby Toulouse, had a tremendous impact in shaping French public opinion, moving it from a previously sympathetic disposition toward the Vichy regime to a more pronounced opposition to its antisemitic measures, including helping Jews to avoid arrest and deportation. Gineste's Paul Revere-like bicycle ride contributed to making this possible.

Having accomplished her mission, Gineste was charged by Théas to care for the sheltering of Jewish adults and children on the run, in local convents – such as Bénédictines du Mas-Grenier and Ange Gardien – or with private persons, as well as provide them with false papers and food ration cards. Until 1943, she got these documents from resistance sources. Then, from that time on, she obtained fake seals from clandestine Jewish sources, including police and municipality seals.

With the war over, Marie-Rose Gineste returned to her prewar social work, with the help of her ever-present bicycle, which she used for her various errands. Finally, after many years, she donated the bicycle to Yad Vashem, and it is proudly displayed in the new Holocaust historical museum in Jerusalem.

In 1985 Yad Vashem conferred upon Marie-Rose Gineste the title of Righteous Among the Nations. On a visit to Israel she planted a tree in her own name in the Avenue of the Righteous at Yad Vashem.

Giorgetti, Ezio
Carugno, Osman
ITALY

*D*r. Ziga Neumann, an attorney by profession, was very much active in the Jewish community of Zagreb in former Yugoslavia. When the Germans invaded, in April 1941 and created the Fascist state of Croatia, Neumann was immediately arrested and kept imprisoned in a Croatian camp. Allowed to leave for a few days, he used the opportunity to escape with his family (wife, daughter, and her husband), with the help of false papers, to Split, a city on the Dalmatian coast held by the Italians, who did not harm the Jews. After a while the Italians transferred Neumann's family, as well as other Jews, to Italy proper, and to Asolo, in Treviso province, where they were allowed to reside as civilian war internees under police supervision. This peaceful spell came to an abrupt end when Fascist Italy capitulated to the Allies, on September 8, 1943, immediately followed by the German takeover of most of the country (a part of southern Italy had already been liberated by the Allies).

The German occupation meant that Jews in Italy would share the fate of their brethren in other countries under Nazi domination – arrest and transfer to concentration camps. Neumann's group decided not to wait, and three days into the German occupation, on September 11, they decided to strike south in the hope of reaching Allied lines. The group, numbering over 30 people, set out in three vans, and after reaching Adris continued to Bellaria, near Rimini, on the Adriatic coast. They carried with them a letter of recommendation from a certain countess in Asolo to a certain Giorgetti family who owned two hotels in Bellaria, one under the management of Mr. Giorgetti senior; the other owned by his son, Ezio Giorgetti.

In Bellaria, Dr. Neumann went to see the elderly Giorgetti and was cordially received. His own hotel being already full of refugees and his son Ezio's hotel already closed for the season, he asked Ezio to help find lodging for the night for Neumann's group. But Ezio Giorgetti, upon hearing from his father that a group of Jewish refugees needed shelter, was at once prepared to reopen his establishment. The group had planned to leave the following morning, heading farther south, but after meeting Ezio Giorgetti and learning of the danger of movement in zones of military activity for a group including women and children, they allowed themselves to be convinced to be taken under his care.

The group paid for their board at the Savoia Hotel, reopened by Giorgetti. This was the "official" part of their relationship with Ezio, and this was paralleled by the man's humanitarian part in caring for his charges. He at once put the group in touch with the commanding officer of the local state police (*Carabinieri*), Osman Carugno, who not only was prepared to help them but augmented the group with four more fugitive Jews, the Fröhlichs and their and two daughters.

Very soon the refugees had to leave the hotel, following a German order for all residents of the coast to evacuate their homes. At this crucial juncture Ezio Giorgetti did not abandon the refugees. With Carugno's assistance he moved the whole group to an isolated, empty hotel near Bellaria, and when this too became impractical he moved his charges together with the hotel furniture to an empty farmhouse. When they had to move again, he settled them in a pension, not disclosing their Jewish identity to the owner but presenting them as refugees from southern Italy, as was borne out by the new identity cards that Giorgetti had arranged for them. All financial arrangements with Giorgetti had by then ceased.

As told by Josef Konforti, one of the Jewish refugees, "Till then we might perhaps have thought that all his actions had been guided by his interest in extending the hotel season through our stay. But daily contact with our people had created such a close ties between us and Mr. Ezio Giorgetti that somehow our destinies became interlinked." Konforti also added, "We warned Mr. Ezio on several occasions that through us his whole family was in serious danger. His parents put pressure on him to stop, but he did not falter even for one moment." He continued to look after his charges, providing them with medicine and establishing contact with underground elements. "All this he did without any remuneration, spending his own money and even neglecting his own family," Konforti stated.

Dr. Neumann, for his part, emphasized, "During all the time Ezio was always available for advice and active help. Despite the rigid control of the Germans he would visit us at our distant hiding places in the hills and would take care of everything." He also used his connections with anti-Fascist elements to arrange the group's flight to the small hilly republic of

San Marino, should it become necessary. The fleeing Jews carried only fake identity papers, and a close inspection of these documents would have revealed they were forged. "The majority of us did not speak Italian at all," Neumann further wrote, "and the few who did had a foreign accent. So Ezio made the contacts and shielded us from the authorities."

When in spring 1944, the fighting moved closer to where the refugees were staying, Giorgetti decided to move them into the mountains, to Pugliano Nuovo, a small place near San Marino. On this occasion, Ezio undertook to cover all payments for food and board to the owners of the farm where the group stayed. After a while the Germans ordered the farm converted into a military hospital and the hidden Jews had to flee again. Again Ezio came to the rescue by using his connections with some peasants in the village of Pugliano Vechio, farther up in the hills. Here they remained until liberated by Allied forces in September 1944.

Earlier, during the group's stay at Pugliano Vechio, the local police commander became suspicious of the new arrivals. On being told of this, Carugno obtained a motorbike and the necessary fuel (which in those days was hard to get), and went to the see the commander, appealing to him to give the refugees all necessary support and representing them as his personal friends. "This," Konforti pointed out, "helped us a lot." Moreover, "Carugo never received any payment whatsoever for his help and he refused even to accept remuneration for his expenses."

After liberation, Konforti decided to look up his benefactor, Ezio Giorgetti, and found him in Rimini, together with his wife and two daughters, in a half-ruined house, sleeping on the bare floor and using blankets given to them by the Jewish Palestine Brigade fighting with the British Army. The Giorgettis had escaped from the war zone, leaving everything behind. This time it was Konforti who tried to help out with the little means at his disposal. In Rimini, Konforti was also told that his group was not the only Jews whom Ezio Giorgetti had helped; he had hidden others as well in the vicinity. Konforti remained in touch with Ezio Giorgetti for many years thereafter and named his son after him: Nuri Ezio Zadik Konforti.

Konforti ended his deposition of 1963 with a list of the names of the 38 people, mostly from Yugoslavia, saved by the tireless efforts of Ezio Giorgetti. They comprised:

Dr. Ziga and Bella Neumann; Ziga's father, the 80-year-old Adolf Neumann; Ziga's sister, Dania Rothmueller; her two children, Ruth and Eli (15 and 13 years old, respectively); Hugo Schwarz (brother of Bella Neumann) and wife Cvijeta; their daughter Mia (then 16), and son Leo (then 10); Bella's brother Eugen Schwarz and wife Zdenka; her 80-year-old grandmother Eugenija Hirschl; Stefa and Erna (Eugenija's daughters); Reuben (14-year-old son of Erna); Joseph and Maja Konforti; Josef's mother Blanca; Ljerka Nadasi (sister of Cvijeta Schwarz) and husband Zeljko; their son Ivica (then 10); Joseph and Blanka Lackenbach (the sister of Cvijeta Schwarz); Stefi (Joseph's sister); Mirko Hirschl (brother of Ljerka Nadasi) and wife Nada; Mr. Fröhlich, and his sister Ruža; Fröhlich's two children (24 and 18); the four Lehrer family members; Leopold and Charlotte Studenti; and Wilhelm Pick.

In 1964, Yad Vashem conferred the title of Righteous Among the Nations on Ezio Giorgetti. In 1985, the Righteous title was also bestowed on Osman Carugno.

Grüninger, Paul

SWITZERLAND

*I*n October 1968, when Switzerland opened its doors to Czech refugees after the suppression of the Dubček regime by Soviet tanks, some journalists recalled the injustice endured by a Swiss man who 30 years earlier had acted similarly, by taking in Jewish refugees fleeing the Nazi terror in Germany. The man was put on trial and convicted. Had the time not come to redress this act of injustice, the journalists wondered, and to rehabilitate the still living victim of Swiss injustice? The government, however, stood by the conviction, refusing to budge. This is the story of Paul Grüninger and of events that took place in 1938.

In that year, after Austria's annexation to Nazi Germany in March 1938, the Swiss government had severely restricted the admittance of Jewish refugees from the now expanded Germany. On March 18, 1938, Switzerland closed its border with Germany to those arriving without proper entry permits, and the Swiss border police were instructed to turn back refugees arriving after that date; even going so far as to hand them to over to the German border police. There is no need to dwell on the treatment awaiting these hapless refugees at the hands of the German authorities. By 1938, the condition of the Jews in Germany had deteriorated severely, a situation that became even more aggravated after the infamous government-instituted pogrom of November 9-10, 1938, known as *Kristallnacht*. It was clear to Jews who had not yet left the country that the future bode more ill tidings and it was consequently in everyone's interest to get out as fast as possible – but where to? At the Evian Conference of July 1938, sponsored by the United States, the 32 countries represented there came up with a host of excuses for not allowing Jewish refugees from Germany into their countries beyond their restricted immigration quotas.

Paul Grüninger (left)

Geographically speaking, one feasible escape route on the old Austrian-Swiss frontier was the area south of Lake Constance (in German, *Bodensee*), in northeast Switzerland. There, at the Rhine River's headwaters, one could even wade across on certain days of the week when the water was only knee-deep. The river at that point constituted the border between the two countries. The jump-off point from the Austrian side was the town of Feldkirch (which also borders on the tiny principality of Lichtenstein), from where, proceeding stealthily at night, the refugees would reach the Rhine River and after crossing it find themselves on the Swiss side, near the Diepoldsau camp – converted by the Swiss authorities in the early 1930s from a textile factory into a temporary refugee internment camp. To the north lay the Swiss customs station and official transit point of St. Margarethen, which the refugees understandably avoided.

After the Swiss government's refugee interdiction came into effect, the police forcibly removed refugees from the Diepoldsau camp – those who had arrived there subsequent to the illegal entry deadline of March 18, 1938, and they were turned over to the German police. Some refugees seeking to avoid apprehension sought refuge in the neighborhood and the Swiss police conducted raids to ferret them out. Those caught giving shelter to Jews were prosecuted and the Jews were sent back into Germany.

At that time, Paul Grüninger served as the border police commandant of the St. Gallen region. His duties consisted of controlling the border sector nearest to him in order to prevent the illegal crossing of refugees, at a time when refugee pressure from Germany had grown to unprecedented heights. Grüninger was now faced with a moral dilemma. Should he obey his government's instructions and turn the refugees back, with all the personal anguish involved in such a step, or should he take the highly unusual step for a police commandant of flouting these regulations and allow free access into Switzerland to all refugees – and face the inescapable consequences? One evening, he confided to his wife, Alice: "I simply cannot send these people back. I know this could cost me my job. But I cannot act otherwise."

Acting on his own, and in the hope that his immediate superiors, not themselves happy with their government's new draconian ruling, would look the other way, the 47-year-old Grüninger decided to disregard the refugee interdiction and not hinder the free flow of people across the border or turn those who had already crossed into Switzerland illegally over to the Gestapo. Having arrived at this decision, the trickle of refugees through the St. Gallen region proceeded uninterruptedly through the summer and winter months of 1938. Soon enough, word had gotten out that the Swiss frontier at the Feldkirch-St. Gallen point could be breached easily and from that point one could escape the Nazi nightmare.

To give his actions a legal veneer, Grüninger's also took the calculated personal risk of falsifying the entry date on the official police seals stamped on the refugee's passports, so as to make it appear that the refugees had entered the country prior to the March 18, 1938, deadline. The Ministry of Interior questionnaire that the refugees were made to fill out was simultaneously stamped in a like manner, so as to synchronize the date with the one on the passport. The forms were then forwarded to the federal agencies in Bern, the country's capital. The refugees, taken to Diepoldsau, were duly processed with the help of local Jewish organizations for a temporary stay in Switzerland, or assisted to leave the country for other destinations. It appeared that Grüninger's immediate superiors were willing to look the other way, as long as Grüninger's tactics did not become public knowledge or known in the higher echelons of the government, or impair the friendly Swiss-German relations.

When the 1938 winter set in earlier than usual and many refugees arrived without proper winter clothing, Grüninger and his wife dipped into their own savings to help defray the cost of additional clothes. Through all this, Grüninger relayed false reports on the number and status of refugees in his sector. Thus he replied in the negative to a government query as to the whereabouts of a Jewish refugee who had jumped a train bound for Dachau and made his way into Switzerland, a query which had originated in the German Embassy. In fact, as it later turned out, Grüninger had allowed the man into the country and had knowingly helped him settle there.

In time, the Gestapo succeeded in pinpointing the refugee leak on the Swiss border after confiscating a letter mailed by one of the Diepoldsau refugees to a friend in Vienna. After the Germans informed the Swiss of this, in January 1939, the latter decided to put a stop to the refugee leak in the St. Gallen region and simultaneously initiate measures against Grüninger. On March 12, 1939, he was dismissed from the police force pending his trial. The charges against Grüninger, as presented by the state prosecutor, included the accusation that during the period from August up to and including December 1938, as a result of false reports submitted by Grüninger, some 3,600 people had been allowed to enter the country illegally.

Grüninger's immediate superior, Valentin Keel, who it turned out had known all along of his subordinate's activity, decided to help Grüninger out by suggesting to him that he submit to a psychiatric examination, so as to be able to plead mental aberration. This, Grüninger was told, would spare him the agony of having all his pension and retirement benefits forfeited in the event of conviction. But neither Grüninger nor the psychiatrist who met briefly with Grüninger would go along with this. In the face of Grüninger's resistance, Keel turned state's witness against him and the trial became a *cause célèbre* in the country. The Swiss government was determined not to allow Germany's persecution of the Jews to unhinge the normal relations between the two countries. By prosecuting Grüninger, the Swiss were signaling to its powerful neighbor that it would not countenance an affair likely to undermine the good relations between them.

Grüninger was specifically charged on several counts: that he had made a false statement when he reported that a Jewish prisoner who had fled a Dachau-bound train in Germany had not passed through his region; furthermore, that he had aided a Polish-born Jewish refugee who had entered Switzerland illegally to take up residence in Zürich on the basis of incorrect information provided by Grüninger to government agencies; finally, that he had indirectly counseled would-be refugees on how to illegally deposit their valuables inside Austria, not far from the Swiss border, before their passage into Switzerland. The most serious charge, however, was Grüninger's personal involvement in the illegal entry of some 3,600 Jews into the country through the false registration of their actual entry dates.

Proceedings against Grüninger, which began in January 1939, dragged on for over two years. But already at the start, on March 13, 1939, he was summarily dismissed from the police with all retirement benefits suspended. On March 14, 1941, the court handed down its verdict. It found Grüninger guilty of breach of duty (*Amtspflichtverletzung*) and fined him 300 francs. He was also required to pay 10,000 francs in court expenses. The forfeiture of all his retirement benefits and the removal of his name from the police register were also confirmed. In its verdict the court recognized the man's altruistic motives but added that these were not excusable, since they conflicted with the proper performance of his duties. When he disobeyed instructions from above on the refugee question, as a State employee he was clearly guilty of a breach of faith.

Without an income, the 49-year-old Grüninger found himself having to provide for his family with odd jobs. He was in succession a rug and lumber salesman, a raincoat store manager, and a life insurance salesman. During all these years, he was heard repeating to all who questioned him about his behavior, "I would do it all over again today!" In 1954, years after his dismissal and a life of hardship, he gave the following explanation of his "rebellious" behavior in the late 1930s:

> *"I am not at all ashamed of the court's verdict. On the contrary, I am proud to have saved the lives of hundreds of oppressed people. My assistance to Jews was rooted in my Christian world outlook ... It was basically a question of saving human lives threatened with death. How could I then seriously consider bureaucratic schemes and calculations. Sure, I intentionally exceeded the limits of my authority and often with my own hands falsified documents and certificates, but it was done solely in order to afford persecuted people access into the country. My personal well-being, measured against the cruel fate of these thousands, was so insignificant and unimportant that I never even took it into consideration."*

So matters rested until December 1970, when as a result of the protests of journalists the government sent Grüninger a somewhat reserved letter of apology. While it recognized the man's moral stature, at the same time the government pointed out that nothing could be done about the forfeiture of pension benefits, for this would entail reopening the whole case and opening old wounds.

While his own country stubbornly stood by its harsh treatment of the man – in 1971 Yad Vashem informed Paul Grüninger that it had decided to confer on him the title of Righteous Among the Nations. The following year he passed away, at the age of 80.

The Grüninger Affair continued to give the Swiss public no rest. In February 1985, 34 members of the St. Gallen regional council passed a motion to accord Grüninger full posthumous rehabilitation. This motion was, however, rejected, with government support, by a majority of the council. Finally, in 1995, the Swiss Federal government, bowing to widening public pressure, annulled its 1941 condemnation of Paul Grüninger and granted him a full posthumous rehabilitation.

Gut-Opdyke, Irena

POLAND

As a professing Catholic, Irena Gutowa went to a church in Tarnopol (today Ternopol, in Ukraine) located on Chopin Street. When her turn came for confession, she took a deep breath and told the priest she had become the mistress of a German officer to save the lives of her Jewish friends. "My child," the confessor priest responded, "it is a mortal sin," "But Father," Irena politely objected, "if I don't do this, eleven people will lose their lives." The priest would not give her absolution. Leaving the church, Irena confidently thought to herself, "I believe I have God's blessing. I was never more sure of it."

Born in Kozlowa Góra, Irena Gutowa was 21 when Germany invaded Poland in 1939. Earlier, she had wanted to be a nurse. "I was trying to be another Florence Nightingale. I had big ideas: I wanted to go to other countries. I wanted to help." She had been attending a nursing school in Radom when the war came. Drafted to treat wounded soldiers, she then fled towards Lwów, which in the meantime had been taken over by the Russians. There she had another traumatic experience – she was raped by Russian soldiers, and hospitalized in Tarnopol. With the end of the Polish campaign, she elected to return to Radom, under German occupation, and be with her family. One day, the Germans stormed into a church during the Mass to seize able-bodied people for forced labor and Irena was taken to work in an ammunition factory. One day, while on the job, she fainted. When she came to, an old German major, wearing thick glasses, was staring down at her. After she had answered his questions in German, he said, "Your German is very good. Perhaps you would be better suited to work in the officers mess." The officer's name was Eduard Rügemer. He was to play an important role in her life during the war years.

Irena Gut-Opdyke

In the officers' mess, Irena served meals to German officers and their secretaries. She also witnessed German atrocities against the ghetto Jews, watching SS troopers randomly open fire on them. In 1942, Rügemer told her that she would be moved to Tarnopol, further east, and there continue her present assignment of serving meals to German officers. Rügemer, too, was reassigned there and placed in charge of the officers club as well as a military workshop facility, including a laundry, serving the German army and known by the initials HKP (*Heereskraftsfahrpark*).

Earlier, when the Germans entered Tarnopol on July 2, 1941, two weeks after the start of the German invasion of the Soviet Union, the city had numbered 17,000 Jews. Within two days, a week-long pogrom commenced, claiming 5,000 lives, with Jews dragged out of their homes and shot. A ghetto was sealed off on December 1, 1941, but that did not prevent the further mass liquidation of the Jewish population – 600 to 700 Jews on March 25, 1942, executed in the nearby Janówka forest; another 3,000-4,000 deported to the Bełżec death camp; a further 600–750 on September 30, followed by 2,500 in November 1942. The remaining 8,000 Jews were concentrated in a labor camp, but that did not stop the executions – 1,000 on April 8–9, 1943, 500 more on June 20, 1943, followed by the remaining 2,000–2,500 Jews two days later, taken out of the camp and shot. Some managed to escape to the forests, where they continued to be hunted by the Germans and Ukrainian collaborators. When liberation came on April 15, 1944, a little over 700 from Tarnopol and environs came out of hiding. Three years earlier, the city had numbered 17,000 Jewish souls.

Returning to 1942, soon after her arrival in Tarnopol, Irena met Helen Weinbaum, a non-Jewish woman married to a Jew, Henry. Irena went with her to a nearby village, and there witnessed another horrific and brutal German killing raid against the local Jews. She was horrified at the sight of an SS officer picking up an infant, shooting it, and flinging it down on the ground beside its screaming mother. Then the officer shot the mother too. Irena was so shocked by this, the "worst thing man can do," that she blamed God for allowing such a dastardly act. "I prayed to God: 'I do not believe in you! You are a figment of my imagination! How can you allow such a thing to happen?'" The next day, on her knees, she recanted: "Forgive me, I don't know what I'm talking about. Thy will be done."

Irena continued to serve officers their meals, and was also put in charge of the laundry facility in the HKP workshop, which used Jewish labor and where Irena's job was to supervise the washing and mending of the officers' and secretaries' clothes. At a later period, the HKP network was removed from Rügemer's responsibility, and as a *Julager* (i.e., Jewish camp) placed under the command of the SS, headed in Tarnopol by the brutal and notorious SS commander Wilhelm Rokita. At the officers club, over dinner, Irena occasionally eavesdropped on conversations between Rokita and Rügemer, usually dealing with coming raids on the ghetto Jews. Irena then passed the word to trustworthy Jewish workers at the laundry, "Expect trouble tomorrow; a raid or something. Spread the word."

In addition, Irena, who had befriended some of the Jews in the laundry facility, hid them in the club building during Rokita's deadly raids on the camp's Jews. Her charges included Fanka Willner, Ida Haller and husband, Lazar, and Moses Steiner. In July 1943, Janina also helped Hermann Morks, one of the professional tailors at the HKP, to flee to the Janówka forest at his request, together with his wife, Pola, and his brother Nathan and wife Miriam. She arranged to pick them up outside the city after their escape from the labor camp, which was next to the HKP facilities, covered them with hay in a horse-drawn wagon, and drove them safely to the forest.

Suddenly a new turn of events unfolded for Irena, when Major Rügemer told her that he was moving out of the officers club and into a villa and wanted Irena to move there too to serve as a housekeeper. This was fine with Irena, as she had already thought of ways to save some of the Jewish laundry workers whom she had befriended; such as Ida and Lazar Haller, Klara Bauer, Moses and Irene Steiner and Fanka Willner. Irena checked out the new residence and noted that villa included servants' quarters, a kitchenette, a bathroom, storage rooms, and a boiler room with a coal chute leading in from outdoors. Good enough, she thought; several people could easily be hidden there.

In the meantime, before the villa was ready for habitation, the curtain was coming down on the last Jews in Tarnopol. On July 15, 1943, Irena overheard Rokita tell Rügemer, "We'll all be celebrating soon, because by the 22nd of this month, Tarnopol will be *judenrein* (cleansed of Jews). Irena immediately alerted her Jewish friends in the laundry. She told them to stay over in the laundry at the end of the working day on July 21 and not return to the *Julager,* and that Irena would find a way to smuggle them over to the as yet uninhabited villa the next day (the building was still undergoing renovations). Her six wards were told to slip furtively into the coal chute on the left side of the villa, which led to the basement, and wait there. "I'll be over first thing in the morning. Stay in the shadows, and God bless you." Irena had first planned to hide them in an air chute in Rügemer's bathroom until the renovations were completed and the workers had left, but then changed her mind and decided to hide her charges in the building's attic. As she finalized this plan in her mind, she overcame her depression at the sight of the horrific killings taking place around her. She now saw herself in the role of a saving angel. "As I fell asleep that night, I felt a surge of triumph: the Nazis thought Tarnopol was *judenrein* tonight. But I had taken action myself. There were at least six Jews in town. As long as I could help it, Tarnopol would never be *judenrein*." Seven persons actually showed up; the six had brought with them another fugitive Jew, Henry Weinbaum.

Quickly moving the seven people into the attic, Irena looked after their needs – mainly food and hygiene. When the renovations were completed, she took the seven back down into the basement; this was to be their new quarters. Eventually three other people joined them: Joseph Weiss, Marian Willner, and Alex Rosen. They were now ten. Later, in November 1943, two more came, Natan and Miriam Morks, who had been hiding in the forest, but when Miriam got sick Irena had smuggled the two back to Tarnopol and to the villa hideout. There were now twelve fugitives in the German major's villa, in the personal care of Irena Gutowa.

Every day when Major Rügemer left the house, Irena locked the front door and left the key in the lock in case he showed up unexpectedly. During his absence, the people hidden in the basement could come upstairs and help themselves to the villa's amenities; to shower, make coffee, listen to the radio, and also help Irena out with the household chores. The basement also had a separate, though more primitive, washroom.

One day, the Gestapo suddenly appeared to check the house, evidently on a tip from an informer that irregular occurrences were taking place there. Irena, who opened the door, said she had strict orders from Rügemer not to let anyone in. In their presence, she phoned him, and he told the Gestapo that they were welcome to conduct a house search. They decided to skip it and left.

Then came the day that almost spelled doom for Irena's humanitarian endeavor. She had forgotten to lock the front door and Klara Bauer and Fanka Willner had left the basement and were helping themselves in the kitchen. Suddenly the kitchen door swung open and the major came in. He was astonished at the sight of two Jewish women in his kitchen and began to shake with emotion. He turned on his heel and walked out. As later related by Irena, she ran after him to the study and pleaded with him. The fugitives downstairs could hear him screaming at her, but could not make out the words. Rügemer: "Irena! What in God's name have you done to me?" Irena: "They are innocent. They've done nothing! Don't turn them in, I beg you. I know you are a good man!" He would listen no more. He was red with fury and fear. Irena grabbed at his hand and kissed it, but he pulled it away and stormed out of the house.

Fearing the worst, namely that he had gone to get the Gestapo, Irena told her charges to move into a special underground space leading from the basement and not known to anyone, and to stay there for three days. "If I don't come back for you, get out through the coal chute at night and try to get to Janówka." Rügemer had only encountered two women; he had no idea there were ten more persons in the basement. That evening Rügemer came back drunk. As related by Irena, he grabbed her arms, pulled her toward him, and said. "I won't keep your secret for nothing, Irena, I want you willingly. That is my price." He took her hand and led her upstairs. The next morning, as she lay in bed filled with shame and humiliation, Rügemer tried to raise her spirits. "I'll protect you, Irena. I love you; you must have realized that before now. I couldn't let any harm come to you. And your friends will be safe here. I won't turn those women in, although I risk my own life. You understand that, don't you?" Irena could never tell her friends how she had bought their safety. They continued to think, even in the postwar years, that she had achieved it by using her female wiles, coupled with his natural pity on the hidden Jews. Irena kept the secret to herself.

Irena took in stride the priest's censure of her decision to allow Rügemer free access to her body. She justified what she had done to save her twelve wards: "They were persecuted. It was a human bond. I did not think of them as different because they were Jews. To me, we were all in trouble and we had a common enemy." As for Rügemer, she did not actually despise him, and even excused his advances. The major was an old man, and not in good health. He suffered from a stomach ailment and she cooked him special meals. After all, she thought to herself, he had always treated her very kindly. "I had always felt that behind the uniform, he was a decent man. But I had used him for too long and now it had apparently come to this accounting. He liked me. I was with him for about three years. In spite of everything, I was already forgiving him for what he put me through because he had helped me save many lives."

Another problem arose in February 1944, when the major told Irena that in light of growing suspicions of what was happening inside his villa, it would be better if she got rid of her charges by the time he returned from a trip of several days to Lwów. However, Irena felt otherwise. With the Russians steadily moving closer to Tarnopol, Irena decided to move the fugitives to the nearby Janówka forest, five kilometers from the city. Dressed as a peasant woman, she led first the men in her group, later the women, to a place deep in the forest with a previously prepared bunker. Back in town, Irena stayed in touch with them, bringing them food and provisions. One of the women, Ida Haller, was pregnant, and two months after liberation gave birth to a son in the forest, named Roman. During the early stages of her pregnancy, while still in the major's villa, Ida had considered abortion, but had been strongly discouraged by Irena, who felt that giving birth to a new life was the correct response to the murderous acts of the Nazis. Ida had followed Irena's counsel.

When Rügemer returned, he told Irena that the Germans were evacuating Tarnopol and moving westward to Kielce, and he would take her along. Irena had other ideas, namely to join her people in the forest hideout. However, on March 18, 1944, when Irena went to speak with a forester, Rügemer suddenly appeared and with the help of another German forced her into the car and off they sped in the direction of Kielce. Five days later, on March 23, 1944, the Russians gained full control of Tarnopol after the city had changed hands several times. The Jews in the forest were free. In Kielce, Irena had to suffer another eleven months of German occupation. In December 1944, she succumbed to pneumonia and remained bedridden for three months. When she recovered in February 1945, the city had been liberated.

After the war, Irena renewed contact with some of her beneficiaries, who had relocated in Kraków, and joined them when they were moved to a displaced persons camp in Germany. There, in 1949, she met William Opdyke, who was part of a United Nations delegation. After hearing her story, he helped her move to the United States, and in 1956 the two married.

Settling down in California, and with a daughter of her own, Irena (presently, Gut-Opdyke) decided to put the war and its horrors behind her. In her words, "I put a 'do not disturb' sign on my mind. I did not want to talk about the war." She rebounded in 1975, when a neo-Nazi organization started spreading the lie that the Holocaust never happened. "Well, that put me on fire. Why? Because I was there; I had the duty to tell the truth." From then on she made it a point to appear before many groups, especially school children, and share with them her message, encapsulated in the following words: "To try and understand that we all belong to one human family and the only way to defeat ignorance of prejudice is to reach out – reach out without nationality, religion, creed or color. This is my will: to do right; to tell you; and to remember." In 2003, she died peacefully, at age 85.

Much earlier, in 1982, Yad Vashem conferred on Irene (changed from Irena) Gut-Opdyke the title of Righteous Among the Nations.

Hammann, Wilhelm
Leitner, Franz
GERMANY & AUSTRIA

The four SS men stormed into the children's barracks, known as Block 8, of the Buchenwald concentration camp and asked the barracks supervisor, political prisoner Wilhelm Hammann, to point out the Jewish children. Hammann knew what this meant – that the children would be killed. He replied that there were no Jewish children in the barracks, as they had all been evacuated several days earlier. Not able themselves to sort out the Jewish from the non-Jewish children, the SS men shouted and threatened, promising that they would be back. Indeed, they soon returned, and this time they ordered the several hundred children in the barracks to step outside and line up at attention. Half drunk, the SS men now shouted, "All Jews, step forward!" The command was greeted with total silence. Hammann had previously warned

Franz Leitner (Gedenkstätte Buchenwald Archiv)

the children not to comply with such a command. The SS were furious. At this point Hammann suggested that perhaps the children, who originated from various East European countries, were not familiar with the German language. "Then get a translator," he was told. It had already been arranged by Hammann and his fellow prisoners that no translator should be available. The SS screamed again, "Jews, step forward." One Jewish boy, originally from Yugoslavia, did so. Immediately Hammann went over to him and said, "But you told me that you're not Jewish," ordering him to get back in line. Fuming with rage, the SS consulted among themselves and left for further instructions. Suddenly the alarm was sounded in the camp – American troops were reported closing in on

Wilhelm Hammann (Gedenkstätte Buchenwald Archiv)

the camp. Next morning, the SS contingent fled. A day later, on April 11, 1945, the U.S. Army entered the Buchenwald camp. The Jewish children were saved.

Buchenwald was one of the largest of the concentration camps. Opened in 1937, eight kilometers north of Weimar – the city where Wolfgang von Goethe wrote some of his country's greatest poetry, in the spirit of the Enlightenment – it saw some 239,000 prisoners pass through its gates, and claimed 43,000 lives. Buchenwald had over a hundred affiliates and sub-camps, where prisoners worked under slave labor conditions for German firms such as BMW and IG Farben. In the main camp, work was mainly either at the nearby quarry or in ammunition factories. First intended for political prisoners (such as Konrad Adenauer, the future chancellor of West Germany), it included a large contingent of German communists. Thousands of Jews were incarcerated there in November 1938 following the *Kristallnacht* (Night of the Broken Glass) pogrom in Germany. Of these, some 9,400 Jews were freed and allowed to emigrate; 600 others had already died inside the camp. Primarily a forced labor camp, it was intended to kill off prisoners through harsh treatment, including torture, beatings, starvation, lack of hygiene, and pseudo-scientific medical experiments, not to mention lethal injections, especially on the many Soviet prisoners-of-war brought there.

In February 1945, thousands of Jews were among the approximately 86,000 prisoners, moved there from other concentration camps in the east, emptied due to the advance of the Red Army – including many children, who were housed in two main barracks, Block 66 and Block 8. Whereas conditions in Block 66 were not much better than in other camp barracks, the situation was different in Block 8, thanks to its supervision by two political prisoners – Franz Leitner and Wilhelm Hammann. These two men belonged to an underground network in the camp, made up of imprisoned German communists who, as "Aryans," were placed by the SS in key administrative positions (previously filled by prisoners with a criminal background) – though naturally under the overall supervision of the SS command. These men took advantage of their preferential status and went to great lengths to ease the plight of other prisoners, especially saving the lives of the many children in the camp. This included exempting them from the tortuous hours-long daily roll calls, and those under the age of 14 from work, as well as transferring 70 Jewish youngsters from Block 66 and other barracks to Block 8, where conditions were much better, relatively speaking.

Franz Leitner, an Austrian communist, had been arrested in 1939, and imprisoned in Buchenwald. In July 1943, he took over the leadership of Block 8, and the number of children there rose from 160 to 400. He assigned those of working age to lighter work indoors so as protect them from inclement weather, and he provided them with warmer clothing. Roll calls were held inside the barracks. An additional innovation, secretly introduced under the watchful eyes of the SS, was an underground school system for the children, with writing paper and pencils and drawing boards clandestinely brought from other places, and also by bribing SS guards with cigarettes. During classes, some of the youngsters stood on guard outside, and when they sounded the alarm on the approach of SS guards the children quickly hid the educational materials under the floorboards. When Leitner was detained in October 1944 for participating in a secret memorial service for Communist Party head Ernst Thälmann, killed in Buchenwald in August, his function in Block 8 was taken over by Wilhelm Hammann. In February 1945, Leitner was released from his Buchenwald cell and given a clerical position in Block 40, from where he continued to smuggle children into Block 8.

As for Wilhelm Hammann, born in 1897, the eldest of nine children, he was raised and educated in Gross-Gerau, near Darmstadt, and served in the German army during World War I. After the war, he joined the Communist Party and was elected to represent it in the local state assembly. He simultaneously perfected his educational skills as a schoolteacher. After the Nazis rise to power, he was confined in prison from 1935 to 1938, and then sent to Buchenwald, where he remained until the end of the war. As part of the communist underground in the camp, he was asked to replace Leitner upon the latter's arrest in October 1944, to head the children's compound in Block 8.

As told by 14-year-old Erich Weiss, originally from Czechoslovakia and one of the Jewish youngsters in that barracks in 1944, Hammann managed to continue to persuade the SS officers not to subject the children to roll calls, since he was personally responsible for them and they were all accounted for. With his educational background, he was especially helpful in furthering the children's schooling, both in Block 8 and in Block 66 – teaching them the rudiments of the German language, math, and geography. It is related that he allowed the younger Jewish children, most of whom came from traditional homes in East European countries, to be instructed in their religion by some of their older brethren. Of even greater importance for the survival of the Jewish children in his compound was his message to them never to declare themselves as Jewish, but as Poles, Czechs, Ukrainians, and Hungarians – in fact, the countries from where they originated. He quickly became a father figure for these children, and they affectionately called him "our old man."

Then came the dangerous confrontation with the SS guards, days before the camp's liberation, when Hammann at the risk of his life faced down the pistol-brandishing SS men while trying to save Jewish children from their murderous intent on the eve of Nazi Germany's collapse. For in April 1945, as the American army crossed into Germany, the SS was ordered to evacuate prisoners, especially the Jews among them. The SS managed to remove some 28,000, of which between 7,000 and 8,000 were shot or died from exhaustion and maltreatment. Thus, when on April 9 the SS threatened to remove the Jewish children from Block 8, Hammann resorted to the blatant lie that these children, some 155 out of over 300 in the compound, had already been removed a few days earlier.

In the words of Erich Weiss: "I would just like to add simply that Mr. Hammann was not tall in stature but on that morning when the SS wanted to separate the Jews from the non-Jews, when the SS man came to our barracks to ask if he (Mr. Hammann) had any Jews in the block, and he said, 'No,' he appeared as a giant to us. Mr. Hammann did this at great personal risk, for there were other, specifically Ukrainian inmates, who certainly, had it been earlier in the war, would have turned in both Mr. Hammann and the Jews he protected." Earlier, when he sensed that with the collapse of the Nazi regime the SS would try to do away with the Jews in the camp, including those under his supervision, Hammann was heard repeating, "I should rather die than be an accomplice in the murder of Jewish children." Among the children saved was the seven-year-old Israel Meir Lau, from Poland, who later rose to fill the position of chief rabbi of Israel. In all, on the day of liberation, there were 159 Jewish children in Block 8, of which 58 were below the age of 16 – out of a total of 328 children (by one account) of various nationalities, including three gypsy children. Other Jewish youngsters also managed to survive in the camp's other barracks, such as Elie Wiesel, the future Nobel Prize laureate.

After the war, Hammann returned to his pre-war passions – teaching and Communist Party activity. He died in 1955. Likewise, his colleague Franz Leitner returned to communist political activity in his native city of Wiener Neustadt, Austria. Both were content to have played a personal role in saving so many innocent young lives – snatched from the grips of the SS under the most intolerable conditions imaginable.

Yad Vashem awarded the title of Righteous Among the Nations to Wilhelm Hammann in 1984 and to Franz Leitner in 1998.

Hardaga, Mustafa & Zejneba
BOSNIA

*M*ustafa Hardaga, a Muslim by faith, lived in Sarajevo, Bosnia (then part of Yugoslavia), where he owned a building next to his home in which Josef Kabilio operated a firm manufacturing sewage and drainage pipes. Kabilio's own family lived on the third floor of a building also next door to the firm. On April 14, 1941, the Germans suddenly struck, invading Yugoslavia after a massive aerial bombardment. Kabilio's family had sought safety in the nearby woods, and when they returned they saw that their third-story apartment had been severely damaged and was in fact no longer inhabitable.

Josef Kabilio, a family man with a wife, Rivka, and two children, Boena-Tova (born in 1938 and today Greenberg) and Benjamin (1927), considered moving into the factory with his family, but Mustafa would not hear of it. Instead, he insisted that they come and stay with him. Zejneba recalled: "We found them destitute. We brought the whole family, Josef, his wife and two children to our home. This was the first time that a strange man had slept in our home. For us women, who veiled our faces according to our religion and tradition – this was forbidden. But we welcomed them with the following words, 'Josef, you are our brother, Rivka – our sister, and your children – our children. Our house is your house; feel at home here just as you would in your own home. Our women will not hide their faces before you, since you are family. Today, when your lives are in danger, we shall not forsake you.'"

Zejneba Hardaga

Along with Mustafa's family, the household also included his brother, Izet, and wife Bachriya.

With the entry of the Germans into the city, conditions for the Jews worsened. The old synagogue was looted by a mob incited by the new authorities and the 400-year-old Torah scrolls were put to the torch. "I watched this terrible sight, hidden behind a curtain in my host's home," Josef recalled. Mustafa consoled Josef and assured him that his family would remain safe in his home. After a brief stay with the Hardagas, Josef, fearing the worst, had his family moved to Mostar, which was under Italian control and relatively safer for Jews, while he stayed behind to liquidate his business, which the pro-Nazi authorities required to be "Aryanized," that is, to be turned over to non-Jews. Bosnia had been annexed to Croatia, which was ruled by the intensely pro-Nazi Ustasha regime, which collaborated with the Germans in the persecution of Jews and equally of its much larger Serbian minority. After a while, Josef was falsely accused by the new proprietor, the firm's former bookkeeper, of sabotage, and Josef was forced to flee. With the help of a friend, he managed to have himself admitted into a military hospital for a pretended illness. However, after a two-month stay, the ruse was discovered and Josef was arrested and taken to jail.

It was now the winter of 1941/2, and a heavy blanket of snow covered all major roads, making it hard for the prisoners to be moved to the infamous Croatian-built Jasenovac concentration camp, where thousands were put to death in the cruelest fashion. Instead, each day they were led out, their legs chained, to remove the snow from the streets. One morning, Josef noticed a veiled woman standing at a distance and weeping. It was Zejneba's sister. She alerted Zejneba to Kabilio's presence and his sorry condition. From that moment, and for a month's time, Zejneba or her sister-in-law brought him food, in quantities which sufficed to feed Josef's fellow prisoners. Josef eventually made his escape and returned to Mustafa's home, where he was again welcomed and nursed back to health. Not wishing to endanger the Hardagas with his stay (their home was across the street from Gestapo headquarters in the city and at night Josef could hear the screams of prisoners being tortured in the prison cells), he decided to escape and join his family in Mostar. An ethnic German, a former business associate of Kabilio's, got him a false paper that stated that Kabilio worked for the German civilian Todt firm and had been reassigned to Italian-administered Mostar – where his family awaited him. Previously, while Kabilio was held in jail, the Hardagas had sent various provisions to Josef's family in Mostar.

Returning to Sarajevo upon the area's liberation, the Kabilios were again hosted in the Hardaga household for about two months before moving on and eventually settling in Israel. Josef Kabilio learned that Zejneba's father, Ahmed Zadik, had sheltered Izidor Papo and his wife for a while. This occurred in early 1942 when Zadik ran into Papo, his wife, and their two children at a train station in Konice. Striking up a conversation with Papo, he learned that they had arrived from Dubrovnik and were heading for Sarajevo. Zadik counseled them not to go there, since all Jews had already been either liquidated or sent away. Instead he invited them to his home, an offer which for lack of other alternatives they gladly accepted. As a result, Ahmed was later betrayed to the authorities, and was apprehended and sent to the notorious Jasenovac concentration camp, where he perished. As for Zejneba, after the death of her husband Mustafa, she remarried and assumed the surname of Susič. A daughter was born to her, named Aïda.

In 1984, Yad Vashem conferred upon Mustafa and Zejneba Hardaga (Susič) the title of Righteous Among the Nations. Also honored were Mustafa's brother Izet and wife Bachriya, as well as Zejneba's father, the martyred Ahmed Zadik. That same year Zejneba Susič visited Israel and planted a tree in her own name and the name of the other family honorees in the Avenue of the Righteous, at Yad Vashem.

The story is not yet finished. In December 1992, as I (Paldiel) was about to wrap up another day's work at Yad Vashem, I turned on the radio to listen to the news and heard of another bombing of Sarajevo by Serb militiamen from the hills commanding the city. I wondered then how Zejneba Susič was faring. Picking up the phone, I called Tova Greenberg (her father, Josef, had by then died) to find out if she had news of her rescuer. She told me that as far as she knew Zejneba was in need of medicine due to her heart condition. At the time, Israel did not have any representation in Bosnia, so I put through a call to the Joint office in Jerusalem, on the assumption that the organization was probably assisting the diminishing Jewish community in that besieged city. I asked a certain Pauline Shumer to allow us to send Mrs. Susič the medicine she needed through the local Joint representative. A little later the JDC man, Bar Chaim, learned that Zejneba Susič had instead asked to be allowed to leave the stricken city together with Jews who were being taken out. For this, a written request had to be addressed to the President of Bosnia, including the assurance that once in Israel she would be taken care of by the state. The Joint, for its part, was prepared to subsidize her trip here. A letter to the president of Bosnia-Herzegovina, issued in August 1993, and at my urging signed by Shimshon Eden, Yad Vashem's Secretary General, stated the following:

From right to left: Zejneba Hardaga and Rivka Kabilio, walking in Sarajevo in 1941. The two walk arm in arm to hide the Star of David on Rivka's sleeve, and their children with Bachriya Hardaga (on the far left), sister-in-law of Zejneba (Courtesy of Sara Pećanac)

"Dear Sirs, Mrs. Zejneba Hardaga-Susič was recognized by the State of Israel as Righteous Among the Nations for saving Jewish lives during the Nazi occupation of Sarajevo. We plead with you to allow her to leave Sarajevo with a convoy of the Jewish community. We invite her as our guest to come to the State of Israel."

Several months passed by before the government there acted, and in the meantime Bar Chaim was told that Zejneba Susič did not wish to leave Sarajevo alone, but insisted on taking along her married daughter, Aïda Pečanač, as well as her husband, Bratomir, who was stricken with multiple sclerosis and their 10-year-old daughter, as Mrs. Hardaga-Susič was totally dependent on them. To make this possible, in January 1994, Mr. Yair Tsaban, Minister of Absorption, committed himself in writing to grant Zejneba's extended family Israeli citizenship upon their arrival here and that care would be taken to ease their absorption into the country. The Susič-Pečanač family landed in Israel on the night of February 10–11, 1994, to a tumultuous welcome by officials of Israel, the Joint, and private individuals. Two weeks later, Zejneba was awarded Israeli citizenship in a special ceremony in the office of Prime Minister Yitzhak Rabin.

On the eve of Passover (April) 1994, I received the following letter from Tovah Greenberg-Kabilio:

"Dear Dr. Paldiel, We wish to thank you for your efforts in rescuing Zejneba Hardaga and her family from the inferno in Sarajevo, and for bringing her to a warm and secure home in Israel. Zejneba wishes to build her future here, in a place where she feels 'at home.' Her feelings of warmth and sympathy toward this country, as a result of the invitation to come here, go back to the period when she was still destitute in Sarajevo. These feelings received added strength from the pleasant reception here. We hope that her further absorption here will be as comfortable and easy as in the beginning. Again, without your help, this would not have been possible."

That same year, on October 22, Zejneba suddenly passed away, at the age of 76. As, according to her daughter, Aïda, she had asked to be buried among Jews, I arranged for her burial in Moshav Beit Zayit, located in a valley at the foot of the Yad Vashem memorial. The burial was attended by the Absorption Minister, Yair Tsaban, who had made possible this brave woman's arrival in Israel.

An interesting addendum to this story is the resolve of Zejneba's daughter, Aïda, to convert to Judaism. She explained her decision in the following terms. "God opened the way for us, and the good people in the Jewish Agency and the Ministry of Absorption gave us our lives back … When we came here, we only knew how to say 'Shalom' in Hebrew … At first, I did household chores and I felt lucky to be able to be with so many Jewish people in this beautiful country, causing me to feel so rich." Asked by the rabbinate why she wished to go through the conversion process, she explained, "If my mother risked her life for Jews – it is only natural that I should want to become Jewish. It is an honor for me to belong to this people. God gave me the opportunity to change religion and to choose Judaism." Today Aïda is known as Sarah, her husband as Moshe, and her daughter as Ruth. Sarah is a religious person in all senses, in dress and in speech. "Jews know how to live and survive under difficult conditions, without a country and home. The hope that I carried with me all this time that the Jewish people will save us, this gave us the strength to go on. Even when

I stood in line, at three o'clock in the morning, to get water, I knew that tomorrow will be better, when we arrive in Israel."

Upon her request to be gainfully employed instead of the recipient of the State's welfare payments, she was admitted for work in the archives department of Yad Vashem (in charge, among others things, of the Serbian-Croatian language section). In her words, "This is a sacred place, a place which knows how to remember the past, the history, for the sake of the future. My work is mainly technical, but I feel that every page that I touch has behind it a story, and every name that I write has significance." She has appeared before audiences on behalf of Jewish organizations. "I try to explain to people about life in wartime conditions, and the tremendous significance for us of Israel's help. Only Israel received us – four people with one suitcase and many difficult experiences. There are still many people who suffer in the world, and it is important to help them. In this way, I should like to continue the work of my mother."

Harder, Loni & Albert

GERMANY

The date is January 31, 1945; the place a village in East Prussia; the weather – subzero centigrade with snow covering the ground; the survivors are three scantily clad Jewish women running for their lives.

As told by Celina ("Zilla") Manielewitz (born Moskowicz), on that day the 23-year-old woman was part of a group of 10,000 Jewish women laborers on a Death March from a German labor camp in the direction of Königsberg. From there, they were moved out of the city to a certain beachhead on the Baltic Sea – supposedly to be evacuated to the interior of Germany in advance of the Russian offensive. Walking in subzero weather without proper clothing and nourishment, with wooden clogs bruising their sore feet, and constantly harassed by SS, Latvian, and Ukrainian guards, many died of exhaustion or were shot for not keeping up. After a night's rest in the village of Palmnicken, where each was given three potatoes to eat, the haggard marchers continued toward the Baltic Sea.

As they neared a cliff overlooking

Albert and Loni Harder

the beach, machine-gun fire was suddenly opened on them from several directions. In the words of Celina: "I was hit in the head and lost consciousness. When I awoke I found myself lying in the icy waters of the Baltic Sea." She probably had been struck by the butt of a rifle to make her fall into the frozen sea. All around, corpses were floating, half draped over the ice blocks. The wounded were moaning; some prayed to God to let them die. A woman next to Celina who raised her head above the water was immediately shot and killed. After the shooting had subsided and the SS had left, a woman named Genia Weinberg came up to Celina and said: "Celina, you're alive!" The two dragged another survivor of the shooting, Miriam Zweig, out of the water and ice. After they waded ashore in their dripping clothes, the three began to walk aimlessly toward the nearest village. Celina's arms and legs were shaking and her teeth chattering. "I was shaking with cold and fever. I'd swallowed sea water, and was pretty sick … I could hardly put one foot before the other… Our ragged clothes froze solid to our bodies and we were soon covered with a white layer of ice. I simply couldn't go on. I wanted to sit down for a just a moment, just to rest." Genia hurried over to her. "If we sit down now we're done for. We must go on."

Continuing, they then noticed smoke coming out of the chimney of a house in the distance and headed in that direction. Approaching the village of Sorginau, they knocked on the door of the first house. "Hide us, please," Genia pleaded with the man who opened the door. "We're the sole survivors from last night. Don't send us away – please." The man's wife nodded to him to let them in. They were given some food and hidden in the attic. However, after a few days the farmer who had taken them in evidently learned that the Russian offensive had bogged down in that area and that the Germans seemed to be regrouping. Fearing that the SS would come in search of those who had escaped from the Death March and the Baltic Sea killing spree, he took fright. He told the three women to leave immediately or else he would report them.

After coming down from the attic and leaving the house, for lack of choice they hid in a shed where coal and firewood were stored. When they went there, they were noticed by someone else – a woman from a nearby house. Soon the farmer came back accompanied by several SS men leading a dog. They rummaged through the area looking for the three women. When the woman in the nearby house saw the dog approaching the yard where the women were hidden, she immediately shouted to the SS, "Oh, yes. I did see something. Three gypsies, I thought. They were making for that forest," and pointed to a wooded area. The SS men left. Loni Harder had saved the three women. As she later told it, "I was pretty agitated. I'd seen those three girls distinctly; they were just skin and bones and looked as if they'd had a ghastly experience. I made up my mind to help them."

When darkness fell, a man approached the shed and introduced himself. "I'm Albert Harder. Remember the woman who didn't give you away this afternoon? I'm her husband. We want to help you. Come out." At first, they feared a trap and did not move. Harder began clearing the bundles of wood away. As he got nearer, he realized that they could hardly move their legs. He took them to the loft of his pigsty, where they stayed for a week and where he brought them food. He then gently carried the exhausted women separately on his back to the kitchen, where, in Celina's words,

"We found three tubs of hot water, three towels and three bars of soap. Our rags were thrown

into the fire. Beds had been prepared for us in the bedroom. The entire night we thought we were dreaming and that it could not be true… When I opened my eyes, Loni was standing next to my bed. She said, 'Why, you're young! I thought you were old women.'"

After a long sleep, they felt well enough to stand up and they were served a hearty breakfast. Eggs, farmhouse bread, butter, marmalade, cheese and steaming hot coffee. "Here, in the midst or our enemies, the Germans, we three Polish-Jewish girls had suddenly found a mother!" Celina thought incredulously to herself. After the hearty breakfast, the three women went back to bed, where they slept off their fatigue during the remainder of the day. When they got up, Loni had them dressed up as German farm women, and told them their new names. Thus Genia became Gerda, Miriam – Maria, and Celina – Elsa. Loni also told neighbors that she had admitted three women refugees fleeing from the advancing Russian army. The women's shaven heads was explained as the result of typhus. The three women stayed indoors most of the time. When they occasionally stepped out, they wore kerchiefs pulled low over their foreheads. In Celina's words, "Thus we lived in almost indescribable tension until the Russians arrived three months later. Loni and Albert Harder treated us as though we were their own daughters and shared their meager rations with us."

After the area's liberation, Celina moved to occupied Germany, where she met the man she married. There, in one of the displaced persons camps, she ran into Loni's sister-in-law, who told her that sadly Albert Harder had died. His last words to his wife were, "Any news of our girls?" Loni also left her village and came to Germany, where she moved in with Celina and her husband in the displaced persons camp. When Celina moved to Israel, she wanted to take Loni along. "I can't," she said. "I'm an old woman. I'd only be in your way; an unnecessary yoke for a young couple like you. You'd have to think of me all the time, and I don't want that." Loni Harder moved into a Bavarian village, and from there exchanged letters with Celina Manielewitz in Israel.

In 1966, Yad Vashem declared Loni and Albert Harder Righteous Among the Nations.

Hautval, Adelaïde
FRANCE

"Since you defend them, you will share their fate," was the curt Gestapo response to the plea of Adelaïde Hautval for better treatment of Jews imprisoned in a Bourges jail. She was then given a label and told to stitch it on her coat. It said: "Friend of Jews," and consigned her to the next transport leaving for Auschwitz. The special sign bore ill tidings for her and could mean only one thing – "special" harsh treatment for her in that notorious death camp.

Born in 1906, Adelaïde, affectionately known as Heidi, had studied medicine and worked as a physician. Her father, Philippe, was a Protestant pastor. All went well for her until, in

April 1942, she was arrested for trying to cross the demar-
cation line, separating the two parts of France during the
occupation, into her hometown in Alsace province, without a permit, to attend her mother's funeral. Imprisoned
in Bourges, she had then protested the inhuman treatment
of Jewish prisoners there. After her sentencing, she passed
through several prisons, and in January 1943 she arrived
in Auschwitz, in a convoy of French political prisoners.
Quickly she became known as "the saint," treating Jewish prisoners for typhus and hiding their illnesses from the
Germans.

Several months later, she was transferred to the notorious Block 10 – a place reserved for pseudo-medical experiments. There a team headed by Nazi doctor Carl Clauberg,
practiced sterilization on women prisoners by introducing
a caustic liquid into the uterus, an operation causing great
pain to the hapless women, who often bled as the stitch-
es came apart. Another doctor, Horst Schumann, irradiated the genital organs of 16-year-old girls, thus causing
their destruction. The ovaries were then removed and sent
to laboratories. Eduard Wirths headed the whole team of
German doctors in Auschwitz and he also participated in
these experiments. This was part of a Nazi plan of mass
sterilization for what they regarded as lesser breeds, a so-
phisticated alternative to their immediate extermination.

Adelaïde Hautval

This horrendous idea was meant to leave races subject to the Germans alive, such as the
Slavs, with the capacity for work unimpaired but with no possibility of reproduction. Thus
they irradiated male and female organs and crudely removed them to see what effect this had
on their capacity for productive work.

Learning that Hautval was a practicing physician – some two to three months after she
arrived in Auschwitz – Dr. Wirths asked her whether she wanted to practice gynecology. At
first, learning of the sterilization experiments that were being conducted there, she thought
of accepting, in the hope that one day, when she was freed from the camp, she could testify
about them. Taken to Block 10, she met a group of 100 Jewish women. She was shocked
when she was asked to anesthetize a Greek Jewish woman in preparation for an ovariectomy
(the excision of part of the female reproductive organ after irradiation). Shaken by what she
saw, she told Wirths she could not participate in this type of work, since she was opposed
to this form of sterilization. Wirths tried to explain to her that the work was necessary in
order to find a better selection method for the preservation of the Aryan race. Hautval: "I
answered that it was very arguable and also that this was a method which necessarily caused
abuse. He talked to me about the Jewish question, and I answered him that we had no right
to dispose of the life and fate of others." Dr. Wirths suddenly shot out: "Can't you see that
these people [the Jews] are different from you?" At this, Hautval answered that there were
in this camp many people different from her, starting with him. Many SS men were present

at this exchange, but luckily for Hautval no one intervened. Shown to the door, she was transferred to the Birkenau camp, where the gas chambers and crematoria were located, and advised to keep out of sight for a certain time. Luckily for her, this was as far as her punishment went. But she feared the worst. She told Dorota Lorska, a fellow inmate: "The Germans will not allow people who know what is happening here to get in touch with the outside world, so the only thing that is left for us is to behave like human beings for the rest of the short time that remains to us."

Assigned to work in the camp dispensary (known as the Revier), she was told by the supervisor, a German woman prisoner (a communist), to submit and take part in the experiments, "for there is an order for you to be returned there tomorrow, when executions will taken place." Hautval responded that this was impossible, since she would sooner commit suicide than accede. Hearing this, her interlocutor took matters into her own hands and arranged with some SS doctors that Hautval not be sent back to Block 10. After the war, Hautval was tormented by the thought: "The only thing that I don't know, and which torments me, is whether another person was executed in my place. I hope that some arrangement was found one way or another." In August 1944, all French women were transferred to the Ravensbrück camp. Liberated on April 28, 1945, she returned to France. Of the original convoy of 230 women, only 50 survived. She returned to her medical practice.

In 1964, Adelaïde Hautval was asked by the defense to testify in the London trial of Wladyslaw Dering vs. Leon Uris. In his book *Exodus*, American novelist Uris had mentioned that Dr. Dering, a Polish prisoner in Auschwitz decorated after the war, had conducted experiments on the bodies of Jewish women without the use of anesthesia. In fact, Dering had administered a painful spinal injection before the ovariectomy operation. As a consequence, Dering had sued Uris for defamation of character. At the trial, Dr. Dering's position was that if he had not performed the operations he would have been killed. If he did perform them, they would at least be done efficiently. The alternative was that they would be carried out by unskilled hands; by butchers. Or again, if he did not operate it would be simpler still for the Germans to kill their victims first, then do the surgery on the corpses. Dering's defense was that in Auschwitz, if you were ordered to carry out an operation, either you did it or you were killed. "When I entered Auschwitz, all law, normal, human and God's, were finished. There was only German law." Dr. Dering participated in salvaging irradiated organs for histological examination. A surgical record of the Auschwitz hospital was disclosed at the trial for the first time. It contained details of castration operations. This was the most important piece of evidence. At the trial, Hautval was asked whether she was ever punished for her refusal to perform these operations. Answer: "No, I was never punished. I refused afterwards to carry out experiments for Dr. Mengele and they said, 'We cannot force her to do what she does not want to do.'" So, contrary to Dering's argument, even in the hell on earth that was Auschwitz, one was not discharged from being bound to moral laws. Hautval argued that this was a place where one's moral commitment was challenged in the most direct as well as frightful way.

In his summation, Judge Frederick H. Lawton stated: "Then there was Dr. Hautval. The jury might think of her as one of the most impressive and courageous women who had ever given evidence in the courts of this country – a most distinguished person – and she stood up to the Nazis four times and made it quite clear what she was and what she was not prepared to do. As a result of standing up on one occasion she had been summoned by

Dr. Wirths and gave him a reply which his Lordship expects will live in the jury's memory for many years – a devastating reply. The jury is asked to infer from the evidence that if Dr. Dering had stood up, nothing would have happened to him at all." The trial ended with the jury coming back with a verdict in favor of the plaintiff Dering – but awarding him the sum of only half a penny – the smallest denomination in the British currency. Uris subsequently described the trial in his novel *QB VII*.

Writing after the war, Hautval said:

"What impressed me in all this Nazi experience was how vulnerable human nature is. We always thought here in France that we were above certain practices, certain theories. But it's not true. You only have to be indoctrinated about something for months, for years, to end up by believing it. And once you believe certain people to be inferior it becomes perfectly natural to subject such people to experiments and no reasoning can touch you. I remember at Auschwitz having a long conversation with an SS doctor who basically was quite a fine man. And he said: 'Look, you don't understand. We're not responsible. We are instruments.' If the elite of a country – and the doctors ought to be in a certain sense the elite – think of themselves as instruments, this is incredibly dangerous … The so-called 'experiments' carried out at Auschwitz had absolutely no value at any time for humanity in general. Anyone who worked in Block 10 must have known from the beginning that the Nazi program was aimed at the mass sterilization of Jews and nothing else whatever. One would have had to be incredibly naive not to have realized this … What I did was nothing. And besides, if I had the luck to be able to refuse, it was certainly not due to myself, but simply because I had in me an instinct which told me that there were more important things in life than saving one's own skin."

Honored as Righteous Among the Nations in 1965, Hautval planted a tree in her name the following year. During the ceremony, she said: "This return of the people of Israel to their own country is an accomplishment which concerns not only you, but the world at large … Israel has always played a gestation, fermentative role, due to which it was hated or respected. Its mission in the world continues to exist, and may Israel remain faithful to this mission. The entire history of this people demonstrates the primacy of spiritual forces, and hence its undertakings cannot but be successful."

Ho, Feng Shan
China

*L*ilith-Sylvia Doron was one of the unhappy people who watched in horror Hitler's triumphant entrance into Vienna on March 10, 1938, accompanied by physical assaults against the city's Jews – the city of Johann Strauss's world-famous and heart-warming waltzes. Next to Lilith stood Feng Shan Ho, a Chinese diplomat in his country's embassy in Vienna. He knew Lilith's family, so on this day he accompanied her home and assured her family he would use his diplomatic status to make sure they were not harmed. When later Lilith's brother Karl was arrested and taken to Dachau concentration camp, he was released on the strength of a visa issued by Ho. Armed with the Chinese visa meant for Shanghai, Lilith and her brother were able to leave the country in November 1939, and instead head for another

Feng Shan Ho

destination – Palestine. When Lilith left Austria, the country had become another province of Nazi Germany, and after the Chinese ambassador there left on another assignment, Ho became his country's consul-general in Vienna, subordinate to the Chinese ambassador in Berlin.

Ho was born into a poor family in Yiyang, Hunan province, in 1901. His mother had converted to Christianity in the Norwegian Lutheran Church. Feng Shan Ho left for Munich, Germany, to further his studies and in 1932 earned a doctorate in political economics. Entering his country's diplomatic service, he was eventually posted to Vienna. There, thanks to his knowledge of German, he cultivated a wide-ranging circle of friends, especially among the intelligentsia, many of whom were Jewish. His appointment as the Chinese consul-general coincided with the severe persecution of the city's Jews by the newly installed Nazi authorities.

The 185,000 Jews then living in Austria were subjected to a reign of terror, unprecedented in its swiftness even when compared to Germany proper. Public humiliation was more blatant and sadistic; expropriation better organized, forced emigration more rapid – with the local populace relishing the public shows of degradation. Soon after Austria's annexation to Germany, Jewish prisoners were sent to the Dachau and Buchenwald concentration camps. They were told that their release was conditional on the presentation of a visa, or other travel document, and their immediate departure from the country. However, most Western countries had strict quotas, and these could not meet the needs of the thousands wishing to leave. At the Evian Conference, convened in July 1938 to discuss ways to alleviate the suffering of Jewish refugees, the 32 nations represented there found various excuses to avoid changes in their countries' restrictive immigration policies. In Vienna, Jews besieged all foreign consulates day after day in a desperate search for visas. As one Jewish refugee, Leo Spitzer, aptly put it:

> *"Visas! We began to live visas day and night. When we were awake, we were obsessed by visas. We talked about them all the time. Exit visas. Transit visas. Entrance visas. Where could we go? During the day, we tried to get the proper documents, approval, stamps. At night, in bed, we tossed about and dreamed about long lines, officials, visas. Visas."*

In contrast to other diplomats, Ho Feng Shan readily issued visas to all who requested them, even to people he knew had other destinations than China in mind but needed to show an end-visa to be able to get out of Nazi Germany. Many of those helped by Ho did indeed reach Shanghai, either by boat from Italy or overland via the Soviet Union, while others availed themselves of the Shanghai visas to head for other destinations, such as Cuba and the Philippines.

Norbert Lagstein was one of these people. He hastened to the Chinese consulate with the passports of his family only to find a throng of people waiting in line. He thought of a way to circumvent the long line, and back home with his fountain pen he carefully copied onto a clean envelope a series of Chinese characters that he gleaned from the family encyclopedia. He returned to the Chinese consulate and told the policeman on duty that he had a special delivery for the consul, flashing before his face the envelope with the Chinese characters on it. The policeman, not able to read Chinese, was impressed and immediately let Lagstein in. Once inside, he stuffed the envelope into his pocket, took out the passports, and applied for the visas. Thanks to Ho, the five younger members of the Lagstein family were able to leave Vienna in time and were saved.

As for 19-year-old Hans Kraus, he also tried desperately to avoid the line of people waiting in front of the Chinese consulate. One day, as he again took his place in the long line, he suddenly saw the Chinese consul-general's car about to enter the consulate's grounds. Noting that the car's window was open, on the spur of the moment Kraus thrust his visa application paper through the window. He then got a telephone call to come and pick up his visa. Hans Kraus and his four family members left Vienna for Shanghai. The same good luck befell the four members of Hugo Seeman's family, who before the Nazi takeover had owned a department story in Vienna. After obtaining visas to Shanghai, on October 12, 1938, they left on the Trans-Siberian Railroad, which took them to Shanghai by way of the Soviet Union.

Soon enough, Feng Shan Ho ran into trouble – not from the Nazi authorities but from his own ambassador in Berlin. The Chinese government, under pressure in the face of the Japanese invasion, was purchasing weapons from the German Krupp works. To counter the Japanese, the government headed by Chiang Kai-shek wished to cement its relations with Germany, and Hitler obliged by sending two German military advisers, including the former chief of staff of the German army, General Hans von Seeck. Chiang, for his part, sent his son, Chiang Wei-kuo, to Germany for military training. In Berlin, the Chinese ambassador was worried that Ho's liberal policy of extending visas to all who asked for them might derail the good relations between China and Germany at the time.

It is worth remembering that a visa was not required for entry into Shanghai, which was under Japanese control at the time, and the Chinese government had no jurisdiction there at all. In issuing visas to Shanghai, Ho was well aware that these visas were not meant for entry into Shanghai but for exit from Nazi Germany. The Shanghai visa was in reality an "exit visa," honored by the Gestapo to free people from the concentration camps, or otherwise allow them to leave the country, on condition that it be done quickly. This was in line with the then Nazi policy of forced emigration of Jews, which lasted even into the second year of the war, coming to a complete halt in October 1941, when the new policy became a combination of ghettoization and extermination. As Ho himself confirmed, the visas were "to Shanghai in name only." As for the Japanese masters of Shanghai, until the latter part of 1939 they allowed the refugees free access to this Chinese city.

Eric Goldstaub's father was another recipient of Ho's Shanghai visa. As he later testified, "I spent days, weeks, and months visiting one foreign consulate or embassy after another trying to obtain a visa for me, my parents, and our close relatives numbering some 20 people." Finally, on July 20, 1938, he received from Ho visas for all of his people. He had not yet left Austria when the Nazis launched the infamous *Kristallnacht* (literally "Night of the Broken Glass") pogrom throughout Germany on November 9, 1938, when synagogues were burned, Jewish businesses and homes vandalized, and thousands of Jews carted off to concentration camps. Eric and his father were among those arrested. In Eric's words, "The fact that we had a visa for China as well as ship tickets for the end of December [via Genoa, Italy] enabled us to be released within a few days and we were on our way by train to Italy and liberty in China." The whole party left Vienna by train on November 12, 1938, for Italy, from where they proceeded on an Italian steamship to Shanghai. As for Eric's uncle and aunt, feeling confident that no harm would befall them, they decided to stay behind in Vienna. By the time they had changed their minds it was too late and they perished in the Holocaust.

Karl Lang was one of the many Jews hauled to Gestapo headquarters during *Kristallnacht,* and then to the Dachau concentration camp. His wife, Katerina, desperately made the rounds of foreign consulates. Then, as their daughter Marion recalled, "Word got out that the Chinese consulate was issuing visas. [Mother] got a visa for my father with an end destination visa to Shanghai. Armed with this, she went and bought temporary transit visas from the consulate of Monaco. I took our passports to the Gestapo headquarters to get them stamped. My father was in Dachau from November 1938 to February 1939. He was released and had to sign a paper that said he would leave Austria within 48 hours. My father left and went to Monaco, from there to Trieste, and then to England." Ho also issued a Chinese visa to Karl's brother-in-law, Erwin Hostovsky, and he left for Shanghai. His wife, Helene, sadly did not make it and she perished in a concentration camp. As for Karl Lang's daughter Marion, she left on the last *Kindertransport* (children's transport) to England right after her father's release. Her mother joined her later, on a domestic help visa, as well as her father a bit later. Ironically, when the war broke out, Karl was for a while interned by the British as an enemy alien on the Isle of Man because of his German passport.

Bernard Grossfeld and his parents, in Vienna, were also granted visas by Feng Shan Ho for travel to Shanghai, thanks to which his father, Morris, was released from Dachau and the family left the country in time. As for Fritz Heiduschka, after his arrest in mid-June 1938, his wife Margarete obtained a visa from Ho for travel to Shanghai. Together with daughter Hedy they boarded an Italian boat in Trieste bound for Shanghai. But when the boat stopped at Colombo, Ceylon, Margarete changed her mind and decided on a different course – to the Philippines; there they stayed through the Japanese occupation until the end of the war.

In the case of Lotte Lustig, when on October 18, 1938, her father retrieved three visas from the Chinese consulate – "just in case" – his mother could not understand him. "Shanghai," she said, "Where in heaven is that?" She was worried, because a friend had told her that "they kill all white people" there. Only after Lotte's uncle was brought back from Dachau for burial, in December 1938, did the family decide to head for that "feared" place, Shanghai, which in Lotte's words had become "an immediate necessity." "We parted from our 78-year-old *Grosspapa* [grandfather] who would die in Theresienstadt in 1942 … I am one of the 4,500 to 6,000 Viennese who arrived in Shanghai between 1938 and 1941."

Ho's charitable behavior did not sit well with his immediate superior, the Chinese ambassador in Berlin, Chen Jie, and he ordered him to desist. Ho countered by claiming that he was only following his country's liberal policy in this regard. Upon which Chen snapped: "If that is so, I will take care of the Foreign Ministry end, you just follow my orders!" However, Ho stuck to his guns, and the fulminating ambassador decided to cause Ho's discomfiture by insinuating that Ho was lining his pockets with the visa business. For this purpose, the ambassador sent an underling, Ding Wen Yuan, to Vienna to investigate fictional claims that the consulate was "selling" visas, a charge which proved unfounded. Nevertheless, on April 8, 1939, Ho was reprimanded, and a "demerit" was entered in his personal file. It is assumed that the reason for this was Ho's issuing of hundreds of visas, and perhaps a whole lot more, in spite of contrary instructions. The Swiss Jewish activist Recha Sternbuch, working out of Switzerland, claimed that in 1939 at least 400 Jewish refugees used Chinese visas to make their way to Palestine via Switzerland.

In May 1940, Feng Shan Ho was removed from his post in Vienna and replaced by another and more compliant diplomat. Ho left with his wife and their 11-year old son, Monto. In 1941, through the efforts of Henry Luce and the China Lobby, the United States moved closer to Chiang's China and began to make large-scale arms deliveries to support China's military struggle against Japan, which led China to sever its relations with Germany and to close ranks with the Allies. At this point, Ho was recalled to China to lend a hand in the war effort against the Japanese.

In the meantime, after Ho's departure, his successor in Vienna, Yao Ding Chen, adhered strictly to the rules laid down by the ambassador in Berlin and reduced the number of Chinese visas to "the utmost minimal number." On May 29, 1940, he reported: "In the period of April 1938 to 1939, the monthly number of visa applicants was extremely high … [about] 400 to 500 [each month] and even higher …. [However], I have adhered strictly to regulations. Presently, this kind of visa has already been reduced to the utmost minimal number." It is estimated that up to the start of the war, in September 1939, an estimated 18,000 Jews made their way to China, many of them with a Shanghai visa issued by Feng Shan Ho. In August 1939, the Japanese overseers of Shanghai began to close the doors to further Jewish entry into the city.

After the war, Ho filled many diplomatic posts for his country, and in 1973 he retired in San Francisco. He died in 1997, aged 96. It was only after his passing and through the efforts of his daughter, Manli Ho, and also through evidence submitted by many of his beneficiaries that the story of his help to Jews was made public. He had once written: "I thought it only natural to feel compassion and wanted to help. From a humane standpoint, that is the way it ought to be." Or, in the words of Ady Bluds, one of Ho's many visa recipients, "I believe Feng Shan Ho was a man of principle and compassion. His actions were all the more noble because it seems he acted against the instructions of his superiors." Had many other diplomats acted like Feng Shan Ho, the number of Holocaust victims would have been much less than they actually were.

In 2000 Feng Shan Ho was recognized as Righteous Among the Nations.

Hulst Van, Jan

NETHERLANDS

*B*orn in 1903, Jan van Hulst, as a trained engineer, worked as the assistant director of public works in Amstelveen, just outside Amsterdam, and was married to Paula, a Jewish woman (born Horowitz). The couple had three daughters. At home, the children, all born before the war, were not aware of anything special concerning their mother's Jewish origin; if they knew about it, they did not ask any questions.

Jan van Hulst with his wife Paula and their daughters, from left to right: Myriam, Hannah, and Alexandra (Coutesy of Hannah Yakin-van Hulst)

Then came the war and the German occupation. In the early stages of the occupation, at school, Hannah, born in 1933, was once taunted by a schoolmate, "You look different. You're a Jew." Until then, Hannah did not know what it meant to be Jewish. At home, she questioned her non-Jewish father, "Lotte says that the one who looks different is the Jew. [Sister] Alexandra and I wear our hair in buns, but [sister] Myriam's hair is frizzy. And she wears glasses. So she is the Jew." At this, father Jan responded, "Look here. There's no difference between Jews and non-Jews. There can only be a difference between good and bad people." Learning that their mother was Jewish did not in any way upset her children, "were it not that the Germans would kill her if they found out," as Hannah put it. In the meantime, Hannah and her sisters went to Sunday school in order to allay suspicions about their half-Jewish status.

When in the summer of 1942 the Germans ordered all Jews to wear a yellow star on their outer garments, Paula van Hulst, as a Jew, had to wear it too. Now that the secret was out, the children were taken out of Sunday school. At this point, Jan was resolved to do something to protect his family; in Hannah's words, he would "un-star Mama by de-Jewing her," and at the same time fight the Nazis by helping other Jews to avoid deportation and stay alive.

But first a pressing problem arose when one night the Germans picked up Paula's mother, Chaja Margolia Horowitz-Zuckerman, her husband, Pinchas, and her sister, and took them to the *Hollandsche Schouwburg* (Dutch

Theater), in Amsterdam – a way station for further transport to the Westerbork camp and from there to the death camps in German-occupied Poland. Jan hastened to Amsterdam and somehow persuaded the Germans that they were making a fatal error. Mrs. Horowitz was in truth a Catholic, Jan claimed, who at the outbreak of World War I had been expelled from Belgium to Holland because her husband held an Austrian passport – a country allied to Germany and at war with Belgium. In the confusion, she had apparently been registered as a Jew without being aware of it. To butter up the Germans, Jan added, "We are much indebted to you for ridding our country of the Jews; only don't overdo it. You might kill an Aryan and that would be murder." Paula's mother confirmed Jan's story and she was released along her husband, since Jewish partners of mixed marriages were, at the time, protected by their gentile spouses. Margolia Horowitz's relatives were by the same token designated as non-Jews and saved from deportation. Jan's wife then automatically became only a half-Jew married to a non-Jew and therefore exempt from deportation. She could also unstitch the yellow star she had worn on the lapel of coat and never put it on again.

From that moment, the Van Hulst home became a short-term stopping place for many Jews on the run. One of the regular and somewhat strange guests, however, was not a Jew. He was Arie de Froe, an anthropologist living in Amstelveen and knowledgeable about certain ideas then current among anthropologists according to which a person's character could be divined by a close study of facial features. De Froe used these criteria to falsify the pseudo-racial records of certain people so as to help them change their status to non-Jewish or semi-Jewish. This was of great help to Jan van Hulst in his rescue activity. De Froe spent long nights with Jan jotting down figures and drawing up tabulations of what he called "characteristics of the Jews." He had a fascinating collection of false dentures, tufts of hair, and glass eyes. De Froe would check Jan's Jewish charges with the help of various instruments, which he bent in all direction in order to measure the most unlikely features of the human body, such as comparing the shade of their nails with complicated color charts. De Froe had numbers and charts to indicate the maximum and minimum length of Jewish ears, eyelashes, and toes, color of teeth, pores per square centimeter of skin, distance between navel and chin, between nape of neck and tip of the tail bone. Jan van Hulst found De Froe's spurious information helpful in making out cases to prove that certain people could not be truly Jewish.

A case in point is that of Emmy Andriesse, a Jewish photographer. To prove that her father was not really her biological father, one needed first a medical statement that her registered father had been sterile when he married Emmy's mother. Jan thought about this and then came up with an idea. He went to have for a checkup with a local doctor of German origin, a pedant who kept all his records neatly arranged in the basement. During the checkup, both talked about health, the war, the weather, and the "good old days." Jan asked him, "Do you really never throw away old files?" The doctor said, "Come and see!" He took Jan down to the basement and said: "Here are the records of every single patient who has ever consulted me. But who gives a damn about history nowadays? Soon my life's work will end up on the rubbish heap just like everything else in this country." When the doctor looked the other way, Jan quickly snatched the case that had the required date and put in it his briefcase. With the help of Dick Elffers, Emmy's husband and an artist, an entry was made in the doctor's handwriting and in faded blue ink saying that Emmy's father had, as a result of a severe case of the mumps, lost his sexual virility. Afterwards, disguised as a gas meter inspector, Jan was able to return the file to its place when only the doctor's wife was in. Now proof was needed that Emmy's real father was a non-Jewish Dutchman, in other words an Aryan. For this, Jan went to Venlo, in southern Holland, stayed over two nights in a hotel, stole some of its old ledgers and wrote in between the lines that 40 years earlier and nine months before Emmy's birth, two guests had registered for a room, one being Emmy's mother and another a man with a clearly non-Jewish name. Then Jan found someone who was willing to identity himself as that person. Emmy was then declared as half-Jewish and exempted from deportation.

Taking additional risks upon himself in acts not always approved by his wife, Paula, who feared for his and the family's safety, Jan used to travel on his bike once or twice a week to The Hague dressed in a long leather or trench coat and a wide-brimmed hat in the style of the Gestapo or collaborators. He would then stop over at the German government compound, entering with shouts of "Heil Hitler," and see the people dealing with questionable cases of Jewish origin – probably in the office headed by Hans Georg Calmeyer. "Look at the case of Mr. So-and-So," Jan would point out. "According to the anthropological findings of Dr. De Froe, this person cannot possibly have more than 12.5% Jewish blood. Don't you think this case needs further investigation?" And that started an investigation into the person's racial background and for the time being prevented his or her deportation.

At the same time, to be credible, Van Hulst had to organize a certain amount of failures. Occasionally a Jew proved to be Jew. Whenever that happened, Jan would congratulate the Germans on a job well done and express the hope that the Jew in question would get what he deserved – this after having ascertained and taken care that these people were properly sheltered somewhere or even in his own home. Soon, with people passing through the van Hulst home all the time, it became necessary to build a hideout.

A double wall was constructed in the attic by smuggling 14 square meters of bricks into the house without attracting the attention of neighbors. Mortar, too, was gotten as well as long wooden boards. As a diversion, a second hideout was constructed between the floor of the attic and the ceiling of the master bedroom. The trap door to this one was sufficiently hidden to be convincing but visible enough to be discovered. In this second place, Jan stored chocolate bars, cigarettes, and cognac – all these to weaken the resolve of possible finders. There he also kept papers, forged especially with a view to sending the enemy on time-consuming wild goose chases.

Of the Jews who spent one or more nights in Jan's house, three stayed on for long periods of time: Anne Petersen (Vera Cohen) and Frits and Kitty Waterman. Frits was a violinist, and every evening after the curtains were drawn he tiptoed downstairs from the attic to play duets with Paula van Hulst. Other persons who stopped over for shorter periods, included a certain Dr. Wolff and wife and Haim Elta. After the war, Haim Eylata (his Hebraized name) wrote that with the help of Dutch people, as a 14-year-old boy he was able to be declared as only half-Jewish, and in the summer of 1943 he spent most of his time in the home of Jan van Hulst, where he helped him bring food to various addresses in Amstelveen and got to know many of his people, who were introduced as "relatives."

Jan's daughter Myriam, who was 13 years of age in 1944, recalls once being surprised to see her father crying. As he explained, he had been trying desperately to persuade a family of four (parents with two children) to go into hiding. They finally agreed, but asked for one more day to make final arrangements. On that very day, they were picked up and deported. Jan blamed himself for not insisting that they not postpone their departure with him.

Rudy Reisel was another person helped by Jan van Hulst. They met in the summer 1944 under the most unlikely circumstances. At the time Reisel was in danger of arrest after Rie Bakker, his underground contact, had been arrested. Rie had previously arranged a hiding place for Reisel with the Nepkens family. It was now feared that under torture she might give him away. Reisel asked the Nepkens to get in touch with Wim Schroeder, the Amsterdam police chief, who was linked to the underground, and he promised to help.

It was 9:30 in the evening, curfew time, when the doorbell rang at the Nepkens home. Dressed in a khaki raincoat and a big hat in the style of the Gestapo, a stranger stood before them. "We had no doubt that our last hour had come," Reisel related. The man asked the woman of the house if her name was Nepkens and whether a man named Rudy was with her. He said he was sent by a certain Wim, who told him that Rudy was in danger. The man was none other than Jan van Hulst. It was now already past 10 o'clock at night and Jan said it was too late to find a hiding place at this hour and he would be back the following morning. But Reisel, fearing that the Gestapo would knock on the door next morning (as indeed happened), insisted that they leave immediately. Jan obliged and took Reisel on the back of his bike, with all the danger involved in being on the street during curfew hours. They rode through Amsterdam in the direction of Amstelveen. At each major street junction, Jan would stop and make Reisel get off and check if the way was clear around the corner. At a certain point, Jan dropped off Reisel behind a billboard and left. A dog kept barking at him. After an hour, Jan returned; he had found a place for him at a pastor's house, but only for a short stay. Then another place was found for Reisel.

Rudy Reisel told another adventure story involving Jan van Hulst. Before the war Reisel had planned to go to Palestine, and in preparation had undergone agricultural training with a farmer named Piet Franzen. During the war, the same farmer headed a farmers' organization, *De Landstand,* that collaborated with the Germans. Franzen was also a black market dealer in farm produce. To get him to cooperate with Reisel and van Hulst and delivering foodstuffs free of charge, Reisel went to see him while Jan hid behind a tree. Franzen was surprised to see Reisel again, but welcomed him warmly. Reisel told him that the war would soon be over and Franzen would be in big trouble unless he helped him and his colleagues with food. In that case, Reisel would testify that he had aided opponents of the Nazis. When Franzen agreed, Reisel called in van Hulst, who introduced himself as a representative of the underground. Franzen agreed to provide an unlimited supply of wheat and oil together with another farmer, items hard to come by in those days, which Jan kept busy distributing to needy Jews in hiding.

In the fall of 1944, Paula van Hulst fell seriously ill from a chronic kidney disease and was taken to a hospital for treatment. It was one of the worst winters in the country's history, with people dying for lack of food. At home, only three people remained in hiding, Frits and Kitty Waterman and Anne Petersen (Vera Cohen). While his wife was in the hospital, in January 1945, Jan learned that one of his Jewish associates, Harry Romp, had been arrested. Jan succeeded in spiriting away the secret transmitter used for sending messages to London in time and taking it to his house – but unbeknownst to him he was seen and followed.

It was January 29, 1945, when Hannah happened to look out the window and a saw a German soldier climbing over the garden fence. At the same time someone rang the doorbell.

"I ran to the kitchen and turned the key to lock the back door. 'Open the door,'[the soldier] shouted, and I shouted back: 'I can't, the lock is rusty; the key is stuck.' I fumbled a little with the key, feigning to do my best, and shouted: 'Wait, somebody is ringing the front doorbell.' However, instead of going to the front door, I went to the staircase and turned the light switch on and off, on and off … That particular switch, working on a hidden battery concocted by Papa, was connected to a buzzer in the room where Uncle Frits, aunt Kitty and Anne lived. The doorbell kept ringing. My mind saw the Jews vanishing behind the double wall in the attic. I opened the front door. The German soldier ran to the kitchen door and he turned the key to let his pal in."

The other was a collaborator who began to question Hannah: "Where is your father?" "I don't know." "Where is your mother?" "In the hospital." "Which hospital?" "I don't know." When Myriam came home, she and Hannah were further questioned. "Who has lit this stove?" Hannah: "I did." "Who has been cooking here?" "Me." "Why such a big pot? Are there any people in the house besides you?" No answer.

After they locked the two sisters in the study, Myriam tore out two pages from a writing pad and wrote in large letters one word on each, "Warn Papa." The two waited by the window until they saw Bernhard Johansen, a trustworthy neighbor, walk by. They pounded on the glass to get his attention and showed him the two pages. He nodded and walked away. Johansen had no idea where to find Jan so as to alert him not to come home. Then little sister Alexandra came home. Sensing that something was wrong, she went over to the house of Johansen, who told her about the message. Alexandra told him that her father was probably in the hospital visiting mother. Calling the hospital, they were told that Jan had just left. Johansen told a nurse to get him immediately, as "it's a matter of life and death! Run, see if you can catch him!" The nurse ran into the street.

Back at Jan's house, the phone rang and Myriam picked up the receiver. One of the soldiers pointed his gun at her. "Say everything is fine." It was Jan. He said, "Shall we talk French, as usual?" "No," said Myriam; "today I'd rather talk Dutch." From this Jan understood that somebody was threatening her. He continued to make small talk and ended the conversation. The Germans locked the two girls in again and began a meticulous search of the house. They were not so much looking for hidden people as for the radio transmitter that they were told Jan had brought home.

Suddenly the Germans roared in triumph. They had uncovered the second hiding place, which produced a carton of cigarettes and a bottle of cognac. They also took the forged papers prepared by Jan to give them false leads, and left. It was past midnight when Jan and his friends felt safe to reappear and get the three hidden people and move them elsewhere.

On February 19, 1945, Paula died. It was Alexandra's tenth birthday. Jan emerged from hiding to attend his wife's funeral at an Amsterdam cemetery. Emmy Elffers was among the cortege following the wagon-drawn casket and carried a gun with her. Jan had made her promise that in case of his arrest during the funeral, she was to shoot him right in the heart.

He had firmly resolved to die rather than risk betraying Jews or fellow underground workers under torture. For years Jan would be saddened to think that while he could save so many others he could not save his own wife.

After the war, Jan returned to Amstelveen and his job with the municipality. For years afterwards Jan refused any honors and tokens of recognition for his wartime deeds. During the war, Jan had gone under many different names and often changed his appearance. Hannah remembered once when on the street with her father, a man said to him, "Please give my best greetings to Mr. van der Stad." It was one of Jan's false names. When Rudy Reisel suggested to van Hulst to be honored by Yad Vashem under the Righteous Among the Nations program, Jan categorically refused. In Reisel's words, "He said, I did not do what I did in order to have my name remembered. My work was an obligation in those days." He died in 1975.

Two decades later, when Reisel learned of Yad Vashem's work in preparing an Encyclopedia of the Righteous Among the Nations, he felt that it would be unforgivable if Jan van Hulst's name were not included. Together with Hannah (married name Yakin), they petitioned Yad Vashem for Jan van Hulst's recognition, and their request was granted in 1997.

Huzarski, Marian & Alfreda, Fryderyk & Zbigniew

Poland

*I*n September 1939, at the start of the war, Avraham Itzhak Rivkind, his wife, Chaya, and their children, Menachem-Mendel and Raaya, all living in Bialystok, fled eastward to Brody ahead of the advancing Germans. Brody was then occupied by the Russians and remained in their control until the German attack on the Soviet Union. When the Germans struck again, in June 1941, Menachem-Mendel, at the time in his thirties, was married to Lonia, the daughter of the chief rabbi of Bialystok, Rabbi Gedalia Rosenman. Acting swiftly to assist his son-in-law in Brody, Rosenman turned to the Catholic bishop in Bialystok, Aleksander Chodyko, and asked for his intercession. Chodyko in turn approached a number of clerics in the Brody region and appealed to them to make an effort to save the Rivkind family. However, before any of the clerics could act on the bishop's appeal, on November 2, 1942, the Germans and Ukrainians staged one of their murderous raids on the city's Jews. Avraham Itzhak Rivkind and wife Chaya were among the victims as was their daughter, Raaya. Only their son, Menachem-Mendel, and his two cousins from the Cygielman family were able to escape by finding temporary shelter and survived the bloody raid. A home-produced pocket Jewish calendar carried by Menachem-Mendel witnessed the elapse of three days following the murder of his family until he was able to ensure burial of his martyred parents and sister according

Marian and Alfreda Huzarski in front of the Rivkind house in Nowogrodzka 1 street, Bialystock

to Jewish rites. At this time, he laid their bodies to rest in the Jewish cemetery in Brody in a specially prepared plot, dug with his own hands.

Brody was one of the many Jewish communities in eastern Poland (today in Ukraine) that was totally obliterated by the Germans and their Ukrainian collaborators. When the Germans occupied Brody on July 1, 1941, the Jewish population there numbered some 9,000 people. Two weeks later, on July 15, the Germans executed 250 persons – many of them leaders of the Jewish community. Several thousand were conscripted for work in nearby labor camps, where many died as a result of brutal treatment and famine. On September 19, 1942, German SS and Ukrainian militiamen deported 2,000 Jews to the Bełżec death camp, while 300 others were shot on the spot. Another deadly raid, on November 2, 1942, cost the lives of the Rivkind family members as well as 2,500 more Jews, most of whom were dispatched to Bełżec. Then, in December 1942, the remaining Jews were locked into a ghetto, but this proved to be only a momentary respite, as all of the ghetto residents were liquidated five months later, on May 21, 1943 – either murdered there (mainly the disabled and children) or sent to death camps. To make sure that no one was left behind, the Germans burned the ghetto to flush out people in hiding; some of those who fled from the burning buildings where thrown back into the flames. The few who had managed to flee into the forests continued to be hunted down by the German and Ukrainians. Only an estimated 250 managed to survive the horrific extermination of a community that had existed for 400 years.

Returning to our story – when during 1942 Father Emil Kobiezyński, in Brody, in response to Bishop Chodyko's appeal, began to make inquiries among his parishioners to help the remaining member of the Rivkind family, Menachem Mendel, and his two cousins, Dr. Julian Cygielman and his brother Avraham, he was able to persuade one of his church members, the Polish-born Marian Huzarski to consider the matter favorably. Huzarski lived on the outskirts of Brody, in the nearby village of Sydonowka, a distance of three kilometers – a village containing a mixed Polish-Ukrainian population. After receiving the priest's request, Marian Huzarski returned home and gathered his family for a serious discussion about how to respond.

There is no written record of this crucial family consultation attended by all the immediate members of the Huzarski family, including Marian, wife Alfreda, and their two sons, Fryderyk, aged 22, and Zbigniew, aged 19. It seems that all were leaning toward a positive response when Alfreda's mother interjected that she objected strongly to taking in of the fugitives, probably for fear of the serious consequences for the family in case of discovery – death to the rescuers as well as to their Jewish wards. Not able to sway the rest of the family, she packed her bags and left in anger to join her relatives in another place. The family consultation ended in a unanimous decision to shelter the fleeing Jews, people whom they had never seen before.

After the war, Zbigniew wrote that on November 25, 1942, he or someone else in the family informed Rivkind of the family's decision and set up a meeting for the next day in Brody. The two Huzarski brothers, Zbigniew and Fryderyk, arrived at dusk and took the three fugitive Jews to their village home through fields and side roads. The three new arrivals – Dr. Julian Cygielman, his brother Avraham, and Menachem-Mendel Rivkind – stayed there for a full 17 months, until the area's liberation in July 1944. The two Huzarski sons, who happened to be active in the Polish underground (*Armia Krajowa* – Home Army) prepared an underground hiding place for the new arrivals in the stable, to which was added an emergency exit in the loft facing the nearby forest for emergencies. At night, the three usually slept indoors, in a corner of the Huzarski kitchen.

The two Cygielmans and Rivkind were very religious and made an effort to strictly observe the Jewish rituals, even in the unfavorable conditions of their new setting. This included daily prayers, with the donning of the obligatory *tefillin* (phylacteries) and *tallit* (prayer shawl) for morning services and eating only kosher food as prescribed by Jewish religious law. Menachem-Mendel Rivkind was a follower of the famed late Hasidic master from the town of Kotzk, known simply as "the Kotzker Rebbe." In consideration of their charges' religious sensibilities, the Huzarskis, themselves religious, purchased special utensils and mother Alfreda cooked her wards' food as prescribed by the Jewish religion. In fact, during prayers, which were at times uttered with intensity and raised voices, the Huzarkis were forced to ask

Huzarski's house in the village of Sydonowka

the supplicants to lower their voices for fear that outsiders might overhear them, with all the risks involved for all. Not at all oblivious to their hosts' own religious obligations, the three Orthodox Jews celebrated the Christian festivals with them.

The fall of 1943, a year after the arrival of the three Jews, saw an increase of internecine strife between Ukrainians and Poles, with the Germans allowing the Ukrainians a freer hand, which led to the burning of Polish homes in the region, including Huzarski's village of Sydonowka. Many Polish inhabitants took to fleeing to the forest at night, returning to their homes only during daylight hours. Over time, the frequency of raids by Ukrainian nationalists in the village intensified, a situation that greatly concerned the Huzarskis – themselves Poles.

In light of this troublesome development, the Huzarskis prepared an underground shelter at the edge of the forest near their home, filling it will all the necessary items to accommodate their three charges. After transferring Rivkind and the Cygielman brothers to the new hiding place, the Huzarski family continued to supply them with all their needs on a daily basis, resolving not to abandon them even after the majority of the Polish peasant population of the village had deserted their homes.

In March 1944, the Red Army approached Brody. Out of fear of the Ukrainians, the Huzarskis advised the three Jews to flee toward the approaching Russian army. In June 1944, during the final German retreat, the Ukrainians set the Huzarski home on fire. The Huzarskis fled to neighbors in the forest, and on the following day the Red Army took over. The Huzarski family had escaped in good time and had headed westward to Lancut.

Rivkind and the two Cygielmans made their way to liberated Bialystok. As a professional textile engineer, Menachem-Mendel Rivkind was inducted into the Red army with the rank of captain and appointed to manage the large textile firm in the city. Once he had located his rescuers, he invited them to Bialystok and ensured their employment in the factory that he managed. In 1946 when he decided to leave Bialystok, Rivkind transferred to his rescuers his big house, which had earlier been occupied by his father-in-law, Rabbi Rosenman, and left for Israel – as did the Cygielman brothers. From there, Rivkind continued to maintain contact with his rescuers and send them food parcels on Christmas. Rivkind's wife, Lonia, who had stayed behind in Bialystok with her father, the rabbi, did not survive.

Remarried to Lusia, herself a Holocaust survivor, Menachem-Mendel had a son named Avraham, born in 1949. At home, the Rivkinds did not divulge to their son anything of their harrowing experiences during the Holocaust – only opening up in the intimate circles of survivors. Choosing the medical profession as a career, Avraham Rivkind is currently head of the Department of General Surgery and the Shock Trauma Unit at the Hadassah Medical Center in Jerusalem. In May 2006, he journeyed to Poland to meet Zbigniew Huzarski, the only surviving member of the original four Huzarskis who, in November 1942, made the fateful decision to take the three Jewish fugitives to their home, and thereby save their lives. Meeting the 83-year-old Zbigniew, Professor Rivkind heard him say, "If I hadn't saved your father, you would not be here today." Still remembering Avraham's father's religious observance and kosher food requirements, Zbigniew refrained from serving him meat at the lavish dinner that he hosted for his Israeli guest.

Asked whether the choice of a medical career and the saving of lives as surgeon had anything to do with his father's rescue by the Huzarkis, Professor Rivkind said that perhaps it had, but only on a subconscious level. "I simply perform my job with complete honesty and dedication as required by my profession. I make no distinction between Jew, Arab, or otherwise – only the health and life of the patient." As for the Huzarkis' rescue of his father and two other relatives, this story symbolizes for him "a narcissus amidst a swamp."

In 1984, Yad Vashem recognized Marian and Alfreda Huzarski, as well as their sons Fryderyk and Zbigniew, as Righteous Among the Nations.

Imeri-Mihaljic, Hayriya
YUGOSLAVIA

*I*n 1991, Josef Josifovic, formerly of Yugoslavia and presently living in Israel, related the following to Yad Vashem:

> *"In 1945, I lived in Prishtina [Kosovo]. One day, we were told by the police that in the village of Ade, near the train station of Obilic, a certain gypsy woman by the name of Hayriya had a Jewish child with her. Several of our Jewish colleagues got together and went out to the village. When the gypsy woman came out, six children followed her, but one of them had a lighter skin. 'Is it true that you are hiding a Jewish child?' 'It is true, but I am not hiding her; she is mine.' 'How can that be?'"*

She then told the following story. The parents of the girl, named Esther, had joined the partisans in 1941, leaving the child with her grandmother. Then the Germans deported all the Jews, including the grandmother and little Esther, to a camp in Kosovska Mitrovica. Hayriya, who had previously worked as a maid in the girl's home, went to visit the grandmother, who asked her to take the child and care for her. According to Hayriya, the elderly woman told her, "Take good care of the child, just as you do your own children. If we return, we'll take her back; if not – may she remain with you as your own daughter." The girl was taught to speak the local gypsy dialect and began to act like other gypsy children. When the war over, and none of Esther's family came to get her, Hayriya told the five-year-old girl, "You know, your name is not Moradia, but Esther Baruch, and I am not your mother. Your mother's name was Bukica Baruch, and she probably got killed fighting with the partisans. If she does not return, you will stay with us. "Bukica did not return, nor the child's grandmother, therefore she is mine," Hayriya concluded her story.

Josifovic explained to Hayriya that what she did was a great humanitarian act, but the child would have to be taken away and turned over to a Jewish orphanage. This proved a bit difficult, for the child refused to leave and her foster mother wailed and cried: "Don't take the child; her parents are not alive; don't throw her away; I am raising her and I love her." It was to no avail. The woman followed them to the police station, where she was told in no uncertain terms to leave. Esther could not hold back her tears. "I reacted by crying uncontrollably. I cried because I loved them; I knew them and only them."

As Esther Baruch told the story, after Hayriya married she left the family's service, but often returned to visit, bringing along her own children. Later, in the gypsy camp, "I always slept together with the other children," Esther recalled, "between them so that nothing would happen to me. That gypsy woman was an honest and trustworthy person." They had no beds, but spread hay and grass and covered themselves with blankets. When she was four, Esther was told that they had found her future groom. "I remember well when they told me, 'When you grow up, this boy will be yours. You will marry him.'" In 1947, two years after Hayriya told the child the truth about her origin, and that her real mother was named Bukica, a fight broke out between Hayriya's husband and another man in the gypsy village over the ownership of a plot of land. The other man, seeking revenge, went to inform the authorities that Hayriya's family was keeping a Jewish child not her own. This led to the police investigation involving representatives of the local Jewish community, and the child was taken away.

The child was taken to Prishtina, where it was planned to place her with a foster family. Little Esther was very dirty and had lice in her hair. When they tried to remove her clothes, "I fought back and refused to have them removed, for I felt good in them." She was washed, fed, and treated for lice, but she refused to touch the food given to her. Before parting with Esther, Hayriya had pushed into the child's hand two boiled eggs, and these she gladly ate afterwards. She was then taken to Belgrade and a Jewish orphanage there. There too it was almost impossible to communicate with her, for no one understood the gypsy language that she spoke. Then, a certain woman volunteered to help out. She said she had picked up some words from a gypsy girl who had worked for her as a maid before the war. The woman took hold of the child and in a broken gypsy dialect asked her name. "So, like a parrot, I told her everything that the gypsy woman had told me, that my mother's name was Hayriya, but that before her I had had another mother who had since died, and her name was Bukica. I also told her my previous family name." On hearing this, the woman fell to the ground in a faint, mumbling, "I have found my daughter. She is my daughter." The girl's mother had survived the partisan phase of her life.

The problems for Bukica had only begun. Esther refused to acknowledge the fact that this unknown woman was indeed her real mother, thinking she was pretending to be her mother. "She tried to take me home with her. I did not want to go; I wanted nothing from her." She made scenes, refused the food given to her. It reached a point where her mother thought she might have a physical defect, an impediment in her jaw that made it difficult for her to eat. She took the child to a doctor. "No blockage in the mouth," he ruled. It took Esther two years to readjust to the new reality.

To make matters easier for the child and herself, Bukica decided to look up Hayriya. At first, she sent her packages, perhaps also money. She then went to see her. Then it was Hayriya's turn, and she came to see the child that had once been hers and the new mother. Esther believed that the reason for her visit was to see for herself that the child had not simply been given away to some stranger but was well cared for and treated kindly. She brought along a basket full of food. "She felt maybe I was hungry. But I did not touch the food. She grabbed me and hugged me, and said I should not be afraid, that she was not taking me back with her." When she saw my mother, she fainted." She then said, "I only wanted to make sure that the child is in good hands, that your mother is alive. I did not believe it. But as it is true, I am very happy, and I can return to my village relaxed, and live there my life."

After that, Esther became better adjusted to her mother. "I got used to the new life, to clothes." When Bukica remarried, Esther took a liking to her stepfather. "He was such a good person, and I adored and loved him more than my mother." Sadly for both Esther and Bukica, the man died at the relatively young age of 52. In 1948, mother and child left for Israel. The child is now herself a mother of three, as well as a grandmother. Then Esther began frantically looking for Hayriya, to find out whether she was still alive, or otherwise.

She asked people in Yugoslavia to help her in her quest, to place an ad in the local press, The advertisement in a Kosovo journal did not produce any results, and the search was made more difficult when the civil war that broke out in Yugoslavia also spilled over into Kosovo. "Perhaps someone will read, perhaps someone will hear, maybe someone will know, maybe someone knows how to locate her," Esther wrote. This, indeed, is the hope.

In 1991, Yad Vashem declared Hayriya Imeri-Mihaljic a Righteous Among the Nations.

Jaromirska, Leokadia

POLAND

"*D*ear Yoram, I will try to fulfill your request and tell you the story of a little girl whose name was Bogusia [pronounced Bogusha], and now is called Shifra. For me, she will always remain Bogusia, for that name was etched in my heart with love and suffering." So began Leokadia Jaromirska's letter to Shifra's husband, Yoram Kotzer in 1966, in Israel, in response to his great interest in knowing more about his wife's background during the Holocaust in Poland.

In her letters to Yoram Kotzer in kibbutz Shaar Hagolan, Leokadia Jaromirska began by relating how she lost her mother at the age of six and her father when she was sixteen. When she married Bolek, the two lived close to the Jewish quarter in Warsaw. In 1938, due to a throat infection, the doctor suggested that she move outside the city. This is how they arrived at nearby Bialolęka Dworska. Then came the war and the German occupation, and soon afterwards, in 1940, Bolek was arrested for political reasons and sent to Auschwitz. She would not see him for five years. Alone, Leokadia did all kinds of work to support herself – laundry and house cleaning as well as child care. Finally, she landed a job in the warehouses of the German army. Armed with a German work permit, she felt protected from the occasional German impressment of passers-by for forced labor in Germany. In October 1942, she visited a friend, and the conversation turned to the com-

Leokadia Jaromirska (left) with "Bogusia" – Shifra Ivri-Kotzer

plete liquidation of the Jewish community in nearby Legionowo. "We cursed these 'Swabians' [i.e., Germans] and took pity on the people." As she was about to leave, her friend suddenly said that she heard the cry of children. "I replied that they're probably beating the children at the Prokopowiczes." She continued on home and took to her bed.

The following morning, Monday, October 4, 1942, Leokadia left early to catch the 6:04 train to work. On the way, she was joined by another woman, and both suddenly heard the cries of children. "We went in the direction of the noise, until we got to the end of the road. On the other side was a long fence surrounding a convent. We looked around and saw something moving. We hurried over and saw two small girls – one blondish, sitting up, and the other, smaller and black-haired, lying down. Both were crying. Their cheeks were swollen, their voices hoarse, they were scantily dressed. We picked them up, I the bigger one, she the smaller one. We stood there wondering what to do."

Leokadia asked her companion, Mrs. Kuklinsky, to take both girls with her, for she had to hurry to work. At work, Leokadia could not get her mind off the encounter with the children. After work, she hurried back to Kuklinsky and met her and the older of the two girls in front of a store, where people were staring at them. Leokadia bent over the girl, "Come to me, little dolly." The girl stretched out her hand; she was holding a bread roll in the other hand and, looking at the people, simply said, "Mommy." Leokadia took the girl in her arms, then remembered to ask her companion what had happened to the other girl. Mrs. Kuklinsky told her that she had taken her to the police station and left her there. "What could I do," she said, "I am an old woman, and scared." Leokadia was upset at Mrs. Kuklinsky for doing something as foolish as involving the police when another solution could have been found. Eventually the younger girl was adopted by a local family.

Leokadia hurried home with her girl constantly crying, "Mommy." For the first days, Leokadia made it a point to return a bit earlier from work, claiming she had not fully recovered from a recent bout of cholera. Sundays were entirely devoted to the little girl. Slowly, the childless Leokadia became intensely attached to her – buying her presents with the little money she had and spending time playing with her. "I gained her confidence, and now too she would call me 'Mommy,'" Leokadia wrote to Yoram. In return, Leokadia named her Bogumila (God's beloved), "for God was with her" – "Bogusia," in diminutive. Leokadia added significantly, "I lived only with her and for her, and as though I had grown wings. My indifference and depression disappeared. I had nothing else to think about but my 'Bogusia.'"

Leokadia began to pamper the little girl – new dresses, a coat and shoes. She was not beyond being wary of her neighbors. "Each bit of news frightened me, not for myself. The interpretations given to the identity of the girl could have ended tragically, had I not known how to deal with people. I was lucky that no one held anything against me and this saved us." At the municipality, they agreed to register both girls as recently born, in the case of Leokadia's as Bogumila Jadwiga Jaromirska.

After a month, little Bogusia had regained her self-confidence; her cheeks turned rosy, she walked around freely and chattered like a bird. "When I returned from work, she was so happy, that while still in my coat I had to hug and kiss her." Soon Leokadia found her a trustworthy babysitter – Irena, or Irka. To supplement her income, Leokadia did some peddling on the side. She also stole a mattress from the German warehouse and sold it on the market. This inspired her to steal other items. "I did not consider myself a sinner, for after all this had been stolen from us by the Germans. Of course, I was afraid, since for such a deed one was sent to a concentration camp." The year 1943 came and went without incident, and Bogumila was developing into a beautiful girl.

One day on her way home from work, Leokadia was told that the Gestapo was close by. "My God, how I ran home. I fell on the way, and blood flowed from my knees through the torn socks." At her building, not a living soul was in sight. She knocked on her door and went in. A neighbor told her not to worry, for the babysitter Irena had taken the child out the window to an acquaintance. It turned out that it was a false alarm insofar as the child was concerned, for the Gestapo was looking for someone else.

With Bogusia constantly on her mind, Leokadia often traveled to Kraków to do some trading, and get items that were in short supply, such as oil, vegetables, and flour. A big problem in winter was heating because of the shortage of coal. Sometimes, she bought coal from a train conductor. Leokadia also had to worry about her husband in Auschwitz and send him packages with food and other items. She occasionally received letters from him. Non-Jewish prisoners in that infamous camp were allowed such "luxuries." Jews there could not communicate with the outside world.

As the Red Army approached, Leokadia was forced to evacuate and move to the rear. This was the start of a most difficult period for her and the child, as they wandered on the roads from place to place, occasionally sleeping in unheated barns as summer turned to fall in 1944. In one such stopover, Leokadia barely was able to save herself when the Germans started burning houses in reprisal for the presence of partisans in the village. On the road, she learned that the Poles had surrendered to the Germans in early October 1944 after a long siege during the Warsaw uprising. During all this time, Leokadia cared for little Bogusia, nursing her through various illnesses, including one frightening bout of whooping cough.

With the liberation of Poland in February 1945, Leokadia's husband, Bolek, returned from Auschwitz. He was weak and exhausted and Leokadia had to care for him until he was able to get back on his feet and look for work. One day, back in Warsaw, Bogusia's father, Geniuk-Gershon Jonisz, suddenly showed up – alone, for Bogusia's mother had not survived. "We happily welcomed him." He brought along many things: gifts for the child and clothing. He also gave Leokadia money to getting more food and she immediately left to resupply the household with bread, sausages, vodka, and cookies. Eventually Leokadia and Bolek moved to Wroclaw, where Bolek hoped to find work.

Jonisz's appearance marked the beginning of a sad and anxiety-ridden period for Leokadia. "I did not believe that any of her parents would return, and I thought that I myself would raise and educate Bogusia … However, 'Man proposes and God disposes.' I lost my peace forever." Jonisz dropped in often to visit, bringing food, while Leokadia's husband went idle. In the meantime, Bogusia was growing into a very sensitive girl. She liked quiet and could not abide shouting and harsh talk. "I always asked her to do things gently." Leokadia was especially upset when Bolek or Geniuk Jonisz talked to Bogusia in a peremptory voice, and she also did not allow them to hit her when she disobeyed. "They had no right to touch her. Jonisz said that he was her father and it was permitted. I answered, 'You have a father's responsibility to care for her needs, but to punish her, only me, for I raised her. If she doesn't listen, then tell me. But I won't allow anyone to raise a hand to her. She listens to me, and if you don't know how to talk to her in a nice way, then she is in the right.'"

As Jonisz stayed on in Wroclaw after his two other brothers came and left, Leokadia hoped, perhaps a bit naively, that he would eventually find someone to marry and settle down near her, making it possible for his daughter to visit him from time to time. But Jonisz had different plans – to take Bogusia away, not only from Leokadia, but far away from Poland and its sad memories. "This created a scene. I told him that I would not give her up." In one of her letters to Yoram, she hinted at the tense situation at home, then added, "I don't want to go into details about Jonisz's behavior, for I don't want to disappoint her with regard to her father. Ask him yourself, but let him tell the truth." Leokadia could not bring herself to part from Bogusia. "I could not imagine my life without her. For whom should I live?

Whom to take care of? Whom to worry about if she was gone?" Jonisz saw her suffer but kept insisting that as her father he had the right and that the law was on his side.

Leokadia consulted a lawyer, but he was of no avail. "I became a nervous wreck." At home – all the time arguments. At one point, to overcome Leokadia's opposition, Jonisz suggested that she leave with him, abandoning her husband. Leokadia at first thought about it seriously but could not bring herself to do it. "For five years he dreamed of meeting me; for me he remained alive, and this kept him going. Now he is helpless like a child (concentration camp syndrome), without work, and not able to think straight." Not knowing what else to do to stop Jonisz from taking her beloved Bogusia, "overwhelmed, I ran into the street. I wanted to end my life. But I could not do it to the child. I wanted to spare her such a shock." Little Bogusia also sensed something wrong in the air, and she would say to Leokadia, "Let's go to Warsaw, but without them."

One day, Leokadia heard Bogusia weeping terribly. "Bogusia, my love, what happened?" "Renia told me I was Jewish and Geniuk [Jonisz] is my father." At this, Leokadia, in an effort to calm the child, told her, "In the meantime you're not Jewish, for your mother is Catholic and we attend church, and when you grow up you'll understand better. Let me kiss you and go out and play." For Bogusia this was nevertheless a revelation, quite troubling for her. At this point, Jonisz insisted that Leokadia reveal the truth to the girl, but she held back and sank into deeper gloom.

"I was the most miserable person in the world. I would go to church and spill out my anguish before the Holy Mother, and asked for a solution to this vicious circle. There, without witnesses, I allowed my tears to flow freely. At home, scenes and hate and pressure from him. Finally, I began to think. If her mother were alive, I am sure we would have agreed to something between us and lived together, or I would have turned over the child to her without hesitation and in complete tranquility. I would have satisfied myself that we could visit one another. We would have educated her together. But to turn her over to a man whom I hardly know, in spite of the fact that he is her father? Who will understand her? Who will have the same patience and devotion? Who will dry her tears during times of sadness and pain? A man would certainly not understand this. Men are egocentric and only think about their own comfort. They lack a motherly feeling – even the best of fathers. But I knew I had to give her up."

If not for Bolek, a concentration camp survivor, Leokadia added in her letter to Yoram, she would have fled with the child to an unknown location and disappeared. But she simply could not abandon her husband. She decided on another gambit, to demand from Jonisz a sum of money that she knew he did not possess; in order to postpone the child's transfer. But to her surprise, he left and returned with the requested amount. "I could not retreat. I took the money. I hated money, the bills burned inside me like the gold coins of Judah Iscariot."

Then came the moment of separation. She had prepared Bogusia for this by telling her she needed to be hospitalized, so in the meantime her father would care for her. Bogusia innocently replied, "Not for long." That day, Leokadia could not hold back her tears. "I had to part from this child forever. I had pleaded with him to allow me to keep the child. 'You can bring other children into the world. I will not deny your fatherhood of this child.' He refused to listen."

He also did not disclose where he was going. As he left, "I went wild with grief." A doctor was called in and gave her some tranquilizers. Not able to control her emotions, she decided to try to find her and went on a search of children's homes where she suspected Bogusia was being kept, but to no avail. Finally, she learned that Bogusia had fallen ill and had been admitted to a hospital. Arriving there, she was allowed to look at the child from behind a window and carry on a little conversation. "Bogusia, how are you?" "Fine, and why did you not come for such a long time?" "Bogusia, why are you scratching your head?" "It is because I have lice and the nurse put on some powder so that they should all die." Leokadia stayed close to the hospital, visiting the child until she had recovered. She could not answer Bogusia's question why she had turned her over to this strange man. "If it hadn't been her father I would not have turned her over to a stranger for any amount of money. It was better if I died, for without her there was no meaning to my life."

After the final parting from the child, she returned to Wroclaw together with Bolek, who had come to visit the child in the hospital. "For a long time I heard her desperate voice. I hear it until now," she wrote to Yoram. "I returned to Wroclaw, a different person. Irena [the baby sitter], when she saw me, crossed herself in shock – my hair had turned white."

Irena brought Leokadia a little dog, but Leokadia kept crying and the dog responded by whining. Everything began to upset her. "I went around the apartment like a wraith. Every item reminded me of the child." She could not get Bogusia out of her mind, and every child she came across in the street reminded Leokadia of her. Twelve years passed. In 1958, she had to undergo surgery and wrote to Bogusia, including photographs, at the address given to her by Jonisz. He had in the meantime taken the girl with him to Israel. From there, he would send her packages. She asked Bogusia to write back, and found a letter from Bogusia waiting for her after her release from hospital, "the first unforgettable letter from my beloved child … I was happy and wept. My eyes were swollen from weeping." This was followed by other letters. Leokadia was happy to learn that Bogusia, renamed Shifra, was living on a kibbutz and was happily married and the mother of three children. "Now that I think of her, I am no longer sad."

"Dear Yoram," Leokadia ended one of her many letters, "I have finished telling my story. It is not my fault that there is not much joy in it … But you asked for it, and I tried to fulfill your request … Now you will not be angry that I am upset that Bogusia is working in the [kibbutz] kitchen … In my eyes she deserves a royal crown. But love is the most important thing. You love one another. You both have treasures of your own, and this is worth much more …. In reading these reminiscences, don't be saddened, for this is all behind us and now you have a beautiful and sweet wife, a mother to three children. You must love her and be good to her forever. You must compensate her for all the suffering that she underwent during her childhood. Many kisses. Mother."

Two years later, on October 21, 1968, Leokadia learned that Yoram, had been called up on reserve duty to the army, and had fallen in an Arab raid inside Israel in 1968. From distant Poland, Leokadia commiserated with Bogusia-Shifra, in one of the letters she wrote her:

"My dear child – what a disaster has come upon us! … I know there is nothing I can do to alleviate your suffering. Nobody is able to do that except your children. My beloved daughter

— my tears have also run dry. I am as full of agony now for my dear Yoram, my good child, as I was in those days when you were taken from me. In twenty-one years, I haven't shed so many tears ... You know what a treasure you are to me. In my life, I haven't loved anyone the way I loved you ... If it weren't for you, I would be miserable – if only I could suffer now instead of you. Don't break, my child ... Life will force you to regain your equilibrium. You will be healthy together with the beloved children. I kiss your gray-green eyes, the sad and tearful eyes. Kisses to the sweet children. And for our beloved – place a flower on his grave and give him regards from a loving mother and grandmother. Leokadia."

She then went to Israel to be again with her beloved Bogusia, and stayed with her on the kibbutz for six weeks, comforting her and holding her children in her arms. When Leokadia got off the boat, in Bogusia-Shifra's words, "I soon recognized her. Everything came back to me ... Words came back to me and I spoke Polish. We had a strong attachment that did not die." Leokadia then was told how Shifra's father had found her after the war, her mother, Golda, having died in the Majdanek camp. As for her father, he had survived several concentration camps, and after the war, believing that his then two-year-old daughter whom he and Golda had left on the road near the convent before being deported had not survived, he had made his way to Italy, to continue from there to Palestine. Before leaving, he consulted a fortuneteller who told him, "You have a little soul in the world waiting for you." He took this as a sign that his daughter was alive. He changed his travel plans and decided to return to Poland for a last effort to find his daughter, and eventually was able to locate her in Wroclaw, with Leokadia Jaromirska. He had not seen her for three years.

Years later, Shifra-Bogusia remarried, to Adam Ivri, a schoolmate of the late Yoram, and raised two more children. She is now a happy grandmother. As for Leokadia Jaromirska, after returning to Poland, she continued to correspond with her beloved "Bogusia" until Leokadia's death in 1979. Earlier, in 1968, Yad Vashem conferred upon her the title of Righteous Among the Nations.

Job, Józef & Wiktoria & Stefania, Edward & Izabela
POLAND

*B*erl Sturm and his nine-year-old daughter, Henia, were walking aimlessly in deep snow, after they had escaped from a German killing raid in Dębica (pronounced Dembitza), Poland. They felt their strength ebbing and that it was only a question of minutes before they would not be able to go on and sink into the snow. At this eleventh hour, a saving angel appeared in the form of a Polish girl – Stefania Job, who brought them to the safety of her forest home.

The story begins in the Dębica ghetto in December 1942, when Berl Sturm and his daughter were caught in the third Nazi raid on the ghetto's Jews. Berl had already lost his wife, Breindla, in an earlier Nazi "action." Now, when the group with Henia and her father was being taken to be shot, one of the Jewish guards designated by the Germans to help them implement their satanic plans told the two in a whisper, "Ratavit zich, ver ken, ratavit zich" (Yiddish for, "Save yourself, whoever can, save yourself"). Thanks to a particularly heavy fog that cut down visibility almost to zero, the two Sturms were able to sneak away and stealthily leave the ghetto. They found temporary shelter with a woman, where they met some relatives in hiding in a cellar beneath the porch. After a few days, feeling their presence there made it too risky for the woman, Berl and daughter Henia left the place. Having nowhere to turn, they returned to the ghetto and hid in a cellar with Henia's brother Izaak. Since danger lurked everywhere, Henia and her father decided to move on, leaving Izaak behind, as he had managed to be taken on as an expert worker by the Germans and felt himself safe of harm from them.

Berl Sturm knew a shoemaker named Wiktor who lived on the outskirts of the town, believing that unlike his other non-Jewish friends, who had turned down his requests for help, perhaps Wiktor would be different. "Wiktor was our only chance," Henia said. Taking off his armband with the yellow star and pulling his collar up and his hat down in order not to be recognizable, the two fugitive Jews walked in the direction of Wiktor's home. After walking in the snow for some time, the two finally came to the house, situated on a hill. Berl explained to Wiktor the dire circumstances of their situation and asked to be allowed to stay in his house in return for payment, and Wiktor agreed to this arrangement. Then, one day, Wiktor's wife came home, perhaps from shopping, and excitedly told her Jewish wards that that the Germans were searching the houses for Jews and she thought it would be best if her guests would leave immediately. "Let me add," Henia emphasizes, "that unlike Wiktor she was not kindhearted and had no sympathy for Jews. Until this day I do not know whether she was telling us the truth or had made up a story to get rid of us."

With nowhere to go, and asked to leave in a hurry, Berl and Henia headed for the woods. Where to go next? Perhaps nearby Tarnow, where it was said that Jewish families were still living in the ghetto. On the way there, they were stopped by a Pole, who told them that if they gave him all they had on them he would not betray them to the Germans. Berl gave him some of his money and other valuables. Satisfied with this, the man was good enough to show the two the way to Tarnow.

It was a very cold winter day. As darkness fell, the two approached an isolated house in the woods. A dog's barking brought two youngsters, brother and sister, out the house. They told them that their father was the mayor of the village. The two children agreed to take in Berl and Henia, give them some food, and allow them to spend the night in their stable. In return, Berl gave them some of the money he still had and some other things. The next day the two continued on their journey in the direction of Tarnow. The weather was turning much colder. Looking for a place to rest and warm up, Berl decided to check out a log cabin in a nearby valley. A friendly old woman invited them in. After warming up near the stove, the woman offered them some bread. Then the two continued on the road to Tarnow. Hitting the main road, Henia felt she could not go on. "It was very, very cold and I had ice in my boots which caused me to take very small steps. At this point I had a talk with my father and we decided that it would be best if he and I would walk separately instead of together on the road." Thinking that this would be safer, her father walked about 50 feet ahead of Henia. As she walked alone, suddenly a Polish girl came over and saw Henia's dire condition. She said to Henia, "I know you are Jewish, but don't be afraid, I won't do you any harm." She then added: "Let's walk together," but soon she saw that Henia was going too slow for her. "She was strong, healthy and rested, and I was knocked out and frozen through and through."

So this unknown girl continued down the road until she caught up with Berl, not knowing who he was. She said to him in Polish: "There is a sick girl back there and maybe it would be a good idea to take her to a house nearby to warm up." She purposely omitted to mention the fact that the girl was probably Jewish, not sure of the man's views on the subject. When Berl Sturm responded that it would indeed be a good idea to do as she suggested, she immediately sensed from the inflection of his words that he was Jewish and soon deduced that the two were related. She then asked, "Aren't you perhaps the little girl's father?" to which he heard himself say, "Yes." She then told him that her own father was willing to hide Jews. As soon as Berl heard this, he grasped at this lifeline and blurted out that he and his daughter were indeed Jews and, not sure of the fate awaiting them farther down the road, he asked her to take him and his daughter to her home. The girl and Berl waited until Henia caught up.

Stefania Job then said that it would be best if she would walk some distance ahead of them; this would be the safest way to go, especially if she ran into someone she knew, who might ask about the two strangers with her. As Henia later wrote:

"The only problem with this was that she walked like a normal person, and I did not because there was ice in my boots and I was frozen and exhausted. After a while I could not walk anymore and my father had to carry me … He carried me a little, then he put me down and I tried to walk, then he picked me up and carried me a little more; and in this way we made slow progress. But we saw that she was getting farther and farther away from us, and since she was healthy and neither my father nor I were strong, we could do little to keep up with her. At one point we were in great despair because we could no longer see her in the distance and we feared that we had lost our last chance for survival… The snow came up to my shoulders. Aside from that, I did not have the strength to walk and my father did not have the strength to carry me. Every time I put my foot in the snow, I found it hard to pull it out. As I struggled with the snow we were no longer able to see the girl, but we followed her footsteps in the snow. All of a sudden I lifted my head and saw a man coming towards me. At first we were scared because we did not know who this man was. When he came closer to us, he told us that he was the girl's father, and that he had come to take us back to his house. Then he picked me up and walked as fast as he could in the deep snow, and in this manner he brought us to his house (which I later learned was a kilometer from the road)."

It turned out that Stefania had purposely walked fast in order to get her father to help the two slow-moving Jews. In Stefania's house, Berl and Henia were introduced to Stefania's parents, Józef and Wiktoria, to her younger sister, Izabela ("Iska"), and her elder and younger brothers, Edward ("Edek") and Zdzisek. Edek and everyone else tried to take off Henia's shoes, but that proved too difficult because of their frozen condition. After several painful efforts the boots did come off, and a layer of ice could be seen in each of them. At this, mother Wiktoria exclaimed in shock, "Oh Lord, oh Lord." She then busied herself by the stove and fixed something to eat and drink for the newcomers. They also removed Henia's clothes to have them dried. Then after Henia and her father had a hearty meal, the two were put to sleep on the floor, which was covered with straw and with pillows. "This is how our stay with the Job family began."

The Jobs then devised a plan to protect their charges from discovery. In the event that anyone came over to the house, Berl and daughter Henia would lie still in the back on top of the oven, which was built high. The family would then place some logs in front for additional security. Afterwards, it was decided to move the two to a half-finished house (begun before the war) on the Job property, with only the walls and roof constructed. There were no windows or floor, and sunlight would filter in through the cracks between the rows of tiles on the roof. But the structure also contained an attic that was quickly built by laying unnailed planks across beams meant to eventually serve as the supports of the attic floor. In Henia's words, "We thought that no one in their right mind would think that someone was there. Actually it's questionable whether normal people could live there because [it was] extremely cold in the winter and hot in the summer." Mother Wiktoria told five-year old Zdzisek never to tell anyone that they were hiding Jews, because if he did the Germans would kill everyone in the family and would burn down the house and the barn. The boy took this to heart and kept the secret to himself. It was shortly before Christmas 1942 when Berl and Henia moved into the attic of the unfinished house. On their way to church, on Christmas Eve, the Jobs came up to the attic to celebrate the holiday with them, "wishing that all of us would live through the war together. This was a very moving moment and everyone was crying because we all deeply felt the danger of this present undertaking." While there, the Jobs provided them with all their basic needs – food and a bucket for use as a chamber pot.

Conditions in the attic were far from satisfactory, to say the least. In the winter, with its heavy snow, the two fugitives would sometimes wake up to find that the snow had covered the quilt under which they slept. This was because of the cracks between the rows of square clay tiles on the pitched roof of the house. "Once the wind was so strong that it actually lifted up the side of the roof (fortunately not the side that we were on). Then the roof fell back and all the tiles on that side were smashed. Luckily, the family had spare tiles, so using ladders they were able to repair the damage themselves." In fact, when it simply became too cold to stay in the attic, the Jobs insisted that Berl and Henia come over to their house and stay for a while in their better-constructed attic.

Of all the Job family members, in Henia's opinion, Stefania (or 'Stefka') was the bravest. When she received a summons to report for forced labor in Germany, her father objected, since he considered her the smartest and shrewdest of all his children. So he decided to go himself instead. After he left, Stefania took over the management of the farm, continuing after her brother Edward was also taken away for labor in Germany. Danger was always present, and one close call occurred when Stefka was grinding corn in a hand mill located in the unfinished house with the help of Berl. Suddenly a friend of Stefania's appeared (it seems that the watchdog had fallen asleep and had not warned them by barking) and saw Berl together with her. At first Stefania was shocked, but she quickly recovered and immediately escorted her friend out of the house. Somehow she was able to convince him that he had seen a gypsy who happened to be passing by the farm and had asked for bread. Since she was tired, she asked him to help her grind some corn in return for the bread. No one knew for sure if the boy bought the story, and this caused all concerned much anxiety for fear that he might alert the authorities. On another occasion, the Jobs were alerted that the Germans would be coming to look for dairy animals that Polish farmers had hidden from them. The Sturms were urged to stay in the woods for a while.

A more serious threat arose when, with the approaching Red Army in late summer of 1944, a German unit decided to encamp in the village and ordered all the inhabitants to leave. At first, Stefania responded by crying hysterically. She then went up the attic and told the Sturms that the reason for her uncontrollable crying was, "because I am very worried about what will happen to you now." To save them, Stefania wanted to help them relocate to a safe place deeper in the nearby forest. The weather was still good, and at first the Sturms fed themselves on the potatoes that Stefania brought them. Then the fall began and the weather turned bad – it started to rain heavily day after day. "We didn't have any shelter, so we were soaked through and through. Aside from that, we were not able to eat the potatoes because normally we would have baked them, using dry branches to make a fire and later concealing the ashes to hide our presence in the woods. Now everything was wet and we could not build a fire. We thought that this was the end." Then suddenly one day they beheld Stefania coming toward them. She told them that she had finally relocated and wanted to help the Sturms with a more weather-secure hiding place in the forest. Her brother Edward had returned home from Germany after about a year's absence, and he together with Stefania went into the woods with tools to help dig a small bunker – a pit large enough for two people to fit into covered with boards. They also promised to return occasionally with food. For the time being Berl and daughter Henia were safe, thanks to Stefania and Edward.

One day, two German soldiers out hunting gave chase to an animal and came upon the bunker, ordering the two occupants out with all their possessions. When one of the soldiers noted the Hebrew prayer book and phylacteries (*tefillin*) held by Berl, he told the other soldier that he knew what these were, and explained: one part was put on the head and the other part on the arm, during prayer. The Sturms were led out of the woods and onto a forest road, where they ran into a large group of soldiers digging bunkers. The Sturms were assured by these regulars that they would not be killed, but Berl was not too sure, since he had heard stories about German soldiers who were polite to Jews and then killed them later on. Berel also noticed some Ukrainian militiamen, known for their murderous rampages against Jews. The Sturms were then led to the village and to their amazement led into the house occupied by the Jobs – their benefactors. The Jobs took fright, thinking that the Sturms had given them away. "Of course we wouldn't do this in a million years," Henia wrote in her testimony. "When we got close to one of them, we signaled with our eyes and hands that there was nothing to be afraid of. They finally got the message that we did not involve them in this."

Paradoxically, Berl and Henia were then led to the unfinished house where they were earlier hidden and which was now occupied by German soldiers, who had fixed up a room for their commander. From them the Sturms learned that the Russians were already in Dębica. The German officer in command gave orders that the two fugitive Jews be treated well (he gave them candy and chocolate that he had received from home) and arranged a sleeping place for them. He also ordered the owners of the house – that is, the Jobs – to feed the two Sturms. There "we ate and drank and acted as though we didn't know the family." This was followed with the two being placed in another Polish home, whose occupants showed their displeasure at having to feed and accommodate Jews. In Henia's words, these Polish peasants felt very much put out when they had to take in Jews and feed them; and they were happy that Jews were being killed.

One afternoon the officer's adjutant told the Sturms that he had been ordered to escort them for their safety to the main road, where they were to be freed. Once liberated, and with nowhere to go, they returned to Stefania Job's home and were hidden in the stable, where the Germans kept their horses. The two hid underneath a long trough that was used to feed the cows and horses with straw, hay, and oats. At night, with the soldiers not around, they crept out of the narrow place and slept in a corner of the stable. One morning, the Germans left the area, and a few days later, Russian troops arrived. The Sturms had survived. They stayed on for a while in the Job home; then left for Dębica.

When the war was over, Stefania's father, Józef, returned from Germany, and immediately asked his family whether the two Sturms had survived the war. When told that they had returned to Dębica, he went to see them. "He was so happy to see us and we were happy to see him; and we were very grateful to him and his family for doing all they could to help us survive the war and the Nazi death machine." When in 1946, Berl and Henia left the country for France, Stefania came to see them off at the train station. "This was one of the most tearful moments I can remember. Stefka and I cried as though this was the end of the world; in fact this parting changed our close and special friendship forever. Though we have exchanged letters since then, unfortunately I have not seen her since that day." Henia's brother, Izaak, had luckily survived several concentration camps and was liberated in Buchenwald on the arrival of the U.S. Army.

In 1980, Yad Vashem conferred the title of Righteous Among the Nations on Józef and Wiktoria Job and their children Stefania, Edward, and Izabela.

Kacherovski, Ivan & Tatiana
UKRAINE

*I*t was February 1942, and the beginning of the end for the Jews in the town of Brzucho-wice, near Przemyslany (today, Peremyshlyany in Ukraine). The town's mayor, with whom the Katz family were on good terms, had come to see them and urged them to leave – right away, for the next day the Germans planned a killing raid on the town's Jews.

The Katz family held a brief discussion. Father Mechel Katz decided that the family should separate. He would go to the still-existing Przemyslany ghetto together with his two daughters, Lea and Sara. Mother Gitel decided to hide with a farmer in the neighboring village of Kosteniv together with her older son, Lieber. As for the other son, the 20-year-old Kalman, he decided to take up the invitation of Maksimovich, a local farmer and hide with him. In fact, this man had extended his invitation to the whole Katz family. "They were people," Kalman wrote after the war, "with whom we had had good relations before the war. They had, in fact, been our best customers." There was one serious hitch: the Maksimovich's only son was a leader of one of the most antisemitic armed elements at the time – the Bandera group.

Ivan Kacherovski

When Kalman arrived there he was told he could stay for as long as he liked. Maksimovich then asked Kalman to give him his trench coat as a present and Kalman obliged. This was already a bad sign of the man's true intentions. Later, when his wife brought Kalman something to eat at night, she told him quietly that her husband had told her that five or six men from the Bandera group would be coming to their place that evening for a meeting and that her husband had decided to get rid of Kalman. In fact, he planned to shoot Kalman and dump his body in the nearby Gnila-Lipa River. She advised Kalman to disappear as soon as he had finished eating. Kalman now understood why the man had asked for his trench coat – so that it would not be stained by bullet wounds. Kalman left and hid in the cemetery, and pondered what to do next.

Some time earlier, another non-Jewish farmer friend of the Katzes, named Ivan Kacherovski, who lived in the village of Kosteniv and with whom the family had done some business, had also invited the family to stay with him. Father Mechel had then pointed to his son Kalman and said to Ivan, "Take him." Now it was time to take him up on his invitation. Arriving there, Kalman was heartily welcomed. Ivan introduced him to his wife, Tatiana, their daughters, Maria (19 years) and Kornella (13), and son Michal (11). To the younger seven-year-old son, Leon, Kalman was introduced as an "uncle."

Before the war the Katz family with their four children had been relatively well to do. Father Mechel was involved in farming, raising cattle, and exports, while mother Gitel ran a general goods store. The family was strictly religious. Relations with local Ukrainians had over the years known its ups and downs – occasional murderous pogroms as well as cordial and even friendly relations. Kalman remembered how during the 1930s Ukrainians on the way to church would greet the Katzes with a loud "good morning," but on their way home some would throw rocks at them or scream, "Jews go to Palestine."

A month after the Germans occupied Brzuchowice – on July 15, 1941– local Ukrainians had burned down the town's biggest synagogue. Kalman remembered one particularly horrific incident, when rioters grabbed three Jews from the street, two of them children of the famed Hasidic rabbi from Belz, and threw them into the fire – alive. Rumor had it that the Belzer Rebbe himself was for a brief spell hidden in the home of a Greek Orthodox priest – Father Kovch. "I knew him personally because I had gone to school with his son." This priest reportedly also saved other Jews.

That same night, when Kalman arrived at the Kacherovski farmstead, Ivan and Kalman began digging a bunker in the stable, where the pigs were kept. They worked through the night, preparing a pit, about one meter in length and width and slightly less than that in depth – barely enough for one person in a crouching position. They spread the excavated earth outside under the manure so that it would not be seen. The entrance into the bunker was from under the trough where the pigs ate. The pit was covered with heavy logs hidden from view by a layer of manure. A small, camouflaged vent allowed for some fresh air to enter. This barely habitable hole in the ground was where Kalman was to stay during daylight hours.

For the evenings Ivan prepared another hiding place for Kalman. This was on top of the stable where he kept the hay in the loft. There were three large buildings on his property all stacked with hay to feed the cattle during the long winter. Kalman's hiding place was in the first building facing the main road, right at the end where the cows were kept. When one looked up from below, one could not tell that there was an opening, as the hay hung down from the loft covering it up. "I stayed in hiding for over two years. It is very hard to understand, to imagine, how a human being could sit in a hiding place, in a bunker or a hayloft, day and night for such a long time. The will to live is very strong."

Ivan's wife, Tatiana, fed Kalman three times a day. Little Leon would see his mother putting food in a bucket and taking it to the barn. "For who are you carrying food in a bucket to the stable," he would ask? "For the geese," she answered with a smile. It was customary among local people to fatten the geese for the Easter or Christmas feasts. "Do the geese also eat with a spoon?" Leon then asked. "Sometimes they do," his mother replied, her face getting red. "Mum," Leon said, "I know everything. My uncle is in there, but don't worry, I won't tell anyone."

As for the rest of Kalman's family, his father was hiding with a local farmer and his sisters hid in the forest, where they were joined by Kalman's mother and brother. For a time, sister Sara stayed in the barn with Kalman, unbeknownst to Ivan – her brother Lieber having brought her from the forest lair because of the extreme cold there. She then decided to return to be with the rest of the family in the forest. "I never saw her again," Kalman sadly wrote.

Ivan dropped over to see Kalman every day, sometimes even twice a day, and talk with him, at times for hours, bringing him up to date on current events. "Ivan always kept my spirits up. He told me not to worry, that it was only a matter of time, and that one day Hitler would get his just reward. He would repeat to me a folk saying, "He who flies too high must fall down; it's only a matter of time." He was always optimistic and he gave me hope and courage to carry on and survive.

Then an event occurred that Kalman would remember for the rest of his life. It was in June or July 1943, after most of the Jews hiding in the village had been murdered, that the local mayor dropped in to see Ivan Kacherovski. He held in his hand a list with names, which he pointed at Ivan, saying to him, "I have been given this list of people suspected of hiding Jews, and your name is on top of the list." Ivan was momentarily taken aback, but then denied that he had any Jews with him. The mayor said that Ukrainian militiamen would be coming the next day to search the village of Kosteniv, as well as Ivan's home, and before leaving added a word of friendly advice, "If you have Jews, tell them to get out for the time being."

That evening Ivan came over to the stable, and after hearing the agreed signal of two coughs, Kalman came down from the hayloft, and Ivan told him of the conversation with the mayor. Kalman asked Ivan what he thought he should do. Ivan nervously puffed on one cigarette after the other. Finally, he said, "Look, I will not tell you what you should do, because if something happens to you, it will be on my conscience for the rest of my life. You will have to make your own decision in this situation. If you want to go into the fields or into the forest, we will provide you with enough food for two-three days, and then you can come back to us after the search. Or if you decide to stay here, make sure you are well hidden. Maybe they will not come." Kalman thought, "If I am caught there, Ivan and his entire family will be destroyed and all his possessions and buildings will be burned." But despite the danger, Kalman's decision was to stay put on the farm, since he feared that if he left it he ran the risk of being caught in the fields by the farmers.

Early the next morning Kalman heard loud voices on the road outside, in German and Ukrainian. "I was at that time hidden in the hay on top of the building. I looked out through the roof, where I used to get air between the straw and I saw two German Gestapo and three Ukrainian police in uniform. They drove straight onto his property and screamed at Mr. Kacherovski, 'Where are the Jews you're hiding here?' I could hear them yelling outside. He answered, 'I have no Jews here, you are welcome to search my place.'" They began to search through all of the buildings on Ivan's property, looking especially for any underground holes. Finally they reached the barn, where Kalman was hidden, and what transpired there is described in precise words by Kalman – when he saw death staring him in the face.

"Leaning against the loft was a tall ladder. Two Ukrainian militiamen climbed the ladder to the loft. One took a pitchfork and began to pitch the hay with the fork. The other began

crawling towards the rear of the building, towards me! I was hiding at the very end of the loft. I could hear them clearly, talking to each other in Ukrainian. One was only two or three meters away from me, and he was crawling right towards me. I held my breath and covered my mouth with my hand. Suddenly I saw his hand reaching towards me, already very close to me. But at this point he stopped. He couldn't see me sitting in the corner on the floor, covered with only a handful of hay. Suddenly I heard him say to the other militia-man, in Ukrainian, 'Tut zhydiv nema' ('There are no Jews here'). You can imagine how I was feeling. All he needed to do was take one more step or push down hard on the hay, and he would have discovered me. This was the most frightening moment of my life, to see the angel of death in front of me. That would not only have been the end of me, but the end of the entire Kacherovski family as well."

After about an hour and a half the armed men left the property to continue their search in other places. That day 11 Jews were caught in the village and all were taken out and shot.

In September 1943, Kalman's father came to join him. He had been hiding in the same village with a Polish farmer. However, due to the internecine strife between Poles and Ukrainians at the time, Mechel Katz had to leave his benefactor's home. Ivan readily welcomed him. As for mother Gitel, she was still in the forest with her two daughters and son Lieber.

The Red Army was steadily approaching, and in March 1944 the important city of Ternopol fell into their hands. Liberation was at hand, but one still had to remain vigilant against local armed men who did not give up the hunt for Jews in the forests. Such a tragedy struck the Katz family. That same month, a group of armed Ukrainians discovered a large group of 74 Jews in the Ostalowice forest and proceeded to murder them all. Among the victims were Kalman's two sisters and brother. Mother Gitel happened to be outside that particular forest lair, and when she heard the shooting she quickly lay down and hid among the bushes. She was the only survivor.

Late that night, she came rushing in from the forest to Kalman's hideout with the terrible news. "She came straight into the barn crying, 'We have lost our children.'... I lost my two sisters, Lea, Sara, my brother Lieber and other relatives. This was on March 7, 1944. My mother, father and I sat huddled together all night in the barn crying. When Tatiana Kacherovski came in, she too began to cry."

Ivan assured them that he would shelter them until liberation and he kept his word. In mid-July 1944 the Russians occupied the village of Kosteniv. Kalman learned that 30 more Jews had hidden in the village but were discovered and murdered. He and his parents were the only survivors.

In 1948, Kalman Katz and his family migrated to Australia, and from there remained in very close contact the Kacherovski family. "Those people were real *Tsaddikim* (righteous person)," Kalman Katz pointed out. "Ivan acted entirely out of good will – no money, no reward, he wanted nothing." Just to save them!

In 1983, Yad Vashem recognized Ivan and Tatiana Kacherovski as Righteous Among the Nations.

Karski, Jan

POLAND

*A*s he sat riveted to his chair in a dark, secret room in the non-Jewish section of Warsaw, Jan Karski was stunned by the impassioned words of his two Jewish interlocutors:

"You other Poles are fortunate. You are suffering too. Many of you will die, but at least your nation goes on living. After the war Poland will be resurrected. Your cities will be rebuilt and your wounds will slowly heal. From this ocean of tears, pain, rage, and humiliation your country will emerge again but the Polish Jews will no longer exist. We will be dead.

Hitler will lose his war against the human, the just, and the good, but he will win his war against the Polish Jews. No – it will not be a victory; the Jewish people will be murdered … Our entire people will be destroyed. A few may be saved, perhaps, but three million Polish Jews are doomed."

It was the summer of 1942, and Karski was preparing for another dangerous journey to England on behalf of the Polish underground. That summer, as the extermination of the Jewish population in Poland reached a crescendo, with thousands of Warsaw Jews taken by train to the Treblinka killing site to be gassed and burned upon arrival, Karski was instructed by the underground to meet secretly with two leaders of the stricken Warsaw Ghetto Jewish community (they are assumed to have been Menachem Kirschenbaum, representing a Zionist faction, and Leon Feiner, a leader of the Socialist Bund movement), outside the ghetto perimeter, in order to relay a message from them to the Polish government-in-exile in London.

Jan Karski

When he met the two leaders, as related by Karski in his 1944 account, "The first thing that became clear to me as I sat there talking to them in the silence of the darkening Warsaw suburb was the complete hopelessness of their predicament." The two leaders were telling Karski that the German extermination of over three million Polish Jews spelled the end of close to one thousand years of the Jewish presence on Polish soil. Asked by Karski what could be done to stop this unprecedented orgy of murder, his interlocutors were at a loss for words. They then ventured the suggestion that if Jewish leaders were to stage a hunger strike in front of the government offices of the English and American authorities, perhaps this would move the leaders of the free world to take some action. Karski sank into his armchair and began to shake uncontrollably. He had not been prepared for such a bleak prognosis and could take no more. As he rose to go, he was stopped by one of the two leaders, who told him, "We did not intend to tell you, but I want you to know ... The ghetto is going to go up in flames. We are not going to die in slow torment but fighting. We will declare war on Germany – the most hopeless declaration of war that has ever been made."

Born in 1914 as Jan Koželewski, Karski had studied law at a Lwów university, hoping to enter his country's diplomatic service. Mobilized by the Polish army at the start of World War II, he was taken prisoner by the Soviets but made his escape and returned to the German-occupied part of Poland and joined the underground. He was assigned as a courier on missions to the Polish government-in-exile in London. To get there, he had to travel through Slovakia, Hungary, and other countries, and for this purpose he chose a new code name for himself – Karski – the name under which he would be known thereafter.

Fearing that his report on the murder of the Jewish population would be received with disbelief, Karski asked to be smuggled inside the Warsaw ghetto to be able to see with his own eyes the mass roundup of Jews there. Still not fully satisfied, Karski asked to be smuggled into one of the camps where the Jews were being moved in cattle cars. Dressed in the uniform of one of the Latvian guards who formed a contingent guarding some of the camps, Karski again witnessed from a safe distance the brutality that accompanied the unloading of Jews from the deportation trains.

Five weeks later, he was in London. As expected, his words were received politely but with skepticism and incredulity. The human mind could not fathom a horror tale encompassing the murder of a whole people by another people – hitherto considered very civilized – for no other reason than having been born. Szmul Zygelbojm, the Bund representative in London, was, however, not surprised at Karski's ghastly report. Karski relayed to him the appeal by the trapped Jewish leaders to world Jewish leaders to stage a hunger strike in front of offices of the major chancelleries of the West. "This may shake the conscience of the world," Karski repeated the words of the two Polish Jewish leaders. At this, Zygelbojm snapped: "It is utterly impossible. You know what would happen. They would simply bring in two policemen and have me dragged away to an institution." The two shook hands and parted. Several weeks later, Zygelbojm committed suicide. Karski was informed that Zygelbojm left a note saying that having failed to save his brethren in Poland, he had decided to join them. Karski was terribly shaken. "Of all the deaths that have taken place in this war, surely Zygelbojm's is one of the most frightening," Karski stated in his book, written one year after this tragic event; "the sharpest revelation of the extent to which the world has become cold and unfriendly, nations and individuals separated by immense gulfs of indifference, selfishness, and convenience." In June 1943, Karski met Anthony Eden, the British Foreign Minister, who told him that Great Britain had already done enough by accepting thousands of refugees.

Shaken but still resolved to carry the message of Polish Jewry to the United States, Karski rearranged his priorities. His urgent calls to stop the Holocaust had taken preference over his other assignments for the Polish underground. A new mission was born. He continued on to the United States, where he arrived in July 1943, and was allowed to meet with President Roosevelt, who listened attentively to Karski's narration of events inside Poland. But when it came to the Jewish part, Karski felt that what he was saying had fallen on deaf ears. Karski told Roosevelt, "The Jewish leaders are totally helpless. The Poles can save only individuals, they cannot stop extermination. Only the powerful Allied leaders can do that." Roosevelt avoided the Jewish issue and closed the one-and-a-half-hour meeting with an assurance that the Poles had a friend in the White House; that the guilty ones would be punished, and that justice and freedom would prevail. Karski also met with the American Jewish leader and Supreme Court Justice Felix Frankfurter. When Karski finished, Frankfurter said: "I am unable to believe you."

Not yet completely discouraged, Karski continued to address audiences and plead for the rescue of Jews. His articles appeared in many publications, such as *Life*, *The New York Times*, and the *Jewish Forward*. "I traveled all over the United States, delivering over two hundred lectures. His book *Story of a Secret State*, published in 1944, became a Book-of-the-Month-Club selection. But frustration soon took over, as he realized that all he was getting was applause, not action. The vision of the terrified Jews in Poland kept haunting him. As his cover was no longer a secret, he could not return to Poland and remained in the United States. In 1952, he earned a doctorate at Georgetown University, where he taught political science, and visited various African and Asian countries on behalf of the State Department. In 1965, he married Pola Nirenska, a former Jewish dancer whose family had perished in the Holocaust. The Holocaust was a forgotten subject for him – buried deep in his subconscious. As he told the *Baltimore Sun* many years later, "I wanted to run away after the war … I saw too much misery, hatred, ruthlessness, human losses. I saw horrible things. What I learned from the war made me silent for 30 years." Then, in 1980, Nobel Prize laureate Elie Wiesel persuaded him to break his silence. In October 1981, he addressed a Holocaust conference in Washington, and the audience was spellbound. There were tears when he described the Warsaw Ghetto in its death throes.

From then on, he appeared in public on numerous occasions. He explained his decades-long silence about the pain caused to him by the silence of world leaders at the massacre of the Jews. "All those great individuals, presidents, ambassadors, cardinals, who said they were shocked; they lied. They knew or didn't want to know. This shocked me. I didn't want to have anything to do with it. I said to myself, 'Karski, you are helpless. Give up the subject.'" He also said: "I have a feeling that the Jews had bad luck with me. They charged me with this terrible mission... I was on hand. For the enormity of my Jewish mission, I was too insignificant to make an impression." As reported by Elie Wiesel, "He is a man of absolute integrity, of extraordinary force of character. But I had the feeling from the moment I met him that he was a wounded person; that he carried secret, invisible wounds in him ... I think that he feels that he failed."

In 1982, Yad Vashem conferred on Jan Karski the title of Righteous Among the Nations. This was followed in 1994 with honorary Israeli citizenship. Responding to the award presentation by the Israeli ambassador, Karski made a personal profession of faith:

"This is the proudest and the most meaningful day in my life. Through the honorary citizenship of the State of Israel, I have reached the spiritual source of my Christian faith. In a way, I also became a part of the Jewish community … Since the early days of my high school in Łódz, I have been getting understanding, friendship or help from the Jews. Now, they took me in. Now, I, Jan Karski – by birth Kożelewski – a Pole, an American, a Catholic,

have also become an Israelite! Gloria, Gloria *in excelsis Deo. Our Lord revealed Himself to many nations in His own ways, but always with the same commandment – Love Thy Neighbor ... He endowed us with a free will. We have infinite capacity to do good, and an infinite capacity to be evil."*

After that, Karski spoke on many occasions of the phenomenon of antisemitism, which he described as rooted in people's feelings of inferiority and insecurity – and especially jealousy at the prominence attained by Jews through the centuries in the fields of science, literature, medicine, philosophy, and economy. As for the uniqueness of the Holocaust, Karski stated emphatically that admittedly not only Jews suffered but other nations suffered as well – such as the Poles and Russians who lost millions during World War II. In fact, all nations under Nazi domination had victims. However, the major difference is that "all Jews were victims." Only Jews were singled out for destruction; other groups were allowed to survive, although with a lower status than the Aryan "super-race." "Let, therefore, no nation, no government, no church appropriate this sacred, this cursed theme. Holocaust is Jewish."

When, in 1981, he first spoke again on the Holocaust after a long silence, Jan Karski said that as a practicing Catholic he considered the Holocaust mankind's Second Original Sin. He added, "This sin will haunt humanity to the end of time. It does haunt me. And I want it to be so." At the same time, Karski warned against instilling in the minds of listeners a message of hopelessness that will cause them to lose faith in humanity; especially in the case of Jewish children, who will be led to think that "everybody hates us ... everybody was against us, so I must be only for myself." Karski warned not to cause them to lose faith in humanity. The underlying message should always remain the biblical teaching of "Love your neighbor as yourself." In 2000, Jan Karski died, at age 86.

Kaszuba, Stanislaw & wife
Stefan, Ryszard & Daniela
POLAND

*I*n 1993, the four Shore children, Philip (born 1917), Sara (1922), Nachum (1930), and Abraham (1933), wrote to Yad Vashem about their miraculous rescue by the Kaszuba family.

The Szoors (spelling at the time) lived in Chmielnik in the Kielce district of central Poland, a bustling commercial center and home to a large Jewish population of about 10,000. The Szoors were among the town's more affluent and respected residents. Father Natan David was a very pious and prominent merchant who owned a wholesale tobacco business that served the entire vicinity. His wife Alte Rifka, mother of eight children, also worked in her husband's business, affording him time to fulfill the religious duties of an extremely Orthodox Jew, which included prayer and Torah study.

Natan David Szoor got to know Stanislaw Kaszuba, who had lost a leg fighting in World War I and had been granted a tobacco license by the government as a reward for his military service. He held this license for the Szoor business, since no such permits were granted to Jews. "They had a warm relationship of mutual respect. When our father built a house for us in town he also built a house for the Kaszuba family in the village where they lived, named Zudów." It was help that would later be repaid many times over.

A few days after the Germans invaded Poland on September 1, 1939, they assembled 30 Chmielnik Jewish community leaders and burned them alive in the synagogue. A ghetto was established in April 1941 and with the arrival of refugees the ghetto population rose to 11,000. But this was a temporary respite, as the mass shootings began in 1942, followed by deportations of the ghetto population to the Treblinka death camp.

On one such occasion, in the fall of 1942, the Germans announced that all Jews in Chmielnik were to assemble on the following Tuesday in the center of town. Stanislaw Kaszuba came to see his friend Natan David on the Sabbath before the roundup and told him that he had heard rumors that all the Jews were going to be taken to their deaths. He told Szoor that he had arranged a hiding place in the annex to his house and that he would welcome anyone from the family. Natan David thanked Stanislaw for this gracious offer, but said he would not desecrate the Sabbath but would wait until nightfall to take up Kaszuba's invitation. Stanislaw agreed to come back with a wagon after dark to take the Szoor family. At nightfall the Szoor parents and their seven unmarried children, aged 9 to 24, and a nephew who lived next door along with his fiancé, all piled into the wagon. "We were covered by blankets," the four Shoor children recalled.

Arriving in the dead of night in Kaszuba's village, Kaszuba hurriedly moved his guests to a room attached to the main house but having a separate entrance. It was small place with a single couch and no plumbing facilities. Stanislaw and his eldest son, Stefan, dug out a space under the house with a trap door leading to the Szoors' room, from which they could escape in case of an emergency. The Kaszuba children helped out by bringing whatever food they could spare twice a day – mostly bread and potatoes. They bought the extra food at various locations, for they could not risk being seen shopping for this many extra people in one store.

After about one month, Stanislaw Kaszuba brought news of a German announcement that enough Jews had been taken away to camps as laborers, and the remaining Jews who were in hiding could safely return to the town and would be left alone. He warned, however, that the Germans were not to be trusted, and the Szoor matron, Alte Rifka, agreed with him. But Natan David, who was by nature a very trusting man, wanted very much to return to his home and to the synagogue that he missed so much. In his children's words, "He felt strongly that we must place our faith in God." The Szoors thanked their rescuers profusely and returned to Chmielnik. As they left, Stanislaw Kaszuba reminded them of his open invitation to them to return to him if anything should go wrong.

Something did go wrong when after a few days the returning Jews were herded into a big warehouse, lined up, and loaded on wagons. The Szoor family were among the hundreds of Jews that the Germans assembled in Chmielnik on November 5, 1942, for the second deportation, including Natan David, Alte Rifka, their daughters Yona and Sarah, sons Abraham and Nachum, and son-in-law Yoel Zilberberg.

Natan David with the two youngest, Bracha and Tova, were put in a different wagon from his wife. They were never heard from again, having probably been taken to Treblinka to the gassed. As for Alte Rifka, the man who drove her wagon turned out to have been a customer of her husband's. Because of his respect for the Szoors, he warned them that they were being taken to their death and that, consequently, they should try to escape. When the convoy passed the first village, some jumped off the wagon, including Alte's daughter and son-in-law. The wagon driver continued to urge the rest of the Szoors to run for their lives, and he turned a blind eye as they jumped off. Alte Rifka and her two children ran to the nearest woods as they heard shots fired at others who had fled. Late at night, Mrs. Szoor and her sons left the woods for the main road. A Pole they met took them into his hut and later brought them to a certain village where another Pole fed them and went to Chmielnik to see what the state of affairs was. He returned with news that some of the Szoors had made it back to town.

Two days later, the Pole led Mrs. Szoor and her sons back to Chmielnik, where Szoor met her other three children. Quite coincidentally, Szoor's nephew, Leib Kozlowski, ran into Stanislaw Kaszuba in the local market, where Leib was wandering aimlessly, and when Stanislaw heard that some of the Szoors were in town he decided to take them to his home under the cover of darkness. The Szoors and Kozlowkis, numbering eight persons, were taken into Kaszuba's home and put into the small room in the annex.

The eight fugitives spent the next 27 months under the protection of the Kaszuba family. "We never left the tiny room, and we rarely opened the windows. At night, we never turned on the lights for fear that this would arouse suspicion. Although the family must have been as terrified as we were, they never stopped protecting us, feeding us what they could, bringing us water with which to wash, removing our human waste in a pail." Taking additional risks upon himself, although illiterate, Stanislaw Kaszuba bought a newspaper for his charges' sake, telling his neighbors as an excuse that he liked to look at the pictures. His young children were warned of the dangers of telling their friends of the eight people hiding in the room attached to their house, and they kept the secret. Mrs. Kaszuba cooked whatever she could spare and also washed the fugitives' clothes. How did they spend their time over this long period? As told by the four Szoor-Shore children:

> "We passed our time playing cards, praying, reminiscing about what life was like before. We lived in constant terror that we would be discovered. Stanislaw would occasionally warn us to go in our underground hole so that he could invite people to come into the room in which we were normally hidden. In this way he diverted any suspicion that neighbors might have about this hiding place. On one occasion he heard that a neighbor had seen a hand in the window in our room. Kaszuba invited her over shortly thereafter, and asked her to come into the room to help him choose a paint color. After looking around, she returned home satisfied that we were not there."

While the woman's suspicions were stilled, danger lurked from another and more threatening direction – from armed men. One day, 18 members of the A.K., the Polish underground, burst into the Kaszuba home looking for the Szoor family, as Kaszuba was known to have befriended them. They threatened to shoot everyone unless Kaszuba told them where the Jews were hiding. When he denied having any knowledge of the Szoors, they beat him mercilessly, as well his wife, his sons, and his daughter Daniela, but the Kaszubas kept quiet. The armed men searched for six hours and came near the trap door, covered with a rug, leading to the underground bunker where the eight people were huddling in fear, but they did not discover the entrance and left.

Some time later, Kaszuba was visited by another group of armed men. Stanislaw wept as he told them he had no Jews in his house; in fact, he added, he had never liked Jews. He was after all an amputee, and asked for their mercy. They searched his house and after finding nothing they left. The Kaszuba daughter Daniela continued to bring a bowl of soup to the bunker every day.

Alte Rifka Szoor related that because of the Kaszubas' fear of detection, Daniela became less friendly toward them and the Szoors began to receive less food. One night, Alte Rifka saw her husband in a dream, and she told him the children were hungry. Natan David told her to plead with Stanislaw Kaszuba for extra food, with the promise that he would be rewarded for this after the war. At dawn, Stanislaw appeared and told Alte Rifka that her husband had appeared to him in a dream and begged him to look after his family. The coincidence of these two dreams has remained a mystery to both families. At any rate, from then on, the whole Kaszuba family remained dedicated to the welfare of the Jews in their care. The Szoor-Shore children emphasized, "We can never forget the special kindness, the extra potato to keep us from being hungry, the moments of conversation to reduce our boredom, the water and soap lugged in by the children so that we could wash."

The last ten days of hiding were possibly the worst. As the Germans retreated they passed through the village. Coming upon the Kaszuba house, they told Stanislaw that they needed a storeroom and that they were taking over the room that was attached to the house. Stanislaw immediately warned his wards to go underground through the trap door, minutes before the Germans entered that room, and piled it up to the ceiling with supplies. When they found a *Siddur* (Hebrew prayer book) that Mrs. Szoor had accidentally left behind, Stanislaw cleverly told the Germans that it must have been a souvenir that the children picked up somewhere.

The fugitives huddled in the underground hiding place for some time, until Stanislaw and his son Stefan managed to dig a hole in the side of the foundation wall to let them out. Stanislaw then snuck them over to his barn across the yard, where they hid in a loft for the last ten days of the German occupation. Then Kaszuba's concealed the place occupied by the fugitives with a pile of manure and moved the ducks there. Liberation came on January 13, 1945, when the Russians entered the village.

Forty survivors returned to Chmielnik after the war. Among these very few survivors were the eight Jews of the Szoor and Kozlowski families, sheltered for 27 months by the Kaszuba family. As antisemitism had resurfaced in Chmielnik and the Kielce vicinity, and the surviving Jews no longer felt safe among local inhabitants, the few remaining survivors left Chmielnik, leaving the town empty of all Jews – a place where Jews had lived uninterruptedly for 700 years, since the 13th century.

In 1993, Yad Vashem recognized the five Kaszubas, parents and three children, as Righteous Among the Nations.

Kiselev, Nikolai

BELARUS

*A*s the battle of Stalingrad was raging in the summer and fall of 1942, pitting several million Russian, Ukrainian, German, Italian, Romanian, and Hungarian soldiers against each other, but mainly Russian against German forces, in a contest that was to mark a turning point in the war – some 800 kilometers to north of the embattled city a drama of much smaller scale was unfolding. A lone partisan commander was leading a group of largely destitute Jewish escapees from German killing raids in a long trek extending hundreds of kilometers, through forbidden terrain in an area held by massive German forces, in an effort to reach safety behind Russian lines.

At the start of the war between Germany and the Soviet Union, on June 22, 1941, Nikolai Kiselev was drafted into the Red Army. In October 1941, when his unit was surrounded by rapidly moving German forces, he was taken prisoner. He managed to hide the fact that he was a member of the Communist Party, which would have doomed him immediately in accordance with Hitler's orders to execute all such personnel. After a few days in captivity, he managed to escape. He wandered through the Belarus region until he arrived in the town of Iliya in the Minsk region, where he found work.

Then he began to organize groups of former Soviet soldiers for clandestine activity and established contact with partisan units that had begun to operate in the region. In May 1942, he joined the "Vengeance" group headed by a certain Voronyanski. His assignment was to assemble Jewish families and individuals who had escaped from Nazi killing raids and were wandering in the forest with no purpose or destination in mind. Some of them were able to get a hold of vintage arms, which they used to raid local farms for food and occasional overnight shelter. The purpose of assembling the Jews was to put a stop to the raids on local farmers, who complained to the partisan commands, some of the raids being perpetrated by organized bandits.

During the summer of 1942, Kiselev was able to assemble close to 300 men from among these forest wanderers, most of them Jews – survivors of German killing raids in Dolhinov in the western extreme of Belarus. On March 28, 1942, the Germans had gunned down some 1,500 Jews in the town's market square and confined the rest to a ghetto. Another 1,200 were executed on May 5 and a further 300 skilled workers on May 22 of that year. The rest had escaped to the forest in the hope of joining the partisans, where they ran into other Jews who had also fled from the towns of Ilya and Borisov – they too survivors of German extermination raids, and had brought along their families, including women, children, the old and the sick. The younger and able-bodied among them were able to take up arms and conducted an armed struggle from the depths of the forests while at the same time tending to the needs of their noncombatant loved ones.

These wandering Jewish bands tried in vain to affiliate with local partisan bands but were turned down by them, since they felt that the noncombatants among these people would hinder the strictly military nature of the partisan activity, not to mention having to care for their day-to-day needs. An additional worry was that in the event of the capture of one of the unarmed people in the group, he or she might give away the partisans' location. It is small wonder that other partisan units in the area considered unarmed Jews an unnecessary burden to be avoided. There were also partisan units that had been infected with the anti-semitic virus and on principle refused to take on even able-bodied and armed Jewish men and women.

While Nikolai Kiselev was pondering what to do with the mixed crowd in his hands, in August 1942 he was ordered to remove the whole group to the rear, which was hundreds of kilometers away. As he started to move out, on August 26, 1942, his group and the other partisans in the area came under German attack. Kiselev ordered the armed men to try to break through the German ring, while the unarmed people were to disperse in the forest and find shelters for themselves. He also told them to reassemble at a designated place in order to continue, or rather start, their long march toward the rear. After four days, with the siege and encirclement over, 218 people showed up.

As it turned out, Kiselev had not been told by the partisan command to take the women and children along, but he had decided on his own not to abandon the noncombatants in his group. Not asking for precise instructions with regard to the women, children and el-derly with him, he would not countenance leaving them behind to an unknown, or perhaps too well known, fate. His guiding principle was to leave no one behind – combatant and noncombatant alike, including the sick among them, even knowing that that this would seriously slow them down.

Led by Kiselev, the people usually marched only at night, until two in the morning. From then until nightfall, Kiselev and his men rested and gathered food for everyone for the con-tinuation of the march. Some villagers were not too happy to share their food with fleeing Jews, and Kiselev had to force them to be generous.

Another problem was that some of the people fell ill and had to be carried. Kiselev insisted that no one was to be left behind – the sick and the exhausted included, as before each march, a roll call was taken, and when someone did not answer to his or her name Kiselev directed his people to see to the missing person. Among the marchers was the Jewish Kremer couple with their four-year-old daughter, who cried a lot, as she was hungry. Her crying endangered the others, to the point that some demanded that she be done away with one way or another. When Kiselev learned about this, he went and got the child and for part of the march carried her in his arms and fed her from his own ration. The girl and parents survived. He then car-ried some of the other small children on his back, so that their parents could keep up.

There was also the case of one-legged Yakov Rubin. He too was not left behind. Or the el-derly Kugel, who lost his way in the forest. Kiselev stopped the rest and went out to look for him and found him. Kiselev went even further than this. Shifra Zamkov told of one man, Melech Kuzinits, who had left his prayer shawl (*tallit*) and phylacteries (*tefillin*) behind in a certain village. Fearing that this loss would hamper the man's marching ability, Kiselev sent out men to retrieve the religious articles.

Moving with his group of mostly noncombatant people on the long trek to the rear, he did not lead them in a straight line that would have shortened the route but involved too many risks. The approximately 500-kilometer distance to the rear was thereby extended by several hundred kilometers. The group zigzagged through rivers (crossing the Dvina River twice), forests and open fields, trails and side roads, and guarded railroad tracks. "On many occasions," Natan and Yitzhak Kuzinits noted in their postwar account, "we found ourselves sleeping while walking." On the way, they were exposed to sudden fire by German troops, and some were killed in these exchanges. The march that had begun on September 1, 1942, reached its destination on November 25, 1942 – in the contested Toropets area near the city of Velikiye Luki in Russia proper. The people led by Kiselev were at the end of their strength – especially the old people and the children. The totally exhausted and undernourished fugitives, trembling from the extreme Russian cold gold, fell into a long sleep but were soon awakened by a German attack, which forced them to get back on their feet and flee the area.

Finally, they were allowed to board trains to be taken further to the interior. Kiselev accompanied some of the people for part of the trip. In their new, but temporary, locations, too, they faced the hardships of a country at war, in subzero weather (reaching 40 centigrade below zero) and not always receiving a friendly reception from local inhabitants, not a few who took umbrage at having Jews in their midst. But at least they were alive. The young and able-bodied were drafted into the army.

Kiselev's group of men, women, and children had reached safety barely three days after Soviet forces had encircled the German and allied troops in the Battle of Stalingrad, which had raged since August 21 and which eventually led to a total German defeat in that sector and signaled a turning point in the war. The German forces vainly tried to break out of the ring and finally surrendered on February 2, 1943. It was a major defeat.

While the Battle of Stalingrad was raging to the south, Nikolai Kiselev had led a ragged band of over 200 Jews, most of them noncombatants and escapees from German liquidation raids, bypassing many German troop concentrations, and after a two and half months, in a trek, extending over hundreds of kilometers, had made it to safety. It was a unique and singular feat. Partisan commander Nikolai Kiselev had insisted that all in his group, the able-bodied and the weak, the young and the old – children as well as adults, the healthy and the sick – all continue together, and he succeeded in that courageous and heroic endeavor.

In 2005 Yad Vashem recognized Nikolai Kiselev as Righteous Among the Nations.

Koen, Peter & Elizabeth, Peter & Joke
NETHERLANDS

*F*ive-year-old Dina Dasberg was surprised by the young man standing in front of her; she had never seen him before. Turning to Dina's mother, he spoke only a few words, "I've come to take the girl." The mother was not surprised at all. In fact, she had arranged the man's visit to take Dina out of their deportation-threatened home in Amsterdam and to a better and safer location. It was January 1943, and the preceding fall Dina had lost her father, who was arrested as he stepped out of the synagogue after the Yom Kippur eve prayer. He was never seen again, having perished in the Sobibor death camp in faraway Poland.

The link with 18-year-old Peter Koen was arranged by Margaret Buscher, a Jewish refugee from Germany who had rented a room from the Dasbergs. She had made contact with an underground man named De Pouw. This man was the head of a teachers' seminar and one of his students was Peter Koen, who lived with his parents, Peter and Elizabeth, and his sister Joke in Haarlem. Peter was also deeply involved in clandestine work and when Buscher told him of Mrs. Dasberg's predicament, he agreed to pick up little Dina and take her with him to his parents' home. Dina's mother filled a suitcase, including the child's toys and also a few apples, and sent her daughter off with this stranger. Peter took her that evening by train to Haarlem. There, things almost went awry. Peter had not told his parents about the new addition to the family – and a Jewish girl to boot. It was a Sunday, and the devout Calvinist parents were at church. When they returned that evening, the Koens were surprised, even shocked, when Peter presented Dina before them. Dina remained glued to her chair as she watched Mrs. Elizabeth Koen almost have a fit. She screamed at her son. He replied that after hearing her say that something must to be done to help the Jews, who were being deported, he decided to take his mother at her word, and here was one threatened Jewish child needing protection.

After the parents calmed down, their attitude changed for the better. "Soon they were good to me," Dina recalls. This was especially so with regard to Peter's sister, 20-year-old Joke, who made Dina her special ward. The father was mostly away at work, filling a clerical position in a firm producing cocoa. Dina stayed in the Koen home until the country's liberation in May 1945 – a full 16 months. She was given a new name, Dientje Stein, and represented as an orphan of the devastating air raid on Rotterdam at the start of the war. She attended school as well as joining the Koens for services in church, but they honored the promise made to her mother not to have her baptized, even if this meant she would not survive.

Occasionally, when there was danger of her discovery, she was moved to another location for a temporary stay, such as with Mrs. Koen's sister in Utrecht; then returned to the Koens. At times, it was too late to move Dina elsewhere, as the Germans carried out sudden inspections in homes, but fortunately for Dina they paid no special attention to her. The danger for the Koens also stemmed from the fact that a Nazi collaborator lived across the street from them. It was a quiet street, so any new resident was immediately noticed. No money was exchanged between the Koens and Dina's mother, who sought shelter elsewhere. At a later stage, Dina's mother was also taken in by the Koens. She was hidden in an out of the way place in the house, kept hidden not only from outsiders but also from her daughter, Dina, for fear that Dina would inadvertently disclose her presence to outsiders. At a later stage, mother and daughter were allowed to see each other again. Dina's older brother, Haim, also stayed there for a while, such as in November 1943, when the Koen home served as a transit point for a group of Jews who were to be sent to northern Holland to be hidden, including Haim Dasberg. As for the young Peter, he was away from home much of the time due to his involvement in underground work. One evening he came home with a bullet wound. A doctor was summoned late at night to remove the bullet from his arm.

During the terrible "hunger winter" of 1944/45, when people starved to death for lack of food, Joke went on long bike trips to Friesland in the north to sell household goods in return for food. Haim Dasberg, today a professor of psychiatry, described the Koens as courageous people, adding: "They saved; they are saints."

In her testimony to Yad Vashem, Dina Dasberg, today Shapira, revealed a dramatic side-light to her story that occurred before she reached her rescuers' home. "In fact," she stated, "my life was saved even before I came to the Koen family," and she went on to explain. It happened in the fall or late summer of 1942. There was a German roundup of Jews on her Amsterdam street. Sensing the approaching danger, her mother had sent her away with two non-Jewish women and their children to play with them. "We sat in a sandy playground near our street .... Suddenly German armored cars raced by with soldiers in it. The two mothers took fright and got their children, and told me: go home, and they left. I was then four years old, and I went home, a few hundred meters away." As the street became filled with German armored vans, Dina went upstairs to her house and rang the doorbell, but there was no answer (afterwards she learned that her mother and brother were on the roof). Returning to the street, she stood frozen in her place and watched the roundup of the Jews by the Germans and noted their green-brown uniforms. She heard a great deal of screaming and crying. As she stood alone, frightened and weeping, a German soldier, SS or otherwise, suddenly came up to her. "He asked where I lived? I showed him. He went up the stairs with me and told me to wait at the end of the hall; not to go down nor leave until the street was totally silent. I did so. I don't know how long I stood there. When everything was over, I knocked on the door, and there was great agitation, for they had thought that I was in a safe place with the gentile friends of my mother. This SS man had saved my life, half a year before I came to the Koen family … Thanks to this brave man, I remained alive and later arrived at the Koen family."

As for Dina's Dutch rescuers, in 2003 Yad Vashem conferred the Righteous title upon Peter and Elizabeth Koen as well as their children Peter and Joke.

Korpershoek, Hein
Florissen, Wibo
Netherlands

"*I* have often wondered what became of the little girl we saved, but so far I have resisted the temptation to try and find out." So wrote Hein Robert Korpershoek in 1985 in Rio de Janeiro to the Israel consul-general there. Korpershoek had been happily settled in Brazil for many years, and just recently had received an invitation to attend an exhibit by the *Rijksmuseum* (National Museum), in Amsterdam, of the posters and pamphlets produced by him during World War II for the Dutch underground. At this crossroads of his life, events of the war years, 40 years earlier, resurfaced in his mind and brought up memories of his underground work, and he suddenly became fixated on an unusual incident – how he and a colleague had saved a little Jewish girl from the Nazi grips – virtually at the twelfth hour. What had become of her, he asked himself?

Hein Robert Korpershoek

The little information he had been able to gather was that the girl had been taken to Israel after the war by her parents. Could the Israel consul help locate her, he asked in his letter, and perhaps obtain from her documents and photos from that period, which he would gladly add to the exhibit to take place in Amsterdam very soon, since, as he further explained, the story of that child far outweighed in emotional terms any other activity of his during the war years? "I would be most grateful," Korpershoek concluded his letter, "if you, through official Israeli channels or otherwise, would be willing and able to help me in this quest."

Without knowing the girl's name and what had become of her, Korpershoek was referring to a dramatic episode in his underground activity that began on Sunday, November 28, 1943. On that day, Ans Van Dam, a medical student, whose semi-Jewish background exempted her from deportation, as well as the wearing of the yellow star, was asked by her friends Nathan and Elisheva Dasberg, who were in hiding in Hilversum, to look up their daughter, Miriam, at the private pension in Amsterdam where she had been being placed, and to bring her a gift on her third birthday. Ans had visited the child several times, and also paid the monthly 150 Dutch guldens for the child's upkeep. When she arrived there this time, Ans learned from the pension's headmistress that several days earlier the dreaded Gestapo had raided the establishment and had immediately identified three-year-old Miriam, from her looks, as Jewish. Taking the woman's husband as a hostage with them, they promised to return in a few days to pick up the child. Miriam's life was clearly in danger.

Instead of returning to the Dasbergs with the bad news, Ans van Dam ran over to Mrs. Morling, one of her underground colleagues, and with tears in her eyes frantically pleaded for help to avoid the child's apprehension. It just happened that Wibo Florissen, a 20-year-old Dutch underground operative, was visiting Mrs. Morling and overheard the story. He immediately alerted his 17-year-old colleague, Hein Korpershoek, and both decided on a daring and risky plan to snatch the child before the Nazis could lay their hands on her. Hein Korpershoek, who specialized in the fabrication of documents, immediately got to work and produced identity papers by which he and his friend appeared to be Gestapo agents.

The following day, the two rendezvoused with Ans Van Dam in Amsterdam, not far from the pension, and she was told to wait there as a lookout. The two men then proceeded to the boarding house. It was an early Monday morning, about 7:15 a.m., when Korpershoek and Florissen sporting dark trench coats, as well as Gestapo-style hats pulled down slightly over their foreheads (also meant as to hide Hein's too youthful look), appeared in front of the pension. Furiously banging at the door, they shouted: "Gestapo! Open up!" They quickly flashed their fake credentials in the face of the frightened lady of the house, and pushing their way past her entered the lobby. Some of the adult boarders had gathered for their customary breakfast and were told by the two men to return immediately to their rooms, or else! Shouting and cursing, Hein and Wibo said that, as promised earlier, they had come to pick up the little Jewish "creep." The headmistress was quite surprised, for she had been told that the child would only be picked in several days' time and had been solemnly warned not to give the child up until the Gestapo returned, and began to suspect that the two men standing before her were impostors. Taking no chances, and with her husband held hostage, she decided to phone the German police. Wibo and Hein immediately grabbed the receiver out of her hand and, swearing at her and threatening physical violence, told her they knew perfectly well what game she was playing – she wished to alert her underground friends. Continuing to shout insults and threats, they got the little girl, had her dressed, and immediately whisked her out of the home. Hastening to where Ans Van Dam was tensely waiting, they turned the child over to her and disappeared. The whole operation had barely taken a few minutes. Mission accomplished!

Linocut by Hein Robert Korpershoek, *The Rescue of Mirjam Dasberg*, 1987, showing the rescue of the 3-year old Jewish girl, Mirjam Dasberg (Collection of the Yad Vashem Art Museum)

Hein and Wibo then hurriedly left the place and remained in hiding for a few days. As for little Miriam, she was turned over to the Nabbing family for hiding in Swolgen, southern Limburg province, where she remained until 1945. Back in Amsterdam, when the real Gestapo agents appeared at the pension to claim their prey, they were furious to learn that men of the Dutch underground had outsmarted them and snatched the little Jewish victim from their hands. Under questioning by the Gestapo, the pension mistress mentioned Ans Van Dam as the woman who had visited her prior to the arrival of the two fake Gestapo agents. Ans was eventually traced in Amsterdam and arrested. Under interrogation, she denied any involvement in the child's rescue operation and only admitted having visited the establishment for the monthly payment for the child's upkeep. Asked by the interrogator why she was at all involved in the care of a Jewish child, Ans timidly responded, because of "compassion." To this, the interrogator replied that anyone who has compassion for Jews is invited to join them. For this "compassionate offense" she was ordered deported to Auschwitz. As a medical student, she was assigned work in the camp's so-called infirmary, which helped her survive. From Auschwitz she was moved to Dachau and Kaufering, two other dreadful concentration camps, and luckily survived there too.

In November 1944, Korpershoek, Florissen, and a third man, participated in another rescue attempt of two Jewish children – this time in Rotterdam. The plan miscarried, with the German police giving chase to the men. Four days later, Hein was arrested, but for other reasons, and was able to talk himself out of detention. He continued his underground activity, including the hand printing of anti-Nazi pamphlets that, together with others, he stuck on walls and lampposts. According to Hein's estimate, he must have produced close to a million pamphlets of this kind.

At the end of the war, Miriam's parents came to get her, as well as their other four children, who were also in hiding, and in 1948 the family moved to Israel. Miriam eventually settled on a kibbutz, married, and in 1986 was the mother of six children. Ans van Dam, born to a Jewish father, and to a mother who had converted to Judaism, also moved to Israel, and under her new and Hebraized name of Hanna-Anna, and married to Meir Drukker, made her home in Jerusalem, where she was a practicing physician.

As to Hein Korpershoek's letter to the Israeli consul-general in Rio de Janeiro, the latter was of course ignorant of the child's real name or her parents' name. Dutifully he communicated the request to his colleague in The Hague, who by a stroke of good luck knew of the Dasbergs' move to Israel, and contact was established between both sides within a relatively short period. Writing to Miriam's father, in March 1986, and introducing himself as one of the two men who carried out the rescue operation, Hein Korpershoek underscored the importance he attached to his participation in the rescue of the three-year-old child. "The kidnapping, if I may say so, of your little girl was the peak of my underground activity, and the most cherished memory of a life filled with many nuances and adventures. If anyone should be thankful, it is I myself – for having had the opportunity to carry this out." Hein continued by speaking of his frustration that the Dutch people had not done more to save its Jewish population (close to 80% of which were deported and killed). "I am thankful that I was privileged to erase something of this disgrace."

In 1987, Yad Vashem conferred on Hein Korpershoek and Wibo Florissen the title of Righteous Among the Nations. That same year Korpershoek was also honored in Amsterdam in a special exhibit of his wartime posters and cartoons, organized by the Dutch National Museum and the National Institute for War Documentation. In anticipation of this special exhibit, Korpershoek prepared a hand-printed linoleum cut depicting the rescue of Miriam – a copy of which was made available to Yad Vashem. Rescuer and rescued, living thousands of miles apart, had found each other again, thanks to a fortuitous event – an invitation to an exhibit of wartime posters.

Koźmińska, Teresa
Koźmiński, Jerzy & Karol

POLAND

With fighting raging close by, between Germans and Jews, Samuel Glazer's group of fleeing Jews stole out of the burning Warsaw ghetto, and began to make their way to the home of persons who had promised them help – in the hope that at this desperate moment in the lives of the fugitive Jews, this promise would be kept. Days before that, the Glazer family had made their way to a family that had survived several deadly raids inside the Warsaw ghetto, by hiding in specially constructed shelters inside buildings. Time, however, was running out, as the Germans had decided on the total elimination of the Jewish population there. Fortunately for the Glazers, they had met a youthful Polish lad who, like some others, had occasionally stolen into the ghetto to barter with the local population – much needed food for the starving people in return for goods no longer considered absolute necessities. Seventeen-year-old Jerzy Koźmiński was one of these audacious Polish youth, known by the Glazers. Samuel Glazer: "We were desperate, and sought contacts. He came to see us several times." On April 18, 1943, the eve of the Jewish uprising in the Warsaw ghetto, Jerzy was again on one of his rounds to visit the Glazers, and decided to sleep over there, leaving early the following morning. He had brought food. As the uprising burst on the following morning, the Glazers urged Jerzy to flee. "We are Jews and we are doomed to die; however, you do not have to risk your life." Before jumping over one of the ghetto fences, Jerzy stopped for a while, and gave Samuel his family's address, in the Wawer section of the city. During those split seconds, he told them that his father was an engineer and was married to a much younger woman, Jerzy's stepmother, named Teresa – adding that she was a decent and courageous person. If the Glazers were to save themselves from the ghetto, surely his family would hide them with them.

It did not happen immediately, as the ghetto erupted in fighting between the heavily armed Germans and the ill-armed Jewish defenders. The die was cast for the remaining 50,000 Jews of the ghetto, who had once counted close to 500,000 souls, but the defenders had sworn to take as many German lives with them before themselves dying in this hopeless uprising. On April 30, with the ghetto up in flames, the Glazers made their escape across to the non-Jewish (or so-called Aryan) part of the city – Samuel, his wife and 70-year old father, and other family relations, include 12 year old Halina Herling, for a total of 14 persons. Stealthily making their way through a city infested with numerous German uniformed men, they were able to send a message to the Koźmińskis. Very soon, Teresa appeared together with her husband and stepson Jerzy, and took the frightened group of fugitive Jews to their home. In truth, the Koźmińskis had not expected that many persons to turn up, but there was nothing to do but admit them all, and this was indeed done.

Such a large group presented a real danger of detection, so a secure hiding place had to be immediately improvised. The Glazers helped with preparing an underground shaft, large enough to hold them all. There, under the Koźmiński home, the 14 stayed from May 1, 1943, for over a full year – to the area's liberation by the Russians, on September 9, 1944. Samuel Glazer especially points out Teresa's courageous spirit in instilling hope into the frightened souls of these fugitives, and even adding more fleeing Jews (forced to leave their hideout due to the danger of detection) to the secret hideout, for a total of 22 persons. The youthful Jerzy Koźmiński was affiliated with the Polish underground, and acquired several pistols, which he turned over to the hiding Jews for their protection, in the event of the hideout's detection by the Germans; he also fetched a secret radio, on which the hiders could pick up news from Moscow and the BBC in London. On one of his clandestine rounds, he was apprehended and taken to the infamous Pawiak prison, where he underwent a grueling and tortuous interrogation, which left him with all his teeth severely damaged, but he did not disclose the secret of his family's hiding of the large group of Jews. Jerzy was then dispatched to Auschwitz and Mauthausen camps, which he luckily survived. After the war, he taught electronics at a university level.

"The interesting thing," Samuel Glazer noted in his deposition, "is that we did not know the Koźmiński family from before; despite this, the whole family including the elderly father, committed themselves to our rescue." At first, the hidden persons helped with defraying some of the additional costs, especially with regard to food. When the money had been spent, one of the hiders, a watchmaker, helped out with fixing watches brought from the outside by Teresa. She explained that she kept at home a sick uncle, a watchmaker, and therefore she was doing the business errands for him. Several more of the shelter's inhabitants were taught the art of watch fixing, and they pitched in. This additional source of income helped in easing the difficult living conditions of both hiders and the hidden. Pushing her baby's carriage, Teresa carefully bought her food supplies at several locations, so as to dispel any suspicions in buying that much food in one place.

In late summer 1944, the Russian army had neared the Wawer suburb of Warsaw, and fighting soared close to the Koźmiński house between the warring sides. At this point, the Germans ordered the evacuation of this section of the war zone. Teresa's husband and her father left, but she decided to stay behind, so as not to abandon the large group of hidden Jews to an unknown fate, and she joined the group with her two-year old child in their underground hiding place. She explained her daring decision: "If I leave, you are lost." As the fighting above them raged for four weeks, Teresa stole out on occasions to fetch food from wherever and, running from place to place under constant shelling, she managed to find additional food. This tense and dangerous situation lasted until the area's liberation by the Russians on September 10, 1944. Warsaw itself remained under German occupation for four more months – until January 1945.

The Koźmińskis, and especially Teresa, had saved the large group of 22 Jews, many of whom eventually moved to Israel. As for Teresa, after the war, she worked as a nurse. After divorcing, she left for Israel in 1964, upon the invitation of her erstwhile wards, and continued her nursing profession in a Tel Aviv hospital. Before remarrying, she converted to Judaism, and assumed the name of Ruth Lindner. Her second marriage turned sour, and ended in divorce. She continued to live in Israel, while at the same time maintaining contact with her son in Poland, a trained engineer, and her stepson Jerzy, and maintaining close contacts with the large group of those she had saved during the Holocaust. She passed away in 1999.

In 1965, Yad Vashem conferred upon Teresa Koźmińska and Jerzy Koźmiński the title of Righteous Among the Nations. In 2005, Yad Vashem responded favorably to the request of the survivors and Jerzy's father, Karol Koźmiński, was also awarded the Righteous title,

Kugler, Victor
Kleiman, Johannes
Gies, Jan & Miep
Wijk van-Voskuyl, Elisabeth
Netherlands

Anne Frank

"'The time has come for us to hide.' These words, spoken by Otto Frank, still ring in my ears, though I heard them back in 1942. I, Victor Kugler, the Mr. Kraler of Anne's diary, will never forget the words that followed. 'The Germans have ordered Margot to report to the assembly point, from where they plan to ship her to Germany. We must use our secret annex sooner than anticipated.'"

Thus spoke Victor Kugler in 1979. He had worked with Otto Frank since 1933. Born in Hohenelbe, Austria, Kugler had moved to the Netherlands in 1920, at the age of 20 and had subsequently received Dutch citizenship.

In the 1930s Otto and Edith Frank and their two daughters, Margot and Anne, escaped from Nazi Germany and began a new life in Amsterdam. Otto Frank then bought two small firms (the Travies and Kolen companies) that imported spices for meats and pectin for preserves, where Kugler worked as general manager. Frank had asked Kugler to continue in the same capacity. The offices and warehouse of both firms were housed in an old four-story house at 263 Prinsengracht, overlooking one of the city's many canals and near the famous Ester church, where Rembrandt lies buried.

Soon Kugler and his wife became good friends of the Frank family and they often visited each other. Kugler remembered Otto as "an educated man who was proud of his Jewish heritage. Mrs. Frank was a religious woman and a devoted wife and mother." As for little Anne, she struck Kugler as already a precocious child at the age of three – lively and outgoing. Her sister, Margot, three years older, seemed more studious, subdued, and introverted.

In 1941, under the German occupation, Otto Frank was forced to give up his business, to sell it to a non-Jew or have the Germans confiscate it, so he decided to turn it over formally to his two trusted aides, Victor Kugler and Johannes Kleiman. The following year, when it became apparent that the Jews in the occupied country were slated for deportation, Otto Frank, coming from Nazi Germany, knew perfectly well what was in store for his family if he allowed himself to be taken there or further east to countries under direct German control. He decided, instead, to go into hiding with his family. Aided by Kleiman and Kugler after working hours so as not to arouse suspicion, he furnished and equipped the upper two floors of the commercial premises. These two floors, located to the rear of the building, were separated by a staircase, which was closed off by a revolving bookcase. For over a year, Frank and his trusted associates stocked the secret hiding place with food, bedding, and essential furnishings.

Victor Kugler at Yad Vashem

On July 5, 1942, when 16-year-old Margot received her deportation notice, the Franks knew the time had come, and the next morning they moved into the hideout. Otto Frank invited another Jewish family he had done business with to join him – Hermann and Augusta van Pels and their 15-year-old son Peter. To give the impression that the Franks had left the country, Victor Kugler took a farewell letter written by Otto Frank and mailed it to himself from a distant border town.

For the next two years, the four walls and roof of the annex were the boundaries of their existence. As a precautionary measure, all windows had to be curtained, blackened, and shuttered. They were to be neither seen nor heard, particularly during the daytime. In Kugler's words, "I used to go up to the secret annex almost daily. Of necessity my visits had to be short because, first, I had to attend to business and, secondly, I was afraid of arousing suspicion … Our greatest fear was that the hiding place would be discovered … We therefore had strict regulations. The occupants of the secret annex could not wear shoes or flush the toilet in the daytime because we had workmen downstairs. I also told them to keep the window shades drawn at all times and never to show their faces at a window."

Over the 25 months that followed, the Franks and the Van Pels, later joined by an elderly dentist named Dr. Friedrich Pfeffer, never left their hiding place. The eight occupants of the upstairs hideout were completely dependent on their Dutch benefactors, who provided them with food, reading matter, and everything else, including news and much-needed encouragement, sometimes even inventing Allied victories in order to counteract the occasional spells of depression of the secluded people.

Miep Gies

Kugler visited them at scheduled times, sometimes before office hours and sometimes at lunchtime when the other employees left the building. Miep Gies, who worked in the firm, and husband Jan, as well as Johannes Kleiman, purchased ration coupons on the black market and, when necessary, sold jewelry belonging to the hidden people with which to purchase other needed items. Miep's background was in some ways similar to Kugler's – they both came from Austria. Born as Hermine Santrouschitz, she moved to the Netherlands in 1920 at the age of 11 as part of a Dutch program to take in Austrian children who had suffered from malnutrition as a result of World War I. She originally came for a three-month period as the foster daughter of a couple with five children of their own. She stayed on, and in 1942 she married Jan Gies and became a Dutch citizen. Since 1933, she had worked for Otto Frank. Now she took on the job of collecting the Franks' list of requests every morning, obtaining the items, and secretly delivering them during her lunch break. Her husband, Jan, was active in the Resistance and would also supply the people with cigarettes purchased on the black market. He also selected books for them from a friend's private library each week. As for Elisabeth von Wijk, she visited the hidden people every day and also helped out by filling their requests.

Victor Kugler remembered bringing Anne the latest magazines, although her mother frowned at this type of literature. "I remember Anne would always be waiting for me at the top of the hidden stairway, saying nothing, but the look in her eyes told me that she hoped I had remembered." To still the insatiable appetite for knowledge of this young girl, Kugler arranged to have her enrolled in a Latin correspondence course – naturally under a fictitious name. "And she did quite well." Years later, Kugler still remembered her as "always inquisitive, sometimes melancholy."

Kugler probably did not suspect that Anne Frank was keeping a diary for the 25 months of her enforced confinement, in which she unfolded the story of life in seclusion for herself and the others, so eloquently recorded as to become known throughout the world under the title *The Diary of Anne Frank*. The revelations of a young girl groping her way into womanhood in the most trying of circumstances have been translated into a score of languages. In the diary, Victor Kugler appeared as "Mr. Kraler," Miep Gies – "Miep van Santen," the Van Pels couple – "Van Daan," Dr. Pfeffer – "Albert Dussel," Jan Kleiman – "Mr. Kophuis," and

Elisabeth (Bep) Voskuyl (later van Wijk) – "Eli Vossen." In one passage, she mentioned that Kugler's (Kraler's) responsibilities were "sometimes so much for him that he can hardly talk from pent-up nerves and strain."

"Then," in Kugler's words, "came that terrible day, August 4, 1944 – a day which has left an indelible imprint on my memory." While working at his office desk, he heard an unusual commotion, and saw four policemen, one a uniformed Gestapo man and three others in Dutch uniform. The Gestapo man was an Austrian named Karl Silberbauer and he was obviously in charge. "Show us all the rooms in the building," he shouted at Kugler, who obliged by opening all the bookcases and cabinets. "Outwardly, I showed great calm, but inwardly I was terrified. I wondered why these men were here. Had we been betrayed?"

Silberbauer then ordered Kugler up to the next floor, followed by the three other policemen. "Now," he said, "let's look for hidden weapons." He asked about the contents of the various cases, boxes, and bales. Next they headed to the corridor in the back. "My heart was in my mouth. We had come to the crucial place. For in this area was the bookcase which concealed the entrance to the secret annex." There was a similar bookcase nearby and some boxes that, in the meantime, had all been moved from their original place. "To my horror I now saw these same men tampering with the bookcase which hid the entrance to the secret annex. However, the bookcase did not yield an inch. Again and again they tried to move it but they failed. Finally, they found the hook which kept the bookcase in its place. The hook was unfastened and they moved the bookcase. The door leading up to the staircase and rooms above was now exposed. My heart sank. The moment I had dreaded for two years had now arrived… The eight people in the secret annex were now doomed; a terrible fate awaited them all."

The four policemen drew their guns and ordered Kugler upstairs. "The first person I saw was Mrs. Frank. She was sitting motionless in the living room. Choked with emotion, I could only whisper, 'The Gestapo is here.' Mrs. Frank did not move." Anne came down slowly. Margot wept silently. "All right," said Silberbauer, "Get your things together." He then shouted, "Who claims ownership of this chest?" Otto Frank responded, "This chest belongs to me!" and added for what it was worth, "I was an officer in the German Army in World War I." Silberbauer's face turned scarlet. "Then why didn't you give yourself up and register? You would have been sent to Theresienstadt, a camp for the privileged?" Otto Frank kept silent. As for Kugler, "I was watching the Nazi Silberbauer struggling with his mixed feelings. I was wondering which was stronger – his ingrown respect for officers or his sense of duty? He had come to attention in front of Mr. Frank and I had the feeling that a sharp command would make him salute."

At any rate, Silberbauer was proud of his catch, and all of the annex's occupants were taken away in waiting vans, including Kugler and Kleiman, who were suspected of being the main accomplices in the rescue operation. Arriving at the jail, Silberbauer told the two, "*Mitgefangen, mitgehangen*" ("Caught with them, you will hang with them"). Then began the interrogation, first of Kugler. He told them he was born in Austria and had served in the Austrian navy in World War I. "I noticed from Silberbauer's dialect that he himself was an Austrian. Maybe the shock was too great for him. First Mr. Frank, a Jew, an officer in the German army and then somebody from the Austrian Navy." Silberbauer leaned back on his chair and said, "That's enough for today."

Kugler and Kleiman were able to persuade their captors that Miep Gies and Elisabeth van Wijk were innocent, and the two were released. A while later, Johannes Kleiman was also released, due to his ill health and the intercession of the Dutch Red Cross. As for Kugler – the "main culprit" – he was in for more severe treatment, and for the next seven months he was rotated among several camps inside the country and put to hard labor.

As for the hidden persons, they were first dispatched to the big Westerbork camp in the north of the country,which served as a way station for further "travel" to Auschwitz. Some among them were later moved to Bergen-Belsen. With the exception of Otto Frank, none of them survived. Anne died of dysentery in March 1945, just a month before the liberation of the Bergen-Belsen camp.

After the Franks' arrest, Miep Gies was sent by a worker to offer the Germans money for the release of the eight Jews. Miep naively went to speak to the Gestapo at their headquarters. Directed to an officer, she was literally thrown out of the room. She was lucky not to have been arrested. Perhaps her "Aryan" credentials worked in her favor. She returned to the annex and carefully collected Anne Frank's diaries and gathered the many loose pages scattered all over the place, and stored them. When Otto returned, she gave him Anne's diaries and said: "This is the legacy of your daughter."

On September 7, 1944, Kugler was moved to a private cell. There he was shocked to see the scribbled messages on the walls from previous prisoners, such as: "I too will be shot, pray for me;" or "I die for the Queen and our Fatherland, God is with me." To Kugler it became clear that he was in a cell reserved for those who had been condemned to death. "I broke into a cold sweat, for I was sure that my last hours had come." But the following day, he was moved out and taken to Amersfoort camp, still inside the Netherlands.

One day he was standing for hours at roll call after a number of prisoners had already collapsed from the ordeal. At this point, "Silently, I addressed myself to God … I said: 'Dear Lord, should I be punished so severely because I tried to save the lives of my friends? What did I do wrong?' Suddenly he saw a bright white light in the dark blue sky, and underwent a kind of mystical experience, "and I knew for certain that I would one day come back to my home, safe and sound."

Amersfoort was actually an assembly center, a way station for prisoners to be sent on to Germany. But luck was with Kugler and he was instead moved to Zwolle, then to Wageningen, close to the German border, where he was assigned various duties, including the translation of messages in the two languages known to him, German and Dutch. In March 1945 he was with a group being marched toward Germany, and as they neared the last Dutch village of Zevenaar the column was attacked by British planes. In the confusion that followed, Kugler made his escape. He found his way back to his hometown of Hilversum, where he remained hidden until the end of the war, over a month later.

After the war, Victor Kugler went back to work for Otto Frank when he reopened his business, but the ongoing conflict between the Netherlands and Indonesia, formerly the Dutch East Indies, disrupted the supply of spices, and in 1948 Frank closed up shop. Opting for a new life in Canada, Kugler settled in Montreal, where he was at various times an electrician, a bookkeeper, a photographer, and an insurance clerk.

In Israel in 1975 for a ceremony in his honor at Yad Vashem, Victor Kugler broke into tears as he addressed the audience. "I tried to do what my conscience dictated," he said.

"I tried to save the lives of my friends. And it is my greatest sorrow that I failed." When a reporter asked him about his motives, he replied, "They were my friends. What else could I have done?… I don't understand what all the fuss is about." When he died in 1981, at the age of 81, an honor guard of Jews and Christians stood outside the funeral parlor in Toronto as his coffin was carried past.

On August 1, 1944, three days before her arrest, Anne Frank had written about herself in a mood of self-criticism:

> *"'A little bundle of contradictions,' can you tell me exactly what it is? What does contradiction mean? Like so many words, it can mean two things, contradiction from without and contradiction from within. The first is the ordinary 'not giving in easily, always knowing best, getting in the last word,' enfin, all the unpleasant qualities for which I'm renowned. The second nobody knows about, that's my own secret. I've already told you before that I have, as it were, a dual personality … I'm awfully scared that everyone who knows me as I always am will discover that I have another side, a finer and better side. I'm afraid they'll laugh at me, think I'm ridiculous and sentimental, and not take me seriously…. Therefore, the nice Anne is never present in company, has not appeared one single time so far, but almost always predominates when we're alone. I know exactly how I'd like to be, how I am too … inside. But, alas, I'm only like that for myself … I am guided by the pure Anne within, but outside I'm nothing but a frolicsome little goat who's broken loose."*

Anne Frank's rescuers were for their part not "bundles of contradiction," but thoroughly dedicated to their charges. Thanks to their selfless dedication, Anne Frank had two memorable years to write the very moving, sensitive, self-revealing and literate words that have become a genre in itself – a masterwork and personal testimony for millions of readers throughout the world for generations to come.

In 1972, Yad Vashem conferred the Righteous title on Victor Kugler, Johannes Kleiman, Jan and Miep Gies, and Elisabeth Wijk van-Voskuyl.

Latte-Brockmann, Ellen
Calogerás-Meissner, Ursula
Poelchau, Harald & Dorothee
Andreas-Friedrich, Ruth & Karin Friedrich
Einem, Gottfried von
Siemsen, Gertie
Harich, Anne-Liese
GERMANY

*I*n May 1944, a man was hired as conductor of an orchestra created by the Nazi regime to entertain troops. No one knew that he was in truth a Jew, passing as an Aryan. A singer in the troupe who suspected this fell in love with him and shielded him from suspicion in the troupe. At the end of the war the two married. This is the fascinating story of Konrad Latte.

The son of Dr. Manfred and Margarete Latte, Konrad, born in 1922, grew up in Breslau in an assimilated Jewish family. In his words, "I wasn't brought up any differently from the other German children. At Christmas we went to a Protestant church, and at Easter we went to the Breslau cathedral, which was famous for its lavish Easter service." His father was proud to have served in the German army during World War I. Then, when the Nazis came to power, Konrad was expelled from public school and forced to attend a Jewish school. He concurrently also studied music with a friendly organist who at first did not mind the boy's Jewishness but quickly had a change of heart. When the family received deportation orders, Konrad persuaded his parents not to report but go into hiding – not in Breslau but in Berlin. In March 1943, the Lattes arrived in Berlin by train, disguised as non-Jews – Konrad sporting a Nazi badge with a swastika. At first, not knowing where to turn, and without valid papers – such as the indispensable identity card and food ration cards, and (of great importance for Konrad because of his age) an army service book, the Lattes approached a distant relative who was married to a non-Jewish (i.e., Aryan) woman and therefore protected from immediate deportation. This man referred them to his friend, Ursula Meissner, a 20-year-old Berlin stage actress at the Prussian State Theater who lived alone, and she agreed to shelter the three Lattes in her home, where they remained hidden for several weeks. When a neighbor became suspicious, it was time to move on.

Through a friend the Lattes were referred to Dr. Harald Poelchau, a Protestant minister, who during the Nazi period served as chaplain at the Berlin-Tegel prison, where many political prisoners were kept, whom he often accompanied when they were taken out for execution, including those implicated in the foiled attempt on Hitler's life on July 20, 1944. From 1941, he also secretly belonged to the anti-Nazi Kreisauer group headed by Count von Moltke and also helped Jews with hiding places. His help to Konrad Latte was to get a blank form from the Volkssturm, the civilian militia created by Nazi propaganda minister Joseph Goebbels, and enter Konrad's name on it, but with the surname Bauer. This document also protected Konrad from being drafted into the army, as he ostensibly was already a member of the militia. He also provided the Lattes with food coupons, some cash and addresses for temporary lodging and work. Konrad's mother became a cleaning woman and his father did menial work. As for Konrad, he was incessantly on the move – to dozens of temporary addresses. Gertie Siemsen, a close collaborator of Poelchau, helped the Lattes with ration cards, money, and occasionally night lodgings. Anne-Liese Harisch hid Konrad for several weeks in 1943, gave him clothes belonging to her son Wolfgang, and provided food for Konrad and his parents. At the home of Ruth Andreas-Friedrich, Konrad could stop over whenever he wanted for a brief rest and a good meal.

At the same time, in spite of the impossible situation he found himself in, he yearned to return to his musical profession, so with great courage and perhaps a modicum of naiveté as a Jew on the run in the capital city of the Nazis, Konrad set out to find teachers who would help him perfect his musical talents. He started by rehearsing with Edwin Fischer, a pianist and conductor who was once married to a Jewish woman. Konrad surmised: "Under those circumstances, he couldn't be too much of an antisemite." Soon he felt confident enough to disclose to the man his true origin, in response to which the man took Konrad under his protective wing and gave him free piano lessons. Konrad then began earning money by playing funeral music at a crematorium and as a backup organist at some of the largest Protestant churches. "In Berlin, church services became almost unthinkable without me," Latte proudly recalled, perhaps with a bit of exaggeration. "The preacher had to plan his sermon around my schedule." Gottfried von Einem, of noble ancestry, was also of assistance; he had just produced a ballet, *Princess Turandot*, and Konrad was invited by the choreographer Tatjana Gsovsky to help with rehearsals. He also received lessons from Leo Borchard, who had once conducted the Berlin Philharmonic, to whom he disclosed his Jewishness. "Now I know, and now I have forgotten it again," was Borchard's terse response. Borchard taught Latte how to conduct Beethoven symphonies.

Then it seemed the end had come for Konrad when, in the aftermath of the arrest of one of Konrad's friends, he himself was apprehended in September 1943 together with his parents and taken to a place of detention on Grosse Hamburgerstrasse (a former Jewish old age home) in Berlin, from where the parents were deported to Auschwitz, where they perished. As for Konrad, the Gestapo held on to him for a while longer, anxious to extract from him information on the people who had assisted him in the underground life. On November 27, 1943, Konrad made his escape together with another Jewish prisoner. He now resumed his fugitive life, and as a man on the run slept a night here and a night there, including the homes of kindhearted people like Pastor Poelchau. His old patron von Einem got him a card from the Reich Musicians' Chamber (Musikkammer) under the name of Konrad Bauer and arranged for Konrad to be again employed at the opera. This membership card was the only document held by Konrad, and in case of emergency it would not have been sufficient.

As most of the organists in Berlin had being conscripted into the army, Konrad replaced them, playing in church services, as in the Annenkirche in Berlin-Dahlem, and at funerals. Friends sometimes brought him food or food coupons. Very rarely, however, would they allow Konrad to sleep over, because of the great danger involved. "I spent my nights in empty basements or attics."

As life became too risky for Konrad Latte – too many people were getting to know him – his instincts told him that it was better for him to find something outside Berlin. In early 1944, he ran into a subway guard who had earlier been at the Grosse Hamburger Strasse, the place from which Konrad had escaped. "He did not arrest me, as I expected, but only said: 'Hit the road.'" It was time to move elsewhere. He then had a lucky break, when he learned at the opera that Bodo Bronsky, the director of the Hessische Volkstheater (Hessian People's Theater), a popular singing troupe, was looking for a band leader for its tours among troops throughout Germany – as one of the many bands created by propaganda minister Goebbels to entertain the weary troops. Konrad consulted with Harald Poelchau, who told him it absolutely necessary for him to grab this opportunity and get out of Berlin.

Introducing himself to Bodo Bronsky under the name of Bauer, Konrad described his musical performances in Berlin and was hired. There remained one serious problem – the lack of proper identification papers. Konrad made the usual excuse also used by others, of having lost them in a bombing raid (a common occurrence in Berlin in those days), being left only with the Music Chamber card. Bronski told him that for the moment this would do. At the same time, since he was working for the Propaganda Ministry, and was considered trustworthy, he told Konrad to submit an application for a new identity card. Konrad cunningly used the following device to protect himself. "Every fortnight I wrote a letter to the military district office in Berlin-Schoeneberg. I threw away the original and sent, by registered mail, an empty envelope. I attached the receipt to a copy of the letter. With these papers every check by the Wehrmacht (army), police, or Gestapo, I passed after long explanations."

Meeting the ensemble in Goslar in May 1944, he met singer Ellen Brockmann and became romantically involved with her. She soon found out the truth about Konrad's background and decided to shield him from suspicion within the troupe. "She stood up for me so staunchly that after a serious discussion with the entire group and its director I was allowed to stay on until September 1944 without having to reveal my true identity." A real danger loomed from the direction of a certain Peggy Duenkler, who suspected Konrad was Jewish and threatened to have him reported. Latte told this woman he would not tolerate the affront of being called a Jew and invited her to accompany him to the Gestapo to have this matter settled once and for all; also reminding her of the stiff penalty awaiting her for denouncing a true German Aryan. The trick worked, and the singer backed off. Latte continued touring with the band throughout northern Germany, with Ellen at his side, ever counseling him to avoid entrapment.

In September 1944, due to the deteriorating military situation, all theaters in Germany were closed and the performers were conscripted into the military. Konrad again faced the problem of where to go, and again Reverend Poelchau came to the rescue. He sent Konrad Latte a fake cable informing him that the State Opera in the small town of Bad Homburg, near Frankfurt, needed him urgently. This gave him an excuse to travel there, where he was joined by Ellen Brockmann, who kept an apartment where both stayed. Konrad still lacked proper papers, including ration cards. In the building where he lived, someone was charged with getting ration cards for all the residents of the house, including about 11 women whose husbands were away at the front. Ellen explained Konrad's non-military status by saying that as a government-approved itinerant artist he was getting special ration cards directly from Berlin, but now he had difficulties receiving them due to the disruption of the regular postal service caused by the incessant bombings. As a result, Ellen was allowed to get food for him, taking care not to have him registered at the police as required by law.

In this small town, Ellen arranged for Konrad whatever musical work was available. Being well-known there, she represented Konrad as her fiancé. "Ellen Brockmann's reputation being spotless, my connection with her proved positive for me," Konrad wrote. "I could fill a book with details." As an aspiring pianist, Konrad gave public concerts as well as recitals in private homes and also conducted the Protestant church choir. On April 28, 1945, soon after Bad Homburg's liberation by American troops (on March 29), but with the war still on, Konrad and Ellen were married. Two days later Hitler shot himself in his Berlin underground bunker and a week after the war was officially over. In November 1945, a baby girl, Gabriele, was born to the happy couple.

Returning to what mattered most in his life, other than his beloved Ellen, Konrad renewed his musical career. In 1953, he put together an ensemble that later became the Berlin Baroque Orchestra and he also directed the Wilmersdorf music school. He remained at the podium for many years, until his final curtain call in 1997.

In 1978, Yad Vashem conferred the title of Righteous Among the Nations on Ellen Latte-Brockman. Also awarded the Righteous honorific were the following persons involved in helping Konrad Latte as well as other Jews on the run: Pastor Harald and Dorothee Poelchau (in 1971); Ellen Meissner-Calogerás (in 1994); Gertie Siemsen, Anne-Liese Harisch, Gottfried von Einem, Ruth Andreas-Friedrich and daughter Karin Friedrich (in 2002).

Lemaire, Jean Severin
FRANCE

*A*fter apprehending him for helping Jews on the run, the Nazis had jailed him in a cell filled with Jews. Sporting a biblical beard, he was mistaken by his fellow prisoners as a rabbi and asked him to lead them in prayer. He consented. He was no rabbi but a Christian Protestant pastor. How had he come to end up in a jail reserved for Jews?

From 1937, Jean Severin Lemaire had served as a pastor in an evangelical community in the French Mediterranean city of Marseilles. From the start of Vichy rule in France, which many clerics in both the Catholic and Protestant camps greeted with much enthusiasm and few reservations, Lemaire was among the minority who stood out in his condemnation of the proto-Fascist style of this regime. He was especially incensed at the regime's accelerating persecution of Jews, which led to the handing over of foreign-born Jews to Vichy's German overlords. "I could not stand by without actively assisting these hunted people whose numbers grew with time."

Pastor Lemaire upon his liberation from the concentration camp

Deciding to act at the end of 1941, Lemaire reversed his original intention of joining the underground and instead joined forces with organizations helping Jews escape arrest. As a first step, he contacted the Jewish Joseph Bass, who went under under several identities but was best known as "Monsieur André" and headed a clandestine rescue operation with the cooperation of Jewish and Christian lay and religious leaders. "This type of work I found to be just," Lemaire wrote after the war, "and I decided to give it my full support. We had many contacts with Christian and Jewish organizations ... We created in Marseilles, and throughout the southern Mediterranean region, an organization where Protestants, Catholics, and Jews of various shades of opinion worked fraternally – including Father de Parceval, a Dominican prior [title of the superior of a convent] who was later interned; Father Brémond, a Jesuit from Aix-en-Provence; Father Marie-Benoît, a Capuchin; Pastor Heuze (interned and deported), who was pastor of the Reformed church in Marseilles; Joseph Lasalarie (attorney); Murzi (attorney); Israel Salzer (chief rabbi of Marseilles); Angelo Donati; Rabbi Hirschler; and many others. We helped many people avoid arrest and deportation, either by hiding them or arranging their passage into the Italian zone, or abroad, or leading them to areas controlled by the Maquis [French underground], chiefly in the Chambon region." In addition, as a religious minister, Lemaire was allowed to visit the internment camps where Jews were imprisoned, with many eventually delivered into the hands of the Germans.

Then tragedy struck Lemaire, involving a most eerie set of circumstances. In his words, "I never dreamed that I would be arrested as a result of the complicity of a Belgian Jewish doctor, Siegfried Levy, who worked for the Gestapo and learned from one our Jewish associates, through no fault of hers, the location of our Sunday meetings." Dr. Levy was one of those cases of Jews whose families were being held hostage by the Gestapo to force spouses to collaborate with the Nazis in pinpointing Jews in hiding or those who helped them.

As also told by the Jewish rescue activist Denise Siekierski (nicknamed Colibri), Lemaire had agreed to place at the disposal of Jewish organizations his prayer hall. Siekierski's role was to interview people, to sort out and make sure that the people asking for help were genuine and not planted by the Gestapo – all this before directing them to Lemaire's place on the corner of Rue Aubagne and Rue des Trois Mages, though without mentioning his name. Dr. Siegfried Levy, originally from Germany, who presented himself as a fleeing Belgian Jewish doctor, came to ask for help, saying that he was being tracked by the Gestapo. "I interviewed him twice (as was customary)," Denise Siekierski recalled. It turned out he was a Gestapo agent. This was relayed to the Jewish activist Joseph Bass by people in the resistance who discovered it through secret channels in the Gestapo. On March 12, 1943, the Gestapo raided Lemaire's temple, which also served as a transit and information center for Jews on the run, on a tip by the traitorous doctor.

It so happened that as the Gestapo waited for people to walk into the temple's precinct, two young men were at the same time waiting close by for a bar to open its door. The Gestapo mistook them for the Lemaire's associates and had them promptly arrested. Undergoing a brutal interrogation, they truthfully claimed their innocence of any clandestine involvements. Pastor Lemaire was not in Marseilles on that day, returning the next morning. Before he had a chance to head back to his temple, he was stopped by Joseph Bass, who pleaded with him to leave the city immediately and not show himself at the temple, where he would certainly be arrested. At the restaurant where Bass and Lemaire were having this dramatic exchange, Bass got down on his knees, begging Lemaire. However, when he learned that two innocent men were undergoing torture for a "crime" not their own, Lemaire's mind was made up. "I felt it a matter of conscience that I had to be there, and if necessary to be arrested, so that two innocent young men might be released." On Sunday, March 14, 1943, he appeared at his temple to lead the afternoon services at 3 p.m., when suddenly the Gestapo had all approaches to the street blocked off. "I was arrested, and the two innocent men were released. I do not regret what took place, nor the decision I made. As a Christian and a Pastor, I had to act without concern for the consequences."

It was now Lemaire's turn to undergo torture at the hands of four Gestapo agents. After each session, he was hauled back to his cell, "with my head on fire, my hands twisted and wounds in my back as a result of truncheon blows." Lemaire stood firm and did not divulge the names of his clandestine associates. He was then led to a cell filled with imprisoned Jews. As the door was locked behind him, the Gestapo man said, "Since you love Jews so much, we're putting you in with them." There he stayed for over two months. Conditions were harsh: some straw on the ground and in the middle a tub in a cell occupied by old and young, women and children, even an 18-month-old baby, "for whom I asked for milk instead of the watery soup which the Germans provided to the prisoners."

Lemaire remembered seeing the arrival of a Jewish family of 13 (the Vigderhaus family), father, mother, son, daughters-in-law, daughters, and a girl. "I must say that this child is alive because I managed to have her freed and the Red Cross came to get her; this was due to my insistence." She was Francine Weil, today Abravanel, then five years old, freed on the pretext that she had measles, which was infectious. However, the mother's fate was tragic. She was suffering from diabetes and begged the Gestapo to be allowed to get the insulin which she had left at home in Nîmes. Instead she was told coldly, "It's unimportant, you'll die sooner or later; you may as well die here." All had to watch helplessly the agony of this woman, who slowly grew weaker from day to day over a period of eight days. She died in front of her husband and children. Her family wanted to have the body washed before burial, but the guards simply dragged her out. "I emphasize," Lemaire underlined, "they did not carry her, but dragged her," and the body was disposed of in an undisclosed location. Of this family of 13 persons, aside from the girl only a daughter-in-law was saved, surviving the camps. All the others perished.

As mentioned earlier, as he awaited his own fate Pastor Lemaire was asked by the other prisoners, all Jews, to lead them in prayer, as they mistook him for a rabbi thanks to his composure and patriarchal beard. In his words, "One witnessed this extraordinary thing, which showed that there were neither Jews, nor Greeks, nor pagans, nor Christians, but we were all the frightful victims of our indescribable sufferings in this extraordinary phenomenon of Jews asking the help of an evangelical pastor to bestow on them God's blessing before commencing their final journey." From a Bible that Lemaire had managed to get smuggled in, he read to the assembled Jews some passages from the Psalms. "Then we read the Psalms together, and together we also prayed to the Lord, the God of the Jews and Jesus Christ; the God of believers – to be with them in their future pilgrimage." In her testimony to Yad Vashem, Francine Abravanel, the liberated child, told of seeing in the cell "a rabbi with a long beard, who prayed with us, observed the Sabbath, who always blessed us when people were taken away for deportation. It was he who raised our spirits and it was this 'rabbi' who liberated me." She continued: "How great was my surprise, recently when I learned that the person who I had always taken for a rabbi was in truth a Protestant pastor, Reverend Lemaire."

Lemaire was also present to witness the indescribably poignant scenes when families were separated amid desperate crying and screaming. One day the infamous Dr. Levy was thrown into the cell. Lemaire had known all this time that it was he who had betrayed him, as well as many of his Jewish cellmates, who now wanted to do him in. "I had to place myself between him and the Jews to keep him alive, for they wished to kill him. He was sent to Auschwitz, where he died at the hands of those he denounced to the Gestapo."

After two months' imprisonment, Lemaire was removed to another cell, filled with non-Jews; then to another prison, and finally, in March 1944, he was deported to the Mauthausen camp in Austria. He was put in a railroad car with 100 people. By the time they reached Mauthausen, some were dead or had gone insane. "We were 2,800 when we left Compiegne [in France], and of this group there were 52 when we returned in 1945." The new arrivals were first quarantined for 12 hours outside in the rain without any food. Three weeks later, Lemaire and the other survivors were moved to Melke camp (also in Austria), an affiliate of Mauthausen. Recalling this terrible period of his life, Lemaire in a postwar statement said the following. "One had to find in oneself each moment the strength to live another second. When one lost one's will, one was on the way to the crematorium within 24 hours. I saw thousands of my friends die. I lived surrounded by the dead – myself not even having the strength to walk, to sleep, to eat scraps that were given to us, or to work – keeping myself on my feet through the constant miracle of divine grace." On December 1, Lemaire was taken to Dachau, where he was placed in a caserne reserved for imprisoned clerics. He recalled that dreadful camp, where many fell victim to a typhus epidemic.

Liberation came just in time. On April 27, 1945, a transport of several thousand Jews left. They were killed in the cars. The following day, several thousand Italians were led on foot to a forest where they were murdered. On April 29, it was the turn of the French. Luckily for them, and Lemaire, on that day came liberation. Lemaire was then suffering from edema, which caused an abnormal swelling of his body. "I was swollen, and weighed 49 kilograms instead of 84 kilograms. We came back sick, tired, asking nothing from anyone and receiving nothing from anyone; only wanting to rest, calm and peace." As for his Nazi persecutors,

"Man may forgive for himself, but man's justice may not always forgive … Only God may forgive everything. But he has not granted man, in their passions, the right to invoke God's pardon, for they know not his ways."

The story does not end here, for there remained another injustice to be rectified. Denise Siekierski, the woman who had through an innocent mistake disclosed to the traitorous Dr. Levy the involvement of Pastor Lemaire in the rescue of Jews, suffered a "blackout" at the war's end. She even forgot having met Lemaire on his return from the camps. When her memory of those days returned, she blamed herself for having inadvertently led to the pastor's arrest and tremendous sufferings at the hands of the Germans. When she visited Marseilles in August 1984, Pastor Lemaire insisted that she come to see him. He had found out where she was staying, and told her on the phone that it was absolutely necessary for her to have dinner with him and his wife. Hearing his voice over the phone, "My throat was completely paralyzed, and I could not pronounce three words." He came to pick her up and on the way to his house, in a suburb of the city, he told her, "I know very well what you feel, and I want to free you completely from this feeling of guilt that you have borne for forty years. Things happened the way it did because God wanted it that way, and it was a mission that I had to accomplish, and you have no reason to feel guilty."

In 1976 Yad Vashem conferred upon Pastor Jean Severin Lemaire the title of Righteous Among the Nations.

Linschoten, Pieter & Maria Elisabeth
& daughter Maria Elisabeth
Rowe, Vivian & Hendrina
Bley, Hendrik & Jacoba
Enck van, Frederik & Hendrika
NETHERLANDS

---

*I*n the still darkness of Utrecht, a city under curfew in the German-occupied Netherlands, Pieter Linschoten rode on his bike with a newborn baby in a sack. It had just been born to Jewish parents in hiding and was to be delivered to a childless non-Jewish couple anxiously awaiting its arrival.

The baby's parents, Mozes and Sophia Bouwman, had already parted with their two other children (Lion and Koosje, aged 4 and 5), hidden with a kindhearted Dutch family. At first, the children were registered, against payment, in an institute for problem children in Oldebroek. However, when someone revealed the children's real identities to the authorities, the two children were taken out of the place in time by an underground operative, who took them to a temporary hiding place. He then spoke to his own parents, Hendrik and Jacoba Bley, who readily took the two children into their home in the village of Elburg, where they stayed until the end of the war. As for the children's parents, the Bleys arranged for them to be hidden with Frederik and Hendrika Van Enck in Oldebroek. The arrangement proved fairly amenable considering war conditions. The Bouwmans were allowed to move around freely and Mozes presented himself as a Dutch army officer on the run from the Germans. The Bleys owned a pharmacy and a paint workshop, and Mozes, a photography hobbyist, opened a photo lab in the pharmacy and thus helped defray the costs of his and his wife's stay there.

The Bouwmans had arrived in the Bley household in May 1943, and early the following year Sophia Bouwman learned that she was pregnant with her third child. This was not a happy occurrence given the circumstances, with the Nazis on the hunt for Jews. A solution had to be found; luckily for all concerned, it was forthcoming. A certain Maria Elisabeth Linschoten had previously worked as a clerk in a firm in Utrecht that had once belonged to Isaac Bouwman, the brother of Mozes, whose misfortune was to have been arrested and deported to the Sobibor death camp in Poland. When she learned of the predicament faced by Mozes and Sophia Bouwman, she immediately told her father Pieter Linschoten. He was no stranger to the Bouwmans, for at the time he was already sheltering the mother and aunt of Mozes Bouwman in his home, where they remained until the war's end. Pieter Linschoten was the managing director of the *Stichting Volkswoningen*, a city-funded foundation housing people with social problems. At the time in question, an institution of this kind was considered the best place for a Jewish child to first see the light of day, and it was therefore decided that the delivery would take place there, under Pieter Linschoten's personal supervision.

That was only the half of it, for it had to be decided what to do with the newborn child. Again a fortunate solution was found. A second daughter of Pieter Linschoten had befriended a certain Vivian Rowe, an Englishman employed as an office manager at the company where she worked. She learned that this man and his wife, Hendrina, were interested in adopting an infant. When told of the coming birth of the Bouwman child, they agreed to adopt it – in fact to fake its birth – accepting the condition that the child would be returned to its real parents if they survived the war. Otherwise, they would keep the child. Mrs. Rowe thereupon began to simulate a pregnancy, down to the protruding belly, and spread the happy news to her relatives and friends; even, with great misgivings to, her own parents.

At the end of July 1944, Mozes and Sophia Bouwman left their hiding place at the Bleys in Oldebroek and moved over to Pieter Linschoten's home, in Utrecht. Close to the child's delivery, the parents were rushed to the institute headed by Linschoten, where it was felt that the delivery could be made in total secrecy. A boy was born on September 2, 1944, and the parents named it Albert Dirk. The following day, the baby was put in a sack and taken at night by Pieter Linschoten to the Rowe home. A day later, on September 4, Hendrina changed out of her maternity clothes and with her husband announced with great joy the birth of a son, whom they named Tommy Franklin. That very day Vivian Rowe had the baby boy duly registered as his own. In the same city, the baby's real mother, Sophia Bouwman, recovered for a while in Linschoten's home before returning with her husband, Mozes, in their permanent hiding place with the Bleys in Oldebroek. Saddened at not being able to cuddle the baby in her own arms during the early period of his life, she was nevertheless happy that he was in good hands and hoped to have him returned to her very soon – for in September 1944 it seemed that the Netherlands would soon be liberated. It was not to be so for another harrowing eight months. In the meantime, Vivian and Hendrina Rowe cared for the baby boy through the terrible winter months of 1944-45, known as the Hunger Winter for the lack of food.

On May 29, 1945, several weeks after the war's end, the child was properly returned to his natural parents. Now began another struggle, having to do with reregistering the child as born to the Bouwmans instead of the Rowes. After many bureaucratic complications, the formal change was made. In gratitude to the child's benefactors, two additional names were given to the child – Thomas and Frank (the Dutch registrar rejected the un-Dutch-sounding "Tommy" and "Franklin"); hence, Albert Dirk Thomas Frank Bouwman. The Bouwmans returned safe and sound with the baby boy and their two other children to their former home in Haarlem.

In 1983, Yad Vashem conferred upon all of the Bouwman family's rescuers the title of Righteous Among the Nations: to Pieter and Maria Elisabeth Linschoten and their daughter, also named Maria Elisabeth; to Vivian and Hendrina Rowe, as well as Hendrik and Jacoba Bley, and Frederik and Hendrika Van Enck.

Lipke, Janis (Zānis) & Johanna
LATVIA

On July 1, 1941, the Germans occupied Riga, capital of Latvia, and this was immediately followed by the mass executions of the city's Jews. By December of that year, Nazi *Einsatzgruppen* and Latvian auxiliary units had murdered three-quarters of the city's 40,000 Jews. Thousands were led to the nearby Rumbuli forest, stripped naked, told to lie face down in deep pits, and executed by German and Latvian firing squads. Each group was ordered to lie naked on the bodies of the previous group. Between 25,000–28,000 people were murdered in this way. Some 5,000 Jews had been killed earlier, synagogues were burned, and homes were vandalized. The remaining Jews were locked inside a ghetto from which all able-bodied people were conscripted for forced labor, mainly at nearby army installations. Over the next years, more were killed, including many from among another 20,000 Jews deported to Riga from Germany and Austria. In summer 1943, the ghetto began to be liquidated, with some spared and sent to the nearby Kaiserwald concentration camp, which held 10,000 mostly Jewish prisoners, including people brought from other places in the country and from nearby Lithuania. Many German firms had their subsidiaries there and the prisoners worked in a variety of facilities: workshops, warehouses, kitchens, etc. On the approach of the Red Army in July 1944, the sick and old from among the thousands of Jewish laborers began to be murdered, a process that continued until the end of September. Spared were only those aged 18 to 30 and in good health. When the Russians reentered the city on October 10, 1944, fewer than 100 Jews were to be found in Riga, and a few more outside it. Forty-two of them had been saved by one man, a dockworker named Janis Lipke.

Janis Lipke

Our story begins on November 30, 1941, during one of the early killing sprees among the city's Jews, which claimed thousands of lives. Janis Lipke looked on in horror at the bodies of dead children on the streets. Turning to his son, he said in an emotion-filled voice, "Look well, my boy, and never forget." This horrific vision out of Dante's *Inferno* spurred Lipke to do something to save innocent lives. He quit his job as a stevedore on the docks for a new one with a civilian-contracting firm that did work for the *Luftwaffe,* the German air force. Lipke took the job because he knew that the firm used Jewish slave labor from the ghetto, people whom Lipke was intent on saving. In the past, he had also done some smuggling. He decided now to smuggle people. With the aid of a trusted companion, Karlis Jankovski, who drove a truck, he was able to help many to escape from the labor camp. Karlis would load the escapees in the back of his van and cover them with wood and furniture. On the way, he would pick up hitchhikers, preferably policemen and even Germans in uniform, as a guarantee against searches. He was thus able to move 28 Jews to three farms in Dobele, a distance of 80 kilometers from Riga.

Lipke began rescuing Jews in December 1941 and he continued until the arrival of the Russians in October 1944. He never asked for any compensation. His job as supervisor of a group of Jewish workers from the ghetto facilitated his rescue efforts. He would usually take them out of the ghetto to the local *Luftwaffe* depots and bring them back in the evening. It is told that one day, two of his workers escaped. To make up for the missing persons needed for the head count on returning to the ghetto, Lipke brought in two Latvians to mingle with the returning group. The following morning they nonchalantly left, passing as non-Jewish contractors.

Zalman Drizin, Haim Smolianski, and Grigori Arensburg are three of those helped by Lipke who gave testimony after the war. Drizin made his escape from the ghetto on October 10, 1943. Lipke took him and his brother to a farm in Miltini, near the town of Dobele, where they hid in a bunker underneath the chicken coop with seven other Jews and were cared for by Lipke's rescue associates. Lipke had leased the farm, which belonged to a Latvian who was serving with the German army. As for Smolianski, he had lost his wife and children during the first large-scale "action" on November 30, 1941. Escaping on December 10, 1941, he hid in a place arranged by Lipke, who then moved him to another place, in a shelter with seven others – until the fall of 1943. Then Lipke added him to those hidden on the Miltini farm. As for Arensburg, he too was helped by Lipke to hide in various places in Riga, eventually being taken to the Miltini farm in January 1944. Another person, Lida Bobe (nee Dolgizer), stated that at the end of 1941 she noticed a man standing outside the fence at her place of work talking to Jews about escape plans. It was Lipke. When Bobe made her escape with her daughter she first remained hidden in the home of her former maid. When Lipke was told of her whereabouts, he and Karlis brought Bobe different clothing and took her and her daughter to Karlis' home, where they met six other Jews in hiding. They were then moved to a cellar belonging to Maria Lindenberga, an elderly non-Jewish woman working closely with Lipke and his associates. She cooked food for all her charges. Sofia Stern and her six-year-old daughter, Hanna, originally from Germany, were also helped by Lipke. He first took them to his home, where his wife Johanna fed and clothed them, before he moved them to a certain farm, where they stayed the remainder of the war.

Janis Lipke also began saving Jews from the ghetto, but he concentrated his main efforts on those in the Kaiserwald camp to which he had access as a work group supervisor. Sometimes he would contact people he hoped to save by means of written messages left at their work places or in some public place like a phone booth; at other times, they would meet at the barbed-wire fence surrounding the camp. Once someone had successfully gotten out of the camp, Lipke would be waiting nearby at an agreed-upon spot and would whisk him away either by trolley or hidden in the back of a truck driven by his friend Karlis. At first, Lipke brought most of the fugitives to his own house and hid them in a specially constructed shelter. His wife, Johanna, helped him. For example, in December 1941 he brought a group of eight Jews from the ghetto and housed them in a bunker next to his house, a place prepared with the help of his wife and eldest son, Alfred, in below-zero weather.

One day, Janis received a message with the words: "To Jan, Blasta Dembis Street." He understood that someone there needed help. He arrived at the location, facing a warehouse, and waited for a while. Twelve men approached him, beholding the man who it was rumored was helping Jews almost as a pastime. "Are you Jan?" one asked. "I plead guilty," Lipke replied, and then: "Well, guys, ready to escape?" They nodded in agreement. "Okay, wait here on September 10, and make sure to wear different clothes under the ones with the yellow star one." Someone said: "The problem is that we have nothing to pay." Lipke: "If you think I'm doing this for your money, don't come. At any rate, you won't have enough to pay for my life. You others, be ready." They waited for him on September 10 at the assigned place. He came and told them he could not take them then, but would return eight days later and wait for them at the ghetto exit. "When you have left for work, separate into two groups. Around the corner, a truck will be waiting for you. Go quietly, as on a regular day." But only three people showed up. Others had either been killed or moved elsewhere. Jan told the ghetto guard he was taking them to work. Outside Riga, he gave them weapons and moved them to his farm in Miltini.

David Fishkin was one of those saved by Lipke. Lipke had a special interest in saving this man, as he had been friendly with Fishkin's family before the war. At first, David worked in a detail cleaning out the homes of Jews who had been murdered and whose household possessions were being turned over to the Germans. He was eventually moved to a *Luftwaffe* installation, where one day Lipke, who had access to the place, came to see him and proposed that David join him, to be moved to his home, where he said he was already hiding six

Jews. At this point, David declined the invitation. Lipke reappeared later and asked him if he needed additional food and clothing, and "when I was ready to leave with him." David's response was that, for the moment, he was satisfied with the food at the camp. As for leaving – he left it up to Lipke. Before leaving, Lipke said he wanted to give him his family's jewelry, which had been left with him for safekeeping. "I wondered what was I to do with the jewelry? He told me that I was to keep it hidden and at an opportune moment, if Lipke could not come to take me out, I was to bribe the guards with the jewelry in order to leave the camp. I would then find the address of the hiding place on the door of the phone booth on Aizmargan Street." Lipke visited David several more times. On July 24, 1944 the Germans began liquidating the weak, sick, elderly, and injured from among the workers. A week later, a German asked David to prepare him a suitcase. Evidently the Germans were edgy and preparing to evacuate, as the Russians were already 40 kilometers away. The time had come to escape, before the Germans decided to do away with the remaining Jews.

Assisted by two Ukrainian workers who refused payment, David was helped to jump over the fence. As prearranged, Lipke was waiting for him on the other side and the two men immediately got on a crowded trolley car. They had to be on their guard, for there were German soldiers on the trolley and David had a clearly Semitic appearance. Lipke quickly told him to turn his face toward the window and look out. In the meantime, to distract the attention of the others, Lipke began railing against the evils of communism and how all true Latvians should help the Germans defeat the Red Army. Distracted by Lipke's fiery words, the passengers paid no attention to David. Approaching their stop, Lipke gave Fishkin a light kick in the leg and the two got off and headed for the home of Maria Lindenberga, where David stayed until nightfall. Lipke then took him to a warehouse used for storing spare parts for machines, where he met another Jew in hiding. There the two stayed, with Maria bringing them food. Lipke had planned to move them to the coast and have them smuggled over to Sweden aboard a fishing boat that took people across in return for payment, but the Red Army had by then severed links to the coast. In the meantime, Lipke, who often visited the two men, spotted a German military vehicle that had been left abandoned in front of the house. It had belonged to Latvians fighting with the SS who had deserted their unit. Before the authorities could lay their hands on the vehicle, Lipke stole a few of the weapons left behind inside.

From there, the two were moved back to Maria's house. She hid them in an underground shelter that had a small window facing the street. After two weeks, the concierge happened to look through the window and noticed David, whom he mistook for a thief. David grabbed the machine gun he had and threatened the man, who ran off screaming that there were armed robbers in the cellar. David and his companion, Willi Nogler, quickly left the cellar and decided to pass the night next to the Dvina River, in a place frequented by homeless people, the poor, and drunkards. Later they learned that Lipke had returned to Maria's home and had told the concierge that the two men were in truth Latvians who had deserted from their unit, hence patriots. He warned the concierge that if he were to inform on them, his life was not worth a cent. The Russians were close by, Lipke added threateningly. That evening the two men returned to Maria's home, where Lipke found them and moved them to Karlis' home to join other Jews in hiding. More Jews were brought there by Lipke, and they were eventually moved to the cellar of the building, where a section had been blocked off for their stay, accommodating ten hidden persons. There they remained until liberated by the Russians on October 10, 1944.

Earlier, Lipke had toyed with the idea of moving some of his charges across the Baltic Sea, to Sweden, and for this purpose he had purchased a boat. However, he and a Jewish colleague were discovered and arrested. While Lipke was able to talk his way out of detention with the help of a bribe, his Jewish co-conspirator was shot, though Lipke had also paid for his release. Tragedy also struck some of the people hidden on the Miltini farm, near Dobele. When the Soviet army first occupied the area, some of those in hiding there were too hasty in coming out into the open and were caught and killed when the Germans retook the hamlet for a short while. The other ten in hiding were more careful and survived. With liberation, Lipke's rescue operation was over; 42 Jews owed their life to this brave man – an unassuming blue-collar stevedore who had turned into a legendary rescuer.

In 1966, Yad Vashem recognized Janis and Johanna Lipke as Righteous Among the Nations.

Łoza, Stefania & Eugeniusz & Irena Nowak Kuropienska, Leopolda Kolska, Stanislawa

POLAND

In 1942, after several Nazi killing raids on the Jews in the Sandomierz ghetto, the Flakowicz family, originally from Kalisz, decided to split up. As with other Jews who lived dangerously in the open, the Flakowiczes had assumed new names and were equipped with false identity papers. Father Moshe-Moniek became Mateusz Filipowski; his wife Cesia – Mirosława Krystyna Łągiewska; their son Yitzhak-Ignaṣ, born in 1935, became Marian Dąbrowski, and their son Joseph, born in 1936 – Marek Wojciech Łągiewski. Cesia and son Joseph moved to several places, finally settling in Brzesko, located between Kraków and Tarnow, while Moshe and son Yitzhak headed for Warsaw. In Brzesko, Cesia rented a one-room basement apartment with a kitchen and supported herself by baking rolls and cookies and selling them in partnership with the landlord, who lived above them with her two children.

Cesia's husband, Moshe, who was deaf from childhood, supported himself by repairing sewing machines after settling down in Warsaw on the Aryan (i.e., non-Jewish) side. He eventually found a secure place for his son Yitzhak-Ignaś in the home of Leopolda Kuropieska, a mother of two children, a boy and girl, whose husband, a former captain in the

Polish army, was a prisoner of war with the Germans. Yitzhak related that at first Kuropieska, fearing for her own safety, hesitated to take the Jewish-looking boy into her home and it took much pleading by his father to get her to change her mind. "I was treated very warmly," Yitzhak admitted; "nothing was denied to me. She was a strict Catholic, but she did not attempt to influence me. Her two children knew the truth about Yitzhak, but they kept the secret to themselves. Having settled his son there, Moshe supported his wife and other son, Joseph, in far-away Brzesko with money sent in the mail taped inside Catholic prayer books. During his few visits to Brzesko, Moshe befriended two deaf-mutes, one of them Eugeniusz Łoza, about 25 years of age and a professional tailor. At first Eugeniusz was not told the true identity of the Flakowicz family; Moshe's wife and son were presented as relatives, and naturally Christians, and Joseph was told to explain to Eugeniusz that his father was a prisoner of war in Germany.

At the end of 1943, Cesia went to her regular place in the market with her baked goods and there someone recognized her from before the war and began to extort money from her. When Cesia's husband learned of the threat, he asked Mrs. Kuropieska to hide Cesia and Joseph in her home temporarily in addition to Cesia's other son, Yitzhak, already there since January 1943, as well as two Jewish sisters also hiding in Kuropieska's home, located in the heart of Warsaw.

Joseph stayed there for three months, when in the summer of 1944 it seemed that Kuropieska's rescue efforts were doomed. A Polish policeman accompanied by two informers raided her apartment and discovered Joseph and the two sisters there. Joseph's brother, Yitzhak, managed to slide under the bed and was not discovered. Leopolda Kuropieska agreed to pay them a substantial bribe not to report her to the Gestapo, using money given her by the two brothers' father, Moshe. She also threatened them that if any harm befell her or her charges, the Polish underground, with which she was connected, would put out a death warrant on the policeman. Joseph was then moved elsewhere, to the home of Mietek Kolski (a nephew of Moshe's wife, Cesia), who was married to the Catholic Stanislawa-Stasia. After a short stay there, Joseph was taken by Stasia to Zofia Kaluszko, who was hiding Mietek's parents (Helena, who passed as Maria Tomaszewska, and her husband Moritz) and their daughter Cesia-Tsirel. Eventually Eugeniusz Łoza, the newfound deaf-mute friend of Joseph's father Moshe, who was told of his friend's true identity, agreed to take Joseph with him by train, in mid-1944, to his family in Słotwina-Brzesko, near Bochnia, in Galicia, where Joseph remained until the liberation a year later.

To get back to Stanislawa (or Stasia, as she was better known), married to the Jewish Mietek Kolski's – her involvement in her husband's rescue efforts was not something she had foreseen when she married him but was the result of totally unforeseen circumstances. Born into the Roginski family in 1912, Stasia had come to Warsaw in 1930, where she stayed with an aunt who owned a butcher shop. In 1940 she had met Naftali Kolski, who went by the name of Mieczyslaw (or Mietek) and represented himself as a non-Jewish Pole. Naftali had fled from Kalisz to Warsaw and supported himself by buying goods produced in the Warsaw ghetto and selling them to stalls and shops on the non-Jewish side. In the course of time he offered to go partners with a policeman named Michal. Michal was a distant cousin of Stasia. On Christmas Eve 1940, Michal invited Mietek for a festive dinner at his home; there, Mietek met Stasia, and the two fell in love. Neither Michal nor Stasia knew that Mietek was Jewish, and that his parents were in fact hiding on the Aryan side of the city. On October 28, 1942, Stasia married Mietek in a church ceremony and they took up residence in a small Warsaw apartment.

All seemed to be going well for them when in March 1942 a 16-year-old girl knocked on their home – frightened, weeping, and seeking shelter. It turned out that she was related to Mietek, and only then did Stasia discover that her husband was Jewish. As told by Rena Skolski, born in 1927, she had originally arrived with her parents in Warsaw in 1941 under the name of Barbara Alicja Smarzynska and was equipped with false identity papers. Rena's mother had arranged a baby sitting job for her, while she and her husband lived elsewhere. After Rena's father lost all his money to *Szmaltzovniks*, professional informers who stalked the streets of Warsaw to pick out Jews passing as non-Jews, then harass and fleece them of their valuables – he moved out of the city with his sister to the small town of Rembertów, where Rena and her mother visited him on weekends. "I was blessed with so called 'good looks,' not looking Jewish," Rena stated, "and spoke Polish without a trace of a Jewish accent." One day, Rena's mother disclosed to her that she had run into a man who looked like a German (in a Tyrol- type hat), but actually was her nephew Naftali-Mietek Kolski, and he told he that he was married to a non-Jewish woman who did not know his background. Mietek's parents, Moritz and Helena (Cesia), Kolski lived in separate hiding places in Warsaw, under borrowed names. Cutting short the conversation, Mietek gave Rena's mother his address, but stressed in no uncertain terms that under no circumstances was she to visit him – afraid his wife would discover the truth about him.

On May 9, 1943, Rena was to meet her mother in town and then go see her father in his hiding place. Her mother never showed up at the appointed place, and after she inquired she learned with horror that both her parents and her aunt (Dora Szeinfeld) had been betrayed and shot by the Germans. As told by Rena:

> "I was then 16 years old and left completely alone with no money or place to stay. The people I worked for were scared to keep me any longer, since I did not stop crying for several days. I started wandering the streets of Warsaw and in despair decided to approach a German soldier so that he should put an end to my misery. Suddenly I felt something hard in my pocket. This was my little notebook. I found the address of Mieczyslaw Kolski. I rang the bell on Grzybowska Street. A young woman answered the door, and I asked for Mr. Kolski. She replied that her husband was not home and asked who I was. She wanted to know. I said, 'I am his cousin.' 'Cousin? Please come in and sit down. What kind of cousin are you?' she inquired. 'He never told me that he had such a young cousin here.' I replied, 'Of course my father and his father are brothers.' Then I started to cry. 'What are you crying about?' 'Why, because the Germans killed my parents three days ago.' 'Jesus Christ, why did they kill them?' 'Why?' I said, 'Because they were Jews.'"

At this, Rena was told to leave the premises immediately, which left her dumbfounded, not understanding what led Mrs. Kolski to react so strongly to what Rena had told her. The only other address she had was of Mietek's mother, who was Rena's aunt – Maria Tomaszewska. When Rena told her what had happened at Mietek's apartment, Maria scolded her, saying that Rena had brought a great tragedy on the whole family by revealing to Stasia that her husband was Jewish.

"How in the world could I have known that Stasia did not know that her husband was Jewish," Rena questioned? To the surprise of everyone, after the initial shock, Stasia came to terms with the reality of her husband's Jewishness and began berating herself for having sent Rena away. Who knows where the poor girl went, she asked? She did not rest until Mietek found Rena and brought her back into their home. Rena: "I was undernourished, neglected, desperate and thanks to them and especially Stasia, I regained my balance." Rena attended church regularly with her benefactors, but this was done for her sake, so as to be seen by the neighbors, to whom she was introduced as a cousin. Stasia herself was a practicing Catholic and a strong believer, but she never made the slightest attempt to try to convert Rena to her faith. In Rena's words, "She not only accepted this with love [the discovery that her husband was Jewish], but decided without hesitation to harbor another Jewish girl – myself."

Stasia's volte-face went even further than this. She began to run errands to help other Jews on the run, delivering messages, money, food etc., and her home was always open to those in need. As recollected by Rena, "I remember among others Moshe Flakowicz, known as Mateusz, who was deaf and mute, who very often ate dinner with us, and when he was sick Stasia cooked and sent me with pots of soup to him or delivered them herself." Other visitors included Moshe's sons, Yitzhaq-Ignaș and Joseph (when their previous hiding place with Leopolda Kuropieska proved no longer safe, as already mentioned) – both of whom stayed there for several weeks, until other arrangements were found for them. Rena continues to describe her benefactress' goodness, "I remember Stasia escorting me to a hospital which was run by nuns when I had an appendicitis attack. She certainly endangered her life after the curfew hour, while coaching me about how to behave with a priest and about possible confession before my surgery."

During the Polish uprising of August–September 1944, Mietek and Stanislawa (Stasia) Kolski were ordered out of the city by the Germans like other inhabitants and arrived in the village of Walka Kosowska and the nearby village of Leśnia Kosowska, where Moshe Flakowicz joined her with another member of her husband's family. As for Moshe's wife, Cesia, she fared badly. Expelled from Warsaw to Pruszkow, she was taken from there to the Stutthof concentration camp and made her escape during a death march. She survived.

In the meantime, in Słotwina-Brzesko, Joseph Flakowicz (under the name of Marek Wojciech Łągiewski) had settled in with the Łoza-Nowak family. The family included the widowed mother Stefania Łoza, who lost her husband during the German bombardment of Poland at the start of the invasion of September 1939. Her daughter, Irena Nowak, also a widow (her husband died of tuberculosis at the start of the war), was the mother of three small children: a son of Joseph's age and two younger daughters. Irena's brother Eugeniusz Łoza was single. Another sister lived in Warsaw and a brother had left for America before the war. The Łoza-Nowak house was quite roomy, relatively speaking, consisting of three or four rooms and a vegetable garden. Joseph, with his non-Polish features (dark eyes and hair, and circumcised to boot), his short-sightedness and his chronic bronchitis, stayed mostly indoors. To strangers, he was represented as a relative from a distant village whose parents had been killed in the war. He behaved as a Christian, with full prayers mornings and evenings that he learned by heart. However, he was not sent to school, nor did he attend church services on Sundays and holidays, for fear that someone would suspect or recognize him from Brzesko. The atmosphere at home was of strong Polish nationalism. "I was taught

Polish national hymns and martial songs from the period of the war of liberation, as well as church hymns."

Danger threatened when, due to the relatively large size of the home, the Loza-Nowaks were forced to billet a German soldier. He was accommodated in the kitchen and slept next to the wall on which opposite side was Joseph's bed in the children's room. After a while, another soldier joined him. Both walked around with weapons and all felt the danger that this presented to Joseph. The situation was exacerbated when one day SS troopers showed up to carry out a house search for hidden weapons, probably based on the tip from an informer that the family had close ties with the underground in the surrounding woods. Several of them even stayed over for the night, and the next day, armed with shovels, they began to dig in the garden looking for weapons. The previous evening, Joseph had seen the elderly Stefania Łoza transfer weapons in her apron to be hidden in the brick stove next to the kitchen – a spot that the Germans had already searched – feeling that the Germans would not check the stove a second time. She was proven right. The SS remained in the house for a full week, and were finally satisfied with the family's denials that they had anything to do with storing weapons.

After they left, the Łoza-Nowak family continued to treat Joseph with great kindness and warmth. They even invested much time in his education, teaching the eight-year-old boy to read and write. They also took Joseph for early morning walks in the lush countryside to counter his cloistered existence. Just before liberation, in January 1945, the two soldiers billeted in the house left for good and everyone was relieved. Soon Joseph's father turned up with son Yitzhak, and with Cesia his wife's appearance the Flakowicz family was reunited. They were the lucky ones – they had all survived. Yitzhak was sent with Leopolda Kuropieska, who left to join her husband, Józef, in London – freed from a German prisoner-of-war camp and on a diplomatic mission on behalf of the new Polish government. She gladly took Yitzhak along on her diplomatic passport and he stayed with them in London for about a month before continuing in 1947 to Palestine, where he joined the rest of his family.

In Israel, Joseph Komem (changed from Flakowicz) learned that Eugeniusz Łoza was married to a deaf woman and became the father of three children (one or two of them unfortunately also suffering from their parents' ailment). After Eugeniusz's death, in 2001, Joseph Komem donated a plaque in his name, placed in the commemoration section of the Helen Keller Center of the Association of the Deaf in Israel.

As for Stanislawa (Stasia) Kolska, moving with her husband, Mietek, to the United States (where he Americanized his first name to Martin), the still strictly Catholic Stasia started to observe all Jewish holidays, preparing all the right foods down to the smallest detail, buying matzos, and eating no bread during the Passover festival, even after her husband died. All this while she continued to celebrate her own Catholic holidays and attend church regularly. She also supported the local synagogue and never failed to send a donation for a *kaddish* (Hebrew prayer for the departed) to be recited in the name of her late husband and mother-in-law.

In 1983, Yad Vashem conferred the title of Righteous Among the Nations on Stefania Łoza, her daughter Irena Nowak, and Eugeniusz Łoza. Earlier, in 1967, Leopolda Kuropieska was also accorded the Righteous title, and in 2005, Stanislawa Kolska, now known as Stella Kolski, was also added to the honor roll of the Righteous.

Majerčik, Michal & Anna

SLOVAKIA

*I*n March 1939, Slovakia declared its independence, with the blessings of Nazi Germany, when the former Czechoslovakia to which Slovakia belonged was dismantled and ceased to exist. A Fascist regime rose in the new state, headed by a Catholic priest, Father Jozef Tiso, and supported by a local militia, the Hlinka Guards. Slovakia joined Nazi Germany in the war against the Soviet Union, and sent a brigade to fight alongside its ally. Some 136,000 Jews lived in the country on the eve of its independence. Between March and October 1942, some 58,000 were deported to concentration camps in Poland. The deportations then stopped, and were resumed in October 1944, when the Germans took over direct control of the country – adding 13,500 to the list of the deportees, not counting the thousands who lived in regions ceded to Hungary, who were also deported. The majority of Slovak Jewry disappeared in the Holocaust.

Janka-Hetty Fisch (hereafter Hetty) was born in 1932 in Bratislava, Slovakia's capital city, to her father, a dentist. Her mother died at Hetty's birth and an aunt came over to help raise the child. Hetty witnessed the antisemitic measures of the Fascist regime, including the expulsion of her family from their home and the confiscation of valuables (jewelry, coats, bank accounts, clothes, etc.) as well as the obligatory wearing of the identifying yellow star on their outer garments. At first she was forced to attend a school for Jewish pupils only, but this too was shut down by order of the authorities. Jews were also forbidden to use certain streets or go to sports facilities and public swimming pools. People were free to taunt, ridicule, and even assault Jews without police intervention. Abusing Jews in the street had become a national pastime. All this, in full view of a young and growing girl.

In summer of 1943, the situation in Bratislava had became insufferable, so Hetty's father sent her to her aunt Beate, who had earlier taken care of her and was now married to Julius Weiner and staying in Zilina with her husband. There, the authorities interned the Jews in a labor camp, and many were assigned to build the city's sport stadium. Those working on this project were allowed, at the end of the day's work, to stay in the city itself rather than in the camp, in

Michal and Anna Majerčik (private collection)

rented rooms. In August 1944, the Germans took over after invading Slovakia to quell a local uprising and decided to liquidate the remaining Jews. All Jewish workers were then forbidden to stay overnight in the city and had to return to the camp at the end of the day's work, falsely promised that no harm would come to them, at least until the stadium was finished.

That same month Gestapo men accompanied by local Hlinka Guard militiamen arrived to take the Jews in the camp to the train station for deportation to Auschwitz. Some people were allowed to retrieve the belongings that they had earlier left in their rented rooms, Hetty, her uncle, and her aunt among them. Accompanied by two Gestapo agents the three went upstairs to their room; two other Gestapo men waited for them outside the building. After getting their belongings, the Weiners went downstairs as ordered and were taken in charge by the Gestapo outside. Hetty followed her relatives downstairs, but suddenly a door opened and a total stranger stretched out his hand, pulled Hetty inside, and shut the door behind him. His only words were, "Don't be afraid, my child; I only want to help you; don't talk and don't shout." The man's name was Dr. Michal Majerčik. Helped by his wife, Anna, they lay Hetty on the board of a small bed and placed a mattress on top of her with a sheet, and then their little baby boy, "I lay there without moving."

Soon the Gestapo came to look for her. They had rightly surmised that Hetty had disappeared between two floors, since she was not seen coming out of the building. They searched everywhere, from the basement to the upper stories. Bursting into Majerčik's home, they turned everything upside down, emptied closets and moved all the furniture – even removing the ashes from the oven. The missing girl could be hiding there. Hetty remembered, "I heard one of the Gestapo men ask Dr. and Mrs. Majerčik whether they knew that the penalty for hiding Jews was death for the entire family by execution? They answered, 'Yes, we know.'" The frustrated Gestapo returned several times to all the places in the building but came up with nothing. All this time, Hetty lay motionless under the mattress of the Majerčik baby.

The first days in the Majerčik house Hetty slept in the bed shared by the Majerčiks. Later she was given the room of her hosts' two-and-a-half-year-old daughter, Miroslava, and the little girl was moved to her parents' room, where the baby also stayed. Hetty's room included a closet, table, chair, and shelves with books. Anna Majerčik made sure that flowers were always on the table. "It is hard for me to find words to tell how much they cared for all my needs, for warm clothes, shoes, even buying me slippers. At night, when I felt terribly homesick, they tucked me in in their bed. They always brought me good and interesting books. They also got textbooks for me and gave me lessons. I really felt their goodness and their love for me. For instance, on Christmas, I received presents like those received by their daughter and son … The family's style of life changed because of me. They stopped visiting friends and did not invite friends to their house for fear of my safety." Mrs. Majerčik gave up the idea of taking the job as a high school teacher for which she had applied, sacrificing the extra money it would bring. "They never left me alone in the house, for they knew that I was afraid. When there were air attacks they did not go down to the shelter but stayed with me." Across the street from their house was a grocery, and the woman who owned it, who was related to President Tiso, had seen Hetty enter the house with her uncle and aunt in the company of the Gestapo, and had noticed that when Hetty's relatives were taken away,

Hetty was not with them. She had duly reported this to the authorities, and insisted that the young girl was somewhere inside the building.

Anna Majerčik's mother, Valeria Majerčikova, lived by herself in a little house nearby, in the middle of a courtyard. Next to the house was a shack where the elderly woman hid seven Jewish people, consisting of Lajos Klein, his wife, daughter, and extended family – with Mrs. Majerčik's mother providing for their needs. One day in March 1945, tipped off by an informer, the Gestapo raided the house and found the hidden Jews. When news spread, Anna Majerčik dressed Hetty up as a farm girl, placed their baby boy in a carriage, and told Hetty to take it down the road toward the slaughterhouse, which was some distance away. "Don't stop, don't talk to anyone, and go fast."

It was a typical winter day, but especially cold, with a heavy snow coming down accompanied by strong winds that made it difficult for Hetty to make any progress. The street lights had dimmed. Hetty lost her way as she pushed the carriage in all directions. The baby started crying; he was hungry but Hetty did not have a bottle to give him. Due to the poor visibility, Hetty did not know where she was. "When I no longer felt the toes on my feet and the fingers on my hands because of the cold and the child had fallen asleep after much wailing, I was at the end of my strength. I despaired, and sat down on a rock beneath a tree. I fell asleep, with my head on the baby carriage, and this is how Dr. Majerčik found me at nine o'clock in the evening." It turned out that the Majerčiks had searched for Hetty and the baby for hours, and almost went out of their minds with worry. Despite this, they did not let Hetty feel that she had caused them pain. In her words,

> "When I asked them why they had turned over the child to me, since had I been caught by the Gestapo, the child would have suffered the same fate as me, they answered, 'We were afraid that if we let you go alone you would be arrested, and we hoped that a young girl leading a carriage with a baby would not arouse any suspicion, and everyone would think she was hurrying to get home.' Today [1981], when I am a mother of five children, I still find it hard to believe how they did not fear for their baby's safety. I am not sure that in their place I would have displayed a similar magnanimity."

Hetty stayed with the Majerčiks until the war's end. When her uncle, who survived the camps, came to fetch her (her aunt also survived) and wanted to pay Hetty's benefactors, they refused to accept any reward. Also, packages of food and clothing sent by the relatives to the Majerčiks were returned unopened, again and again. The only thing asked by them was for Hetty to maintain contact. Two years after the war's end, Hetty happened to be visiting the Majerčiks and she took this occasion to ask Dr. Michal Majerčik how was it that he had opened the door of his apartment at the precise moment when Hetty passed by? He answered that he had just gotten home and saw two Gestapo men guarding the building's entrance, so he immediately surmised that they were taking away some people for deportation. The Majerčik had only a few days earlier moved into their apartment, and had not yet gotten to know the building's tenants. As he went into his house, he decided to stand near the half-open door. Suddenly he heard some people coming down the stairs. As Hetty summarizes Majercik's account of events, "He stuck his head out and saw my uncle, my aunt, and me very close to his door. He did not see the Gestapo men, since they were still busy sealing the detainees' apartment. In that moment he decided to try and save my life." Janka-Hetty Fisch survived thanks to this courageous spur-of-the-moment act of Dr. Michal Majerčik, accompanied by the help of his wife, Anna. Hetty's father was less fortunate, perishing in the Holocaust.

In 1981, Yad Vashem conferred the title of Righteous Among the Nations on Dr. Michal and Anna Majerčik.

Málková, Hana & Eva
Czech Republic

*O*n March 15, 1938, Germany tore up the Munich treaty of September 1938, which it had signed together with England and France, committing itself to guaranteeing Czechoslovakia's independence within its reduced borders, and invaded the country. The Czech lands of Bohemia and Moravia were declared a German protectorate, with Slovakia detached and declared an independent state with Fascist rule installed there. While Czech president Emil Hacha remained in office, real power was in the hands of Nazi-appointed governors. The German occupation lasted until the end of the war, in May 1945. The officially registered 88,000 Jews still there in late 1941 experienced the full force of the Nazi persecutions and 77,000 lost their lives in Nazi concentration camps; a few others luckily survived the depredations of the camps. When liberation came, there were only 2,800 Jews left, and an undisclosed number survived in hiding. One of these was Heda Kaufmannová, along with three other Jewish women. They were hidden in the home of Hana Málková and her daughter Eva, born in 1922.

Heda Kaufmannová and her brother Viktor had both been active in a Czech clandestine cell since her country's takeover by the Germans in March 1938. Heda became a messenger in this secret cell and carried out assignments given to her mostly by her brother, such as arranging places for meetings of the cell and looking up people willing to shelter individuals sought by the Gestapo. In February 1939, she lost her job as a secretary at the State Health Institute, since she was Jewish, and was forced to move with her mother and other Jewish families to a special house reserved for Jews. On September 5, 1942, summoned to report for deportation, she instead went underground. From that moment on, with the Gestapo looking for her, she found shelter with various people. In her postwar memoirs, she listed 22 people with whom she stayed for a day or two or other short spells. In some of these places she managed to flee in the nick of time, just before a Gestapo raid.

Jarka Maiwaldová and Heda Kaufmannová had known each other since their Girl Scout days. During the German occupation, Heda gave private lessons in German to Jarka's daughter Sylva, born in 1931. One day Heda came to Sylva's apartment and gave her two books and a fountain pen. In Sylva's words, "I realized that this was the end for her. She would not have given me her fountain pen had she not been going away like all the other Jewish people. I was told that Heda and her mother had gone away on a transport." Sylva was therefore surprised when towards the end of the war, in the second half of April 1945, her mother took her to Hana Málková's flat and there she met Heda again. "It was a very emotional encounter. We were all very happy."

As Heda Kaufmannová related in her postwar memoirs, in July 1943 she had run out of hiding places. At this point, her close friend and helper, Mrs. Čizková, got in touch with Mrs. Málková and asked her whether she was prepared to shelter Heda. Hana Málková decided to come over for a first impression of the stranger before deciding. Heda wrote: "She came to see me at my other place, at Mrs. Čizková's. I stood face to face with a tall gray-haired woman whose age contrasted with her very lively brown eyes and youthful smile … Her figure suggested someone active in sports. She stretched out her hand and chuckled. There was something direct and spontaneous in her smile and movements, as though it was a matter of course for her to welcome me as one of her own … She said, 'Oh, it's you. I've heard plenty about you. You can come to our place.'"

When Heda arrived at Málková's home, in accordance with the instructions given to her she came quietly through the front door of the building. "I closed the door behind me and as luck would have it a woman stood at the basement door." Heda had been told to avoid the basement, where other people lived, and head straight for the upper floor, where Hana Málková and her daughter Eva resided. Now, before even the start of her stay there, another person in the same house had apparently already taken note of her. "But the person came straight toward me, with a young and lively face and white teeth – with a smile, and with a finger on her lips. She had planned to get me upstairs right away and that is why she had hidden on the steps to the basement." It was none other than the 17-year-old Eva. "Silently we went upstairs, toward the open door, which she closed behind me. It was July 13, 1943."

"But what awaited me," Heda continued, "was a cat's life, or rather life with a cat. And not just any cat." Heda would later explain the significance of this cat's presence. She first met the beautiful Angora in the living room. "How beautiful you are," Heda exclaimed in an almost too loud voice. "The cat got up slowly and majestically led us to the kitchen." Later, when Málková returned from work, the two women greeted each other like old friends. "I sat down on a footstool as though I was used to sitting there, and 'hop,' the cat is in my lap … The Málková women stared at me in total bewilderment, and I wondered why? This had never happened, they said. The animal never approaches a strange person, and certainly does not sit on his lap. She does this with us only when she is in the right mood." Heda continued, half jokingly, half seriously, "Thus Isolda [the cat's name] … herself provided the best reference to the Málková family and welcomed me, a homeless person, like an old friend. It was for them and me the beginning of 22 months of a clandestine life."

Hana Málková's daughter, Eva, gave a slightly different account of Heda's arrival at her home. When Mrs. Čizková came to their house and said there was need to hide a Jewish woman for several days, "I said, of course." Then, when Mrs. Čizková continued and said the woman was Jewish. "I said, so what?" Čizková then added that the Gestapo was after her, and "I said, great! This gives me another chance to do the Nazis in. Mom will be home later, but I think it will be okay." When her mother arrived, she said, 'Well, you've already agreed, I cannot be denied. One must help." Heda came that same day, or the next day. When Eva's mother returned from work, Eva told her, "Well, how could I have left her in the lurch? And in any case where would she go? She must stay with us." Telling this later to Heda, Hana Málková told her, "I ask you, how could I have said no when my own daughter said yes?" Heda hid there from July 13, 1943 to Prague's liberation, on May 5, 1945, three days before the war's end. Heda's sister-in-law, Irma Kaufmannová, wife of Heda's brother Viktor, also hid there.

For Heda this was almost like paradise on earth after six months of running from one place to another. As she wrote in her memoirs:

"It goes without saying that after a long period of lack of security, improvisations, sleepovers in barns, among strangers, on dirty hay, on floors no less dirty, washing in the morning at a courtyard water well or river, and continuous running to and fro; after all this period of homelessness, to be able to sit down at a table covered with a table cloth, having an endless amount of good food, fresh bread; to wash in warm water, and the miracle of a bed with sheets – knowing that all this was not just for one day, but repeated the next and the following days. The feeling of belonging with the two Málkovás – the sense of security."

At the same time, security required that rules be strictly obeyed. It goes without saying that there was no question of stepping out. Indoors, walking was on tiptoes; there were neighbors downstairs. When the Málkovás were at work, Heda and Irma were to tiptoe in slippers or sneakers with the least movement possible. Irma passed most days in the study and Heda in the kitchen, where she had already stacked up books on the table. Conversations between the two were to be in a whisper; indeed everything was to be done silently. Water faucets were not to be opened when Heda and Irma were alone, neither was the water to be flushed in the toilet. Málková's apartment faced a German army barracks. But, as Heda quipped in her memoirs, it is often dark under the candlestick. In all this, Isolda, the cat, wittingly or not, played an important role. As revealed by both Heda Kaufmannová and Eva Lutovsky (her later married name):

"The cat's noise helped us. Its noise served as a cover for our movements, which nevertheless caused us much concern. When [Hana and Eva] were out, only the cat could jump freely on the furniture and walk around, going through the half-open door between the kitchen and the hallway and thus creating for the downstairs neighbors some noise for us. If there was any noise heard downstairs, it was attributed to the cat, Isolda. Of course, Isolda could not draw the water from the tap or pull the chain in the toilet. People in the building wondered from time to time why the cat was making such wild jumps that sounded like people walking. And sometimes the cat even turned on the water tap. But a little cat is an intelligent creature indeed and can manage all sorts of things."

For almost two years, until the end of the war, the downstairs neighbors never knew that someone was living upstairs illegally. Of course, the hidden persons were not to answer the downstairs doorbell. These would usually be the mailman and people from the gas and electric company. There were almost no other visitors, since in those days it was not customary to drop in unannounced. Relatives lived far away, about 150 kilometers from Prague, and did not visit. During unannounced visits, Heda and Irma would be quickly hidden in the locked study or under a pile of bed covers in a side room formerly occupied by the maid. Once an aunt and her granddaughter came to visit and Heda and Irma remained hidden in a back room.

Hana Málková worked in the telephone department of the Supreme Court and her daughter Eva worked for a time as a secretary for Emil Hacha, the half-senile President of the Czech Protectorate who stayed in office after the German takeover but had no power. Eva also did secretarial work in the main Social Security office. The situation took a critical turn when Hana suffered a heart attack on her way to work, and had to rest for a few days at home. Her immediate supervisor was an ethnic German who pressed Hana to register as a German based on her mother's birth, although she had married a Czech man and had since declared herself as Czech. He then tried to force her to return to work prematurely by making her appear before an office doctor. Not yet satisfied with this, he continued to harass her, transferring her from the convenient telephone center to an administrative post that required her presence every day. This made it difficult for the hidden persons, for now Hana had to spend longer hours at work, and when she came home she was totally exhausted. Her supervisor continued to harass her and caused her early retirement, achieved in March 1945.

On April 15, 1945, weeks away from liberation but with the Nazis still in full control in Prague, Hana and Eva admitted another fleeing Jewish person. It was Hana Weisbergerová, who with her sister Lucie were among a group of 10 women who had escaped from a Death March from Kurzbach to Gross Rosen. Making their way to Prague, friends from before war cared for them, and Weisbergerová was sent to Málková. Somewhat later, her sister Lucie also joined her. The stories told by these two newcomers were frightening. "From them, we learned what took place in Auschwitz," Heda Kaufmannová related; "words like 'selection,' 'gas chambers,' 'crematorium,' and other concentration camp terms." There were now four Jewish women hidden in Málková's Prague home, and they saw liberation on May 5, 1945 – only days before the official end of the war. Sadly for Heda, she learned that her brother Viktor Kaufmann, the husband of Irma, had been executed by the Germans in February 1945 on the charge of high treason.

In 1999, Yad Vashem recognized Hana Málková and her daughter Eva as Righteous Among the Nations.

Mamen, Hans-Christian
NORWAY

Germany invaded Norway on April 9, 1940, and within a month completed the occupation of the country. A puppet government was set up under Nazi supervision, headed by Vidkun Quisling, leader of the local Nazi Party. There were some 1,700 Jews in the country, toward whom the occupying power applied restrictive measures. Then, in October 1942, the Germans decided to deport them; they succeeded in laying their hands on 760 Jews, who were taken by boat to Stettin; then by train to Auschwitz, where most were gassed. About 900 Jews survived by fleeing to neighboring Sweden, an undertaking impossible without the active participation of the Norwegian underground, one of whose operatives was Hans-Christian Mamen.

As told by Mamen, one day in November 1942 he received an urgent phone call from a Jewish family that had been referred to him. The father and a son were hiding in a small apartment in Oslo but could stay there no longer, while the wife was hiding elsewhere. The family had managed to flee Nazi Germany just a few days before the German invasion of Norway. The wife's aged father had already been arrested and, as a German Jew, knowing what to expect from his captors, he had taken his life with poison. The family asked Mamen's help to flee to Sweden. Hans-Christian's parents agreed to take into their home in Asker the father and child – Dr. Winterfeld and his 16-year-old son Gerhard. However, this could only be a temporary arrangement. In the meantime, Hans-Christian went to see the man's wife to assure that her husband and son were in good hands. He then made contact with what he termed an "export-route" to Sweden. It was not a simple matter, and one had to act quickly. First, one had to reach Mysen, and from there the Swedish border with the help of underground operatives. Since the Winter-

Hans-Christian Mamen

felds were not familiar with the country and its language, Mamen had to accompany them himself to Mysen. For the trip, he took a bus that also transported milk. Mamen and the three Winterfelds (the parents were reunited with their daughter) went first, while their son was to follow later. While on the bus, they were told to pretend not to know each other.

Arriving in Mysen, the Winterfelds continued to Orje. From there the party proceeded to Rodnes Lake, which they crossed in a small boat. Then they continued in total darkness past fields, barbed wire fences, and streams. "Those few kilometers felt like an eternity," Mamen recalled. Close to Klund Chapel on the eastern shore of the Rodnes Lake was the farm that was their next stop. The party then entered a dense forest that extended into Sweden. Before starting on this last leg of the journey, the party was told to get some sleep, fully dressed. Before sunrise, they started again, and soon crossed into Sweden. The Winterfelds were safe. But Mamen's mission was not over. Mrs. Winterfeld looked at him with pleading eyes as they parted: "Please take good care of our boy!"

Back in Norway, young Gerhard Winterfeld was moved to Morro, near Asker, and there he luckily avoided arrest, thanks to the friendly disposition of a policeman, who one morning stopped the youthful Gerhard and asked to see his identity card. It had the large eye-catching "J" on it. When the policeman saw the Jewish mark on the card, he excused himself for having frightened the young Gerhard and said that he had actually come from the Asker police station to look for a certain thief. "Don't be afraid," he comforted the boy, "nobody will know you are staying here." It was a lucky break for Gerhard. It is told that this policeman was later arrested for helping the underground and imprisoned. Gerhard was moved by Mamen to his home in Asker, and eventually taken across the border to Sweden. "I stood on the Swedish border and waved goodbye to him, glad on his account, and for his father, his mother, and his sister."

Mamen continued to help other Jews on the run to reach the Swedish border. At first, the fleeing fugitives remained temporarily hidden in houses, staying indoors during daylight hours and only at night being allowed to step outside and stretch their legs a bit. As for Dr. Zellner, over 80 years old, he began exercising indoors. He filled a knapsack with old books and heavy objects and walked back and forth, practicing he said for the trip to Sweden. "However, we dared not let this old man make this arduous journey," Mamen noted, "and we got him to Sweden on a fishing boat." When, for instance, it came time to take Dr. Neumann and his wife, they were told to board a bus heading for the frontier zone together with another fleeing Jew. Mamen also got on, but they pretended not to know each other and even sat quite far apart. Suddenly, as the bus was ready to leave, a police car pulled up in front and two constables from the Norwegian state police got on the bus and asked the passengers to show identification. One started from the rear; the other from the front. And there, next to the driver, sat the third Jew... He cast a frightened glance in Mamen's direction. Mamen turned white. "My hands were damp." The man was typically Semitic looking. That was why Mamen had not prepared a false identity card for him, for fear that if he were caught he could implicate others under pressure. The man had trouble finding his card. The policeman got impatient and said, "I'll be with you later." Then came the turn of the Neumans, who were equipped with false identity cards. The two constables met in the middle of the bus, having finished their inspection, except for the Jew who still hadn't produced an identity card. At this point, one constable said to the other, "Okay, let's leave." Says Mamen: "I was sitting with theology books in my hands and had told the police I was going to Mysen to visit a friend who was ill. Now I folded my hands and thanked God for the constable who had done his duty to humanity and sabotaged tyranny."

On another occasion, Mamen carried the three-year-old son of a dentist across the border to Sweden. As the boy sat on Mamen's shoulders, he began to sing. He naturally did not understand the importance of being silent as they walked through the woods. Mamen related how he handled the problem:

> *"We managed to silence him by telling him not to disturb the birds who were sleeping. I still remember his strong grip in my hair, and how he bent down and looked at me with his dark eyes. A son of Abraham, and a good Norwegian boy he was. The meaning was that this little boy and all of his race were to be killed. But he was saved from the gas chamber. It was my privilege to see the boy's family safely across the border where they were received by Swedish soldiers, and could start speaking out loud again, just as it was time for the birds to awaken. But we heard no birds singing. It was November 1942, and darkness reigned in Europe."*

Felix and Edith Adler were another couple helped by Hans-Christian Mamen. Early one morning, in November 1942, when the Germans arrested all Jewish men between the ages of 15 and

65 – men at first and not their wives – Edith Adler succeeded in warning her husband, Felix, at the factory where he worked not to come home. For a short time he stayed hidden at a friend's house, but he could not stay there for long. Edith herself had to report to the local police station once every 24 hours. She tried to get in touch with an underground group that might be able to help her family cross the border into Sweden and went to see the Reverend Per Faye-Hansen, who was a friend of the family, but was then ill and in a hospital. When she visited him there, he phoned Professor Hallesby, who at the time headed the illegal leadership of the Norwegian Church, and he in turn introduced Mrs. Adler to Hans-Christian Mamen – who took over the assignment to save the Adlers. In Edith's words, "Mamen immediately made a very good impression on me. I could see that he was utterly reliable, kind and helpful." He told her she and her husband should meet him that same night at a place outside Oslo. Edith packed two knapsacks and after meeting her husband at the train station rode with him to the designated station, where Mamen was waiting for them.

Mamen first settled the Adlers in with a Norwegian family who lived at Valstad, near the farm of Hans-Christian's parents, and where they were warmly welcomed and given a room to themselves. From there, Mamen moved them to several places, including his parents' home. Finally, the day of their escape to Sweden had come. For that, the Adlers had first to go back to Oslo by train, where they sat in different compartments, and meet in the middle of Oslo. They were instructed to take a bus going toward the Swedish border, but not actually up to it. At that time there was a restricted zone of several kilometers between the Norwegian and Swedish border. To enter the zone, one had to have a permit, which the Adlers naturally did not have. They had been told that if – contrary to their expectations – there should be a police raid on the bus, they were to give them the address of a family living outside the forbidden zone, whom they were supposedly planning to visit. The family really lived there, but didn't know anything about the fugitives. When the bus was just about to leave, two plainclothes policemen got on and everybody on the bus had to identity himself – a repeat of the earlier incident with the Winterfelds. In Mrs. Adler's words, "We two had only our own identity cards with a large red 'J' (= Jew) on them. But luck was with us. The policemen were Norwegians and not Germans and seeing our identity cards they got a real shock, and so did we. We started to tell them the story of our intended visit and they studied our passes for a considerable time, saying nothing. Then they gave the passes back to us and left. The bus started on its way." Edith's husband told her it was better to get off the bus, since the police would probably alert others to arrest them when they got off, "but I knew somehow that the policemen had at once realized that we were on our way out of the country and that they wanted to help us. I was proved right and nobody came after us." Through these tense moments, Mamen sat up front, watching closely as the drama unfolded in the back of the bus, and glad that nothing serious took place.

The Adlers had been told to get off the bus when Mamen got off, and they followed him without talking to each other. He led the two to the house of a bus driver, where they met around half a dozen other Jewish fugitives. The bus driver had put his bus at the disposal of the underground. With the group on his bus, he drove at night without his lights in the direction of the Swedish border, through a dense forest. When they got off the bus, they were already inside the restricted zone. It was a beautiful and clear night, with a full moon, and therefore the greater the danger of being spotted by border patrols. Mamen and the bus driver led them through the forest to a lake, where another man took them across in his boat. Disembarking on the other side of the lake, they quietly crossed a road that was patrolled by the Germans and the group was told to keep absolutely still. There were some with children, who had been put to sleep with tranquilizers. The group approached a farmer's house, a stone's throw from the Swedish border, where they spent the night. The two mothers and their babies got a room for themselves. Edith and Felix Adler, being the oldest in the group (they were then in their early thirties) were allowed to sleep in the farmer's bedroom, which he shared with his wife.

Early next morning, after a hearty breakfast, the farmer guided the group through the forest and into Sweden. Once over the border, Mamen and the bus driver bid the fleeing Jews farewell, and the two returned to the Norwegian side, to continue with their help to fugitives – many of them Jews. As for this particular group, when they approached a Swedish military camp, they were admitted and given something to eat and then taken by lorry farther into Sweden.

Back in Norway, Hans-Christian Mamen eventually had to go into hiding, as the authorities were looking for him. His sister Judith, who had helped him care for the refugees, was arrested by the Germans and spent several years in prison. Their parents had to abandon their farm, which the Germans confiscated. "Both my husband and myself owe our lives first of all to Hans-Christian Mamen and then to all the other people who helped us," Edith Adler noted in her deposition. "None of them got paid for their help. Hans-Christian Mamen has saved not only us but many other people and he has done so at the risk of losing his own life. We will never forget this as long as we live." His was part of a larger team of Norwegians in the underground that made it possible for over half the Jewish population in the country to survive, by smuggling them across the border into Sweden.

In 1979, Yad Vashem conferred on by then Pastor Hans-Christian Mamen the title of Righteous Among the Nations.

Meerburg, Pieter
Musch, Jacobus (Jaap) & Gerard
Woortman, Johannes (Joop)
Voort van de, Johanna (Hanna)
Voûte, Henriëtte (Hetty)
Söhnlein, Gisela
and dozens more
NETHERLANDS

*T*he persons mentioned above were among the leading figures in three organizations or cells, two of whom were made up of university students, which arose spontaneously in the summer of 1942 with one purpose in mind – to save Jewish children from deportation to the death camps. These mostly young men and women were not part of any institutionalized underground network, although they sought such assistance to facilitate their own specific activities. They are to be credited with the rescue of over one thousand children from the hell of the gas chambers. Today these children are themselves parents and grandparents, and consequently progenitors of thousands more. They are thankful for the help received from a group of people filled with youthful fervor combined with deep humanitarian commitment.

It all began in the summer of 1942 when the leaders of a student group in the city of Utrecht that called itself Utrechts Kindercomité (Utrecht Children's Committee, henceforth UCC) contacted another student in Amsterdam, Pieter Meerburg, to suggest to him the establishment of an Amsterdam-based student group for the purpose of saving Jewish children from deportation. The idea was that the Amsterdam group would pick up the children in the city with the largest Jewish population and spirit them out to Utrecht, some 35 kilometers to the south, where the other student group would then disperse them to various places in the country.

Pieter Meerburg

The UCC already knew that Meerburg was toying with the idea of a similar group in Amsterdam. The idea had germinated in his mind earlier in the occupation when as a law student he had refused to sign the so-called loyalty oath to the German occupation administration and thereby lost the right to study at the university. At about the same time, he also happened to be sitting with a Jewish friend when the man was called to the phone. He then told Pieter that had been ordered to proceed to a labor camp for Jews in North Holland province. Pieter Meerburg was greatly upset by this development in his country, and this strengthened his determination to do something about it. Learning in the summer of 1942 of the start of the deportation of the Jews, he was led to respond favorably to the UCC invitation.

Meerburg gathered a group of students around him, and they began to plan ways to save Jewish children. At the same time a certain Dr. Philip Fiedeldij Dop operated a pediatric practice in Amsterdam with two Jewish pediatricians – one of whom committed suicide and the other of whom went into hiding. As a result, Dop took over the care his partners' clientele, most of whom were Jews. Anxious himself to save his patients' children, when he heard of the Meerburg group, in August 1942, Dop got in touch with Meerburg and assured him that as someone trusted by the Jewish community, he could convince a large number of families of the urgent need to save their children by placing them in the hands of the unknown Piet Meerburg organization made up of young students and calling itself the Amsterdam Student Group (henceforth ASG).

The founders of the ASG were four in number: law student Pieter Meerburg, mathematics student Jur Haak, his sister Tineke Haak, and Tineke's boyfriend Wouter van Zeytveld. Piet's fiancée Hansje van Loghem, succeeded in recruiting members via her student debating society. Soon this small group of young people was devoting all of its time to the rescue effort. The young age of the rescuers heightened their sense of identification with the children. Meerberg's student organization also took care of the necessary financing of food and clothing, supplying his wards with forged identity cards and food ration coupons. By the end of August 1942, the students had already managed to bring 70 children to safe havens outside Amsterdam with the help of the Utrecht-based UCC.

As the number of children from Amsterdam exceeded the number of safe houses available to the UCC, Meerberg decided to branch out. This was especially so during the six months after January 1943, when the ASG smuggled approximately 140 children out of the Crèche (a former day care center in Amsterdam for children of working parents, converted by the Germans into the main children's assembly point on the eve of their deportation). In January 1943, he enlisted his 31-year-old cousin, Mia Coelingh, who lived in Sneek, Friesland province, where she worked as an assistant minister in the Liberal wing of the Protestant church and taught religion in public schools. She used her connections with the local clergy to lay the groundwork for finding hiding places, such as with Father Gerard Jansen and the Baptist minister Willem Mesdag, whose spacious home because a haven for new arrivals. The three branched out in the Friesland area while Meerbug and Wouter van Zeytveld scoured the Leeuwarden region, the provincial capital of Friesland, where chaplain Felix van der Wissel helped out. Piet Meerburg went under the alias Piet van Doorn

One of Wissel's parishioners was Krijn van den Helm, a tax official active in the underground, who became one of the main stalwarts of this operation, both in raising money and bringing children from Amsterdam to the Friesland region. He enlisted Pieter Wijbenga, the head of the city's ration distribution office in nearby Drachten – an obviously important position for the resistance. Other persons enlisted included Sjoerd Wiersma and Uilke Boonstra, both of Joure near Sneek and both devout Calvinists. Wiersma, in his early thirties, had a laundry business and owned a large truck. Once a week he drove to Amsterdam, returning with a truck full of Jewish fugitives – understandably a very risky undertaking. As a result of these endeavors, shelter was provided for dozens of Jewish children in and around Sneek, a number that steadily increased over the months to a total of several hundred children who found refuge in this part of Friesland.

In May 1943, Meerburg began to explore places in the southern province of Limburg in order to create a network there too. He made contact with Johanna van de Voort in Tienray, through whose efforts 123 Jews, mostly children (the youngest one only two weeks old), found shelter in the area. Arie van Mansum, a salesman from Maastricht who had set up an illegal network of his own, also joined Meerburg's organization, and through him 33 children found shelter in the area. Women like Iet van Dijk, Tineke Haak, and Marie ("Mieke") Mees served mostly as couriers, accompanying children to safe havens. Nearly all of Piet's female couriers registered babies as "theirs" and acted as if greatly embarrassed that they did not know who the father was. From early 1944, the so-called evacuation certificate protected many of the hidden children and their foster parents. These documents, issued by the Central Evacuation Bureau in Rotterdam, indicated that the child in question came from the bombed-out area of Rotterdam and was therefore living with a foster family. It is estimated that some 350 Jewish children were saved by the ASG under Peter Meerberg's leadership.

A few more words about some of the major activists in Meerburg's ASG. Dr. Philip Fiedeldij Dop delivered between 100 and 200 Jewish children to the ASG until far into 1944. Sometimes, in times of emergency, Dop acted independently, as in September 1943, when he hastened to the Amsterdam Jewish hospital, which was about to be shut down, to smuggle out four-year-old Georgine van Voolen and take her to Sneek, Friesland. Georgine's mother, Henrietta, survived Auschwitz and was happily reunited with her daughter; her husband, Maurits, did not survive the camps.

Krijn van den Helm with his wife, Johanna, found dozens of addresses. Krijn was a wanted man for his additional armed resistance activities, and in the summer of 1944 he left the Friesland region and moved to Amersfoort with his wife. On August 25, 1944, the Sipo (German security police) came to arrest him. In the ensuing exchange of fire, Krijn van den Helm was killed. His wife fled with her son to Bakhuizen, Friesland, and remained in hiding. As for Abraham and Trijntje Nijdam, they worked closely with Krijn in hiding Jewish children. Abraham worked as a supervisor for the Dutch railroad system and refused German orders having to do with the railroad, which forced him to go into hiding.

Mia Coelingh, together with Baptist Pastor Willem Mesdag, were charged with dispersing an estimated 80 children and providing them with clothing. Before placing the children with a foster family, Mia bleached the hair of those who had typically Jewish features. Mesdag, a pastor with the Mennonite Church, and wife Sjoukje hid some people in his church. Overall, the Coelingh and Mesdag team cared for about 80 Jewish children with the help of the Baptist, Reformed, and Catholic communities in the Sneek vicinity.

Jaap van Meer (today Yaakov Agmon), born in 1939, was one of the children helped by the Mesdags in 1943. In a 1991 letter to him from the Mesdags' daughter, Nine Treffers-Mesdag, born in 1925, she affectionately recalled the young boy's stay with her family:

> *"At the moment of your arrival I was in school. During the first days you were very quiet and shy. In your hand you held part of an Amsterdam streetcar ticket. This was precious to you. Your mother had prepared a suitcase with clothes for you. On Sunday we dressed you with nice clothes and you said: 'Sabbath?' We had to say: 'It is Sunday' – not to convert you! Just for safety reasons. We were a family with 5 children…. We did not hide you. That would have been impossible for a lively child, interested in what was going on. Moreover, you were [represented as] an orphan. No questions. So you played in the garden in the backyard with my young brothers. You played in the sandbox, with the swing. All of us were supposed to take care of our 'little one.'… My parents knew that your parents were hidden somewhere in the southern part of the Netherlands. For reasons of safety they did not know where…. You were an inquisitive boy, eager to know what was going on. You wanted to see what happened outside the garden … Now and then you slipped away … Then my parents decided that it was safer for you to go to a farm. We were told that it was for your good health, and that it was nicer for a small boy to be able to run about in the fields around a farm than live in a small town. We were not told where you went and we all knew: don't ask any questions."* [At the end of the war, when Jaap's parents came to fetch him], *we had dinner together, but we did not eat so much – emotions! And we had no kosher food of course. In the evening your father brought his tallit [prayer shawl] and we had a prayer meeting. My father had a prayer book translated into Dutch … It was moving, tears running down our faces … Your parents invited my parents for a meal on Sabbath as soon as your family should be settled again. They managed to find a house in Amsterdam … I still remember the blessing of you three by your parents. Again tears running down our cheeks. We thanked Adonai – it was a Sabbath fulfilled with thanks and gratitude."*

As for Sjoerd Wiersma, he owned a laundry in Joure, Friesland, and was also active in the resistance. He helped to find hiding places, bringing Jews to the region from Amsterdam, and his home served as a transit point for one- or two-night stays. His wife, Trijntje, escorted many children on the back of her bike to their new addresses. She was a nurse and also took care of children with serious cases of scabies, nursing them back to health. In 1944, Sjoerd was forced to go into hiding. After the war, the couple adopted a Jewish girl whose parents had perished in the camps. Finally, Jan Evenhuis, a tax inspector in Leeuwarden, was principally involved in raising funds to assist people hiding in Friesland. Also active in resistance work, he and wife, Johanna, were arrested and imprisoned. Jan was executed by a firing squad in the Vught camp on August 18, 1944.

Moving to the ASG associates in the southern Limburg province – in Maastricht, Arie van Mansum and his sister Margaretha received some 60 Jewish children brought to them by couriers. Arie himself picked the children up at a local train station and sometimes even went to Amsterdam to get them. Arrested, he remained imprisoned until the end of the war.

Johanna, or "Hanna," van de Voort lived in the town of Tienray and was well known in the area because of her midwife practice. It is told that she was present at practically every birth. Hanna's main job was to find new addresses for new arrivals. Meerburg's couriers would escort the fugitives to nearby Venray by train, and the children would then stay at Hanna's house to acclimatize themselves and learn the customs and traditions of this largely Catholic region. They would also be provided with false identity cards and an evacuation certificate, and then taken to foster families. It is estimated that 123 fugitive Jews, mostly children, passed through her hands. On the night of July 30, 1944, the Germans raided the van de Voort house and Hanna was taken to Gestapo headquarters in Eindhoven and interrogated. Hearing of her arrest, Meerburg, in Amsterdam, sent the beautiful Marie (Mieke) Mees (later married to Peter Louwers) to try to obtain Hanna's release. Mieke immediately left for the Gestapo office, and using her female wiles she made advances to the officer in charge. The man took a fancy to Mieke and she promised to go out with him in exchange for the release of "that silly little woman from Tienray." Hanna was released, but Mieke did not turn up for the date. After the war, an exhausted Hanna van de Voort suffered from a heart ailment. She died in 1956, at the age of 52. Her closest aide was Nico Dohmen, whose task was to maintain contact with all the children at their different locations and solve problems arising from the fears and bed wetting of the frightened and disoriented children. On July 30, 1944, he narrowly escaped arrest, and remained in hiding.

On one occasion the beautiful Marie Mees mentioned above, together with a girlfriend, picked up nine Jewish children from the Central Station in Amsterdam and took them by train to Geleen, Limburg. Colleagues of Arie van Mansum were supposed to collect the children at the station, but there was no one there. After some discreet inquiries, they were sent to a miner's family who took in all nine children and gave the two exhausted women a hot meal. Until late 1944, Mieke repeatedly made risky train trips to addresses in Limburg, Friesland, and sometimes Overijssel province. Mieke often got Jewish children from the Crèche in Amsterdam, escorting those who looked Jewish to Tienray, Limburg, where Hanna van de Voort and Nico Dohmen found places for them.

We turn now to the Utrecht Children's Committee. As earlier mentioned, the group's original purpose was to find safe hiding places for Jewish children in the Utrecht region. Jan Meulenbelt was the driving force behind this group with mostly students members, such as Henriëtte (Hetty) Voûte, Gisela Söhnlein, Frits Iordens, Rutger Matthijsen, and Geertjan Lubberhuizen. Söhnlein had the job of maintaining contact with the Amsterdam Student Group (ASG), where the children came from at first. After a short time, the UCC expanded its operations and began to arrange for the shelter of children nationwide. Several hundred Jewish children and a small number of adults were hidden at addresses across the country. Affiliated groups were formed in Arnhem, Rotterdam, and other places. Jewish parents who could afford it paid money. Money was also received from numerous individuals as well as from various institutions. In the first year of the UCC's existence, the Catholic Church, especially the Archbishop of Utrecht, Joannis de Jong, provided the organization with required capital through a secret fund. Much clothing was also collected and distributed from a small depot in Utrecht.

Right from the start, Jewish parents had it made clear to them that any contact with the children was forbidden and that they would never know their whereabouts. After the war, Hetty Voûte learned that a man had followed her from Amsterdam, where she had picked up the child, to her parents home, near Utrecht, to find out about his sister's placement. "I never had any idea that I was being followed." In addition, most foster parents were not told the real name of the children. An estimated 400 persons, mostly children were thus aided by the UCC.

During the war, Hetty Voûte was one of the UCC principals. She had studied biology at the State University in Utrecht and was active in student activity, many of the students being in the resistance. Late in August 1942, she joined the Utrecht Children's Committee. Previously she had, with the help of fellow student Olga Hudig, found addresses for Jewish children in and around Noordwijk, South Holland. In the second half of 1942, Hetty combed the whole country in search of ration cards for the many Jewish children sheltered by her organization. In a short time, she set up a network of 12 distribution offices where cooperative officials supplied the required ration coupons against the children's registration cards. From November 1942, Hetty Voûte also took charge of the UCC's administration, which consisted of an innocent-looking notebook containing the names of the Jews in hiding and – in code – their hiding addresses. Hetty's third job consisted of escorting children to their safe houses. Most of these trips were to villages or towns in southern Netherlands. Whenever there was no hiding place available, Hetty would find a temporary shelter at her parent's home or at Geertruida van Lier's Kindjeshaven, a children nursing home, in Utrecht.

As for Gisela Söhnlein, she was studying law in Amsterdam when after the summer vacation of 1942, Hansje van Loghem, Pieter Meerburg's fiancée, asked her to find safe houses for Jewish children. She agreed and soon became an important link between the UCC and the ASG. She could also travel by train for free because her stepfather was employed by the Dutch railways. Initially, Gisela's job was to pass on information from Meerburg's group in Amsterdam about the number of children to be delivered to the Utrecht area so that the UCC could then start arranging the required hiding places. As she traveled from Amsterdam to Utrecht, Gisela would also bring children with her. In March 1943, when the UCC and the ASG began to operate independently, Gisela moved to Utrecht. From then on, escorting Jewish children to their safe houses (particularly to those in the south of Holland) became her main task – sometimes alone; at other times in the company of other UCC operatives. When she and James van Beusekom traveled together, they often posed as a married couple traveling with their children. On one of these trips, Gisela took young Anita Meyer to Eindhoven, north Brabant, where she stayed until the end of the war. As recalled by Anita Budding-Meyer:

"I go back to a day in May of 1943, the day my family decided we could no longer live safely in the Jewish ghetto in the eastern part of Amsterdam…Gisela had secured a hiding place for me earlier with a family in the southern part of Holland and had promised to take me there when the time came … My father was met and left the house at 7 a.m. My sister left a short while later, to be escorted to her new address. When it was my mother's turn to leave, she had a hard choice to make. Here she was leaving her youngest child – I was 13 at the time – not knowing what my fate would be. The choice was difficult, but the result inescapable. So I had to wait alone, knowing, and hoping, that Gisela would not let me down …I was only 13 years old at the time. I can't remember all the things that came to my mind during those long hours of waiting. But I do know that … there would have been no today for me had Gisela not arrived later that afternoon of May 23, 1943."

Others involved in the UCC work included Geertruida (Truitje) van Lier and her assistant Henriëtte Macey-van Berlekom. The two women, who studied law at the Utrecht University, had set up a children's day care center known as the Kindjeshaven. In July 1942, they decided to clear as much space as possible for extra Jewish children who came to the center before being moved to permanent shelters elsewhere. Two of them, Judith and Deborah Schavrien, twins, stayed there for the duration of the war. Whenever there was the threat of a raid on the home, Van Lier threatened to evict all the children, which included a number of illegitimate children fathered by German soldiers. This would have caused the soldiers to be reprimanded by the German local military commander, who acted as the guardian of these children, and the truth about such children was not what the German command wished to have publicized among the conquered population. This threat usually put them off. In late 1944, Van Lier went into hiding, and her assistant Macey-van Berlekom took over the center until February 1945, and then moved the children to various safe houses.

A native of The Hague and before the war an instructor in the girl scouts, Adriana (Adri) Knappert sheltered children in a summer house in Nieuwebrug, Overijssel province, that belonged to a baron who had been introduced to Anna (Ankie) Stork, who coordinated the UCC's activities in the region. Later Adri and her charges moved to a country estate near Hellendoorn, where more Jewish children were added. Altogether, Adri cared for 13 children in hiding. Later, she herself had to go into hiding, after Anna Stork was arrested. As for Anna Stork, she lived in Nijverdal with her parents, Johan and Guretta, where Johan was the managing director of the Dutch Steam Bleachers. Anna found hiding places Jews in and around Nijverdal and escorted Jewish children from one place to another.

Rutger Matthijsen was another UCC affiliate. Before joining up, in the summer of 1942, he had studied chemistry in Utrecht. His job included raising funds and acquiring supplies for the numerous Jewish children in hiding and locating new venues for the UCC's office, which was constantly being relocated. In February 1943 he was apprehended, suspected of dealing on the black market when he was caught carrying a suitcase full of food earmarked for fugitives. Also discovered were ration cards taped to his body. In despair, he jumped out of a first-floor window, causing him to be hospitalized for his injuries. Luckily, he was released four weeks later. He continued his work, producing false documents, principally for the UCC. Geertjan Lubberhuizen worked closely with Matthijsen forging identity cards and from time to time escorting Jewish children to safe houses.

As for Paul Terwindt, in Arnhem, Gelderland province, he was mobilized for UCC work by Frits Iordens, who asked Paul to look for safe houses for Jewish children as well as for adults on the run. Paul was a religious Catholic and he had some hidden Jewish children baptized. Mary van Gelder was one of the children helped by Terwindt. She was born in Amsterdam in July 1939, the third child of Rosa Marks and Abraham van Gelder. In April 1943, Paul Terwindt took her to the Guillaume and Maria Mulleneers family of six people. Father Guillaume worked at the mines. In Mary's words:

"I was number seven. They explained that I was a little niece from Rotterdam; name – Ria Gerritsen. I talked so much and told everybody that my Oma [mother] was picked up by the Germans … After a short time I had forgotten all those things and my real parents and sisters. As luck would have it, I looked like these people. I was dark, my foster family too.…

Across the street there lived people who were pro-German. They were always asking me a lot of things. That was very frightening and so my foster parents forbade me to talk to those people. They suspected something … I did not know all that time that I was a Jewish child that was hidden … When the war was over, my parents came to pick me up but I cried and would not go with them. So they left without me and after a short time they came again.… It was very, very difficult for me to get used to my own family. Often I was homesick for my foster family … At school holidays I always went to my foster parents … I could not forget them."

Returning to Hetty Voûte, in February 1943 she narrowly evaded arrest. It happened after one of her co-workers had been caught with a large bundle of ration cards, and under interrogation she revealed Hetty's address and alias, Jet Juttink. Shortly afterwards, the Gestapo appeared at the house of her parents and asked for Jet Juttink. Hetty's mother had no idea to whom they were referring, and the men left. Hetty was upstairs in her room at the time. She hastily gathered all incriminating materials, including the notebook, and fled the house. She went into hiding with Adrie Knappert in Ommen, Overijssel. A few weeks later, after the coast had cleared, she resumed her resistance work.

Then, when it was learned that two of the UCC workers were in fact working as agents for the Germans, it was decided that two men would eliminate them while Hetty and Gisela Söhnlein got the children that the two traitors had placed with foster families. Hetty and Gisela carried out their assignment and returned to Utrecht by train, and then checked the bicycles they had taken along in the station's baggage room. That evening they were told that the traitorous man had been killed but the woman was only wounded and she informed the police. This was on June 11, 1943. The following day was Hetty's 25th birthday, which she celebrated in Noordwijk. In her words,

"Holding a large bouquet, I returned by train to Utrecht. I wanted to go to my parents for my birthday, and from there to my hiding place. I hurried to the baggage section to pick up my bike, and there stood a Gestapo agent. I was arrested next to my bike. They took me to the Utrecht police station and showed me a photo of the murdered man. I was shaking all over. I leaned my foot against the leg of the table, but the whole table began to shake. I continued saying, 'Yes, I was there now, what bad luck for these people.' I pretended that I took this whole matter to heart. The following day, I was taken to Den Bosch. As for Gisela, a day afterwards she also came to pick up her bike, from Amsterdam, and was also arrested."

The interrogations were terrible. As Hetty Voûte recalled, "Sometimes, out of decency, they took off my eyeglasses before slapping me, but this did not upset me. It was worse when they were kind. Then it was more difficult for me to keep quiet." Voûte and Söhnlein were moved to the Vught camp. Then, on September 6, 1944, the two were taken to a train and packed into a car with about 70 people. The trip lasted two full days, until the train stopped at the women's concentration camp of Ravensbrück, in Germany. As soon as Hetty arrived, she fell ill with a throat and ear infection. "I had fever. I thought this is the end; now I'll die." Taken to the dispensary, she was placed with other sick people; the sanitary conditions were terrible and people were dying all around her. Luckily for Hetty, she managed to recover and was assigned work at the Siemens plant, assembling radio parts, and she was moved to a different barrack. "When I arrived there I burst out crying for I could not stand up on my feet. This situation lasted for about a month. During the time when I could not walk, the other women dragged me between them. Fantastic! During roll call someone always arranged a stand-in for me."

Hetty and Gisela were with the group freed by the Swedish Red Cross and arrived in Sweden on April 28, 1945. In 1946 Hetty returned to the Netherlands. That same year she married and began raising a family. "At first I did not talk about it, as my husband did not wish to talk about these things after sitting in a Japanese camp in Indonesia … But, somewhere in the back of my mind, there always lingered the question – had I done things right. What had become of all those little children I first took away from their parents? I should have taken all those parents too, but we were not equipped for that task."

In 1988, Hetty Voûte and Gisela Söhnlein (married name Wieberdink) visited Israel and planted trees in their name. Hetty and Gisela had together prepared words to be spoken at the ceremony in their honor:

"As young girls we entered the unknown homes of unknown people. We did not mention our names, but the parents gave us their children in confidence. We thanked them for that confidence. We urged them to hide themselves also, but in most cases they did not want to do that. If only their children were in safety!… Their own State of Israel, that must have been the ideal that those parents had in mind who entrusted their children to us … We could not have done this alone. We were part of a group … the Children's Committee. Each one of these people assisted by searching for addresses where the children could disappear, by transporting them, and by supplying the ration cards … We do not know how many children we were able to shelter. Perhaps a few hundred, but what is the meaning of this number when you realize what you have not been able to do. Here we remember our and your dead. We believe in building a future. Planting our tree is, in our eyes, a symbol of this belief."

Hetty Voûte had earlier compiled a list of the 360 children that the Utrecht Children's Committee had saved. Of these, only 13 were discovered and apprehended, but they were liberated from the Crèche, in Amsterdam, to where they were taken, by underground operatives. Only three children died while in hiding. This is quite a remarkable achievement by a group whose nucleus was mostly made up by youthful and inexperienced university students.

The third large-scale independent and spontaneously created group dedicated to the rescue of Jewish children went by the code name NV group, which stood for *Naamloze Vennootschap* (NV-LTD). It is credited with saving at least 226 children and 28 adults, and its main theater of operations was the province of Limburg in the south of the country. The NV commenced its activities in Amsterdam in July 1942 when Jacobus (Jaap) Musch, his brother Gerard,

Jaap Musch

and their friend Dick Groenewegen van Wijk created the nucleus of a cell dedicated to hiding Jewish children. In October 1942, the organization made contact with Johannes (Joop) Woortman (alias Theo de Bruin) and his wife, Lena (later Riekerk), in Amsterdam. Woortman was known and trusted in the Jewish community and could be relied on to supply the fledgling NV

Joop Woortman

with a constant supply of Jewish children. It worked as follows: Woortman would search for Jewish families who wished to send their children into hiding. Simultaneously, the two Musch brothers, Jaap and Gerard, as well as Dick Groenewegen were locating addresses in Heerlen, Kerkade, and other places in Limburg province. When sheltering places had been satisfactorily located, Dick, Gerard, and several confreres journeyed to Amsterdam to pick up the children and escort them to Heerlen by train.

In early January 1943, Joop Woortman made contact with Walter Süskind, a German Jew who held an administrative position in the Hollandse Schouwburg, a former theater in Amsterdam which served as an initial assembly point for Jews under arrest. Süskind arranged for Woortman to meet with Henriëtte Pimentel, the director of the Crèche, which was located opposite the theater. In cooperation with these two individuals, Woortman established a system for smuggling out as many Jewish children as possible from the Crèche. In the first five months of 1943, the NV succeeded in hiding approximately 100 children. As more manpower and expanded territory was essential, in June 1943 Jaap approached Reverend H. Bouma, the Calvinist vicar of Treebeek and Brunssum, and as a consequence a large number of reliable addresses were found.

Additional strength came with the enlistment of the Willem and Truus Vermeer family in Brunssum, to whose home the NV leadership eventually moved its headquarters. The NV succeeded in evacuating approximately 110 children from Amsterdam between June and September 1943. With the deportation of the last Jews from Amsterdam, the Germans closed down the Crèche and at the last moment the NV managed to spirit out 14 children and bring them to Brunssum. To avoid apprehension, and also due to instances of a host family's change of mind or mistreatment of the child, NV operatives were always on the alert and children had to be moved from place to place, from one home to another. The average number of places that any child hid was four, and some were rotated to over a dozen places.

Jaap and Gerard Musch went under the name of Jacob Vogel; Dick Groenewegen's alias was Richard Hoffman. All three were registered as miners. Danger always had to be taken into account. On November 6, 1943, Willem Vermeer in Brunssum was tipped off by a friendly policeman of a large-scale raid the following day. That night, all the Jewish children in the area were taken out of their foster homes and temporarily sheltered at an outdoor swimming pool not in use at the time. Two cold, anxious days later, the NV received word that the raid had been called off. However, a large number of foster parents were too frightened to take back their former wards. The NV concluded that other places needed to be located and many children were transferred out of the Limburg area, many of them to the Nijverdal region in Overijssel province. By end 1943, the NV had grown into a large organization with several centers scattered across the country.

Johannes (Joop) Woortman, who had been working as a waiter and was married to Lena (Semmy), and went under the name of Theo de Bruin, was mainly responsible for pirating about 160 children out of the Amsterdam Crèche. Woortman also combed the Jewish quarters of Amsterdam to convince Jewish parents to save themselves and put their children into the care of the NV. His associates would use the password, "I come from Theo de Bruin," a name that inspired confidence among many Jews. He was able to secure money, ration cards, and goods. In May 1944 a former classmate betrayed Joop Woortman. He managed to evade arrest, but was arrested on July 19, 1944, and transferred to Bergen-Belsen camp in Germany on September 4, 1944. There he succumbed to spotted fever in mid-March 1945, and died.

Lea Nenner-Winnik gave a vivid account of how she was helped by Woortman. Arrested with her sister in Amsterdam in the summer of 1943 (aged 11 and 13, respectively), they were taken to the Crèche. There, with the help of Walter Süskind, they escaped and wandered the city streets, not knowing where to go. Finally they decided to look up the family's former maid. However, she took fright and did not know what to do. She went over to the window and looked out, then told the two disoriented sisters to look down at the street. "There's a man who helps children hide." They went down and approached him. "He asked for our name. He said, be quiet and don't be afraid. After the *razzia* (raid), go back to the Crèche and I will take you out from there. At first, we did not believe him, for how could he tell us to go back there without any explanation; we were sure he was a Nazi." With nowhere else to go, and night having fallen in a city under curfew, the two made their way back to the Crèche. After a few days, the two sisters were called to the office and told that soon some people would come to take them, and so it was. One day, two persons came; one of them was "Theo

Herman Flim with Lea Nenner-Winnik

de Bruin," the man they had met earlier. They took the two sisters separately with another group of girls to a train going to Limburg. "Thanks to Theo de Bruin, I am alive, and sadly he is not," Lea noted in her testimony. Her sister was hidden with Joop's wife, Lena. "Woortman found for me my first hiding place, out of 20 places that I passed through, one of which was the home of Herman Flim."

As for Gerard Musch, he was an Amsterdam office worker when he and his brother Jacobus decided to help – at first adult Jews in flight. The experience with the Brauns, who at a certain point left their hiding place unannounced and thereby risked their arrest and the betrayal of their helpers under torture, made the Musch brothers and their colleague Dick Groenewegen van Wijk change direction and start helping children. Together with Joop Woortman, the NV group was created. Limburg province was chosen as the target area. Gerard Musch took it upon himself to find safe houses in and around Kerkrade and he also distributed ration cards, clothing, and footwear to the families who had already taken in Jewish children. He also got children from Amsterdam, and on such occasions he entertained the children with his skills as a clown, ensuring that the train ride was never boring.

Gerard's brother, Jacobus (Jaap) Musch, was a lab technician at the Free University in Amsterdam. When the NV was created, Jaap answered a newspaper advertisement for a lab technician at the State Mines in Heerlen, Limburg province. Jaap was hired, which protected him from being seized for forced labor in Germany (coal was considered a vital war material). This also afforded him the opportunity to explore the region for hiding places. In August 1942 he visited Calvinist pastor Gerardus Pontier in Heerlen, who provided him with a list of reliable members of his congregation as well as the address of a boarding house owned by the Harmen Bockma family, in a hamlet near Heerlen. Much later into the rescue operation, in early 1944, as part of the plan of spreading out from Limburg province, Jaap Musch took several children with him to a small country house in the woods near Nijverdal, Overijssel province, that belonged to the Flim family. Among the children was the earlier mentioned Lea Nenner, who up to that point had had a miserable experience in her several hiding places. Lea described the eight months she spent in the country house as the happiest time of her hiding period. Tragedy struck in September 1944 when police wandering through the Nijverdal forest happened upon the isolated country house and saw four Jewish girls, including Lea, suspiciously flee into the forest on Jaap's order. When they approached and asked Jaap to identify himself, he mistakenly blurted out, "Jaap Musch, uh, sorry, Jaap Vogel" (his false name). He was interrogated and brutally tortured. After 36 hours he was executed, shot dead in the forest near Erica. After the war, he was re-interred with military honors in the Ommen cemetery. All four girls survived the raid.

On May 9, 1944, Dick Groenewegen and Gerard Musch were also arrested. Gerard was caught at the Amsterdam railroad station with five forged identity cards in his possession. It transpired that a Gestapo agent had been following him. Gerard was brutally interrogated. He was eventually sent to the Sachsenhausen-Oranienburg concentration camp, Germany, which he luckily survived. He returned to Holland very weak and in a poor physical state. As for Dick Groenewegen van Wijk, one of the original NV trio, on May 9, 1944, he was arrested by the *Landwachters,* the Dutch collaborationist militia, when they suspected that the papers on him were forged. He was imprisoned in several camps and eventually sent to a camp in Burschied near Cologne in Germany, from which he made his escape. Making his way back to Brunssum and the Vermeer home, he met Ida Roose, who worked in supplying ration cards to foster families. After the liberation the two married.

As for Willem Vermeer, an electrician and the NV's principal man in Brunssum, he was married to Geertruida (Truus) and the family numbered 11 children, two of whom, Wilhelmina (Mien, later married to Gerard Musch) and Pieter (Piet) were active in the NV. The Vermeer home served as a first stop for many children on their way to their hideouts. Pieter at times escorted children from Amsterdam to his parents home in Brunssum, which was always full of fugitives – Jews, downed Allied pilots, and others. Mien assisted Piet in accompanying the children on the train to Limburg and looking for families willing to shelter them. Enlisted in this dangerous work was Heike Meines, who was engaged to Pieter Vermeer, who also persuaded her brother Tette (Ted) to join the NV group, where he was known under the name of Josephus Alphonsus Meex and had good connections in the Gelderland region, to where he moved some of the fugitive children.

Harmen and Sara Bockma were Calvinists and lived with their eight children in an old farmhouse outside Heerlen that served as the NV's headquarters for a time. Many Jewish children passed through that home. Daughter Rins, 18 years old when the war began, helped out as a courier for the family, distribution of ration cards and fetching Jews from Amsterdam. As for Berend and Gerarda Flim, and their son Herman, we have already noted Lea Nenner's stay at the Nijverdal home – one of her twenty stops – taken there with other children by Jaap Musch. More children moved into the area, and they were first taken to the bakery, where Gerarda Flim instructed them in local customs and manners, before being taken to their hiding place. After Jaap Musch was arrested, Herman rounded up the three other Jewish girls who had fled in time (Lea Nenner was also arrested, but she managed to persuade the captors that she was of Dutch East Indian descent and was released), and took care of their subsequent hiding places. The Flims also hid several Jews in their home.

The future mayor of Amsterdam, Eduard (Ed) van Thijn, born in 1934, a Jew in flight, was arrested with his parents in May 1943 in Amsterdam. On the way to the Westerbork camp, the father jumped from the train and somehow managed to have his wife and son released and turned over to the care of the NV organization. Ed van Thijn was brought to Limburg province and the home of the Vermeer family in Brunssum. This was his first stop, to be followed by eight different places before being moved out of the Limburg area and taken to Overijssel province on August 17, 1944, where he stayed at nine different addresses, most of them in Oudleusden, not far from Nijverdal. After having passed through 18 places, in November 1944 he was arrested again.

Ed remembered well this second arrest. It was the home of Hendrik and Gerritgje van de Vegt on a farm in Nieuw-Leussen, Overijssel province. Neighbors probably had betrayed him to the police. In Ed's words:

"On the evening of November 26, a couple of police vans stopped in front of the door. The farm was searched from top to bottom without any results. I sat together with railroad striker who was hiding at the same address, in a stuffy and cramped hiding place that we were able to reach just in time. The next day they came back and headed straight for the hiding place, informed as they were in the meantime."

Ed was interned in a detention house in Zwolle, where he was the youngest prisoner, before being transferred to the Westerbork camp in January 1945, where he stayed until liberation. By then, transports to Auschwitz had ceased, as the camp was evacuated by the Germans in the face of the approaching Russians. This probably saved the life of the future mayor of Amsterdam. The Vermeer and Flim families are the two he remembers best. He is especially grateful to Herman Flim: "He was the first person to come see me in Westerbork after liberation."

In closing, one may also mention Joseph Hendriks, a municipal clerk in the Brunssum municipality who helped with false identity cards, food coupons, and other documents for the hidden children, as well as advance warnings of imminent police raids. Also, Jacobus (Koos) Postuma, who worked as radio technician for the national mines and resided with his mother in Treebeek, Limburg. His home became a favorite way station for NV children, and he also checked out families willing to shelter children and brought ration cards. Moving into the Flim house in Nijverdal, he made regular bicycle trips to a large number of foster families in Almelo, Hengelo, and Enschede. He died during an Allied air bombardment of Nijverdal. Also, Anne-Marie van Verschuer, from Utrecht, who fetched many children in Amsterdam, sometimes howling infants, and took them to safe houses. Last but not least, Calvinist pastor Gerardus and Dora Pontier, in Heerlen, whose story appears separately in this volume. This couple too was of great help to the NV organization.

Page from the secret NV notebook of hidden children

The price paid was high. Jaap Musch, Joop Woortman, and other members of the NV cell lost their lives. Others, such as Gerard Musch, "Aunt" Truus Vermeer, and many children sustained mental or physical traumas as a result of trying to stay several steps ahead of their German and local collaborator persecutors. But what the three groups achieved is nothing short of miraculous – the rescue of over a thousand Jewish children as well as some adults to boot. These were three separate, mostly youthful groups, born on the spur of events in the summer of 1942, with one common goal in mind – to save the lives of children threatened with destruction simply because they had been born – or rather because their grandparents had been born Jewish. That was their only "crime." But they're alive, thanks to the dedication of the dozens of activities of the three aforementioned rescue networks.

Following is an alphabetical list of the 57 rescuers mentioned above who were honored with the Righteous title by Yad Vashem, including year of recognition:

Bockma, Harmen & Sara & Rins, 1967; Coelingh, Mia, 1993; Dohmen, Nico, 1984; Evenhuis, Jan & Johanna, 1982; Fiedeldij Dop, Philip, 1976; Flim, Berend & Gerarda & Herman, 1981; Groenewegen van Wijk, Dick & Ida, 1981; Helm van den, Krijn & Johanna, 1982; Hendriks, Joseph, 1995; Knappert, Adriana, 1988; Lier van, Geertruida, 1992; Louwers-Mees, Marie, 1977; Lubberhuizen, Geertjan, 1974; Macey-van Berlekom, Henriëtte, 1992; Mansum van, Arie & Margaretha, 1969; Matthijsen, Rutger, 1974; Meerburg, Pieter, 1974; Meines, Tette, 1992; Mesdag, Willem & Sjoukje, 1993; Mulleneers, Guillaume & Maria, 1980; Musch, Gerard and Wilhelmina, 1981; Musch, Jacobus, 1981; Nijdam, Abraham & Trijntje, 1982; Pontier, Gerardus and Dora, 1968; Postuma, Jacobus, 1981; Stork, Johan & Guretta & Anna, 1994; Terwindt, Paul, 1980; Vegt van de, Hendrik & Gerritgje, 1992; Vermeer, Willem & Geertruida & Pieter, 1983; Verschuer van, Annie-Marie, 1985; Voort van de, Johanna, 1984; Voûte, Hetty, 1988; Wieberdink-Söhnlein, Gisela, 1988; Wiersma, Sjoerd & Trijntje, 1983; Wijbenga, Pieter, 1975; Woortman, Johannes & Lena, 1981; Zeytveld van, Wouter, 1974.

There are many other people who were associated with the rescue work of the three networks and whose cases merit further study and evaluation.

Meier, Albert & Maria & Katharina Weeg, Ludwig & Elisabeth
GERMANY

*B*efore her marriage, Maria Meier (then known as Henseler) had worked as a governess for the Jewish Erwin and Nanny Bernauer and their daughter Karola, born in 1920, in Troisdorf, located between Cologne and Bonn, where Erwin owned a popular photo lab. After her marriage to Albert Meier, Maria moved to another town, Donrath, where a daughter, Katharina, was born in 1926. The two families continued to maintain a friendly relationship. In the fall of 1944 came the turn of the Bernauers to be arrested and taken to the Cologne-Müngersdorf transit camp, from where they were to be deported to the Theresienstadt camp. Their daughter Karola, also confined in the transit camp, was assigned work as a nurse to care for the sick and was therefore allowed to leave the camp to get the necessary medicines. She decided to take advantage of this golden opportunity to escape. Karola headed straight for her family's former governess, Maria Meier. Her request was simple; extra food for her parents, who were to leave on a transport to Theresienstadt, and an overnight stay for herself. The Meiers readily agreed to host her for the night.

Next morning, the Meier daughter Katharina volunteered to go the Cologne-Müngersdorf transit camp with a parcel of food, and was told by Karola where she could find her parents. Before leaving, she said jestingly: "I shall bring them out of there!" Everyone took this as a joke, but in Karola's words, "This incredible thing became reality; she brought out my parents. For us, this meant a chance to survive." Snatching two imprisoned Jews from the camp was no simple matter, as the camp was well guarded by SS troopers. As Katharina approached the dreaded place, she searched for a sure way to get herself admitted inside. The answer came quickly to her mind – by flirting with the guards.

As she related in her postwar testimony, "Without any difficulty I started up a conversation with one of the guards. I was blond and just 18 years old. From Karola I knew that the people working in the kitchen were not Jews. Therefore I pretended to wait for my parents who were both working in the kitchen." After a little flirting, she told the guards that she suddenly remembered the purpose of her visit – to bring food to her parents. She then asked one of the guards whether she could go into the camp to bring them the food. She was allowed in, but was told to use the same exit so as to avoid difficulties. Katharina quickly located Mrs. Bernauer. "She began crying when she saw me." At this point Katharina decided to turn her joke into reality and free the Bernauers. It was a dangerous gambit. How was she going to accomplish this? She gave the answer in her testimony to Yad Vashem:

> "I had the sudden idea to act as if the Bernauers were my parents and to take them with me. I went back to the soldier and told him that my parents would come in a few minutes. I started flirting and made a date to come back one evening. After a while I told him I didn't have any more time to wait and asked to be allowed back in to get my parents. I went in for the second time and gave my coat to Frau Bernauer to put over the yellow star, and with my long scarf I covered the shoulders and upper torso of Herr Bernauer. I was able to pass the control in the same place as before."

Katharina went on to say that she was in a kind of trance as she maneuvered herself and the two Bernauers out of the camp. Once on the outside, it was of vital importance to get as far away from the camp as possible. Afraid that the alarm would soon be given that the two Bernauers were missing, Katharina decided to avoid the nearby train station entrance where SS soldiers would probably be posted at the check-post. She took her charges to a railroad embankment at the end of the station, climbed it and crossed the many railway tracks to reach their train from the opposite end, and climbed inside. Arriving at their stop, the three got off, and using detours they reached the Meier home; a place that would not be suspected as Katharina had not divulged her address to the SS guards. For four to five months, Maria Meier, the Bernauers' former governess, and her daughter Katharina hid and cared for the three Bernauers. Maria's husband was at the time away in the German army.

In the meantime, some people in the vicinity began to show signs of suspecting that something was amiss in the Meier household. This was principally due Mrs. Bernauer, who had a hearing problem and did not listen clearly the necessary precautions told her not to be seen. To add to Maria's worries, her husband, Albert, came home on leave from the army with the intention to desert and hide. He was well known as an anti-Nazi and had already been arrested twice for his anti-Nazi remarks, so he was afraid that the military police might have his house under surveillance. For the moment, he gave up on the idea of deserting and reported back to his unit, but not before finding another place for the Bernauers; this was especially necessary as neighborhood rumors spread about the strange goings-on in the Meier household.

Albert Meier, still officially on leave, contacted the family's good friends Ludwig and Elisabeth Weeg, the owners of a farm at Scheiderhöhe, who readily agreed to host the Bernauers in their farmhouse. To inquisitive villagers, the Weegs said their guests were refugees from air raids in a nearby city. Later Karola's sister, Erna, also joined the family at the Weeg household. There they stayed until the war's end.

In 1990 Yad Vashem recognized as Righteous Among the Nations Albert & Maria Meier, and daughter Katharina, as well as Ludwig and Elisabeth Weeg.

Mendes, Aristides de Sousa
PORTUGAL

It was a momentous event, without precedent in Portugal's history. On March 13, 1988, the parliament in Lisbon officially threw out the verdict against a former diplomat who had since died and had been punished for disobeying orders from above by granting thousands of Portuguese transit visas to Jewish refugees in World War II. The man was cleared of all charges and his name was restored to the rolls of the diplomatic corps. The vote was unanimous.

Born in 1895 into an aristocratic Portuguese family, Aristides de Sousa Mendes entered his country's diplomatic service and was posted in various places. In August 1938 he was appointed consul-general in Bordeaux, France. Two years later, in June 1940, Bordeaux was flooded with thousands of refugees, among them many Jews who desperately wished to leave a defeated France, and escape the war-torn continent of Europe via Spain and Portugal in advance of the German army, whose troops were within striking distance of Bordeaux. Mendes' home country was then ruled by dictator António de Oliveira Salazar (who also served as Foreign Minister), whose regime increasingly exhibited Fascist-style behavior.

Already earlier, in November 1939, two months after the start of World War II, Mendes was instructed by his government that no visas were to be issued to certain categories of people, and especially Jews, without prior approval by the Foreign Ministry. When it was learned in Lisbon that Mendes was disregarding these restrictions in some individual cases – he was reminded in April 1940 by Luiz Teixeira de Sampayo, the Foreign Ministry's Secretary General, not to repeat these irregularities and warned "that any new fault or infraction in this regard will be considered disobedience and give rise to disciplinary proceedings." Mendes evidently attached no importance to this warning, for he continued to issue transit visas to certain small groups of people, acts that were recorded in his file back in Lisbon. Then came the unexpectedly sudden collapse of France and with it an avalanche of refugees filling the streets of Bordeaux, with many stampeding the Portuguese consulate and literally begging for visas that would allow them to cross into Spain. A month earlier, on May 21, before the flood of refugees had turned into an avalanche, Mendes had asked Salazar for instructions on how to deal with the refugees seeking Portuguese transit visas. The answer received was a plain and simple no.

Aristides de Sousa Mendes and his wife Angelina, with some of his children (courtesy of John P. Abranches)

During his nightly rounds of the refugee encampments on the streets, Mendes had met Rabbi Haim Kruger and invited him to the consulate, which also served as the consul's residence. The rabbi related to the diplomat how he had fled from Belgium at the start of the German invasion and was now stranded in Bordeaux together with thousands of other Jewish refugees. As in the past, Mendes offered Rabbi Kruger and his family transit visas, but only them. The rabbi, however, turned down this friendly gesture. He would not take advantage of his position and leave his brethren behind, parked on the streets. Instead, he urged Mendes to grant visas to all the others before it was too late. As told by Rabbi Kruger in a postwar account, Mendes had also told him that he believed he was a descendant of the Marranos (Jews forced to convert to Christianity in the 15th century). Kruger continued, "I thanked him for his generosity and returned to our brothers stranded outside. I then went back to him and explained that there was only one avenue of escape – to give all of us visas to Portugal." This presented Mendes with a moral challenge of incalculable proportions. Should he acquiesce to the rabbi's request and thereby violate the instructions received from Lisbon, or should he throw these instructions to the wind and freely issue the transit visas? Such a step – the issuing of visas to hundreds and thousands of persons, was a transgression that could not be passed over lightly in Lisbon, as was the case with the small number of visas issued earlier.

To ponder his decision, Mendes secluded himself for several days in his bedroom, where he was heard tossing and turning and occasionally groaning. His family wondered what had become of him, as he alternated between states of great agitation and self-imposed silence. His son Pedro Nuno noticed this change. "All of a sudden my father seemed terribly weary, as though he had been struck down by a violent disease. He just looked at us and went to bed." Another son, Sebastião, remembered the change in his father's eyes and hair: "His eyes had blue circles around them; his hair had turned completely gray, as white as snow almost." After three days of isolation, Mendes announced he had made up his mind. As recalled by his son Pedro Nuno,

"My father got up, apparently recovering his serenity. He was full of punch. He washed, shaved and got dressed. Then he strode out of his bedroom, flung open the door to the chancellery, and announced in a loud voice: 'From now on I'm giving everyone visas. There will be no more nationalities, races or religions.' Then our father told us that he had heard a voice, that of his conscience or of God, which dictated to him what course of action he should take, and that everything was perfectly clear in his mind."

It was June 16, 1940, the day when French Prime Minister Paul Reynaud resigned and turned over the reins of government to Marshal Philippe Pétain, who told the nation that France had capitulated to the Germans. An unknown general named Charles de Gaulle flew off to London to continue resistance against the Germans from there. A chaotic situation prevailed in Bordeaux, as all expected the German army soon to be within the gates of the city. Large crowds besieged the foreign consulates, especially the Portuguese consulate-general.

That same day, Mendes began to sign visas with no questions asked. Consular secretary José Seabra tried to dissuade him from this new course in flagrant violation of instructions from above. "For the sake of your wife and children please stop! You're ruining your life and your family." But Mendes paid no attention to this. It was the start of one of the greatest rescue operations carried out by a single individual. As also reported by Rabbi Kruger, "I sat with him a full day without food and sleep and helped him stamp thousands of passports with Portuguese visas." To his staff, Mendes explained:

"My government has denied all applications for visas to any refugees. But I cannot allow these people to die. Many are Jews and our constitution says that the religion, or politics, of a foreigner shall not be used to deny him refuge in Portugal. I have decided to follow this principle. I am going to issue a visa to anyone who asks for it – regardless of whether or not he can pay ... Even if I am dismissed, I can only act as a Christian, as my conscience dictates ... My desire is to be with God against man rather than with man and against God."

As the word spread outside, a long line of people thronged outside the consulate, anxiously awaiting their turn to have their documents stamped with the Portuguese transit visa. As also witnessed by the consul's nephew, César Mendes, "the closer I got to the consulate the larger the crowd. They wanted desperately to get visas to go to Portugal. Inside, the dinning-room, the drawing room, and the consul's offices were at the disposal of the refugees – dozens of them of both sexes, all ages, and mainly old and sick people. They were coming and going: pregnant women who did not feel well and people who had seen their relatives die on the highways killed by air fire. They slept on chairs, on the floor, on the rugs. The situation was out of control. Even the consul's offices were crowded with dozens of refugees who were dead-tired after waiting for days and nights on the street."

When Mendes learned that Faria Machado, the consul in Bayonne, on the French-Spanish border, a city under the jurisdiction of the Bordeaux consulate, was refusing visas to refugees there, Mendes hurried there to bring the consul into line with his new policy. He lectured vice-consul Manoel Vieira Braga: "Why do you not help those poor refugees? How would you like to find yourself, your wife and children in the same circumstances as the refugees? You say you're here to carry out the instructions you receive from your superiors. Very well, I am still the consul at Bordeaux and, consequently, your superior. I therefore order you to pass out as many visas as may be needed."

Mendes stayed on in Bayonne to make sure that the refugees were given visas so they could immediately cross over to Spain, ahead of the June 22 armistice agreement between Germany and France that would immediately be followed by the German occupation of the French-Spanish border. Mendes even decided to help refugees with the crossing itself and directed some to avoid the direct route between Hendaye, in France, and Irún, in Spain and instead use a side road, farther uphill, on the assumption that the border guards would create less problems, since they probably had yet not been told not to honor the visas issued by Mendes, as the Portuguese government had most likely requested. Mendes knew that he was in deep trouble with his own government.

Infuriated, indeed, at Mendes' insubordination, dictator Salazar ordered one of his aides, Armando Lopo Simeão, to go immediately to Bayonne to see with his own eyes what exactly was happening there and to report directly to Pedro Teotónio Pereira, the Portuguese ambassador in Spain. Not waiting for a report from his diplomats on the scene, on June 23, 1940, Salazar took the first punitive step by stripping Mendes of most of his authority and in particular the right to issue visas. The next day Salazar ordered Mendes' immediate recall to Portugal. A day later, Pereira, accompanied by two aides (Simeão and Machado), met Mendes and began to berate him: "Orders must be obeyed." To this, Mendes responded: "Not if those orders are incompatible with any human feeling." Three days earlier, in a communication to Lisbon, Simeão termed Mendes' behavior an "act of madness" caused by the tragic circumstances of the war.

Returning to Madrid after his encounter with Mendes, Pereira, acting as Portuguese ambassador to Spain, informed his Spanish counterparts that all visas granted by Mendes had been declared invalid. In a telegram to his superiors, several days later, Pereira lashed out in vicious language against "giving shelter to the scum of the democratic regimes and defeated elements fleeing before the German victory." He added, "I spent time today in San Sebastian watching the border crossing closely and can say that Spanish authorities are quite clear as to our government's intentions. It is understood that we have declared visas issued by the Portuguese consul in Bordeaux as being null and void." Pereira later related that when he met Mendes in Bayonne he was struck by the man's appearance. In Pereira's words, "His disheveled aspect gave the impression that this man was disturbed and not in his right mind. He appeared not to have the slightest idea of the enormity of the acts committed … The behavior of Mr. Aristides de Sousa Mendes implied such confusion that … I had no doubt in stating my conviction that said consul had lost the use of his faculties."

More trouble awaited Mendes after his return to Portugal on July 8, 1940. Resting with his family on his country estate in Cabanas de Viriato, Mendes prepared his defense before the disciplinary board convened by Salazar against him. On August 2, Mendes was handed an indictment, which included charges relating to both the period before June 17, 1940, when he issued visas to individual persons without prior approval by the Foreign Ministry, and to the period after that date, when he issued thousands of visas to fleeing Jews. He was accused of having acted in a way "that was dishonorable for Portugal vis-à-vis the Spanish and German authorities."

On August 12, 1940, Mendes submitted his defense against these charges in a 20-page document. Regarding a certain Harold Wiznitzer, who was granted a visa, Mendes explained: "He was going to be interned in a concentration camp … I considered that it was a duty involving basic humanity to spare him such an ordeal." Turning to the many others who were also given visas, Mendes emphasized:

"It was indeed my aim to save all those people whose suffering was indescribable: some had lost their spouses, others had no news of missing children, others had seen their loved ones succumb to the German bombings which occurred every day and did not spare the terrified refugees. How many must they have had to bury before continuing their frenzied flight! This filled me with commiseration for so much misfortune. There was another aspect that should not be overlooked, the fate of many people if they fell into the hands of the enemy … Many were Jews who were already persecuted and sought to escape the horror of further persecution … Add to this spectacle hundreds of children who were with their parents and shared their suffering and anguish … Because of the lack of accommodation this multitude slept in the streets and public squares in all weather. How many suicides and how many acts of despair must have taken place. I myself witnessed several acts of madness! All this could not fail to impress me vividly, I who am the head of a large family and better than others understand what it means not to be able to protect one's family. Hence my attitude, inspired solely and exclusively by the feelings of altruism and generosity."

Mendes did omit also to answer the charge of his so-called "strange" behavior as a diplomat. "It is obvious that the attitude I took could not fail seem strange. However, it should be noted that everything was strange at the time. My attitude was in fact a result of the totally abnormal and insuperable circumstances, of force majeure." Finally, "it may be that I made mistakes, but if I did so it was not by design, for I have always acted according to my conscience. I was guided solely by a sense of duty, fully aware as I was of my responsibilities." Mendes ended his defense by stating that "I could not differentiate between nationalities as I was obeying dictates of humanity that distinguish between neither race nor nationality." Also, to his knowledge none of the refugees have disturbed the public peace or abused Portuguese hospitality during their stay in Portugal, which they hoped to leave very soon.

At the disciplinary hearing, Ambassador Pereira's evidence was the most damning against Mendes. Pereira tried to impress the disciplinary board that the accused had gone out of his mind. "I got the impression of a deeply disturbed man who was not in his normal state. Sousa Mendes's attitude suggested such a degree of disturbance that I hastened to draw it to the attention of the Spanish authorities. And I asked them to regard any visas that had already been issued as invalid. There was not the slightest doubt in my mind when I told the Spanish authorities that the consul had taken leave of his senses." Count Tovar, the rapporteur, added derisively that the defendant "glories in having acted the way he did;" that he "does not confess to infractions … The defendant shows neither repentance nor the intention to mend his ways – only bafflement and boasting."

The disciplinary board's ruling was that Mendes was guilty of insubordination and pre-meditated unacceptable behavior; it also rejected the extenuating circumstances surrounding the refugee situation at the time. At the same time, it recommended that the punishment should be limited to demotion in rank. Salazar, however, decided on a stiffer punishment. On October 30, 1940, he ruled that Mendes should be dismissed from active service for one year on half pay; then be forced to retire and forfeit any benefits due him after his long diplomatic service to his country.

After his dismissal, Mendes reportedly told Rabbi Kruger (whom he met again in Lisbon): "If thousands of Jews can suffer because of one Catholic (i.e., Hitler), then surely it is permitted for one Catholic to suffer for so many Jews." He added: "I could not have acted otherwise, and I therefore accept all that has befallen me with love." With a family of 12 children to feed, and without any other income, Mendes was forced to sell his estate in Cabanas de Viriato. Soon he was reduced to poverty, and he died in 1954 a broken-hearted man. Two of his children were helped by Hias, a Jewish welfare organization, to move to the United States. The man himself seemed to have been forgotten.

In 1966, with Portugal still ruled by Salazar, Yad Vashem declared Aristides de Sousa Mendes, posthumously, Righteous Among the Nations. In 1987, Mário Soares, President of a now democratic Portugal, bowing to pressures by children of the late diplomat and concerned organizations, awarded Mendes the Order of Liberty. A year later, the Lisbon parliament took the final step of restoring Mendes' name to the roster of Portugal's diplomatic corps. Subsequently, the government ordered damages to be paid to his family. Presently many streets and a secondary school in Portugal bear the man's name, and in 1994 the city of Bordeaux, where Mendes made his fateful decision to help the refugees, paid him tribute by inviting Portugal's President Soares to unveil a statue of Mendes on a major roadway.

Adriano Moreira, who served as a minister in the Salazar government, stated that the significance of Mendes's action is that he "attacked a principle which had hitherto been absolute: that orders must be obeyed. The Nuremberg tribunal established that people are also responsible to obey certain principles and that they cannot act against human values. The great quality of Sousa Mendes was that he obeyed the values of mankind."

Micko, Vladimir
Kateneva, Olga
Latvia

*T*welve-year-old Karolina Knoch (born 1929) and her parents were among the lucky ones; they had survived the first massacre of the Riga ghetto Jews in late 1941, which took place in the Rumbula forest. Located eight kilometers from Riga, Rumbula was the main killing ground for Jews in Latvia, with thousands led there, told to strip naked, lay face down in the pits, on top of the dead and dying, and await their fate at the hands of German and Latvian execution squads firing down at them from above the pits. In November–December 1941, the Rumbula forest pits claimed 38,000 Jewish lives – 28,000 from inside the Riga ghetto and an additional 10,000 brought there from distant places – Germany, Austria, and the Czech lands.

The German occupation of Riga, on July 1, 1941, was followed by a pogrom staged by local antisemitic factions which claimed 5,000 lives and was accompanied by the burning of synagogues and vandalizing of Jewish homes. Some 20,000 able-bodied people were conscripted for backbreaking labor. In August 1941, the ghetto was created, holding some 30,000 Jews, including persons brought in from Germany, Prague, and Vienna. With the ongoing massacres, mainly in the Rumbula forest, the ghetto population was reduced to several thousand, including 200–300 seamstresses, who were spared for the time being. In the summer of 1943, the ghetto was liquidated, with the remaining Jews transferred to other labor and concentration camps. The Red Army liberated Riga on October 13, 1944.

Returning to our story – it was November 1941 and the ground was covered with snow. "It was four o'clock in the morning and the Jews were driven from the ghetto with sticks and whips," Karolina recalled. When they arrived at the pits in the Rumbula forest, the order was given to halt. To Karolina it seemed that the last moments of her life had come. "We could see that a mass grave had already been dug for us. We were told to undress. People screamed. I will never forget the snow mixed with blood, the children who were shot … Naked, the people were shot by machineguns and fell in the grave."

Slowly the line progressed to where Karolina and her family were standing. The end had come. Suddenly the Germans asked if any of the women in the line were seamstresses, and Karolina instinctively grabbed at the opportunity, feeling that with death so near there was nothing to lose. Several Jews, including Karolina and some members of her family, were told step aside and were led back to the Riga ghetto. It was a lucky break; Karolina had been saved, but not her father and brother, who died in the massacre. She had to find a way to save herself, but how and where?

It suddenly came to her mind that if she could find a way to her old nursemaid, a Baptist woman, perhaps she would agree to hide her. It was dangerous to try, with the roads filled with armed Germans and Latvians and others who might turn her in, but Karolina's mind was made up. She was determined to make a supreme effort to save herself.

Dressed in men's clothing with the obligatory yellow star, and her head covered with a cap with earflaps, she joined a group of men on their way to a day of hard labor and managed to get past the guards of the ghetto. Once she had distanced herself from the ghetto, Karolina began to scan the houses around her. She noticed a house with some logs piled up for firewood and hastened there to hide between the logs until the day had passed. At nightfall, Karolina decided to try out the occupants of the house. As she approached, two dogs barked fiercely at her. She then heard a woman's voice from inside the house, "Who's there?" The dogs' barking stopped as the door swung open. A man and a woman stepped out and looked at this strange girl. "I told them my story, that I had run away from the ghetto, that I was trying to get to my maid, a Baptist, who perhaps would hide me." Would they help her at least by letting her spend the night there, or would they turn her away? Filled with fright and anxiety, Karolina waited for the answer. "Come in, my child," the man responded. Inside, he told her an unbelievable story. "My child, last night I had a vision. I heard a heavenly voice speak to me, saying, 'You will save someone who will come to you in need.'" He was convinced that the forlorn girl standing before him was the person God had sent to be saved. Karolina could not believe these words, and she breathed a sigh of deep relief! The man's name was Vladimir Micko (born 1911) and the woman beside him was his sister Olga Kateneva (born 1905).

Since it was very dangerous to keep Karolina openly in the house, Vladimir decided to build an underground shelter for her. To do this, he removed the floorboards and dug out a small space where she could stay in emergencies. While preparing the shelter, he had to be careful how he disposed of the earth that he dug out so that people would not notice it. Getting rid of the earth in buckets or a cart was too risky. Vladimir found a different method: filling the pockets of his winter clothing with small amounts of soil and making numerous trips from his house to places where he could dump it without being seen.

Karolina normally spent most of her time in the house, but when danger threatened, or when a neighbor suddenly dropped in for a visit, she would jump into the underground shelter in seconds and secure the cover with a lock from the inside. The entrance to the hiding place was concealed by a carpet, above which stood the dinner table. In Micko's words, "It was impossible for Karolina to stay a long time in the pit, which was without ventilation and lighting, was cold and damp. Therefore, normally the pit was open with the cover nearby and Karolina was always ready to jump in in case a stranger approached." People caught sheltering Jews, Micko added, were hanged in Riga's marketplace, "and the corpses were left hanging for weeks in order to warn the local population not to provide help and shelter to the persecuted and doomed Jews."

Vladimir also volunteered to bring provisions to Karolina's mother and sister, still inside the Riga ghetto, by passing food, clothing, and medicine to them through the ghetto's barbed-wire fence. "Without his unselfish help, which was extremely dangerous to his life, both my mother and my sister would have starved in the ghetto," Karolina wrote.

On several occasions, to meet Karolina's family inside the ghetto, Vladimir would sew a yellow star on his coat, so as to be able to make his way inside. "I was petrified by his behavior and begged him not to do such things any more. But he went often to the ghetto, past the Nazi guard post, and brought to my mother and sister bread, sugar, butter, cheese, etc. His pockets were filled with food, and in many cases he indiscriminately distributed foods to every Jew who came his way … It was a truly divine miracle that the Nazis did not stop him." Vladimir bore all these extra expenses himself in spite of the fact that he earned a meager income as a stoker in a nearby kindergarten.

Karolina stayed with Vladimir Micko, his sister Olga Kateneva, and their family for a full three years, until the area's liberation in October 1944. In her post-war deposition, Karolina (presently, Carolina Taitz) stated emphatically, "They cared for me as a member of the family and never demanded any payment or monetary reward for their kindness. Without their selfless love, their courage, and their humane actions, I would never have survived." Carolina Taitz was one of the few lucky survivors not claimed by the fearsome Rumbula forest death pits – thanks to her two brave rescuers.

In 1991, Yad Vashem conferred the title of Righteous Among the Nations on Vladimir Micko and Olga Kateneva.

Mitzeliotis, George & Magdalena
Korfiatis, Stefanis & Magdalena
GREECE

*A*s Jacques Leon stepped off the boat on the island of Skopelos, he was greeted by Magdalena, wife of George Mitzeliotis, who invited Leon to her home. There she asked him to sit down. "What for," he asked? "So I can wash your feet," came the response. "This is not necessary," Jacques hesitatingly said, not sure what was behind this act. "Yes, it is," Magdalena responded, and she wanted to do it personally. It was an old tradition on the island, she explained. "It is a way of expressing our hospitality to our friends." Jacques could hardly believe his ears.

The story begins in Thessaloniki, or Salonika as it is better know by the Jewish community, one of the oldest in the eastern Mediterranean basin. In March 1943, the Germans decided to destroy this ancient Jewish community, which numbered 60,000 souls. Starting on March 15, 1943, thousands left by train almost every day, heading north to the death camps over hundreds of kilometers away. To deceive them, they were told that a new life was waiting for them in Poland, and for this purpose they were even given Polish currency. The trains, however, went to Aus-

Seated left to right: Magdalena Korfiatis and Magdalena Mitzeliotis. Standing left to right: George Mitzeliotis and Stefanis Korfiatis (Private Collection Yvette Leon, Athens)

chwitz, where, with the exception of a few, they were led directly to the gas chambers upon arrival. By August 19, 1943, the last Jews had been cleared out of the city. A 2,000-year-old community had been liquidated, its inhabitants murdered. A few managed to save themselves, including Jacques Leon and his family.

It was April 1943, just before Passover, and the deportation of Jews was in full swing. Leon's parents and other relatives had already made their escape and were on their way to Athens, then under Italian occupation, where under the umbrella of Fascist Italy, Jews felt safe. Leon was left alone, and he was desperately looking for a way out. Suddenly he remembered an old acquaintance, George Mitzeliotis, the mayor of Glossa, a village on the island of Skopelos. Leon decided to send him a telegram of two coded words – "*Sotirios Mitzeliotis.*" Sotiris, in Greek, is a familiar first name, but it also means "rescuer." As there was only one Mitzeliotis in Glosse, Leon had no doubt that the telegram would reach him. Three days later, Mitzeliotis arrived to help Leon out. He had understood his message and had leased a small boat, similar to the ones used for conveying grain, and had docked the boat in Epanomi, a village 50 kilometers from Thessaloniki.

In the meantime, Jacques Leon had succeeded in escaping from the ghetto and was hiding with friends who maintained contact with Mitzeliotis, so he knew where to find Leon. The two met, and Mitzeliotis gave Leon a new and legally produced identity card under the name of Demetrios Papadopoulos, supposedly a resident of Glossa – a document that Mitzeliotis, as the mayor of a village, had no problem issuing. Mitzeliotis' intention was take Leon with him to that island village. The two took a bus to the harbor in Epanomi and boarded the boat. Night had fallen and the departure was postponed to the next day. At dawn, the boat passed near Iraklia, where Mitzeliotis was supposed to pick up some wheat. For Leon's security, Mitzeliotis had him get off the boat and taken to a deserted place on the coast, where Leon remained hidden in the bushes. Late that afternoon, Mitzeliotis showed up, after he had gotten his wheat (as a cover for coming all that distance to an area held by the Germans), and brought Leon back to the boat.

The boat left the village harbor and sailed in the direction of Moudhania. As it started getting dark, the boat had to stop, for military regulations forbade sailing at night. The captain of the boat wanted to stay overnight in Moudhania. But since there was a German military base there, Mitzeliotis felt it was dangerous to dock there. The captain insisted and a heated argument ensued between the two. Then, as the local fishing boats, which had permits to sail with lamps at night, turned on their engines and were preparing to leave the harbor, Mitzeliotis felt this was an opportunity to join them, and he was able to persuade the boat captain to do so. As the sun set, the boat slipped in among the fishing boats, which sailed out in the open under their night fishing permits. After two hours, the flotilla reached their fishing grounds. The fishermen cut their engines and began working on their nets. At this point, Mitzeliotis also had his engine turned off, and his boat slipped out of the flotilla, quietly continuing with the help of the sails.

George Mitzeliotis was then close to 50 years of age; he was a man of the sea, strong and sturdy and very cool-headed. Giving the captain a rest, Mitzeliotis took charge of the boat's rudder. "I will not forget his optimistic spirit," Jacques Leon wrote after the war, "when he told me, 'You can go to lie down. In a few hours we will sight our island.'" The boat was bobbing on waters that had turned choppy as Leon fell asleep. When he woke up, it was six in the morning, the captain was back at the helm and the shoreline of the island could be seen. At noon, the boat docked in Glossa. "I was saved."

Magdalena, Mitzeliotis's wife, was waiting for them on the beach. The party headed to Mitzeliotis' home, where they were served by Magdalena with fresh spring water. She then washed the feet of Jacques Leon. "Out of a real nightmare, with the Mitzeliotis family I slowly regained the calm that I needed so much," Leon wrote. George's sister was married to Stefanis Korfiatis and was also called Magdalena. She came to see Leon together with her husband. "They were very simple people," Leon recalled, "but with superior feelings. Since I was a friend of Mitzeliotis, I was unquestionably their friend as well, in spite of the fact that they had only met me a little while ago." Stefanis Korfiatis said to Leon, "We helped hundreds of English and New Zealanders who fled the Germans after the defeat at the front [in April 1941], and they hid in our village. We therefore helped them, and they were able to reach the Middle East. It would therefore be unthinkable for us not to help you – you, who are a friend. Here, with us you have nothing to fear. You are under our protection." Leon was very touched by this manifestation of friendship and hospitality. He felt that it was probably the same on almost all the small Greek islands, where one finds very simple people with very noble feelings.

Jacques Leon's mind, however, was not fully at rest, since he wanted to know if his family had reached safely in Athens, and there was no communication between the island and the city. Seeing Leon's anguish, Mitzeliotis decided on an additional mission and left with a sailboat for Piraeus. A week later he was back. "He had seen all my relatives; they had arrived safely in Athens, which was then under Italian occupation."

Soon afterwards the situation in Athens changed for the worse, when after Mussolini's downfall the Germans swept into the city and made plans to lay their hands on the city's Jews. For the third time, George Mitzeliotis took to the sailboat to rescue Leon's extended family in Athens. This time he took along his brother-in-law, Stefanis Korfiatis. The two brought all of Leon's extensive family of 13 from Athens safely to Glossa on Skopelos Island. There were now 14 persons under the care of the Mitzeliotis and Korfiatis families. The two rescuers dispersed the large group of their charges in little country shacks outside the village. The two Magdalena women baked fresh bread for them which their children delivered to them with other dishes. "They took care that we lacked no food," Jacques Leon made sure to point out.

Again danger threatened when the Germans set up a military position on the island. For the rescued peoples' safety they were told to stay indoors and cease all activity during daylight hours. The Germans had installed themselves in the little harbor and did not go out at night. "We reversed day and night. We slept during the day and with the coming of night we got up, ate, and washed." For added insurance, Mitzeliotis had people who kept a lookout on the movement of the Germans.

Jeanne Cohen, brother of Maurice Leon, related that one morning the rescuers sent over a young priest who kept a revolver under his frock. "He stayed with us the whole day, playing cards and backgammon with us." The hidden people could not understand the meaning of all this. The next morning they learned that the Germans had started a search in the mountains. The young priest was sent to be at the side of the fugitive Jews in case the Germans came across their mountain shacks. In that event, he would try to mislead them by explaining that they were old friends; the proof being that he had come all the way to have a game of cards and backgammon with them. Luckily for all, the Germans did not penetrate the area.

One night, at about four in the morning, there was suddenly a knock on the door of one of the shacks. "The Germans have left; they abandoned everything," was the happy announcement. The Germans had begun to withdraw from Greece. The enlarged Leon/Cohen family breathed a sigh of relief. In Jacques Leon's words, "We were again free and without any fear." The people saved by the Mitzeliotis and Korfiatis families included Isaac Cohen, Henriette Leon, Juda Leon, Victoria Leon, Nina Camhi, Nicos Leon, Jacques Leon, Elie Cohen, Jeanne Cohen, Maurice Leon, Berthe Matatias, Sarina Saltiel, Isaac Rousso, Salomon Molho – 14 souls in all. It had all started with two words, "*Sotirios Mitzeliotis*" – Jacques Leon's coded message to George Mitzeliotis.

In 1981, Yad Vashem recognized as Righteous Among the Nations George and Magdalena Mitzeliotis, as well as Stefanis and Magdalena Korfiatis.

Myrgren, Erik
SWEDEN

On Christmas Day, December 1944, Reverend Erik Myrgren of the Swedish Lutheran Church was standing in front of the altar in the Berlin Swedish Victoria Church and reading from Isaiah 9:2ff.: "*The people who walked in darkness have seen a great light; those who dwelt in a land of deep darkness, on them has light shined. Thou hast multiplied the nation, thou hast increased its joy; they rejoice before thee as with joy at the harvest, as men rejoice when they divide the spoil.*" At this point, Myrgren stated, he "felt that the words left the page of the book and entered the present reality. They were transformed into people I knew, into events of a terrible reality. Everything was there: the sound of war, the camps of torture, the despair of the people, the bloodshed, but also the beam of light, the hope of the final victory, of love in spite of all, the hope of a great day of reconciliation and salvation when the kingdom of God will become a reality." Reverend Myrgren happened to be in Berlin by chance during the almost daily air raids on the city in the final months of the Nazi Third Reich.

A month earlier he had been on his way home from his ministry as the Swedish pastor of his country's sailors in Stettin, which had by now become a frontline city. The church there was in ruins, and no Swedish sailors docked in the harbor, so Myrgren was no longer needed there. He was therefore hoping to celebrate Christmas with his family in Sweden. Passing through Berlin, he was met by the Swedish vicar, Erik Perwe, who asked him to stay on for only two weeks, since Perwe was needed in Sweden for consultations. "So it happened, that for the first time I met Jews that Reverend Perwe was hiding in the cellar of the church," Myrgren noted. "I had no objections. I would still be able to go home for Christmas, if nothing would happen. But something happened, the worst thing possible!"

Officially Perwe was leaving in order to collect food and clothes for needy Swedes in Berlin. In reality, however, he was planning a substantial evacuation of Jews who had succeeded in escaping the Gestapo net and were in the care of the Swedish church in Berlin. Generally known as *Untertaucher* – divers – the fugitive Jews also called themselves *U-Boote*, submarines. Erik Perwe was, according to author Leonard Gross, "the brains and guts of the most organized effort in all Berlin to save its remaining Jews." He had arrived in Berlin in September 1942 with his wife, Maria, sent there by Swedish Archbishop Erling Eidem with the specific mission to save Jews after the preceding minister Birger Forell had been expelled by the Nazis. Perwe considered it a religious duty, as he noted in his diary: "God calls, I must obey." The Swedish Lutheran church was located on Landhaustrasse in the Wilmersdorf section of Berlin. With the help of his dedicated staff (which including Sister Wide Ohmann, a trained nurse), the church gave refuge to fugitive Jews – twenty at a time on some occasions. Perwe also provided false baptismal certificates, and maintained contact with the Gestapo, some of whom were ready to "sell" their Jews in return for payment.

Among the Jewish people helped were Martin Weissenberg and wife Margot. Both had managed to elude the Nazis with the help of a sister of Nazi hero Horst Wessel, who before his death and his apotheosis by the Nazis (they named the Nazi anthem after him) had been a friend of Margot. Perwe arranged for them to stay in a retirement home near the southern outskirts of Berlin. In March 1943, after the home had been destroyed during an allied bombing, they moved into the Swedish church.

When Myrgren passed through Berlin on his way to Sweden, he knew nothing of Perwe's rescue work. "I knew nothing of all this when I took leave of him on the morning of November 29." A few hours later there was a telephone call. The plane with Perwe and the other passengers had disappeared into the Baltic Sea. The news of his death spread rapidly, especially among those who were counting on his continued help, the *U-Boote* Jews whom he had hidden, people for whom he had been the difference between life and death. As Myrgren recorded after the war, remembering his first encounter with the anguish of these people, "I can still hear their cries of despair. Trembling old people, youngsters with despair in their eyes, hunted for years and now – so they believed – they had lost their last hope." Myrgren was soon plunged into Perwe's work in Berlin, including continuing to help the Jewish people in the care of the Swedish church. Myrgren's vacation plans had at that moment evaporated; he was now the man in charge.

> *"Slowly, slowly, I myself became part of the machinery which Perwe and his famous predecessor, the vicar Birger Forell, had built up so carefully, the purpose of which was to save lives and to help persecuted and bereaved people. My own work was humble compared to that of the others, but it lasted six intensive months ... Together with the others in the church, Wesslén, Vide Ohmann ... I did what had to be done. People needed help – that was all. Help with food and clothing, a place to hide, transportation to a secure place, some money, maybe medical care, or just some words of comfort and hope."*

The only person who to a certain extent knew of Perwe's many activities was his close assistant Erik Wesslén, also from Sweden. His part was to try bribe guards and policemen to let arrested Jews go free; Jews for coffee, liquor, chocolate, money, and jewels. In the Swedish church, many Jews came to stay for either a few days or two to three weeks and were then placed elsewhere the moment a safe alternative was found for them. Countess Maria von Maltzan, surnamed "The Lion of Berlin," was one of the great and active helpers in the Swedish church's rescue operation. She came from the high aristocracy and had a quite haughty personality and spirited temperament. She knew judo, swam, and rode a horse like a man, and, even better, knew how to handle a pistol if necessary. At the same time, she was a woman through and through, charming, elegant and very attractive. She had a way to deal with party functionaries, generals, and SS officers. Her sister was married to the Nazified Field Marshal von Reichenau. Her activities were incredible. Occasionally she had dozens of Jews hidden in her apartment in the Detmolderstrasse, and lived with one of them, whom she married, divorced, and remarried. Through the sewage system of the city she smuggled Jews whom Wesslén had managed to free and led them aboard trains to the harbor city of Lübeck, where she managed to have them smuggled aboard merchant ships sailing for Sweden.[1]

A case in point was that of a totally destitute individual, Herbert Friedemann, who had once had an important job and was fifty but looked like seventy – extremely thin and frightened. "He was living like a shadow, afraid to be caught and sent away." Perwe had promised to take him to Sweden. When that hope was swept away, he was in despair. "Is there a place for me here in the church?" he kept on asking. Myrgren had checked on him and was satisfied that Friedemann was staying in a relatively secure place, so he told him, "We have already far too many here in the church. Be patient, maybe we will find something." "*Aber lieber Herr Pfarrer, ich kann nicht mehr. Bitte, bitte, lassen Sie mich bleiben!*" ("But dear Mr. Pastor, I can't hold out any longer. Please, please, let me stay here"). In order to calm him, Myrgren promised to reconsider the matter and invited him to come back in a week. The following day, Friedemann was back, standing before Myrgren, with the same plea. Myrgren reminded him of his request to return only in a week's time. "After a week I may have a solution." But the man came back again the following day. As Myrgren was again going to ask him not to come every day, the man fell down on his knees and crawling up to Myrgren, cried, "Let me stay! Let me stay! I ask you!" Myrgren was taken aback; he had no previous experience in these matters. It was painful for him, so he looked away. At first, he felt ashamed of himself at not being able to respond immediately to the man's pleas. Then he felt a volcano bursting from within. As he later wrote:

> "I was so ashamed. But within me came a burning hatred against that system which so deeply humiliated a people and crushed its dignity so that an old man found it necessary to beg a young man for his life at his feet. It was terrible. But it was good for me. It strengthened my inner resolve. It was there before. Now it received maturity and strength. What had I to fear? Death was always close. The bombs were falling day and night. To take an additional risk meant so little. But to some people it was a matter of surviving.
>
> Friedemann could stay some days in the church where a few other Jews took care of him."

As the days passed, the Gestapo did not let up in its search for Jews in the open during these last months of Nazi Germany's existence, and the stream of people passing through the church increased. Sometimes 30, 40, 50 spent the night there, filling every corner. Some of these were non-Jewish Swedes desirous to leave the country, members of the Swedish church whose homes had been destroyed, fugitives from forced labor, army deserters, and, of course, Jews. Only a few Jews had their permanent residence in the church; most were taken to secure hiding places with the help of trustworthy local Berliners.

The passage at the Berlin Tempelhof airport was like the eye of a needle. There were all kinds of policemen and Gestapo people examining passports. The passports of Martin and Margot Weissenberg, for example, were written in the names of the Swedes Martin and Margot Bley ("One of our contacts there left before us and went to Tempelhof equipped with some bottles of good cognac," for use as bribe). The night before, Martin Weissenberg had not been able to sleep due to his state of tension. That evening Myrgren had arranged a little feast for them to raise their spirits. The next day, at the airport, Myrgren's contact confirmed that all was in order; the local Gestapo men had been bought off. Still there was always the danger of a mishap at the last moment. At the airport to make sure that the Weissenbergs were safely off,

"I can still see how the smoke from my cigarette trembled together with my hand. I smoked one, two, three ... We tried to speak, but we could not. The throat was dry. The heart was beating and the heat rose in the neck and the head. It was like fever. 'Why didn't he [Weissenberg] come?' Then, finally, he stood there, discreetly waving the passports in his hand. The coup had succeeded. We went calmly toward him. Everything must look normal. It was a silent farewell, but filled with joy ... With my eyes covered with tears, I saw the aircraft disappear in the morning haze."

But many times, Myrgren added, it was a matter of tears of disappointment and fright during this time of agony. For many help came too late. Others were caught on the very doorstep to freedom.

On April 25, 1945, during Berlin's siege by the Red Army, the Swedish church suffered a direct hit. Several days later, the church burned down. All the people and important items had already been removed and dispersed. There was nothing to do but wait for the final days of Nazi Germany, a week later.

Responding to his elevation to the Righteous title by Yad Vashem in 1987, Pastor Myrgren downplayed his role in the rescue of Jews: "I feel very humble ... Whatever I did during my time in Berlin, I had no idea there was something extraordinary about it. On the contrary I always had a feeling of not doing enough. Still I tried to act as much as I could in the way my pious parents taught me: bring help to your fellowman, whoever he is, whatever he needs."

Neff, Dorothea
AUSTRIA

"*T*he Lord gave me friends who were destined to stand by my side to help me when the need, the terrible need, arose … Hitler." So began Lilli Wolff's dramatic account of her rescue in Vienna by a famous stage actress – Dorothea Neff.

Born in 1903, in Munich, to a father who had come to Germany in his youth from Switzerland, Dorothea Neff's life dream since childhood had been to appear on the stage. Fulfilling her ambition, in 1931 she appeared on stage at the Munich State Theater, but two years later was dismissed because she was considered "politically unreliable," that is, anti-Nazi. She then moved to Cologne, where she continued her stage appearances. There, in 1934, she met Lilli Wolff, who in partnership with Meta Schmitt designed ladies costumes and dresses (employing 40 workers) that Dorothea used for her stage appearances. Then, in 1939, Dorothea moved to Vienna, where she was invited to appear at the prestigious Volkstheater, where she played leading roles such as Lady Macbeth and Iphigenie (Goethe). In the meantime the Nazi regime ousted Lilli Wolff, as a Jewess, from her studio, but the business continued to operate with the help of Meta Schmitt and another employee, Martha Driessen – both close friends of Lilli Wolff.

Dorothea Neff (Dokumentationsarchiv des Österreichischen Widerstandes, Wien)

Lilli renewed her acquaintance with Dorothea Neff when she left for Vienna in September 1940 (then part of Germany), mistakenly believing that Jews would be treated better in the former Austrian capital than in Germany proper. She turned up at Dorothea's fashionable apartment on Annagasse in Vienna's Inner City. Dorothea was only too happy to see "Lillichen" again, but shocked at her appearance. In Dorothea's words, "I hardly recognized the penniless, emaciated poor soul." As a Jew, Lilli had to register with the police and live in the city's Jewish quarter on Ferdinandgasse, second district, where she knew no one, but Dorothea managed to find her a room with a family there. It was quite cramped. Lilli had to share a two-and-a-half-room apartment with 10 other people who slept on mattresses on the floor. Jews were prohibited from leaving the quarters except for a few hours each day, to do some shopping, but Dorothea often visited Lilli, bringing medicines and other necessities, and invited Lilli to spend daylight hours in her three-room city center apartment. On these occasions, before the night curfew began, Dorothea would accompany Lilli back to her apartment. Nearing the street where Jews were restricted, Dorothea helped Lilli rearrange her clothes, marked by the obligatory yellow star as required by law. "How dangerous this was," Lilli wrote after the war; "It could have cost her her life."

As a Jew, Lilli was forced to do work for the Nazi regime, and was assigned the job of making flaps for the uniforms of women postal workers. During this period, Dorothea began to pay money each month to a certain man to take Lilli off the employment rolls, and this also served as a temporary guarantee against deportation to the camps.

One day, in the summer of 1941, Lilli Wolff received the dreaded summons to report at a certain schoolhouse, from which she was to be deported. On this occasion, she alerted her friend Meta Schmitt, who happened to be in Vienna, and both went by train to Berlin, where Lilli's father lived, to explore the possibility of going into hiding in the sprawling capital city. The two women could not find anyone willing to take Lilli in, and both returned to Vienna. Back in the city, Lilli found out that the authorities had been told about her trip to Berlin and she was required to appear for questioning. Taking along Meta Schmitt, Lilli was interrogated, then released after being warned not to leave the city without an authorization. "God helped again!"

Then, in October 1941, Lilli received her second summons to report for deportation to Poland, for the purpose of "work." With the summons came instructions about the size and weight of the two suitcases it was permitted to take along, with the name of the owner to be clearly written in white. Little did Lilli or the other Jews suspect that all this had no meaning – it was a ploy to get the deportees to believe that they would indeed be starting a new life. Once inside the concentration camps, the suitcases were taken away and the items inside were recycled in the German war economy. Lilli, of course, could not have known this. Having decided to show up, she was concerned that her carry-on bags not be over the permissible weight. She recalled that Dorothea had a scale in her apartment, so Lilli showed up there with the things she meant to take along.

The two women sat on the floor with the scale between them and began to weigh and pack – food supplies, a pair of fur-lined boots, a small heater with kerosene cubes to warm the food, and medicines. "It was one of the darkest hours in our lives," Lilli later said. Then, in the midst of this surreal scene, the women looked deep into each other's eyes, and in Lilli's words, "We both felt that something else was going on." Suddenly Dorothea said, "Let's stop … you are not going. I'm going to hide you." Lilli was going to disappear – right there in Dorothea's apartment in the heart of Vienna; she was going to hide there and not be seen by anybody from that day forward. Asked after the war what had prompted her to make this momentous decision, Dorothea Neff said the following.

"While we worked, squatting on the floor, I looked into Lilly's pale, gray face across the kitchen scales, I saw in her eyes only helpless surrender. At this moment, I felt my heart wrench at the sight of this human being giving way to a brutal system. Suddenly I heard a voice, 'You must not permit this.' It came from somewhere. I grasped Lilli's hand. 'Enough of this, put away the stuff; all this is nonsense; you are not going back to that place tonight. You are staying with me – now and for good.' I'll never forget the expression on her face. The tear-filled eyes and trembling lips. We got up from the floor, and I put her in my guest bed, where she soon fell asleep. But I didn't sleep that night. I knew what I was risking, and it took me time to come to terms with my decision."

Looking back on this momentous turn of events many years later, Lilli could only think of divine intervention; God had fulfilled for her the promise made in Isaiah 43:2, as stated by the prophet: "When thou passest through the waters, I will be with thee … and through the rivers, they shall not overflow thee; when thou walkest through the fire, thou shalt not be burned, neither shall the flame kindle upon thee." Lilli stayed in one of Dorothea's back room for a full three and a half years.

Every evening, Lilli counted the 32 minutes that it took Dorothea to come home after a performance. Dorothea would rush home, her heart pounding as she turned the key and opened the door for fear something might have happened to "Lillichen," but no one found out about her, not even the guests that Dorothea occasionally entertained after openings and on other occasions, as she was professionally expected to do as a leading stage actress. Then Dorothea stayed up with Lilli, filling her in on the days' events so as to keep her spirits up, repeating tidbits from her conversations with people on various subjects as well as news of the war and the outside world.

Dorothea was losing weight the whole time because she shared her food rations with Lilli. In 1944, the Nazis severely curtailed theater performances and actors were mobilized for war work. Dorothea worked half-day shifts in a factory sewing uniforms. There she met an aspiring actress, Eva Zilcher, who helped with black-market food. Once, she brought Lilli a heavy bucket of potter's clay so that she might do something to occupy her mind and try to forget her underground life filled with fear, trembling, terror, and air bombings all around them. Fear was everywhere, especially of Gestapo informers. Dorothea Neff was careful when talking to others, lest she inadvertently let a word slip out about the woman hiding in her apartment. As she later ironically told it, "People stopped talking to each other. In a way one started eavesdropping on oneself." During air raids, when the two women clung together in the shelter, Dorothea introduced her to others as a friend from bombed-out Cologne. Lilli wrote: "Sitting in the basement, a friend's hand was holding mine, telling me not to be afraid … the flames of the bombs did not kindle upon me, the rivers of hatred did not overflow me, and the fires of Hitler's ovens did not burn and consume me. I escaped irreparable hardship, but relatively small hardships came and went – they were easier to take because somebody shared the burden." When Dorothea was out, and the doorbell rang, Lilli did not answer.

"I trembled. How long would this fearful hardship go on? What would happen in the next hours? It went on for FOUR YEARS. In spite of all of this, the friendship and care I received gave me a glorious balance in my otherwise completely shattered life. The Lord provided; and how thankful I was and will ever be! We needed each other – we were hungry together, we endured the cold and had no way to heat the place. When the war reached Vienna, we went down to the basement every night, seeking protection from the bombs. We never knew if somebody would recognize me or if the walls would come down on us or if fire would break out. Yes, it broke out in a neighbor's house and underneath our living room."

In February 1945, Lilli developed a lump in her breast, and she had to be taken to a hospital to decide whether she needed an operation. But no Jews could be admitted. So Dorothea arranged for Lilli to be smuggled in under a false name by distributing free theater tickets to the right people in the hospital. To explain away Lilli's lack of papers, Dorothea said they had all been burned in Cologne during an air raid. Dorothea's former name (she had been widowed from her husband for many years), Schmitt, was affixed to her bed. It turned out that her lump was a benign cyst, and was excised.

Lilli stayed shut up in Dorothea's apartment, "like a pearl in its shell, hidden from the light," Dorothea related. "She never complained or had a bout of despair" in the nearly four years the two women were together. "But I was in public, and I was dancing on eggs." When the Russians entered Vienna in April 1945, Lilli sighed, "Now no one can harm me anymore." She decided to leave Vienna, with all its traumatic memories, and head for America, and she settled in Dallas, Texas. There she resumed her career as a dress designer, designing costumes for the Miss Texas pageants. From there, she corresponded regularly with her wartime friends, Meta Schmitt and Martha Driessen (who were also helpful to Jews in need), but especially with Dorothea Neff, who had resumed her acting career. "In those years in Vienna, under the force of our fate, I observed in deep thankfulness Dorothea's nobility of mind and heart."

Summing up her deposition to Yad Vashem in 1979, Lilli Wolff wrote that "love your neighbor as yourself" is the basic law for peace and harmony in this world. She then added that as she finished writing her testimony she happened to read an interview with Israel's prime minister, David Ben-Gurion. Asked by the interviewer what was the most important passage in the Bible, Ben-Gurion said, "And God created man and woman in his own image ... God created man and woman, not Christian or Jew or Moslem or others. He created people in his own image. People have created the divisions and people are the cause of the problems they have today. If we understood this one passage and observed it, people would have peace and care for one another." What a happy coincidence, Lilli thought? It was the same idea that ran through her mind as she wrote her story.

That same year, Yad Vashem conferred on Dorothea Neff the title of Righteous Among the Nations. The following year, a ceremony was held in her honor in the Viennese Burgtheater in the presence of Israel's ambassador and Austrian government and Vienna city officials as well as stage luminaries, on which occasion Ambassador Yissachar Ben-Yaakov decorated the now partially blind Dorothea Neff with the Righteous medal and certificate of honor, both bearing her name. In her response, she said, "The greater the darkness of a period, the brighter is the light of a single candle." In her deposition, Lilli Wolff had written, "God chose Dorothea Neff to save my life ... When she was born, the world became more bountiful, and part of that bounty was bestowed on me."

Nickel, Maria

GERMANY

*I*t was November 1942, and Ruth Abraham was on her way to work as a forced laborer for the Nazi regime, in a pharmaceutical firm producing medicines for the German army in Berlin's Tempelhof district. She wore the obligatory yellow star, displayed on her overcoat. She was also in the seventh month of pregnancy. Four months earlier, in July 1942, her parents, Meyer and Frieda Fromm, had been deported to the death camps, where they perished. As she neared her place of work, Ruth suddenly noticed something strange. As she later related:

> *"One day, walking up the hill, I had the oddest feeling that I was being followed. This feeling continued for a few days, but I thought this must be my imagination. Then one day I turned around; there she was: the stranger who would end up playing such a huge role in my life. She looked to be in her early thirties, a typical German woman, plain and quite motherly. She was wearing an old coat and a thick wool hat. Although she looked perfectly harmless, there was nothing really harmless to a Jew in these times, nothing so safe that it could not turn instantly into a danger. When you are being hunted, you want to be invisible, to blend into the scenery like a sidewalk or a tree. Maybe this woman was a spy. 'I want to help you,' she said. 'Go away,' I said, running as fast as I could."*

Ruth rushed into the Starke pharmaceutical factory, relieved when the door closed behind her. But the strange woman did not give up, and kept following Ruth on her way to work. Then one day she came up to Ruth and looking her in the eyes while holding her breath, she said. "Don't be afraid, nearby is a cloister. Come with me. It will be safe." Ruth later explained what made her follow the strange woman. "Whatever God had decided was going to happen anyway, and besides, I just didn't have the strength to go on resisting." They went into a convent. When a nun came out to inquire, the strange woman said, while looking at Ruth, "This woman is Jewish."

Maria Nickel (center with striped blouse), on her 90th birthday; with Reha and Ruth Abraham (to her left) (Private Collection Reha Sokolow)

The she pointed to Ruth's belly, and said, "She is expecting. You must help her." The nun responded, "I cannot endanger the other Sisters." With that the women left, and Ruth ran off to work.

About a week later, the woman showed up again. This time she walked into the factory, and went right over to where Ruth was working, handing her a basket piled high with food – flour, margarine, milk powder, potatoes, and rice. She explained that she was turning over the special Christmas ration that the German government had distributed in its efforts to curry favor with the population at a time when the Germans were beginning to suffer military reverses. She wanted Ruth to have it. "Take this, I cannot enjoy Christmas with my family, knowing that you are carrying this baby and don't have enough to eat." Ruth was stunned. These items were precious, difficult to find – even on the black market. The other Jewish women workers also stared in disbelief, the head pharmacist as well. After the strange woman left, Ruth answered their un-asked question. "Do you believe in miracles? I've just seen the hand of God." The woman's name was Maria Nickel. She was married and the mother of two sons.

A few days later, on a bitter cold night, she reappeared again, knocking on the door where Ruth and her husband, Walter, lived in their assigned cramped Jewish dwelling. Maria had a bunch of flowers, lilies of the valley. Ruth was again stunned. "This was unbelievable. It was really like a fairy tale." She asked her the reason for her willingness to befriend and help a Jewish person, behavior strictly forbidden by law. Maria answered that she had always been well disposed toward Jewish people. The incident that had triggered her present resolve oc-curred when she had recently got a notice of a special distribution of grapes by the authori-ties – a delicacy at the time. Fresh fruit was rare during the war, so this was a big treat. She had taken her children to pick up her family's allotment. She then noticed a group of Jewish children passing by; evidently they were among the last, not yet deported. They stopped to see if they could get some grapes too, but Nazi officials turned them away with a shout, "These grapes are for German children, not Jews!" Maria immediately went over and gave the grapes meant for her children to these children. She then made a momentous decision – she would risk her own safety to help the next Jewish person she ran into. That person turned out to be Ruth Abraham.

Maria added that she was prepared to take in the baby after its birth and care for it. The baby could be left on her doorstep, and she would pretend that the baby was a foundling and raise it as her own until its parents were free to take it back. January 19, 1943, was the day the baby was born. That night, Ruth and Walter were out visiting a Jewish relative when suddenly the pains began, the beginning of labor. The two ran out into the street to get a doctor or a midwife, but to no avail. The streets were still smoldering from the Allied aerial bombardment the night before. Hastening back to their house, Ruth was now in ac-tive labor. Walter tried to help, but he was a furniture salesman, not a doctor. As Ruth kept screaming in pain, Walter ran out to bring over a relative, Aunt Marta, who in turn called a Jewish doctor, who helped to deliver a little baby girl. She was named Reha.

"Reha was no 'mistake,'" Walter Abraham later said as he explained the reason for bring-ing a child into the world in such unpropitious times for Jews in Germany. "We wanted a child. That was the one way we had of fighting Hitler. To bring a new Jewish child into the world would be like spitting in Hitler's face. And God willing, the child would live."

When Ruth had recovered sufficiently to get back on her feet, she and her husband planned their next step. They decided to forgo Maria Nickel's charitable offer and instead stay together as a united family, including little baby Reha. But in Nazi Germany in January 1943, this could spell doom for the entire family. Something had to be done quickly before the Gestapo came to seize them all. Earlier, Walter Abraham had met a certain man, named Jahn, who in return for payment was prepared to take the Abrahams to a farmhouse owned by an elderly woman where they would be safe from deportation. The homeowner would not be told that the newcomers were Jewish, but bombed out Berliners – a phenomenon becoming more common in those days. The Abrahams decided on this option. However, for travel on the train, they would have to somehow be armed with new papers – false ones with borrowed names. Ruth contacted Maria Nickel, who immediately decided to help. She took a picture of Ruth with her to the post office to get a new identity card. The clerk looked at the photo suspiciously, then stared at Maria for a long time. "This is not your picture," he said. "This is how I looked before the war," Maria replied curtly. "If you want I can bring your another picture." "Oh, never mind," the embarrassed clerk replied, and gave her a new card. As for Walter, Maria stole her husband's driver's license right out of his wallet. But the picture on it was of husband Willi, who did not look at all like Walter. Perhaps, Maria reasoned, no one would notice the difference.

With their new documents, Walter, Ruth, and little Reha joined Jahn on a three-hour train ride in the middle of the night to a farmhouse in Streitwalde, where Jahn introduced them to the old women. She, too, had to be paid. It was a most primitive house, with no indoor plumbing, no running water, and no electricity. On the other hand, the woman fed them with freshly baked bread, butter, eggs, and potatoes. They lived in that house for five months. Inside, it was bitter cold, but it was a safe and secure place, or so it seemed.

In June 1943, the Gestapo raided the village in search of opponents of the regime, and they also visited the house where the Abrahams were staying. Examining their papers, they began to suspect that something was wrong. In a split-second decision, when the Gestapo stepped outside for a moment, the Abrahams made a run for it, streets, all the way to the train station, where they snuck onto a train and made it back to Berlin. However, they had left the incriminating documents in the name of the Nickels in the hands of the Gestapo. Arriving in Berlin, the Abrahams immediately went to Ruth Nickel and warned her of the danger facing her. Maria dismissed these fears and assured them that she would find a way to talk herself out of everything if and when questioned. Soon enough she was called in by the Gestapo to explain the presence of her family's papers on the persons of fleeing Jews. She gave her interrogators the following unbelievable story. One day, she said, she was sitting on a park bench with her children when a woman with an infant approached her and with tears in her eyes asked her to lend her identity card so she that she could buy a baby carriage. Maria admitted that she foolishly commiserated with the woman and had no idea that the woman would take off together with her card. As for her husband's driver's license, she explained that she had probably kept it together with her identity card and must have inadvertently given both to the strange lady. Luck was with Ruth Nickel. The Gestapo bought the story, concluding that the woman facing them was terribly naïve and not too bright. She was set free, but not before being lectured to be wary of Jews and not fraternize with them in the interest of racial purity.

The Abrahams then sought alternative hiding places. Walter moved in with a prewar friend who lived on a farm outside Berlin, where he stayed until the war's end. As for Ruth and baby Reha, they moved through several places in metropolitan Berlin and Ruth occasionally dropped off Reha with Maria Nickel for temporary stays between her stops in Berlin. When the baby fell ill, and Ruth panicked at not being able to see a doctor, Maria again came to the rescue, taking the child with her to a clinic treating infants and children, where Reha received proper medicine. "Maria soothed me," Ruth wrote after the war. "She was like a mother, all strength and comfort in a crisis." The three Abrahams survived the dark night of the Nazi regime until the end of the war in May 1945.

After the war, the Abrahams settled in New York, from where Ruth corresponded fairly regularly with Maria. In 2000, on Maria Nickel's her 90th birthday, Ruth Abraham's expanded family, including Reha's (now Sokolow) own children, flew to Berlin to celebrate the birthday of the woman who had made it possible for them to survive and later beget more children and grandchildren.

Years before that joyous occasion, in 1971, Yad Vashem conferred on Maria Nickel the title of Righteous Among the Nations.

Nicolini, Giuseppe
Brunacci, Aldo
Niccaci, Rufino
ITALY

*T*he little picturesque town of Assisi is located in the foothills of the Apennine Mountains in central Italy. It is best known as the home of Francesco di Bernardone, better known as St. Francis of Assisi, who was born there in 1181, and for the Order founded by him and bearing his name, whose monks are devoted to poverty. It is told of St. Francis that he had a special loving affinity for birds (to whom he preached) and animals. One story told is about how he tried to rescue a wolf that was ravaging people and sheep near the city of Gubbio. He went out in a search of this predatory wolf, and having found him he lectured him, as follows, "Brother wolf, you do much harm in these parts and you have done great evil. All the people accuse you and curse you. But, brother wolf, I would like to make peace between you and the people." The wolf nodded his head in consent, and St. Francis arranged a pact between the inhabitants of Gubbio and the wolf, which stated that because the wolf had "done evil out of hunger," the townsfolk were obliged to feed the wolf regularly. In return the wolf would no longer prey upon them or their flocks.

Giuseppe Nicolini

In September 1943, when the Germans swept into Assisi and began to hunt Jews there, a reenactment of the pact between the wolf and the local inhabitants 700 years earlier would not have helped. For the Nazis' voracious killing appetite was not grounded in any physical "hunger" but in pseudo-religious zeal to do away with every living Jew, whatever that person's deeds and beliefs might be. St. Francis' disciples realized that no bargain was possible with the Nazi wolves who preyed on Jews, and turned their city of Assisi into a refuge for fleeing Jews.

In 1943, Assisi had a population of about 5,000; not one of them Jewish. Pilgrims came to pray at the shrines of St. Francis, founder of the Franciscan and the St. Clare Orders (Poor Clares). Then, with the German occupation of Italy, which started on September 8, 1943, several hundred Jews, as well as others fleeing the Germans – anti-Nazi Italians and downed Allied pilots – found shelter in that community. The signal for this was given by Giuseppe Nicolini, the town's bishop. One day, soon after the German takeover, Nicolini called Father Aldo Brunacci to him and said, "We have to organize ourselves to help those who are being persecuted, especially the Jews," adding: "Everything must be done with the greatest secrecy and prudence. No one, not even the priests [those not involved], must know anything about this." As the bishop's residence had already been used earlier as a center for help to refugees, it was now extended to include fleeing Jews as well as their religious objects – hidden in a walled-up enclosure in the basement. In Brunacci's words, "The work was not done by workers but by the Bishop himself, who used the trowel to build the walls while I held the lantern. When a wall had to be broken through, I would wield the pick while the Bishop held the light for me. These operations were performed whenever we had to restore objects to individuals who were leaving Assisi even before the end of the war." Nicolini also authorized the use of monasteries and convents to hide hundreds of Jews and presided over an aid committee that provided essential items, especially clothing.

Aldo Brunacci at Yad Vashem

Father Aldo Brunacci, who headed the rescue operations in Assisi on behalf of Bishop Nicolini, was posted in the San Rufino Cathedral. Brunacci arranged sheltering places in monasteries and convents, even those that were *clausura* – strictly closed to others by monastic regulations. The canonical laws regarding the enclosure of the cloistered monasteries, and always rigorously enforced, were in this case lifted in the name of charity and solidarity. Hidden Jewish men were reportedly dressed as monks and women were taught to behave like pious Christians. The important Jewish holiday of Yom Kippur was observed inside these monasteries and convents, with the nuns, on one occasion, preparing a meal for the Jews at the end of the fasting day. In Brunacci's words: "When the guests sat down to take their first meal after the fast and looked around, they no longer felt like strangers and they understood that they had been welcomed in a bond of love as brothers and sisters. I recall what a day of intense emotion that was!"

One Jewish woman fugitive who died while in hiding was buried in the local cemetery without the necessary Catholic rites. On the way to the cemetery, Brunacci and his entourage passed a German patrol, "whose members immediately stood at attention, never knowing that the coffin they saluted contained a Jewish lady." After the war, the inscription on the tombstone, headed by a Star of David, read: "Kerfa Feld Clara, widow Weiss, born in Vienna on 15 September 1887 and peacefully died in Assisi on 9 November 1943, where she had found loving hospitality during the Nazi persecution." The Viterbi family was among those helped by Brunacci – including chemistry professor Emilio Viterbi, who went under the name of Ernesto Vitelli, and wife, Margherita, both from Padua, as well as their daughters Grazia and Mirjam. They, and many other Jewish fugitives, lived openly in Assisi but under assumed names, and even attended local schools. The locals, who suspected the truth, kept their silence.

Planting a tree in honor of Don Rufino Niccaci (center), on the right is Hanna Hirsch

Father Rufino Niccaci, a Franciscan cleric and Father Guardian of the St. Damiano monastery (where traditionally St. Francis had his first mystical experience), also played a role as part of the clerics' rescue team that saved approximately 200 Jews scattered in 26 monasteries and cloisters around Assisi. He, as well as others, made efforts to supply his charges with some of their religious needs, including kosher food (causing one postwar journalist to observe that "at one point, Assisi could boast of being the only convent in the world with a kosher kitchen."), and also arranged classes for their children.

Among the churches, and monasteries that opened their doors to fleeing Jews, one may number the Basilica of St. Francis, Saint Quirico, the Church of St. Francis, the Laboratorio Saint Francesco, the Cathedral and the Diocesian Seminary, and among the convents: German Sisters, Stigmatique, and Poor Clares. One Jewish child was born soon after liberation to one of the hidden people in Poor Clares convent. The mother was the daughter of a Belgian Jewish family, also hidden in the convent. The Abbess at the time was Mother Hélène, from France. As for the clerics associated in this rescue conspiracy, they included, besides Brunacci and Nicacci, Michel Todde, Federico Vincenti, and Monsignor Minestrini.

The sisters Rachel (Hella) Lev and Mira Barsiah (both born Baruch) were among those sheltered in Assisi. Until 1942, they had lived in Fiume together with their parents. Now they found refuge in the Stigmatique Nuns convent in Assisi, where they remained from the end of 1943 until the town's liberation in June 1944. They testified to meeting other Jews in hiding there, and that Niccaci often came to visit, bringing food and false papers. Hanna Hirsch (born Gelb in 1925), also testified to Niccaci's help, to her as well as to

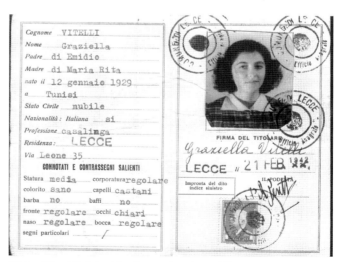

Mirjam Viterbi's false identity card under a different name

other Jews passing through the town. The rescue operation lasted from September 1943 until Assisi's liberation on June 17, 1944.

On May 15, 1944, two policemen came to arrest Father Brunacci on orders of the prefect, as Brunacci was about to enter into his house. Brunacci asked them to please wait outside while he went to get some things and his breviary. Stepping into his study, he saw Emilio and Margherita Viterbi waiting for him. They had come to ask Brunacci to help them move to another place, because they no longer felt safe in their present location. "I told them not to move, I took my breviary, and I closed the door after me, said goodbye to my parents and went off with the policemen." Brunacci was tried by a Perugia court for sheltering persons sought by the authorities. He was eventually released through the intervention of the Vatican authorities on condition that he did not return to Assisi but stayed in the Vatican.

After the war, Brunacci remarked that "in all, about 200 Jews had been entrusted to us by Divine Providence; with God's help, and through the intercession of St. Francis; not one of them fell into the hands of their persecutors." Brunacci ended his recollections of that period with the words: "Jews and Christians venerate the same book, the Bible, whose opening chapter reminds us that we are created in God's image and likeness. God is our Father, and we are all brothers and sisters."

In 1947, Father Aldo Brunacci attributed the Assisi rescue epic to the spirit of St. Francis, and the determination of the town's bishop, Giuseppe Nicolini, who withstood the threats directed at him. As Brunacci wrote:

> "I will never forget how insistent those threats were, yet how determined the Bishop remained. He would not let anyone intimidate him from performing what he, as pastor, was required to do. I recall very well the strength Monsignor Nicolini showed in the face of the repeated alarms of the 'big shots' who felt it was their duty to suggest prudence and moderation. There are times in everyone's life in which it is easy to confuse prudence with a calm life; there are times when heroism is required. Monsignor Nicolini took the path of heroism."

In 1977, Yad Vashem recognized Bishop Giuseppe Nicolini and Father Aldo Brunacci as Righteous Among the Nations, Earlier, in 1974 Father Rufino Nicacci was also accorded the Righteous title.

Nowinski, Waclaw & Janina
POLAND

*A*lexander Bronowski turned to the sergeant on duty in the Warsaw prison: "Perform an act of grace on me. I know I am going to die. I have no hope of remaining alive. The Gestapo will turn me into a crumpled rag. They will force me to reveal where other Jews are hidden, how it happened, where I was hidden, who arranged it…. I am only human. I don't know if

I'll be able to withstand it." "So what are you asking?" Sergeant Waclaw Nowinski snapped back? "Do me a favor, take me out to the toilet in the courtyard; I'll pretend I'm trying to escape, and you will shoot and kill me. It will be a coup de grace. Do this for me. Do me this favor." Nowinski stood up, "I cannot do such a thing. I never killed, and I shall not kill. I will try to help you." He indeed did.

Born in Radom, near Lublin, Alexander Bronowski studied law in Kraków and humanities in Vilna universities. He then moved to Lublin, where he practiced law. In 1938, he was surprised when the local Catholic diocese asked him to represent it in a real estate case, knowing he was Jewish – a very uncommon thing in those days. As he recalled, "When I appeared in court on behalf of the bishopric I could see the surprise of the Polish attorneys present in court that a Jewish lawyer was representing the Church." Indeed, soon afterwards the Lublin diocese was taken to task in several newspapers on this point, where it was asked why the diocese had found it necessary to assign the case to a Jewish attorney in a city numbering 200 non-Jewish lawyers. This, and other antisemitic occurrences, such as the resolution adopted by the Lublin lawyer's association, in which Bronowski was a member, to no longer to admit Jewish lawyers, and the harassment of Jewish students at the university, who were forced to sit in segregated places – all convinced Bronowski that there was no future for him in Poland. He went to Palestine to make preparations to emigrate there and returned to Poland at the end of June 1939 to settle his affairs, when the war intervened.

With the coming of the Germans, Bronowski first escaped to Bialystok, then under Soviet rule; then returned to Lublin, was arrested, interrogated by the Gestapo, and released. A friendly non-Jewish woman named Kazimiera Sadzikowska who worked in the Social Security office in Warsaw provided him with a false identity card, as well as cards for his wife and daughter.[1] Bronowski survived several German killing raids on the Jews in Lublin and was taken to the nearby Majdan Tatarski labor camp, from which he escaped and fled to Warsaw. With the help of a certain Irena Muniowska, temporary lodging in return for pay was found for him, separate from his wife and daughter. When Alexander's landlady suspected he was Jewish, she told him to leave, and he moved with his wife to the Praga section of the city, and with the help of Kazimiera Sadzikowska, a new dwelling was found for Alexander, again separately from his wife and daughter. Alexander presented himself as Catholic seminarian whose studies were suspended as a result of the war. His wife posed as the widow of a Polish soldier killed in the war and found work in a German firm producing telephone parts. Alexander made it a point to visit the St. Florjan church in the Praga section, where his neighbors could see him and be impressed by his religious zeal. His landlady was also proud of him; that a near-priest was living at her place, and spoke to neighbors about the man's religious devotion.

In spite of this relative security, Bronowski could not rid himself of the fear of sudden arrest and interrogation by the Gestapo, an experience he had already had in Lublin. "I decided that if arrested I would jump from the fourth floor of the building and commit suicide." The methods of the Gestapo were known: terrible torture to extricate from the hapless victim all sort of information; all the places he had been hidden, and his helpers. They would then kill the person. "I had decided to avoid this torture."

---

1 Kazimiera Sadzikowska was also honored with the Righteous title.

Then came the day, in April 1943, that almost sealed his fate. On that day, Bronowski stepped out to buy tobacco and cigarettes, to which he had become addicted, smoking 100 cigarettes a day. As he boarded the trolley car on his way back to his Praga apartment, he noticed two men staring at him. He got off the trolley before reaching his destination and the two men got off as well. He jumped back on and so did the two men. There was no doubt about it – he was being followed. "Suddenly an idea flashed through my mind. I knew that on this day, in the afternoon, a Mass would take place. I therefore decided not to return home but get off at the next station, next to the St. Florjan church. When I entered the church, the two men followed me. I mingled with the crowd." Leaving the church through a side exit, he found the two men waiting for him. One of them said, "*Sicherheitspolizei* [Sipo, or Gestapo]. You are a Jew; come with us." Bronowski showed them his *Kennkarte* [identity card] and labor permit. They replied that they're probably fakes, "and I was under arrest." He failed to persuade them that there was a misunderstanding. Also his attempt at bribery with 500 zloty did not work.

They told him that it was up to a Gestapo interrogation team to decide whether he was Jewish or not. If it turned out that he was really Aryan, no harm would come to him. "I was trapped, and they paid no attention to my additional words of explanation." Since it was already late, Bronowski was taken to a local Polish jail, where he was duly registered as a Jew under arrest by the Gestapo. When they left, they said they would return at 7:00 o'clock the next morning to pick him up. Bronowski was locked up in a cell. Terrified at the thought that his end had come, he desperately wanted to call a friend so that the man would alert Bronowski's wife to take precautionary measures. He asked the guard on duty to allow him to use the phone and gave him the 500 zloty he had on him. The guard took the money but refused to let him use the phone. At 10 in the evening the guard left and was replaced. "I had no doubt that these were indeed my last hours; I saw no way out... I cannot describe the state of mind I was in. I became conscious that death was close, and I suddenly felt a kind of strange indifference to my life. I thought, 'What will become of my family?' ... I was not afraid of death, only of the torture. As I did not wish to place my family in danger and cause them anguish, nor my benefactors outside, I prepared the story I was going to give the Gestapo. It went as follows. Yes, I am indeed Jewish. As for my wife and daughter, they were taken away in a roundup in Majdan Tatarski, outside Lublin, and their traces were lost." Alexander would continue that he had fled into the forest and hid there until January 1943. As for his false papers, he had gotten them while still in Lublin.

Bronowski decided to make a final try. He asked his guard to bring him a few cigarettes that the Gestapo had taken away from him and left somewhere in the jail. When the guard returned with the cigarettes, Bronowski learned from him that the sergeant in charge who had refused to let him use the phone had finished his shift and had been replaced by another man. Bronowski then complained about the terrible cold in his cell, and asked for permission to step out into the bigger room to warm up a bit. The guard agreed and took Bronowski into a large hall in the middle of which sat a man behind a desk – the night sergeant on duty, Waclaw Nowinski.

Bronowski looked up at the clock on the wall; it was 11 p.m. He stood there for a while. The man behind the desk invited him to sit down. "Why were you arrested," he asked? This led to a conversation between the two that stretched into the night. "At first I did not tell him I was Jewish, only that I was suspected of being Jewish." Nowinski did most of the talking, berating the Germans for what they were doing to Poland, also the terrible things they were doing to the Jews. Bronowski looked at the face of the man in front of him. "I felt that this was not a trap, but that he was sincere." After an hour of such talk, Bronowski blurted out, "I admit that I'm Jewish." At this, Nowinski began to question him more, while he kept repeating to himself, "How to help you, how to help you?" Bronowski then ventured to ask him the same favor had asked earlier of the prison guard, to let him phone a certain Julian Frankowski, so as to inform him that he was under arrest by the Gestapo and there was no more hope for him, as his luck had run out. This was followed by Bronowski's extreme request – for Nowinski to shoot him in the back as he was being led toward the toilet in the courtyard. Nowinski, as mentioned, turned him down.

It was 2:00 a.m. when Nowinski suddenly got up and said, "I have to save you." He asked another policeman to replace him and left Bronowski sitting in the hall under guard while he stepped out of the police station. Bronowski watched the clock ticking away. Only five hours remained until the Gestapo would come to get him for the feared interrogation. "I did not shut an eye; I thought of my wife and daughter." The hours passed, and it was already five in the morning and Nowinski had not come back. Bronowski was convinced that Nowinski had rescinded on his promise to help him and this explained his continued absence. "My fate was sealed."

Suddenly, at about 6:00 a.m., "when I had already given up hope," Nowinski reappeared with a broad smile on his face. He told the startled Bronowski, "Everything's okay – you will be freed." He handed the prisoner 5,000 zloty in cash and instructed him that when the German agents took him out to the courtyard, Bronowski was to give them the money and he would be set free. Nowinski, who was linked to the underground, had managed to arrange this through them. "I was shocked by the news," Bronowski related. "When I asked him what made him sure I would return the money to him, he answered, 'There's no need to return it.' I was stunned! A miraculous rescue!"

The last hour of waiting seemed like an eternity for Bronowski. The two Gestapo agents appeared at 7:00 a.m., went over to the registrar, and wrote down that there had been a mistake in the prisoner's identity and that he was in truth an Aryan. They took Bronowski out to the courtyard, where he handed them the 5,000 zloty. Before parting, they told the still stunned Bronowski that he would have had no chance under interrogation, for his arrest was brought on by a Jewish man from Lublin who was collaborating with them, and it was he who had pointed Bronowski out as a Jew from Lublin.

After his release, Bronowski hurried over to his wife, who was shocked by his appearance. He told her everything that had happened and began to organize the money to pay back Nowinski. When Bronowski returned to Nowinski, he had added 2,000 zloty to the original 5,000 as a bonus for the man's great help to him. When Nowinski saw the money, he got angry. "Only with great difficulty did I manage to persuade him to take the 5,000 zloty, so at least he could use it to help save some other Jew. As for the bonus, he refused to touch it. He was even hurt by the very idea." From then on, the two developed a lasting friendship. Bronowski later learned that policeman Waclaw and his wife, Janina, had also sheltered in their home some more Jews; such as the Rapoport family, Dr. Berlowicz, and Janina Penska; all these with no compensation.

Bronowski then resumed his life in hiding, moving to another dwelling equipped with a false identity card. At a later period, he was snatched off the trolley for forced labor to Germany and taken to the Trawniki camp, where he served as an interpreter from Russian to German. He made his escape and returned to Warsaw, where he stayed in hiding until the Polish uprising of August–October 1944. He was then evacuated with his family, like the rest of the city's population, to a camp in Pruszkow; from there to Wolbrom, and further to several villages. There he faced again the antisemitism of local people. They had been helpful to him until they discovered that he was Jewish. A certain Mrs. Makowska had asked Brownowski's daughter what they were eating on the holiday and she had innocently answered that on Easter-Passover they ate only *matzot* (unleavened bread) – for it was forbidden to eat bread then. She had let out their secret and the Bronowskis were turned out and forced to move on. In another village, on January 18, 1945, the Bronowskis witnessed the liberation by the Red Army.

Returning to Lublin and his law practice, the sight of a city emptied of its Jews was too much for Bronowski to bear. He moved to Gdansk (formerly Danzig), and practiced there as an attorney, but his mind was set on leaving Poland and settling in Israel, which he achieved in 1950. He was then active in several survivor organizations and on the Yad Vashem board of directors, as well as being a member of the Commission for the Designation of the Righteous.

In 1987, he made possible the placement of a monument at Yad Vashem in honor of the Unknown Righteous Among the Nations from among the non-Jewish rescuers of Jews during the Holocaust. One of the "known" Righteous honored by Yad Vashem, in 1970, was Alexander Bronowski's rescuer, literally hours before what could have proven Brownowski's last moments alive – police sergeant Waclaw Nowinski along with his wife, Janina.

Oldak, Apolonia

POLAND

A Jewish child was found abandoned by a Polish forester in a forest hideout and the mayor of the nearest village asked the inhabitants who was willing to care for the child on a permanent basis? No one volunteered and some even wanted to do away with the child – except for one woman who was not from the village but had come from Warsaw to live there with her husband to avoid his arrest by the Germans. In the face of the hostility of most of the villagers, she and her husband cared for the child, treated its recurrent illnesses, and eventually moved with her to Israel, where the child is herself a mother of children.

This is the story of Apolonia Nowicka, born in Sosnowice, Warsaw region, to Józef and Józefa Nowicki, who also brought four more children into the world, two girls and two boys. After finishing elementary school, Apolonia entered a nursing school in Piotrków Kujawski. When the family moved to Warsaw, she proceeded to Wloclawek, where for three years she studied sewing; then, for two years, she was in charge of an orphanage in Mieczysław. Moving to Warsaw herself in 1932, she eventually worked as a nurse in a Jewish-run hospital, until the start of the war. In that place Apolonia met her future husband, Aleksander Oldak, who worked as a mechanic on medical equipment before moving on to a government engineering firm that dealt with military equipment. The two married in 1935 and had two children, but both tragically died at a young age.

Apolonia Oldak

Late one evening, during the early part of the German occupation, an acquaintance visited the Oldaks in their Praga apartment and told them that he had seen Aleksander's name on a German black list together with others who were to be arrested, and urged them flee immediately. The Oldaks decided to head for the village of Dzieźkowice, about 22 kilometers from Kraśnik, where a good friend of theirs lived. There, Aleksander worked as a mechanic and Apolonia kept busy as a nurse. At the time, there were still some Jews there. When, one day, Aleksander heard from a Jew that he was leaving for the Warsaw ghetto, he tried to dissuade him. "Whoever can flees from Warsaw to the countryside, and you who are here agree to be imprisoned inside a ghetto?" The man changed his mind and instead took to the nearby forest with his family, where he joined up with other Jews in hiding there. From local inhabitants, the Oldaks learned that as many as 400 Jews had camped inside the forest.

Then in September 1942, during the potato harvest, shots were heard from the direction of the forest – a battle not involving the Germans but between Poles and Jews, both armed partisans, with the Poles having the advantage of more men and weapons. The Jews were overpowered and many fled in disarray. According to one version, a forester on his rounds in the forest and surveying the place of the recent battle suddenly discovered an abandoned baby girl in a man-made pit. He ran to the village mayor with the news, emphasizing that the child was still alive and one had to get her from the pit. The child was lying on a bullet-ridden sack; the bullets apparently having missed her. The village council decided that, in light of the unwillingness of anyone in the village to take in the child on a permanent basis, the girl would be rotated each week among the farmers. It is told that villagers knew exactly who the girl's parents were – that her father was Nehemiah Tenenbaum – and that she was eight months old; they also knew her mother. In another version, the uncles of the child who survived the battle found the baby girl and turned it over to a Polish peasant, threatening that if any harm befell the child, then the still-armed Jewish group in the forest would wreak revenge. The farmer kept the child for a while; then passed it on to others, and finally the child landed in the lap of the village mayor.

Then, as reported by Apolonia Oldak, one day a Jewish woman suddenly appeared at her home. After she made sure that no one was around, the woman said to Apolonia, "Take the girl, and may God bless you." Apolonia replied that she would have to ask her husband and would have an answer the next day. "I don't know what made her decide to turn to me," Apolonia related. "Perhaps the fact that I was not one of the villagers but had come here from Warsaw, or perhaps the fact that my husband had contacts with the people in the forest." At any rate, the Oldaks decided to take the child and keep it for an indeterminate period as their own.

Having made the decision, Apolonia went to the village mayor, who was at the time keeping the child. She saw the child lying on the floor under a chair and holding a raw potato, which she kept sucking. Taking the girl with her, she noticed that the child kept scratching herself. It turned out that she had lice and was suffering from dysentery. For her young age, the child was underfed and quite weak and could hardly sit up. Lacking hygienic products, Apolonia asked her landlady for some soap. She adamantly refused, saying she did not want to waste it on a Jewish child. A friendlier neighbor lent Apolonia a washtub.

"Everywhere I was met with refusals," Apolonia recalled. "All claimed that a Jewish child does not deserve milk. I received only skimmed milk." With the local farmers refusing to provide but the barest food, Apolonia prepared porridges for the child. The farmers could not come to terms with the fact that a Jewish child was being cared for right in their midst. "Once some farmers came and demanded that we turn the child over to them. I was very frightened, I could not move from my place; I felt paralyzed. It took a long time until I regained my senses." Faced with Apolonia's refusal, the intruders finally relented but continued to treat Apolonia with no little hostility.

Someone must have reported all this to the Germans, for soon they told the village mayor to have Apolonia report to the German police in nearby Kraśnik and bring along the little girl. The Gestapo began to cross-examine Apolonia on the child's origin. "I claimed that the child was a foundling and that she may be either Polish or even German. At any rate, she does not resemble anything Jewish." The Germans examined her closely and then asked the local farmers about the child, but they too did not tell the truth. According to Apolonia, they feared retribution from the Jewish partisans in the forest who were in touch with Apolonia's husband. The interrogation continued for three months, with Apolonia having to walk repeatedly a distance of 22 kilometers with the child in her arms to the German police station in Kraśnik. Finally, the investigation was over and Apolonia was allowed to keep the child with her. "Still, the farmers refused to deliver milk for the girl, claiming that Jews do not deserve milk."

Apolonia decided to give the child a name – Barbara, or Basia for short, her real name, as it later turned out, being Zelda Tenenbaum. One neighbor told Apolonia that she had seen the child's father, roaming through the village, looking disheveled and in pitiful state. Soon after, he was murdered and thrown in one of the pits in the village. A few days before that, a man had appeared at the Oldak home. "I was holding the girl in my arms, and he said to me: 'Feed the child.' 'I am feeding her,' I replied. The man left. A neighbor told me this was the child's father. I was told that the child's mother was also murdered."

One night, at about 11 o'clock, three Poles burst into the house; one was wielding an axe. They looked a bit deranged and insisted on having the child turned over to them. They said they were going to behead her. One of them shouted, "Why waste a bullet, we want to kill her with the axe." Aleksander, who was present, did not lose his composure. He grabbed a gun, pointed it at them, and shouted: "Hands up!" The robbers took fright and raised their hands. "My husband took the axe from one of the men, promising them [to be rid of them for good] that he would himself kill the child. He told them never to return. The robbers went back to the forest."

After this incident, the Oldaks decided to have the child baptized and thus diminish the hostility toward them from the local inhabitants. This took place in the summer of 1943, and the girl was officially named Barbara. After this, the farmers stopped bothering the Oldaks, but they still refused to provide them with fresh milk. The child was still weak and suffered from many ailments, including a lung inflammation. For the first two years with the Oldaks, she could hardly walk or speak; it was only at the age of four that she began to utter words. Her uncles, her father's brothers, were all that time hiding in the forest.

Aleksander's work as a medical equipment mechanic also led to his repairing weapons for use by people in the forests, Jews and others. This caused some problems, as the armed men in the forest were in the habit of forcing the two Oldaks to be of service to them, as in the following example, related by Apolonia. A group of armed men came to their home, blindfolded her, and told her to follow them. After a walk of perhaps several kilometers, the blindfold was removed and she saw many wounded men. She was asked to attend to their wounds, was then blindfolded again, and returned to her home. This happened several times.

In the summer of 1944, as the fighting approached village area, the Oldaks decided to leave and hide in the fields to avoid the shelling. "As we left, one of the villagers, passing by, said: 'Throw away the Jewish child!' My husband replied, 'Why don't you throw away your own child?'" Finding protection in a ditch, they awaited the coming of the Russians, after which they returned to Dzieźkowice. There the situation had completely changed. The farmers' attitude had undergone a total transformation. "They began to take an interest in us, coming to us occasionally and asking whether we needed milk. Now I did not want to receive anything from there." Barbara's two uncles who had hidden in the forest also appeared and embraced their niece, who did not know them. The Oldaks then moved to Lublin, where Apolonia informed the Jewish committee of Barbara's real origins. The committee provided them with a one-bedroom basement apartment. Eventually the Oldaks returned to Warsaw, where Apolonia returned to her nursing profession.

The Tenenbaum brothers, Shraga, Arieh, and Avish, left for Israel, and in 1950 Aleksander died. In 1953 Apolonia remarried, but she kept the truth about Basia from him. Occasionally, people from the Jewish committee came to see her to persuade her to part with the child, even offering her a large sum of money. "I answered that I never traded in horses and children, and would for no money in the world part from the child." As for the child's uncles in Israel, they too began to implore her in letters to come to Israel. It was not too long before Apolonia's husband found one of these letters, which led him to wonder who really was the Jew in his family – his wife, Apolonia, or the little girl, Basia-Barabara. "He went into a rage and screamed at me – Jewess! I did not answer nor did I correct his mistake." At the time Basia had no doubt that Apolonia was her mother. Then the principal at Basia's school learned the truth, and rumors began to fly. "So I told her the truth; she was then 15 years old, and she burst out crying terribly. She repeated that she had no other mother but me."

Again, people from the Jewish committee urged her to move to Israel. Her husband's hostility towards her and the child, as well as to Jews in general, began to affect Apolonia's health. "I began to think seriously of going to Israel, where I felt Basia would be close to her relatives and her future best assured." She parted from her husband and before leaving the country was required to waive her Polish citizenship. Coming to Israel in 1958, Apolonia and Batya (the Hebrew rendering of Basia) first stayed with Shraga Tenenbaum in Tel Aviv. The child's uncles tried to give the child an Israeli education by sending her to a kibbutz, but Batya refused to part from Apolonia. Eventually, Basia was turned over to an educational institution, where she stayed for two years, while Apolonia moved into a small apartment in Bat-Yam, near Tel Aviv, and found various jobs. After completing her studies, Batya registered in a nursing course. In Apolonia's words, "The profession she chose was not incidental. After suffering so much in her life, she wanted to help others." She became a practicing nurse in an institution for mentally disturbed people. In 1964, she married and became a mother of children.

In 1966, Yad Vashem conferred on Apolonia Oldak the title of Righteous Among the Nations.

Olt, Mária

HUNGARY

*H*urrying to a doctor's appointment, Mária Olt made her way to Dr. Laszló Kuti's office in Budapest. The first thing that struck her as she entered his office was the yellow patch on his doctor's coat – the telltale star that all Jews had to wear on their outer garment when leaving their homes. Coming to the big city from a distant village, Mária Olt was not sure what this really meant and began to ply the doctor with questions. He began to tell her about his newborn daughter and how he and his wife, Miriam, were worried about the future of the infant under the current conditions of the German occupation. It is hard to tell what went through Mária's mind, but suddenly she forgot the reason for her appointment and heard herself saying, "Please let me save the child." This was the beginning of Mária Olt's initiation into rescue operations that grew beyond any ordinary bounds for a young 21-year-old woman – recently married.

For the Kutis, the bells had begun to toll on that fateful day of March 19, 1944, when the Germans occupied Hungary. Three days later, Miriam Kuti, wife of the doctor, gave birth to a daughter, named Anna, in the Budapest hospital where her husband was employed. The atmosphere in the hospital and throughout the city for Jews was grim and depressing. Miriam related that some of her Jewish friends on the hospital staff, totally depressed, had committed suicide. She added bleakly, "My husband and I thought about it too, but several days after Anna was born, Mária Olt appeared on the scene." With Mária's arrival a new and fresh spirit of hope had replaced The Kutis previous mood of despair now that there was a distinct possibility of saving their newborn child.

Dr. Laszló and Miriam Kuti agreed the very day that Mária Olt visited the doctor to place their trust in their patient and hand over their young daughter to her. Mária left Budapest with the child and returned to her native village of Hosszúvólgy in the Zala region in southwest Hungary. Several days later Mária Olt returned to Budapest; this time to get the child's mother, Miriam, so she could continue to care for her baby

Mária Olt (Private Collection)

daughter. To explain her presence in the village and her connection with Anna, Mária told everyone that she was a gypsy friend who had become pregnant and run away from home to escape punishment. Miriam's curly black hair and dark complexion made the story credible.

Mária did not stop at this, and the following week she also brought Miriam's husband to the village, but he had to be hidden – in the tiny cellar of her father's winepress, since there was no other way to explain his presence in the village. Every day, Mária Olt slipped in to bring him food and remove his wastes. Paradoxically, their roles had been reversed, as she was now treating him and caring for his health.

When little Anna developed a whooping cough, Mária Olt brought her back to Budapest, where Miriam's sister, Vera Rozsa, was waiting for her at the train station. With no taxis available to take the child to the hospital, Mária took the bold step of going to the police office at the train station, and they obliged by driving the two women and the baby straight to the hospital. Mária Olt seemed to have been emboldened by this act to take further risky steps to keep any harm from befalling the Kutis.

Back in the village, unfortunately for Miriam, after a while she was recognized by the village midwife, who had trained in the hospital where Dr. Kuti had worked, and had even been present at Anna's birth. It turned out that she was not well disposed toward Jews and she began to threaten to tell the police. At this point, Mária Olt quickly moved Miriam to relatives in another village, but without disclosing to them Miriam's true identity. When these people regaled in the gory account of how the local peasants had torn a Jewish shop-keeper limb from limb, Mária felt it was time to take Miriam elsewhere. In the meantime, Miriam's daughter was moved to her sister, who by then was going by the name of Ilona Hilak, which Mária hold arranged for her. She in turn gave her into the care of a family living near the Slovak border. The child, too, appeared under a borrowed Christian name – also arranged by Mária Olt.

Returning to Miriam Kuti, Mária planned to get her away from her relatives, but there was a problem. Neither Miriam nor Mária had proper identity papers on them. Miriam could not show the papers on which her previous name appeared. As for Mária, she had given her own identity card to the wife of a friend of Dr. Kuti's. Mária decided that she and Miriam had no other alternative but to move from place to place until a better solution was found.

The days and weeks that followed were a grueling ordeal, for the two women could never stay anywhere long. "We wandered from village to village," Miriam recalled. By that time, the Jews from the provinces were being deported on a daily basis, in sealed railroad cars, to the Auschwitz death camp. Miriam Kuti's state of mind at the time can be gathered from her own words: "Once we came across a train packed with Jews heading for Auschwitz. I was so depressed that when the train stopped for a moment I felt a terrible urge to climb aboard and put an end to my suffering. But Mária said she would go along with me, so I dropped the idea."

In time, Mária managed to borrow some money, with which she was able to rent a room for Miriam. She then returned to her village of Hosszúvólgy to get Dr. Kuti and brought him to Miriam's place, concealed beneath a load of hay in the wagon of Mária's father. Soon afterward, she was also able to get a set of papers for him.

Mária's ever deepening involvement in help to the Kuti family was too much for her husband to take. It seemed to him that she took more of an interest in others than in him, but she would not give up her care of the Kutis' extended family. The marriage was irreparably damaged, and the two divorced. Mária was by then 22 years of age. In a way, the breakup of the marriage may have given Mária a freer hand, for she soon found others to help, now that Miriam and Lazsló Kuti were provided for.

Over the next ten months Mária Olt looked after Miriam's parents as well as spiriting Dr. Kuti's mother, Mrs. Nandor Klein, and a friend of hers, Mrs. Antal Gál, out of the Budapest building assigned to Jews and placing them in an abandoned house in the non-Jewish section of Buda, telling the neighbors that they were relatives. She made it a point to visit the two women regularly to allay any suspicions.

Mária now seemed to have entered into a frenzy of rescue activities, as she began to collect documents from her non-Jewish relatives and friends, such as birth certificates, identity cards, and others documents, in order to distribute them among those who needed them badly. How she managed to do this without jeopardizing herself has never been fully explained. Miriam's sister, Vera Rozsa-Nordell, testified, "My own life was saved by false papers, under the name of Ilona Hilak, which she gave to me. She gave her papers to another woman, the wife of a Dr. Béla Laszlo, and took the great risk of going without papers in the most dangerous circumstances." In addition, she frequently traveled from Budapest to a small village near Fot, where Vera's parents were in hiding, to furnish them with necessary documents that had to be renewed from time to time, such as ration cards.

A further example mentioned by Vera Rozsa-Nordell is Mária's help to a friend of Vera's sister, Anna Gruenberg, who in the fall of 1944 was being assembled with thousands of other Jews at a factory, ready to be deported. Mária Olt appeared on the scene and at the last moment succeeded in getting this woman out of the place with the help of a police officer, a friend of hers.

All this, Mária performed gratuitously, asking nothing in return. What could possibly have motivated her, to sacrifice her marriage and the care of her immediate family for the sake of others? According to Miriam Puti, it was linked "to a deep religious feeling, for she believed with all her heart that God commanded her to help every persecuted person." Mária Olt was and remained a devout Catholic.

After the war, Mária Olt remarried and gave birth to a daughter. Here again her marriage floundered, as her husband left her, left the country, and took up with another woman. As for little Miriam Kuti, she moved to Israel, where she became an actress and drama instructor under the name of Miriam Nevo. She and Mária kept in touch, and in 1979 she invited Mária to attend the Passover Seder celebration together with her.

After being honored by Yad Vashem with the planting of a tree in her and her father's name (Jozsef Lang), she was asked about the reasons for her involvement in the rescue of so many Jews on the run – all by herself, Mária Olt replied that her first contact with the yellow star had jolted her like a bolt of lightning. From that moment, she added,

"I felt an urge to help the persecuted. An inner voice spoke to me in those days and guided my every action without consideration of the dangers surrounding me. I would never have forgiven myself if I had done anything else. Those were certainly days of fear and terror. But since I had no time to worry about what would happen to me if I was arrested, I just went on without stopping to think."

It had all started with a routine visit to a doctor's office in Budapest. The yellow star on the doctor's robe and the dispirited look in his eyes as he worried about his newborn child had triggered something in her and launched her on a far-reaching humanitarian adventure affecting the lives of others. Many Jews owe their survival to this self-effacing but quite enterprising village woman.

In 1979 Yad Vashem recognized Mária Olt, and her father Jozsef Lang, as Righteous Among the Nations.

Oppenheim, Friedrich Carl von
GERMANY

*I*n 1938, Friedrich von Oppenheim had decided that it was high time for the Griessman and Lissauer families, with whom he had close business connections, to leave Nazi Germany. He helped them to emigrate to the Netherlands, where through his financial contacts he assisted them in setting up a business that dealt in metal production and continued to maintain contact with them. In May 1940, came the German invasion of the Netherlands, and the Griessmans and Lissauers were again in danger, and for a second time Von Oppenheim came to their rescue. In September 1940, after much effort, he succeeded in obtaining exit visas for them to Portugal and from there to South America. To make sure that this would go off without a hitch, Von Oppenheim went to the Netherlands to part from his friends and arrange the details of their escape. He achieved something quite spectacular for those days – he got them a special German bus, commanded by *Abwehr* (German military intelligence) officers, which left on September 7, 1940, with the two Jewish families – 11 persons in all – through occupied Belgium and France to the safety of the Spanish border at Irún. Crossing safely into Spain, the fugitive Jews continued by train to Lisbon, and from there traveled by ship to Brazil. How was this German businessman able to carry off such a remarkable achievement?

Baron Friedrich Carl von Oppenheim

Friedrich Carl von Oppenheim, born in 1900, was a descendant of the German-Jewish banker Salomon Oppenheim (1772–1828), who had established in Cologne his famous banking house under the name of Sal Oppenheim. The bank played an important role in the industrial development of the Rhine-Ruhr region, especially through the financing of the construction of railway and waterway communications and the development of the coal and steel industries. The government ennobled Salomon Oppenheim's sons, Simon and Abraham. Simon's sons, Albert and Eduard, converted in 1858 and 1859, respectively, and married non-Jewish women. With the Nazi assumption of power, Baron Friedrich Carl von Oppenheim and his brother Waldemar – Salomon Oppenheim's great grandsons – were classified as quarter-Jews, or in Nazi terminology, "*Mischlinge* of the second degree."

Although excluded from holding positions of power, quarter-Jews were still allowed greater degrees of freedom than those classified as *Mischlinge* of the first degree, and naturally than those who were fully Jewish. On the other hand, the Oppenheim banking firm in Cologne and its employees were subjected to some harassment from Nazi Party circles. However, other than having to change its name to *Pferdmenge,* after Dr. Robert Pferdmenge, a non-family banking partner, the bank was by and large allowed to carry on its normal business. While Friedrich von Oppenheim was subjected to special Gestapo surveillance, he continued, at the same time, to enjoy certain privileges by virtue of the economic importance of the banking firm's indispensable business connections abroad.

After the outbreak of the war, in September 1939, both Friedrich von Oppenheim and his elder brother, Waldemar, were inducted into the *Abwehr,* which entitled them to virtually unrestricted travel abroad. In addition, disregarding the risks to himself, Friedrich von Oppenheim continued to maintain close business contacts and friendly relations with Jews, as evidenced by his help to the Lissauer and Griessman families, in disregard of his own heightened vulnerability as a so-called *Mischling.*

After the Germans began deporting the Dutch Jews in 1942, Von Oppenheim was active in a largely unsuccessful attempt to save the lives of the Jewish workers of the Oxid firm in Amsterdam. This firm, which had previously belonged to the aforementioned Lissauer and Griessman families, was taken over in 1940–41 by the Oppenheim bank together with another German company. Since the Oxid firm was engaged in the production of certain metal alloys that were of importance to the German munitions industry, its Jewish workers – most of them former German-Jewish refugees – enjoyed protected status for the time being. Von Oppenheim exploited this situation to lobby other German agencies with whom he had financial ties, such as the *Reichsbank* (Central Bank) and the Ministry for Military Production, to exempt these workers from deportation. Unfortunately, these efforts largely proved unsuccessful, as the Germans intensified their anti-Jewish measures in the Netherlands. In 1943, Von Oppenheim personally met with Ferdinand Aus der Fünten, the SS Chief in Amsterdam, to plead for the exemption of Dr. Hugo Weil, the former Jewish director of Oxid who had been incarcerated in Westerbork pending his deportation. This, too, proved of no avail, and Weil was deported to Bergen-Belsen, where he perished. In the end, only ten Jewish Oxid workers (out of an estimated 80) survived the Holocaust.

There is also considerable evidence regarding Friedrich von Oppenheim's efforts on behalf of other Jewish individuals who were either in hiding or under arrest. Thus, in November 1941, he dispatched an employee, the Swiss national Ernst Gut, to Switzerland for the sole purpose of phoning friends in New York to raise money for immigration permits for certain Jewish individuals. Von Oppenheim also extended help to the Cologne police chief Karl Winkler, of Jewish ancestry, from the time that he and his family went into hiding at the beginning of 1944, which coincided with the Nazi decision to arrest the *Mischlinge* and deport them to labor camps inside Germany.

Following the abortive attempt on Hitler's life in July 1944, Friedrich Carl von Oppenheim, who had long been targeted by the Gestapo, was arrested and thrown into prison pending his trial on charges of treason. In an attempt to frame him, the Gestapo produced, in August 1944, fabricated evidence to prove that his mother was of Jewish descent and therefore downgrading him to the status of half-Jew, or "*Mischling* of the first degree." This by itself could have had fatal consequences for the outcome of his trial. Fortunately for him, the interrogation dragged on until the end of the war, and Von Oppenheim was able to survive in prison until he was released by the American military. After the war, the Oppenheim firm, which reverted in 1947 to its original name, resumed its banking activity, to become one of the largest private banking concerns in Germany.

In 1996, Yad Vashem recognized the late Baron Friedrich Carl von Oppenheim as Righteous Among the Nations.

Ozarchuk, Anton & Pelageya & Nadezhda, Mariya & Marta
UKRAINE

When the Germans entered Tuczyn (today Tuchin in Ukraine) on July 6, 1941, a town with a large Ukrainian population, they immediately staged a pogrom on the town's 3,000 Jews. Sporadic killings continued until the final liquidation date, set for September 24, 1942, two days after the Yom Kippur holiday. Some persons had prepared themselves for this and put up resistance with arms gotten from the partisans. During the fighting, a sizable group, numbering 2,000, managed to flee to the forest, two-thirds of the ghetto population – quite a feat! Sadly, half of them were eventually caught and killed. An additional 300 women with their children, who could not withstand the cold in the forest, returned to Tuczyn and were shot. When liberation came on January 16, 1944, there were only two dozen Jewish survivors.

All these terrible events took place during the German occupation. Before the war, however, Yaakov and Esya (probably a diminutive of "Esther") Zilberberg, owners of a grocery store, had entertained fairly good business relations with their non-Jewish neighbors in Tuczyn. The Zilberberg family included three sons, Joseph (born 1933), Itzhak (1927), and Aaron (1931). Then came the war and with it the organized killings of the town's Jews, initiated by the Germans and aided by local armed Ukrainians, who hoped that as a reward for killing Jews their country would be granted independence under German protection. At first, the victims were people whose names appeared on a special list – mostly the intellectual and professional leadership of the Jewish community. They had been asked to take along some provisions with them for a trip elsewhere. They were then taken out of the city to a secluded spot, told to undress, and shot next to open pits.

Some Jewish people felt that if they could get work with the Germans their lives would be spared, but this proved expedient only for the short term. For added protection, Yaakov Zilberberg had built a bunker under his home, where he and his family sought shelter whenever there was a rumor of an imminent killing raid. On other occasions, the Zilberbergs sought safe havens with local Ukrainians in a nearby village in return for a huge payment, but these "rescuers" were not all trustworthy. One spread the news among his neighbors that he had Jews in his house. No sooner was the news out than armed men came to get the Zilberbergs, who were able to flee in time, saving their lives by the skin of their teeth.

Fortunately for the Zilberbergs, they had known a Ukrainian with a heart of gold – Anton Ozarchuk. He and his wife, Pelageya, were devout Baptists and owned a farm in the hamlet of Pustomid, not far from Tuczyn. Before the war, Ozarchuk had often sold the surplus produce from his farm to Jewish traders, among them Yaakov Zilberberg. First, Ozarchuk agreed to receive some of Yaakov Zilberberg's valuables for safekeeping. In the meantime, word had gotten out that local Ukrainians were urging the Germans to wait no more and liquidate the Jewish community immediately, arguing that they could do the same work for the Germans that the Jews were doing. At this critical point, in August 1942, Yaakov Zilberberg turned up at the Ozarchuks' home and asked if they would be prepared to hide him and his family should it become necessary. When on September 20, 1942, the eve of Yom Kippur, the sacred the Day of Atonement, the town's Jews were ordered to assemble in a specific place, it was deemed a bad sign. The Zilberbergs decided instead to flee to the Ozarchuks. It was a Sunday, and when the Poles in town were leaving church the Zilberbergs mingled with them and thus made their way out of the city.

However, Yaakov felt miserable that he was not able at this late hour in the life of the Jewish community to at least participate in the *Kol Nidrei* prayer being said in secret in another Jewish home. On the way to the Ozarchuks, Yaakov felt a terrible urge to return for this important prayer, but his family stopped him and urged him not to take any unnecessary risks. The Germans might be waiting at the home where the Jews had assembled for prayer. Before entering Ozarchuk's home, Yaakov put on his *tallit* (prayer shawl) and led his family in the *Kol Nidrei* prayer under the open sky. The whole family wept. They were all depressed; they felt that they might not survive for next year's Day of Atonement.

They were warmly received by the Ozarchuks and promptly hidden under a haystack in the threshing room. Two days later, the Zilberbergs were told that the ghetto in Tuczyn had been totally burned down. On the night that the ghetto went up in flames, the Ozarchuks took in another fleeing Jewish family – Eliyahu Shtaingold, his wife and children. There were now nine people hiding in Ozarchuk's haystack.

Winter soon set in and Anton Ozarchuk dug a bunker for the two Jewish families that he was sheltering. Dug out under the floor of the barn, it measured three by two meters and one-and-a-half meters in depth. The entrance was from inside the barn and was concealed by a haystack. Inside, the floor was lined with straw. The women and children slept on a low bench and the men on the straw beneath the stool. A small opening allowed fresh air to penetrate. It was, nevertheless, stifling inside and the heat caused the people to wear a minimum of clothing with no considerations of modesty. Also in matters of personal hygiene; people took care of their needs unashamedly next to each other. Survival was what counted.

Every day before sunrise, Anton Ozarchuk brought his wards soup and bread that they divided sparingly among each other. Joseph Zilberberg, nine years old at the time, said, "I kept my slice of bread for two days, even three days. When the bread had completely gone stale, I would suck it like candy. Thus I also kept myself occupied. When the bread fell apart, I would eat the crumbs." Anton's three daughters, Nadezhda, Mariya, and Marta, even helped with the unpleasant task of emptying the people's toilet bucket. Anton's wife, Pelageya, frequently visited them and paid particular attention to the Zilberbergs three sons, aged between nine and thirteen. The Ozarchuks' other children – some very young and others who were married and living away from home – were not told about the hidden Jews. The rule in those days was that the less people who knew about someone's hiding Jews, the safer it was. A slip of the tongue could bring tragedy to all concerned.

The feeling among the rescuers was that it was a matter of only a few weeks. No one thought the fugitives would stay in hiding for a year and a half. Had they been told of this at the start, they might have given up on the whole undertaking. Anton's disposition was of great help. He was by nature a quiet person with an encouraging demeanor. He would appear each evening and tell them that the Germans were getting beaten on the battlefield, whether that was true or not. His wife, Pelageya, also pitched in with encouraging words. She was a bit more devout than her religious husband and had confidence that God would help them out – to the extent that once she suggested that the fugitive children move into the house. However, Anton objected, feeling that this was too risky and could lead to detection. He had to be careful of roving Ukrainian nationalists of the Bandera faction, known for their appetite for killing Jews, who on occasions suddenly appeared in his home and took with them whatever supplies they needed. When these armed bands stayed too long near his home, Anton cautioned his charges that he might not be able to visit them for a few days and not to worry about it. In such cases he left them food to last for two to three days. He also told his wards to make sure they did not to talk in loud voices. He himself always spoke in a low voice, to the extent that, in Joseph's words, "When we left the hole, I was surprised that people were speaking in a regular voice." Anton's married daughter and her family were among the victims of a German punitive raid in the village in retaliation for the failure of some villagers to make their obligatory contribution of wheat to the Germans.

During the winter of 1942–43, Anton came to tell his wards about a local Ukrainian family that had been executed with the Jews who had been discovered in their home. This alarmed him very much and he took fright. In Joseph's words, "He was a very religious person, and could not understand how such frightful things were taking place with the indifference of everybody. He once told my mother that he was not afraid to die, and the same for his wife, but the small children who did not even know that he was hiding Jews – what was their guilt?"

Joseph especially remembered a certain serious incident that occurred between Anton and his parents in the spring of 1943. It happened after Anton had been ordered to bury Ukrainians who were executed for sheltering Jews. Returning from this awesome personal experience, Anton was greatly upset and asked his charges to step out of their hole. He was beside himself as he related what had taken place. He then asked them to kneel together with him and pray that no such tragic event befall them. Joseph's mother, Esya, explained that it is not customary for Jews to kneel in prayer, similarly to their not eating pork. As Joseph told it, "Anton felt deeply insulted. He replied that he was risking the life of his family, and we were not willing even to do such a simple thing. He ended by telling us to get back in the hole and get out of his house that night." After he left, the fugitives had a terrible argument among themselves. Some said that it was a small thing to kneel and they should not damage the good relations with Anton, who was afraid and worried about his safety. What would happen if he stood by his word and everyone would have to leave? Esya Zilberberg, however, stood fast, saying it was anyway not certain that they would come out alive, and if not, then it was better to go to heaven without having violated an important Jewish religious prohibition. "To mother, kneeling in prayer was like changing one's religion," Joseph Zilberberg explained.

Later that evening, Anton returned and conferred with Esya. She spoke to him gently, explaining that there was only one God in heaven and that all prayed to him, but everyone prayed according to one's ancestors' customs and one should not be forced to diverge from this. Anton had probably thought about this himself, and following his talk with Esya he came to terms with it and told his charges that they could stay. The incident was over.

In January 1944, the Russians approached the Tuczyn area. The fugitives were overjoyed; liberation was at hand. But Anton would not let them leave for several weeks due to the chaotic situation outside, with armed bands killing Jews who came out of their hiding places. He insisted that they remain in his home until the region had stabilized. When they eventually left their hideaway, Anton Ozarchuk had a surprise for them; he returned a gold ring that the Zilberbergs had left with him for safekeeping at an earlier period, before they moved in to hide with him. After returning to Tuczyn, the Zilberbergs were met with an angry and threatening populace and saw that their home had been vandalized. They returned to Anton Ozarchuk, who took them in again and supplied them with food. In Joseph Zilberberg's words, "I shall never forget the beautiful attitude of Anton. After having suffered us for a year and a half, he felt it necessary to look after our needs and saved us this time from famine and encouraged us to keep on." Fearing for his safety after his village neighbors learned of his help to Jews, Anton took his family away and moved to the city of Rovno, where the Zilberbergs had also gone. He took up shoe repairing. This time, it was Yaakov Zilberberg who helped him out with money and other necessities. On the Passover eve *Seder* of 1944, Anton Ozarchuk was a guest at the Zilberberg home.

Eventually the Zilberbergs moved to Israel. To this day, the parents on both sides having already passed on, the Zilberberg children continue to maintain close contact and a warm relationship with the Ozarchuk children.

In 1991, Yad Vashem recognized as Righteous Among the Nations Anton and Pelageya Ozarchuk, and their children, Nadezhda, Mariya and Marta.

Pają̨k, Genowefa
POLAND

"*I*t was a hot day at the end of that July 1942," so begins Henrietta Altman's 1982 account of conditions in the Będzin (pronounced Bendzhin) ghetto during the height of the deportation of Jews to Auschwitz, and the rescue of one Jewish child by a Polish woman – Genowefa Pają̨k (pronounced Payonk). At the time, the ghetto was seething with rumors. In her litany of the doomed ghetto, Henrietta wrote:

"People were weary, recovering from the recent and exceptionally severe 'action.' We were moving on the unpaved streets, crying, calling out to friends and relatives: 'Are you still here?' The tears were hot, almost scalding. Tears for the ones that went and tears for the ones who would go next – us, the survivors. Rumors, like rumors, grew by the hour, nobody knew who started them, nobody knew what was true, everybody wanted to believe – maybe it was the last action. After all, how long can it last?"

Genowefa Pają̨k (left) with Tamara Cygler

Genowefa (also known as Genia) Pają̨k, a Polish woman who lived in the city was aware, like all of Będzin's non-Jewish population, of the terrible things taking place inside the ghetto. She was married and the mother of three children and had gotten to know Henrietta Altman's mother through the barter trade between the two populations – goods and valuables (such as linen and fur coats) in exchange for food (flour, buckwheat, lard, and beans) for the famished ghetto dwellers. On that July afternoon, she came to Altman's room, saying under her breath, "I want to save you." She had a friend, a woman whose lover was a German soldier and who had disclosed to her that soon "it will be all over" for the ghetto Jews. Genowefa's woman friend was willing to hide Henrietta in her attic until the end, provided Genowefa would provide the additional food. It seemed an ideal solution, since the woman made no secret of having a German soldier visiting her and therefore was beyond suspicion in the eyes of the Germans.

Henrietta quietly replied to this kind invitation: "Geniusiu, my dear, I am young and healthy, I'll survive. But there is a child in my family whom I love dearly, the six year-old daughter of my beloved aunt." Genowefa did not know the aunt, but she had heard of her, for the aunt was a dental surgeon and before the war had many Poles as her patients. Genowefa acceded to Henrietta's plea. Henrietta's aunt, Rachela Cygler, however, had certain doubts, since she did not know Genowefa, but finally she acquiesced to Henrietta's pleading to place her daughter, Tamara, in Genowefa's care for at least a few days to save the child from sure death at the hands of the Germans in one of their deadly raids. As Henrietta explained in her postwar testimony, "I think that every child in the ghetto was taught that a day may come when they'll get a new name, a new 'mama,' they shouldn't cry or talk about their real parents and never, never admit that they lived in the ghetto and are Jewish."

When Genowefa came to get Tamara, her mother told her, "This is your aunt Genowefa, you'll go and stay with her for a few days." Genowefa put the crucifix she was wearing over the child's head. She bent down, smiled, kissed the child's head, and took her by the hand. The child, well trained as she was, did not turn around. Genowefa, smiling with tears in her eyes, looked back and said to Rachela Cygler, "Don't worry, Mrs. Doctor, I'll look after your child." A few days later, Genowefa returned with the child for what turned out to be the last visit. It was the last time she was to see her parents. In her few moments alone with Genowefa, the child's mother scribbled on a piece of paper the address of her sister in Palestine and a request to anyone in the family who remained alive after the war to compensate Genowefa Pająk with five thousand zlotys or their equivalent when she returned the child. She also slipped into her hand all the money she had in the house – a thousand German marks. Genowefa named the child "Bogusia" – a gift from God.

Soon after, the Germans staged another deadly raid on the ghetto's Jews, where thousands paid with their lives, including the child's parents, Rachela and her artist husband, Samuel Cygler. Before this, Rachela had told others about Genowefa, and consequently a woman who had fled from the German raid came up Genowefa's street with her little daughter calling out her name. Genowefa did not dare answer, afraid that her neighbors would discover her involvement in the rescue of a Jewish child. To protect Tamara-Bogusia, she told her to run quickly to one of the three non-Jewish people whose names and address were embedded in the child's memory, given to Genowefa in case she should need help. The first on the list was Jadzia, the child's former governess, who had lived with them for about five years had been adored by the child. Bogusia ran the short distance to where Jadzia lived. It was in a big block of flats and Bogusia did not know her apartment number, so she began knocking doors. It was obvious that the child was Jewish. Some slammed the door in her face, not wishing to get involved; some said they did not know who Jadzia was or where she lived. By that time the whole town was swarming with German soldiers looking for Jews hiding among Poles. In the meantime, some hours later, Genowefa was frantically looking for the child. She went to Jadzia only to be told that Bogusia had never come. Desperate and broken-hearted, she returned home, and there was Bogusia at the house. The child told her about her unsuccessful attempts to get help. She was sent upstairs to hide beneath the roof among the rabbits, who kept her warm. After this incident Bogusia was sent away to a farm in a village where Genowefa thought she might be safer, and subsequently underwent movement from place to place and from family to family – with consequences for the child's mental health.

Inside the Będzin ghetto, a small contingent of only 30 people, including Henrietta, was left behind by the Germans to work in a factory still producing uniforms for the German army. Whenever she could, Genowefa smuggled some food and letters to Henrietta, assuring her that Bogusia was well. Henrietta: "I had my misgivings, but what could I do?" Then, late one evening, there was a faint but persistent knock on the door of the workers' dormitory. Henrietta relates: "I heard my name called. Someone quickly got the keys, secretly made by our men to open the door, in front of which on the side of our room was an iron grill that could not be moved. Genowefa and Bogusia squeezed themselves into the narrow space, shut the door behind them, and laughing and crying we embraced through the grill. Now you can see with your own eyes that she is well, said Genowefa, as if she was reading my thoughts. After the first moments of excitement we all realized the danger both to them and to us." Genowefa and Bogusia quickly left the place, but not before agreeing on another meeting. During this next encounter, almost all the workers wanted to be present.

> *"They all wanted to touch, to embrace a Jewish child – the only hope of a future. This child has a chance of survival. Everybody wanted to say something to this child – like leaving an important legacy in her childish hands. Words that were beyond the comprehension of a child's mind, but maybe they would remain in a small cell, maybe they would be stored in the memory until such a day that they would burst out of the depths of the nightmare and cry out loud and clear for the whole world to hear: 'Do not let it ever happen again – to anybody.' Little did we know that in years to come the only way for the child to live and survive would be to bury and forget any memory of that time... Bogusia was terrified, people were rushing towards her, touching and kissing her, throwing names and words at her. She looked at them with her huge brown eyes, frightened by the intensity of the words whose meaning she could not grasp, horrified by the yellow Star of David sewn into our garments. Her little face was wet with the salty tears of these strangers who behaved as if they had a claim on her. She clung to me convulsively and whispered, 'Promise me, promise me I'll never have to be a Jew again.'"*

To further protect the child, Genowefa concocted a story that she had had a child out of wedlock, that the child had been placed in a village with her old aunt and that her husband had not known about it. Now that her aunt died, she had to take back the child. Her husband, having discovered his wife's infidelity, had at first beaten and abused her, but finally agreed to adopt the child. So went the story. She then went to the police and, with tears in her eyes, convinced the officer there to issue her the necessary papers for the child, now renamed Bogumila Pająk. The child's existence had been legalized.

Before and after, Tamara-Bogumila had been moved to various places, for her own protection, such as to the small town of Wojkowice-Komorne, where the woman of the house, in Tamara's words, "was a very bad person and I had to work very hard. I did the cleaning, cooking and worked in the garden. I also had to learn to play piano and to speak German. The lady was a teacher of German and her husband was an orchestra conductor. They were Poles, he was Mr. Pająk's brother. This man was very good to me." She stayed there for eight months, and Genowefa Pająk came to visit her from Będzin twice each week. She then returned to the Pająk household in Będzin . Once the Gestapo raided the house looking for hidden partisans and found a German military cape. Genowefa was able to convince them that the cape belonged to a German who had taken his meals there. They also found some drill material with 1,500 German marks and some parts from a motorbike. Suspecting that Mr. Pająk was a partisan, they handcuffed him and threatened to shoot him on the spot, but instead decided to take him in for interrogation. There he was able to exonerate himself, and after two weeks of imprisonment he was freed after much physical abuse. This happened just one week before the Russians arrived.

In the meantime, Henrietta was transferred to another camp and managed to survive the horrors of the Holocaust. After moving to Sweden, it was only toward the end of 1945 that she received word that Tamara-Bogumila was alive. She was eventually turned over to Henrietta's mother and the child was taken to Warsaw, from where she moved to Israel. As for Genowefa Pająk, in Henrietta's words,

> *"The woman who gave 'birth' to the child's existence and future and who, for nearly three years, lived the pain and fear of it every hour of every day, this woman had to make yet another sacrifice. She had to give up the child not only physically but also emotionally. She had to relinquish all claims to her. She had to be denied the pleasure and joy of participating even from afar in her growth and development to womanhood and motherhood. 'Bogusia' could not deal with what had happened to her childhood and repressed all memory of both the time in general and Genowefa in particular. She had neither the wish nor the capacity to communicate in any way with Genowefa and did not. It seems as if the only way for her to resume her life was to deny the past."*

This was for Genowefa the hardest thing to take. She could not understand it. Yet she did not question it or bear a grudge, but in her letters from Poland to Henrietta she constantly asked about Bogusia. Henrietta: "I have tried to explain to her that though in a sense she gave her the gift of life for the second time, she must now stand back, so the child can fully profit from it. I am not sure if she ever understood the complexity of the situation, but I know that to the very last day of her life Bogusia was in her heart and mind. I know because her last letter to me was written a day before she died – and all she wanted was to see a picture of Bogusia and her children. And I also know that she would have endangered her own life again if it would have meant saving another human life."

In 1982, Yad Vashem conferred upon the late Genowefa Pająk the title of Righteous Among the Nations. The story does not yet end here, for some two decades after Pajak's induction into the Yad Vashem Righteous Hall of Fame, Tamar (hebraized from Tamara) underwent a slow but steady reawakening and a coming to terms with her past. In April 1993, eleven members of her family attended the opening exhibit of Tamar's father paintings, hosted by the city of Będzin. Tamar walked again through the streets of the former ghetto, and visited the others spots in Będzin linked to her childhood. Tragically, that same year, she died, at age 58, after suffering a stroke. However, before that, she had managed to put her new thoughts on paper. In her memoirs, she related some of her feelings when she was a hunted child:

> *"I am a Jewish child and children like me are condemned to death by the Germans. I don't know why this is so and I don't understand it. All I know is that I must never disclose the truth about who I really am to anyone if I want to stay alive. And I want to live so very much!"*

Then, there was that terrible night, when the Germans were looking for Jews in hiding, and

Genowefa Pająk put a cross around Bogusia's neck and sent her to seek temporary shelter with another person, who refused to admit her. She finally passed the night in the attic of Genowefa's home, in the company of a rabbit. "I felt the beat of his heart and the warmth of his trembling body penetrated my skin." The warmth of the rabbit's body put her to sleep. Returning home, Genowefa exclaimed: "You were lucky; the cross saved you." Tamar thought to herself: "No, the rabbit did." Summarizing her thoughts before passing from this world Tamar gave expression to a new sense of confidence:

> "Life can be seen as a continuous chain of links between people. There are some who give you love, friendship and warmth, and there are others to whom you in turn bestow these feelings... I did not lose my love for, or faith in, humanity. On the contrary, I have always encountered wonderful human beings everywhere. My faith in humanity has been strengthened by years of experience... All that I have received, I have passed on in my own way to others."

Paukštys, Bronius
LITHUANIA

Bronius Paukštys

When after the war, Masha Rabinowitz came to thank Father Paukštys (pronounced Paukshtys) for helping her to survive, and also asked him for his blessings for her soon-to-be marriage to Eliezer Eisenbod, who accompanied her – the last thing she expected from the Catholic prelate was to be counseled by him on the observance of Jewish rituals. In fact he told the two, "If you wish to respect my feelings, please marry according to the law of Moses and Israel, with my friend Rabbi Oshri." Masha granted his wish and was married in the synagogue court, on Maironus street.

Earlier, in 1943, in the Kovno (Kaunas) ghetto, Masha Rabinowitz had learned from someone on the possibility of escaping from the ghetto and its terrible conditions with the help of a Catholic priest, named Bronius Paukštys. Mustering the necessary courage for such an unknown adventure, she decided to seek out this cleric. Slipping through the ghetto fence, she removed the tell-tale seeing and incriminating yellow star, once outside the ghetto perimeter; she mixed with the crowd, and arrived at the priest's church. When her turn came to see him, she stood in front of a table, behind which sat a tall man, that seemed to her about 50 years old. Responding to his question what it was she wanted, she answered that she had been referred to him by a certain Dr. Kisin. "He offered me to sit, to rest; offered me a meal, and asked me to talk about myself." Afterwards, he told her that her outward looks, her use of an accented Lithuanian, and her sad eyes, in spite of their blue color, ruled out any chance that she could circulate freely under a different name. While she needed new credentials, she also had to be hidden somewhere. The name given her was Maria Paukštite – supposedly a relative of his. He offered her refuge with his sister in a village. Masha thanked him but declined, since she insisted that any arrangement also include her mother, whose looks were even more Jewish-pronounced. She eventually found another arrangement, a hiding place with a farmer. From there, she occasionally visited Paukštys, who always received her with great friendliness. He once asked her if she prayed. "When I answered in the negative, he remarked: 'Too bad. It's unimportant to which God one prayed. But I appreciate you telling me the truth.'"

Avraham Tory estimated that Father Bronius Paukštys probably saved some 200 Jews from the Kovno ghetto, including many children. He was born in 1897 into a farming family, one of eleven children. Entering the priesthood, he joined the Salesian order and lived the life of a monk. Tory remembered him as a modest and shy person, goodhearted, friendly and kind. Stationed in Kaunas, he had at his disposal an office in the monastery building, and a bedroom nearby. During the Nazi period, both the office and bedroom served as temporary sheltering places for many Jews. He saw in the Nazi conquest a tragedy to his people and country, and in the persecution of Jews, plain and simple genocide that one had to oppose. Tory contrasted him sharply to Archbishop Vincentas Brizgyz, head of the Catholic Church in Lithuania, who turned down a petition to help Jews on the ground that this may jeopardize the Catholic Church vis-à-vis the German occupiers. Tory added: "Father Paukštys revealed to me in my place of hiding, after my escape from the ghetto, that he was reprimanded by his superiors for jeopardizing the church and for raising doubts in the eyes of the occupation authorities concerning the credibility of the church."

Rachel Levin-Rosenzweig was another of Paukštys many Jewish beneficiaries. In 1943, on behalf of the Kovno ghetto underground, she was sent to him to receive from his hands false identities for several of Rachel's ghetto companions. "He always received me with much friendliness, inquired about myself and my family and asked why I was not asking for Aryan papers for myself." She answered that she had other plans. In July 1944, the Germans began the liquidation of the Kovno ghetto, and the remaining Jews were marched off to the train station. Rachel managed to sneak out of the column, and hide in the bushes. She then decided to look up a Lithuanian family to which she had been earlier referred, but they refused to admit her in spite of her urgent pleadings. At her wits end where to turn, she decided to look up the kindhearted Father Paukštys, whose church was far away from where she was at the moment. Making her way stealthily through the streets of a city filled with German soldiers, she finally arrived at Paukštys' residence.

"With a heavy heart I mounted the steps leading to his room and in my heart a sole prayer 'if only he were there.' The moment I entered he recognized me; he did not ask whence I

came and for what purpose. That moment my self-assurance gave way and I burst out in bitter weeping, for my whole family was still with the Germans. He then turned to me with great warmth and said: 'At least, it's good you're here, my daughter; I will protect you; be no longer afraid.' I received a room adjoining the church, which I did not leave for two weeks. Food was brought to me, water to wash, and clean clothes. Father Paukštys visited me every day; he would bring me books and talk with me. He told me about his life and studies, his life as a monk in Italy, his family and his work. He discussed moral issues: love of fellow man, religious tolerance, and non-violent resistance… He was a very religious person, but not once did he raise the religious question, and he respected me for my outspokenness. I gave him to understand that I was not religious, but that Jewish values were sacrosanct to me. Outside, the Germans distributed fliers that the house where Jews would be found will be destroyed and its owners killed."

A little later, Paukštys arranged her placement in a woman's home, where she stayed until liberation. After the war, she visited Paukštys on occasions. "He urged me to leave Lithuania because of my Zionist outlook. When I came to part with him, in March 1945, on my way to Palestine, he was very happy; he blessed me and gave me a monetary gift and a pair of shoes."

Penina Tory, another of Paukštys' beneficiaries, was the mother of a young girl, named Shulamit. She desperately sought ways to save her, especially after the Children Action of March 1943. She too was referred to Father Paukštys. The plan was for the girl to be brought to him by her Lithuanian nursemaid, Veronica, who would be waiting to pick her up near the ghetto's gate. Paukštys did not disclose to Penina that the pick up person would be his brother, Juozas Paukštys, a professor in agriculture, and owner of a farm. After the failure of this initial escape attempt, Penina brought her himself early the next morning, after an adventurous escape from the ghetto. Paukštys had not expected her, and at this early hour, he was in fact still at his prayer in the chapel. Penina was terribly concerned that the priest would react badly at the sight of two Jewish escapees waiting outside the church, in full view of passers-by.

After a while, that to Penina seemed an eternity, the door of his office opened, and Paukštys welcomed her with a broad smile. He told her that the man who originally was to take Shulamit had already left the city, so Paukštys suggested that Penina and her daughter be accommodated in his living quarters behind the office, until an alternative solution would be found. "He took us to his room, gave us his bed, while he settled down on the sofa in his small office." There, mother and daughter stayed locked in for ten days. "I thought a lot of the danger and the annoying situation this placed him in. Thrice a day he brought us our food, cared for our comfort, and comforted us." An additional problem was the care taken by him to allow his charges the use of the church's rest rooms, which to Penina seemed to add to the unpleasantness of Paukštys' burden. "However, I never noticed any sign of displeasure on his face." Finally, the decision was to move Shulamit to his professor brother who lived at the other end of the city. To go there by bus was dangerous, so the three, Penina, Shulamit and Paukštys went by foot. Penina and Shulamit stayed on the man's farm for a week.

Then, when the child came down with an ear infection, Penina wished the child be removed from the village; at least, until she was completely healed, and Paukštys agreed for the child to be brought to him in Kaunas. Due to certain complications, this could not be carried out, and when Penina appeared at Paukštys' office, she learned from him that the girl had been sent back to the village. At this news, she burst out in a terrible weeping. Paukštys came over to apologize, and she heard him murmuring to himself, "I wanted to do good, and here now I am causing pain to others." He then explained to her that he had to send the child back, for had he waited just a little longer, the Nieman River would have frozen, and passage by boat would have been impossible. After calming down, Penina stayed overnight in Paukštys' office, settling down on his couch, and the following morning before leaving, she left him an address of a relative in Tel Aviv, to whom the child was to be turned over should Penina not survive. She then returned to the ghetto.

Later, when informed that her daughter was down with an ear inflammation, Penina again left the ghetto and moved in with her daughter on the farmhouse owned by a certain Marijona Jurksaiatis and her son Juozas. There she stayed together with her daughter until the area's liberation, eight months later – with Father Paukštys occasionally dropping in on visits to see if additional help was needed. Throughout this lengthy period, Paukštys secretly forwarded letters from her to persons in the ghetto, mostly on matters of medicine for the child. After she had been on the farm for a few months, Paukštys himself fled there as a fugitive. Apparently, the Gestapo after trailing him for a while, discovered his help to Jews, including the fabrication of false identities, and he went underground. He then moved to other locations, where he remained in hiding.

Immediately after the liberation, Penina went to see him in Kaunas. "He welcomed us with such joy, as though he was seeing his brother and sister just returning from hell. Out of deep emotion, he even kissed me. He then opened a drawer and removed an envelope, which she gave him the day that Shulamit was sent to the village, and which contained the only valuables left with Penina, so that he would use them for Shulamit's upkeep. The envelope also contained a ring. "I begged him to accept it as a token and modest remembrance of us. He stubbornly refused. He would remember us even without a memorabilia." Later, Penina and her friends tried to persuade him to join them in their flight from Lithuania, in light of the danger facing him from the communists for his outspoken pro-Lithuanian sentiments. He declared: "I cannot abandon my flock; here I belong, and I must fight the Bolsheviks as I fought the Nazis."

When Masha Eisenbod-Rabinowitz learned that he was arrested, she assembled other Jews who had benefited from his aid and were still in Lithuania, and petitioned to the authorities to show him special consideration, in light of his rescue of dozens of Jews. Their request was not honored, and he was sent to Siberia. When he returned in 1956, he was forced to live in seclusion. He died in 1966, aged 69. Many of his Jewish former beneficiaries attended the funeral.

Recalling the charitable priest, Penina Tory, in Israel, wrote of him:

"Of all my terrible and hair-raising memories of the Holocaust, one ray of light shines forth – the image of a wonderful person – Father Bronius Paukštys. The very appearance of a man like Bronius Paukštys instilled in our hearts the hope that not all was lost, that not all men had turned to predator animals or cowards. That there are still people with morals and conscience, goodhearted and compassionate, and on top of that, gifted with a unique courage and urge to combat evil."

To which Rachel Levin-Rosenzweig added:

"I recall his memory, after a lapse of 31 years, his image appears to me in the form of a noble patriarch; a cultured person, lively, a lover of music; a man filled with a belief that his duty is to help all the oppressed and downtrodden, without prejudice. In the despondent darkness of the Holocaust; at a time of the dimming of the world's lights, the image of the Lithuanian priest Paukštys rises as a shining star, and this noble Christian person is worthy that his memory not be forgotten."

After the war, Paukštys wrote to a priest friend in the United States: "I did what I could at the expense of my family [i.e., the monastic order to which he belonged]. At times, I had nothing in my pockets, not even a few cents to buy the most basic foodstuff for my family. To help others, I was forced to flee my home three times from the Gestapo... How many worries? How many sleepless nights? How many exhausting wanderings? How many fears were my portion?... I did not pride myself, nor did I kneel, neither to the Right nor to the Left. When Stalin learned of this, he gave me a 'dividend' (i.e., ten 10 years of exile in Siberia), but I was encouraged by the one single thought: "Work in the cause of others, and love."

In 1977, Yad Vashem conferred on the late Father Bronius Paukštys the title of Righteous Among the Nations. Also honored with the Righteous title were Juozas Paukštys, Juozas Jurksaitis and his mother Marijona.

Paulavičius, Jonas & Antanina

LITHUANIA

---

*O*n August 10, 1944, Miriam Krakinowski was with a group of forced workers, being driven from a labor camp toward Panemune, a suburb of Kaunas (also known as Kovno) in Lithuania. As they crossed a bridge, one of the workers tried to escape. In the commotion that followed, Miriam decided to make her escape too. Luckily for her, she succeeded. She then walked aimlessly along the Niemen River when she saw a man in a boat, who called to her in Lithuanian and asked her if she had seen what had happened on the bridge. Not sure of his intentions, Miriam ignored him and kept on walking. A few minutes later, the man called out to her again, adding that she looked like she needed help. "I unequivocally answered that I did not need of any help and told him to please stop following me." The man then warned Miriam that the Germans were checking papers and she would surely soon be arrested. "The man asked me to trust him. I didn't really trust him, but I had no place to go." She followed him to his house, which stood high on a hill facing the river. He then took her into the cellar, where she noticed a carpenter's bench with wood shavings all over the floor.

Taking a broom, he swept the wood shavings aside and knocked on the floor. "I saw a small door being pushed up. He told me to go down the steps. I couldn't see where I was going, but I didn't say anything. Gradually the room became lighter, and I found myself in a very small, hot room filled with half-naked Jews. I began to cry as they asked questions about the fate of the ghetto."

Miriam remained in that bunker with seven adults and a four-year-old boy for three weeks until liberation by the Red Army. "My savior's name was Jonas Paulavičius. Every morning he would knock and one of us would open the little door. Jonas would bring us coffee and some bread. Every few days, he would allow us to go upstairs into the house and wash ourselves. He would bring us any news he had about developments in the war … After the Germans were driven back by the Russians, we were free. Altogether, we were twelve Jews and two Russian prisoners of war who were saved by the Paulavičius family: father Jonas, mother Antonina, son Kestutis, and daughter Donute."

Born into a poor farm family, Jonas Paulavičius only finished several grades of schooling and

Second and third from right, Antanina Paulavičius and Jonas Paulavičius (Private Collection Jochanan Fein)

at the age of 14 began to work at an upholsterer's to learn the trade. He was strong and robust and he built his house with his own hands, a two-story frame house. To earn a living he worked as a carpenter in the railways workshops. Before the war he had leaned toward the clandestine Communist Party, but never formally joined it. Then came the German occupation, and one day he learned that the Shames family inside the Kovno ghetto was looking for a way to save their three-year-old son. After consulting with his wife, Antonina, the two agreed to shelter the boy. However, due to the child's constant crying, Jonas asked that the child's parents join him in the Paulavičius household. The Shameses insisted on bringing along the child's grandmother, and Jonas agreed.

At this point, Jonas made a fateful decision; to try to save as many as he could, and especially people belonging to the professional elite of the Jewish community so that, in his words, the Jews would have leaders when the time came to reconstitute a viable community. So he chose educated people, physicians, and engineers. One of the lucky chosen ones was the Ipp couple, both doctors. At first they turned down the offer, fearing a trap. When Dr. Haim Ipp met Jonas at Haim's work place outside the ghetto, Jonas told him: "I want to save you and your wife, because both of you are physicians." Haim begged off: "But we have no money with which to pay you." Jonas said: "I am not asking for money. It's for free." "Free, but why?" Jonas explained in a halting voice his interest in saving Jews.

To accommodate an ever-larger group of Jews, Jonas began constructing a bunker beneath his home. The soil was collected at night in sacks, taken by boat to the middle of the river (on the pretext of going out fishing), and dumped in the water. Inside the hiding place Jonas boarded up the walls with wooden planks, with a narrow opening for ventilation. The entrance was through the cellar. The hiding place housed among others the four Shameses, the Ipp physician couple, and an engineer named Aaron Neimark.

Another fugitive Jew joined them quite by coincidence. This happened when Jonas, who wanted his son Kestutis to learn to play the violin, found out that a certain Johanan Fein, a former Jewish schoolmate of the boy, now in the Kovno ghetto, might be able to teach Kestutis to play. Neimark was sent to see Fein in January 1944, with the unbelievable news that a stranger wanted to save him simply because he played the violin. Hesitating at first, 15-year-old Johanan Fein then decided, on his sister's urging, to take up the magnanimous offer – especially after the violent Children Action in the ghetto on March 27. In his words: "At Jonas's home, I was greeted with a hearty meal. Afterwards, Jonas took out a violin and commanded me: 'Now, play something for us! I bought this violin especially for you.' I played the tune 'Dear Lithuania, Beautiful Homeland,' a sad and sentimental song." Tears welled up in the eyes of Jonas Paulavičius. Johanan was hidden in a small corner of the upper story in a space that served as a storeroom and was covered by a slanted roof. Meals were brought to him. During visits by Kestutis, Johanan also taught him to play chess. At the time, Johanan did not know about the other people hidden by Jonas on his premises. Jonas did not want them to know about each other, so that if caught they would not give each other away. In addition, Jonas refrained from having visitors over. For his added safety, Johanan was later moved to an underground bunker in a tomato field. He was then moved back to the Paulavičius home and secluded in the attic.

Once, when Jonas visited him, he found Johanan in a depressed state. Jonas said: "Perhaps you want to return to the ghetto? There you had many friends." "I replied without hesitation: No! He then embraced me, saying: I was only kidding; I would not send you back at any price." He then said he had something important to discuss with Johanan – he wanted to rescue Johanan's sister, Judith, still inside the ghetto. For this purpose, Jonas asked Johanan to draft a letter to his sister, in Yiddish, not Lithuanian, so that she would not suspect foul play. However, Judith decided not to abandon her surviving relatives in the ghetto, and declined the offer. For his security, Johanan was again moved; this time to a storage pit for potatoes. "My closest companions were rats and I was eaten by lice."

One day, Jonas brought in an escaped Russian prisoner of war. A third man joining them in that hole in the ground was David Rubin, a religious Jew who had escaped from a nearby German labor camp. When Jonas had first run into Rubin on a river boat, he had said to him: "I know you're Jewish." Rubin tried to deny it, but Jonas insisted: "Your looks betray you; come and I will hide you with me." Rubin was at first afraid to place his trust in a stranger, but for lack of an alternative he accepted the offer.

When the place was liberated by Russian soldiers, Johanan was surprised to see 13 additional rescued persons. In his words, "We then realized that Jonas had saved a total of 16 people. They all looked terrible; unwashed, unshaved, dirty clothing with blood stains and sores all over their bodies." Of the 16, 12 were Jews (the four Shameses, Doctors Haim and Tania Ipp; Aaron Neimark, Musia Gershenman, David Rubin, Miriam

Krakinowski, Johanan Fein, and a Mrs. Feinsilver), two were Soviet POWs, and two were Lithuanians.

Afterwards Jonas's fame spread throughout the neighborhood. He was derisively dubbed "Father of the Jews," and many resented him for this. Nonetheless he continued to look after his former Jewish wards in a country still ridden with violent antisemitism, with roving bandits waylaying and killing Jews. In 1947, Jonas even turned over a substantial sum of money to some of his wards to help them flee the country – for they wished to go to Palestine. At first, he cautioned one of the Jews, Musia Gershenman: "I suffered much in order to save you all, similar to a woman during birth pangs. This is one of the reasons why she loves her children so much. I underwent all these pains in order for you to remain alive. I gave you life, just as if you were reborn. You are like my children, and I worry that nothing bad befalls you. I should like for your group to think carefully before each step, for the risks are great… If you decide to go through with the plan, come back in several days, and by then I will have the money needed by you." His former wards left with his blessings. Much later, it was learned that on May 1, 1952, during May Day celebrations, Jonas was murdered by an antisemite.

In 1983 Yad Vashem recognized Jonas and Antanina Paulavičius, as well as their two children, Kestutis and Danute, as Righteous Among the Nations. The following year, during the visit by Antanina to Yad Vashem, she planted a tree in the family's name in a ceremony attended by many of those saved by the martyred Jonas.

Perlasca, Giorgio

Italy

One evening in 1987, Dr. Blitstein Willinger, an immunologist originally from Hungary, assembled her small circle of former Hungarians presently living in Berlin for their monthly get-together during which they reminisced about seminal events in their lives and read from their own and others' works. That evening, as the conversation turned to events in Budapest, Hungary, during the war years, someone recounted her work for the International Red Cross there, where she had known an extraordinary person, an Italian named Giorgio Perlasca. At the next meeting, Irene von Borosceny, the former Hungarian countess who had known Perlasca, described the man's rescue activity in Budapest. "As Irene spoke, I began to shake," Dr. Blitstein Willinger said, and took the initiative of investigating whether the man was still alive. Finding his address in Padova, Italy, she wrote to Yad Vashem of a man who, while posing as the chargé d'affaires of the Spanish legation in Budapest, managed to save some 3,000 Jewish lives during the worst phase of the Holocaust in Hungary. "To my astonishment, nobody knows his name, nobody thanks him for what he did. He was really sincere, he didn't do anything for personal advantages, he never tried to make a profit ... We are asking you to honor this great man with a noble soul before it is too late." In fact, mentioned by historians of the Holocaust in Hungary, the man's origins and biography remained unknown, and now began to unfold.

Giorgio Perlasca

Born in 1910, as a young man Giorgio Perlasca served with the Italian military contingent fighting alongside Franco's fascist forces in the Spanish Civil War. Demobilized, he joined an Italian firm importing livestock and frozen meat products. Sent first to Yugoslavia with his wife, Nerina, he witnessed the German invasion there in April 1941, and the roundup of Jews immediately thereafter. "I can still hear the sound of their voices. I remember those women very well; they were fully aware that they were going toward a dark destiny, but they were also very proud. The hymn they were singing was not a song of desperation. And yet they knew full well that they were being taken away."

Sent later to Hungary, he witnessed another German invasion – in March 1944. Fearing arrest for refusing to return to Italy as demanded by the new Nazi-installed Mussolini regime after Mussolini's re-investiture by the Germans in September 1943, he headed for the Spanish legation and presented to the ambassador Angel Sanz Briz a document he carried with him, a kind of certificate given to him by the Franco regime at the end of the Spanish Civil War. It read, "Dear Brother-in-Arms, no matter where you are in the world, you can turn to Spain." After a ten-day stay in a Spanish-owned villa, arranged by Sanz Briz, Perlasca turned himself in and was held in confinement by the Hungarian authorities, from which he escaped on October 13, 1944 – two days before the pro-Nazi Arrow Cross takeover. With nowhere to go, Perlasca returned to Sanz Briz, who handed him a Spanish passport and a letter addressed to the Hungarian Ministry of Internal Affairs approving Perlasca's request for Spanish citizenship. He now appeared under the Spanish-sounding name of Jorge instead of Giorgio.[1]

Perlasca was presently invited by Ambassador Sanz Briz to join his staff, and specifically to deal with Jews who claimed Spanish descent and were sheltered in Spanish protected houses. This included the risky job of visiting police headquarters to protest unlawful break-ins at these houses by marauding Arrow Cross gangs. In one such confrontation with Arrow Cross strongman József Gera, the latter shouted: "But why isn't Franco fighting against the Jews?" Perlasca explained that Spain was protecting the Jews because of the need to maintain a balanced foreign policy. When the war is over, it would be time to show its appreciation to certain people. Gera understood by this that Spain would take care of him after the fall of the Arrow Cross regime. At this, Gera changed his position, and in the words of Perlasca, "He let me know how fond he was of Spain and assured me that our wards would be treated

---

1 Angel Sanz Briz was also honored with the Righteous title.

with all due respect. In the end, he shook my hand. I remember how uncomfortable I felt during that handshake. I was shaking hands with someone who would sign a death warrant as easily as he would a greeting card."

On November 29, 1944, with the Red Army closing in on Budapest, Sanz Briz informed Perlasca that his government had instructed him to leave for neutral Switzerland to await further developments. Then, looking Perlasca in the eye, the Spanish ambassador said: "Listen to me, Perlasca. You have been invaluable, and I appreciate everything you've done. I've been able to get you a German visa. You can leave too. I'm going to Bern, and I can assure you that, from there, I'll make sure you receive a visa… Wait here for a few days and then come to Bern. Believe me, unfortunately there's nothing more we can do here." At this point, Perlasca made a fateful decision – to stay on in Budapest, come what may, so as not to abandon the thousands of Jewish people whose safety and survival under the chaotic circumstances then prevailing in Budapest depended on the presence of an accredited Spanish diplomat. So the next morning Perlasca presented his credentials to the Hungarian authorities. He remained on his post from December 1, 1944, to January 16, 1945, when the Russians occupied the larger Pest section of the city where the Spanish protected homes were located. The Italian-born Perlasca had made himself the official representative in Budapest of the Spanish government without Madrid's knowing a thing about it.

"At first, I didn't know what to do," Perlasca admitted after the war, "but then I began to feel like a fish in water; I continued giving out protective passes and looked after the Jews in the 'safe' houses flying the Spanish flag. As the proverb says, 'Opportunity makes the thief.'" As the representative of Fascist Spain, Perlasca had access to the highest Hungarian authorities, who in the country's desperate situation were anxious for Spanish support. More than once, Perlasca had to confront Arrow Cross men who ransacked houses flying the Spanish flag. As reported by Edith Weiss, one of the residents of these protected houses, "It happened often in those days that the Hungarian Nazis would come and march Jews down to the Danube and kill them there and throw their bodies into the river. One day they came and took us downstairs and were going to march us to the river. But Perlasca arrived. He was mesmerizing. In this forceful, powerful way of his, he told them to go away and leave us alone. The leader of the Nazi group – there were eight of them – was so stunned he couldn't even talk. Perlasca had such authority, he was so strong, that there was no way anyone could defy him. They simply went away." As also reported by Avraham Ronai, when a group of Arrow Cross men tried to take away the residents of one of the Spanish protected houses one day, Perlasca walked up to them and peremptorily said: "How dare you behave like this on the property of a friendly country? I insist that you release these people, otherwise you will have problems with your superiors. If I have to cable Madrid about this violation of Spanish interests there will be grave consequences." The Arrow Cross men withdrew.

The following is taken from Perlasca's diary: December 2: "New raids this morning. They rounded up everybody who didn't have a Spanish safe conduct letter. I succeeded, though, in getting them all into our houses on the promise that, by the end of the day, I would have issued each of them one of our letters of protection." December 3: "Total success! At noon I was received by the Vice Foreign Minister … The Vice Minister accused Spain of not regularizing its relations with the government. 'Don't be surprised, then, if the Hungarians take retaliatory measures.' Perlasca: I reminded him that there are thousands of Hungarian citizens living peacefully in Spain, but if, for any reason whatsoever, the Spanish embassy and the Hungarian government were to fail to reach a satisfactory solution concerning conditions for the Jews under Spanish protection, the Spanish government, albeit with great regret, would have to put its relations with Hungary under review. The Vice Minister asked me if he was to consider this a threat. Yes, I answered." The Vice Minister then left, and came back with greetings from [Foreign] Minister Gábor Kemény, "and assured me that, as far as they were concerned, a way to an agreement would surely be found. I thanked him and repeated our requests. We thus reached an understanding that was also put in writing … obligating all units of the Hungarian military to respect the letters of protection issued by the Spanish embassy." December 25: Perlasca to his wards, in all the houses: "A month ago I asked you to put away your arms. Now I am asking you to keep them ready. In case of attack, defend yourselves!" At that time, law and order in the besieged city had disintegrated, and roving armed Arrow Cross gangs shot and killed Jews at will.

In addition, Perlasca joined the other diplomats stationed in Budapest in a joint effort to stop the deportation of Jews by appealing to the conscience of the Hungarian regime. In a meeting with the Vatican nuncio, Angelo Rotta, Perlasca told him the truth about himself. "At the beginning he refused to believe it, but then he enjoyed hearing how I had succeeded in tricking the Germans. He was happy to hear that I was a Lombard like him. He told me that in the interest of the common good my deceit could be forgiven … If they should find me out, I could always ask for refuge from the Papal Nuncio or the Swiss legation."

When the Russian troops entered Budapest on January 16, 1945, they arrested Perlasca and briefly put him to work cleaning the streets of rubble and corpses. He managed to escape and took shelter with friends in the capital. Before making his way back to Italy, he was handed several letters of thanks and appreciation by his former wards, such as the one from the residents of 35 Szent Istvan Street–Spanish house, of April 18, 1945, which reads:

> "We have regretfully learned that you are leaving Hungary in order to return to your homeland, Italy. On this occasion, we wish to express the affection, recognition and high regard of thousands of Jews, persecuted by the German Nazis and Hungarian Fascists, and who found themselves under the protection of the Spanish legation. We shall, never, never forget that not only did you work incessantly days and nights for our shelter and nourishment, but you also looked after those needing to be fed, the elderly and sick – with a kindness that we find hard to express in words… Your name will never, never be missing from our prayers, as we pray to God to bless you, for only he can properly reward you."

Asked whether he was religiously or politically motivated, he replied: "Neither. I found myself in a given situation and I reacted to it. I couldn't ignore it … I couldn't stand the sight of people being branded like animals ... I don't think I was a hero ... All of a sudden I found that I had become a diplomat, with a lot of people who were depending on me. What do you think I should have done? As it turned out, I think being a fake diplomat was a big help, because I could do things that a real diplomat couldn't do. I mean … There's etiquette, there are formalities, hierarchies, people to answer to, your career. A lot of things, a lot of constraints that I didn't have." Then, perhaps naively: "Anyone in my place would have done what I did."

In 1988, Yad Vashem conferred upon Giorgio Perlasca the title of Righteous Among the Nations. The Italian government also honored him by naming him *Commendatore Grand'Ufficiale* and granted him a lifetime annuity. He died in August 1992, at the age of 82.

Perrone, Lorenzo
ITALY

*M*any would agree that to survive in the hell on earth that was Auschwitz one needed more than perseverance, one also needed good luck. Most of those who passed through the gates of that camp were not that fortunate. For one Jewish prisoner from Italy, the well-known post-Holocaust writer Primo Levi, his lucky star was another Italian in the camp – but actually not really of it, for the man was not a prisoner but a civilian worker by the name of Lorenzo Perrone. Primo Levi, a chemist by training and involved in clandestine activity in Italy, had been arrested by the Italian Fascist police in Turin in December 1943 and eventually deported to Auschwitz in February 1944. In his many postwar writings, Levi described at length the inhuman rigors of the camp, as well as the man whom he credited with his survival.

It happened in June 1944, when Primo Levi and a fellow prisoner were assigned to help out an Italian team of construction workers in the Monowitz complex of the camp, also known as Auschwitz 3. The man to whom Levi was to report was Lorenzo Perrone, by trade a bricklayer, presently working for an Italian construction company, that had been contracted to build a number of structures in the Monowitz subsidiary of the camp. In general, the Italian workers were given certain privileges forbidden to the ragged prisoners of Auschwitz. They slept on cots, had days off on Sundays, enjoyed one or two weeks of vacation, were paid for their labor, could exchange letters with people in Italy, and received food and clothing packages. By pure coincidence, or luck, Levi was picked by his Kapo (prisoner supervisor) to help out two Italian masons, one of whom was Lorenzo, who were working on a scaffold and putting up a wall. At first irritated by Primo Levi's clumsy handling of the cement, Lorenzo began to lecture him, and in the brief exchange

Lorenzo Perrone (courtesy of Emma Barberis Bard)

learned that the man was from Turin, Italy, not far from Lorenzo's hometown of Fossano. At that moment, something was kindled in Lorenzo's mind and heart, not only a liking for the affable Levi but something more – a commitment to help him survive Auschwitz, a hell on earth that could serve as the backdrop for Dante's *Inferno*.

This, initially, took the form of supplying Levi with additional nourishment, with food stolen from the Italian kitchen. Every day, for the next six months, in the morning Lorenzo brought Levi a military mess tin full of soup, carefully hidden under some boards, and told him to bring it back empty before evening. Late at night, when all the Italian workers were sound asleep, Lorenzo sneaked into the kitchen and scraped the leftovers from the cauldrons, and this is what he brought the next day to Levi at the work site. A slice of bread was sometimes added to the daily soup. Once Lorenzo apologized to Primo for the dirt in the soup, caused by a Russian shell from the previous day's air raid on Monowitz that had scattered debris. What Lorenzo omitted from the story was the damage caused to one of his eardrums by the exploding shell. "But he didn't tell that to me – he was half deaf that day – he didn't tell it to me so that I would not feel indebted to him."

One very pressing matter in Primo Levi's mind was how to communicate to his mother, in hiding back in Italy, that she need not worry too much, for he was alive, albeit in a German concentration camp. In *Moments of Reprieve*, Levi explained how this was done. "I had gotten hold of a sheet of paper and a pencil stub, and for many days I had been waiting for the opportunity to write the draft of a letter which I meant to entrust to [Lorenzo] so he could write it, sign it as if it were his, and send it to my family in Italy ... We were strictly forbidden to write ... If I could think about it for a moment, I would find a way to devise a message that would be sufficiently clear to the recipients but at the same time innocent enough not to attract the censor's attention." Lorenzo agreed to this device, and Levi penned a message to his mother, but carefully addressed it to a non-Jewish woman friend of his named Bianca Guidetti Serra. One of the messages read:

> *"Dearest Miss Bianca, greetings. I am keeping very well, indeed with the good weather I am better, I get on well in German now and this is a great advantage in the work; recently I heard that Luciana is working not far from here* [a friend of the Levi family – she was also arrested and deported]. *I have no news of Franco* [also arrested and deported. He was engaged to Primo's sister. He did not survive]. *Please say hello to Molina [code word for "my family"], if you see him. Communications are difficult and take a month. Don't worry about me, try to send me news of everyone and stay full of hope and courage as I do. Best regards and much love from someone who never forgets you. Your Lorenzo* [actually Primo Levi]."

Surprisingly for a Jewish inmate in Auschwitz, in August 1944 Primo Levi received, via Lorenzo Perrone, a letter from home, followed by a package sent by Primo's sister and mother, both in hiding in Italy. The package contained ersatz chocolate, cookies, and powdered milk. "To describe its real value, the impact it had on me ... is beyond the powers of ordinary language," Levi wrote after the war. "That unexpected, improbable, impossible package was like a meteorite, a heavenly object, charged with symbols, immensely precious, and with an enormous momentum." It goes without saying that if the real purpose and the author of these letters had been uncovered, both Levi and Perrone would have been in dire danger of their lives, not to mention the fact that it was strictly forbidden for a prisoner to even speak with a contracted civilian laborer, let alone for both to conspire to communicate with the outside world.

Lorenzo also gave Primo a "rag of clothing" to wear under his prison uniform. (In return, the first thing Primo brought Lorenzo after the war was a vest knitted especially for him.) Lorenzo's simple humanity came forth when he adamantly refused to discuss any kind of reward for his help to Primo, not even a promise of help after the war. He finally acquiesced to Levi's pleas to allow his worn boots to be repaired at the prisoners' cobbler's shop. This is as far as he would go in benefiting from his magnanimous help, because, in the words of Levi "he was good and simple and did not think that one did good for a reward." Levi is sure that without Lorenzo's aid, he, as someone not inured to physical labor under the conditions of the camp, would not have survived.

Primo Levi was, to put it mildly, dumbfounded by Lorenzo's goodness – of all places, in a camp where civilized conduct and moral behavior had been ground into dust. "A man helping other men out of pure altruism was incomprehensible, alien, like a savior who's come from heaven." Levi found it difficult to penetrate Lorenzo's inner thoughts, for he kept to himself and was not effusive with words. At times, he could also be irate and unresponsive. "I offered to have some money sent to his sister, who lived in Italy, in exchange for what he did for us, but he refused to give us her address."

When the Germans dismantled the Italian labor camp on January 1, 1945, due to the approaching fighting, Lorenzo together with a colleague decided to walk back to Italy with the help of a railroad map and by following the stars. After a four-month trek they made it through the Brenner Pass. In mid-May 1945 (the war having just ended), still on foot, Lorenzo reached Turin and went directly to Levi's mother, to whom he brought unhappy news about her son. He told her to be prepared for the worst. Before leaving Auschwitz, he had heard that Levi had fallen ill, and was sure that the Germans would not allow the sick prisoners to taste freedom. However, unbeknownst to Lorenzo, the Germans in their hasty evacuation of the camp somehow overlooked, or disregarded, the presence of a group of sick prisoners in the camp's so-called dispensary – and they miraculously saw freedom a lot sooner than the other, "healthy" prisoners who were forced on a Death March. Primo Levi was one of these lucky prisoners, released by the Russian liberators. A month after the end of the war, Levi wrote to a friend in Italy with regard to his rescuers. "I've had no news of the marvelous Lorenzo Perrone... No one knows what I owe that man; I shall never be able to repay him."

In the meantime, Lorenzo returned to Fossano, where he had lived before the war, and took up collecting scrap metal and rags in the street. He had always been a lonely, silent figure, but after Auschwitz he seemed to be even more withdrawn. Primo, who met him again, sent him clothes and medicines and regularly visited him and constantly urged him to give up his drinking. It did not help.. Finally committed to a hospital, he succumbed to a serious case of tuberculosis. In Levi's opinion, Lorenzo died because he no longer wanted to live – after he saw what he saw in Auschwitz. He had grown weary of this world. "He had seen the world, he didn't like it; he felt it was going to ruin. To live no longer interested him." Before passing away, Lorenzo confided to Primo that back in Auschwitz he had helped others, but he had not thought it necessary to talk about it. "We are in this world to do good, not to boast about it," he told the startled Primo.

Lorenzo's goodness left a deep mark on Levi's thinking, which may be understood from the author's words in *If This Is a Man*:

"Why I, rather than thousands of others, managed to survive the test, I believe that it was really due to Lorenzo that I am alive today; and not so much for his material aid, as for his having constantly reminded me by his presence, by his natural and plain manner of being good, that there still existed a just world outside our own, something and someone still pure and whole, not corrupt, not savage, extraneous to hatred and terror ... for which it was worth surviving ... His humanity was pure and uncontaminated, he was outside this world of negation. Thanks to Lorenzo, I managed not to forget that I myself was a man."

Throughout the postwar years, until his mysterious death in 1987, Primo Levi never failed to mention his debt to Lorenzo Perrone, the man "to whom he owes his life," his profound goodness and compassion, and his compulsion to help. In a letter to the writer of these lines, Primo's son, the biophysicist Dr. Renzo Levi, wrote that as a token of gratitude his father gave him and his sister names derived from Lorenzo's – Renzo for the son and Lisa Lorenza for the daughter. Author and biographer Carole Langier aptly added, "Without Lorenzo Perrone we would not have had one of the greatest of witnesses and writers about the Shoah, perhaps the greatest of all," having in mind Primo Levi.

In 1998, Yad Vashem conferred the title of Righteous Among the Nations on the late Lorenzo Perrone.

Peshev, Dimitar

BULGARIA

*A*lone, in his office, Vice President of the Bulgarian Parliament Dimitar Peshev began slowly and laboriously, but determinedly, to compose a letter of protest that he hoped would be countersigned by many members of parliament and would shake and undermine the foundations of his government's plan to deport Bulgarian Jews. He chose his words carefully to achieve the right effect:

"Recent actions taken by the authorities make clear their intentions to institute new measures against persons of Jewish origin. What is the precise nature of these steps? On what basis are they being taken, and what is their purpose and scope?... The right of the state to remove all obstacles that might stand in the way of its policy cannot be contested, as long as its actions do not go beyond what is truly necessary or fall into excesses that qualify as needless cruelty. Yet how else is one to describe measures taken against women, children, and the aged, people who are guilty of no crime whatsoever? It is impossible for us to accept that plans have been made to deport these people ... Such measures are unacceptable, not only because these – who are still Bulgarian citizens – cannot be expelled from their own

country, but also because this course of action would be disastrous, with grave consequences for our country. Our nation's reputation would be stained forever, its moral and political standing forever compromised.... What Bulgarian government would be willing to accept this responsibility? … The use of exceptional and cruel measures, measures that may expose the government and the entire nation to accusations of mass murder, are unwarranted and excessive. The consequences of this policy would be particularly grave for the government, but they would weigh upon the Bulgarian people as well.... We cannot share any responsibility for it whatsoever. Good government requires basic legal principles, just as life requires air to breathe. The honor of Bulgaria is not just a matter of sentiment; it is also and above all a matter of policy. It is of immense political capital and no one has the right to jeopardize it without good reasons approved by the whole nation."

As Vice-President of the Subranie, as the Bulgarian parliament was officially known, during the war years, Dimitar Peshev, like other political figures in the country, had favored Bulgaria's alliance with Germany in the hope of regaining territories lost during the Balkan wars of 1912–13. Germany indeed rewarded Bulgaria by handing her chunks of lands from defeated Yugoslavia and Greece – Macedonia and Thrace – without the Bulgarians having to commit troops in the German campaign against these two countries in April 1941. For centuries, thousands of Jews had been living in these two provinces. Their fate was now in the hands of the Bulgarians.

In his postwar memoirs, Peshev pointed out that in the years prior to World War II, Bulgaria had no Jewish question, with the exception of a few incidents provoked by small groups that modeled themselves on the German Nazis and took to the streets in Nazi-style uniforms, spouting borrowed slogans. But all this amounted to little more than a grotesque and pathetic vaudeville that was laughed off the stage and was soon forgotten. In spite of this, Peshev as a representative of the government majority in parliament supported in late 1940 the cabinet's draft bill – the Law for the Defense of the Nation – which was designed to curry favor with its German ally by restricting Jewish participation in the country's economic and social life. The proposed law called, among others things, for a special tax on the Jewish community; Jewish rights were drastically circumscribed; they were required to wear the yellow star; their freedom of movement was limited; and able bodied Jewish men were required to perform forced labor.

The bill produced shock waves among intellectual and professional circles in the country. The Lawyers Union protested, calling the bill unnecessary, socially harmful, and running counter to the traditional spirit of the Bulgarian people, "who in all the longs years of the [Turkish] Ottoman yoke and its miseries, misfortunes, and injustices never considered the Jews their enemies or oppressors." The Bulgarian Writers Union also condemned it in the name of civilization and Bulgaria's good name. The Physicians Union added its voice of protest. At the other end of the spectrum, the Students Union supported the Bill, as did the Bulgarian Youth League.

Peshev was among those who halfheartedly supported the bill as a concession to Bulgaria's alliance with Nazi Germany. "I was of the firm conviction that all this was indeed about bringing Bulgaria's policies in line with those of Germany … No one imagined that the measures would become permanent, let alone that they would take the same forms and proportions as those that were being carried out in Germany." A sacrifice was necessary in the interest of *realpolitik,* and the hope that Germany would restore the lost territories of bygone years to Bulgaria. Peshev and others persuaded themselves that the restrictions on the Jews, however painful, were nonetheless temporary and would not be taken to extremes.

Two years after the passage of this discriminatory law, in early March 1943, rumors began to circulate of certain harsh measures meted out against the Jewish population in Thrace and Macedonia, both regions under full Bulgarian control. "I heard that what these new measures entailed was nothing more and nothing less than the mass roundup of men, women, and children, who were then taken away somewhere – but we did not know where. What was the nature of these measures? Where were all the Jews, regardless of age or sex, being sent? And for what reason? Everything was shrouded in mystery."

As he was trying to remove the veil from this mystery, Peshev received a visit from Dimitar Ikonomov, the parliamentary deputy from Dupnitsa. He told of desperate and powerless Thracian Jews, old people, men, women, and children, begging for help as they crossed the town on foot, dragging themselves towards some unknown destination. At about the same time, Peshev met an old Jewish acquaintance from his youth in Kyustendil. This man, Baruch, told Peshev of preparations taking place in Kyustendil, a city inside Bulgaria, for the deportations of its Jews. According to Baruch, Peshev could not believe that all these things were going on without his knowledge. He decided to see for himself.

He went to Kyustendil and met with the local assistant chief of police, who confirmed to him that preparations were under way to assemble all local Jews in a single location, in some empty tobacco warehouses. The operation was to take place under cover of night; special convoys were already starting to get organized; their departure times had already been set. Peshev: "I could not remain passive." Up until that time, the anti-Jewish measures had been explicitly or tacitly sanctioned by the parliament, which had earlier passed the Law for the Defense of the Nation. All these measures, in the words of Peshev, "did not include the extermination of the Jews. But that was exactly where we were heading if the operation that was now being prepared, and that needed only to be set in motion, was not halted."

As Peshev was pondering his next steps, on the morning of March 9 he received a delegation from Kyustendil headed by Ivan Momchilov, Assen Suichmezov, and Vladimir Kurtev, with a plea to intercede on behalf of Bulgarian Jews to prevent their deportation. This was followed by visits of other concerned citizens, Jews and non-Jews, as well as several parliamentary delegates.

At the head of a parliamentary delegation, Peshev went to see Petur Gabrovski, the powerful Minister of the Interior, known for his strident antisemitism, to inform him of their disapproval of these measures and make an urgent request that the deportations be canceled. Gabrovski, blatantly lying, responded that the delegation had nothing to worry about, that no new anti-Jewish measures were being contemplated, and, feigning ignorance, he promised to find out what exactly was happening. Peshev noticed that the minister was tense and nervous and found it hard to believe that Gabrovski knew nothing, since this completely contradicted the unimpeachable information received from the minister's police subordinates. "I really did not suspect that he was trying to trick us with outright lies … but that he was speaking with the kind of platitudes one might use to extricate oneself from an awkward situation." At the time, Peshev had not been told of the secret agreement of February 22, 1943, hatched between Aleksandur Belev, the Commissioner for Jewish Affairs, and Adolf-Heinz Beckerle on behalf of the SS, for the immediate deportation of an initial group of 20,000 Jews – an agreement approved by the Bulgarian government, with Gabrovski's support.

The following day, Peshev learned that the deportations had been suspended, literally at the last moment – but not canceled. In some places, Jews were already on board trains when the order was rescinded. But it was only temporary relief, and the order could be reactivated at any given moment. Only then was Peshev apprised of the Belev-Beckerle agreement, approved by the government. He was shocked by this revelation. "A hard blow had been dealt to Bulgaria's honor, to its international prestige, and to the moral force of its foreign policy."

Something had to be done urgently to avoid the renewal of the deportations, an act that in Peshev's estimation would tarnish Bulgaria's good name forever. There was also a moral dimension to take into consideration. "I could not twiddle my thumbs and sit back quietly when at stake were matters that would have such grave consequences both now and in the future. To remain silent would have been a breach of conscience; it would have been contrary to my sense of responsibility both as a deputy and as a human being."

Peshev struggled with himself. "I decided to act, but how? A solitary act, though possible, seemed to me both inadequate and ineffectual; it could easily be brushed off and dismissed by the government," claiming "the nation's higher interests which, for reasons of state, could not be divulged." However, there was no time to lose. The deportations could resume at any time, given the likelihood of pressure from the Germans. There was only one way out – "I believed it was necessary to bring the question to the parliament and draw on as large a base as possible within the government majority. The action had to be of a parliamentary nature, it seemed to me, if the government was to get a sense that it was facing a difficult situation in the parliament, that its majority hung in the balance, and that it had to take this new situation into account." Peshev had decided to use his leverage as vice president of the parliament to force the government to back down. It was a gamble fraught with serious consequences for himself. "I felt that the initiative had to come from the government majority … It had to be made clear that stopping the deportation of Bulgarian Jews once and for all was paramount. Inaction by the majority on this question would have made it an accomplice not to a crime of state, a violation of the Constitution, but to much more – to criminal felony plain and simple: the mass murder of thousands of human beings."

At the same time, for the challenge to have any chance to succeed, it was "politically correct" that the initiative be led by members of the majority, by strong supporters of the government who would not challenge the government on its domestic and foreign policy but rather give it its full support on these two agendas – the only disagreement being on a single issue, as phrased by Peshev, "the deportation of Bulgarian Jews and their delivery to a foreign power whose intentions in their regard no one could claim not to know."

On March 17, 1943, he penned his letter of protest and had 42 deputies add their signature – all, with the exception of two, from the government's own benches. Not wanting his action to be viewed as a conspiracy hatched behind the back of the majority leader, Peshev first showed the letter to Christo Kalfov, president of parliament, and read its contents, word by word. When Peshev finished reading, Kalfov got up and left, heading straight for the office of Prime Minister Bogdan Filov. A short time afterwards he returned and told Peshev that the prime minister requested that he not submit the letter at this time but wait until the next meeting of the majority caucus. Peshev did not respond, but left to reflect on the hidden motives behind this request. "Was he [the Prime Minister] attempting to foil our action by trying to gain time in which to exert pressure on the deputies who had already signed it, as well as on those intending to sign it?" … I did not rule out the possibility of institutional pressure, some of it against me … It was obvious that the government was enormously irritated and annoyed."

At any rate, Peshev decided to ignore the prime minister's request and, wasting no time, he hurriedly submitted the letter with its 42 signatures the first thing next morning, even if it meant foregoing more signatures. On that day, March 18, 1943, he sent the letter of protest to the prime minister and the minister of foreign affairs. The die was cast. Several days passed without anything happening. Word, however, had gotten out that the cabinet had discussed the protest letter and that the prime minister had let it be known in so many words that he intended to take severe measures against nearly all the majority deputies. As a first step, the cabinet had decided to convene the majority caucus, which met on March 23, 1943. Every cabinet minister attended. Peshev knew he could expect trouble as the prime minister himself decided to chair the meeting – a highly unusual step.

Prime Minister Filov immediately took the floor and announced that he had received the protest signed by 43 deputies, and then proceeded to read it aloud in its entirety. He spoke in scolding and disapproving tones and accused Peshev of having violated his word not to submit the letter before the caucus meeting (Peshev: "I categorically deny ever having made such a promise"). Filov's words amounted to an accusation that Peshev and his associates were fomenting an open rebellion, words that unnerved several deputies. Not once did the prime minister address the letter's contents, its substance and purpose. "All we heard was reproach and rebuke – how was it possible that certain deputies had broken ranks and taken part in an action that damaged relations with the government?"

Peshev then responded to Filov's frontal attack. He began by taking full personal responsibility for the letter. "I stressed the fact that I had initiated the action, that I had written the protest letter myself, and that I was willing to accept all the blame – insofar as one could speak of blame. … I also pointed out that, for me, the letter was not about the government's general policy, whose implementation, as mentioned in the letter, enjoyed our approval and our support, but rather about the national policy for the unification of the Bulgarian people." The prime minister responded by asking each deputy present point blank, in a brutal display of political pressure, to stand up and answer the following questions: did he approve of the sending of the letter signed by the 43 deputies from the majority and did he support the government's overall policies? This was immediately put to a vote. The deputies were called upon one by one, and each had to stand while answering the questions. Filov, pencil in hand, took notes. "Never in my life had I witnessed such a scene," Peshev recalled. "It was a brutal procedure, a cowardly breach of trust, and completely incompatible with the deputies' function." Not a word had been said at this stormy meeting about the issue at stake – the government's agreement to deport Bulgarian Jews by turning them over to the Germans for a fate no one doubted.

Only 30 of the original 42 signatories stood fast and refused to recant, whereas all deputies, to a man, declared their support for the government's overall policies. On the question of censuring Peshev, 66 voted yes and 33 no. There were 11 abstentions, and four members had left the hall before the ballot. Peshev: "It was a defeat for me and a victory for the prime minister. I was disappointed by the lack of conviction, the docility, and the opportunism of some of my colleagues, who had failed to defend their prerogatives as deputies and had yielded under pressure." As Peshev left the room, Filov turned to him derisively, "*Tu l'as voulu, Georges Dandin*" ("You asked for it, Georges Dandin") – taunting him with this famous line of the French writer Molière.

The prime minister was not yet finished with Peshev; he had to humiliate him further by forcing his resignation as vice president of Parliament. The minister of justice was given the job of persuading Peshev to step down, but Peshev categorically refused. The government turned to parliament for this final act in Peshev's political downfall. On March 25, a majority deputy rose from his seat and asked to place on the agenda Peshev's removal as vice president, "since Deputy Dimitar Peshev no longer enjoys the confidence of the majority of the deputies." This was agreed and on March 30, 1943, Peshev was demoted. The session was set for March 30, 1943. On that day, Peshev requested to be allowed to speak. This was denied. "I rose in protest and stood at the foot of the speaker's rostrum, practically howling that this flagrant violation of the rules must not be allowed; that a deputy was being denied his basic right of expression – an elementary right." The chairman declared that there was a majority in favor of taking up the motion without debate. Peshev was censured and removed as vice president. The government had taken its revenge, as Peshev was politically ostracized.

However, due to the public commotion created by Peshev and his 42 colleagues, the government could no longer proceed with its deportation plans in total secrecy, as had been the case up to then. In fact, the government found it difficult, if not impossible, to proceed with this fiendish plan at all. "That had been the goal of my letter," Peshev wrote after the war; "the vote of censure against me and the vindictive attitude of others towards me could not alter the fact that the goal had been achieved … It was my firm belief that I had done my duty as a deputy and had acted in the name of my country's interests and its reputation, and for the sake of humanity." Peshev had set in motion a galvanizing movement that others would join, such as the heads of the Bulgarian Church, to thwart the government's intentions to do away with its Jews, mostly for reasons of political expediency – in order to please its German allies.

Two years later, with Bulgaria under new leaders, and many of the previous government on trial, Peshev, as an important political figure before the events of March 1943, was also being tried for treason by the newly installed communist regime. While Bogdan Filov and Petur Gabrovski were sentenced to death and executed, Peshev escaped the death sentence on the basis of his role in preventing the deportation of the Jews, as well as his intervention, as minister of justice in 1936, in saving the communist Damian Velchev from a death sentence. Velchev was now the new minister of justice. While many other political figures of the previous regime were sentenced to death, Peshev was condemned to 15 years' imprisonment, but was released after only one year.

In his memoirs, Peshev wrote: "I feel that I belong to an unfortunate generation that lived through a series of upheavals and saw its most cherished ideals crushed in the end." At the same time, he was proud that, "Of all the European countries under German control or influence, Bulgaria was the only one where the Jews had been rescued, where they had been spared the tragic fate that awaited the deportees." Dimitar Peshev died in 1973, the year he was recognized as Righteous Among the Nations.

Petényi, Géza
Hungary

*D*r. Géza Petényi was professor of pediatrics in the children's ward in the Feher Kereszt hospital in Budapest. During the Holocaust phase in Hungary, he hid many Jews, adults and children, in his hospital wards. The Gordon family was one of the beneficiaries of Dr. Petényi's gracious aid. He had been a friend and the family physician of the Gordon family before the war. As told by Maria Gordon, born in 1932, when the Germans invaded Hungary in March 1944, Petényi placed her for a while in a sanatorium under false documents as a tuberculosis patient; then he took her home when it seemed at first that the Germans

Géza Petényi

were not about to institute severe anti-Jewish measures in the capital city of Budapest. He continued helping them with food and supplies which he brought to their home, paying for them from his own pocket, as well as arranging for them Swiss and Swedish safe conduct papers, documents known as *Schutzbriefe* – Protective Letters. These documents offered protection to their holders from deportation to the concentration camps.

When in October 1944, the newly installed pro-Nazi Arrow Cross regime took the reins of power and launched a reign of terror against the city's Jews, Petényi again swung into action to help the Gordon family. Starting with the arrangement of false papers for them, he then placed Maria, her 15-year-old brother, Otto, and their mother, Irene, in a private room in the hospital on the pretext that they were suffering from various infectious diseases, such as tuberculosis for Maria, using for this subterfuge the X-ray results of another patient. The Gordons noted that many other rooms and wards in the hospital were filled with Jews admitted there by Petényi, and who posed as gentile refugees from the Russian- occupied areas in eastern Hungary. Maria Gordon remembered that at a certain time all the private rooms in the hospital, including Petényi's own office and waiting room, had Jewish families hidden there, whereas the wards were full of Jewish children under false names.

In an ironic twist, Petényi made contact with a certain Leo Hochner, a Jewish architect from Vienna who happened to be living in Budapest and was able to pose as an SS officer and hide Jews in an attic. Petényi received Jewish children from him for hiding in the hospital, and in return Petényi referred adult Jews to Hochner, including Alex Gordon, the father of Otto and Maria, who up to then had been sheltered elsewhere, since Petényi felt they would be safer in Hochner's place rather than in a hospital meant for children only.

Otto and Maria Gordon estimated Petényi to have thus saved about 20 Jews. These included several well-known surgeons, such as a certain Dr. Makay and Dr. Alfred Berendorfer. Other beneficiaries included the pianist Paul Urbach and the Nagel and Meisner families. In light of the atrocious Arrow Cross rule in Budapest during that chaotic period (starting October 15, 1944 and lasting until January 17, 1945), Petényi placed himself at considerable risk in case of apprehension. What saved him is described by Otto Gordon as follows: "His enormous prestige and integrity were his only safeguards and his personnel (many of them aware of his activities) dared not denounce him, because they did not wish to destroy him." It should be mentioned that all his good deeds were done without ever taking money from his wards.

In 1983, Yad Vashem conferred upon Dr. Géza Petényi the title of Righteous Among the Nations.

Pontier, Gerardus & Dora
NETHERLANDS

One day, in July 1942, 20-year-old Salomon-Shlomo Silber was walking the streets of Heerlen with his younger brother Hanan, both wearing the obligatory yellow star with word *Jood* (Jew), when a man pedaled up to them on his bicycle. He looked at the two boys and their yellow star, got off his bicycle, and greeted them kindly. Salomon looked at the stranger and wondered what he was up to. As Salomon recalled, the man looked to be about 50 years of age, was very tall and heavily built, with blue eyes and short gray hair. He smiled and asked them how they were faring in these difficult days for Jews? Salomon: "I told him that we were in danger. The Nazis could pick us up any day and send us to a concentration camp. God knows what will happen with us." At this, the stranger snapped back, "They are doing satanic work, and it is terrible to hear about it." He closed his eyes for a minute as though in silent prayer and then told them, "If you need help, I can put up two people at my house." Stunned at this impromptu offer by a total stranger, the two brothers thanked the man. In return, he left them his address, got back on his bike, and pedaled off. The man's name was Reverend Gerardus Pontier, the Protestant Calvinist pastor in the city.

Heerlen is a town located in Limburg province, at the southern tip of the Netherlands, tucked in between Ger-

Gerardus Pontier (courtesy of S. Silber)

many and Belgium. At the start of the war, it had a very small Jewish community of about 160 people out of a total population of 50,500. Pontier was the shepherd of the relatively small Calvinist community, of about 500 souls in a predominantly Catholic region, where he lived with his wife, Dora, and their four children. After the German invasion, Pontier preached incessantly against the occupiers and also alluded to the obligation of unarmed resistance. As for the Silbers, they were Orthodox Jews and included the parents, Gershon and Mirla, and their four sons: Salomon, Abraham, Bernard-Hanan, and Aaron.

Barely a week later, the Silber family received the dreaded deportation order. Mrs. Silber urged her eldest son, Salomon, to seek out Reverend Pontier, to find out whether he still stood by his word. Salomon was a bit hesitant, not wishing to force his family on this cleric because of the risks to him in case of apprehension. He was looking for a way to circumvent the matter of shelter and find an excuse to visit the man at his home. "I finally got the idea to go to him with some books that were very dear to me and ask him to keep them until the war was over. In the back of my mind I thought that perhaps these books would also interest a clergyman." When Salomon finally mustered enough courage to go the him – a man he had met randomly on the street and about whom he knew nothing other than from a few brief words – he walked up the front door and rang the bell.

Reverend Pontier opened the door himself and invited Salomon in, leading him to his upstairs study. He told Salomon to sit down, then asked why Salomon was so pale and looked so sad. "I told him about our present situation and the deportation order and asked if he would kindly take care of my books." Pontier readily agreed and asked of Salomon to put his name in the books. "Not your real name, one never knows." Salomon wrote "Sieg" and was about to get up and leave when Pontier stopped him and asked – perhaps he could be of more help? "He assured me that he was our friend and that I should tell him everything. This man emanated so much confidence and warmth that one felt immediately that he was a protector. To tell the truth, I really waited for his offer to help us. I then told him that the police had brought the deportation order and that we had to leave our house on August 25, 1942, for an assembly point near the railroad station for deportation to Germany."

After listening to Salomon's story, Reverend Pontier left the room for a few minutes and returned with his wife, Dora. Salomon looked at her and was struck by her kind and noble face. She was a brunette and her blue eyes bespoke much tenderness. "She looked at me with pity and her lips started trembling and tears filled her eyes." Her husband took on a serious demeanor, mingled with some sadness, and told Salomon that he had discussed the matter with his wife and they had decided to take two boys into their home until the war was over. Salomon stood still, searching for the proper words.

> *"Words failed me and I felt like choking. It was like a dream, but somehow I managed to blurt out, 'It is very dangerous for you to have Jews into your home.' [Pontier]: 'Don't worry, my child. We decided to do so and God will protect us. Son of Israel, we are happy to give you any help we can. It is the duty of every Christian to help people in danger.' He then took me upstairs and showed me the room in the garret with two beds, saying that the room will be waiting for us when we come on Monday night, and that it would be comfortable and secure."*

Before leaving, Pontier gave Salomon a small book – the New Testament, in Hebrew. "I wondered why he gave it to me, but I saw that he was happy that I accepted and took it with me." Salomon hurried home, where the whole family was waiting to learn the outcome of their son's meeting with the reverend – their faces pale and tense. He told his anguished family what had happened and especially Pontier's words, "I am your friend and I feel your pain. I can take two of you into the house." At this, Salomon's mother burst into tears and said that they had met a guardian angel, sent from heaven. Then she looked at each of her children for the painful decision – which of them was to go into hiding and who would report for deportation. She looked each in the eye, but kept silent.

Saturday night, when the Sabbath was out, father Gershon made the traditional *Havdalah* prayer, including the words, "In you I trust, O God." He had tears in his eyes; he felt that this was the last Sabbath that the family would be together. Now came the time for the bitter decision. When it was mentioned that Salomon would have to report for deportation, since he was the oldest, his brother Abraham stood up and said he would not let him go and that he would go in Salomon's place. He stated his reason for this: he had a better chance to survive because of his better physical appearance. So it was decided that the two who would benefit from the reverend's hospitality would be the eldest and the one next to the youngest of the brothers: Salomon and Bernard-Hanan. As for the youngest, Aaron, a sheltering place was eventually found for him with a host family.

After a tearful farewell from their family, Salomon and Bernard headed for the Pontier home. They were heartily welcomed and given their unmarried daughter's upstairs room. Lies Pontier vacated her room and moved in with reliable neighbors. Pontier cautioned the two boys, "You must obey me, and I beg you to be careful. Don't open the window; don't go downstairs before asking me or my wife. Danger is in every place, even in the house itself and also outside. Never go out by yourselves." The two brothers nodded in agreement.

Salomon and Hanan were naturally not privy to Reverend Pontier's other clandestine activity, which placed him in at even greater risk of arrest. The same July 1942, when Pontier offered his hospitality to Salomon Silber, a certain Jacobus (Jaap) Musch visited the Pontiers. Musch, a laboratory assistant in Amsterdam, had created with his brother Gerard, Dick Groenewegen van Dijk, and other committed friends a clandestine cell known by the acronym NV (in Dutch the acronym for NV-LTD) for the sole purpose of saving Jewish children, who would be spirited out of the SS-controlled assembly point for children known as the Crèche, in the center of Amsterdam. With the help of a team of helpers, these children were quickly taken to the train station and most of them were moved to the southern part of Holland and dispersed among trustworthy host families. This is where Pontier came into the picture. Jaap Musch has come to solicit the pastor's help in providing the NV organization with a list of parishioners who could be asked to take Jewish children on the run into their homes. Musch showed Pontier a letter of recommendation from Constant Sikkel, the Amsterdam vicar known to Pontier. Jaap Musch also asked the pastor to find him a place to live. This was arranged. Pontier sent him to the Harmen and Sara Bockma family, who lived in a nearby hamlet.

Musch's first request was more problematic and very dangerous for Pontier, since it meant exposing himself to the risk of betrayal by one of their parishioners, or through an accidental slip of the tongue. The Pontiers nevertheless agreed to help, and together with Jaap Musch they visited many of the Calvinist families and tried to persuade them to to help out. The first batch of children began arriving in Heerlen in October 1942. In order to speed up the process of locating safe addresses, Jaap Musch's team, including his brother Gerard and Dick Groenewegen van Wijk, moved to Heerlen, where they set up a base in a colleague's home. By late April 1943, approximately 80 children were already hidden in and around Heerlen.

Then adversity struck the Pontiers. On November 6, 1943, when it seemed that everything was running smoothly, the Pontiers were informed by underground channels that the Gestapo was on its way to arrest the pastor. The Pontiers tried to remove incriminating evidence as quickly as possible, but it was too late to remove the Silber family, which by now included the parents of the two brothers, since they would most likely have been immediately recognized by Gestapo agents, probably already staking out the house, and they would be caught. Consequently, to save his charges, Gerardus Pontier decided not to flee but to stay put and wait for the Gestapo's arrival.

Sure enough, they came within minutes and were about to start a search of the premises when Pontier, who was sitting behind a desk, told them that a search was not necessary, since he was prepared to come with them. The Silbers, who were waiting tensely in an upstairs room, were saved. Reverend Pontier was incarcerated for six months in a notorious Gestapo building in Scheveningen. He was interrogated on the clandestine activities of the NV group and at times placed in solitary confinement. Not able to extract any evidence from him, they released him to his family in May 1944, weakened and emaciated.

In the interval, Mrs. Pontier, fearing a return visit by the Gestapo, had the Silbers move in with a neighboring family, from where they moved to other sheltering families, and the whole family fortunately survived, including Abraham, who returned from the concentration camps. As for Reverend Pontier, after regaining his strength, he continued his work for the NV group. It is estimated that some 200 Jewish children were saved through the cell's endeavors. Unfortunately the group's leaders, Jaap Musch and brother Gerard, were eventually betrayed and arrested. Jaap was executed and Gerard sent to a concentration camp, which he survived. Likewise Dick Groenewegen van Dijk, who was arrested and sent to a German camp, from which he escaped and made his way back to the Netherlands also survived.

Salomon-Shlomo Silber emphasized in his deposition, "The man who saved our lives and those of many Jewish children brought us this wonderful message of keeping faith in mankind." In 1968, Yad Vashem recognized Reverend Gerardus and Dora Pontier as Righteous Among the Nations.

Pop, Nicolaie & Maria & Aristina
ROMANIA

*O*ver the years a friendly relationship had developed between Nicolaie Pop, a prosperous and hardworking farmer in the village of Lăpuşul Românesc in northern Transylvania, and Samuel Dub, who resided in the nearby town of Lăpuşul. Before the war the area, which contained a mixed Romanian-Hungarian ethnic population, had been part of Romania. Then, in September 1940, when both Hungary and Romania had allied themselves with Nazi Germany, on orders of Hitler, Romania ceded Northern Transylvania to Hungary, and it remained in Hungarian hands until the end of 1944, when it reverted to Romania. When Germany occupied Hungary on March 19, 1944, Northern Transylvania was slated to be one of the first provinces in the overall master plan to empty all of Hungary of its Jewish population. The first transport from Transylvania left for Auschwitz on May 16, 1944, and within the space of six weeks the Hungarian authorities had handed over to the Germans 131,600 Jews out of an original population of 165,000. These were taken to Auschwitz, where the overwhelming majority was gassed upon arrival.

Before and during the Hungarian phase of his village, Nicolaie Pop worked as chief forester in the area, and although a resident of Lăpuşul he stayed most of his time with his wife and six children in a spacious home in the forest, about 25 kilometers away, and only spent weekends in the village. He also tended a flock of 120 sheep and had a team of four shepherds to look after them. As for Samuel Dub, he operated a sawmill in the village for trees felled by Nicolaie Pop. The Dubs' only daughter Hanna was married to Baruch Mendel Marmor, who operated his own sawmill in the village, and by 1944 the Marmors had brought into the world three children. Baruch Marmor had been conscripted into the Hungarian Jewish-manned but not Jewish-officered labor battalions, like other able-bodied Jewish men in Hungary, for various hard labor assignments with the Hungarian army, and was away from home. He returned to his family only in 1948, after he was freed from Soviet captivity.

Soon after the German occupation of Hungary, Nicolaie Pop came to see his friend Samuel Dub and told him of rumors rampant in the village that the Jews in Lăpuşul would soon be rounded up and taken away to an unknown destination. In Hanna's words, "He came to tell us that under no circumstances were we to go to the ghetto [a temporary assembly point before being boarded on trains], for he would hide me, my children, and my parents, and would care for all our needs. He added that as long as he lived, no one would harm us." At about the same time, Hanna had a chance encounter with her husband in his labor battalion camp, and he told her of the frightening things done to Jews in Poland and Ukraine that he had witnessed, and he too urged her not to follow the other Jews into the sealed ghetto, but do everything to escape.

Pop's plan was to take his friend's family deep in the forest for hiding. He sent his 12-year-old daughter, Aristina, to guide the Dub/Marmur family into the forest. She arrived at the

Marmor house on Friday, April 28, 1944, and was to take the Dub/Marmor family the following night. On Saturday, Hanna faced an unforeseen problem – her mother refused to go along, claiming she would not be able to make it on her feeble legs and would only become a burden to the rest. Nothing could persuade her to change her mind, so it was decided that her daughter Hanna and the children would go first and then the mother would be fetched with a horse-drawn wagon. But it proved to be too late, for four days later, on May 3, all the village Jews were rounded up and taken to the city of Dej in preparation for their deportation. Hanna never saw her mother again.

Using side roads, Aristina led the Marmors on foot until they were outside the village; then they continued with a horse-drawn carriage, taking along a cousin, Gedaliah Dub. When they reached a stream, they discovered to their chagrin that due to the snow melting in the hills the waters had risen, and it was feared that the horses would not be able to make it across. At this point, Hanna adamantly refused to back off and return to the village. "If my husband ordered me to hide in the forest," she stated, "then he knew what he was talking about. If we have to die, then let us die here. At least here the Gentiles will give us a burial [as opposed to the rumored disposal of bodies in the camp crematoria]." She managed to sway the others to continue, and they led the horses through the rushing waters and made it safely across. Aristina then led her charges in total darkness to the place in the forest designated by her father for building a shack.

Nicolaie Pop waited for the party's arrival and showed them how to construct the shack with the boards and other materials and implements prepared by him, but urged them not to use noisy tools, so as not to attract the attention of other foresters who might be passing through. He left one of his trusted workers with them to help out. Hanna Marmor, her father, Samuel, and the three children moved into the shack. Nicolaie and his wife, Maria, "the angel," in Hanna's words, looked after all their needs. "They did everything from their heart, without any other considerations, with love and kindness, out of true and sincere friendship and a deep humanitarian feeling, in spite of the dangers to them." Aristina often came over to play with Hanna's children, and on these occasions she would pass the night with them in the shack. Nicolaie would also on occasion spend the night in the company of his charges.

After a three-month stay in relative security in the forest shack, Samuel Dub asked of Nicoalie to allow him to use proper tools to cut trees down to size to better his family's living conditions. Pop counseled against this, fearing that the noise and commotion would attract attention, but he finally gave in and brought Samuel the necessary tools. Then the inevitable happened. On August 13, 1944, the noise attracted two Hungarian gendarmes, who had the Dub/Marmor family arrested. Taking Gedaliah Dub with them, they headed for Pop's home, where their unit was reconnoitering, and then returned in a wagon driven by Nicolaie Pop, who was careful to indicate to the gendarmes that he did not know about the fugitives' presence in his area. One of Hanna's children managed to escape, as well as Gedaliah Dub. Nicolaie Pop and Hanna's father were also able to make a run for it deep into the forest. There they stayed until liberated by advancing Soviet forces on October 16, 1944. As for Hanna and her two remaining children, they were taken to Lăpuşul, and she too later managed to make her escape and survive.

After the war, Nicolaie Pop ran afoul of the new masters of Transylvania, the communist regime of Romania, when with the start of the Cold War they forced the incorporation of the Greek Catholic Church, to which Pop belonged, into the Romanian Orthodox Church, in an attempt to sever the ties of Greek Catholics with the Vatican. Hundreds of protesting priests were arrested and this time Pop sheltered one of these priests in one of his forest lairs. Samuel Dub counseled him not to take unnecessary chances with the new and harsh communist masters, but Nicolaie would not listen. For years, he hid with his son Itim and daughter Aristina in the forest. Arrested in 1950, Nicolaie Pop was shot by the Romanian secret police. Aristina (married name Săileanu) was released after an eight-year prison term – a sick person. The Marmors had by then moved to Israel and kept in touch with the members of their benefactor's family.

In 1966, Yad Vashem recognized Nicolaie and Maria Pop and their daughter Aristina as Righteous Among the Nations.

Popovici, Traian
ROMANIA

*M*r. *Governor, the French Revolution that gave mankind the gift of justice and freedom took a toll of 11,800, while with the winter coming soon, you are sending 50,000 to their deaths....Do you really want to go down in history along with someone like Robespierre? I for one do not want history to soil my name. Think about it. There's still time. Get in touch with the Marshal [Antonescu] and entreat him, in your capacity as governor, to at least put this off until the next spring.*

Traian Popovici

This is not, as one might imagine, a Jewish person entreating a high Romanian official not to sanction the deportation of Jews in a particular city. It is the mayor of that city cautioning his immediate superior in somewhat impertinent language not to add his name to the roster of history's infamous malefactors – in a country ruled by a dictator who had allied himself with Nazi Germany. The risks for that person were serious. His name was Traian Popovici (pronounced Popovits) and he was mayor of Cernauti, otherwise known as Czernowits and presently called Cernovtsy. The man he was addressing was General Calotescu, the Romanian governor of Bukovina province.

There were about 50,000 Jews present, close to half of the city's population, when the Romanian army occupied Cernauti on July 5, 1941. For the next three days, in a murderous orgy, Romanian soldiers killed 600 Jews. Then the Germans came in to help out, sending in *Einsatzgruppe* D under Otto Ohlendorf (hanged after the war) to take over 2,100 more lives, including many Jewish community leaders and intellectuals, in a city officially under Romanian control.

Born in 1892, Traian Popovici, the son of a Romanian Orthodox priest, studied law in Cernauti, earning a doctorate; then in June 1940 he settled in Bucharest when Cernauti reverted to the Soviet Union under the Ribbentrop-Molotov pact of August 1939 that launched World War II. At first, he supported self-declared marshal Ion Antonescu, who promised to lead the country to a more glorious future, but he was quickly disappointed as new laws were, in Popovici's words, despoiled, banned, and oppressed people, "and I realized he'd started off on the wrong foot on the road to moral renewal he was claiming to inaugurate. Through him, the dignity of an entire nation was sacrificed to a lack of culture, boorishness, and savagery." One of Antonescu's major error's was to join Nazi Germany in the attack on the Soviet Union on June 22, 1941, on the promise of being given newly conquered lands beyond the Dniester River – known during the war as Transnistria – as well as recovering the lost province of Bukovina and the city of Cernauti.

The war had barely started when Popovici was summoned by the Ministry of the Interior and told he had been selected as mayor of liberated Cernauti. At first Popovici declined this dubious honor, but was told he had no choice but to accept, otherwise his refusal might be considered an act of sabotage. The allusion was clear. By the time he arrived there, on July 8, 1941, he learned that he was to be deputy mayor under Dr. Octavian Lupu. However, the governor, Colonel Al Riosanu, Antonescu's friend and henchman, soon had Lupu removed, and on August 1 Popovici was officially installed as the city's mayor.

Before that, some anti-Jewish measures had already been taken, such as the imposition of the yellow star and prohibition from dealing in certain economic fields. As recalled by Popovici, "I had no way to protest at the time, as the dignity of mayor was still vested in Dr. Octavian Lupu … So I couldn't take any stand until after my installation at City Hall as mayor." Soon after the governor asked him to mark out an area for a Jewish ghetto. "I frankly told him my view about it and emphasized the absurdity of such a medieval measure, particularly as applied to the highly cultured Jews of Cernauti [most of whom had absorbed German culture when, for over a hundred years, the city had belonged to Austria, up to the end of World War One]." In addition, Popovici argued that technically he could not accept responsibility for a section of the city to be fenced off with barbed wire and boards. "Cernauti, which looked so much like a western city, would not tolerate such a profanation of its beautiful appearance."

However, orders from Bucharest enjoined the creation of a ghetto. So Popovici came up with an expedient to postpone the directive – to study how ghettos were installed in other places through a commission chaired by himself or another municipal official, which was to travel to Germany to study how ghettos were organized in Lublin, Kraków, and Frankfurt am Main. "Since I was hardly about to visit the German ghettos and the governor's health was failing," Popovici added, "the problem of the Cernauti ghetto remained in limbo. In fact, except for a short period from October 11 to November 15 when a ghetto was used as part of the deportation procedure, no other ghetto was organized in Cernauti during my term or afterward."

Governor Riosanu died during surgery on August 30, 1941, and was replaced by General Corneliu Calotescu. Under his tenure the situation of the Jews took a turn for the worse. Under pressure from the military, new restrictions against the Jews were issued virtually every day. They were barred from practicing their professions; Jewish physicians could only treat their coreligionists; Jewish youths were banned from public schools, and religious services were forbidden even on major Jewish holidays. Public institutions such as banks and post offices were prohibited from making any payments to Jews, who were ordered to hand in foreign currency under pain of death. Cars, radio sets, and various other items were also to be handed in. Jews had no right to ration coupons and had to pay double for bread. They were barred from access to open-air markets for their shopping and were forbidden to go out except for three hours a day, from 10 a.m. to 1 p.m. Jewish patients were thrown out of hospitals and sanatoriums. To cap it all, Jewish mental patients, even the violent ones, were expelled from mental institutions and moved to a place where they were kept in filth and poverty beyond description. Popovici was outraged. "And there were many more such humiliations that I can't remember right now … Not even the great Dante would have been able to depict the beastly state to which they were reduced. But worse still was the madness that had infected the thinking of the decision-makers, twisting their minds and making them participate in the terrible disgrace that senseless people had visited upon the history of our nation."

Through all this, there was one "oasis," in Popovici's words, the city hall, where Jews could file complaints and petitions; where their pensions were regularly paid, where they were not abused, and their suffering was treated with respect. "Its gates like those of ancient temples were open to anyone fleeing from persecution, seeking a place to rest their martyred souls, looking for comfort and encouragement." In his postwar account, Popovici took pains to remind the reader that during his term as mayor no Jew was ever evicted for failing to pay his rent and the city continued paying pensions to its Jewish employees despite gubernatorial orders to the contrary. This lasted until Popovici's removal from office in spring 1942. "My attitude was hardly meant to strengthen my relations with the governor, who dissociated himself more and more from me." A local Romanian journal jeered at Popovici for extending his protective mantle over the city's Jews, who were mockingly termed "Traian's people" (an allusion to Trajan, the Roman emperor whom the Romanians claim as their ancestor).

On October 10, 1941, Popovici was summoned to the governor's office and told to prepare additional loaves of bread for the city's Jews, who were to be deported to Transnistria. While the governor's men termed it an "evacuation," Popovici corrected them; it was rather a "deportation." "Let's get this straight. Evacuation means the partial or mass removal of inhabitants from a place or area in danger from military operations, fires, floods, epidemics, and other similar disasters, and taking them to a safer place – regardless of the evacuees' blood, religion, or ideology. Evacuation never stems from hate but rather, on the contrary, from love of one's fellow humans. 'Deportation,' on the other hand, is prompted by hate and is meant to get rid of them, in fact by destroying them," and this is what was really meant by "evacuating" the city's Jews.

As part of this horrific plan, the goods left behind by those deported were to be collected and handed over to the state for "safekeeping;" the valuables they had on them were to be seized, and they were to embark on trains – men, women, and children; the old, the young and the sick – 50 cars in each convoy and under military guard to the border points on the banks of the Dniester River, and across it to a dreadful fate.

Upon hearing this, Popovici was beside himself, petrified with horror and barely able to utter a word. Then suddenly he burst out, "How could you come to this, Mr. Governor?" "What could I do," the governor responded? "It is the Marshal's order." At this, Popovici lost control of himself and, as related in his memoir, began to utter "violent words, which I admit were rather uncommon as addressed by a mayor to his governor, the marshal's proxy." Popovici spoke about the difficulties Romania will face at the final peace conference where the civilized nations will call Romania to account. "I spoke about mankind and humanness … against savagery, cruelty, murder, and disgrace … I mentioned the disgrace of Spain, which had never managed to cleanse its history of the stain of Torquemada's anti-Jewish persecution of 1492." When he finished his tirade, there was a moment of silence, as the governor and the two other military officers present were at loss for words. Then the governor said, "It is exactly what I was telling these gentlemen … Let me think about it." Then, one of the officers, Lieutenant Colonel Petrescu, turned to Popovici and said, "Who's going to write history, Mr. Mayor, we or the *Yids*? I'm coming here to weed your garden and you won't let me do it?" "I weed my garden myself, colonel," was Popovici's response. "As for history, it's not just the *Yids* that will be writing it, for they don't own the world. Historians of all nations will. We, too, will write it even sooner than you think. I fear you'll get to read that history yourself, to which you want to make your contribution." The colonel's face turned crimson, but he dared not moved against Popovici in the governor's presence.

From there Popovici went back to his work at city hall. There, waiting for him, were leaders of the Jewish community, hoping for words of relief from the mayor. "I had no assurance to give them. Silently, I contemplated their anguish: their instinct had told them all there was to tell. Their leave taking was poignant. They thanked me for everything I'd done for them and vowed that, wherever their suffering would take them, they would remember me as the only man that had sympathized with their sorrow, and that their memory of Cernauti would always be associated with my name. They left in tears as if they were gong to a funeral." That day, Popovici could hardly concentrate on his work. "I was exhausted, beaten in my heart and body. To avoid seeing all this tragedy and taking any part in it, I decided to step down." However, his aides discouraged him from this step, cautioning him that it would prove that the champions of what they termed "Romanianism" were right to call him "Judaized." Besides, "it would be cowardly of me to leave the Jews at their time of grief." He decided to remain at his post.

On the morning of October 11, 1941, a cold, wet day, Popovici looked out the bedroom window, attracted as he was by the first flakes of an early snow, and couldn't believe his eyes. "Out there a great column of people was going into exile: old men leaning on children, women with babies in their arms, cripples dragging their mangled bodies, all bags in hand; the healthy ones pushing barrows or carts or carrying on their backs coffers hastily packed and tied, blankets, bed sheets, clothes, odds and ends; all of them taken from their homes and moved into the ghetto," especially set up to facilitate the deportation process.

Next morning, Sunday, October 12, Popovici was invited to a meeting of all public officials in the governor's office, where all the assembled were told of the start of the deportation. None of the gathered civic leaders uttered any words of protest. "Lacking civic courage,"

Popovici derisively characterized them in his memoirs. "None of them was bold enough to protest against that act of major historical consequence for our nation." Popovici was the only one who, when his turn came, stood up and spoke at length on the issue on hand:

"I stressed the merits of the Jews, their valuable contributions to the economic development of the country, their achievements in every professional and cultural area and, in my capacity as mayor of the city, I protested against this act. I asked for mercy for those who had joined the Church through baptism [there were an estimated 1,500], *or else I said we would be undermining this foundation of Christianity that is its missionary vocation. I asked that those who had devoted their lives to high culture and fine arts be spared. I asked for the reward of the pensioners, officers, invalids, who had earned the gratitude of our nation. I asked that foremen in every branch of industry should be allowed to stay. I asked, for the sake of humanity, that doctors be exempted. I argued for keeping back the engineers and architects that would be needed for the work of reconstruction. I pleaded for exempting magistrates and lawyers, showing we owed that much to the intellect and civilization."*

The governor was momentarily moved by these words and authorized Popovici to draw up a list of those who, according to Popovici, were needed for the city's economic maintenance, but the list was not to exceed a maximum of 100 to 120 persons. "As I was leaving, I clearly felt my fellow officials had tacitly joined the chorus of those who branded me 'Judaized.'"

At this point, Popovici decided to take matters into hand so as to be able to save from deportation much more than the 120 allowed by the governor. With the aid of persons whose names Popovici preferred not to disclose, he was able to reach the ear of dictator Antonescu, and to his total surprise, on Wednesday afternoon, October 15, Marshal Antonescu called the governor on the phone and told him to exclude a much larger group that in his estimation was needed for the city's economy – as many, but not more than, 20,000 Jews, comprising the professional categories Popovici had mentioned during the earlier Sunday meeting.

The governor gave Popovici four days to draw up the list and in the meantime he ordered the deportation suspended, except for three trains that had already left on the night of October 13. Popovici began feverishly working on the process of selection, sorting the people allowed to remain behind. He decided to do this in cooperation with the Jewish community and asked them to help him compile such a list. The military command provided 48 men to help with the filling out of forms and the issuing of authorizations to be delivered to the security service. Not fully trusting the military, Popovici decided that this work would take place at city hall rather than in the military command post, "so that I could keep an eye on everything and intervene whenever necessary."

He then did something that was also highly irregular for a government-appointed mayor in a regime whose official policy was to persecute its Jewish inhabitants – he visited the ghetto to inspect conditions there. This almost cost him not only his job but, in his words, his "neck … and became the subject of many reports against me, some carefully preserved in the military office safe, others posted directly to the presidency." He wanted to convey to the Jewish community leaders the reassurance that the Jewish community would be spared. He then told what happened as the assembled Jews listened to his words of reassurance and hope:

"The dramatic moments when I broke the hopeful news to them I think have been the most solemn and moving in my life so far, and I doubt if there will be anything more glorious in store for me in the future. Old rabbis, intellectuals of all ages, leaders from all areas of social life, merchants, workers, in short, every living soul, burst into soothing tears, went down on their knees blessing their God, thanking heaven for its mercy … and trying to kiss my hands and my feet and the tails of my coats … Moved by that natural outburst of gratitude, tears came to my eyes, and I, the 'father of the city,' wept along with them."

Hermann Spasser remembered well Popovici's ghetto visit that was meant to comfort the people, distribute monies and food, and plead for patience, for help would surely come. "I worked together with another attorney in Popovici's office as one of his secretaries. He hid Jews in danger of deportation in his own home. I saw that personally with my own eyes." For some of the Jews slated for deportation, Popovici came to the station and released them from the cars, including Spasser's brother, his wife, and their small boy.

Still working on his list, he struggled hard to persuade the governor that some categories had to be added to avert serious disruptions of everyday city life. For example, except for one Christian tinsmith ("I even remember his name: Basaraba") – all others tinsmiths in Cernauti, a city with over 11,000 buildings, were Jews, and so they were absolutely indispensable and could not be deported. He found more and more excuses to delay the operation, hoping by his protracted work that any further deportations would be suspended at the beginning of the winter. Many non-essential names were added to the exemption list that Popovici presented to the governor for his signature.

After the list was closed, whoever came and begged for the rescue of their relatives (parents, brothers, nephews, cousins, and in-laws) did not walk away empty-handed. For these cases, Popovici would enter a notation, "Also applicable to X, a dependent of Y," who is disabled, or paralyzed, or for various other reasons, and he then confidently signed and put the mayor's stamp on it. "This procedure alone, which was later turned against me and nearly got me charged for abusing my power, saved not just tens but hundreds of souls." Popovici had succeeded in saving some 20,000 Jews from deportation, and they were permitted to return to their homes, which in the meantime had been vandalized.

His "abuse" of his mandate on the exemption list, in granting permits to persons who did not qualify from a professional point of view, the so-called "Popovici authorizations," eventually cost him his job, and in the spring of 1942 he was removed and he returned to Bucharest. For a while, the authorities contemplated court proceedings against him, but no action was taken. Popovici's departure was just in time for the Romanian authorities, who planned to resume the deportations with the coming of the summer. A total of 28,000 had been deported in October and November 1941 to Transnistria. On June 4, 1942, the deportations were resumed, claiming some 5,000 more victims. The fatality rate among the deportees was high – 70 to 80 percent did not survive. The remaining Jews in Cernauti remained unharmed, and were saved by the arrival of the Soviet army in February 1944.

In his postwar account, Popovici characterized the deportation of the Cernauti Jews a tragic chapter in the history of mankind "that will forever remain the most serious injury ever brought to the concepts of culture and civilization." He castigated his country's dictator Ion Antonescu, who posed as the "builder of a better destiny" but who "actually served a heathen Christ and tarnished our history." The deportation of the Jews to the Transnistria region was a callous, cruel, and savage act.

"The deportation lowered us in the eyes of all civilized nations and stigmatized us as barbarians ...Callousness was a virtue; charity a debasement. Anyone who tried to protest or reason with the crazed ended up a target for contempt by the public and persecution by the powerful ... I was turned into an outcast and suffered many humiliations for three years ... As far as I'm concerned, the fact that I was strong enough to resist and fight the trend, that I kept my head, challenged the powerful, and remained a man, I don't owe it to myself. I owe it to the long lineage of priests from whom I am descended and who taught me to love my fellow humans."

Traian Popovici lived to see the end of the war, and died soon thereafter, in 1946.

In 1969, he was posthumously recognized by Yad Vashem as Righteous Among the Nations.

Potesil, Maria

AUSTRIA

Born in 1894 in Vienna, Maria Potesil was widowed when her husband, Adolf, died in Russian captivity during World War I. She was left with two children, Anna, born in 1913, and Adolf, born in 1915. To supplement her income, in 1927 she became the foster parent of two-year-old Kurt in return for childcare payments from the city. He had been born out of wedlock to Johanna Franziska Martinez, who died four weeks after giving birth. The father's identity was unknown. Five years later, when Kurt entered the second grade, Maria was informed that a certain Jewish person named Berco Berkowitsch had acknowledged his paternity. Maria continued to keep Kurt and care for him like her other children.

Then the Germans marched into Austria, in March 1938 and the country became a German province, and with it the introduction of Nazi racial laws. That same year Maria Potesil was invited to appear before the children and youth office of the municipality, where she was told that since the now 14-year-old Kurt was half-Jewish, she would no longer be paid for his upkeep. He was also expelled from school and forced to attend a Jewish school. In 1941, he was also made to wear the Jewish star. The Nazis were frustrated that Maria Potesil did not get the message, as she refused to give up the boy, so they took things a step further. Maria Potesil was told that she and Kurt had to move into a house reserved for Jews only, on Josefinengasse, and she was made to bear all the inconveniences and harassment suffered by Jews in that street, under Gestapo surveillance.

As she no longer received financial support for Kurt's maintenance, Maria decided on a gambit of her own – to apply for legal adoption under existing law, not mere guardianship. She also asked that he be classified as *Mischling* (half-breed) 1st grade, thus exempting him from immediate deportation, but her request was denied. She was told at the time that since when Austria was annexed to Germany she was still listed as a Czech citizen (that region had belonged to Austria before World War I) rather than German, she could not make an adoption application. She did not give up and applied for German citizenship, while her two children remained listed as Czech nationals. After the change of nationality, she again applied for Kurt's change of status to half-Jew, but was again turned down. As for life on Josefinengasse she related:

> *"I refused to part with the boy and moved over to Josefinengasse 6/18. I then constantly approached various authorities to prevent Kurt's deportation. When the purpose of my visit was announced, I was treated with utter disrespect and insulted. Once I faced a certain SS man named [Alois] Brunner who was responsible for the deportation of Jews. I remember his words to me: 'Aryan swine.' On another occasion, an SS man made me wait for three hours. This man was especially rude. Suddenly he stood up and threw the chair he was sitting on across the room. I suffered a heart attack."*

Maria Potesil (center) (courtesy of Dokumentationsarchiv des Österreichischen Widerstandes, Wien)

Maria did the utmost to keep Kurt indoors, allowing him to go out only in her company. When she walked the streets together with Kurt, who wore the Jewish star, as no one suspected that a non-Jewish Germanic, that is Aryan, woman would show herself in public in the company of a Jew, she was in constant danger of being either harassed or, worse, arrested as a Jewess for not wearing the obligatory star. When arrested, she had to prove that she was indeed an Aryan. To add to her difficulties, in order to acquire food she was made to shop at stores reserved for Jews, where there were constant searches. In addition, during air raids, she was not allowed the security of public air shelters, but had to remain indoors with Kurt and sit out the bombardments with all the consequent risks of being injured or killed.

Another problem was the situation in her "Jewish" house on Josefinengasse 6. The non-Jewish caretaker of the house knew, of course, that Maria had a half-Jewish child living with her. Not only was she subjected to continual lack of courtesies and insults but had to purchase, with her reduced income, gifts for neighbors and the housekeeper to secure their "kindness" and keep them from harassing her in derision and contempt as an Aryan woman prepared to live as a Jewess when she had the choice of making her life much more comfortable by giving up the boy.

In the fall of 1944, when the Nazis decided to arrest those qualifying as half-Jews, known as *Mischlinge,* Kurt was forcibly removed from his home at midnight and taken away for deportation. Maria interceded for him and was able to have him released after a period of six weeks of running from one office to another and asking friends and acquaintances to intercede on her behalf. Kurt returned with a high fever and at times suffered from temporary losses of consciousness, but thanks to the continued treatment of a doctor he regained his health. To protect the boy from further deportation attempts, Maria arranged for him to stay with trustworthy friends most of the time.

This situation lasted until the end of the war. Thanks to Maria Potesil's stubborn determination, Kurt survived the Nazi period unharmed. For eight long years, 1938 to 1945, she had to face continual harassment, humiliation, and deprivations, but would not part from Kurt, since she felt that he had a right equal to others to be allowed to exist – a privilege questioned by those in power at the time.

After the war, Maria Potesil faced another problem. Since, during the Nazi period, she had elected to annul her Czech nationality (which she had acquired when the country was under Austrian rule) in favor of German citizenship, now with Austria having regained its independence, paradoxically her pension as a World War I widow was canceled. It took Maria 18 months of complicated red tape to get this cancellation revoked. In addition, she was invited to the Russian headquarters in Vienna and told that since she had chosen to be a German citizen she was hereby expelled from the country and had to leave for Germany. Only after her explanation of the reason of her status change was the expulsion order canceled.

In 1978, Yad Vashem recognized Maria Potesil as Righteous Among the Nations.

Pritchard-van Binsbergen, Marion

NETHERLANDS

*I*n 1943, four Germans, led by a Dutch Nazi policeman, raided the house outside Amsterdam where Marion van Binsbergen had been hiding four Jews for a year: Freddie Pollak and his three young children, aged one to five. The raiders did not find the hiding place under the floorboards of the living room, where the frightened fugitive Jews were huddling. The searchers left, but Marion knew from experience that sometimes they would wait a little while and then come back when the hidden persons would have come out of their hiding place, so she cautioned the fugitives to stay put for a while longer. But then the baby started to cry, so the children were let out. At this point, the Dutch policeman showed up again – he had caught them. Marion moved over to a chest supposedly to get a comb. In the drawer was a revolver that a friend had given her. "I felt I had no choice except to kill him. I would do it again, under the same circumstances, but it still bothers me, and I still feel that there 'should' have been another way." She alerted Karel Poons, a Jewish ballet dancer who lived on the outside with the help of false identities. He undertook to find an undertaker who would agree to bury the body in a coffin together with someone who had died a natural death and had been prepared for burial. "I hope that the dead man's family would have approved," Marion later remarked as she told the story. To this day, the family of the "real" corpse is not aware of the other body placed in the same coffin. The Jewish family of four was safe and secure, and this was one of many rescues by 22-year-old Marion van Binsbergen.

She was born in 1920 to a Dutch father and an English mother. Her father was a judge in Amsterdam, and Marion claimed to have learned tolerance from him. "He was more accepting of all people and their differences than my mother, who was tiny, tough, cheerful, critical, self-confident, very British and class-conscious." From her mother, Marion picked up her trait of being "action-oriented." In general, Marion had a good and loving upbringing. "I was never punished and always encouraged to express my feelings, both the negative and positive ones, in words. And when I asked questions I got answers. I was never told I was too young or anything like that. I was treated with respect and consideration from the time I was born." At a very young age, she learned four languages; English from her mother, Dutch from her father, French from a governess, and German from several maids. Wanting to become a therapist, at 19 she entered the school of social work in Amsterdam.

Then something happened that changed her course of her life during the war, with her country under German occupation. One morning in 1942, on her way to school, she passed a Jewish children's home and saw the Germans loading the children on trucks. The children appeared aged from infants to eight-year-olds; they were frightened and crying. When the children did not move fast enough the Nazis picked them up, by an arm, a leg, the hair, and threw them into the trucks. "To watch grown men treat small children that way – I could not believe my eyes. I found myself literally crying with rage." Two women coming down the street tried to interfere, and the Germans pushed them as well into the truck. "I just sat there on my bicycle, and that was the moment I decided that if there was anything I could do to thwart such atrocities, I would do it. Before this I had known of the threats but I hadn't actually seen the Germans in action. When I saw that, I knew that my rescue work was more important than anything else I might be doing." The die had been cast for Marion van Binsbergen; she was going to forgo her studies and dedicate herself to helping Jews, and especially children avoid Nazi entrapment.

She joined a group of about 10 friends, including two Jewish students, who organized themselves informally for this purpose. The group obtained Aryan (non-Jewish) identity cards for the Jewish students; they helped find hiding places and accompanied people there, providing them with food, clothing, and ration cards. They registered newborn Jewish infants as gentiles and provided medical care when possible. In one case Marion took a two-year-old boy to her parents' home without telling them that the boy was Jewish. He stayed there for several months until Marion found him a safer place outside Amsterdam. "His name was Jantje Herben, and I don't know what happened to him after that."

Then there was the story of Lientje Brilleslijper, the daughter of a lively Jewish family of circus artists, small businessmen, and musicians – a dancer and singer who lived with her non-Jewish common-law German musician husband, Eberhard ("Piet") Rebling and her daughter Kathinka. Lientje and Piet had invited all her Jewish relatives (her parents, brother, sister Jannie with her husband, and two small children) to join them in a rented house. On July 12, 1944, during breakfast, the SS and police burst in. While a Dutch policeman questioned Lientje's relatives, she decided to simulate a fit. She began to shake her entire body up and down on the floor; she rolled her eyes and screamed: "Just don't take the children to prison, don't take the children!" Clearly taken aback, the Dutch policeman agreed to move little Kathinka to a village physician, who was made to swear to release her only to the Nazi authorities.

The adults were taken to Amsterdam, where they were interrogated by the Gestapo, but Lientje was not forthcoming with any information, and she was deported to Auschwitz, then Bergen-Belsen, which she luckily survived, while Piet succeeded to make his escape and alert a friend to help free Kathinka. Karel Poons and Marion von Binsbergen volunteered to kidnap the two-year-old girl. Early in the morning, the two went to the village. It was agreed that Marion would enter through the back door and pick up Kathinka while Karel tried to distract the policeman at the front door. Moving quickly upstairs, Marion grabbed Kathinka, ran down the stairs, placed her on her bike, and pedaled off. "She was so small, so scared, and so brave, but did not utter a sound." In the meantime, Karel, at the front door, kept the doctor and guard busy with idle talk. A while later, the Gestapo appeared, and were enraged that their small victim had escaped, and arrested the doctor. They also put up posters all over the village, offering a reward for information leading to the capture of Kathinka; date of birth: August 8, 1941 – a most wanted "criminal"!

In yet another rescue, Marion had been handed a Jewish baby, stolen from the Crèche, the day care center opposite the *Hollandsche Schouwburg* (Dutch Theater).

Marion Pritchard-van Binsbergen in her UNRRA uniform, 1946 (from Gay Block and Malka Drucker, *Rescuers: Portraits of Moral Courage in the Holocaust,* Holmes & Meier, New York, 1992)

Both places served as assembly points for Dutch Jews before their dispatch to the death camps, the Theater for adults and the Crèche for children. Marion had been asked to take the baby to a certain village. When she arrived there after a 12-hour trip by train that normally should have taken three, a man approached her and said, "If you are on your way to the Gerritsens, don't go. They are in trouble." This meant that they had been arrested. The baby was hungry and exhausted and so was Marion. "I just wanted to drop the baby and run." The man clearly wanted no part of Marion or the baby, and felt he had done his duty by warning her that the family had been betrayed. Finally he said, "Well, why don't you come to my house, you can rest, and maybe we can find some milk for the baby before you go back". He led her to a small house at the end of the village, where she met the man's wife and their four or five children. Totally worn out, Marion immediately fell asleep in her chair.

> *"When I woke up, his wife had taken the baby, changed it, fed it and was telling the children that they should pray for me because I was a sinner; I had had this baby out of wedlock, could not take care of it, and that they were going to keep it. That my punishment was that I would never see my baby again. Walking me back to the station, Mr. van Dyke apologized, but said that this story made it possible for them to keep the baby and protect themselves. When asked by neighbors where this new baby came from, the children would tell a credible, convincing story."*

One more touching story Marion likes to tell is about Esther, a 16-year-old girl for whom she arranged a hiding place. Esther had to stay in a small, windowless room in the upstairs apartment of a middle-aged couple who ran a small clock repair business downstairs. Marion visited her regularly. Early in 1944 she told Marion she wanted to have a baby. She was quite convinced that she would not survive, but she wanted to leave the world a Jewish baby. Her boyfriend, who was passing as a gentile, agreed with her idea wholeheartedly, and their son was born in the fall of 1944. Marion took him to the gentile couple who had agreed to register him as their own child until the end of the war, and promised they would make the best arrangements they could after the war to provide him with a Jewish environment. Esther was caught, deported, and perished in a death camp. Her son lived. Esther's grandson was born in somewhat similar circumstances to his father's – in a cellar in Israel, during the blackout in the Persian Gulf War of 1991, with Scud missiles flying overhead and the people in attendance wearing gas masks.

With the war over, Marion volunteered to work with the UN's Displacement Persons Operation (UNRRA) in Germany to help concentration camp refugees build a new life. In one of the DP camps she met her future husband, Anton ("Tony") Pritchard, an officer in the U.S. army in charge of the camp. The two married in 1947, moved to the United States, and settled in Vermont, where Marion became a professional psychoanalyst. The couple had three sons, "and I never even told them about the war … We didn't talk about that until the letter came from the Israeli embassy in 1983 saying they wanted to give me a medal. I have come to agree with Elie Wiesel, who believes in remembering and telling. But it's difficult; I still find myself weepy when I retell a story."

Then she decided to talk before groups of adults and students about the war, the Holocaust, and the need of the church to change its negative attitude toward Jews and Judaism. As she stated, "It has taken a long time to realize that if I am going to keep the faith, as an Anglican/Episcopalian Christian, I have to do that in the full knowledge of how the Christian Church has preached, practiced, and condoned the persecution of the Jews, starting 2,000 years ago. Except for the technology, all the indignities the Jews were subjected to by the Nazis are repetitions of the past. Christians have burned their synagogues, made them wear identifying clothing, forced their children to be baptized, ghettoized them, forbidden them to enter schools and universities. A Methodist, Franklin Littell, has underlined in his book, *The Crucifixion of the Jews*, that Jesus, Paul and Peter would have perished at Auschwitz, a fact that latter-day gentile Christians dare not forget … If it is our Christianity which gave the artistic and intellectual impetus to the period in history known as the Renaissance; then it is our Christianity which also sponsored the Inquisition. If it is our Christianity which saved learning through the so-called "Dark Ages," then it is also our Christianity which counseled expropriation of Jewish property in various centuries." Some steps have admittedly been taken to redress the situation, Marion makes it a point to say, especially with Pope John Paul, who on a visit to a synagogue in Rome, the first ever by a reigning pope, called God's covenant with the Jewish people "irrevocable." But, Marion noted, much more remains to be done, especially at the grass roots level of believing Christians.

Reflecting on her wartime deeds, she asked herself whether she was afraid? "Of course the answer is 'yes.' Especially after I had been imprisoned and released." This happened after seven months of imprisonment for listening to Radio London together with a group of student friends; someone had betrayed them. She then added, "There were times that the fear got the better of me, and I did not do something that I could have. I would rationalize the inaction, feeling it might endanger others, or that I should not run a risk, because what would happen to the three children I was now responsible for, if something happened to me, but I knew when I was rationalizing." At the same time, these occasional moments of fear did not diminish her resolve to help. "It did not occur to me to do anything other than I did. After what I had seen outside that children's home, I could not have done anything else. I think you have a responsibility to yourself to behave decently. We all have memories of times we should have done something and didn't. And it gets in the way the rest of your life."

Still the wartime moments of fear have left an indelible strain in her postwar life. As she explained, "The Germans always picked up people at night after curfew. They were the only ones who had motorized vehicles, so if you heard a truck at night, you knew what it was. When we moved up here to the Vermont woods – we live on a dead-end road – for the first several years we lived here, if a truck came up here at night, I got up and looked out the window. I was scared."

As a psychoanalyst, also counseling parents on child education, she has strong opinions of how to implant altruistic feelings in the minds of children.

"It worries me that people have such disregard for children, that they put them in day care so easily. If you want to raise an altruistic generation, a generation of people who will care about one another and be willing to make some sacrifices – to use that dirty word – for one another, then the first people who should make sacrifices are the parents. The mother or father may have to sacrifice one of their careers for a few years and stay home with the child to demonstrate that the child is important enough to stay home for. If the parents don't think so, why should anyone else? Children must be helped to develop their own sense of what is right by questioning. Blind obedience is a disaster."

Through a variety of efforts, Marion estimated that she managed to save approximately 150 Jews, although she felt she could have done more.

What she achieved was more than required for Yad Vashem, in 1981, to confer on Marion Pritchard-van Binsbergen the title of Righteous Among the Nations.

Profir, Grigore
Pântea, Nona
Nicopoi-Strul, Elisabetha
Beceanu, Dumitru
Simionescu, Constantin
Sion, Mircea Petru
Agarici, Viorica
ROMANIA

*R*omania's record during the war is quite dismal considering its treatment of Jews living within its sphere of influence. Romanian apologists claim that no Jews living in Romania proper – the country in its prewar boundaries – underwent the type of persecution and killings known elsewhere, and especially in neighboring Hungary. This is a debatable point when taking into account the fate of the Jewish population in the province of Bukovina, thousands of whom were deported to the newly annexed territory of Transnistria, with many dying on the way, and thousands others shot or perishing as a result of various illnesses and malnutrition. Whatever the verdict, there can be no doubt about a government-inspired pogrom perpetrated by the Romanian army in the heartland of Romania, which claimed the lives of thousands of Jews. In the city of Iasi (Jassy), province of Moldavia, Romanian soldiers participated in a horrific killing orgy among the city's Jews in June 1941, acting upon orders of the fascist regime of Ion Antonescu, the country's dictator and ally of Nazi Germany.

When Romania sided with Germany in the war against Russia, which started on June 21, 1941, Iasi numbered 33,135 Jews. Already a year earlier, the antisemitic Iron Guard Legion – both a political movement and a militia – declared Iasi a Legionnaire city. This was followed with the tearing down of two synagogues on the pretext that their location was endangering the public. On October 14, 1940, Jewish pupils were expelled from government public schools and Jewish-owned shops were boycotted and their owners forced to sell out to the Iron Guard Legionnaires.

Then, on June 28, 1941, hardly a week into the war against the Soviet Union, Romanian and German soldiers began a pogrom against the city's Jews, many of whom were shot in the streets. Others were rounded up and taken to the police station where they were charged with signaling to the Russian airplanes counterattacking from the air. When the air-raid siren sounded that afternoon, this signaled the beginning of a massacre of the imprisoned Jews.

The pogrom continued and even intensified on the following day, June 29, when thousands more were shot in the police courtyard. The remaining 4,330 Jews were herded into a train to be taken to various labor camps, with many expiring of suffocation and thirst during the trip in sealed cars under the scorching sun. When the pogrom was over, after several days, over 10,000 Jews had lost their lives (some estimates place the figure at 12,000). A month later, the remaining Jews were ordered to move to designated neighborhoods and to wear yellow badges. The diminished Jewish population lived in fear and under severe restrictions until the city fell to Soviet forces on August 21, 1944, followed two days later by the fall of the Antonescu regime and Romania's exit from the war on the side of Nazi Germany.

While this murderous orgy was taking place, with Romanian soldiers rampaging the streets to pick up whatever Jews they ran into, Grigore Profir, an engineer, was at his post as manager of the Dacia flourmill in the city. Jews worked at the flourmill as forced laborers, some painting the mill to camouflage it against air attacks in addition to loading and unloading sacks of flour. When, on May 29, 1941, Profir learned that Jews were being rounded up and taken to police headquarters where they were shot, he decided to add more Jewish laborers to the work of unloading flour from a military train, and thereby to save their lives. He picked them up outside the mill, took them with him, and assigned them work, thereby avoiding their arrest and maltreatment.

Soon a group of Romanian and Germans soldiers arrived at the mill to pick up Jews, but were met with Profir's opposition. He even threatened to complain that they were hindering him from carrying out the orders of the Romanian army and that their interference with his work would cause a shortage of bread in the city. The soldiers proceeded to beat him, even threatening to shoot him, but he stood his ground and refused to let them onto the mill's premises.

Dr. Gedalya Leizer was one of the 100 Jews whose life was saved on June 29, 1941, by Profir during the pogrom. He recalled being present in the yard of the Dacia flour mill when a group of German and Romanian soldiers arrived in order to collect the Jews that worked there, and saw Profir being beaten, with blood running down his head, for refusing them access to the mill, as well as hearing the threats that he would be shot.

With the Romanian and German soldiers returning several times to try again to pick up the Jews at the mill, Profir stayed at his post around the clock, the whole day and night, preventing the soldiers from taking away his Jewish workers. Taking additional precautionary measures, he also allowed his Jewish workers to hide behind bales and sacks of wheat in case the soldiers should force their way in.

After the pogrom, Grigore Profir continued to help Jews by sending flour to the beleaguered Jewish community as well as to the orphans and widows of the deadly pogrom. Profir paid his Jewish laborers, including those he "conscripted" for work to save them, for their labor. He reportedly also helped others with food and medication, and in addition he hid in his home a Jewish family that was in danger of being deported. The authorities eventually brought charges against him, and according to unconfirmed reports he was even tried, but exact details are not known. What is left in no doubt is Grigori Profir's courageous act, and personal risk, in saving 100 Jewish workers from being murdered during the killing spree of several days' duration ordered by the Romanian authorities and which claimed close to 12,000 lives.

In the context of the Iasi pogrom and its aftermath, notice should also be taken of other brave Romanians who either helped Jews to avoid arrest or assisted them in other ways and were consequently honored by Yad Vashem with the Righteous title. Nona Pântea, by profession an attorney, lived in a one-room apartment. During the pogrom, she sheltered a group of six neighborhood Jews in her home, placing them where they would not be seen from the street. Herself sitting on a chair by the door of her apartment and smoking a cigarette, she blocked the way to rampaging soldiers, claiming there were no Jews there. The soldiers finally gave up and left. Elisabetha Nicopoi (later Strul) worked in a textile plant, where she hid some 20 people in a storeroom for two weeks during and immediately after the June 29, 1941 pogrom, and provided them with food.

Dumitru Beceanu, who trained in pharmacology and operated a pharmacy, hid in his home above the pharmacy the Jewish pharmacists Dr. Leon Zisu and Dr. Simion Caufman – both employed by him. About 20 other Jews also found shelter there. To shield his charges, Beceanu donned the uniform of a captain in the Romanian army, to which he had been inducted as a pharmacist. Some of his wards stayed in his home for up to a month in fear of a renewal of attacks against the Jews.

Constantin Simionescu, an attorney and head of the bar association in the city, helped Jewish members during the pogrom. He made sure that they had a place to live and a means of livelihood after they were forced to move out of their homes. Mircea Petru Sion, a legal counsel for foreign trade enterprises, hid two Jews in his home, as a result of which, he was arrested and beaten by the Iron Guard men, but released owing to his status. He also served as a judge in a military court and helped obtain the release of Jews from labor camps. During the war years, he reportedly also hid 15 Jews in his home and on his family estate outside the city.

Finally Viorica Agarici, president of the Romanian Red Cross in the city of Roman – during the night of July 2–3, 1941, while at the city's train station to serve refreshments to Romanian soldiers on their way to the front, she suddenly heard moans and calls for help coming from sealed railroad cars parked far from the station. These sounds were of surviving Jews of Iasi (Jassy) who for several days had been moved back and forth between stations while the people inside the cars were left without food, water, or medical supplies. When Agarici heard the shouts, she insisted that the people be allowed to get out of the cars to be supplied with food and drink. Thus they regained their strength, which helped them to survive their journey to Romanian labor camps.

All these brave people, by their courageous acts, helped maintain a measure of personal and national dignity and offset their country's blighted record during the Holocaust. They were recognized by Yad Vashem as Righteous Among the Nations: Grigore Profir, 1991; Nona Pântea, 1986; Elisabetha Nicopoi-Strul, 1987; Dumitru Beceanu, 1987; Constantin Simionescu, 1991; Mircea Petru Sion, 1986; and Viorica Agarici, 1983.

Proosdij van, Jaap
Kotting, Adriaan
Teutscher, Cornelis
Mom, Antonius
Nijgh, Ysbrand
NETHERLANDS

*T*he Nazis considered the Dutch pure Aryans and a lost Germanic tribe which, based on racial principles, should be "reintegrated" into the bosom of the Third Reich, where it rightfully belonged. Hence the need to "purify" the conquered Netherlands from all non-Aryan elements, foremost among them the Jews. This also created the need to examine carefully cases of persons registered as Jewish but claiming to be either fully or semi-Aryan by birth, so as to weed out from the population all non-Aryans. For this purpose, from among all the occupied countries only in the Netherlands, considered by some Nazi anthropologists to have been the pristine genetic fount of the Aryan race, was a special administrative unit created to examine doubtful cases so as to decide whether they were to be considered Aryans and spared or Jewish and deported to their death.

Hans-Georg Calmeyer was the man chosen to head the special racial reclassification unit, in a country under the most rigorous German civilian and military occupation in Western Europe. The son of a judge and a lawyer by profession, and not a Nazi Party member, Calmeyer headed a section in the German Administration and Justice Department of conquered Netherlands dealing with doubtful racial cases. As it turned out, Calmeyer's bureau was the single anti-Nazi cell within the occupation government. Calmeyer found certain loopholes through which Jews might be assisted in escaping from the German registration trap, based on the 1935 Nuremberg Laws. Soon petitions began to flow to Calmeyer's department requesting that the status of a parent or a grandparent be changed from Jewish to half-Jewish or even fully Aryan. Baptismal certificates, most of them forged, were readily supplied to support such claims. Calmeyer realized that he was skating on thin ice as the SS leadership in the Netherlands became increasingly suspicious of his work, terming it *Abstammungsschwindel* (genealogical fraud) and demanding a case-by-case review of all his approvals. However, with room to maneuver between the SS and the Nazi administration in the Netherlands, Calmeyer had enough leeway to continue his work, though he had to be very careful not to make a fatal slip that would not only undermine all his work but also jeopardize his own position and personal freedom.

Dutch lawyers specializing in Aryanization helped produce false records testifying to the non-Jewish origin of their applicants. Out of a total number of 4,787 petitions for racial reclassification, Calmeyer's team recognized 2,026 as half-Jewish and 873 as fully Aryan, while 1,868 were rejected. Also of help to the petitioners was the delay while applications were being processed, which enabled them to plan to go underground if their requests were denied. At any rate, 60 percent of all applications were approved – the majority on the basis of clearly fictitious documentation. Consequently, it can be said that at least 3,000 Jewish lives were saved.

Calmeyer's work is an example of one of the greatest feats in the art of deception practiced by a German official in a high position in the attempt to save as many Jews as possible from deportation. At times he made decisions on the basis of the flimsiest evidence, such as classifying a person as semi-Jewish who claimed that his real father was a Dutch non-Jew (i.e., Aryan) with whom his mother had had an out-of-wedlock liaison, or allowing a claim that someone was not Jewish on the basis of records only available in far-distant Dutch colonies (such as Indonesia), where the claimant was born, and which were not accessible due to prevailing war conditions in the Pacific area. In this he was seconded by several trustworthy Dutch attorneys who helped draw up false papers and by German aides in his own section, such as Gerhard Wander. Nazi governor Arthur Seyss-Inquart, for reasons of his own (to secure his "territorial" domain in an occupied country against SS encroachments), permitted Calmeyer to continue his operation but cautioned him to bring it to a swift conclusion. When the roundup of Jews started in 1942, those whose names appeared on the exemption list received a stamp in their identity papers that precluded arrest and deportation while their cases were examined.

In the meantime, the deportation of the Jews that had gone into in full swing in the summer of 1942 continued without a letup. In Amsterdam, Jews were assembled in a former theater known as the *Hollandsche Schouwburg*, where SS *Hauptsturmführer* Ferdinand Aus der Fünten was in charge. From there the people were moved to the big transit camp of Westerbork in the north of the country, where SS *Obersturmführer* Albert Gemmeker was in command. From there, almost every Tuesday, cattle trains carried around 1,000 people to the death camps in the East. Of the country's 140,000 Jews at the start of the occupation, 105,000 met their deaths, mostly in the Auschwitz and Sobibor death camps.

Jaap van Proodsij was one of the young Dutch attorneys on Calmeyer's otherwise German-manned staff. Certified as a lawyer in 1942, the 22-year-old Proosdij had worked as an assistant to Dutch attorney Adriaan Kotting. There he learned of Kotting's help to members of the Portuguese Jewish community of several thousand in Amsterdam, the descendants of Jews expelled from Spain and Portugal in the 15th century for refusing to convert to Christianity. To save themselves, the Portuguese Jewish community had invited a team of three professors to prove that genetically they were not Jews. In the meantime, they were exempt from wearing the yellow star, but all other restrictions applied.

Calmeyer instructed his staff to examine the file of each applicant to establish whether he or she was qualified to be on the privileged deportation exemption list, based on proof of grandparents of Portuguese descent. Since his staff was able to investigate only one or two people per week out of the hundreds of applicants, Calmeyer was in need of additional secretarial help. When Calmeyer turned to Kotting for additional help, the latter recommended his young assistant Jaap van Proosdij. In Proosdij's words, "It provided a golden opportunity to infiltrate Calmeyer's office, whose staff consisted of a Dutch pubic servant, De

Waard (a lawyer), a German, Dr. Wander [later shot by the Germans after he defected and joined the Dutch resistance], a retired German, Miessen, a German private secretary, and three Dutch secretary-typists." Kotting introduced Proosdij to Calmeyer. At their first meeting, the young Dutch attorney placed the German on notice as to his thinking on the whole racial issue. "I told him that, despite not agreeing with the persecution of the Jews, I was prepared, as a lawyer, to go through the files and sort out those cases that were unfounded. But I stipulated that if I had conscientious objections I would be free to approach him, and he would release me. Needless to say, what I did was never in conflict with my conscience." Calmeyer agreed to this condition and gave him the use of a room, with all the Portuguese files. A mole had been planted inside this sensitive German office.

Using his youthful imagination, Proosdij handed the full Portuguese list to the still-functioning Jewish Council in Amsterdam and requested it to mark the names of those who had either passed away, were deported, or were protected by marriage to a non-Jewish spouse. In the meantime, Proosdij befriended Calmeyer's German secretary and this helped him ease his way into all of Calmeyer's files. "All this information was very valuable for what we were to do later with other applications."

After three weeks, Proosdij handed a corrected list of names to Calmeyer and told him that the examination of the files revealed that, based on the racial criteria in use, such and such people did not qualify for the exemption list – and all the others did. Calmeyer was impressed by Proosdij's "honest and loyal" work, and from that time he trusted the young man fully. In Proosdij's words, "Little did he know that the names we gave him [of those who did not qualify] were of people who no longer existed. Even after the war, when my partner Kotting told him how we had regularly misled him, he said, 'But Van Proosdij was always honest and had no part in those lies.' I had the advantage of being blond, innocent-looking, and 22 years old."

The issue of the Portuguese Jewish community was not yet resolved, as Calmeyer sought ways to save this large group of people, which numbered several thousand and, in desperation to avoid deportation, claimed to be of non-Semitic origin, but of Iberian stock, with a certain influx of Germanic blood, based on the Visigoth settlement of Spain over a millennium earlier, and therefore to be excluded from the bitter fate awaiting all other Jews. Alternatively, they asked to be allowed to leave and return to Portugal, from which they had left four centuries earlier. Calmeyer upheld their cases, but was overruled by Nazi race "experts," who after much procrastination decided that the Portuguese of "Mosaic faith" were no less Jewish than their brethren of East European origin. If approved, this would have exempted an additional 4,304 persons.

When Kotting and Proosdij finished their work on the Portuguese Jews, Calmeyer asked them to help examine cases of Dutch Jews who claimed they were not fully Jewish by birth. The two befriended the personnel in Calmeyer's office and a relationship of trust developed between the two sides. They also knew who they could bribe. One secretary helped them get the necessary seals and they copied them, including Calmeyer's signature. Kotting spoke with Calmeyer only on justified claims; otherwise, he falsified seals and signatures and inserted into the requests approved by Calmeyer also those not seen by him.

As for Proosdij, from 1943 on he concentrated more and more on individual cases, proving by way of false birth certificates that the grandparents were non-Jews, declaring children to be illegitimate, and using other genealogical documents. Each case had to be different and Calmeyer's decision depended on what Proosdij terms Calmeyer's *Fingerspitzengefühl,* his intuition or mood. Proosdij and Kotting were especially assisted by the anthropologist Arie de Froe and the medical student Cornelius Teutscher, who was an expert in faking certificates and signatures. The Underground helped with financial assistance in those cases where a fee had to be paid for services rendered.

In many cases, in order to protect himself from sabotage by diehard Nazi elements in the occupied country, and especially from the all-powerful SS establishment, Calmeyer coordinated his decisions with Westerbork's camp commander Gemmeker, and for this purpose Proosdij served as Calmeyer's special emissary to Gemmeker, who would then "view" the applicants and give his opinion.

When this had been arranged, Calmeyer selected the files to be examined. He also had notes typed, summarizing the application and stating that as the documents were not conclusive; an opinion on Jewish or non-Jewish appearance would be needed. He then handed the files to Proosdij and asked him to arrange a meeting with Gemmeker on these cases. Before he left for Westerbork, Proosdij consulted with Dutch attorney Kotting, who could write German in Calmeyer's style and would prepare fabricated memos, concluding that the documents were convincing and only needed confirmation as to the applicant's appearance. Proosdij then switched the memos. It was a most dangerous undertaking for the two Dutch men.

Starting in September 1943, Jaap van Proosdij went from Calmeyer's office in The Hague to the Westerbork camp every second week, usually staying in the camp from Tuesday afternoon (after departure of the train) until Thursday morning. From Calmeyer, he had an authorization permitting him to carry classified documents; from Gemmeker – a permit to make enquiries in the camp on behalf of Calmeyer. The result: Calmeyer secured his flanks by obtaining files with positive recommendations from the SS and thereby avoiding criticism of his autocratic rule. As for Kotting and Proosdij, they had the satisfaction of freeing many people, often personally unknown to them, from Westerbork.

The following cases illustrate the problems involved in this work. Mr. Pollak was safe from deportation since he was married to a non-Jewish wife, but he had a foster daughter about eight years old. In the beginning, Calmeyer refused Proosdij's petition in her behalf. As told by Proosdij,

"It was the week before Christmas. I could not think of any further argument to persuade him except by saying that he reminded me of Herod who had killed little children. Calmeyer, who had distanced himself from the consequences of his decisions, reacted emotionally. He said that he could not make another decision, but was prepared to have the file destroyed so that there would be no (death) sentence … I took the file and Calmeyer never saw what happened to it afterwards. Kotting drafted a decision, Calmeyer's signature miraculously appeared on it, and that was that. The family survived the war.

Calmeyer was probably aware, without saying anything about it, that Proosdij and his Dutch associate attorney had worked things out behind his back.

Another case in point was that of Mr. and Mrs. Hart, with their two children, who petitioned for an exemption on the basis of their grandparents' supposedly non-Jewish names. Calmeyer wanted confirmation that the grandparents were non-Jews. Proosdij: "I discussed the file with him and he fell for it. If we obtained proof of the race of the grandparents, he could decide favorably." Calmeyer proved adamant, sticking to his ruling that he needed additional proof. He then wrote his decision in longhand refusing the application and signed it. Proosdij related what happened:

> *"I was sitting there helpless, and as I had had a harrowing time in Westerbork the day before, I could not control myself anymore. I began to weep almost hysterically. I tried to hide my shame in vain and Calmeyer, embarrassed, started to pace the room. Finally he gave me the file saying, 'If tomorrow you bring me another opinion that convinces me, I will reconsider.' That evening Kotting drafted an opinion for me and the next day I went to the Hague. Calmeyer was again in his own office and when I entered he greeted me with, 'Ah, there is Van Proosdij. Let's see whether he can convince me.' He read the paper, said, "Yes, that is also possible," signed it and crumpled his own written decision and threw it (amounting to death sentences) into the wastepaper basket. I have never hated a man as on that occasion ... For the rest of the time we got on well."*

Finally, the Elsa d'Oliveyra case. A friend of Kotting, she had studied medicine and was on the Portuguese list. Early in 1944 all those who appeared there were apprehended and brought to Westerbork for further investigation. Kotting and Proosdij made a special effort to get her out. To get around Calmeyer the two decided to construct a file from fake documents and then falsify Calmeyer's signature. This, however, would take some weeks. On a Sunday afternoon, Proosdij received a secret message from Westerbork that on the coming Tuesday all the Portuguese Jews would be deported. Early on Monday, Proosdij secretly phoned Westerbork from Calmeyer's office telling them that Calmeyer was considering a special application for her and that she should be kept in Westerbork until he had decided on the application. An hour later Proosdij was in Calmeyer's office discussing other matters with him when one of his two telephones rang. While he was talking, his other phone rang and Proosdij answered it. It was the Westerbork commander's office requesting confirmation of the supposed request from Calmeyer that Elsa should be kept in Westerbork. "I quickly confirmed it and rang off. When Calmeyer had finished his call, he asked me what the other call was, and I explained that it had been a personal call for me. This was the only time that there had been two simultaneous calls and that I answered a call for Calmeyer. Had he answered that call, neither Elsa nor I would have survived the war. Actually that Monday when I took that call, the train was loaded and Elsa was taken off it just in time." When Kotting and Proosdij had finally completed the file, they processed "Calmeyer's" decision and Proosdij went to Westerbork to obtain Elsa's release.

Then there was also the Sinek case. He was a Czech Jew, a very pleasant-looking man of about 35. One night during a roundup of Jews in Amsterdam, Calmeyer suddenly turned up. He had heard that a former German Jewish secretary of his had been caught and he wanted to help her. He could not find her, but he saw Sinek and said to him, "You can't be a Jew, you don't look like one. Why don't you make an application to me?" Sinek managed to escape that night, but his wife and son were sent to Westerbork. The next day Sinek came to Proosdij and told him what had happened, and Proosdij promised that he would try to help him. The difficulty was, however, that as he had escaped he was on the black list of the SS. Calmeyer could help him only if he gave himself up and went to Westerbork. Proosdij: "I went to Calmeyer, who confirmed the story and I told him that Sinek was indeed not a Jew, but that the evidence hinged not so much on documents as on photos in a family album. I explained the risk for Sinek if he went to Westerbork and Calmeyer promised to consider an application favorably if he got a positive recommendation from Gemmeker."

Sinek decided to take the risk. Before he went to Westerbork, Proosdij drafted the application, saying that Sinek was an illegitimate child of a non-Jewish father and produced a baptismal certificate of a grandparent on the maternal side. In the specifically made "old" family album Proosdij substituted the father's photograph. The photograph of his official and legal father became the photograph of a very Jewish-looking friend of Proosdij, and on the outside of the album was affixed the cherished photograph of his Jewish but not Jewish-looking real father, who was now said to be his illegitimate father, bearing a non-Jewish name. Of the course the likeness of Sinek to his "illegitimate" father was striking. Sinek went to Westerbok, while Proosdij submitted the application to Calmeyer, who for once wrote a positive memo for Gemmeker. Everything had gone well so far, but the trouble started in Westerbork when Proosdij showed the evidence to SS chief Gemmeker, who considered himself an expert in family likenesses. When Sinek appeared in the flesh, Gemmeker compared his face with the photographs of the Jewish-looking friend of Proosdij inside the album.

> "To my horror he was of the opinion that part of Sinek's face showed a likeness to the 'official' father, who was in fact my non-related Jewish friend. It was utterly ridiculous, but there it was. Sinek remained remarkably calm, with a military bearing so impressive that Gemmeker commented on it to me. When Sinek had left we discussed the case and I could argue that Calmeyer was positive about the evidence. Ultimately, Gemmeker was persuaded to say that although he did see a likeness with the official father (the picture we had chosen because there was no likeness at all), the bearing of Sinek was impressive and he would defer to Calmeyer's judgment … Sinek got his decision and he as well as his wife and son were released. For many years I received Christmas cards from Sinek."

Another somewhat humorous story shows that one cannot always foresee the consequences of one's actions. The possession of a baptismal certificate often gave protection during a roundup, and some Christian churches were prepared to assist in providing such documents. Proosdij and Kotting printed letterheads of fictitious churches. As Proosdij related how this ruse worked:

> "As the Germans had great respect for rubber stamps, we invented a real beauty from an imaginary Dutch Ecumenical Council of Churches, with a cross and several Latin words. All our certificates were embellished with this stamp. All was well until I got a call from the Jewish Council asking where they could find the office of this Council. It appeared that the Germans refused to accept genuine certificates unless they carried the confirming stamp of the "Council." I offered to assist them as I was often in contact with the "Council" and from then on we had to authenticate every genuine certificate with a fake stamp. We never had any complaints, but enabled some threatened people to disappear in time."

Proosdij's partner in falsifying records, Adriaan Kotting, was a young lawyer married to a Jewish woman, Renee Menko, and friendly with the Jewish Rodrigues Pereira family, whom he helped save from deportation. As told by Paul Rodrigues Pereira, a neighbor and friend of Kotting, his mother was born in Paris into the Levi family and was not of the Portuguese community. She also happened to be a very beautiful woman. Kotting showed her picture to Calmeyer when he was in a good mood and said to him: "Look what a beautiful woman; don't you agree that she cannot be Jewish?" Calmeyer agreed and signed the document that she was Aryan. This also saved her children's life. As for Paul's future wife, Elsa Jesurum Doliveira, who was of Portuguese extraction, Kotting prepared a document testifying that she was born out of an affair of her mother with a non-Jewish lover. A supposedly former housemaid signed an affidavit stating that she saw the two together intimately and a hematologist (blood expert) certified that Elsa's blood did not match that of her father. She too was placed on the exemption list.

Proosdij and Kotting also sought the help of Cornelis Teutscher, who had studied medicine but also dealt in genealogy as a hobby and for extra income. As a result, he befriended a certain Mr. Groesbeek, an archivist at the Public Records Office in Haarlem, who allowed him to work independently in the archives. Teutscher first assisted people in tracing great-grandparents, and he was very creative in using blank spaces in old baptismal registers, which he filled in with false data. He developed ink that could pass for old, got a hold of old paper, duplicated handwriting, and forged Calmeyer's signature. The concept of "full Jewish grandparents" meant that it had to be certain that the four grandparents of these full-Jewish people all had been demonstrably Jewish. For middle-aged individuals this meant that many of their ancestors had lived in the latter part of the 18th century. But the Registry Office in the Netherlands had been created only in 1811. So the solution was to show that in the generation of the great-great-grandparents there had been someone baptized. Teutscher was allowed to take records home at the end of the day, and entered the registration of baptisms in places where there was an empty line, putting the records back in place the next morning. Teutscher then told the Jewish applicant to ask for his ancestor's documents, and the latter accordingly received a confirmed statement of ancestral baptism from the relevant clerk, who was completely ignorant of Teutscher's insertions. The applicant then turned to Calmeyer's office.

Another case was of Salomon Mendes Coutinho, the sexton of the Portuguese Jewish synagogue in Amsterdam, who was married to Elisabeth Sarphati and was childless. With them lived Elisabeth's sister, Marianne Sarphati. Teutscher was able to have Marianne registered with Calmeyer as only part Jewish. Her sister Elisabeth refused to change her Jewish identity. "I won't renounce being Jewish." When the Coutinho couple was taken away in May 1943, Teutscher tried to intercede by pointing to Marianne's semi-Aryan origin. Once in Westerbork, Elisabeth agreed to Teutscher's suggestion, and she and her husband were released. Now came the problem of her father, Joseph Sarphati (a widower). He was deported to Theresienstadt. He stated to the camp commander that he was not Jewish, as evidenced by his daughter's semi-Aryan origin, and he was allowed to emigrate to Switzerland. In yet another case, Teutscher fabricated false Paraguayan passports for a Jewish family. They were deported to Bergen-Belsen, and held in a special compound. They survived.

In the meantime, a Central Office for Genealogy was founded in Apeldoorn by Ludo ten Cate, who was a firebrand Nazi, and one had to watch one's step. The Germans then decided that all of Calmeyer's requests first had to go through ten Cate's office before they could be acted on. Ten Cate was impressed with Teutscher's work and summoned him to his office. He "praised my acuteness and offered me a job." For a while Teutscher considered accepting, for the opportunity it would offer to sabotage ten Cate's work. He finally turned him down because of the long distance between Amsterdam and Apeldoorn and the limited freedom of action involved in working under ten Cate. The man did not get along too well with his SS superiors and he was eventually removed from his post, to the relief of Calmeyer and the Dutch attorneys.

As for Antonius Mom, he worked for the Registry Office in Amsterdam, a position that afforded him the opportunity to forge documents. He helped Cornelis Teutscher, who altered the cards that Mom stole. Mom then put the forged cards back and instructed the Jews in question to lose their identity card so that they could subsequently be provided with a new Aryan card based on the falsified data. His fraudulent work was never discovered.

Ysbrand Nijgh was another Dutch attorney who used his considerable historical genealogical knowledge to manipulate records to prove that Jews were in fact non-Jews. Initially, he took identity papers belonging to non-Jews and replaced the photos with those of Jews. Later he gave the bearer a completely imaginary identity. He took the forged papers to Calmeyer and explained to his staff that the person's Jewish registration was a mistake. In dealing with Portuguese Jews, he often claimed that an error had occurred at the time of the Inquisition, four centuries earlier, when sloppy work had been done in registering certain people as Jewish, and that many of these people were consequently not descended from Jews.

Opinions are still divided with regard to Hans-Georg Calmeyer, the man in charge of the whole racial investigation and reclassification project on behalf of the occupying Germans. The Dutch-Jewish historian of the Holocaust in the Netherlands, Jacob Presser, wrote of him: "Though he knew that many Jews were trying to pull the wool over his eyes, he nevertheless let all of them go unpunished ... He went to endless trouble to be helpful to all petitioners. There is no doubt that hundreds of Jews owe their lives to him ... He once described his position to that of a doctor in a lonely post, cut off from the outside world, and left with a mere 50 phials of medicine for the treatment of 5,000 critical cases... Since he could not save all, he did what he could for the few." In most cases, where doubts arose on the authenticity of the documents, he relied on his own intuition to accept or reject them.

Jaap van Proosdij has a more guarded opinion of the man. "He considered that he was doing his duty and it did not occur to him that he might be prosecuted after the war ... He knew that a negative decision would have serious, probably fatal, consequences for the persons involved ... [and this] sudden confrontation with reality fortunately shocked him ... Calmeyer was not a bad person although he was temperamental. One was never certain what he would decide ... Sometimes he positively wanted to help ... He was not evil, but mostly the objective, neutral officer. His positive quality was that he was not anti-Jewish. But he was not specifically pro either. Many people are grateful for the decisions bearing Calmeyer's signature, not knowing that the signature was often made by someone else."

As for himself, Jaap van Proosdij came out of the war after three years intensive work in Calmeyer's office, in the heart of the German occupation administration, undiscovered and unscathed. Likewise for his partner Adriaan Kotting. The two, aided by other trustworthy

Dutch attorneys and genealogical "experts," such as Cornelis Teutscher, Ysbrand Nijgh, and Antonius Mom, and with the silent consent of Calmeyer's German staff, and especially of Gerhard Wander, were able to save hundreds of Jews from deportation and death by having them reclassified as only partial Jews or full non-Jews – based on the flimsiest and clearly forged documentation. From all the evidence, it appears that Hans-Georg Calmeyer, the man that Nazi governor Seyss-Inquart had charged with making sure that this work was done in line with the strict application of Nazi racial principles, knew of the dubious origin of many of these documents but acted as though he was not aware of it. In this charged atmosphere, with the SS breathing down their necks, a handful of Dutch and German officials (with the Dutch attorney Jaap van Proosdij planted in a highly placed German office) were able to play the Nazi racial card to their advantage and save many lives.

In 1997, Yad Vashem recognized Jaap van Proosdij as Righteous Among the Nations; likewise for Adriaan Kotting in 2006, Cornelis Teutscher in 1983, Antonius Mom in 1983, and Ysbrand Nijgh in 1992. The German Hans-Georg Calmeyer was also awarded the Righteous title in 1992.

Puchalski, Jan & Anna

POLAND

Since the German occupation of Grodno (today in Belarus), in June 1941, young Felix Zandman (born in 1927) had expected only the worst from the occupiers – murderous raids, one after another, on the city's 30,000 Jews. In one such "action," thousands were led, accompanied by bursts of machinegun fire and whipping and clubbing, toward the nearby Kielbasin labor camp, where many died of dysentery and others were shot, beaten to death, or hanged. Felix managed to escape and return to the ghetto, where he was momentarily reunited with his family. In January 1943, another Nazi *Aktion* claimed 10,000 more lives – sent to die in Treblinka. With only 7,000 Jews left, Felix watched helplessly as his father and mother, Aaron and Genia, succumbed to despondency and indifference to their fate. Grandmother Tema, once a tower of strength, had resigned herself to the worst. "She was waiting for death to come to take her."

Friday, February 12, 1943, seemed to the 15-year-old Felix like just another day of forced labor as he made his way to his work assignment outside the ghetto. Suddenly all Jewish workers were ordered to return immediately to the ghetto. Felix knew what this meant – another Nazi *Aktion*, perhaps the final one. He decided to start walking, but in a different direction from the ghetto. At first, he was at a loss where to head. He first stopped at the home of a Polish woman who had sold him vodka a few hours earlier, thinking to stay there until the storm had passed. "My husband would kill me," she answered in fear. Felix pleaded with

The Puchalski children kneeling to recite a prayer in the Hall of Remembrance at Yad Vashem in front of the Eternal Flame

her, but to no avail. Removing the identifying yellow star from his jacket, Felix then headed for the home of the former nanny of his uncle's family. She allowed him to hide in the stable, but just for that evening, adding, "If anybody finds you, I didn't have anything to do with it." In the morning, the nanny fed him with hot porridge before sending him away.

At this point, Felix decided to head for Lososna, a name that brought back pleasant memories; a wooded place where his family owned several cottages and would spend the summer months. Since the arrival of the Germans, these cottages were off limits to Jews, but the local caretaker kept an eye on them. His name was Jan Puchalski and he had remained there with his wife, Anna, and their five children. Felix fondly recalled Anna, a strong-willed and determined woman who had been especially nice to him. "She would give me a kiss when she saw me and hold my hand when we went out." During an earlier Nazi raid on the ghetto's Jews, in January 1943, relatives of Felix had managed to hide for two days in the Puchalski home. Coming back to the ghetto, they told of the warm reception received from the Puchalskis and of their commitment to continue to help. "I therefore decided to go to the Puchalskis and ask them to hide me for a few days, and then I would go deeper into the countryside to join the partisans." The Lososno cottages seemed to him an ideal solution, as a way station.

Arriving there, he asked the Puchalskis to let him stay over for just one night. "You'll go nowhere," Anna told him in a commanding voice. She added that no one knew where exactly to find the partisans. Besides, they could be those who fought the Germans but also killed Jews. Anna concluded that it was best for Felix to stay with her family. She gave another reason. "God sent you to me as a gift." Later that evening, she explained what she meant by this. Years ago, when she was pregnant with her second daughter, Sabina, her husband had come home drunk one night and a row ensued which ended with Anna on the street. She had nowhere to go, so she headed for Felix's grandmother, Tema, in Grodno, who took her in and arranged for Anna to give birth in Grodno's Jewish hospital. "So you see," Anna told Felix, "I prayed that one day I could repay her, and here you are, God sent you. I will not let you perish, Felix. If you perish, we will all perish together ... You're not going anywhere." That evening, five more people showed up – escapees from that day's Nazi murderous raid on the ghetto's remaining Jews; among them Uncle Sender Frejdowicz, who had made his escape with bullets whizzing all around him; Mordecai (known as Mottel) and wife Golda Bass, and two more Jewish fugitives, Borka Shulkes and Meir Zamoszczanski. The Puchalski household now numbered 13 people: Jan and Anna and their five children and the six fugitive Jews.

At first, the six were hidden in a cellar near the house used for storing potatoes. The fear of detection then led to the decision to dig a bunker under one of the two Puchalski bedrooms; a space about 1.5 meters in width and length and one meter in height. The entrance was through a narrow opening under the Puchalski's bed. "To me it looked like a grave," Felix recalled. An air pipe leading to the garden, covered with bushes, allowed some air to penetrate. For added security, Jan Puchalski moved the doghouse nearer to the house, so that the dog's barking would give sufficient advance warning of any approaching strangers. The six fugitives soon realized that the space was too small to contain them all, so Shulkes and Zamoszczanski left, hoping to join up with friendly partisans. The four remaining Jews included Felix Zandman, his uncle Sender Frejdowicz (both of whom had lost their entire families), and the couple Mordecai and Golda Bass. The Basses had come with some money to help defray the additional expenses of the Puchalskis, whose sole income derived from Jan's poor-paying job in a tobacco factory.

In the hiding place, no outside light penetrated. "Like some nocturnal creature, I began to get used to living in dark," Felix recalled. In addition, during the hours when their benefactor's family was up and about, they had to keep absolutely quiet so as not to arouse the suspicions of the two youngest Puchalski children (Wladyslaw and Wanda, aged three and one), who were not told of the fugitives' presence. The three older children, Irena 16, Sabina 13, and Krystyna 11, were privy to the secret and knew to keep their silence. To minimize the terrible discomfort – only three people able to lie abreast at one time, with one sitting up on the toilet bucket – the fugitives decided to rotate positions every few hours. An additional rule, imposed by Sender, was for the recently married Basses to abstain from sex, to avoid complications with four bodies pressed so close to one another. There was to be total abstinence and almost total silence in that grave-like hole in the ground for as long as it would take – in fact, for the 17 months that the four stayed there. Anna would tap on the trap door to bring food once or twice a day and remove the bucket. Totally cut off from the outside world, their only companions were worms and fleas which caused everyone to itch and scratch. Felix even became adept at catching the fleas. When Anna tapped on the floor, it was a signal that Germans were approaching. On such occasions, no one moved a muscle. Outside, the dog could be heard barking. In Zandman's words, the Puchalskis were aware of the terrible danger, of certain death for themselves, perhaps also for the children, in case of discovery. "Yet at no time did they ever hint that we should leave. In moments of despair, Mrs. or Mr. Puchalski and even the children tried to raise our morale and prayed for us."

Inside the dark hole, each of the fugitives was enveloped in his private thoughts, shattered as the four were by the tragic events of the times. "We were absorbed in our pain," Felix wrote, recalling the recent losses of their loved ones. Would they in turn also fall victim, or hopefully survive? "Each knock on the front door, each strange sound in the house, each bark from the yard could mean an informant or the Germans." Uncle Sender, who had lost his wife and two children to the Germans, began to assume a paternal attitude toward the orphaned Felix. To keep from dwelling on their terrible conditions, Sender decided that one should focus one's mind on a subject that would require all of a person's attention; a subject removed from subjective feelings – such as mathematics. Crouching in the dark hole, Sender began by questioning Felix: "A triangle has three sides; do you know Felix what a right angle is?" Then they named the three angles: alpha, beta, and sinus. Sender continued: "The tangent is the ratio of the first side to the second side." This was followed by more difficult questions, such as equations of the second degree. If AX squared plus BX plus C equals 0 – find X1 and X2? The answers to this and other difficult problems had to be worked out mentally – no textbooks, scrap paper, or writing implements. With Mordecai Bass, a lawyer by profession, Felix trained in remembering important historical dates and geography. These mental exercises, especially in math, developed in an underground bunker and in almost total darkness (occasionally they were allowed the use of an oil lamp), were to prove handy to Felix after the liberation.

In the meantime, in light of the Russian army's constant advance, the fighting had moved closer to the Puchalski home and German soldiers stationed themselves around the house and in the barn. Soon the Puchalskis were evicted. Fortunately, the five hidden people (a certain Esther Hajdamak-Shapira had joined the others a short time before the liberation) were able to slip out quietly, wandering for several days, feeding on the tall corn stalks in the fields (it was July 1944), and occasionally running into German soldiers to whom they presented themselves as refugees fleeing the Russians – until they caught up with the advancing Russians on July 24.

With everything around them constantly reminding them of the terrible loss of their loved ones, Felix and Uncle Sender decided to move westward and settled in France. Sharpened by the mathematical skills practiced while in hiding, Felix had no trouble catching up with his schooling and was admitted into one of France's most prestigious engineering schools (*École Nationale Supérieure d'Eléctricité et de Méchanique* in Paris), where he earned a diploma in engineering. This lead to a job with a company that manufactured electric generators and to experiments in photoelasticity; that is, how much stress glass could undergo at any given point. Zandman's solution, helped along by his mathematical skills, landed him an appointment as lecturer in the French Academy of Aeronautics. This was followed by employment in several French companies as well as in the United States, where he arrived in 1956. By 1961, Felix was toying with the idea of making a resistor that would be virtually insensitive to temperature changes by bonding together several kinds of metals, with one neutralizing the other. In 1962, he started his own company to manufacture the new product, naming it Vishay after the town where his beloved grandmother Tema was born. The company soon expanded its activities by acquiring other companies in the United States and elsewhere. In 1993, *Fortune* magazine listed Vishay among the top 500 – ranked 15.

With each business success, the memory of the Holocaust continued to torment and haunt Felix Zandman. "I am a person who should have been dead in 1943," he wrote in his autobiography. "Four or five times I escaped death by a hair's breadth – why me rather than the twenty-nine thousand Grodno Jews who did not escape, I cannot begin to say." At the same time, Felix was deeply conscious of the need to acquit himself of his moral obligation toward his rescuers, and in 1986 his testimony as well as of several of the other rescued person, was received at Yad Vashem.

That same year Yad Vashem conferred the title of Righteous Among the Nations upon the late Jan and Anna Puchalski. Felix Zandman makes it a point to have the managerial staff of his company's affiliates visit Yad Vashem to learn what took place during the Holocaust. Also, to stand beside the tree planted by Zandman in honor of his rescuers and be told of the courageous humanitarian behavior of Jan and Anna Puchalski.

Rakevičius, Jaroslavas & Česlovas, Juozas, Zenonas & Algimantas
Mozuraitis, Jonas & Ona & Mefodia & Alfonsas & Suzana & Zenonas
LITHUANIA

One of the most terrible pictures to come out of the Holocaust is of Lithuanian armed vigilantes clubbing Jews to death on the streets of Kovno (Kaunas, in Lithuania), with German soldiers standing by and gleefully watching the murderous mayhem. On the eve of the German occupation of the city, on June 24, 1941, Kovno numbered some 40,000 Jews. Local Lithuanians, armed with whatever weaponry was on hand, immediately took to the streets and began a massacre of Jews. This was augmented by other random killings, including those at the nearby military installation known as the Ninth Fort, which during the first two months claimed the lives of around 10,000 Jews. The remaining Jews were ordered into a crowded ghetto, from which people were taken out to be shot from time to time – 2,000 that same year and 9,000 in further "actions." By March 1944, the Jewish population had shrunk to a little over 14,000. Children still remained, and the Germans decided to deal with them as well. On March 27, 1944, some 1,800 were seized and murdered. Four months later, on July 8, 1944, with the approach of the Russian army, some of the remaining Jews were moved to other camps and the ghetto was torched, with about 2,000 Jews perishing in the flames and smoke.

Jaroslavas Rakevičius

While this murderous carnival was taking place, a Lithuanian farmer named Jaroslavas Rakevičius regularly hitched his horse to a wagon and drove from his village a distance of 90 kilometers to Kovno, to pick up fleeing Jews and bring them to safety to his village home. He managed to save up to 30 Jews. One of them was the eight-year-old boy Aharon Barak, future president of the Supreme Court of Israel.

Leah Brik-Meyerowitz and her son Aharon, eight years old in 1944, had lived through the worst days inside the Kovno ghetto, and survived, including for Aharon also the murderous "children's action." It was April 1944, and spring was settling in. But Leah felt that the ground was burning beneath her feet, and she must find a way to save her son before it was really too late. The only possibility was to have him smuggled out of the ghetto and find a

Lithuanian willing to shelter him. Being part of a work detail, she managed to meet some Lithuanians on the outside, and she took the opportunity to contact some the people she had studied with at the university, but they were not prepared to take the risk. Lithuanians caught with Jews in their home were immediately put to death. She then met Jaroslavas Rakevičius, whom she described as "a brave and courageous man" and who agreed to come and get the boy before the next "action." However, when he arrived in early May, he insisted that Leah join him, since his wife had just died and someone was needed to look after the eight-year-old Aharon.

Česlovas Rakevičius (left) and Aharon Barak (the former president of the Israel Supreme Court)

"With my facial features, I look typically Jewish," Leah wrote in her deposition. "I nevertheless decided that come what may, I have to save my son." Aharon was placed in a sack, and put to sleep with some barbiturate, and the sack was concealed in a pile of sacks on its way out of the ghetto and filled with clothes and shoes that had been repaired in the ghetto workshop. The German guards at the gate were paid off, as well as the German who received the sacks and brought Leah and Aharon to the place where Rakevičius was waiting for them. Jaroslavas then drove the mother and child in a horse-drawn carriage on a busy road filled with Germans, with Leah sitting next to him and the sack with the sleeping boy between their legs, until they got to his home in the village of Keidžiai, near the city of Raseiniai. There they stayed for a while. Jaroslavas had four boys; three were of military age, and Germans occasionally came by to see why they had not reported for duty in one of the Lithuanian units fighting alongside the Germans, now that the war had turned bad for them and they needed every available man – even from occupied countries. During these visits, Rakevičius hid Leah and Aharon (as well as his sons, and the Zarkin family, whom Rakevičius kept with him for three years) in a ditch, covered with big branches. The Germans failed to find the hidden people, but they discovered Zarkin's Hebrew prayer book in Rakevičius' home. They then insisted that he disclose to them the hideout of his Jews, but he vehemently denied any involvement. It was clear that it was in the best interests of the Zarkins as well as Leah and Aharon to move elsewhere, before the Germans returned for further questioning. Zarkin, who knew some of the neighbors from before the war, was able to find for himself as well as for Leah and Aharon another hiding place. It was the home of a poor farmer named Mozuraitis.

In total darkness, the group made its way to Mozuraitis' home, where Leah and Aharon remained hidden until liberated in October 1944 by the Red Army. While there, the Rakevičius children came often to visit and suggested that they return to their home. The Zarkins took up the invitation and left, but Leah decided to stay where she was with her son. Mozuraitis was a woefully poor farmer living in a rundown house. He had the task of providing for his wife and their four children. Leah described him as a bit naïve, for he did not understand the danger he was in keeping Jews, but he loved people and was a kindhearted man. "He was sure the Germans would not come to his house, for what would they find there – some scraps of food – sour milk, potatoes and bread; bread bought with the money I gave him." She further wrote:

> *"He and his family surrounded us with much love. They cared for us and everything they did was out of love of their fellow man, and to make life easier for us. They especially adored my son Aharon, and called him Algirdas (in Lithuanian). They would take him at night to the nearest river to wash, on the children's favorite horse. The farmer, when he noticed my loneliness, would comfort me, saying, 'See here, madam, your son will one day be an outstanding person. Whenever it is very bad – it will be good!'"*

Little did he realize how true his prophecy would be. At Leah's request, Mozuraitis dug a bunker underneath the floor of the house for her and Aaron to hide in when neighbors suddenly dropped in to visit. The place was also used as a shelter during the bombardments that preceded the arrival of the Russian army. Leah recalls the joy of Mozuraitis at having pulled through and saved the mother and child. "How great was the pride of this farmer, that he, a simple Lithuanian, had saved a boy and his mother from the Nazis! He took my son and showed him off from house to house, to pride himself on the greatest achievement of his life."

After the liberation, Leah returned to Kovno and was reunited with her husband, Zvi Brik, and other relatives. When she left Lithuania, she turned over to the Mozuraitis all her belonging, including a sewing machine. From Israel, she continued to send him packages. "He lives with his family in Lithuania," Leah Barak wrote in 1973, "and cannot understand to this day why we have not forgotten him and continue to help him."

As for the Rakevičius family, the Briks left them their three-room apartment with all the household items. Based on information from survivors, it turned out that this family saved close to 30 Jews, with all the four sons participating in the rescue operation. One son was assigned to pick up fleeing Jews from the Kovno ghetto; another son – to find hiding places for them; a third – to keep watch over the house for approaching strangers; the fourth son – to help the others in their various rescue operations. Son Česlovas, for instance – when the danger of betrayal threatened one of the hidden persons, little Henia Meltz – went to get her and carried her in his arms to another hiding place. The people saved by this family, other than Leah Brik and her son Aharon, include members of the Meltz, Zarkin, and Tulishevitz families as well as the families of Moshe Kulshe, Leah Gutshtein, Sarah Liebman, Sheina Raz, and Feiga Shapir (Kuleshaite).

Jonas and Ona Mozuraitis (seated) with their children (standing)

In 1976, Yad Vashem conferred the Righteous title on all members of the two families: on Jaroslavas Rakevičius and his four sons, Česlovas, Juozas, Zenonas, and Algimantas; on Jonas and Ona Mozuraitis and their four children, Mefodia, Alfonsas, Suzana, and Zenonas.

Reynders, Henri (Dom Bruno)
BELGIUM

*I*n July 1938, on a visit to Nazi Germany, Father Henri Reynders was shocked at the intense antisemitism he saw in that country. As he later recalled, when in Frankurt, "everywhere in the street… defamatory signs: *Jude-Judas, Juden heraus, Hier sind Juden nicht erwünscht* ["Jew-Judas, Jews Out, Jews Not Welcome Here"]. This shocked me terribly." What, in his words, especially horrified him was seeing an old bearded man, dressed in a caftan, wearing a black hat, walking half bent, not daring to lift his eyes, hiding his nose with his hands, and the people moving away from him as if he were plague-ridden, abusing him, and sneeringly pointing their finger at him. "This upset me very much. This segregation, this contempt, this conceit; this cruel stupidity – no, this was intolerable! I still retain this memory, and it still makes me feel sick."

Father Bruno Reynders in a war time photo with some of the Jewish children that he saved

Born in 1903, Henry Reynders was ordained a priest in 1928 and joined the Benedictine Order in Louvain/Leuven. In 1931 he earned a doctorate in theology from Louvain University. As a chaplain in the Belgian army he was taken prisoner by the Germans during the brief 1940 campaign, and after his release he returned to his priestly duties. In 1942, his superior assigned him to minister to a group of 20 people in a small home for the blind in Hodbomont. Arriving there, he learned that the home's "blind" director, Mr. Walter Bieser, and several other occupants were not blind at all, but Jews in hiding, though some of the other occupants, including five or six children, were indeed blind Jews and had been moved there from a Catholic institution in Banneux. Later that year, with the assistance of a clandestine network in Liège headed by Albert van den Berg, he dispersed the Jewish residents of the home to avoid their arrest and deportation. This led him into further rescue activities, especially in locating sheltering homes in various parts of the country for Jewish children on the run. He was known to ride on his bicycle to make the rounds of possible hiding places. He once quipped that he estimated he had pedaled 40 to 50 times the equivalent of the *Tour de Belgique.*

Father Reynders, also known religiously as Dom Bruno, was always busy improvising, and caring for the nourishment, clothing, false identities with new non-Jewish-sounding names, and financial support for host families, some of which was covered by the Van den Berg network as well as the clandestine Jewish Defense Committee (CDJ} organization. He placed Jewish children in many religious homes in various parts of the country, including his sister's (Marie-Louise, known as Mother Thérèse) Benedictine convent in Liège and the home of his parents and his brother, the dentist Jean Reynders, in Ixelles. An estimated 350 Jews (some place the number at 390), mostly children but also 90 adults, were helped by him, many of whom were referred to him by the CDJ organization. It did not take long for the Gestapo to realize that Reynders was one of the principal people impeding their work of rounding up the country's Jews, and they decided to track him down, which forced him to leave his base at Mont-César to avoid arrest. Moving from place to place, he changed his name several times (Gustave De Laet, Georges Blanchart, and Hubert Renard).

After the war, he dedicated himself to place on record his many rescue activities involving children, based on secret notations made by him, which included the person's original name, borrowed name, placements, and upkeep. For one such child he wrote:

"With Gielen, 600 [Belgian Francs] per month + 12.50 per day for meals. The child is then moved to P.J. (240 per month), and finally with Delhaize (payments + pension, 300 per month). Or: "Woman originally placed in Hodbomont home for blind children by Mr. Van den Berg. In November 1942, the wife is placed with Alois Antoine, a lawyer, and his wife, Thérèse, in Wisley-Theux. Then, following an alarm (real or false), sent to Miss Lisette Bisset, 63a rue Joseph Stallaert, Brussels; then with Reussens, 68 Longue rue d'Argile, Antwerp. Finally, [as a] domestic and cook with Mrs. Hollander, 45 rue de Namur, Louvain."

He also recorded some of the problems encountered, such as with the 16-year-old Fernande, placed as a maid with Mrs. Tallon in Louvain, who left after a short eight-day stay to join her brother-in-law, giving as a reason that she did not feel comfortable with "your priests" – perhaps a reference to subtle attempts at conversion. In another entry, Bruno recorded a convent in Bellegem where he was told by the Mother Superior to take back the children only recently placed there, since they spoke French instead of the local Flemish language. On the eve of the country's liberation, in August 1944, when he learned that five of his charges had been moved to a Gestapo-supervised Jewish children's home in Linkebeek (still in existence, to lure Jewish children there), Dom Bruno frantically tried to have them spirited out of there, and succeeded, before the Gestapo had them removed on the eve of the anticipated German withdrawal from Belgium in the face of the Allied advance from France.

After the war, Reynders was unfortunately involved in a bitter debate with Jewish organizations about the fate of children who had been baptized not in line with Catholic teachings, which require the consent of parents or guardians. In line with Catholic belief, Reynders felt that the two dozen out of close to 400 children rescued through his endeavors should not be placed in Jewish children institutions that had leftist-Marxist orientations and were aloof even from any practice of the Jewish religion. If baptized children were to be released to such homes, he argued, it should only be done on condition that those among them who wished to continue practicing their Christianity be allowed to do so, under the guidance of Christian tutors. Reynders admitted that some Christian rescuers may have acted over-zealously in having the children in their care baptized without proper Catholic procedures; however, the baptismal act could not be undone. At any rate, he argued, it was necessary that their training should continue under Christian inspiration, especially those who had already become passionately attached to the Catholic religion. Jewish leaders countered by rejecting the thesis of the age of seven as an age of understanding and argued that in the special circumstances of the Nazi period such considerations were not applicable and that the Jewish people could ill afford to lose more Jewish souls after the terrible loss of millions of lives during the Holocaust.

In fairness to Bruno Reynders, the Jewish children under his care testified to his neutrality in questions of religious observance. Herman Krygier related how Reynders had taught him the genuflections he was to practice, but only as to make him unnoticeable. "In no instance did he seek to convert me." Similary for Bernard Rotmil, who stated that he and his brother Charles had once asked Reynders to have them baptized. "To my great surprise, he told us to wait until the end of the war, when we would be reunited with our parents," and only then to reconsider freely their position. Nathan Zygrajch recalled that when Reynders was pressed by host families to have the children baptized, his response was: "We are responsible for the life of these children, but their soul does not belong to us." Equally for Leon Leiberg, who emphasized: "He never made the slightest effort to introduce religion as a *quid pro quo* in our relationship, but insisted on the need of maintaining my hope for my family and conducting myself in such a way as not to shame them." His struggle was limited to children already baptized by others, however the circumstances attendant on this act.

With the war over, Reynders filled many religious posts and also found time to pursue his study of the theology of the second century Church Father Iraneus, translating some of his works before finally retiring as a vicar in Ottignies, where he died in 1981. Before that, in 1964, he visited Israel and planted a tree in a ceremony at Yad Vashem in the presence of many of "his" children, after being proclaimed Righteous Among the Nations.

The children whom he saved remembered him with great affection. Bernard Rotmil, writing to Dom Bruno in 1969, recalled his "friendly smile … After 28 years, you remain the most venerated and truest friend we have ever known." After the war, Bernard Rotmil found the following passage in Bruno's journal: "I recall Bernard's appetite as a sixteen-year-old boy, and the difficulty I had in this regard since I paid for his upkeep at the place where he stayed in Louvain. One day, I dared tell him to try to control his appetite, and I recall his distraught face as he replied, 'But I am always hungry.' I was completely disarmed and I did not cease reproaching myself for my intervention. But nourishment was at that time a difficult and expensive thing." Bernard was finally taken to a farmhouse where the food was plentiful, and he remained there until the end of the war.

Bernard Rotmil saw his benefactor for the last time during the High Holiday services in a Brussels synagogue, on the morrow of the liberation in September 1944. When the rabbi announced the presence of Dom Bruno, the audience cheered him. "The children hung on his hands and the parents tearfully thanked and blessed him. It took some time before calm was restored in the synagogue and the religious services could continue." Esther Krygier equally recalled him as "very kind and fatherly. He gave us a certain security ... He would lead us by hand and explain that where we were going one must not say that one was Jewish, not even trust another child ... He was the only one who had the gift to remove from us the fear which we had." Her brother, Herman Krygier, added: "He was reassuring ... He did not influence anyone with his ideas. He sought to help, to understand. He calmed my anxiety and I must say that he is the only person in my whole life who inspired in me such trust."

In 1991, friends and former charges of Reynders gathered in Ottignies, Belgium, the place where he lived out the last years of his life, to dedicate a memorial, which reads:

> *"Father Bruno Reynders, Benedictine (1903–1981). Hero of the Resistance. Risking his life, he saved some 400 Jews from Nazi barbarism. Israel has proclaimed him Righteous Among the Nations, and in his memory a tree was planted at Yad Vashem, Jerusalem."*

Řiha, Jozef
CZECH REPUBLIC

Jozef Řiha belonged to the Czech community of farmers that had settled in the 18th century in the Volyn region of Ukraine to farm the land. The Czech farmers were known for their deep evangelical religiosity and their high regard for the Jewish people. After World War Two, the Soviet government had them repatriated to their original homeland in the Czech regions of Czechoslovakia – currently the Czech Republic.

Good relations existed between Jozef Řiha's family in the village of Mirohoshcha and Simcha Shtibel in the nearby city of Dubno. The connection had its origins in the business relationship between the two families; the Řihas had been customers of long standing of the Shtibel drapery store in Dubno. But the connection went beyond business and had begun to develop into a real friendship. However, never in his wildest dreams did Simcha Shtibel, born in 1911, ever imagine that a day would come when this evolving friendship would be tested in the Dante-like hell of the Holocaust that swept over the Jews in the region.

The German occupation of Dubno on June 25, 1941, was followed with the random killing of Jews, who originally numbered 12,000 souls. This reached a crescendo on August 21, 1941, with the execution of over 1,000 Jews in the town's Jewish cemetery. Further sporadic killings continued, and the last Jews were liquidated on October 5, 1942. Slightly over 100 Jews are estimated to have survived in hiding.

During the early and pre-ghetto phase of the German occupation, Jozef Řiha already had begun to show the true measure of his feelings of friendship toward the Shtibel family. This took the form of providing them with food and vital necessities at a time when these basic items were cut back by the Germans, forcing Řiha to get them in the market at inflated prices. The help was given gratuitously. When Simcha's parents wished to pay Řiha for his benevolence with valuables in their possession, such as gold jewelry, Řiha stated emphatically that he would only take it for safekeeping, to keep it from falling into German hands, and would return it the moment the Germans were gone. So it was agreed.

On April 7, 1942, all Jews were ordered locked inside a ghetto and all outside communication was forbidden. This was followed by the mass murder of all "non-productive" Jews on May 27, 1941, in which Simcha Shtibel lost his parents and the rest of his family. He was left with his wife, Genia. Contact with Řiha was maintained through Genia, who worked in a sewing shop operated by the Germans outside the ghetto that served the army and the local population. On the excuse of checking out the company's products, the Řiha daughters would visit Genia Shtibel and use the occasion to converse with her. They encouraged her not to lose hope, for a way would certainly be found to save her and her husband. At the same time, they did not in any way indicate how precisely this was going to come about, nor did they suggest that the Řiha family would have a hand in rescuing the two Shtibels. But from the friendliness of the two sisters and their encouraging words, Genia felt instinctively that one could count on that family's aid if it should ever come to that.

The opportunity came when the German labor department made an exception to the rule and allowed Jews to leave the ghetto to assist local farmers near the ghetto with the harvest. The Shtibels took advantage of this to escape and headed straight for the Řiha farm in Mirohoshcha. At the time, spirits in the ghetto were at their lowest ebb, as the surviving Jews realized, even among the most optimistic, that the Nazi Final Solution was an accomplished fact. The clock was steadily ticking away, and it was time to flee, moments before the final curtain came down on the ghetto Jews. At this low point, the Shtibels headed for Jozef Řiha's farm wondering what sort of reception awaited them, as their previous contact had been only with Jozef's daughters who had visited Genia at her work place.

In Simcha Shtibel's words, "We were received with great warmth, and the first words of Mr. Řiha and wife, Yulya, gave proof to the purity of their motives and their noble-minded spirit." Jozef Řiha's opening words, which would remain emblazoned in the Shtibels' memory for years to come, were brief, highly meaningful, and to the point: "Now we will not let you go from here anywhere." This, Simcha Shtibel wrote years later, was in contrast to many others who, while professing their readiness to help, when the time came found excuses not to keep their word. This perhaps was due to fear of the Germans, who threatened death to the entire family of anyone who dared to shelter a Jew in his home. It seems that the Shtibels hesitated at first in the face of Řiha's gracious invitation because of the risks to his family, which included two daughters and a grandson. Jozef Řiha ended the discussion with a peremptory, "Let God's will be done."

For the first few weeks, the two Shtibels were allowed to move around more or less freely inside the house and help out with the farm chores. Then, when Jozef Řiha heard that the Germans were preparing big ditches for the execution of the last Jews in the ghetto, he felt that the time had come for his charges to be hidden. Jozef and his wife took the two fugitives to a big haystack in their yard adjacent to a small pen where two sheep were kept. The entrance to the haystack, a foot above ground level, was concealed and Řiha showed them how to get in and out. In the haystack, the two Shtibels could only remain in a reclining position – for a full eight months! Significantly, when the two Shtibels were about to move to the haystack, Jozef Řiha stopped them for a moment. He wanted to return the gold jewelry that Simcha's parents had left with him since, as he explained, he did not want any expectation of reward to stand between him and his charges.

The Řihas would furtively feed them when they tended their two sheep, so that their going out to the barn with the bowl of food would not arouse suspicion if anyone happening to be passing by. Jozef kept the secret of the Shtibels' stay with him even from his married daughter, who lived nearby. The fewer the people who knew, the less fear there would be of a slip of the tongue and a tragic end for all concerned.

Within the Řiha family the situation was made worse by their Polish son-in-law's habit of fraternizing with the Germans and frequently inviting them to Jozef Řiha's home for relaxation and drinks. This increased the risks for Jozef Řiha, who had to be extra careful when going out to feed his two charges. It happened once that the German visitors were so drunk, that they insisted on lying down and resting on the haystack. On another occasion, the sheep were rubbing themselves against the haystack, which caused one German to facetiously ask, "Are there any Jews hiding inside?" There is no need to underline the heart pounding fear such words instilled in the Řiha couple.

To add to the Řihas troubles, two more people suddenly started showing up, usually late at night, to get food for themselves and their families who were hiding in the community center. Moreover, the news of German victories during that summer of 1942 created a depressed mood among the Řihas and a feeling that they were in for a long haul, with liberation not close at hand. Řiha's son-in-law added to his in-laws depression by predicting an eventual German victory. The fact that he was a graduate of a medical school gave his pronouncements more weight among the less educated people of the village.

News also circulated of how the Germans had found out, with the help of informers, of Jews in hiding in the Dubno region, and of the punishment meted out to their rescuers. Hearing one such story, Jozef's young daughter, Emilia, became hysterical, threatening to kill herself if her parents did not remove the two Jews. No one, she added, would believe that her family's motives in keeping these two strangers had been pure, and it was better for her to die than bear the stigma of having kept the Jews out of greed.

All these circumstances led the Řihas to gently and regretfully tell their two charges that they could no longer keep them. The two Shtibels understood, thanked their benefactors for the eight months hidden with them, and were about to get up from their reclining position and move out when they realized to their shock that they could not move their limbs; that is, stand up and walk. At this point Jozef Řiha surprised them by changing his mind, and took them to another hiding place, where they could stand and thus regain the use of their feet. Řiha then spoke with Shlomo Wowak, one of the two men who had been visiting him at night for food, and asked him to admit the two Shtibels to their hideout in the village community center.

Shlomo Wowak was a resident of long standing in Mirohoshcha village, where he managed a flourmill. His family of five as well as Menachem Feierstein's family were hiding under the stage of the big auditorium in the village community center, a place that Jozef Řiha had helped prepare. There Simcha and Genia Shtibel hid for seven months, from May to November 1943, while at the same time leaving furtively at night to visit the Řihas to get food for themselves and the other people in hiding. Shlomo Wowak also went out on these night forays to Řiha's house. In his postwar account, he related how this was done. "I would quietly wake him up at night without fear that he would turn me out. On the contrary, he always arranged it that the dog would be tied at a distance and not attack us, and the food was ready to be turned over to us. He also prepared potatoes for cooking and wood for heating. We also drew water from his well." Řiha asked nothing in return. "In fact, he would feel insulted when we began to mention this." When his son-in-law entertained Germans, Wowak and Shtibel had to return empty-handed.

Then something happened that again threatened the relative security of the people hidden in the community center. In 1944, as the Germans were retreating, some of their soldiers camped in the auditorium of the community center together with a unit of the renegade Russian general Andrei Vlasov, who had gone over to the German side and had created his own collaborationist army made up of Russian prisoners of war. To show their loyalty to their new masters, the Vlasov troops stood out for brutality toward the local population. Fortunately, for the hidden Jews, Vlasov's men left after a three days. The fugitives took advantage of this respite to restock basic necessities in case enemy soldiers returned. Řiha, of course, helped replenish them.

When, on this occasion, Simcha and Genia Shtibel arrived at the Řiha farm to get food they asked to be allowed to stay the night. Jozef agreed without even consulting his wife. The following morning, he told the two Shtibels that they could not return to the community center, since he had learned that Germans had again occupied the place. Then, suddenly, soldiers on horses arrived at Řiha's farm, bringing their horses into the barn, where the two Shtibels were hiding in the loft. The danger for Jozef Řiha could not have been greater. He had two Jews in his barn, this time without his wife's knowledge.

In the words of Simcha Shtibel, "It is difficult for us even today to describe the feelings and motives at work in this man at these moments." However, he did not panic, but devised a plan. "He invited the [German] officers indoor, and the soldiers he steered to another corner of the yard. He then got us out of the barn and led us under the windows where the officers were busy feeding themselves and took us through the house to his attic. It goes without saying that if discovered he could not have claimed that the people had stolen into his farmhouse without his knowledge."

When Yulya Řiha learned quite by accident that her husband was "stealing" cooked potatoes, meant to feed the pigs, for the Shtibels hiding under her roof in a house also hosting German officers, who were quartered downstairs, she had a nervous breakdown. At that point, the two Shtibels decided that they had caused enough trouble and grief to their benefactors and wanted to leave, come what may. Řiha stopped them from leaving. "I will not let you go anyplace; I will not allow this." In Simcha's words, "We were again privileged to discover – on one more of many occasions – the elevated humanitarianism of Mr. Řiha, that strengthened us in our belief in the existence of supreme values shared by every person … that even a most criminal and evil regime was not able to remove from the world." Eventually the German and collaborationist Vlasov troops retreated from the area, followed by the arrival of the Red Army. Everyone could once more breathe freely.

Jozef Řiha could now return to his farming chores and wait for the outcome of the war, which was still raging, as well as prepare himself to be repatriated with the rest of the Czech community to his native country, which his ancestors had left two centuries ago to seek a new life in the vast expanses of the Russian empire. His Jewish beneficiaries left for Israel, from where they kept in touch with their rescuer in his new home in Czechoslovakia. In 1966, Yad Vashem recognized Jozef Řiha as Righteous Among the Nations.

Rodziewicz, Wiktoria

POLAND

*S*arah Krynski was only 21 months old in September 1941 when her mother, Rachela, in the Vilna ghetto, entrusted her to the care of Wiktoria Rodziewicz. Sarah's father, Joseph Krynski, had been killed earlier with thousands of other Jews by the Nazis in the nearby Ponary forest killing grounds. Two months later, on November 18, Wiktoria and Sarah were betrayed to the Gestapo. During the interrogation, Wiktoria denied any knowledge of the child parents' whereabouts since, she insisted, they were already dead. Wiktoria was released and told to return the next day to continue the interrogation. Instead, she picked up a few things in her room and fled to a friend. The next day the Gestapo came to look for her, questioned her landlady, and sealed her room. Wiktoria got in touch with the child's mother and both agreed that it was best for all sides that the child be returned to its mother while Wiktoria left the city for a safer location. Rachela Krysnki promised that after the Gestapo had given up looking after Wiktoria, the child would be returned to her care. Sarah had then just passed her second birthday. Wiktoria fled to the village of Grauzyszki, some 80 kilometers from Vilna (today, Vilnius), where her brother and his family lived.

Three weeks later Wiktoria was back in Vilna, resolved to save little Sarah. This sudden move came about as a result of the revelation by a drunken Lithuanian policeman in the village that their next assignment would be an "Action" in Vilna – a killing operation to be carried out by the Lithuanian and Latvian police under the supervision of the Gestapo. On a cold December night, after the ghetto curfew, Rachela took Sarah to the ghetto gate. With the

Wiktoria Rodziewicz holding the child Sarah Krynski

help of the Jewish ghetto police chief, the Lithuanian guard had been bribed, and he allowed the mother and child through. Wiktoria and a friend then appeared out of the shadows of the courtyard of the nearby Church of All Saints pushing a baby carriage. Not a single word was uttered as Rachela put the two-year-old Sarah in the carriage, and the two other rescuers disappeared in the still of the night.

After the experience with the Gestapo, Wiktoria was afraid to return to the village without proof that the child was Aryan; also she couldn't stay in Vilna, where the Gestapo was still looking for her and kept her apartment under surveillance. She then went to see a priest, telling him that she had given birth to an illegitimate child two years ago and now wanted to baptize her daughter. This is how Sarah Krynska became Irena Rodziewicz. In the words of Rachela Krynski, "for a religious girl like Wiktoria to lie to a priest was a sin; to come to her native village where she had the best reputation with an illegitimate child was the greatest stigma." In the years that followed, Wiktoria never had peace of mind.

In Grauzyszki she stayed with her brother and sister-in-law, Antoni and Wladyslawa. To add credibility to her story, they even accused her in public of bringing a "bastard" into the world and sullying their good name. As the villagers often spoke ill of the Jews, whenever somebody started asking questions about the child and eyed Sarah with suspicion, Wiktoria would take off for another village and stay there for a while. To support herself and the child, Wiktoria sewed aprons and also cooked up hamburgers and sold them on market days. She kept the pieces of jewelry that Rachela had given her, so that Sarah would have some mementos from her parents if the mother did not survive.

In the summer of 1942, Wiktoria Rodziewicz had herself smuggled into the Vilna ghetto with a column of Jews returning from work and urged Rachela Krysnki to flee the ghetto with her, but Rachela declined so as not to increase the risks that Wiktoria was running. In December 1942, Wiktoria made another attempt; she was back in Vilna and, this time, had a close brush with disaster when she tried to enter the ghetto with a package of meat, which she intended to give to Rachela. A passing Lithuanian policeman saw her talking to the Jewish ghetto guard and arrested her for helping Jews. On the way to the police station Wiktoria tried to convince the policeman that she had no intention of helping the Jews; she only wanted to make extra money for Christmas and she heard the Jews pay very well. She pointed out to him that he had nothing to gain by taking her to the police station. With the scarcity of food in the city and the approaching Christmas holiday, he would be doing a favor to his family and to her if he took the meat and let her go. The policeman relented, took the meat, and happily went off.

In summer 1943, rumors were rampant that the ghetto would soon be liquidated. Rachela wanted to see Sarah "for what could have been the last time." She sent word to Wiktoria to come with Sarah if possible. Wiktoria knew where Rachela worked outside the ghetto and came with the child. Rachela was satisfied with her daughter's healthy appearance.

"Irena Rodziewicz [Sarah's new name] was a lively and very friendly little girl. She talked, walked and behaved like a real peasant child. Her hair was lighter than I remembered; Wiktoria bleached it so she would blend in with the other 'Aryan' children. Irena knew nothing about me, of course, or herself. The meeting lasted only 20 minutes because I was

scared and frightened to keep my visitors longer. For me the worst was yet to come, but I was sure that Sarah would survive, that she had all the love and devotion a child needs."

In Rachela's words, by keeping Sarah, Wiktoria also saved the mother's life, since during the liquidation of the Vilna ghetto in September 1943, all women with children were sent to Majdanek camp while the rest went to a less deadly place, relatively speaking – a labor camp in Latvia. Sarah was 5 years and 8 months old when Rachela saw her again in July 1945 after she luckily survived the depredations of the Stutthof concentration camp.

In Sarah's words, written many years later under the heading "The Woman Who Gave Me the Gift of Life," Wiktoria lived in constant fear in the event that one of the villagers would find out that she was hiding a Jewish infant.

"I remember our flights often in the middle of the night to some other village, where she felt we would be safer for the time. A child growing up in such circumstances might reasonably be expected to have suffered traumatic effects owing to these turbulent early experiences. Yet not only did Wiktoria save my life, which certainly would have been enough to ask of anyone, but she gave me so much love and yes, security as well, that I never felt the fear and danger that she faced daily. She hid these from me so well that I looked forward to our midnight flights as adventures and not as ordeals. Not only did she save my life but she gave me a life worth living. She never transferred her fears to me and I never suspected that my childhood was anything else but normal … My own character has been shaped by two women both of whom played the role of mother to me at different times. I am far richer for being the product of these two remarkable women: my mother Rachela Krynska and my nurse Wiktoria Rodziewicz."

In her testimony, Rachela Krynska praised Wiktoria's wisdom and good judgment; her resourcefulness and, above all, the courage she displayed "that are beyond description."

In 1977, Yad Vashem conferred on Wiktoria Rodziewicz the title of Righteous Among the Nations. In 1979, her brother Antoni and wife Wladyslawa Rodziewicz were also named Righteous Among the Nations.

Schindler, Oskar & Emilie

GERMANY

*O*n November 18, 1939, not long after the German *Blitzkrieg* that conquered Poland, a German civilian came to visit a friend, in occupied Kraków at a firm recently confiscated from a Jewish owner. Running into Itzhak Stern, a Jew working there as a bookkeeper, the German held out his hand. Stern was taken aback and quickly reminded the German, "I am a Jew," since under Nazi regulations it was forbidden for a German to shake hands with a Jew. "Nonsense," replied the German. "Why do you tell me this? Do you think I don't know myself? Why do you remind me that I am a German?" The man was Oskar Schindler, and from that moment an especially warm relationship evolved between the two, which was eventually to lead to an unprecedented giant rescue operation in which 1,200 Jewish lives were saved from the Nazi Holocaust by this German.

Oskar and Emilie Schindler

Born in 1908, in Zwittau (today Svitavy), Moravia, then part of the Austro-Hungarian Empire (after 1918 part of Czechoslovakia), Oskar Schindler had lived an uneventful life until he decided to work for German military intelligence, the *Abwehr,* and became a professional spy. Soon after the German occupation of Poland, in September 1939, Schindler appeared in Kraków, a city he knew well from before the war, to reap the dividends of his connection with the *Abwehr* by choosing an expropriated firm to his liking as a paid trustee of the occupation authorities. His choice fell on the Rekord enamel-producing company, which, on the eve of the war, had been undergoing bankruptcy proceedings. Deciding to purchase the firm rather than manage it as a paid trustee, he changed its name to DEF (*Deutscheemailfabrik*) to manufacture enamel products such as mess kits, kitchenware, and shell casings. Its location in the Zablocie section was close to the Jewish ghetto erected by the Nazis, facilitating Schindler's use of Jewish labor in ever-increasing numbers, and thus ensuring their survival.

When the Nazis commenced the liquidation of the Kraków ghetto in early 1943 by sending most of its inhabitants to the death camps, they transferred the remainder to the newly created Plaszów labor camp, noted for the brutality of its commander, Amon Göth. Schindler used his irresistible charm and manipulative skills with highly placed German officials in the Armaments Administration and other government agencies to allow him to set up a so-called branch of the Plaszów camp on his factory grounds for the ostensible purpose of increasing production. Schindler was not beyond bribing officials with expensive gifts, with all the risks involved in this dangerous game. In truth, the real purpose of the special barracks on his company's grounds was to protect his expanded 900-strong Jewish labor force from the horrors that awaited them when they returned to the notorious camp after a day's work in Schindler's factory.

Taking things a step further, in late 1943 Schindler traveled incognito to Budapest, still free from direct German occupation, to meet with Dr. Rudolf Kasztner of the Jewish Rescue Committee to report on the liquidation of Polish Jewry. On that occasion, he agreed to serve as a funnel for the distribution of money to Plaszów camp inmates and also arranged for pictures of the camp to be smuggled out to Hungary – both highly risky undertakings for Schindler. Itzhak Stern, himself a prisoner in Plaszów, remained his main confidante for events inside the camp – a man he often consulted on ways and means to alleviate the plight of Jews inside the camp and better the conditions of his workers in his own firm.

In many instances Schindler was able to get his way by putting to use his good connections with highly placed officials, aided by his jovial and good-natured disposition and matter-of-fact approach to the issues that concerned him. This stood him in good stead in extracting valuable favors, such as ameliorating conditions and mitigating punishments for offenses against Jews under his care. His genuine camaraderie, coupled with the judicious distribution of expensive gifts (liquor and jewelry as well as money) to the right people made it possible for him to save the large number of Jews under his care. These bribes landed him in jail on several occasions, as the Gestapo accused him of corruption, only to be released upon the intervention of his connections in Berlin chancelleries.

In October 1944, with the approach of the Russian army, Schindler was able to talk his way into getting permission to reestablish his now defunct enamel firm as an armaments-producing company in Brünnlitz (today Brenĕnec), Moravia, and take along some 1,100 Jewish workers from the Plaszów camp – to where many of his factory workers had been relocated – in an operation unequal in the annals of the rescue of Jews within Nazi-occupied Europe. Over 700 men were rerouted to the new location of Brünnlitz via the Gross-Rosen concentration camp, as well as some 300 women, after a harrowing several weeks-long stay in Auschwitz. In Brünnlitz, the Jews were given the most humane treatment possible under the circumstances (food, medical care, and religious needs).

Informed that a train with evacuated Jewish detainees from the Auschwitz-affiliated Golleschau camp was aimlessly stranded at nearby Zwittau, Schindler received permission to have them transferred to his newly established factory. His workers had to force open the iced-over car doors and remove some 100 frozen and emaciated Jewish men and women, who were then swiftly taken to his Brünnlitz factory and nursed back to life, an undertaking to which his wife, Emilie, lent herself with much devotion with her specially prepared porridge and medicine. A dozen or so of the corpses found in the train were buried with proper Jewish rites, led by Rabbi Menashe Lewartow, one of Schindler's workers, in a plot purchased by Oskar Schindler in a nearby Catholic cemetery.

In the words of Justice Moshe Bejski, one of Schindler's many beneficiaries, and years later chairman of the Yad Vashem Commission for the Designation of the Righteous: "He was the first German since the beginning of the war whose presence did not instill fear in me." This was in sharp contrast to most of the other German-appointed trustees and civilian carpetbaggers who supervised Jewish labor in Nazi-occupied Poland. "Not only were we not afraid of Schindler, but whenever he entered the plant [in Brünnlitz], everyone expected him to stop by. It so happened that whenever he stopped by, he always forgot a package of cigarettes, and in those days even a cigarette butt was of great value. Sometimes, at night, he was seen walking and whispering for hours on end with Itzhak Stern." During his first visit to Israel, in 1962, Schindler told Bejski: "What do you know about the lessons in Talmud I received from Stern?" And he added: "But do you know how every Talmudic elaboration ended? With another request for an additional half loaf of bread for everybody! He certainly could have told me point blank that he was talking about bread, and we could have saved time."

Schindler stayed on with his Jewish workers to the very end of the war, which came on May 8, 1945, supplying them with additional food, clothing, and even weapons in case they needed to defend themselves against marauding SS units. When news came of Germany's surrender, he had the following words read over a loudspeaker to his Jewish wards:

> *"You who worked with me from the very beginning and through all these years know how, after the liquidation of the [Kraków] ghetto, I had to intervene personally countless times, intercede on your behalf with the camp administration, or go to great lengths to bring about the cancellation of orders that had already been issued … I always strove to show humanity and to protect [you], to act humanely — which was the primary concern in all my decisions … I took every possible action, spared no effort, to secure extra food for you … I conclude by asking you for three minutes of silence to commemorate the countless victims from among you who perished in this cruel enterprise.*

He ended his words with a request "for three minutes of silence to commemorate the countless victims from among you who perished in this cruel enterprise." These were his parting words.

What is remarkable in the Schindler story is that a man who, by his own admission, arrived in Poland merely to enrich himself, hoping to exploit the vast reservoir of cheap Jewish labor available under German rule to extract quick profits; a man who at first impressed the Jews who met him in Kraków in 1939 as no different from many of the other German civilian carpetbaggers in the occupied country — then underwent such a tremendous transformation to become the single biggest German rescuer of Jews; constantly risking his life and freedom for the sake of "his" Jews. Previously noted for his pur-

Oskar Schindler (second from left) and a group of his Polish and Jewish employees in Kraków (1940)

suit of pleasure and material gain with very little thought of the needs of others, he ended the war penniless and looked after by his former Jewish charges.

In the words of Justice Bejski, during the testimonial in Schindler's honor in 1962:

My dear friends, each one of us can conjure memories and innumerable stories, and still we shall not encompass all that should be said about this man Schindler, about his deeds and his attitude towards us. But from all things, always the humanitarian in him stands out. He made an indelible mark not only because of a single rescue operation, but for his constant fatherly attitude and self-sacrifice, which are indescribable; he passed a test which has no equal. And he stayed with us to the very end.

Itzhak Stern recalled that he "never encountered any reservations from Schindler to any plan of action I suggested, not even to the most dangerous one. He was ready for anything. He never said no. I cannot grasp this to this day." In a ceremony in Schindler's honor, Stern ended his tribute with the following words: "My brothers, in the Hebrew language there are definitions of three stages: a man, a person, and a human being. I think there should be an additional one: a 'Schindler.'"

Schindler admitted that he arrived in Poland on the coattails of the German army, not to save anyone, but to make money. "But I happened to meet Jews… I always had Jewish friends," and slowly his set of priorities changed – from only making money and enjoying the pleasures of life, to saving Jews while continuing to make money, and finally saving Jews, even if it meant spending all the money amassed by him. In 1944, when the authorities closed his plant in Kraków, he could have taken the easy way out, and leave with his fortune either back to Germany, or escape to a neutral country. As he frankly admitted, during the testimonial in his honor, in 1962, "It was not hard for me to escape with my fortune, but I stayed with you until the end." Then, when the end came, "I was left with much less than I had possessed before. I kept my promise."

Perhaps the clue to this metamorphosis is his profound horror at the immensity of the Final Solution, to the brutality of which he was a constant witness, and the effect this had on his thinking and behavior. In his words: "I hated the brutality, the sadism and the insanity of Nazism. I just couldn't stand by and see people destroyed. I did what I could, what I had to do, what my conscience told me I must do. That's all there is to it. Really, nothing more." The man's true character and his motives are still a mystery to his many beneficiaries – the 1,200 Jews who owe their lives to this singular person.

After the war, his Jewish wards did not forget their rescuer, and in the following years they exerted themselves to help him out whenever he was in financial straits – right up to his death in 1974. Before that, in 1962, Schindler planted a tree in his name in the Avenue of the Righteous at Yad Vashem (his wife Emilie was later also added to the Righteous roster). When he died, as previously requested by him, his body was brought to Jerusalem for burial in the Latin cemetery on Mount Zion, a stone's throw from the traditional burial site of King David. In 1993, his beneficiaries gathered at his tomb for a final shot in Steven Spielberg's monumental film *Schindler's List*, which told the story of this one German; of a man, with some questionable personal traits, but with a passionate heart – large enough to encompass and embrace 1,200 living souls, in defiance of all dangers and risks to himself.

Schivo, Beniamino

ITALY

*I*n 1935, Paul and Johanna Korn and their ten-year-old daughter, Ursula, fled from Nazi Germany to Italy. Although a Fascist state, Italy still refrained from any open anti-Jewish measures and thus seemed a temporary safe haven for fleeing Jews. By the time Italy joined the war, in June 1940, on the side of Nazi Germany, it had already begun to restrict severely Jewish civil rights in the country. As for the Korns, they were taken from their home in Alassio and kept interned, Paul in Salerno and Johanna with daughter Ursula in Collazzone, Umbria province. There a local priest befriended the two women. In 1941, as the three Korns were to be moved to Città di Castello, the priest told them to look up a friend of his by the name of Beniamino Schivo, who was at the time the rector of a religious seminary.

After meeting them, Father Beniamino decided to take the Korn family under his protective wing; in Ursula's words, he was "our one and only best friend." The 31-year-old cleric placed 16-year-old Ursula in a convent so that she could continue her schooling, otherwise not permitted by law for Jews. He also provided her parents with extra food to supplement the meager nourishment at their disposal. In the meantime, no further danger threatened the Korns, as the Italian regime stopped short of handing over Jews to their allies, the Germans, for deportation to concentration camps. Italy adamantly turned down German requests in that regard.

Events, however, changed tragically for the Jews in Italy on September 8, 1943, when the Germans invaded the country and prepared to implement the Final Solution there. "Our worst moment came," Ursula recalled, "when all of Italy was taken over by the Germans and they persecuted us interned Jews with a vengeance, and many were deported to the death camps." A week after the German occupation, the Korns escaped from their internment in Città di Castello with the active help of Father Schivo. Removing his habit, Schivo and another priest took the three Korns on an eight-hour night march around German patrols and up into the hills to a summer villa belonging to the Salesian nuns. There the two clerics forced open a door and hid the Korns for a full month in a dark cell, with the Korns having to sleep on the bare floor. Schivo also told the building caretaker to feed the fugitives, and he furtively brought them soup every day at midnight.

When danger threatened the hidden Korns there, Father Schivo moved them to different locations, in the surrounding woods and in the dark corners of a convent, where on Christmas Eve 1943 Schivo came to bring them something to eat. "He had walked for nine hours in the hills avoiding German patrols, without his priestly robe, so that he could bring us some comfort, and he stayed with us until dawn."

As Allied troops moved closer they began to bomb the area where the Korns were hiding. It was then decided to move them out to safer places. Paul Korn was taken by a friendly priest high up in the mountains; his wife, Johanna, and daughter, Ursula, were placed in an area controlled by Italian partisans – always under the watchful eye of Schivo, who supervised all his wards' moves through a group of partisans. When the Korns ran out of strength, Schivo took in them in the middle of the night back to Città di Castello, where he hid them in the Convent of the Sacred Heart. The Korns were dressed as nuns and locked in a room, and only the Mother Superior knew the truth about them. When alarming news came that the Germans were going to break into the convent looking for partisans, Father Schivo moved the Korns to his seminary, where he hid them in a locked upstairs room and personally brought them food every night.

By then, fighting between the British and the Germans had spread to the town's streets. Father Schivo was himself in danger, as the Germans had learned of his association with the partisans and his help to escaped internees, and a warrant was out for his arrest. In Ursula's words, "Thank God, on July 14 [1944], the British 8th Army moved in – we were liberated, and Father Schivo was safe." Before parting, Schivo returned to the Korns all their personal papers and other documents that he had buried in the garden of the seminary. The Korns and the kindhearted priest, who eventually donned a bishop's mantle, maintained contact in the coming years. In the words of Ursula Selig-Korn:

> "I have never met a more wonderful man in my entire life; he is humble, and does not think for a moment that he did anything great by saving us. He helps all who suffer and are persecuted, and will do it over and over again … He is the kindest man I have ever met in my life …My friendship with Monsignor Schivo is a lasting one; as long as I live, he is my best friend; we speak often over the phone. When in Italy, I visit him."

Responding to Mrs. Selig-Korn's request, in 1985, Yad Vashem conferred on Monsignor Beniamino Schivo the title of Righteous Among the Nations.

Schmid, Anton
AUSTRIA

*I*n the winter of 1941, at a time of continuous German killing raids on the Jews of Vilna (today Vilnius, capital of Lithuania), a rumor began to make the rounds of the Vilna ghetto of a strange German army sergeant who was helping Jews to the extent of sheltering them in his home outside the ghetto. It was too good to be true. People began to ask who was this Sergeant Anton Schmid who in contrast to his fellow soldiers, instead of participating in the killings tried to save as many as any one person could?

This story takes place during the most tragic phase of Jewish history in Vilna, one of the oldest Jewish communities in Eastern Europe. It is told that when Napoleon marched through Vilna, during his invasion of Russia in 1812, he was so impressed with Jewish life there that he coined the term "The Jerusalem of Lithuania." It was a city that produced great Jewish scholars in many fields, religious and secular. When the Germans occupied it on June 24, 1941, there were some 57,000 Jews living there. Immediately, all hell broke loose on the streets, as Jews were seized and murdered and homes looted. The following week, on July 4, 1941, German SS units and Lithuanian militia carried out a mass execution of the city's Jews in the nearby Ponary woods – shooting them at the rate of 100 an hour next to open pits. By July 20, 5,000 Jews had been murdered, with 8,000 suffering similar martyrdom in the following month. Some 40,000 Jews were then locked into a ghetto and the remaining 4,000 Jews also done away with in the Ponary woods. The killing continued in the following months and years, with the ghetto slowly but surely being emptied of its inhabitants. Some fortunate people, such as handymen and blue-collar workers, were spared together with their families – for the time being. Roundups and executions continued unabated. By the end of 1941, 34,000 Jews had been murdered, and by September 1943 only 12,000 Jews remained. They too were executed, with smaller groups sent to other concentration camps; others managed to make their way to the forests and fight the Germans as partisans. Of the 57,000 Jews present when the Germans arrived in June 1941, there were only between 2,000 and 3,000 survivors (in hiding or in the forests) to be found when Vilna was liberated by the Red Army on July 13, 1944. The centuries-old "Jerusalem of Lithuania" of Napoleon had come to a sorry end, in an unprecedented orgy of murder staged by the Germans and their Lithuanian associates. This was the place where that strange German soldier Anton Schmid tried to save as many Jews as he could.

Sergeant Schmidt was born in 1900 in Vienna. He always made it a point to say that he was not a German but an Austrian, but during the days of the Third Reich this mattered little, as the Austrian Germans were part of Nazi Germany and many Austrians were in the upper echelons of the SS and the Gestapo. Before being mobilized, he operated a radio equipment business. He was married and the father of a daughter.

Drafted as a German soldier, the 41-year-old Schmid was stationed in Vilna and responsible for a unit whose job it was to deal with German soldiers returning from leave and needing to be reassigned to new units due to the exigencies of the war. His unit was aptly called the "Straggler Assembly Point" (*Versprengten-Sammelstelle*) and was assigned three buildings to house soldiers until their reassignment, as well as a Jewish labor force of up to 300 people from the Vilna ghetto. In the basements of these buildings, located near the main railroad station, the men worked at various assignments, such as metalwork, upholstery, shoe repairs, and tailoring.

Dr. Mark Dworczecki, who met Schmid in the Vilna ghetto, describes him as sort of "folk hero … the antithesis of the Germans and Austrians whom we saw in the ghetto, all blindly obedient to Hitler. In the ghetto, he became a legend and a source of strength." His legendary feats included freeing people jailed in the notorious Łukiszki prison, which served as a way station to the killing site in the Ponary woods, on the pretext that he needed them for army-related work. He had a van at his disposal and generally enjoyed greater freedom than usual for men of his rank in the German army, due largely to the special tasks assigned to him.

His main contact for people inside the ghetto was Hermann Adler, whose wife, Anita, had formerly been married to a man known by Schmid. Anita Adler accidentally met Schmid in Vilna and pleaded with him to get her husband released from the Łukiszki prison. Schmid obliged, using his influence to get Adler out of jail; then invited the couple to stay in a hideout that he prepared in his office. Hermann Adler, who was also associated with a clandestine Zionist organization, arranged for Schmid to meet Mordecai Tenenbaum-Tamarrof, head of a Zionist youth organization known as the Hehalutz-Hatza'ir–Dror group, and a friendship developed between them.

At first, the two discussed ways of getting Jews out of the country on boats to Sweden, but nothing came of it. They then planned even greater exploits that went beyond sheltering Jewish activists in Schmid's home, actually helping them maintain contact with clandestine groups in distant ghettos. After meeting Schmid on several occasions, Tenenbaum described him as a sworn anti-Nazi and openly sympathetic to the Zionist cause; a joyful and friendly person by nature, cordial, and with a kind of childlike charm, who took pleasure in helping Jews outsmart their persecutors. Some of Tenenbaum's underground operatives met, planned activities, and slept over in Schmid's house.

His exploits included spiriting Jews out of the ghetto and taking them in his military van to various locations – in the number of 300 such escapees (some taking this to mean actually 300 families) – sheltering his workers in the three buildings under his supervision during SS killing raids inside the ghetto, and warning ghetto Jews through his workers of similar Nazi-style "actions" in the offing. In October 1941, when the Germans decided on the distribution of 3,000 yellow-colored permits to blue collar specialists, which meant that these people and their families (wife and two children only) were guaranteed not to be harmed, Schmid tried to get as many such yellow permits for his Jewish workers as possible. Shlomo Bernovsky, one of his locksmiths, related that Schmid once told his Jewish laborers not to be fooled by their yellow permits. "The yellow and white permits, they're both the same garbage. Anyway all the Jews will be murdered."

At the same time, the yellow permit was a life safer. Those of his workers who did not get such a permit Schmid tried to get out of Vilna, and move in his van to Lida, in Belarus, which was then under a different and, for the time being, a slightly more lenient German command than in Vilna. In Lida the situation was not so bad, or so the rumor went, since there was as yet no ghetto and no "actions." Several times a week, when Schmid was out in his van collecting wood for fuel in the surrounding forest for his three apartment houses used by German soldiers, he would take several Jews with him, and after loading the necessary wood would continue in the direction of Lida, where he would drop off his Jewish charges. Others he took to Bialystok, in German-occupied Poland, where Jews were working in the many factories that supplied military equipment to the army. Work at the time was considered a life saver. This proved true only in the short run.

Schmid took tremendous risks in using military vehicles belonging to his army unit to transport Jews to these places and putting signs on them saying that they were carrying explosives in order to discourage searches by the border guards and soldiers at the roadblocks. At the beginning, five or six Jews were transported in each truck. Later the number rose to 20–30 Jews per "delivery."

Then in December 1941 Schmid told Tenenbaum that he was prepared to transport some of the Jewish activists in his van all the way to Warsaw, disguised as regular Poles, so that they could report to their clandestine colleagues in the ghetto there of the terrible events taking place in the Ponary forest and warn the over 400,000 Jewish residents of Warsaw not be fooled by German promises but to make preparations for armed rebellion when the time came, as it certainly would. Schmid made similar trips to Bialystok, dropping off Tenenbaum and a dozen of his colleagues, who began to organize a clandestine militant group in the ghetto. Tenenbaum eventually returned to Bialystok and lost his life in a gun battle with the Germans during the liquidation of the Bialystok ghetto in the summer of 1942.

Before that, on several occasions Tenenbaum cautioned Schmid that his exploits were known to too many people in the ghetto, and this did not bode well for Schmid's safety. On New Year's Eve, December 31, 1941, Schmid hosted a party in his apartment attended by Tenenbaum and other Jewish underground leaders. On this festive occasion, Schmid gave vent to his abhorrence of Nazism and everything it stood for. Tenenbaum responded that after the war, in the independent Jewish state that was hopefully to arise, Schmid's name would surely be honored for his rescue of Jews. To this Schmid replied that he would wear this honor with pride.

Then, as suddenly as he appeared on the scene, he disappeared. To this day, no one knows for certain what it was that led to his arrest and execution. A rumor in the Vilna ghetto spoke of Schmid's being arrested in the second half of January 1942, apparently after the Germans discovered Jews from Vilna who had suddenly appeared in the Lida ghetto, and after an intensive investigation as to who had made this possible, the finger was pointed at Anton Schmid. He was arrested and imprisoned, then court-martialed and found guilty of high treason and executed on April 2, 1942. Considered a disgrace to his country, his body was refused interment in Vienna, where his wife lived, so as not to be buried on German soil, but rather in a local Vilna cemetery.

In his last letter to his wife from his prison cell, Anton Schmid wrote among others things, "I have come to terms with my fate; it has been so decreed by our dear God, and this cannot be altered. I am today so calm as to find it difficult to believe. God has so willed it and this has made me strong. You know me with my soft heart. I only acted as a human being and desired doing harm to no one."

Back in Vienna, his widow suffered abuse from her neighbors at her husband's "treachery" to the Nazi cause. Some of them broke the windows of her house and burned some of her possessions, including her husband's letters. Only very recently has the Vienna municipality undergone a change of heart, and a street was named for Anton Schmid – a lone German sergeant who tried to impede the giant killing machine his country had become, and paid the ultimate price for his bravery. The many hundreds he saved continue to cherish his memory.

In 1964, Yad Vashem recognized Anton Schmid as Righteous Among the Nations.

Schroedter, Hedwig & Otto
GERMANY

*K*urt Reich married Ursula in the worst possible of times. For the modest-style wedding took place on May 22, 1942, in Berlin – at the height of the Holocaust there. His father had died the previous year and Ursula's widowed mother, Klara, was deported to Latvia three months later and murdered there. "All our other relatives were also picked up and deported in 1942," Kurt sadly recalled. Before his marriage, Kurt had been forced by the Nazis to do menial work, such as cleaning up at an old age home, road construction, and garbage disposal. Then, on December 14, 1942, a daughter was born to the couple in the apartment they shared with Kurt's mother and his younger brother, Ismar. The daughter was named Monica. With the Germans deporting trainloads of Jews to their death, it was the most unpropitious time to bring a Jewish child into the world. How was the infant girl to be saved?

Two weeks after their daughter's birth, Kurt and Ursula went underground to save themselves and their child. This was the start of a painful and deadly game of hide-and-seek with the Gestapo, with their little girl hidden for short periods of time with various kindhearted people. As for themselves, the Reichs also moved from place to place, having to switch locations as many as ten times to be a step ahead of their persecutors. On one such occasion, walking back to their hiding place in the company of a friendly non-Jewish German woman named Frida Bredlow, the three were stopped by the military police – two men who asked to see their identity papers. When one of the Germans started questioning another man in a wheelchair, Mrs. Bredlow managed to keep the other one from questioning Kurt, who could not produce an identity card (*Ausweis*), saying that he and his wife were relatives whom she had invited for a cup of coffee. The Germans detained the man in the wheelchair but waved the other three through.

Another close call occurred at the empty basement apartment of a brother of one of the women who was keeping little Monica. In Kurt's words, "We lived there for two days, when we suddenly heard loud knocking on the door. Two tall SS man in their black uniforms asked us if they could check the walls in the cellar apartment to see if they could be broken through to the next building as a possible escape route in case the building was hit in a bombing raid. We naturally allowed them to check." The SS men were in a hurry and did not bother to check the identity papers of Kurt and Ursula – the incriminating ones with the big "J" for "Jew" stamped in red.

Finally, in September 1943, the Reichs had run out of hiding places. In total despair, "we had no choice but to give ourselves up to the Nazis, but wanted at least a safe place for our child." Frantically searching for some outlet, they recalled someone's telling them that the Schroedters, who resided in a one-family house on Hohenschonhausen Strasse, had once said that they would like to save people hunted by the Nazis. So Ursula went with little Monica to these unknown people to find out if this was indeed true. She was pleasantly surprised when the Schroedters agreed, without much ado, to take in the little girl, promising to return her to Ursula if she survived the war.

It seemed, to all intents and purposes, that Ursula had achieved her principal aim and was about to leave. As she bid a tearful goodbye to her child, she suddenly heard Mrs. Hedwig Schroedter say that there was a youth bed in the house, just in case she also wanted to stay there. Ursula timidly asked whether she could bring along her husband to sleep there, perhaps on the chair near the bed, asking gently whether any payment was involved for the Schroedters' generosity. As Ursula later told her husband, the Schroedters were quite incensed by this suggestion. "If we would never offer money again, we could all stay," was their response. Ursula was beside herself with delight, unable at first to believe that these strangers were offering all three of her family shelter for an indefinite period – in Berlin, of all places, the center of Nazi power. "And so began the most important nineteen months in our three lives at the Schroedters one-family house," Kurt continued. "They even fed our child at their dinner table many days. We lived there with short interruptions from September 1943 till the end of April 1945, when we were liberated by Russian troops." Otto and Hedwig Schroedter kept a sheep, goat, rabbits, and chickens, and grew many vegetables in their garden.

Not yet fully satisfied with having just three persons added to their household, in December 1943 the Schroedters' took in another Jewish family on the run, Robert and Eva Sachs and her 63-year-old mother, Johanna Hirsch. There were now six Jewish fugitives in hiding in the Schroedter home.

A problem arose in February 1944 when the Schroedter's only child, Herbert, aged 19, a soldier serving in the German army on the Russian front, came home on leave. His parents were not sure of his political sentiments – had he become a Nazi while under fire? It was best not to take any chances and have the Jews moved out of the house until the son's leave was over – and so it was decided. However, to everyone's surprise, Herbert showed up a day ahead of schedule and found his house occupied mostly by Jewish fugitives. When he was told their story, he insisted that they stay. As told by Kurt, "He would not allow us to leave our safe haven on his account. He insisted that we stay. He knew the risk, and did not mind sleeping uncomfortably in his own home. A righteous son of more than righteous parents who risked their lives daily by defying the Nazis and hiding six Jews." The Schroedters, it is told, also invited forced laborers to come and listen to the forbidden BBC radio station beaming news of the war from England in many languages. Kurt Reich testified to this fact, although without explaining how the Schroedters were able to make contact with these forced laborers and invite them to their home.

Another problem arose when the elderly Johanna Hirsch suddenly died in April 1944 and the body had to be disposed of. Calling in a doctor to write out a death certificate was out of the question in light of the departed woman's illegal presence, let alone the existence of the other Jewish people in the Schroedter home. It was decided to have her secretly buried in the yard. She was placed on an ironing board and wrapped in tarpaper. In the dead of night, Otto Schroedter and Kurt Reich dug a grave in the back yard. As Kurt recalled it, "Taking down the body on the stairs gave me a particularly terrible feeling, as her feet pushed into my back."

After this problem was solved, there arose yet another one, in the form of a threatening letter by an informer. One day the Schroedters received a postcard with no return address saying: "Clean your eyes from foreign objects or you run the risk of going blind." This threat had to be taken seriously before the Gestapo came pounding on their door, so the Jewish wards were moved out for a few days to take temporary shelter with friends of the Schroedters, until they felt the danger had passed. Thus, with the gracious aid of their German benefactors, the five Jewish fugitives survived the war and the Holocaust unharmed.

Writing of their rescue almost 50 years later, Kurt and Ursula stated,

"They not only gave us refuge free, but tried too keep our spirits up and our hopes alive … They also fed our baby from the garden and their ration card; and the goat milk and apples from the garden gave our child a healthy look. In the 20 months of hiding in their home, the Schroedters never lost their patience with us or the other family Robert & Eva Sachs and their mother."

Moving to the United States after the war, Kurt and Ursula Reich maintained contact with the Schroedters. As for themselves, they brought into the world two more daughters. Their eldest daughter, Monica, the little baby who, totally unaware, was the immediate cause of her parents' meeting with the Schroedters, is married and the mother of two children.

In 1993, Yad Vashem conferred the title of Righteous Among the Nations on Otto and Hedwig Schroedter.

Seduls, Roberts & Johanna
Latvia

*V*isitors at Yad Vashem gaze in horror at the photograph of a group of Jews of all ages, male and female, standing on a sand dune waiting for a Nazi-led firing squad to end their lives, their backs to a ravine where they are to fall and be covered with sand. The place is Liepaja, a Baltic seaport in Latvia, known for its beauty and peaceful commercial life – until the dreaded arrival of the German army on June 22, 1941, at the start of the German-Soviet war. Right away, the killings began, with executions taking place every day and over 1,000 Jews led to the seashore and shot. By the end of the year, another 3,000 Jews had been murdered – reducing the Jewish population to less than half its former number. The rest were herded into a ghetto, and this too was liquidated in October 1943, with the remaining Jews deported to other concentration camps. Local Latvian militiamen and auxiliary police assisted the Germans in their murderous orgy. When Liepaja was liberated on May 9, 1945, there were to be found there only 30 Jews from the over 7,000 originally there. Eleven of these lucky survivors were saved by one Latvian individual – Roberts Seduls. One of his wards, David Zivtson, before going into hiding had taken advantage of working for the Germans to secretly have copies made of photos taken by the SS of the killings on the seashore, and hiding them in the ground in sealed cans. These were recovered after the war and have since been widely displayed in museums and books.

Roberts Seduls, a former seaman and boxer, was the janitor of the building where he lived with his wife Johanna and two daughters. A cellar served as storehouse for coal and heating equipment. When the killings began in Liepaja, Roberts and his wife, Johanna, decided to make an effort to save their pre-war friend David Zivtson and his family, who had once lived

Roberts Seduls, in the hiding place, with some of his rescuees (courtesy of Ada Israeli-Zivcon)

in the same building as the Seduls. Zivtson had saved himself from the recurrent killings by serving the Germans as an electrician. Roberts managed to enter the ghetto and contact David on the on the pretext, as a locksmith, of having to repair a broken lock. On October 7, 1943, on the eve of the ghetto's final liquidation, David fled the ghetto together with his wife, Henny, and took along another couple, Mikhoel and Hilda Skutelski, apparently without warning Seduls about the two additional people. The four stealthily made their way to the Seduls home. The Seduls were surprised to see the two other people but nevertheless agreed to hide the four. Roberts had prepared a hiding place in the cellar, the entrance to which was through a hole in the wall beneath a table, camouflaged with all kinds of tools. Another entrance was through the bakery in the courtyard above ground. Seduls made sure that his wards enjoyed whatever comforts could be arranged; such as water, electricity, and gas for cooking, drawn from pipes used by the bakery. The four fugitives built two double-decker bunks, where they slept. The hiding place, which lay obliquely beneath the bakery, also used by the Germans, solved the problem of bread, cautiously stolen by Seduls for use by his wards.

In the meantime, the Germans declared Liepaja *judenrein* (purified of Jews), but in fact they kept a small groups of Jews for specialized assignments, such as electricians, shoemakers, and – most important for the Germans – silversmiths, who were told to make assorted items of jewelry from what was taken off the dead bodies, for use by SS men as gifts to their families for the coming Christmas celebration. Earlier, Misha Libauer, one of these jewelers, had been told by his friend Zivtson of Seduls hiding place, so when it seemed that the SS no longer needed them, and they were thus in danger of being shot, Libauer and two of his friends, Josif Mandelshtam and Shmerl Skutelski, made a daring escape and arrived at Seduls' home, where they were welcomed. There were now seven people in Seduls' hiding place under his floor. To help out with the additional costs of feeding them in addition to Seduls' own family, the Jews took to repairing electrical appliances that Roberts brought them from various customers after advertising himself as a former electrician who was looking for additional income in these difficult wartime days.

Taking courage and gaining confidence with the seven persons under his care, Roberts thought of adding still more fugitive Jews. Making contact with Kalman Linkimer, who was part of a work detail kept by the Germans for clean-up assignments in a military base some 30 kilometers from Liepaja, he invited him to hide at his home. At first, Linkimer suspected a trap, but when it became clear that the Jews on his work detail would soon be liquidated, he decided to give it a try, taking along two friends – Zelig Hirshberg and Aharon Vesterman. The three arrived in Seduls' home on April 28, 1944. A week later, Seduls admitted an additional person – Riva, a relative of David Zivtson, who had fled from the Riga ghetto. Riva came along with her four-year-old child, Ada. For the sake of the others, as well as the little girl, Seduls arranged for her to be hidden elsewhere, by Otilija Schimelpfenig, a Latvian woman of German extraction known to Seduls and considered trustworthy.[1] To assure the mother of the child's well-being, Seduls made it a point to visit the child, and take photos of her, showing her well disposed and in good spirits. There were now eleven people in Seduls' hideout, all of whom survived until the war's bitter end, which came on May 9, 1945, the day Soviet troops entered Liepaja. While the rest of Latvia had already been liberated much earlier by the Russians, Liepaja and the surrounding area, known in military accounts as Courland, where German divisions were encircled and trapped, held out until literally the end of the war. To be prepared in the event that the hiding place was discovered, Seduls had also managed to get revolvers for the hidden Jews, who were resolved to go down fighting if it should ever come to that, as well as a radio for clandestine war bulletins from transmitters in countries at war with Germany.

Danger also threatened from the direction of the bakery, located in the courtyard, which was subjected to German searches on the suspicion that the bakers were skimming for themselves more of the bakery's goods than was permissible – at the expense of the German troops. To distract sniffing German hound dogs from the presence of the hiders, they spread gasoline and garlic around the hiding place, and it worked. The eleven survivors (some of whom remained hidden without seeing daylight for 500 days) were among the 30 Jews found in Liepaja on that day – less than one percent of the original Jewish population. They had also kept with them a diary of the hiding period, written mainly by Kalman Linkimer, supplemented with photos of the hiders, taken "live" by David Zivtson during their stay in Seduls' cellar, and developed immediately after the war.

In October 1944, Seduls was summoned for military service in a Latvian unit fighting alongside the Germans. Fearing for the welfare of his wards, he thought of ways to avoid

Roberts Seduls's hiding place, where he sheltered several Jewish people (courtesy of Ada Israeli-Zivcon)

being conscripted. A prewar wound in his leg had by now healed, so Seduls asked his friend Zivtson to spread vinegar acid on the wound, which caused it to reopen, thanks to which, he was exempted from military service. But then, in a tragic twist of fate, Roberts Seduls' life ended suddenly. On March 10, 1945, when stepping out of his house, he was struck by a Soviet shell. The job of caring for the eleven hidden persons was taken over by his wife, Johanna, and her two children. Also lending a helping hand was another woman – Roberts' mistress. It seemed that the two women agreed to lay aside their mutual animosity and try to get along for the sake of the Jews. After the war, this second woman in Roberts' life married one of the hidden Jews.

In 1981, Yad Vashem conferred on Roberts and Johanna Seduls the title of Righteous Among the Nations.

Semeniuk, Domna & Nadezhda
UKRAINE

At the start of the German occupation in June 1941 Anna Hurwitz lived in Dubno, in the Volyn region of Ukraine, where she worked as a nurse, her husband worked in a printing house; and their two children, a son and daughter, were at school. Then, during the Nazi action of May 27, 1942, Anna lost her 15-year-old son and the rest of her family, which included her mother-in-law, her husband's sister and brother, their spouses and children.

Anna and her 15-year-old niece, Frieda Goldberg, managed to survive and were sent to the nearby village of Studinka, where they joined other Jews working in peat bogs under the severe and brutal watch of Ukrainian militiamen. This period of relative respite lasted for several months. Around them, all other Jews had already been killed off. From those who had fled and joined the labor group, Anna and Frieda learned that one after another Jewish settlement had been systematically wiped out. "Our turn would surely come," Frieda feared. Her aunt Anna began to explore the possibility of hiding among farmers whom, as a nurse, she had earlier cared for. She found a forester who was willing to hide the two women in return for money. They felt relieved.

Anna and Frieda left the labor camp in Studinka at night and went to the forester's place. He took them to a cave at the entrance to the forest near his home. Two days after the two women left Studinka, they learned that the labor camp had been liquidated and the Jewish workers taken away to be shot. A few managed to escape but were hunted down in the forest, and only a handful survived.

The two women stayed in the cave for three weeks. The wife of the forester would bring them some food and water at night, under the cover of darkness. She also told them of the final liquidation of the Dubno ghetto on October 5, 1942. The nights in the forest were turning cold, but Anna and Frieda felt secure and safe not having to contend with strangers, who might be hostile to them.

After three weeks, the forester's wife came on her evening rounds with some food and also told them that they had better leave their hiding place in the cave and move deeper in the forest, as far away as possible from her home. The reason for this? One evening her husband, the forester, had had too much to drink and in a jovial mood told his fellow drinkers of a Jewish woman and her "daughter" who were hiding near his home. "Until today," Frieda is not sure, "if this was the real truth or simply an excuse to be rid of us." At any rate it was better to leave immediately.

For the next few days, the forester's wife still came out to the two women in their new makeshift hideout bringing them a little food; then she stopped coming. In the next few days Anna and Frieda kept themselves going by sucking sugar cubes they had brought along. That week, the first snow fell, and the two almost froze. They decided not to move out, for fear of leaving traces in the snow, but rather wait for the snow to melt before heading else-where. Left to themselves, they were afraid they would starve to death in the forest, as they already had gone three days without food. With no alternative, they decided to return to Studinka, whose inhabitants were known for their antisemitism, and seek out a home that Anna Hurwitz had visited in her rounds as a nurse.

Then something happened that might have proved fatal for the two. A day before their planned departure from the forest, they suddenly heard approaching sounds. "We thought that the woman had changed her mind, took compassion on us and was bringing us some food." Instead, they saw from afar a farmer wielding a frightening axe as he made his way through the thick trees. "It was clear that he was looking for us to kill us." It also dawned on them that either he had been sent by the forester, or that his wife had really told the truth about her husband's spilling the beans while under the influence, and someone else had come out to kill the two women.

Whatever the truth, it was better not to take chances, and to move out. Anna and Frieda quietly distanced themselves from the place, and for a while walked aimlessly in the for-est, finally reaching a clearing where the fields of Studinka became visible to them. Anna remembered the Semeniuk family, and the father Ivan, who had been down with bronchitis and whom she had treated, and she decided to approach the family at nightfall and ask for shelter, even a one night sleepover. Perhaps remembering Anna's dedicated care, the fam-ily would take pity on the exhausted women and allow them in. In Frieda's words, "If not, then let what has happened to other Jews happen to us." They were at the last ounce of their exhausted strength.

The house was located at the far end of the village. When it turned dark, the two women went toward it. Ironically, they found their way there with the help of the Semeniuk dog barking at them, louder and louder with each step. They had to be careful not to err in the total darkness of the hamlet and knock on the door of another family. The village of Studi-nka was notorious for its deep-seated hatred of the Jews, and many of its sons had enlisted in the Ukrainian militia, which stood shoulder to shoulder with the Germans as they wiped out the Jewish population of the region.

When Domna Semeniuk, the woman of the house, heard the wild barking of the dog, she stepped outside to investigate. Perhaps she thought the dog was barking at thieves coming to steal some poultry from the chicken coop. As she walked around the house, she suddenly beheld the two women in a crouching position, and almost fainted. Frieda: "We said nothing, but waited for her reaction."

At first, Mrs. Semeniuk seemed to hesitate, but then she told them to enter the nearby barn, for she had a woman guest at home. She added that when her guest had left, the two fugitive women could come in, and then she would decide what to do next. That evening, Anna and Frieda had a full meal after a month on a starvation diet. They were then told to stay over in the barn, where a place was prepared for them in the loft. They slept on hay spread over the bare ground and covered themselves with blankets. For the moment, they were safe.

As for the Semeniuk home, it was one of the poorest in the village. It had no floor but the bare ground and the roof was covered with thatched hay. The interior consisted of one big room divided into several sections with a big oven for baking bread, beds, a table, two benches, and a large chest for storing clothes. There were five children in the family, aged five to sixteen: four girls – Elena, Nadezhda, Viera, and Mina, and a son, Vasili.

In light of the great danger to the family in case of detection, Domna Semeniuk decided on extreme precautionary measures for her family. The children were told to keep quiet about the Jewish women's presence; otherwise, she told them, they faced the danger of being killed. They understood. As for Anna and Frieda, they were told not to move from their place in the loft, for their own security, and to come down only in the evening to join the Semeniuk's in their poor home, where they would be fed and could spend some time warming themselves beside the stove. In the loft, they had to contend with the cold, as with winter settling in, it got colder with each passing day.

Each morning the Semeniuk children brought them food in pails, ostensibly meant for the chickens. Their second meal was in the evening, together with their benefactors. When guests arrived, Anna and Frieda had to manage with just one meal for the day. The Semeniuk family existed on the subsistence level, and the harvest was not sufficient to bring in additional income. "Many times we asked ourselves what motivated these simple people, who hardly knew how to read and write, to share their meager food with us, as well as to share with us the constant threat and danger of betrayal and death?"

As mentioned, the village of Studinka was full of Ukrainian militia and collaborators. Anna and Frieda were also told of several cases where farmers of the village who hid Jews, after being paid off, turned them over to the Gestapo. There were constant searches for fleeing Jews in the vicinity, to the extent that at times it proved dangerous for the two women even to stay in the barn and they had to move into the forest until the danger passed.

For emergencies, when there was no time to flee to the forest, the Semeniuk children prepared a big pit under the oven for Anna and Frieda to hide in. They worked at this at night; the oldest children digging away at the soil and the younger ones removing the dirt. The children also instinctively began to keep their distance from other children in order to keep them away from their house. On many occasions, when Domna saw villagers near her house, she feared that they were spying on her. From such anxiety she was often sick. According to Anna, their benefactress was once on the verge of a mental breakdown from the tension. However, she regained her equilibrium and not once did she hint to the two women that they should leave. In Frieda's words, "One cannot sufficiently describe in words this period, the fear, the danger that increased from day to day at a time when the Ukrainians increased their resistance to the Germans and the Germans in turn began to burn down houses and send people to Germany for labor. We had to be wary of the villagers, the militia, the Germans, and every small child that was prepared to betray us."

To add to the Semeniuks' troubles, Ivan's bronchitis got worse from day to day and he was confined to bed. In the spring of 1943, he died and his wife was left alone, a poor, fragile woman with five children on top of the two Jewish women in hiding. It is related that before passing on Ivan made his wife promise that she would continue to shelter the two fugitive women.

Of all the children, Domna's 15-year-old daughter, Nadezhda, did more than anyone to help. It was she who led the two fugitive women into the forest when there were searches. On many occasions she stayed with them in the barn, brought them food, and also removed the chamber pot while her mother was busy tending her sick husband, the farm and the smaller children. "Without Nadezhda we would not have survived," Frieda emphasized. As mentioned, the other children also helped out, especially the eldest, Elena, who sometimes brought warm food to the two women when they had to stay in the forest during searches. For this purpose, she removed her clogs and walked barefooted, so that the neighbors would not hear her going out in the night.

For 20 months, from September 1942 to April 1944, when the Studinka area was liberated by the Russians, Anna Hurwitz and Frieda Goldberg (later Binshtok) remained in hiding in the Semeniuk household, in a village known for its many collaborators who willingly participated in the hunting down and killing of Jews. Anna and Frieda hid in this most dangerous place, with one of the poorest farming families, who took every care and precaution to make it possible for the two women to survive, with all the attendant risks to themselves. Fortunately for them, they were successful in outwitting their would-be betrayers.

In 1963 Domna Semeniuk was recognized as Righteous Among the Nations. In 1996, her daughter Nadezhda Loseva was added to the Righteous honor.

Sendler, Irena
Schultz, Irena
POLAND

*I*t was a date that Irena Sendler would remember for the rest of her life. October 20, 1943, was her name day; that is, the day traditionally attached to the name Irena, and a cause for celebration. Taking a few hours off from her exhausting undercover activity helping Jews, she went over to her mother's house in Warsaw, where people had gathered for the celebration. That evening there was loud pounding at the door – it was the much-feared Gestapo. Irena Sendler was arrested and committed to the notorious Pawiak prison. She recalled, "Every day at dawn the doors of cells were opened and names called of people who never returned. One day I heard my name among those called." Irena was sure that the end had come for her as a Gestapo agent led her to the Gestapo headquarters nearby for her execution. "I realized that this was my last journey." Then something unbelievable happened. Un-

Irena Sendler

expectedly, another Gestapo man appeared with an order to take Irena "for additional interrogation." He led her to a quiet corner, unobserved by others, and told her in Polish, "You are free, get away as quickly as you can." Irena Sendler: "I was so overcome with emotion that I couldn't move. I asked him for my papers and in response he dealt me a powerful blow. I felt blood running down my face." But she was free. Someone in her clandestine organization had managed to bribe this Gestapo man, minutes before her scheduled execution. "That same night, notices were posted on the walls of Warsaw proclaiming that 'for treason against Third Reich the following had been sentenced to death by shooting,' and among those who had been executed was my name." Apparently it had been too late for the Germans to correct the announcement.

How did this young woman of 33 (born 1910) become involved in trying to undermine the Nazi efforts to root out all Jews in the Warsaw area? Before the war, Irena Sendler, as a trained social worker, worked for the Social Welfare Department of Warsaw. During the German occupation of Warsaw, which lasted from September 1939 to January 1945, this department was the only official Polish social welfare organization, beside the Polish Red Cross, that was allowed to operate. During the occupation, the Social Welfare Department maintained canteens that served food to the poor, the dispossessed, old people, and orphaned children.

Sendler took advantage of her job also to assist Jews, but her work was stopped when all of Warsaw's Jews were ordered inside a ghetto. Up to that time, Sendler's department had about 3,000 people in her care, of which 90% now found themselves behind the ghetto walls. As the ghetto closed its gates, it seemed that all of Sendler's assistance would be stymied. "We had to find a way to get inside the ghetto."

Warsaw, the country's capital, had the largest concentration of Jews in Poland, and the Germans planned to do away with them in stages, first by concentrating and isolating them in a walled ghetto. In mid-November 1940, the ghetto was sealed off after 138,00 Jews were uprooted from their homes and 113,000 non-Jews were forced to leave their dwellings to make room for the ghetto. At that point the ghetto held 350,000 Jews. Up to 100,000 more were added from surrounding communities, as well as from distant places – and the ghetto population rose to 450,000. Conditions were stifling, with up to six people in a room. There was also a severe shortage of food and medical supplies. By June 1941, 4,000–5,000 people were dying every month of malnutrition and various epidemics, mainly typhus. About 2,000 were employed at menial labor in German army barracks and other work places outside the ghetto. On July 22, 1942, in what the Germans termed the "Great *Aktion*," mass deportations of the ghetto Jews to the gas chambers in nearby Treblinka commenced, at the rate of 6,000 to 7,000 a day, stuffed into cattle cars. By the time this huge *Aktion* was over, on September 6, 1942, some 300,000 Jews had been sent to their death. There remained 55,000 people in a smaller ghetto. Resistance to the Germans began on January 18, 1943, and erupted into a full-scale uprising on April 19, 1943. The Germans responded in full force, burning all the buildings in the ghetto. At the end of the operations, in early May, the Germans reported having either killed or deported all the remaining Jews. However, during and before the Warsaw ghetto uprising, many Jews had managed to flee to the other side of the city, known as the Aryan side, and it is estimated that some 20,000 were in hiding in the greater metropolitan area of Warsaw.

Returning to Irena Sendler, when the ghetto was shut off to the outside world she did not throw in the towel but tried to think of ways to get inside the ghetto on an ongoing basis. She came up with the idea of getting a permit from the municipality for a special sanitary service to combating infectious diseases in Warsaw, which were rampant inside the ghetto. She asked that such a permit be issued by the municipality to her and her closest collaborator, Irena Schultz, giving them the right to enter the ghetto without hindrance – just to report on health conditions, nothing else, the two women emphasized, but while there intending to look up old friends. Sendler's partner, Irena Schultz, was by profession a journalist. During the war years, she also worked in the city's Social Welfare Deptartment.

Once inside the ghetto, Sendler and Schultz looked up Ewa Rechtman, who told them of a secret section operating in the ghetto comprising women employed by the Jewish Centos charity organization. "We renewed old contacts and made new ones to give assistance." Sendler and Schultz brought in food, clothing, medicines, and money to the ghetto, which they got from the Social Welfare Department and with the help of forged documents. Inside the ghetto, they succeeded in getting several tenement building administrators and porters to cooperate with them. As entire houses were afflicted with tuberculosis and other infectious diseases, the German controllers, ever frightened by the prospect of getting infected, avoided going to these addresses – the same places where the two Irenas met their collaborators and planned further aid projects.

The two Irenas often passed through the gates of the ghetto two or three times a day carrying goods or money. They entered the ghetto by different gates. Once inside, Irena Sendler made it a point to put on the yellow star armband. "I did this to show my solidarity with these people. But there was also a practical reason, for in this way I did not differ from the other inhabitants and wasn't asked for my documents and questioned about being there." Once she was stopped by the police when she had large sums of money on her meant to be distributed to people in her care. She explained that the money was for sanitary improvements. The police was not satisfied with her answer and proceeded to phone the sanitary-epidemiological department. A certain Dr. Majkowski picked up the phone at the other end of the line. In Sendler's words, "He had no idea what was going on, but he guessed what was involved and fully corroborated my story."

Events took a decided turn for the worse when the Germans launched their mass evacuation of the ghetto's Jews to the death facility of Treblinka in the summer of 1942. Irena Sendler's plan was now to spirit out of the doomed ghetto as many Jews, adults and children, as possible with the help of her colleague Irena Schultz. At that time, she already had a list of addresses in Warsaw where the Jews who had managed to escape from the ghetto, particularly children, could stay until she and Schultz had produced Aryan documents for them and arranged for their safety elsewhere. Sendler and her colleague issued hundreds of such fake documents with forged signatures.

As the deportations continued without a letup and given the increasing need to help Jews survive, Irena Sendler decided to join the newly founded Council for Aid to Jews, better known by the codename Żegota. This organization was created by representatives of the political movements within the Polish underground for the purpose of helping Jews survive within the general population. Created in the summer of 1942, it started to operate only toward the end of the year, when most Jews in Warsaw were no longer alive. But there were thousands in hiding in Warsaw and smaller numbers in other major cities. Żegota had the infrastructure and funds that could help Irena Sendler's rescue work, and she decided to join it and subordinate her activities to it. In September 1943, she was appointed head of Żegota's Department for the Care of Jewish children and received the codename Jolanta. In that capacity, she supervised a team of workers that was responsible for the 2,500 children in Żegota's care.

Before that date, and afterwards, Irena Sendler continued to play a personal pivotal role in the rescue of both adults and children. As far as adults were concerned, she and Irena Schultz were able to spirit them away as they left the ghetto for work outside, after the guards at the gates had been bribed to omit them from their count of workers. This worked. Each person hiding on the Aryan side was looked after by a certain liaison girl, whose task was to keep in touch with the person and solve problems arising from living a fugitive and illegal life. "I myself," Sendler said, "had eight or ten flats where Jews were in hiding under my care." Żegota paid some of the sheltering families for their Jewish charge's upkeep and they also received aid from the city's Social Welfare Department in the form of clothing, food parcels, and coupons for milk.

A case in point illustrating the day-to-day problems that suddenly arose and had to be solved involved Mrs. Maria Palester, one of Irena's rescue colleagues, who came to her with a certain Dr. Roman Bazeches. She had saved him in time, on the point of his committing suicide. She could not keep him in her home as her flat was being taken over by a public agency. Irena Sendler took him to one of her apartments in the Świder section of the city before arranging another hiding place for him.

Sendler usually placed young Jewish women as governesses or nursemaids. They were given a new name, and in the very religious Catholic atmosphere of Poland the women had to know by rote the fundamentals of their assumed faith. "We taught them the Ten Commandments and prayers and gave them prayer books and medallions," also the list of "deadly sins" and instructions not to miss out on church attendance. Religiously overzealous behavior, if not carried off with tact and care, could be counterproductive, as in the following case reported by Irena Sendler. A young, blonde Jewish woman who looked every inch an Aryan and was above all suspicion, was sent to a family and performed well as a maid. The woman's host, however, complained, "Our new maid is very good, she cooks quite well, doesn't steal, doesn't run after the boys, but she has one fault – she goes to church too often." This wasn't to the liking of these people, for as Sendler found out later, they belonged to the Jehovah Witnesses, and the maid's religious ardor did not sit too well with them. The woman had to be moved elsewhere.

Children on the run presented a special problem. To spirit them out of the doomed ghetto, Sendler and Schultz led them through the underground corridors of the public court buildings and the train depot in Muranów district. The courthouse on Leszno Street was on the border between the ghetto and the Aryan sector and was used for illegal traffic to and from the ghetto. Once on the other side, the children were placed in apartments especially prepared for this purpose. After some time, they were turned over to the care of host families or to religious institutions. Some children stayed permanently (Sendler: "if one can speak of anything being permanent in those days") with the families found for them by Sendler's service, living with them under various disguises.

In this major rescue effort, many convents helped out by taking children under their protective wings, such as the Family of Mary, headed by Mother Superior Matylda Getter, and the convent in Turkowice, headed by Mother Superior Stanislawa (Aniela Polechajłło) and with the aid of two trusted nuns, Sisters Irena (Antonina Manasczuk) and Hermana (Józefa Romansewicz). To this convent were sent children who stood out by virtue of their distinct Jewish appearance. The Turkowice convent was chosen because of its remote location, in the Lublin area. Receiving a coded message the Sisters would come to pick up the children in Warsaw, handed over to them by Sendler and Schultz.

In her postwar account, Irena Sendler listed the many people in the Warsaw area who helped her and Irena Schultz, such as Janina Grabowska, a teacher, and Zofia Wędrychowska and Stanislaw Papuziński, "who exposed the lives of their own children to danger to save the lives of other people's children." Important help was also received from Stanislawa Bussold, who was a midwife by profession and director of a municipal health center in a Warsaw neighborhood. She had joined Żegota and took into her home pregnant Jewish women hiding on the Aryan side of the city who were close to delivery. She took no payment for her services. She also arranged for the newborn to be taken in by Christian orphanages without disclosing their identity. She herself adopted a child left in her care by parents who eventually perished. The child was registered as Elzbieta Bussold – her mother's name was Henryka Kopel.

Another person who rendered an important service was Professor Andrzej Trojanowski, who provided medical care. He also hid Jews in his home and performed plastic surgery on Jews to make them look less Jewish, such as on noses. He also operated on males to remove the signs of circumcision. Persons suspected of being Jews were often told to pull down their pants to see if they were circumcised – a telltale sign that only Jews bore in that country and which could make the difference between life and death. Also meriting mention is Jan Dobraczyński, a writer and a prewar member of an extreme Catholic political movement with strong antisemitic overtones. During the war, he headed the Warsaw Department of Health and Social Welfare. He supplied Irena Sendler and Żegota with forged papers for Jewish children attesting that they were orphaned, destitute, or learning impaired, to qualify for admission to various Christian institutions. He reportedly was able to place up to 300 Jewish children through his efforts.

Of all her associates within Żegota, Irena Sendler worked best with the organization's head, Julian Grobelny (under his codename Trojan), whom she described as a big-hearted man who was completely devoted to the cause of saving those for whom death lay waiting at every corner. It appears that there was good chemistry between the two. Grobelny had been a socialist activist in Łódź in the 1930s. He was not healthy, suffering from advanced tuberculosis of the lungs, which was to take his life in 1944. Sendler gave an example of Grobelny's dedicated work and of how the two worked closely to solve urgent problems, in the following case:

> "Once Grobelny called me away from some very important work, and himself cut short a meeting of the presidium of Żegota, only because he had received news that in the vicinity of Wawer there was little girl whose mother had been murdered in such a bestial manner that the child had been in a state of shock for several days … We were going to Wawer by train when the Germans staged a roundup at the train station. We managed to escape arrest, but it was a near miss … I then begged 'Trojan' to go back. I explained that I would try to find the child myself, that he should not take any risks. He was most indignant. 'What's that, do you think I'm such an old good-for-nothing idiot that I can't fool the Germans?'… When we found the girl, he stroked her hair, petted the child and kissed her fondly till she cuddled up to him and said, 'I don't want to stay here, take me away with you.' We took her with us. This time, too, he asked me to find the best possible home for the child and care for her like a mother. That was the sort of man 'Trojan' was."

Irena's wide-ranging rescue work was no mere pastime. Danger lurked at every corner. As she said, "At every step, in all public places, thousands of copies of warning notices were posted to say that anyone hiding Jews was liable to the death sentence. Very often the occupiers murdered entire families for committing this 'crime.'" Outside, crooks, underworld figures, and black-mailers cashed in on the plight of others by trying to identify Jews on the run, then squeezing them and their rescuers for money, and in many cases this was followed by betrayal to the Germans for an additional reward.

Irena Sender kept some of her Żegota-coded files of Jewish children in convents, in a secret cache. As a smokescreen, moonshine vodka was also distilled there. This was done with the thought of getting out of a possibly sticky situation, for it was easier to explain away the production of moonshine vodka than files on hidden Jews, or so she thought. In truth, both categories of offenders were treated harshly by the Germans. As Sendler admitted, she later realized that this was rather naïve thinking on her part. "But at the time we acted like a drowning man who clutches at a straw."

As related above, on October 20, 1943, the Gestapo arrested Irena Sendler in her mother's home. Fortunately for Irena, she and a friend had managed to stash away incriminating documents, such as coded addresses of persons in the care of Żegota written on narrow strips of tissue paper, as well as a bag with a large sum of money from Żegota destined to help the Jews. The search lasted three hours. Nothing was found but Irena was arrested. This was due as a result of one of her rescue colleagues who had been arrested and under torture had given Irena's name. Her rescue from execution was made possible by a huge bribe paid by Grobelny through a third party, and Sendler was released in February 1944 after a three-month stay in Pawiak prison.

Irena Sendler could no longer stay in her apartment, for the Gestapo would surely be looking for her again, as indeed was the case in the following days, and she had to live under cover. Even when her mother died, she did not attend her funeral.

After the war, Irena Sendler returned to her work as a social worker for the city of Warsaw and later for the Ministry of Health. Asked frequently for her motives in volunteering for the highly risky undertaking of helping Jews in a city swarming with thousands of Nazi security men, she was at a loss of words. She frequently mentioned the fact that her father, a doctor, lived in Otwock, a city with a large Jewish population, and that most of his patients were poor Jews. "I grew up among these people. I knew the customs and the poverty of Jewish homes. I had many Jewish friends." Was it merely her affinity to Jews that prompted her to later try to rescue them, or something more – her unique personality?

In 2005, Irena Sendler celebrated her 95th birthday. She still makes it a point to see young people and school children, in whom she tries to instill her message of love, care, compassion, and hope.

In 1965 Yad Vashem recognized Irena Sendler as Righteous Among the Nations. Four years later, in 1969, Irena Schultz was added to the Righteous roster. Also recognized as Righteous were the following rescuers mentioned in this story: Sister Matylda Getter, Aniela Polechajłło (Sister Stanislawa), Antonina Manasczuk (Sister Irena), Józefa Romansewicz (Sister Hermana), Stanislawa Bussold, Andrzej Trojanowski, Jan Dobraczyński, and Julian Grobelny.

Sharp, Waitstill & Martha
United States

*A*s the news kept trickling in from outside, in late May and early June 1940, it was apparent that France was losing the war against Germany, and many of the imprisoned men in the St. Nicholas internment camp, near Nîmes in southeastern France, among them Jews, anti-Nazi refugees from Germany, were deeply concerned about the outcome of the war. With them was the famed author of historical novels Lion Feuchtwanger, who, in spite of his pronounced anti-Nazi views and status as a Jewish fugitive from Germany, had been interned by the French government as an enemy alien, because of his previous German nationality, even though Germany had stripped him of his citizenship. Then came the news of the French debacle, and with it the infamous Article 19 of the humiliating armistice agreement of June 25, 1940, under which France obligated itself to turn over to the Germans "upon demand" any former German national currently in France and wanted by the Gestapo. Lion Feuchtwanger was number six on that fateful "most wanted" list.

Luckily for him, he was spirited away from the camp, dressed as a woman, with the help of Myles Standish, a diplomat in the United States consulate in Marseilles. Secretly hidden in Marseilles, where his wife, Marta, joined him, he had to be gotten out of the country before the French authorities, now under orders from the new pro-German puppet regime headed by Marshal Petain, again laid their hands on the man. Marta Feuchtwanger was able to obtain a U.S. emergency visa for her husband, meaning that he would be allowed into America – that is, if he and his wife made it to Lisbon, Portugal, by whatever means, and then managed to sail to the United States. But how to get out of France without being apprehended? And then, how to cross Spain, a country just over a prolonged and bloody civil war and presently under the sway of the victorious Fascists led by General Franco and edging closer to an alliance with Nazi Germany? Feuchtwanger turned for help to Varian Fry, the emissary of the American-based Emergency Rescue Committee in Marseilles, but Fry had his hands full helping many other fleeing refugees so he asked Martha and Waitstill Sharp to take this specific rescue mission on themselves.

Martha and Waitstill Sharp departing New York for Europe, Feb. 1939 (courtesy of Artemis A.W. Joukowsky III)

Waitstill Sharp was a minister in the Unitarian Church, based in Wellesley, Massachusetts, and married to Martha since 1928. Both were highly educated people – Waitstill had a law degree from Harvard and Martha a master's degree from Radcliffe. On February 4, 1939, they sailed for Europe on assignment from the Unitarian Service Committee, leaving their two children, six-year-old Hastings and three-year old Martha, in the care of members of their congregation. They left on a mission of rescue, principally of Unitarians, but also of others in need, trapped in Prague a month before that city and the Czech lands were to come under direct Nazi rule. They stayed on in Prague well into the Nazi takeover, on March 15, 1939, and were able to get many Nazi-targeted persons out in time. By August 1939, the Gestapo had decided to move against the Sharps, but luckily for them they left Prague in time – Waitstill having left on August 9 and Martha following him on August 16. Two weeks later, on September 1, 1939, the lights went off in Europe, as Germany invaded Poland and World War II began.

Back home in the United States, the Sharps were asked to return to Europe, this time to a country embroiled in a large-scale war. Landing in Lisbon, on June 20, 1940, they learned of the French military collapse. They nevertheless headed for France, bringing along milk and food for refugee children in the south of the country. Once there, they helped set up an underground railroad to help refugees cross the border into Spain and Portugal in collusion with Varian Fry's Emergency Rescue Committee. From the Unitarian office in Marseilles, Martha and Waitstill Sharp focused on securing U.S. visas and necessary travel documents for refugees wishing to travel overseas. At this point, Varian Fry asked them to help get the Feuchtwangers out of the country before the French and their German overlords could get their hands on them. What followed is an adventure that could have come out of Hollywood.

At first, the Sharps put the two fugitives in a Marseilles hotel, very close to the main railroad station. Then, in September 1940, armed with a new identity card in the name of Wetcheek, an English translation of the German "Feuchtwanger" a name already previously used by the author, Lion was fetched by Martha Sharp, herself also appearing in disguise clad as a French fisherwoman. Both entered the train station from a secret underground passage of the hotel leading directly into the station, thus avoiding police inspection at the main entrance. The train took the Feuchtwangers and Martha Sharp to the French border town of Cerbère, where Waitstill was waiting for them. He cautioned them that though he had already bribed the border guards a day earlier, there was no guarantee that the same people would be on duty when the Feuchtwangers made their crossing. It was decided that Marta Feuchtwanger would go first, ahead of her husband, on the passport that bore her name, whereas Lion would go separately on his U.S. emergency visa under the name of Wetcheek. The Sharps, who had preceded them, taking along the Feuchtwangers' luggage, waited for them in Port Bou on the Spanish side of the border.

Continuing by train to Barcelona, they planned the next step. The fastest way to reach Lisbon was by air. But since the only airline flying that route was the German Lufthansa, controlled by the Nazi state, it was decided to go there by train, with all the attendant dangers. The plan was for Lion to travel separately from his wife, in first class and carrying a briefcase given to him by Waitstill Sharp and embossed with a large Red Cross marking. The Spanish police, ever on the lookout for suspected German anti-Nazis wanted by the Germans, would probably make more stringent inspections of third-class passengers and not bother with those traveling in first class – usually high officials. Reaching Lisbon, a city teeming with refugees as well as Nazi spies anxious to pick up persons wanted by the Gestapo, the Sharps took measures, including getting a passenger to sell them his ticket, to get Lion immediately on a boat, even ahead of his wife. That September, in 1940, Lion Feuchtwanger arrived safely in New York.

Not giving herself any rest after this marvelous feat, Martha Sharp headed back to Marseilles to continue her work of getting out stranded refugees, many of them Jews, by various means. This is how she met the 14-year-old Eva Esther Rosemarie Feigl, originally from Vienna, whom she was able to add to a list of children for whom permission was given to leave France for the U.S. After overcoming bureaucratic obstacles, including having to travel to Vichy to get *laissez passer* – French exit permits, Martha Sharp was able to organize of group of 27 children, including nine who were Jewish, such as Eva Feigl and the Diamant triplets (Amalie, Evelyn, and Marianne), and the group left Marseilles by train for Lisbon on November 26, 1940, and sailed from Lisbon the following month, arriving in New York on December 23, 1940. Mrs. Sharp, who had sailed ahead of them a few days earlier, met them at the dock and arranged their continued further stay in the United States.

Returning to the United States with America's entrance into the war, the Sharps traveled abroad on international relief missions. After the war, in 1948, Martha Sharp ran for Congress on the Democratic ticket but was falsely smeared as a suspected Communist by FBI head J. Edgar Hoover, who had her put under surveillance. As a result she lost the election. The war and later developments had probably taken their toll, and the Sharps drifted apart.

The two divorced in 1950 and both remarried. Martha continued her philanthropic activity and was deeply engaged in work for the Jewish Hadassah organization, the Girls Clubs of America, and other non-profit organizations. She died in 1999 at the age of 94. Waitstill, who returned to the ministry and was posted in various locations, was also active in civil rights and antiwar activities, and died earlier, in 1984.

Returning to the Feuchtwanger story, in October 1940 he publicly thanked the Unitarian Service Committee and the Sharps for his rescue. Referring to Waitstill Sharp, Feuchtwanger lauded him in exemplary terms:

"For four months I had lived in isolation from the outside world. And when I had found a first refuge, I still had to live, for many reasons, in strict concealment. Then, on day, a man appeared … and he told me, as though it were a matter of course, that everything had been arranged for my escape. He was a man whose name I had never heard before and of whose existence I was entirely ignorant … And from then on, this stranger looked after me like a brother. He comforted me with understanding; he found the right words to encourage me. During the whole dangerous enterprise, he did not deny the danger, he did not belittle the risk; but, in his matter of fact way, he also pointed out the possibilities and chances of success. But what he did and what he said were truly the deeds and words of a brother … That a stranger, a total stranger, acted in such away, was an unexpected blessing … Even today, it seems like a dream… He took my fate into his hands … I do not exaggerate when I tell you that you lent me even more important and valuable help, manifesting to me that pity and encompassing love, independent of all selfish interest, are still in this our world."

Ten years later, in 1950, Feuchtwanger returned to the theme of his rescue by the Sharps:

"The French Fascist government had put me in a concentration camp, and now the Nazis demanded my extradition. I was in danger of my life … You, my friends, your delegates, Mr. and Mrs. Sharp from Boston, you saved my life and the lives of many others. But you did even more. We, all of us who were endangered, had heard many great words about the 'Brotherhood of Men' and 'that you love one another' and so on. But if you are interned in a camp and waiting for help, and weeks are passing, months, almost a year, and death comes closer every day, and no help is coming, then you begin to believe that all these fine notions are but mere words and empty sound. To learn then, all of a sudden, that men, absolute strangers, from somewhere beyond the ocean, rushed over – in the face of a hundred difficulties – to help you just because you were in danger, believe me, that is an overwhelming and lasting experience."

Learning of the Yad Vashem requirement of testimonies by the rescued party, the Sharp grandchildren, Artemis Joukowsky III and brother Michael ("Misha") Joukowsky, hired a private detective to track down any surviving children whom their grandmother had rescued, and found Mrs. Feigl, still alert and with a sound mind at age 79, living in Manhattan and willing to testify. With the assistance of the Jewish Foundation for the Righteous in New York, headed by Stanlee Stahl, which aids needy Righteous honored by Yad Vashem, voluminous material on the Sharps' rescue activity was made available to Yad Vashem for its consideration.

On October 19, 2005, Yad Vashem conferred upon the late Waitstill and Martha Sharp the title of Righteous Among the Nations – the second and third Americans (after Varian Fry) to be awarded this honorific title. On June 13, 2006, in a ceremony at Yad Vashem – in the presence of Charles Jones, U.S. ambassador to Israel; Yaakov Türkel, chairman of the Commission for the Designation of the Righteous; Avner Shalev, chairman of the Yad Vashem Directorate; and Dr. Mordecai Paldiel, head of the Department of the Righteous – the honorees daughter, Dr. Martha Sharp-Joukowsky, was presented with a medal and certificate of honor bearing her parents' name. Also, together with Mrs. Feigl, she unveiled the honorees' names on the honor wall in the Garden of the Righteous. On this occasion, grandson Artemis W. Joukowski III, who campaigned vigorously to have his grandparents recognized by Yad Vashem, and probably reflecting on the circumstances that had caused his grandparents to part, said he was pleased to see his family brought together again by this posthumous honor. "What they did, they did hand in hand, so it's appropriate they be brought back together by this honor." A day after the Yad Vashem ceremony, Dr. Martha Sharp-Joukowsky, a Brown University archaeologist, flew off to Jordan to continue the dig at a Nabatean temple in Petra, of which she is in charge.

Šimelis, Mykolas & Jadvyga
LITHUANIA

*M*ykolas Šimelis (pronounced Shimelis) was a forester who lived in the village of Tarpumiške, and before the war he supplied pine tree roots to Meir Korn, who owned a turpentine factory in the town of Vievis. Meir, who often stopped over at Mykolas' house, had learned to know him well since 1929 and was impressed by the man's honesty, friendliness, and kind-hearted disposition as well as by his friendly attitude towards Jews, something not very common among Lithuanians.

After the Germans invaded Lithuania, in June 1941, at first Meir was told to train non-Jewish locals to operate his turpentine factory, which was, of course, taken away from him. Then suddenly on October 6, 1941, the Germans and Ukrainian guards staged a killing raid on the Jews in Vievis. Meir and his three children (two sons and a daughter) were able to save themselves by hiding with local people, but he lost his 39-year-old wife, Feiga, and her family in the raid. All of the town's other Jews were likewise murdered. During the follow-

Mykolas Šimelis

ing months, Meir Korn and his children wandered from place to place, and finally in July 1942 he succeeded in contacting his brother, Tanchum, through a messenger, in the Kaunas (Kovno) ghetto – and begged him to come and get him and his children in whatever way possible. Tanchum was able to get ahold of a van from work and bring his brother and family to the Kovno (Kaunas) ghetto.

Life in the Kovno ghetto was no paradise with the ongoing killing raids that reduced the ghetto's population. All-able bodied persons were conscripted for hard labor. As they left in the morning for work, they were never sure whether they would return in the evening, or wind up in the nearby Seventh and Ninth Forts to be shot; these two forts were the horrendous killings grounds of thousands of Jews. At work, Meir Korn often thought of his friend Mykolas Šimelis. "I was sure that he had remained the same decent and good person. I was not mistaken."

One day, while Meir was doing forced labor outside the ghetto, someone tapped him on the shoulder. He turned around – it was Mykolas Šimelis. He said only a few words: "There is room for you at my place." Mykolas disappeared as quickly as he had come. Then through a friend, Šimelis left a message for Meir, urging him not to wait until it was too late but come over right away with his family to his place. Meir debated how to make the passage to Šimelis's house, which was some 45 kilometers away. Going by foot was too dangerous and therefore out of the question. Meir Korn then turned to Moshe Musel.

As told by Moshe's wife, Paula, in fall of 1943 Meir Korn asked her husband, Moshe, to help him organize an escape from the ghetto to the home of a Lithuanian villager. Musel was then in charge of Jewish mechanics in a German auto repair shop and with the help of a trustworthy Lithuanian could arrange to get a van. So it happened that one cold night, in November 1943, all nine members of the Korn and Musel families slipped out of the ghetto to a waiting truck and then drove the 45 kilometers across the Lithuanian countryside to the town of Vievis. They included Meir, his two sons and daughter, his mother-in-law, Moshe and Paula Musel, and Alter and Etel Aranovsky. Meir wondered how Šimelis would react when instead of the original four Korns, he would see five additional people.

Parking at a safe distance from the Šimelis house in order not to leave any incriminating tire tracks in the snow, they advanced slowly on foot and knocked on the door. Mykolas Šimelis stepped out and seeing Meir Korn he embraced him and gave him a hearty handshake with his usual broad smile. His wife, Jadvyga, and her five children were also there to greet the large group. The children, aged one to seven, were told that these people were war refugees, or had reason to flee from the Germans – not in any way that they were Jewish fugitives. Korn told Šimelis that there were eight people with him. Never mind, was Šimelis's response. His door was open to all who had come.

Since Moshe Musel was also active in the Kovno underground, he decided to return that same evening, leaving the eight other Jews behind, who were now in the hands of the Šimelis family. In the words of Paula Musel, "Their fate was now bound with the fate of the eight escapees." For the first two months, they all stayed in a side room, but this proved too risky, so Šimelis decided to build a bunker under his house and move his charges there. All participated in the work of removing the soil at night. Šimelis helped out by carrying the soil up the attic; there was plenty to drag upstairs, so much that the soil's weight in the attic caused cracks to show in the walls. The entrance to the bunker was through two secret trap doors; one behind a closet in a small room next to the hallway; the other from one of the bedrooms. The underground bunker was four square meters in size. Šimelis had taken care to install a small oven as well as electricity. Jadvyga brought them bedspreads and pillows to place on the hay, so as to make their sleep as comfortable as possible under the circumstances.

Then there was the problem of feeding eight additional mouths. Buying more food in local stores would have aroused suspicion. Here too luck was with Šimelis, as he found a village friend who willingly took it upon himself to buy, once a week, the additional food, which included potatoes and meat. In January 1944, Musel brought over Meir Korn's brother Tanchum and wife Judith, as well as ten-year-old Haim Kaplan. There were now 12 persons in the Šimelis household.

Every time the hidden persons expressed regret at causing him so many problems, Šimelis would say, "The world is not without good persons. I would have helped anyone that had knocked on my door." In Paula Musel's words, "He knew perfectly well what awaited him and his family in case we were found at his home, and in spite of this he risked his life and his family in order to save us from extinction." Late each night, after he had locked the front door, he would knock softly at the bunker's trapdoor as a signal that the fugitives could step out and come upstairs to stretch their arms and legs. He would invite them to listen to Russian news bulletin on the war's progress or take them to the attic to get a breath of fresh air. "He did everything to raise our spirits."

Then something unexpectedly happened that placed the whole rescue undertaking in serious jeopardy. In April 1944, at the age of thirty-eight, Jadvyga Šimelis suddenly took ill and was rushed to a hospital in Kaunas, where she died of blood poisoning. Mykolas took his three eldest children with him to the funeral, leaving the other two with a woman neighbor. Before leaving, he cautioned his charges to be extra careful due to the presence of a strange woman in the house. On the very day that Mykolas was expected home, German soldiers and Ukrainian auxiliaries staged a raid in the area in search for hidden Jews. When they stopped at the Šimelis house, the hidden persons could hear the soldiers' footsteps above them and their questioning of the woman babysitter about to the people living in this house. She answered that she did not know as she was only there for the day to look after the small children, and the owner had left to attend his wife's funeral. The soldiers proceeded to search every room in the house. One of them entered the small room with the closet and already had his hand on one of doorknobs and was about to discover the trapdoor to the bunker when suddenly Šimelis appeared with his other children. He greeted the soldiers warmly with handshakes, and distracting their attention from the small room he invited them to the dining room for drinks. The Germans forgot about the search, and after several drinks they left.

After the babysitter had left, Šimelis knocked on the trapdoor and told the frightened people what had happened. As he stepped off the train at the station, on his return trip, someone told him that the Germans were meticulously searching every house in the village. Šimelis's face dropped, as he was sure that his charges had not been too cautious and the woman babysitter had probably found out about them and given them away to the inquisitive Germans. "What I shall do now?" he thought to himself as he stood frozen in the station wondering what his next step should be: to go back home and face arrest or drop everything and flee, taking along the children with him? Then a thought struck his mind: "A man dies only once; perhaps I will be able to help them somehow." And he headed home with the children, arriving just in time to stop the soldier from opening the telltale closet.

Alone with five children, Šimelis needed a maid to help out, with all the risks that this implied for him and his Jewish charges. He found such a woman, but she said she wanted to work for a few days at the household chores and dealing with the children to see if she could cope with her responsibilities, and then would decide if she wanted to stay on. Šimelis urged the hidden people to be extra careful during this short trial period so that the maid would not accidentally discover their presence. And just at this most unpropitious period, Paula Musel's sister, Fania, fled from the Kovno ghetto with her husband, Salomon Nechmad, and showed up at Šimelis's home. He managed to get them to the bunker without the maid noticing. There were now 14 people in hiding.

A few days later, the maid told Šimelis she would stay on. Then a serious mishap occurred, as Meir Korn, not too careful, had allowed himself to be seen by the new maid, named Elena. She immediately told Šimelis about it, adding that she knew who the man was and she wished to leave. It looked like the end of the rescue operation, just when liberation was close at hand with the Russian army not far away. However, if the maid left, she might spill the secret to outsiders. The people in the bunker consulted among themselves and then decided that they did not want to further endanger their benefactor by their presence, and therefore they were going to leave and hope to join up with friendly partisans. But Šimelis refused to hear it. He told them that their chances of survival were next to nil, as they would be immediately caught and killed. Instead he said he would try to convince the woman to stay. Šimelis also asked Judith Korn to help him persuade Elena not to leave, and after long talks by both with her, she changed her mind and decided to stay on.

Two months later, on July 13, 1944, the area was liberated as the Red Army took over. All were overjoyed at having survived, Šimelis included. However, there were people in the village who were not happy with Šimelis's role in saving 14 Jews and hatched a plan to have him killed. A year later, on July 10, 1945, long after the Jewish fugitives had left, a forester who had worked for Šimelis invited him to examine a plot of land in the forest. The killers had hidden themselves nearby, and when he appeared at the appointed time they murdered him. Then they vandalized his house, telling the frightened maid that she would never see him again. "That's what happens to someone who saves Jews," they screamed before leaving. Paula Musel lamented him, "So passed away a most wonderful person, a great humanitarian, a friend of Jews, a man who paid with his life for saving 14 Jews from the Kovno ghetto."

In 1983 Mykolas and Jadvyga Šimelis were recognized as Righteous Among the Nations.

Skobtsova, Yelizaveta (Mother Maria)
Klepinin, Dimitri
RUSSIA

When the Germans, in France, made it obligatory for Jews to wear the Star of David, in the spring of 1942, a nun in the Russian Orthodox Church in Paris penned the following poem:

Yelizaveta Skobtsova

> *Two triangles, a star,*
> *The shield of King David, our forefather;*
> *This is election, not offense,*
> *The great path and not an evil.*
> > *Once more is a term fulfilled,*
> > *Once more roars the final trumpet;*
> > *And the fate of a great people,*
> > *Once more is by the prophet proclaimed.*
> > > *Thou art persecuted again, O Israel;*
> > > *But what can human malice mean to thee,*
> > > *Thee, who has heard the thunder from Sinai?*

She was born Yelizaveta Pilenko in 1891, to Yuri and Sofia Pilenko. Her father was chief prosecutor for the government in Riga, then part of the Russian Empire. After his death, in 1905 in Anapa, a town on the Black Sea, the family settled in St. Petersburg. There, Yelizaveta wrote poetry (such as *Scythian Shards* and *Ruth*) which were well received in literary circles. Her first marriage to Dimitri Kuzmin-Karavaev in 1909, a lawyer by profession and a Social Democrat (who after the Revolution became a Catholic priest), produced a daughter, Gayana, in 1913. When the Russian Revolution broke out in 1917, Elizabeth was a member of the Socialist SR Party. Angry at Trotsky for forcibly closing the party's congress, she wanted to assassinate him, but was instead dissuaded by her party colleagues and sent to Anapa to further the revolutionary cause there – and was elected the town's mayor. With the capture of the town by the White forces of General Denikin, she was arrested and put on trial for her involvement in the revolution. Her defense swayed the president of the court, Danilo Skobtsov (a former schoolmaster), to dismiss all charges. To the surprise of all, the two eventually married and fled to France via Turkey and Yugoslavia, where they arrived in 1923. In the meantime she bore Danilo a daughter and a son.

The year 1932 saw a profound transformation in her life when, upon the premature death of her four-year-old daughter of meningitis, she decided on a radical change – to become a nun in the Russian Orthodox Church. Taking her vows, she chose the name "Maria." Her aim was not to withdraw from the world into a life of spiritual seclusion, but to dedicate herself to the cause of the needy, especially among the many Russian emigrants in France. She opened a dormitory for them in Saxe, near Paris, which included a free kitchen, and then another building in Paris, on Rue de Lourmel, which became the base of her charitable work. Another home, at Noisy-le-Grand outside Paris, served as a convalescent home. In these activities, she was seconded by Father Dimitri Klepinin, also a Russian emigrant, who was ordained in the Russian Orthodox Church in Paris in 1937 and was already married to Tamara, who gave birth to a daughter named Helen and another son, Peter.

With the German invasion of France, she decided to turn her attention to Jews in distress and help them – first by making the free kitchen available to them, then by providing temporary shelter at her center for those in need until other arrangements could be made for them as well as issuing false baptismal certificates (such as the one given to Anne Wellers, wife of future Holocaust historian Georges Wellers, thanks to which his deportation was postponed for over a year). Lourmel soon became known as a "Jewish Church," and the overcrowding there was great. An entire Jewish family was huddled in Klepinin's private room, another in Skobtsova's son Yuri's. During the big roundup of Parisian Jews at the Winter Sports Stadium in July 1942, Mother Maria succeeded in penetrating the closely guarded stadium and snatching away two Jewish children (hidden in trash cans). At night, in her small, modestly furnished room, she expressed her innermost thoughts in a diary in which she alluded to her charitable work, such as the following entry: "There is a moment when you start burning with love and you have the inner desire to throw yourself at the feet of some other human being. This one moment is enough. Immediately you know that instead of losing your life, it is being given back to you twofold."

Warned by friends that the Gestapo was on her trail, she rejected all pleas to cease helping Jews; she could no longer change course, she said, since her work was dictated by an invisible hand. As feared, she was arrested on February 8, 1943, together with her son, Yuri, and Father Klepinin. Under interrogation, she readily admitted to helping Jews, to issuing of false baptismal certificates, and to transferring funds to Jews in hiding. Gestapo officer Hoffmann told Maria's mother: "You educated your daughter very stupidly. She helps Jews only." The old woman replied: "This is not true. She is a Christian who helps those in need. She would even help you if you were in trouble." The Nazi replied, "You will never see your daughter again." On April 24, 1943, Maria Skobtsova was deported to the Ravensbrück camp, where she helped the destitute however she could, with a morsel of food, a kind word, or a prayer. Ravaged by hunger, disease, and torture, she finally succumbed on March 31, 1945, and was committed to the crematorium, only weeks before the collapse of the Third Reich.

As for Dimitri Klepinin, he too was interrogated by Hoffman, As recorded, Hoffmann questioned Klepinin: "If we release you – will you undertake never again to aid Jews?" Klepinin: "I can say no such thing. I am a Christian, and must act as I must." Hoffmann struck Klepinin across his face and screamed: "Jew-lover! How dare you talk of those pigs as being a Christian duty!" Recovering his balance, Klepinin raised the cross from his cassock and, facing Hoffmann, quietly said: "Do you know this Jew?" Another blow by Hoffmann sent Klepinin to the floor. Klepinin and Skobtsova's son, Yuri, were ordered sent to the Dora camp, where they both died in Feburary 1944.

In her private notes, the following entry was found: "At the Last Judgment, I will not be asked whether I satisfactorily practiced asceticism, nor how many genuflections I have made before the divine altar. I will be asked whether I fed the hungry, clothed the naked, visited the sick, and the prisoner in his jail. That is all that will be asked." After the war, on October 12, 1945, a memorial service was held in a Parisian synagogue for Yelisaveta Skobtsova, where cantor and congregation were in tears at the mention of her name.

In 1985, Yad Vashem conferred the title of Righteous Among the Nations on Yelizaveta Skobtsova and Dimitri Klepinin.

Slachta, Margit
Salkaházi, Sára
HUNGARY

*S*ister Margit Slachta stood her ground as she faced off against one of the pro-Nazi Arrow Cross men who were raiding her religious home in Jankovits Telep near Lake Balaton in southern Hungary, where some Jews were hidden. As recorded by Miriam Gross-Shlomi, one of the hidden people, in response to the man's questioning as to the racial origin of the children there Sister Slachta angrily snapped back, "Sir, why are you asking such unimportant questions? Are we raising bulls here, where one is required to know a lot about its lineage? We are merely saving souls. Here, take this brochure (a religious booklet) and read there what constitutes a sin. You will see it is written: 'A person sins when he agrees with a sinner, when he aids a sinner, when he does not raise his voice against a sinner.'" Slachta's interrogator retorted: "You are all sold to the Jews," but stopped the questioning and left the place. She then told the hidden people: "We are in God's hands and we follow his way as he commands us."

Born in 1884 in Kosice, today in Slovakia but during the war years, known as Kassa and part of Hungary, Margit Slachta took an early interest in the conditions of working women and their children. In 1923, after ordination as a nun, she founded the Benedictine Sisters, or Society of Social Service – also known as the "Gray Nuns," due to their simple gray religious habits. Three years earlier, she had been

Margit Slachta (courtesy of Sisters of Social Service, Budapest)

elected to the Hungarian Parliament, where she spoke up on behalf of the underprivileged among the Hungarian population, especially women laborers. To ease their plight, she urged help for these hard-working people in the form of free meals and rest homes as well as vocational schools for women.

Sára Salkaházi (courtesy of Sisters of Social Service, Budapest)

In 1943, in the midst of the war, with Hungary on the side of Nazi Germany, she aroused resentment when she wrote in a Catholic monthly urging Catholics to pray not only for their sons who were fighting on the Russian front but also for the unarmed Jews conscripted into so-called labor battalions, whose labor assignments included clearing minefields ahead of the regular army. A year earlier, news of the start of the deportation of Jews from nearby Slovakia prompted her to travel to Rome to see Archbishop Francis Spellman of New York, who was on a visit to the Vatican, and he arranged for her an audience with Pope Pius XII that took place in the spring of 1943. She pleaded with him to intercede on behalf of the 20,000 Slovakian deportees who were facing untimely deaths in the camps, such as by providing them with food and proper shelter (she may not have been aware at the time of the real deadly nature of these "camps"). As she recorded later, "He [Pius XII] listened to me to the end. He expressed his shock. I can say the following: he listened to me but said very little." She also urged the pontiff to intercede with the Slovak authorities. According to some, it was largely through her efforts that Slovakian bishops took a strong stand against the deportation of the Jews, which indeed was temporarily halted.

Her true test of personal courage came after the German invasion of Hungary on March 19, 1944. Soon thereafter, Sister Slachta called the Society Sisters to a conference in the Society's training center in Oradea, Transylvania. There she implored the Sisters to help the local Jews. She asked her religious colleagues:

> "Is it the conviction of every Sister of Social Service that a moral organization can be safe for the future only when it lives up to its moral convictions? Are we willing in the name of fraternal love to take the risk of being interned, or carried away, of the Community's being dissolved, or even of losing our own lives? If so, even if all these things were to happen, yet if in the soul of every Sister of Social Service, the ideal of Christianity still lived, the Community will be found worthy to have a future and will deserve life even if only one Sister of Social Service were left alive. What does it help us if our work, our property, our lives are left to us but when we come to give account we have to hide our face shamefully before the eyes of God."

According to one estimate, the Society of Social Services harbored between 900 and 1,000 Jewish men, women, and children in its houses in Budapest and elsewhere; some of them converts, others not – before placing them with reliable private persons. The Society enlisted other Catholic institutions to issue baptismal certificates to Jews to save them from arrest, in the full knowledge that the reason for this act was not belief in Christian faith but avoidance of persecution. One method was for parish priests not to enter "deceased'" on the baptismal certificates of parishioners who died. The Sisters then matched the certificates of the deceased with Jewish candidates of similar ages. Then they copied the name and year from the old certificates onto new certificates. Finally, the Sisters gave the doctored certificates to the Jewish families, and in some cases performed some kind of ceremony.

Dr. Gabor Markus was one of the beneficiaries. He was a third year medical student in 1944 when that same fall, after the Arrow Cross coup of October 15, 1944, Gabor was admitted into one of the Society's homes in Máriaremete, a small community just outside Budapest. In his words:

"I was immediately accepted with a warmth and kindness that made me believe they had been waiting for me. I soon found out that in the two houses that made up the convent there were approximately 90 men and women hidden ... Every care was taken to keep our presence invisible. I was overjoyed to find there an aunt and uncle of mine and two cousins, both young girls ... They did not try to convert those of us who were not Christians [some of the sheltered persons were baptized Jews] ... but they offered consolation, hope and guidance to us, and the door of the chapel was always open to anyone who wished to pray, or just to meditate."

Dr. Magdalena-Miriam Gross-Shlomi, born in 1909, another hidden person, had lost her husband in a Hungarian labor battalion in Bor, Yugoslavia, where his unit had been sent for back-breaking work. Moving to Kosice-Kassa in 1943 with her four-year-old son, Menachem, she was admitted to one of the houses of the Society through the intercession of Sister Sára Salkaházi, who had known her husband when both worked with a local journal before Salkahazi joined the Society. During searches, Gross-Shlomi was hidden by other nuns in one of the Society's buildings. In summer 1944, when the Gestapo searched all of the Society's premises in the city, Sister Salkaházi moved her and her son to Budapest, then to a Society home in the town of Jankovits Telep, near Lake Balaton, where Miriam was provided with false identities, dressed as a nun, and assigned work in a rest home for women workers. As a cover she attended religious services with the other nuns. In one of the Society's premises, she met other Jews in hiding. While there, she witnessed from up close Sister Slachta's confrontation with the Arrow Cross raiding party mentioned above. When the situation there proved too dangerous, Salkaházi brought her back to Kosice, where she was hidden in one of the Society's buildings. Dr. Gross-Shlomi recalled that Sister Slachta once talked to her about converting to Christianity. When Miriam declined, Slachta apologized and expressed her admiration for Miriam's stalwart position, and never brought up the subject again.

As for Sister Sára Salkaházi, she was one of Slachta's principal aides in the Society's rescue endeavors. She was born in 1899 in Kosice-Kassa and her family owned several hotels. Before her ordination, she had done work as a journalist, but soon gave it up as she became gradually more attracted to a religious life, which led her to join the Society's order. At the time of the Arrow Cross killing rampage against Jews in Budapest, in late 1944, Sister

Salkaházi was in charge of one of the Society's houses in the city. When the Arrow Cross raided the premises, on December 27, they discovered hidden Jews; three of them with Salkaházi were led away and were marched that same night to join a larger group of Jews assembled from elsewhere to the banks of the Danube River. The Jews were shot and their bodies dumped into the frozen river. As for Salkaházi, her body was found riddled with bullets lying on the riverbank. Earlier, Sister Salkházi had composed a prayer, which included the following words: "If the persecution of the Church or the Sisters takes place, and my death should not be in the plans of Thy Divine Wisdom and Providence, yet deign to accept it, with all its suffering, as a ransom for my Sisters, especially in place of the life of the aged, the sick, and the weak."

Following Salkaházi's tragic death, Sister Slachta sought refuge in a Carmelite convent and remained hidden until the city's liberation. After the war, Sister Slachta was again elected to Parliament, but soon the Society was outlawed by the Communist regime, and its members were forced underground. The Society, and Sister Slachta, moved its base of operations to the United States, where she died in 1974. In 1969 she and Sára Salkaházi were recognized as Righteous Among the Nations.

As this story goes to press, it was announced that the martyred Sára Salkaházi had been declared a saint, and her beatification was to take place in September 2006, at St. Stephen's (St. Istvan's) Basilica, in Budapest – the first such beatification in Hungary in a thousand years; the last one having taken place in 1083.

Socha, Leopold & Magdalena Wroblewski, Stefan
POLAND

*T*he 1972 film *The Poseidon Adventure* tells the fictional story of a pleasure boat suddenly struck by a tidal wave and capsizing. A certain Reverend Frank Scott leads nine survivors from the grand ballroom through steam, fire, and rising water to the bowels of the upended ship (the propeller shaft), now the highest point. On the way, they meet other groups going in the opposite, and wrong, direction, who do not make it. But a few survive. Little did the viewers of this film realize that a similar story had been enacted some 30 years earlier, but under even more harrowing circumstances, resulting not from a freak upheaval of nature but from one of the most horrific chapters in human history, from acts perpetrated by human beings against their fellow human beings – by non-Jews against Jews.

The story takes place in Lwów (formerly in Poland and today in Ukraine and known as Lviv), where a group of survivors of Nazi atrocities were led by a Pole and his companion through the rat-infested sewers of the city, struggling against the waters of a river running through them. Some of them survived, including their rescuer, though he died in a road accident soon after liberation.

When the Germans captured Lwów on June 30, 1941, there were approximately 160,000 Jews in a city that numbered some 310,000 inhabitants (the two largest ethnic groups were the Poles and Ukrainians). The murder of Jews commenced on the same day in a large-scale killing spree carried out by a special German unit (*Einsatz-gruppe C*) and Ukrainian nationalists. It lasted four days and claimed 4,000 victims. Killing raids on the city's Jews continued without letup, with thousands of lives lost on each occasion. Thousands of others were sent to work on roads and bridges and in military camps and were subjected to unrelenting abuse. Synagogues and cemeteries were systematically desecrated and destroyed. On November 8, 1941, the creation of a ghetto was ordered and simultaneously 5,000 old and sick people were murdered. The following year saw the reduction of the Jewish population to a fraction of the pre-invasion figure as 15,000 were deported to the Bełżec death camp in March 1942, followed by 7,000 mostly women and old people taken to the nearby Janowska camp to be murdered. During the Great *Aktion* of August 10 to 23, 1942, 50,000 more victims were sent to the Bełżec death facility. There now remained only 50,000 Jews. These too were disposed of in swift killing operations, and on June 1, 1943, the Germans, in their killing frenzy, decided to liquidate the remaining Jews in the ghetto. In random shootings and with the use of hand grenades, some 3,000 were killed

Leopold Socha (private collection, Kristine Chigen Keren, New-York)

on the streets of the ghetto; the rest were sent to the Janowska camp. Children were savagely murdered, their heads smashed or thrown bodily into burning buildings. At the same time small groups of fleeing Jews were groping their way through the city's underground sewers; and a few more were hiding with friendly non-Jewish rescuers. The Janowska camp was itself liquidated in November 1943. Officially there were no more Jews in the city, and the jubilation among the Germans and their Ukrainian collaborators was great.

As told by Ignacy Chiger, one of the survivors, on the eve of the Germans liquidation of the last remnants of the Lwów ghetto in the spring of 1943, he and some others had already thought of hiding in the sewers of the city. Before the war, the Peltev River had been diverted to flow into and under the city, so it could carry with it the refuse and garbage in the sewers and flush them out on the other side of the city. It was quite an engineering feat, with a labyrinth of tunnels leading from various city locations to the main riverbed, which flowed beneath the city. Now Chiger planned to dig his way to the underground sewer system from the basement of a man named Weiss and get as near as possible to the Peltev River without actually entering it, for fear of being dragged by the river and drowned in its rushing waters.

After eight days of laborious digging, Chiger and his group completed a narrow tunnel of several meters, and found themselves standing on a very narrow ledge with the vaulted ceiling of the sewer high above them. As Ignacy Chiger recalled that moment many years later, "Total darkness surrounded us and the noise of the rushing water below us. The first descent of ours into the subterranean darkness reminded us of Orpheus' descent into Hades." The group stood momentarily paralyzed.

As they moved forward into the unknown holding aloft some lanterns, suddenly a beam of light from the opposite direction blinded them. Unknown voices demanded of them, "What are you doing?" The fugitives realized that they had run into some of the sewer workers. "They threatened to turn us over to the Gestapo. We began slowly and calmly explaining our plight to them. We told them of plans to seek shelter in the sewer and begged them to help us. We saw their three faces in the lantern's light. One with a chubby, round face appeared quite curious about our undertaking. He apparently admired the work we had already done and he and the others decided to accompany us back to our basement to learn more about our project."

The three unknown sewer workers followed the Jewish fugitives to their basement, and there they saw Ignacy's wife, Paulina, huddled in a corner with her two small children. Ignacy observed one of the sewer workers, the one with the chubby face, who appeared the most sympathetic and deeply moved by the appearance of Ignacy's family. "It seemed as if he was involved in some deep inner struggle." His name was Leopold Socha. Much later he confessed to them that it was the sight of Chiger's wife huddled with the children that moved him to help them. Finally he told the people in the basement that he would help them find a suitable shelter in the sewers. But, he said, it would cost them some money. It was to be a business transaction, fraught with many risks for all concerned. But Chiger and his group were prepared for this. In fact, they had no other choice, if they wanted to survive.

Socha returned to the basement through the sewers several times with reports of his search for a suitable sewer with a concealed entrance. Chiger took note of the man's kindness and soft speech, and also that when speaking to them he would usually hold Chiger's four-year-old son, Pavel, on his knees, and the child seemed to grow fond of him. Finally, Socha invited the group to follow him and help him clear the mud and dirt which is usually found in sewers. They thus spent several days working to clear the entrance of the chosen sewer. Then came the evening of May 31, 1943 – the night of horror – the ghetto's final destruction. They heard above them SS men, Gestapo, and Ukrainian militia, flushing out the remaining ghetto Jews, as some who escaped the shooting outside came down in panic to the small basement and asked to be allowed to join Chiger's group into the sewers. Slowly but surely they all moved through the darkened sewers to the edge of the Peltev River flowing underneath the city. Suddenly Ignacy's knapsack slipped from his shoulders and was carried away by the rushing water together with all the provisions packed inside. Above them, their ears picked up the frightening echo of human screams, children's cries, while close by the rushing waters mercilessly pounded in their ears. "All of us pushed forward in a paroxysm of fear. Most of the people surged unconsciously forward not knowing where they were or where they were going." Finally, they came upon an underground bridge. On the way there, in the darkness, some of the people had wandered off in a different direction in one of the underground tunnels, not knowing where it would lead them. It was later learned, that many had followed the river to its exit, where SS troopers had waited for them and shot them dead.

With Socha leading the way, they arrived at the entrance to a tunnel, and as their feet plunged into mud, with rats running all around them, they beheld dense spider webs hanging from the walls. They stood there with a small flickering candle, frightened and lost. From above, they heard shots and exploding grenades. They were soon joined by others, some of whom in their blind rush to find safety in the sewer lost their footing on the narrow ledges and were swept away by the rushing current. After regaining a foothold, they begged to join Socha's group. Socha agreed provided they all stay close together. Chiger looked at Socha's face, illuminated by the carbide lantern held by Socha, and saw his despair. He now had on his hands some 70 people who were frantically seeking a safe place. He knew he could not keep such a large group together for more than a day and that a way had to be found to divide them up into smaller groups of 15 to 20 people. In the meantime, for three or four days Socha and his co-worker Stefan Wroblewski brought food for the whole group while a third worker, Jerzy Kowalow, stood guard at the tunnel entrance, right above them. To continue to feed such a large group in secrecy would be impossible, so Socha decided to transfer part of the group to another hiding place and have them try to survive as best as they could on their own. From the original group of 70, Socha selected 21, among whom were Chiger's family of four, his brother-in-law Kuba Leinwand, and others, some of whom had brought along money and valuables, which it was felt would be helpful.

Socha led the smaller group along the narrow ledge of the tunnel roof in single file. The group resembled a procession of ghosts led by Socha's glimmering carbide lantern. One had to watch one's step and not slip on the sewage flowing down from the houses above ground. At each precarious spot, Socha passed back a warning. In a big tunnel constructed of concrete pipes, the sewage rose almost to hip level. Socha climbed through a hatch and extended his hand to pull each of the fugitives after him as Wroblewski boosted them up from below. They entered a clear, wide area. They had completed the march. They were beneath the Church of our Lady of the Snows.

The people sat down amid the stench and the rats. "We were all shivering, being soaked to the bones." Ignacy Chiger looked around him to take the measure up the people with him. He saw a young girl clinging to his wife, begging her to let her stay with her family. The rest of the crowd was unknown. "There, below the Church of Our Lady of the Snows, we delivered our fate into the hands of the three sewer workers." Two of them, Socha and Wroblewski, bought them bread, sausages and fresh water. Socha also reported how people in the streets above them were looting the remaining possessions of the Jews.

Chiger wondered how long they could survive in the primitive conditions of their underground cavern. "I held our little seven-year-old daughter [Krystyna], and my wife held our little four-year-old year old son [Pavel]. We also slept this way, huddled together." Overcome by thirst, Ignacy dipped his hands into the sewer waters and drank from it. He as well as the others contracted very painful cases of diarrhea, from the water, or the food, or the air – or of them all. Chiger asked Socha to bring some alcohol and an empty sardine tin. He ignited the alcohol and boiled the small amount of water for the children.

In that dark place Socha told them to be as quiet as possible. "We were only several meters below the church. We could hear worshippers coming in and out of the church above us and could hear their voices murmuring prayers. Our voices would also be amplified through the pipe and we tried never to talk above a whisper." On June 10 there was a procession on the

Feast of Corpus Christi. The people below could make out the voices of children singing and would have remembered such festivals from the past, with the children entering the church with their clothes garnered with flowers.

Socha and Wroblewski came to them each time from a different street entrance so as not to arouse suspicion. This caused them each time to increase their underground journey by at least half a mile before reaching their charges. They always brought two bags filled with food; at times, holding the heavy bags with both hands so that they had no choice but to keep the carbide lanterns between their teeth to light the way. They always arrived breathless and exhausted. Two young girls from among the group could take it no longer and pleaded with Socha to let them leave. He gave in and led them out of the tunnel. They were captured and killed. Three others also decided to leave the tunnel on their own, and they too were captured and shot. Mrs. Weiss, the mother of the man from whose basement they had originally dug the tunnel to the sewers, was an elderly woman. Her son had abandoned her, leaving the group. She died in the sewer. There were now only ten left in the group.

Zipporah Wind was one of the remaining ten. Originally from Turka, a town in the foothills of the Carpathian Mountains in southern Poland, she had lost her whole family to the Germans (except for one brother who had fortunately left for the United States before the war). Sensing the end, her parents had placed a Catholic religious medallion around her neck. Her Hasidic father told her, "Remember, your name is Halina Naszkiewicz. You must forget us, your home, your real name." On November 10, 1942, Zipporah boarded a train for Lwów; she never saw her parents again. For a time she lodged with a family. On Christmas Eve of 1942, at services in her landlord's flat, she inadvertently gave herself away by reaching for the communion wafer instead of receiving it on her tongue. The others gasped. The secret was out: Halina was Jewish. Betrayed to the authorities, she was arrested and brutally beaten and imprisoned in the ghetto jail. She was told she would be shot. It was February 1943. At the last minute, a stroke of good luck saved her. Ordered to fetch the prisoners' toilet bucket and take it across the yard, she noticed that the prison gate had been left unguarded. Quickly darting out of the prison compound into the ghetto proper, she found streets and houses almost deserted. Some friendly Jews quickly snatched her off the streets and into their basement hideout. There she was given a new identity and registered as a seamstress in a German-operated establishment where army uniforms were mended and the clothing of murdered Jews was deloused and reprocessed for shipment to Germany. She then joined the group of people who descended into the sewers.

To add to the fugitives' woes, June came with its heavy rains that lasted for several days. The Peltev River overflowed its banks and torrents of water cascaded through the pipes. The people below were in constant danger of being carried away by a sudden influx of water from above with no avenue of escape. Earlier the sewer workers had shown them a place where they could get fresh water from a well. Just like Kuba Leinwand, Ignacy's brother-in-law, was filling the bucket from the leaking well, a torrent of water engulfed him and he was carried off. Ignacy lamented his death: "And so drowned Kuba Leinwand, the husband of my sister; she had perished with their little daughter Inka in a prior killing action."

The group could not remain much longer in this cavern-like hiding place and asked of Socha to find them another one. One of the problems there was the fight with the rats. While Chiger's wife would hold on to the children, warming them with her own body,

Ignacy would try to chase the rats away with the light of his candle. Socha decided to bring them to another niche. Leading the way with his carbide lantern and the young Pavel Chiger in his arms, and with Wroblewski bringing up the rear to make sure no one slipped and fell into the river, he brought them to a different place.

Arriving at their new underground hideout, they noticed that the walls were wet and covered with mold and cobwebs and a there was layer of mud on the ground. The group laid planks of wood on rocks to serve as benches during the day. At night the planks were pushed together to improvise beds. There too, they could not stretch to their full height and spent most of the day sitting hunched over on the benches. The sewer workers supplied them with bread, a coffee substitute, and potatoes. The bread had to be carefully hidden to keep the rats from getting at it. Socha and Wroblewski would usually arrive at 9 o'clock with some food, carbide and benzene to boil water to make substitute coffee and soup.

Socha once obtained a full truckload of potatoes and drove the truck to a point where he could dump them through a manhole into a dry part of the sewer. To inquisitive passersby he explained that these were rotten potatoes that he was discarding into the Peltev River. He then returned to his charges and showed them where the potatoes were and the men collected them in buckets. The rats also had a taste of the potatoes, but they soon got tired of eating only potatoes and started to attack the supply of bread. They also began to become accustomed to these strange newcomers in their dwelling places and got friendly. In Ignacy Chiger's words:

> "My children would feed and play with the rats that lived among us like family pets. Often during the night they would crawl over us as we slept and I was at times awakened by a rat licking my ear or staring at me as if waiting for me to play. We fought a constant battle with the rats to protect our bread … The keen-wittedness of the rodents worked to their advantage and against us. They climbed the tunnel walls with their sharp claws. They were clever enough to avoid the glass of broken bottles which we spread on the floor to deter them."

Then there was the problem of lice that infested all their ragged clothes. Socha often took the clothes home to his wife, Magdalena, who boiled them in hot water to get rid of the lice.

During the winter of 1943-44, the snow on the street above the sewer tunnel where they were hidden began to melt in the shape of the letter L, following the configuration of the tunnel. Socha explained to curious observers that this was because of the heat coming out of the kitchen in a nearby monastery. The Germans, however, suspected that the pattern indicated the presence of people below. Sewer workers were dispatched to reconnoiter but did not find the hidden people.

The fugitives were always glad to see Socha each morning with his bright smile and gleaming teeth. He and Wroblewski would sit with the people and relay to them news from the outside world. The two men tried their best to cheer up the fugitives with light-hearted conversation and jokes. "The part of the day that they spent with us was the most pleasurable part for us because they always dispelled the gloomy atmosphere." Furthermore, when Chiger's daughter Krystyna fell into a state of melancholy, Socha sat with her on his lap and tried to cheer her up with amusing stories day after day until she finally regained her former healthy and happy frame of mind.

As for the other fugitives, their health was rapidly deteriorating since they had to live and breathe in constant damp air. Their sight was also failing because of the darkness of the tunnel and their legs were swollen and the joints stiff. The height of the sewer was at best only a little over a meter and a half, forcing everyone to sit bent over causing their backs to become crooked.

Ignacy Chiger learned from Socha something of his background. It was anything but encouraging – in fact quite troubling and a cause for concern. Socha had had a very difficult childhood, and partly because of conditions at home he had begun to steal when he was 10 years old. One thing led to another and he was arrested several times for burglary and theft and had a record of three prison sentences, one for a notorious bank robbery. Socha was also responsible for the theft of some silver and jewelry from Ignacy's wife's aunt's house, a crime that remained unsolved but was now cleared up. During the brief Russian interlude in Lwów, between 1939 and 1941, the Communist regime had considered him an innocent victim of a corrupt capitalist system, and as a downtrodden member of the proletariat they gave him a job in the city's sanitation department, maintaining the sewage system.

At the same time, Leopold Socha had some redeeming qualities. For one, he was loyal to his partners in crime, never betraying them. But it went further than that. He was, paradoxically, a very religious man, and a staunch Polish patriot. He must have regretted his past life, for he considered his undertaking to rescue the group of Jews an act of repentance for his past crimes; a quest for redemption for the wrongs he had done from early childhood and throughout his stormy and immoral life – a plea for the forgiveness of God, in whom he firmly believed. Socha was convinced that his sins would be forgiven and his past crimes atoned for though his redemptive acts of saving people from death. He considered his current help to the fugitive Jews his greatest mission in life. He attended church diligently, constantly praying for his wards' salvation. He gave charity and even lit candles in church as an expression of thanksgiving. While in church, he like others dutifully recited the Lord's Prayer, but after the words, "And forgive us our sins," he silently added to himself, "as we are rescuing the innocent, the abandoned and the threatened." Socha was also pleased when he saw Mrs. Chiger light the traditional Sabbath candles every Friday evening – candles that he brought to them with the other supplies – and also that at least the Chigers fasted on Yom Kippur, the Day of Atonement. Leopold Socha remained the moving force behind the rescue operation. In this respect, Ignacy Chiger considered him to have preserved within himself an exalted sense of moral values.

In another torrential rainstorm, which flooded the streets above them and ran into the sewers, the underground Peltev River overflowed its banks. The waters almost reached the chins of the fugitives. "We stood on the tips of our toes. Suddenly, as quickly as the storm had begun, it stopped and the waters began to recede." Socha was so delighted that they all had survived that he lit a candle in his church. This latest flood was to Socha a reaffirmation of his divinely guided mission to save his people.

The will to live kept the people restrained and well disciplined under the leadership of Ignacy Chiger. When their money had dried to pay off Socha and his two colleagues, Chiger told Socha where he had hidden a small fortune in gold coins and jewelry beneath the basement in the house where he used to live. When Socha and Stefan returned with radiant smiles and the valuables in hand, they gave everything to Ignacy. Ignacy gave it all back to Socha to sell to pay for their maintenance. After a time, when this source also dried up, Socha decided to forgo further payment and simply continue to care for his wards, come what may.

In June 1944, as the Russians approached Lwów, the Germans began to set up defenses in the city, including laying mines on the streets just above the hiding place. Socha and Stefan were able to persuade the Germans not to mine that particular area, since, as they told the Germans, the sewers below were filled with pockets of explosive gas and this might get their soldiers blown up. The trick worked.

Then, to the surprise of all, during the first days of July, Socha brought a stranger – Tola, a Russian prisoner of war who had escaped and found refuge in the house of a woman who turned out to be Socha's sister-in-law, Michalina. The two had fallen in love and Michalina had asked Socha to save him. Not used to living several meters below the street amidst mud and rats, the man became very nervous and restless and wanted to leave. Socha told Chiger not to allow this at any price, and gave him a gun with orders to shoot Tola if he tried to escape.

Above them they heard the sound of shooting and the rumble of tanks, as well as the voices of German officers as they shouted their commands. Tola began to rave like a maniac; he was losing his mind and had to be kept under constant watch. Above them the fighting raged for several days. Finally, on July 27, 1944, the Red Army completed the occupation of Lwów. On that day, Socha banged overhead: "Come out! Everybody out! Out!"

As they exited in a yard near a building, a small crowd began to gather around Socha. At first, the hidden people could not see at all, since their eyes had gotten used to darkness and the sunlight now blinded them. Gradually they started to recognize shapes, but in a red-orange color. Socha stood with the crowd and some Russian soldiers, explaining how he had kept these ragged-looking people alive. "This is my work," he said proudly.

"We emerged from the sewers like cavemen," Ignacy Chiger said. "We had nothing. People were frightened by our appearance since the clothes we were wearing were nothing more than rags. My children were very, very pale and their cheeks were almost transparent. Their feet were wrapped in rags, since they had no shoes. We still could not straighten up and walked stooped over." Chiger's little son Pavel was unaccustomed to seeing so many people. He became frightened and pulled at his mother's hand for her to take him back to the sewer where he was used being. Socha tried to calm him by hugging and kissing him. He eventually quieted down. Socha had quickly requisitioned a four-room house just recently occupied by the Germans and together with Stefan they got together tables, chairs, beds, and bedding to furnish the house for his liberated charges.

To avoid questioning by the Russians about his too ardent Polish loyalties in a city that had reverted to the Soviet Union, Socha left for Przemysl, Poland, in February 1945. A month later, the Chigers also went there, staying with Socha for a few days before moving on to Cracow. On May 13, 1945, they learned of Socha's tragic death, when he was accidentally run over by a Russian truck. In Chiger's words, "The memory of his compassion and love will remain with us always as well as his bravery and courageous deeds. We will forever admire and respect this man as our savior and honor his memory."

In 1957, the Chigers left for Israel. There, Krystyna studied dentistry and eventually moved to the United States, where she opened a dental clinic in New York. She is married to Marian Keren and has two sons, the eldest, Doron, also a dentist. In a recent interview,

Kristine (her Americanized first name) said, "At each [family] wedding and birth, I am so happy. I always say to myself, 'Aha! Hitler didn't succeed.'" Halina Wind also moved to the United States and was active in creating a Holocaust memorial center in Wilmington, Delaware, where she planted a tree in the name of Leopold Socha. Her son, David Perston, is a journalist. The story has also been told by the BBC on film, under the title "Light in the Dark," and narrated by Susannah York.

Of the many people who had descended into the dark sewers on the night of the ghetto's liquidation, only a handful crawled out upon the city's liberation. Leopold Socha's Jews were among the few who survived in the rat-infested caverns of the city's sewers – for 14 harrowing months. The Peltev River continues to flow underneath the city of Lwów-Lviv, carrying with it the secret of the many others who tried to find a haven amidst its rushing waters but did not make it.

In 1978, Yad Vasem recognized Leopold and Magdalena Socha and Stefan Wroblewski as Righteous Among the Nations.

Soroka, Tadeusz
POLAND

*F*or many years, Lisa Derman had frantically searched for Tadeusz Soroka, a former Polish railroad worker who had saved her and a group of other Jews. Nothing seemed to help until 1981, when she was told to turn to the Polish Interior Ministry in then communist Poland, who through their secret service would surely locate him. And so it did. The following year, Soroka's former charges had him flown to Chicago, where they lived (especially in the suburb of Skokie), to arrange a royal welcome for him.

Tadeusz (or Tadek, as he was affectionately known) worked in Grodno as a railroad man. During the German occupation of Grodno, which began in June 1941, he was in the habit of secretly sneaking into the work place of the Jewish forced laborers outside the ghetto in order to trade with the starving workers and their families – food in exhange for clothing and other articles which were less important to them at the time. Aron Dereczynski (later changed to Derman) and Hershel Zvi Lipsczyc (later Lipshitz), two of the ghetto Jews who worked at that site as carpenters, noted that on many occasions Soroka gave his trading partners food but took nothing in return, although by his very presence there he was risking his life. The man had a heart, they concluded.

Aron Dereczynski was born in Slonim, Poland, in 1922, and survived the massacre of the city's Jews perpetrated by the Germans after they occupied the city on June 25, 1941. Escaping to the Grodno ghetto in summer 1942, he was reunited with his girlfriend (later wife) Lisa Nussbaum, her father Hirsh Nussbaum, and her brother Berusiek (later Robert Ness).

One day, on their return from work to the ghetto, fellow worker Lipszyc related to Dereczynski that Soroka had told him: "Listen, the ghetto will be your death. If you wish ... I can get you to Vilna by train where it's much safer." He had asked for nothing in return. Dereczynski was somewhat hesitant regarding Soroka's motives. It could be a trap, he suspected, to turn a fleeing Jew over to the Germans, and be rewarded by the Jew's captors. One had to be careful these days. One fatal mistake could be the last one. Dereczynski begged off, but Lipszyc decided to go along with the plan. Soroka kept his word and smuggled Lipszyc and a friend aboard a train to the Vilna (today Vilnius) ghetto. Soroka had, however, forgotten to secure from Lipszyc a previously agreed upon note confirming his safe arrival in Vilna. So when Soroka met Dereczynski again at his work place and told him that Lipszyc and his partner had successfully arrived in Vilna, he could not produce a note and Aron's doubts about the man were not quashed. His confidence in Soroka was somewhat restored when he brought Dereczynski food.

On several occasions Soroka again broached the subject of Dereczynski's escape from the Grodno ghetto with his help. Aron, who had lost all his family to the Germans, decided to wait. But after narrowly escaping another German "action," by hiding in the synagogue's coal room, he felt that the risks of staying on in Grodno far outweighed those of fleeing to Vilna with the help of Soroka. Vilna, 180 kilometers away, seemed a safer place; its ghetto was larger; it had an underground, and in case one had to flee from there, the partisans known to operate in the surrounding woods offered an escape route. Still Aron could not make up his mind, and he decided to wait a while longer.

One afternoon soon thereafter, Soroka returned to Dereczynski's place of work and warned him that he had seen German police units surrounding the ghetto, and this could only mean that the liquidation of the ghetto was about to begin. In Dereczynski's words, "He suggested that I follow him to his house, from where he would take me to Vilna at the first opportunity. I accepted his offer. I told him that I had no money nor anything else to give him in return. He answered, and I quote him: 'I did not ask you for money: I do not need your money; I want to help you.'"

However, Dereczynski did not follow through, as the other men at work had taken note of Dereczynski's lengthy conversation with Soroka. Correctly suspecting that the two were planning an escape, they were understandably worried that when they returned to the ghetto and one of the members of the work force was missing, the Germans would punish, or even execute, the rest. "I was watched. Soroka followed our work group to the ghetto just in case I managed to get away from the group, but I could not." Dereczynski's escape had been foiled on this occasion.

In the meantime, Soroka helped two other men reach the Vilna ghetto. As told by Berusiek Nussbaum, in February of 1943, as a thirteen-year-old boy, he had left the ghetto to meet with Tadeusz Soroka and listen to his plan to smuggle out a certain number of inmates to Vilna. Berusiek conveyed the information to his sister, Lisa, and her boyfriend Aron Dereczynski, but they declined to join for the moment. The next day, Berusiek and his father sneaked out of the ghetto to rendezvous with Soroka, but was told by his sister that he had left a message for them to return the next day. So Berusiek and his father slipped back into the ghetto, spending the night in one of the abandoned buildings. The next day they met Soroka, who undertook to join them for the ride, all the way to Vilna. As told by Berusiek (Robert Ness),

"My father and I followed Tadeusz Soroka to an embankment next to some railroad tracks and following Soroka jumped on a slowly moving railroad train. Once on the train, all of us entered a small vestibule attached to one of the boxcars. We rode like that until we arrived in Orany, the then border town between Germany and Lithuania. The train stopped. While all three of us were in the boxcar tower (the vestibule), a German guard approached it and tried to open the door. Unable to open it, the guard started to knock and simultaneously asked who was inside. He was very persistent and would not give up. Tadeusz Soroka finally answered. He went out of the other side of the enclosure and faced the guard, while my father and I remained in the tower. We heard the guard asking Soroka in German whether anybody else was in the tower. We heard Soroka replying that nobody was there but him. Tadeusz Soroka and the guard left the place together."

After a few hours, Soroka reappeared and told the two frightened fugitives that he had learned that this particular train was going stay in Orany for a long time, so it was better to jump on another train leaving shortly for Vilna. Berusiek and his father left the vestibule and, following Soroka, jumped onto another moving military personnel train with Red Cross markings. They sat out the ride on the small platform between the cars until the train arrived in Vilna. Soroka then brought them close to ghetto's gates. "We parted and thanked him for his help. I don't remember whether my father gave him anything for helping us escape from Grodno. It may be that my father gave him a gold watch. I know that I gave him nothing."

Ruby Lubicz (later changed to Loren), was another person helped by Soroka. Born in 1921 in Grodno, Ruby had seen his family killed by the Germans in several liquidation raids in the ghetto. By March 1943, there were fewer than 1,000 Jews left, out of the original 25,000 who had lived in Grodno when the Germans took over. Then, at the end of February 1943, Ruby befriended Aron Dereczynski, who told him about the young Pole, Soroka, who worked on the railroad; his job allowing him to travel on German trains going from Grodno to Vilna, about 180 kilometers away. Ruby had heard of the Jewish underground operating inside the Vilna ghetto, and its plans to join up with friendly partisans in the not-too-distant forests, so he wished greatly to be able to join them. So did Dereczynski. The two decided to take up Soroka on his offer. As a precaution, Aron's girlfriend, 16-year-old Lisa Nussbaum, who was blond and blue-eyed blond, and did not have a "Jewish look," was chosen to seek him out and arrange a time and place for the meeting.

As further related by Lisa Nussbaum, in early March 1943 Aron, Ruby, and some other relatives and friends of Ruby, and herself – all left the ghetto to rendezvous with Soroka. Lisa went ahead to meet him at his sister's house where she spent a good part of the day before returning to the other escapees, who were hiding in a bombed-out house. She relayed them the bad news that Tadeusz would be unable to take the group that Sunday and it would be better to wait until the next Sunday. All returned disappointed to the ghetto.

On the night of March 6–7, 1943, Aron, Ruby, a cousin of his, another friend, and Lisa escaped again from the ghetto and headed for a prearranged empty house to pass the night. The following day, Sunday, March 7, Lisa left to meet Tadeusz Soroka and his sister in their neighborhood church. Again Soroka excused himself, saying that he would be unable to take the group that day, as it happened that no trains were departing from Grodno to Vilna, but that the escape would be possible in two days' time – on Tuesday. The group was to meet Tadeusz outside the public washrooms of the market place. Lisa returned to relay the disappointing message to Aron. There was nothing to do but spent two idle days in hiding in that empty house.

Tuesday evening, all five left the hideout on the outskirts of the former ghetto and proceeded to the market place to meet Tadeusz. He was there on time to meet them. He stated emphatically that under no circumstances could he take more that two people with him as a large group would become too conspicuous for safety reasons. He finally agreed to three: Aron, Ruben, and Lisa, with the understanding that the other two would be taken on the coming Thursday. Tadeusz Soroka and Lisa proceeded from the public washrooms to the railroad station with the other two, Aron and Ruby, close behind, and with Soroka looking back repeatedly to see that the two were at a safe distance from him. Approaching the train station, the group hid by an embankment next to the railroad tracks. Soroka then pointed out the train that would be leaving for Vilna. At this point, Soroka seemed to hesitate, telling the others that it was an ammunition train full of Germans and that perhaps another delay would be in order. Lisa remembered: "The three of us, Aron, Ruby, and I, turned down the suggestion, pointing out to him that we had no choice, that we could not return to the ghetto anymore and that we would have to take our chances with this train. He agreed." Lisa then related what happened:

> *"Tadeusz told us that when the train started moving we were to jump onto the steps of any of the boxcars and climb the ladder to the roof. Once we reached the roof he told us we were not to panic, that he would be there to look after us. I, then sixteen years old, missed a step while trying to jump onto the moving train and was left dangling with my feet off the ground and with one hand holding on to the door handle of the boxcar. Tadeusz, realizing that I was missing on the roof, ran and jumped from one roof to another of the boxcars on the moving train until he found me. He formed a human chain with Aron and Ruby, who had joined him by then, holding on to his legs so that he would not fall from the roof of the boxcar as he was bending over with his body and both hands to pull me up. He pulled me up to the top of the boxcar as the train was gaining speed."*

Soroka was with them throughout the long night ride, handing out food and also, heaven knows how, hot drinks. He showed them how to conceal themselves from the lights of the train stations. "He comforted us generally."

As the train neared Vilna, Soroka had them blacken their faces with coal dust to give the impression that they were railroad workers finishing the night shift. As the train slowed down, they all jumped off and crouched down near the wall of a shack not far from the station, where he told them to wait until he returned. He was going to try to find a Jewish working group that would be returning to the ghetto after the night shift. After a little wait, he returned and had his charges infiltrate a marching group of Jews returning to the ghetto. The operation was a success. "Neither Aron nor I gave anything to Tadeusz Soroka for his help," Lisa underlined. All in all, 20-year old Soroka made the journey with escapees from the Grodno ghetto to Vilna on four different occasions, saving a total of nine persons.

After surviving the Holocaust, Lisa married Aron and both moved to the United States, settling in Skokie, Illinois, but they could not forget Tadeusz Soroka. "After liberation,"

Lisa said, "we all split up, but we all remembered Tadeusz. When we left Eastern Europe we vowed that we would see each other again and that we would find some way to have him recognized for what he did." In 1950, the Dermans and Lipszyc (in Israel) began a concerted effort to find "Tadek." They sent letters to the address where they had contacted him in Grodno, which had become part of the Soviet Union after the war. The letters were not returned. Nor did they receive answers to their letters of inquiry to various offices of information in the Grodno area. Added to the difficulties was the fact that none of the survivors knew for sure how to spell the man's last name. Was it Soroki or Sorota or Soroski, or what? Nevertheless, they kept on, writing to bureaus of missing persons, the Red Cross, and religious organizations, but without results.

Then, in 1981, the Dermans attended a worldwide reunion of Holocaust survivors in Jerusalem and were told by one of those attending to try an agency in Warsaw operating under the Polish Ministry of the Interior. Returning to the United States, Lisa wrote to the agency, including all the details and the different possible spellings of the name Soroka. In October 1981, the Dermans were stunned when the Warsaw agency wrote back: "We have located the person you are seeking." For a fee $15, payable at the Polish consulate, the bureau would send all the pertinent information. And so it was. It turned out that Soroka had moved to Tarnowskie Góry, a town in the smoky coal region of southwest Poland. Lisa, a bit apprehensively, wrote to the man, not sure he was the right person. A reply came in January 1982: "Yes, I am the one." He added that when he learned that a certain American woman was looking for him, he knew it was the little Jewish girl he had pulled to the top of that freezing boxcar outside Grodno almost 40 years before. He had since married and was the father of four children and two grandchildren, and was recently retired.

In late 1982, the Dermans and four other survivors living in the Chicago area flew him to Chicago for a tearful and long-awaited reunion. Lisa immediately recognized her rescuer as he stepped out into the arrival lounge at O'Hare airport. For the next six weeks, Soroka was feted by a host of civic and religious organizations, including a personal audience with Chicago Archbishop Joseph Bernardin. The archbishop said: "I am very happy to meet with you and I will pray to the Lord to bless you for your goodness." To which Soroka responded: "God has already blessed me in many ways.

Rescuer and rescued spent hours together reminiscing about the terrible times of the past. Throughout, Soroka downplayed his deeds in Nazi-occupied Poland. Answering one of the questions concerning his motives, he explained what led him to help Jews on the run. "I experienced poverty and suffering myself. My mother died and my own brother was sent by the Nazis to do slave labor. I ran away for a time and lived on false papers. When I returned I did work for about three months in various houses. It was there I came in contact with the Jews. Knowing the tragedy of the people, seeing them locked up behind bars and fences, I felt pain and wanted to help them." Why did he choose to help when so many others remained passive? "I was brought up in a religious home and I went to school with the Sisters of Nazareth. We were all taught the second great commandment: 'Love your neighbor as yourself.' So I knew what I must do. Others did as much or more. It was no big thing." His father had been a train engineer and his brother-in-law a conductor, so it was relatively easy for him to get a railroad uniform and a schedule of trains leaving for Vilna. The danger, he said, never deterred him, since "we were all in danger under the Nazis all the time." He adamantly refused to be called a "hero." "No, no!" he said animatedly, "I never did anything heroic in my whole life, unless it was raising my four children... No, I never did anything special. I lived by my religion and I still do." In his first letter to Lisa, a year earlier, Soroka had written: "I believe a good deed always remains in human history, and neither time nor distance nor race can erase it."

Lisa's long and determined quest to find her rescuer and acknowledge and thank him for his brave deed had been fulfilled. Tadeusz Soroka was also thankful. In his words, "I am overwhelmed that the people, after so many years, remember me."

In 1983 Yad Vashem honored him as Righteous Among the Nations.

Spiliakos, Dimitris
GREECE

*T*hessalonika or, as it is better known in Jewish history, Salonika, claimed one of the oldest Jewish communities, going back to pre-Roman days. Many Jews had also fled there after 1942 after being expelled from Spain, and the Jewish influence in the city was conspicuous to the extent that on Saturdays the city's port, where many Jews worked, was shut down. In 1913, the city, until then part of the Turkish Empire for hundreds of years, had reverted to Greece. Thessalonika numbered some 50,000 Jews when the Germans occupied it on April 9, 1941, and immediately began to institute severe anti-Jewish measures, including the looting of Jewish property and the destruction of the ancient Jewish cemetery. On July 11, 1942, an especially hot day, thousands of Jewish men were forced to stand for hours in Freedom Square under a scorching sun. Many of them were sent to forced labor, with some 200 dying from exhaustion and maltreatment. The remaining Jews were slated for deportation to the concentration camps that began on March 20, 1943 and lasted until August 18, 1943, during which 19 transports took 43,850 Jews (95% of those still present) mostly to Auschwitz, where with a few exceptions they were conveyed to the gas chambers upon arrival. In the macabre setting of that camp, some of the unfortunate arrivals were

Dimitris Spiliakos (left)

made to undergo pseudo-medical tests on their sex organs; others were consigned to a special unit charged with loading the gassed bodies into the crematoriums. One of the most ancient and continuously existing Jewish communities had been totally decimated within a matter of a few months. A few were saved with the help of their non-Jewish friends, as in the following story.

Albert Simantov, born in 1924, had known Dimitris Spiliakos since childhood, as Spiliakos had served as the family's attorney and advisor on economic and other matters. In July 1942, when the Germans ordered all Jewish men to assemble in Freedom Square, ostensibly to be registered, Spiliakos told Simantov not to go. "Unfortunately, I did not follow his advice and, as a result, I was taken for forced labor for over six months." Released afterwards, Simantov returned to Thessaloniki and soon afterwards, in March 1943, all Jews were confined in a special ghetto to await their deportation. Most Jews assumed that they were going to Poland to start a new life while doing work for the Germans – and not to be immediately killed in gas chambers. This time Simantov listened to Spiliakos, who arranged for him to be smuggled aboard an Italian military convoy wearing an Italian uniform. It was leaving for Athens, then under Italian administration. Italy, although allied to Nazi Germany, did not harm the Jews in their occupation zones. In addition, on April 7, 1943, Spiliakos hid Albert's mother in his home, keeping her there for two weeks before also smuggling her over to Athens. In May or June 1943, during the intensified deportations of the city's Jews, Spiliakos literally forced Albert's sister and her husband to abandon the line that was obediently marching to the train station for deportation, and he provided shelter for them. He also helped Albert's nephew flee to Athens.

In September 1943, after Italy capitulated to the Allies, the Germans took over in Athens and prepared to deport the Jews there as well. At this point, and from then until the city's liberation in October 1944, through his contacts in Athens, Spiliakos arranged hideouts for Albert's entire family, in ten different places, and also got them fake identity cards. He represented Albert and his mother as members of his family who had left their homes due to the constraints of the occupation. In Albert's words, few people believed the story, given the strong Jewish accent of Albert's mother. But Spiliakos' appealing personality was so strong that no one dared do harm to his charges. Spiliakos, moreover, covered all of his charges' expenses, particularly for food, as Albert's relations were left with no resources of their own. After Greece's liberation, Spiliakos refused to accept any payment and insisted that they owed him nothing for his charitable aid. As for Albert Simantov, who had interrupted his university studies in 1941, Spiliakos encouraged him to resume them and took him into his home to help him rebuild his life. In Albert's words, "The fact that I could graduate in 1948 from the university is due, to a very large extend, to his untiring efforts. I owe him not only my life but also my professional development. In 1986, when Albert Simantov submitted his deposition, he was as an agricultural economist and director of Food, Agriculture and Fisheries for an international organization located in Paris.

Isaac Covo, another of Spiliakos' prewar clients, was also saved together with his family by his attorney. In fact, already at the start of the German anti-Jewish measures in 1941, Spiliakos constantly urged Covo's family to leave the city immediately. Isaac Covo was then head of a Jewish orphanage and a leader in the Jewish community. When the deportations started, each day, late in the night, Spiliakos risked his life by sneaking into the enclosed Jewish area and literally begging Isaac Covo to allow him to plan the escape of his family. In Mrs. Ida Covo's words, "He had no trust in the promises of the Germans [that Jewish leaders and the orphanage would be spared] and he did not doubt that they would not keep their word. He told us that if we were deported he would join us in the deportation." Covo declined to leave, fearing retaliation by the Germans on the children in the orphanage. Then, in April 1943, distressed at not having convinced them, one evening he presented the Covos with, in Ida's words, a *fait accompli,* by procuring a false identity card as well as a ticket on the special Italian train for Ida's son, the 17-year-old Albert. That same evening he took Albert with him, in spite of his parents' objections, and that same evening he placed him on the train for Athens. "This is how I was saved," Albert Covo wrote after the war.

In August came the awakening for Isaac Covo, as the Germans ordered him to prepare the children in the orphanage for deportation within two hours. That same day, Spiliakos sensed that something bad was in the offing, and he sent his sister to alert the Covos to expect him that same evening, to take them away. She was able to pass the message to him that her brother would be waiting for him on a side street at the orphanage. "As for me," Ida related, "she tore off my yellow cockade [yellow star], taking advantage of the commotion among the children and the staff, and both of us sneaked out of the orphanage." Her husband could not follow them at that precise moment, and only much later at night when the children had been boarded on trucks, did he meet Spiliakos, who waited for him at the designated place. "That same evening he took us to an acquaintance of his to pass the night." From that moment, the Covos were in Spiliakos' charge, and he moved them to three different hiding places. "Every evening, he came to see us and bring us provisions, at the risk of his life." He then planned their escape.

As Ida had been born an Italian, Spiliakos took care of all the formalities with the local Italian consul to allow her and her non-Italian husband to leave for Athens. He then led them to the train station to board the special Italian train, with Spiliakos swaying the German guards to allow the Covos get on, although they did not appear on the German list, as they had fled the Jewish ghetto. "We were saved." But only provisionally, for a month later the Germans took over in Athens as well. "There, for the second time, attorney Spiliakos was at out side," in Ida Covo's words. He entrusted one of his married sisters, living in Athens, to shelter the Covos. "We owe our lives, my husband, my son and myself, to Mr. Dimitris Spiliakos." Ida Covo, whose husband died in 1949, emphasizes that Spiliakos acted out of friendship and humanity, "and has never accepted anything from us, except our thanks."

Laura Nissim's family was also among those saved by Spiliakos. As told by her, her forefathers arrived in Thessaloniki in the 15th century, having fled during the expulsion of Jews in Spain at the time. The family consisted of Laura's parents, already of an advanced age, two sons and two daughters, one with a husband and two young children. Spiliakos was the family lawyer, "a generous and disinterested man whom we found a real friend and courageous sustainer." He found people who took the Nissims out of the ghetto, in separate installments, and conveyed them to Athens. They were all saved, except for the brother-in-law who unfortunately was seized and deported. Their rescue happened late one night, when Spiliakos, together with two men, entered the ghetto to get Laura's parents, who were hiding in a cellar after their building had been emptied of its inhabitants for deportation. Spiliakos and his companions pretended to be drunk after a late night drinking party and crossed the emptied ghetto section that was under curfew and guarded by German soldiers – or was it the SS? The Spiliakos entourage were "singing like drunkards," in Laura's words, as they led the two elderly Nissims out of the ghetto. Spiliakos then hid Laura's parents for a week before arranging their flight to Athens with the help of false papers.

In 1987, Yad Vashem conferred on Dimitris Spiliakos the title of Righteous Among the Nations. A year later, during a tree planting ceremony at Yad Vashem, he was asked the reason for the enormous risks he took to save so many Jews. He responded jestingly that he was after all a lawyer, and all he did was to save his clients, since he figured that after the war he hoped to continue to represent them. He failed to say whether this was reason enough to risk his life over and over again. Everyone present understood that before them stood a great humanitarian who, in all modesty, dismissed his many rescues as nothing more than part of his professional business.

Stakauskas, Juozas
Žemaitis, Vladas
Mikulska, Maria
LITHUANIA

*A*lfred Rosenberg was the leading Nazi Party ideologue and one of its earliest members. His book, *The Myth of the 20th Century,* was considered a Nazi classic. During the war, he created a special team to loot and collect Jewish and non-Jewish historical publications and artifacts for the purpose of exhibiting in a postwar Nazi museum the "inferior" quality of these items, representing lower cultural levels in contrast to the "master race." One such team, known as the Rosenberg *Kommando* (Special Unit) had its main base for the Baltic region in the former Lithuanian Main Archives building in Vilnius (Vilna), where Juozas Stakauskas was the archives director. Little did Rosenberg suspect (he was hanged after the war) that 12 Jews, representing the primary *bête noire*, the pet hate, of his writings, matched only by Hitler's own hatred, were hiding literally under his team's office floor, in a special hideout arranged by Juozas Stakauskas and two trustworthy aides.

Born in 1899, Juozas Stakauskas had studied theology in Innsbrück, Austria, and philosophy

Juozas Stakauskas (left) with Dr. Aleksander Libo

in Vienna, earning a doctorate. Returning to Lithuania, he was made head of the State Archives, a position he continued to hold in Vilna when the city came under German occupation in June 1941. He was also an ordained priest, but he kept this fact to himself and only after the war did some of his associates learn of it. Under German rule, he had no choice but to work closely with Rosenberg's team of looters who emptied archives from cities in nearby Belorussia, such as Vitebsk, Minsk, and Smolensk, and brought huge crates to the archive center in Vilna, where the books and files were unloaded and registered, and temporarily stored.

To help him with this tremendous work, Stakauskas asked for additional hands, especially of Jews from the Vilna ghetto; not merely for the physical labor of unloading the written material that arrived there from other cities but also because he claimed that among the Jews were to be found many with a knowledge of languages – a vital necessity for the proper registration and classification of the tons of material. Stakauskas' underlying motive, something that he kept to himself, was to try to ease the plight of the Jews in his city and perhaps save them from eventual death by keeping them as indispensable long-term workers.

This is how he met Nina Gawronska. She had had the bad luck to travel from Tel Aviv to visit her mother in Vilna in 1939 when the war interceded and she could not get back. Three years later, she was among the special work force assigned in the archive building, and when Stakauskas was told that she was a professional teacher of English he asked her to teach him the language. Through Nina, he also became acquainted with her brother-in-law (her sister's husband), the physician Dr. Aleksander Libo, who instructed him and provided him with needed medicines still in Libo's possession. One day, Stakauskas told Libo, "If the situation in the ghetto becomes unbearable, come to me in the archives. Perhaps I will be able to hide you [in the plural]." This was in the spring of 1943 and the future looked bleak and ominous as the Vilna ghetto had already been emptied of most of its Jews, most of whom were shot at pits in the nearby Ponary forest. The talk in town was of a ghetto that would soon be fully liquidated.

In the meantime, due to the huge amount of incoming archive material, the Germans asked Stakauskas to find additional storage space, and he chose a nearby former Benedictine monastery that had been shut down by the city's earlier Soviet masters. On German demand, he produced a diagram of an archival annex in a special section of the unused convent, but left out a section that he wanted to set apart as an eventual hiding place for Jews who might ask him to save them. In this he was to be helped by Vladas Žemaitis, a trained physics teacher who worked for Stakauskas as a carpenter. Žemaitis was later to construct the hiding place that was already on his boss's mind.

On September 23, 1943, the Germans liquidated the Vilna ghetto by killing off the last Jews. At the time, Aleksander Libo with his wife and daughter were among the workers spared until now for their work in the German-run Keilis fur factory located outside the ghetto. It was high time to run for their lives; any day could be too late. Seeing the ghetto go up in flames, Libo and others snuck out two days later. Making their way in the evening hours through empty streets, they arrived at the archive building's main gate, where Stakauskas had his office. They were met by the building's cleaning woman, Joasia. She was frightened by their arrival, as she could hear in the distance the explosions and see the smoke rising from the doomed ghetto. She hurriedly took them to Stakauskas's office, telling them to spend the night there and wait for his arrival the following morning.

When Stakauskas appeared early the next morning and saw the fugitive Jews waiting for him, his face grew pale, as he had just left a Gestapo interrogation at their headquarters across the street. As the Rosenberg *Kommando*, which also utilized Polish and Lithuanian workers, was to arrive soon, Stakauskas rushed his unannounced guests up to the attic and told them to lie low and keep quiet. There they stayed for a while, with Stakauskas visiting them after working hours with news of what was happening on the outside. From one of the windows, Libo could see groups of Jews being led from the burning ghetto to the Gestapo building, from where they were to be dispatched to their final destination. A trustworthy former housekeeper of Libo's named Jadzia Markowska secretly brought them food she got by selling items left in her care by Libo. After about a month's stay in the attic, Stakauskas' cleaning woman Joasia reappeared and led them to nearby St. Catherine Church on Wilenska Street.

As they entered the church, they saw that it was full of worshippers. Libo's group kneeled at the entrance, as customary and, after a few minutes, another woman appeared to take charge of them. It was Sister Maria Mikulska, a Benedictine nun, who since the closure of the convent had stayed behind as the caretaker of the unused building and went around without her nun's habit. She signaled to the group to follow her. In Libo's words, "We entered a dark corridor. She told us to take off our shoes and via the corridor we came upon a place already occupied by the engineer Jakub Jaffe with his wife." Libo and his group had arrived in the basement of the former convent, now used by the German team whose office was right above the place where fugitive Jews were to stay. Two weeks earlier, Jaffe's wife had died in there and Žemaitis had buried her beneath the floor of the basement. After the war the body was removed and reburied in a Jewish cemetery.

The hiding place prepared by Žemaitis was behind rows of files stacked up to the ceiling against a newly built makeshift wall, giving the impression of closing off the room. In fact, behind the files and the fake wall was the former extension of the room, a space large enough to hold a sizable group of people. Entrance to the hiding place was gained by pulling a rope which raised a number of files and exposed a hole barely wide enough for a single person to pass through. Once on the other side, the files were lowered by pulling another rope. The hiding place was divided into two sections; a dark room where food and coal was stored and a lighted room with four beds and a closet with kitchenware. A stove in the room allowed for the warming of food. At night, some of them would climb on top of the files, open several of them and sleep on the pages. They sometimes joked among themselves, "Tonight we'll sleep on new mattresses," and would open the thick files to new pages. The Rosenberg team's office was located on the floor right above the hiding place. Food was arranged by Libo's maid, Jadzia, who brought it to Stakauskas in the main archive building on Teatralna Street, and after working hours he would bring it in a suitcase to his charges and sit with them and pass on information about what was happening on the outside.

Above them, when the Rosenberg *Kommando* had finished work and left, Sister Mikulska would give the "all clear" sign by stamping on the floor three times. It was the sign that they could head upstairs and use the toilet facilities and wash up, as well as stopping over at Mikulska's quarters to pick up the food sometimes left with her. Earlier Stakauskas had asked Mikulska, in Libo's presence, whether she would agree to participate in assisting the Jews he was sheltering. She responded: "If his honor is prepared to face hanging, so am I." She kept her word throughout the rescue period.

Grigori-Grzegorz Jaszunski also gave an account of how he was admitted into Stakauskas's hideout. He first had different plans for himself and his wife, Irena. Escaping from the Vilna ghetto, he had arranged to rendezvous with a certain Polish woman who had undertaken to help them. But she was not to be found in her house. The two Jaszunskis, at a loss what to do next, headed for the archive building where Grigori had earlier done some work. They met Maria Mikulska, who had them wait for Stakauskas' arrival. Stakauskas was impressed with Grigori's knowledge of languages and told the two: "You will stay here in this building under my protection and I will take care of both of you." He added that he was already hiding a large group of Jews close by. "He then led us (together with Mikulska) downstairs to the basement's long corridor. He knocked on the wall. The people behind the wall knew the signal and opened it. Six to seven huge binders concealed the entrance to the room." When they went in, they met the ten other people in hiding, people the Jaszunskis did not know, other than Dr. Aleksander Libo. Jaszunki remembered Stakauskas's words to his charges, "We will either survive together or perish together." Stakauskas struck Jaszunski as "a strange person; not a practical person, but very dedicated, I should say an idealist. He considered it his duty to save people, particularly Jews."

There were now 12 people in hiding. They included Yakov and Sara Yoffe and daughter Monika, Yakov's sister Esther-Fira Kantarovitch, Aleksander and Vera Libo and daughter Luba, Grigori-Grzegorz and Irena Jaszunski, Miriam Rolnik, Mita Markovska and her 10-year-old son Samuel Bak. They were assigned shifts for cooking and cleaning. The cooking was done with wood brought by Žemaitis.

When winter settled in, it proved very cold in the hideout. Stakauskas had already provided for that earlier, acquiring a full load of coal in exchange for the fur given him by Aleksander Libo through his former maid, Jadzia. The fur was meant to be sewn on Stakauskas' winter coat. Instead, with his charges constantly on his mind, he exchanged it for the coal, a scarce item in those days. Libo had also wanted him to take a gold watch, but he refused. Warming up the hiding place could only be done at night, when traces of the rising heat would not betray their presence upstairs. As for the fumes, Žemaitis had an excuse; he had stayed behind after work to heat glue for his carpentry work; hence the smoke coming out of the building's chimney. It was an excuse fraught with danger for all concerned, but no one in his right mind suspected that Jews would be hiding literally under the noses of Nazi officials.

As the fighting moved closer to Vilna, shells began to fall on the city, causing Žemaitis and Jadzia to leave. The hidden people were left to their own devices, tensions ran high and arguments broke out among them on trivial matters, such as what kind of soup to prepare for the day. Then, about two weeks before liberation, the smoke from the cooking alerted people outside, including firemen who were called in to extinguish what seemed to be a fire that had broken out inside the unused convent, with the danger of its destroying the important documents stored there. The firemen broke through one of the windows to locate the fire's presumed origin and a curious crowd assembled outside to watch. At this dangerous juncture, Jaszunki decided to step out and speak to the fireman in charge, a person whom he apparently knew. However, the fireman found it difficult to recognize Jaszunki with his bedraggled appearance, unkempt hair, and unshaven face. When he finally recognized him, the man took his men away and told the crowd to disperse; it was a "false alarm."

As the Red Army edged ever closer, the Germans set many public buildings on fire and the fugitives prayed that the archive annex where they were hiding would be spared. Then on July 14, Žemaitis and his wife appeared and began kissing and hugging everyone. They had brought homemade pastries. Russian soldiers were already inside the city. The 12 people could breathe freely again, after being cooped up and hidden for close to 11 tense months. It had all been made possible by Juozas Stakauskas and his two principal and trustworthy aides, Vladas Žemaitis and Maria Mikulska, who hid a dozen Jews under the noses of a top-ranking special Nazi task force.

In 1974, Yad Vashem recognized as Righteous Among the Nations Juozas Stakauskas, Vladas Žemaitis, and Maria Mikulska.

Stefan (Stoyan Popgueorguiev)
Kiril (Konstantin Markov)

BULGARIA

"*B*oris, my son, I am not at all satisfied with you," *Metropolitan Stefan, head of the Bulgarian church, told the all-powerful King Boris III of Bulgaria, the virtual ruler of the country, over the phone on May 25, 1943.* "One hears lately of many things done to our Jewish brethren. Think very hard; it is unworthy of you and of the Bulgarian people." *The King asked:* "But what – what did you hear and from whom?" Stefan: "Things have come to my knowledge which I would rather not believe. They are a disgrace and shame to you and to the Bulgarian people … Boris, let it not be too late. Pull yourself together, my son."

The preceding words, unheard of in any country allied to Nazi Germany – were spoken by the head of the country's dominant church in confrontational language to the country's ruler. It happened in Bulgaria, and it is one of the major factors that prevented the country's Jews from sharing the fate of their brethren in the rest of Europe. They were saved.

On January 1, 1940, a new government headed by Professor Bogdan Filov as Prime Minister took office in Sofia, the nation's capital. Real power, however, remained in the hands of King Boris III, who since 1934 had enjoyed near-dictatorial power. On March 1, 1941, Bulgaria officially aligned itself with Nazi Germany. With the backing of a victorious

Germany, Bulgaria hoped to regain territories lost during the Balkan war of 1912–13 to her neighbors, Serbia and Greece.

Barely a month later, in April 1941, Germany rewarded Bulgaria by turning over to her a major chunk of dismembered Yugoslavia, the province of Macedonia, and from occupied Greece the region of Thrace in the south. The Dobruja region in the north, detached from Romania (which was later compensated with lands taken from Ukraine, known as Transnistria) was also given to Bulgaria – all these lands, gratis! Bulgaria was not asked to send troops to fight alongside Germany in its war against the Soviet Union; in fact, Bulgaria continued to maintain diplomatic relations with the Soviet Union. Bulgaria limited itself to declaring war on the United States and England – an official act without military consequences.

Metropolitan Stefan

However, when it came to the Jewish issue, Bulgaria was asked to fall into line with the policies of Nazi Germany. This was start of a drama that to the surprise of many ended with the survival of the Jewish community in Bulgaria proper, though not in the annexed territories. There were then a total of 63,400 Jews under Bulgarian control, of which 51,500 were living within the pre-1941 boundaries. The Bulgarian church, a division of the Greek Orthodox Church, played a major role in preventing the deportation of the country's Jews. At the head of the church stood Metropolitan Stefan, the country's Patriarch as well as Bishop of Sofia.

The German connection began even before the official declaration of the alliance. In October 1940, the Bulgarian government tabled a wide-ranging antisemitic bill in parliament – the Law for the Defense of the Nation. Under this law, all Jews were required to register, to make it easier for the government to impose restrictions on them in the country's political and economic life. This included restriction in various occupations. Jews were required to submit to the Ministry of Finance a statement of their total wealth within seven days of the law's publication, and taxes were imposed on Jews with property valued over $2,430. Exceptions were provided for Jews who had converted to Christianity, were married to non-Jewish Bulgarians, or served in the military.

Members of the Bulgarian Writers' Union, Union of Lawyers, Union of Doctors, student and worker groups, as well as the much-revered Holy Synod of the Bulgarian Orthodox Church, protested against the law. Other organizations (trade and business groups, certain student groups, right-wing organizations) supported it. King Boris signed the law and it went into effect on January 23, 1941.

A year later, on August 26, 1942, the government also dealt with the definition of who is a Jew, and decided that a person was to be considered as Jewish if he or she had two or more Jewish grandparents, irrespective of the person's current religious affiliation. A month earlier, the government had ordered Jewish men between the ages of 20 and 45 to report for labor service, for work on roads and railroad lines. To streamline and control the anti-Jewish measures, a special government office was created, on September 30, 1942 – the Commissariat for Jewish affairs – and at its head a known antisemite – Aleksandur Belev. In effect, he became the Czar of the Jews, controlling their lives and property. Several months later, he ordered the confiscation of all Jewish-owned automobiles, motorcycle, and bicycles. Jews were forbidden to appear on the streets except for four or five hours a day to shop. In February 1943, Jews were no longer admitted to non-Jewish schools. The stage was set for the deportation of the country's Jews.

In January 1943, SS officer Theodor Dannecker arrived in Sofia to help with the implementation of the deportation plans. The Germans even insisted on the payment of 100 marks a head as an absolute minimum for its help in ridding the country of its Jews. The plan agreed upon with Belev was that an initial 20,000 would be deported, starting in March 1943: 8,000 from Macedonia and Pirot (in former Yugoslavia), 6,000 from Thrace, and 6,000 from Bulgaria proper. Point eight of the February 22, 1943, agreement stated "in no case will the Bulgarian government ask for the return of the deported Jews." On March 3, 1943, the cabinet approved the agreement. Dannecker happily informed SS colonel Adolf Eichmann that the green light had been given, and the Bulgarians began the deportation process on March 4, 1943, targeting at first the Jews in the annexed territories, in Thrace, Macedonia, and Pirot.

Metropolitan Kiril

As Belev prepared to add the Jews in Bulgaria proper to meet the figure of 20,000, the Jews of Kyustendil were also targeted. When the news reached Dimitar Peshev, speaker of the Subranie, the Bulgarian parliament, and representing his city Kyustendil, he was shocked by the revelation of a secret deportation agreement between his government and Germany. On March 17, 1943, he presented a petition, countersigned by 42 parliamentarians, to Petur Gabrovski, the Interior Minister (to whom Belev was subordinate), denouncing the deportation plan. Peshev's protest was unexpected and threw a kink into the government's scenario. Although he was reprimanded and lost his high position in parliament, it was the first step, followed by the Church's intervention, which eventually caused the deportation plans to be scuttled; the first of a series of countermanding actions that saved the Bulgarian Jews.

Two months later, the Bulgarian government, still under pressure from the Germans, decided on the expulsion of the Jews of Sofia, where most of the country's Jews lived, to the provinces, where it was hoped it would be easier, at a late date, to deport them quietly from the country. The expulsion order was approved by King Boris on May 20, 1943, and by the cabinet on the following day. That day, Sofia Jews began to receive orders to leave the city within three days to certain designated towns in the provinces. May 24 was an important Bulgarian holiday, the day of Saints Cyril and Methodius, marked by parades and celebrations in the capital. It was also the day scheduled for the first expulsions.

On that fateful day, Rabbis Daniel Tsion and Asher Hananel went to see Metropolitan

Stefan to ask for his intervention to cancel the expulsion order. He told the rabbis to wait in his home while he went to the palace. The king was not there. Later Stefan spoke to Prime Minister Filov but was unable to get him to change the order. Filov told him that the operation was politically necessary. Stefan objected that he opposed the action on moral, not political, grounds.

The eviction order was carried out, and from May 26 to June 8, 1943 – 25,743 Sofia Jews were evicted to some 20 towns in the provinces – this on top of the 11,000 Jewish men aged 20–26 already assigned to various labor camps. Then, on August 29, 1943, King Boris III suddenly died under mysterious circumstances. The Germans were also in full retreat on the Russian front. With an eye on the restoration of friendly relations with its powerful Slavic neighbor, the government saw fit to further postpone the deportation order. By July 1944, the anti-Jewish laws had been gradually annulled. On September 10, 1944, three days after the Red Army crossed into Bulgaria, a newly installed government declared war on Germany, its former ally. The Jews could breathe freely again; they were saved.

"No other institution with comparable influence so consistently opposed the government's antisemitic policy as did the Holy Synod of the Bulgarian Orthodox Church," wrote historian Frederick Chary. "No other man with comparable influence so opposed the government's antisemitic policy as did Metropolitan Stefan" (Chary, p. 188). It is worth mentioning that even before the government's fiendish plan to hand over its Jews to the Germans, Metropolitan Stefan was already an outspoken critic of the antisemitic policy pursued by the government. On September 27, 1942, for example, Stefan caused a flurry of excitement by denouncing the government's antisemitic policy in a sermon. The essence of his sermon was that God had already sufficiently punished the Jews for the rejection of Christ, and man therefore had no right to persecute them. "It is in God's hands to punish twice and three times, but it is forbidden for Christians to do such a thing." Stefan spoke in the language of his congregants, who still saw the Jews as Christ killers. The sermon was not well received by the SS leadership in Berlin, and SS general Walter Schellenberg, in a message to Martin Luther of the German Foreign office on November 21, rebuked Metropolitan Stefan for exerting pressure on Interior Minister Filov with regard to the yellow star to exempt baptized Jews from wearing it. Schellenberg also pointed to Stefan's general anti-German stance. One was to keep an eye on him!

In a letter to the Holy Synod on September 14, 1942, Metropolitan Stefan's main concern remained the plight of the converted Jews, whom the government had placed on an equal footing with other Jews. At the same time, he also deplored the general antisemitic policies of the government. It should be noted that not only Stefan but the entire Bulgarian Church, represented by its highest governing body, the Holy Synod, had opposed the government's Jewish policy already from 1940, when the Law for the Defense of the Nation was being debated. On November 15, 1940, the Holy Synod wrote to the government protesting that the proposed bill was misguided on several points. First, it did not differentiate between Jews and those who had converted to Christianity. Secondly, insofar as the Jews were concerned, some of the law's provisions were simply unjust and harmful to the nation. "Let no steps be taken to pass laws against the Jews as a national minority," the Holy Synod letter stated, "but let purposeful steps be taken against all the real dangers to the spiritual, cultural, economic, public, and political life of the Bulgarian people, from whatever direction these dangers come." The government ignored this protest and went ahead to approve the bill.

On December 10, 1942, Stefan wrote to the Holy Synod in regard to the Jewish issue. "The persecution of Jews, whether or not converted, has not become less intense," he indicated, "it has been escalated and aggravated."

> *"This occurrence is uncharacteristic of and adverse to the Bulgarian people ... This phenomenon throws the dark shadow of barbarity and brutality over the good reputation of the Bulgarian people as a tolerant and benevolent nation. It is the holy duty of our church to discuss in depth this phenomenon and employ all its divine means to help the oppressed and the underprivileged to get mercy and peace ... I sincerely and eagerly ask the Holy Synod to take in gentle hands the fate of those who the Law for the Defense of the Nations has placed outside the protection of the laws in our country, outside the supreme Law of Laws – that of God's love!... We cannot be callous to the pain of Jews as if we were some strangers or spectators."*

Stefan, furthermore, again referred to the anguish of the converted Jews, as well as of Jews married to non-Jews. He reported that in his conversation with Prime Minister Filov, the latter agreed that converted Jews need not wear the yellow star on top of wearing the cross. This was indeed officially announced on October 5, 1942.

The Jewish issue had been placed in the back burner for a while, but with the start of the deportations in March 1943 the Bulgarian Church was again called into play. In his letter to the Holy Synod of March 16, 1943, Stefan made it clear that "the Holy Synod in its capacity as a supreme church authority should help the Bulgarian citizens of Jewish origin who are subjected to persecutions by virtue of a special law and denied the protection of the basic laws of the state – the constitution and the laws of our church ... We are deeply moved by their desperate tears and wails ... [when they] ask for our intervention with the state authorities for a more humane and just attitude to them ... We are not allowed to hate, to persecute, to punish ... If we do not do what is required of us, every Christian will have the right to question the validity of the Christian teaching ... The Holy Church ... should speak up for the oppressed and persecuted Jews, regardless of whether they are converted or not, and it should insist that the Law for the Defense of the Nation be enforced in a strict but humane way ... Our main concern is the fate of Bulgarian Jews in general and of converted Jews in particular."

In March 1943, Stefan called for a plenary session of the Holy Synod, which assembled on April 2, 1943. The bishops unanimously decided to send a letter of protest to Prime Minister Filov, in which they made clear their displeasure that the Law for the Defense of the Nation had been turned "into a means of restricting and persecuting the Jewish minority in our country," which is deprived of the most elementary rights, such as by "sending them to camps and deporting them from the country. Our people ... cannot tolerate injustice, cruelty and violence against anybody. It cannot accept what is being done now to the Jewish minority.... [We] demand righteous and a humane treatment of the Jewish minority in the country. The Holy Synod of the Bulgarian Church cannot ignore its divine command and its holy duty. [It must] raise a compassionate and protesting voice in aid of the suffering and wronged people

... so that the measures in general against the Jews may cease or at least be eased ... The Holy Synod cannot accept the principle that any race be deprived of the human right to live."

The king made an effort to sway the opinion of the clerics in a private meeting with the Holy Synod in his palace on April 15, 1943, in the presence of Prime Minister Filov. At this unusual gathering, Boris III launched an attack on the Jews. As taken down by one of the metropolitans, "the King pointed out the great damage" the Jews had caused "to mankind throughout the centuries. It has created hatred among people, spread unbelief, moral decay and treason among nations. This spirit of speculation and negation has degenerated into discontent, arguments, conflicts, war and disasters in societies and states. The present world cataclysm is in part due to this speculative spirit." The king further stated that some nations have taken measures to defend themselves against the Jews. "They have come to believe that the sooner they free themselves from the Jewish influence and exploitation, the stronger their national consciousness and patriotism will be. This could be achieved by lawfully taking from them the reins of economic, financial, commercial, and industrial enterprises. The whole of Europe has started to adopt legislation to this effect. So have we – the Law for the Defense of the Nation. Known for its patriotism, our Orthodox Church could hardly challenge this opinion." The clerics were not impressed by the king's argument.

On May 27, 1943, Metropolitan Stefan reported in writing to the Holy Synod of the dramatic events during the annual festivities of Saints Kiril and Methodius, of May 27, 1943.

"Very early in the morning the bishopric was flooded with the tears of frightened and desperate Israelites – of three groups: converted Jews: Jews who had submitted applications for conversion; and unconverted Jews. The third group was the largest. I assured them that they would not be deported from Bulgaria and that their fears of being transported to Poland were unjustified. They were panic-stricken and their laments and hopeless wringing of hands were heart-breaking. Rabbi Hanannel said, 'If we did not fear deportation to Poland, we would not be ill at ease. We have no other homeland than Bulgaria ... Let them draft all of us fit for work, as many are already in work groups, and send them to internment camps, but we need confirmation that we will not be deported from Bulgaria.' ... I promised them that if I saw His Majesty at the service and could speak with him I would ask him to honor their request. My soul was torn in dark foreboding and my heart was weeping for lost national values and imminent hardships and misfortunes because we enrage God and harm ourselves when we persecute the defenseless."

Not able to see the king on Saints Kiril and Methodius Day, Stefan left a written message with the king's secretary.

"My heart is broken! I have had this feeling that we will be punished severely for what we have done to the Jews because our acts are disrespectful of God and harmful to the nation. The blood of the innocent thirsts for revenge ... Jesus Christ says we should not persecute so that we not be persecuted 'measure for measure.' I apologize for the boldness of my words through which I am giving vent to immense pain."

Stefan did not stop at this, but addressed the king in the words quoted at the outset of our story

– words seldom spoken by a church leader to a head of state. Two days later, on May 26, 1943, in the presence of Solomon Mashiach of the Jewish community, Stefan called the king at the palace and Mashiach heard him say the following:

> *"Boris, you forgot yourself. You elude me and hide … You know that one time I saved your father's head and your throne. But it is doubtful whether I, after these acts of yours, shall be able to save your head. Give the matter serious thought and uproot this demonic influence from your heart."*

He then put down the receiver. Afterwards the telephone began to ring. Maschiach said to Metropolitan Stefan: "They are calling you." He replied: "I know; he wants to speak to me over the telephone but I shall not answer him unless he comes personally to apologize to me. You will see that he will not dare to cause you evil." He then sent the following telegram to the king, based on a passage in Matthew 7:2:

> *"Do not persecute, so that you may not be persecuted. With what measure ye mete, it shall be measured to you again. I know, Boris, that from heaven God will keep watch over your actions."*

Abraham Alfassi, a leader of the Jewish community in Sofia, reported that Stefan had also told the King that in the event the Jews were handed over to the Germans he would give instructions to open the gates of the churches and monasteries to shelter the Jews there. As is well known, Stefan's strong words did not stay the government's resolve to expel the Jews from Sofia to outlying towns in the country, but there is hardly any doubt that the strong stand of the head of the Bulgarian Church, speaking in the name of all the metropolitans, swayed the government to delay plans to deport the country's Jews.

On May 27, 1943, Stefan went a step further by making public the Church's opposition to the government restriction of recognition of Jewish baptisms to a certain cutoff date. This led to the local fascist religious movement, named the Father Paisii Union, to ask that Stefan be put on trial for allowing Jews to convert to avoid persecution, and accusing him of Masonic tendencies. It called on the people, to "go to churches to see the blind conversion of Jews. They so hastily took the decision to do it when driven into a corner!"

Stefan's office was raided by the police on May 28, 1943, and church material confiscated, including close to 500 applications for conversion. On June 1, 1943, the receipt book with certificates of baptism issued on May 25, 26, 27 of 1943, was also confiscated. In his June 23, 1943 report to the Holy Synod, Stefan mentioned the attacks on him by members of the Father Paisii Union. "The mob swayed by the forces of darkness did not show mercy to our Savior, let alone me, His humble and weak servant. I have committed the sin of being unconditionally devoted to the Church and to my country, having refused to be pragmatic and accommodate the winds of change. I have chosen to be the antithesis of the silent resignation of the middle way and selfish conformity.… People should be told the truth and shown the lie. People should know that the State cannot be good to some and harsh to others."

In his postwar memoirs, Stefan wrote sadly of the period of the persecution of Jews in his country, which he termed a "black page in the history of our country." He added: "For the peaceful Bulgarian people it was like a bolt from the blue!…The majority of our people were bitterly asking the question: Why this slavish subordination and blind imitation of Hitler's wild march against the Jews? In Bulgaria, the Jewish question as a thorny and dangerous question has never existed and there is no reason for it to exist. Like the other minorities, the Jewish community has deservedly enjoyed prosperity and borne the burden of civil equality in the life of our country … In the spring of 1943, on my way to the holy Rila monastery on the Dupnitza-Kocharinovo road, I saw a train full of displaced Jews from Kavala in Aegean Thrace. Nothing can describe the horror and the inhumanity of that sight; everything pales by the side of it. I saw the old and the young, the sick and the healthy, mothers with new-born babies and pregnant women packed like sardines into cattle cars. They were all standing, exhausted, uttering desperate cries for mercy, for help, for water, for air, for a little bit of humanity … I was grief-stricken and as soon as I reached the monastery I sent a telegram to the Head of State with the personal request to order the Aegean Jews transported through Bulgaria to be treated like human beings, not like animals, and also to ease the unbearable conditions and prevent their being sent to Poland." In his message to the King, Stefan had stated that "the Christian principle obligates its followers to love all people … even your enemies … The persecution of Jews is a negation of the Christian teaching… Therefore [the Holy Church] insists that the persecutions be terminated and the law concerning the Jews repealed…. I mentioned the thousands of wretched Armenian refugees who during the massacre of Armenians under Sultan Hamid fled to Bulgaria and were welcomed by our people and given full rights as Bulgarian citizens. I have noted the patriotism and integrity of the Jews concerning our country … I am begging your Majesty, king of Bulgarians, to stop the enforcement of the anti-Jewish law and eventually order its nullification. This royal act would dismiss the doubts that Bulgaria has become a prisoner of Hitler's anti-Jewish policy and free our country of the greatest crime – hatred of mankind… The Prime Minister warned us to give up our mission… The Attorney General has been investigating our activities concerning the Jews to indict us for seditious acts."

As for Metropolitan Kiril of Plovdiv, he played a major role in saving the Jews of his city. When the police began assembling the Jews in Plovdiv on March 10, Kiril (who after the war became the patriarch of Bulgaria) sent a telegram to the king threatening a campaign of civil disobedience, including personally lying down on the railroad tracks before the deportation trains if the planned operation was carried out. As he reported to the Holy Synod on April 2, 1943:

"On March 10, some 1,500–1,600 people from Plovdiv were arrested and detained in a school before being deported to Poland. In the morning I was told what had happened. I sent a note to His Majesty the King, in which I pleaded with him in God's name to show mercy toward these miserable people. After that I asked to speak to the police superintendent, who was in Plovdiv that day, but couldn't get in touch with him. I looked for the district police chief, but was told he was also absent. Then I called out his deputy and asked him in a rather civil manner to tell the Government that so far I had always been loyal to it, but now will act at my own discretion as my conscience as a Bishop dictates to me. Then some converted Jews came to see me. I comforted them and told them they could find shelter at

my home. They can arrest them in my home! Later on, an order was received at about noon, much to the delight of those arrested, to let them go."

As told by Suzanna-Shoshane Behar, Metropolitan Kiril entertained friendly and warm relations with her father, Shmuel Benyamin Behar, chief rabbi of Plovdiv. Both often met in the rabbi's home, or in Kiril's residence. Kiril never missed an opportunity to congratulate the rabbi on Jewish holidays. On March 10, 1943, very early in the morning, the Behar family was driven to the Jewish school with nothing but a bag with a few items of clothing and half a loaf of bread. On the way, Rabbi Behar met with the synagogue sexton Ruski and told him to wake up Kiril (it was 3:00 a.m.) and tell him of the arrest. At about 8:00, the sexton returned and told him that Kiril had contacted Stefan in Sofia and they had taken matters in hand and that all efforts were being made for the cancellation of that horrible order. By 11:00, the sexton returned with the good news that the deportation order had been canceled. "When we came back home, there was a knock on the door and Patriarch Kiril appeared, dressed in his ceremonial vestment, a smile on his face. He and my father hugged each other. They spoke for about 20 minutes."

Sarina Victor Molho reported that on that fateful day, as a ten-year-old child, she remembers Kiril arriving at the school where the Jews had been assembled and heard him say, "I will not allow any one of you to leave Plovdiv. If necessary, I will take you into the Metropolitan residence. The Orthodox Church and I have made contact with Sofia and King Boris and we believe that God will be with you." In the afternoon all were freed. Albert Leon Alkalai, 19 years old at the time, reported that Kiril, in his telegram to the king, had threatened that if his city's Jews were to be deported, "I will lie down on the tracks in front the train."

In all of Europe, the Bulgarian Orthodox Church, headed by Metropolitan Stefan, was the sole mainline church that took a unified and unrelenting stand against the government's plan to hand over the country's Jews to the Germans for deportation – with the support, it should be added, of the majority of the Bulgarian people. Metropolitan Kiril's heroic stand in Plovdiv is also unique in the annals of humanitarian behavior in those dark days.

In 2001, Yad Vashem recognized Metropolitans Stefan and Kiril as Righteous Among the Nations.

Strobos-Buchter, Tina & Buchter, Marie

Netherlands

*B*orn in 1920, Tina Buchter was in medical school in 1940 and lived in an apartment with her mother, Marie, near the Royal Palace in Amsterdam, when the Germans invaded the Netherlands. She had read Freud when she was 16 and had then decided to become a psychiatrist. But the Nazi invasion unavoidably caused her to postpone these plans to a later period.

Her first act of resistance began on that very day, when together with her mother she decided to hide Henri Polak, a well-known Jewish socialist columnist and writer who had everything to fear from the invading Germans. He was hidden for several weeks in the home of Tina's 80-year-old grandmother, Maria Abrahams. She had an extra room, and the story told to outsiders was that she had rented a room to a stranger – a not uncommon thing.

Some time later, Tina joined a clandestine cell headed by a certain Johannes Brouwer. For a few months Tina did courier work for this resistance group, but found it too violent for her taste. As a fully independent person, she also did not fancy military-style orders. During one confrontation with Brouwer, he lectured her, "You're in an army now. You either obey the rules or you're thrown out!" Tina responded, "Well, I can't obey orders," and she was ousted from the group but continued to do errands for her former associates, including hiding in her home weapons stolen from the German army. "This frightened me to death. They went into action making bombs. They were very impetuous, very heroic and brave. I was none of those … I separated myself from them because I'm nonviolent."

Tina soon moved on to work for a more peaceful group involved in non-violent activity, such as finding hiding places and accompanying Jews, adults and children, to safe addresses in the country. "I remember spending a lot of time each week on my bike." Tina traveled all over the countryside to visit the people she had hidden, sometimes accompanied by her mother.

Tina's house also served as a transit station. With her mother, she used the second floor, with bedrooms being on the third floor. A carpenter from the underground had installed a small hiding place. Throughout the war years, dozens of people passed through there, "Some we knew, some we didn't; some for a couple of nights, some for a couple of months." The house was also used for meetings of the underground, illegal classes of the medical school, and as a place where people could secretly listen to broadcasts from London with the help of a transmitter.

The Gestapo often visited Tina's house but left empty-handed. They searched for hours, ripping up rugs, knocking on walls, and removing pictures, but did not discover the secret hiding place that could hold only two people at a time. A friendly policeman at Gestapo headquarters often tipped them off about a coming raid, so they could take the necessary precautions. All in all, the Gestapo visited the two women's home eight times, and Tina was arrested three times and her mother twice. Mother Marie Buchter was always terribly frightened whenever the Gestapo visited. In Tina's words, "She would tremble, really tremble … I would hiss at her out of the side of my mouth. 'Don't show them you're afraid.'"

In addition, Tina did everything in her power to procure identity cards for fugitive Jews, to the extent of stealing documents from the coats and pocketbooks of others:

"I usually stole passports from people I knew. For example, when I went to my aunt's funeral in the spring of 1941, I noticed that a lot of people were leaving their pocketbooks beside their coats and jackets in the hallway. I stole a couple of passports by going through the pocketbooks. No one saw me. It was very inconvenient to have had your passport stolen. You had to go through a lot of misery to get a new one but this was small potatoes compared to

not having one at all, or worse, having one that had a 'J' [for Jew] on it. There was no way to get that 'J' off."

A certain Leah Gitter was seven months pregnant when Tina took her and her husband, Seig, with her sister and brother-in-law across the Belgian border and turned them over to another underground cell that took them to the Spanish border. She delivered her baby just after she crossed the border.

Then there was the case of a 14-year-old boy named Lou who was placed with people who were quite strict with him. They were at first not too eager to take him, also because of a certain Nazi who lived in their building. They finally agreed, but he was told always to wear slippers and not to make the slightest noise when his hosts were away or flush the toilet. All the boy's rebellious instincts at such an age had to be suppressed. Tina supplied his hosts with money and ration cards from the underground. Lou stayed with them until the war's end. By then he was eighteen. After the war he got meningitis and died. Tina was especially saddened by this postwar loss. "I felt a little bit cheated. Look at all the things we went through – he went through. Then he dies. I really think that life was just too hard for him."

Hans de Jong, who had hidden in Tina's house for a whole year, during 1943 and 1944, caused her not a little trouble. In fact, the Gestapo was on the man's heels, and learning that he had spent time in Tina's home, they called her in for an interrogation. "When I was interrogated," Tina related after the war, "I was always afraid, because they'd seize you by the wrists and slam you against the wall. First, I'd ask for an interpreter in order to have time to organize my defense, even though I spoke fluent German." The interrogation went as follows.

> ***Gestapo:*** *"Do you know Hans de Jong?"*
> ***Tina:*** *"Hans de Jong? Sure I know him. He rented rooms from us. Did he do anything wrong?*
> ***Gestapo:*** *"He's a Jew"* (Tina to herself: "as if I should know that that was a terrible thing").
> ***Tina:*** *"But he has blue eyes and blond hair. How could he be a Jew?"*
> ***Gestapo:*** *"Some Jews are like violets in the woods. They hide by having blue eyes and blond hair.*
> ***Tina:*** *"Really? I can't believe it."*
> ***Gestapo:*** *"I will show you pictures."* [He showed Tina some sixteen pictures that he carried with him, displaying corneas.] *"That's what we're looking for in the streets."*

It was summer and Tina was wearing shorts. "I had nice legs, fortunately, and he was noticing them. That helped to relax me, because I realized that he was just a man and he was interested in my legs. So that gave me a sense of power. I got cocky, and would say, 'I didn't know he was a Jew' in a stronger, more convincing way." She was released. That, unfortunately, did not help de Jong much, as the Germans kept up the search for him and he was finally caught in 1944 and executed.

Abraham (Bram) Pais had special meaning to Tina. During the first years of the occupation, she had been engaged to him, but they broke it off in 1943. Pais belonged to the Sephardi Jewish community, descendants of Spanish Jews who had sought refuge in the Netherlands several centuries ago from persecution in their home country. He happened to be the last Jew allowed to complete his doctorate in physics before Jews were banned from Dutch universities, and was later to become a prominent professional of theoretical physics. Now Tina found him hiding places as well as for many of his relatives – parents, a cousin and sister-in-law. As he testified: "Tina always knew where I was. She would see to it that I had books to read or to study. She got these from the library or through friends." Tina also tried to persuade Bram's sister and her husband to allow her to find a hiding place for them. Her husband refused, claiming, "I'm young. I'm strong. They'll select me to work in a factory." They remained adamant. They were picked up and died in a concentration camp. Bram's parents, Jesajah and Kaatje Pais were hidden on a farm, and Tina visited them frequently.

In 1944, Bram, together with three other friends, all leading members of the Dutch Zionist organization, had had enough of secluded living and decided to rent their own apartment, in the hope that with their false papers they would not be caught. Bram's friends included Lion Nordheim, his wife, Jeanne, and Jeanne's sister, Tirtsah van Amerongen, who also happened to be a close friend of Tina's and had earlier stayed in her house. In February 1945, all four were arrested, betrayed by a former girl friend of Bram's. When Tina was told of this, she immediately rushed to their apartment to find out what exactly had happened, and unknowingly entered the lion's den. The Gestapo grabbed her and pulled her inside. Tina quickly made up a story that she was selling potatoes, going from door to door. Gestapo: "So! You're in the black market!" Tina: "Well, we have to eat." After lengthy questioning, they let her go.

The next day, Tina visited Tirtsah at the jail and left for her a package with food and clean clothes. Because Tirtsah and Jeanne had such credible false papers on them, Tina was able to convince the Gestapo *Sachbearbeiter,* the man dealing with the case, that the two women were indeed non-Jews, and they were released after a week's imprisonment. It was February 1945, and the Gestapo man knew that his country was losing the war. "He wanted to do me a favor. I noticed that. He let them go."

As for Abraham Pais – through connections with influential people, Tina presented a letter to a highly placed German from the famous physicist Niels Bohr inviting Bram to postdoctoral studies in Denmark. The man ordered Bram's release, fully aware of his being Jew. This was already in March 1945, with defeat staring the Germans in the eyes. Maybe the German official was shoring up his credentials with a good deed. Tragically for Lion Nordheim, here the Germans stuck to their guns and had him executed.

With the war over, Tina just wanted to forget everything. She married and left for the East Indies in 1947 (later Indonesia), where she practiced psychiatry for two years, then went to England to study neurology, and back to Holland, where her husband began residency as a doctor, and eventually to the United States, where Tina trained at Valhalla and Cornell and became a family therapist. Pursuing her career in addition to raising three children, she had left the past behind her – or so it seemed. "I had nightmares about being arrested, so who wanted to remember it?"

It took Tina (now Strobos) some 40 years to "come out of the closet" and speak of her wartime deeds. Frequently asked about her motives, she said that while she does not believe in a personal God she believes in the sacredness of life. Her grandmother Maria Abrahams had sheltered people in her house during World War I, refugees from Belgium. "She was my model," Tina emphasized. "My family were Social Democrats and atheists; they were people who acted on their ideals of education and helping people. Likewise for Tina's mother, Marie. In Bram's words, she was a woman of deep conviction but she didn't make speeches. She translated her convictions into actions, without making a fuss about it. As for the family's help to Jews, in Tina's words: "I wouldn't call what I did a sacrifice because we believed so strongly that we were doing the right thing."

Tina has always remained committed to the needs of others, to the less advantaged. In the 1960s, she joined a group to help improve poor neighborhoods. It was a project called, *I Give a Damn*. "We cleaned up streets in the South Bronx, had block parties."

Tina's message is that one can make people better by teaching but also by treating one's children well. "Don't hit them, don't be cruel to your children – that still happens. People who have been treated with cruelty will be cruel." She is glad that people are now becoming interested in the rescuers, "because we have paid enough attention to the bad guys – Hitler, Himmler, Goering. And we don't think as much about the good people who helped. I think that's true in our personal lives, too. We remember much more who did us harm than who did us good."

Hopefully, Tina Buchter's (Strobos's) goodness and that of her mother, Marie, will be better remembered through this story of their deeds.

In 1989, Yad Vashem conferred on Tina Strobos-Buchter and her mother Marie Buchter the title of Righteous Among the Nations.

Sugihara, Chiune-Sempo

JAPAN

*I*n late 1939, the heads of the Japanese military establishment were in a quandary. Not yet militarily allied to Nazi Germany, which had just signed a non-aggression treaty with the Soviet Union, the Japanese were nevertheless led to believe that a German attack on Russia was in the offing. The question was when? For the Japanese military, the answer to this question was important, in light of its huge inactive army stationed on the Chinese-Russian frontier, which in the event of a German invasion of Russia might be freed for use in Japan's main sphere of interest – Southeast Asia and the Pacific island countries. Information from intelligence sources was, therefore, of great importance; to pinpoint as closely as possible the expected date of the attack. Lithuania, tucked between two giants, Nazi Germany and the Soviet Union, appeared an ideal place to set up an intelligence-gathering post keeping tabs on troop movements in the vicinity.

So in late 1939, Japanese career diplomat Chiune-Sempo Sugihara was directed by his superior, General Oshima, the ambassador in Berlin, to leave his post in Finland, and open a consulate-general in Kaunas (Kovno), the capital of Lithuania – a place with no ostensible Japanese interests save for intelligence gathering with the help of spies. In Sugihara's words, "My main task was to establish the date of the German attack on Russia quickly and correctly." In November 1939 Sugihara arrived in Kaunas, a place without a single Japanese citizen, and began enlisting Polish spies. "I soon learned that my main task was to provide to the General Staff, and not merely the Foreign Office, information based on hearsay about the concentration of German forces on the Lithuanian border and Germany's preparations for an invasion of the Soviet Union."

Born in 1900, Sugihara entered his country's diplomatic service and spent many years in Manchuria (known since 1931 as Manchukuo, a Japanese puppet-state) where, due to his expertise in the Russian language, he helped in various negotiations with the Russians across the border. Now, in his new assignment in Lithuania,

Chiune-Sempo Sugihara (seated right) with his wife Yukiko (left) and family (Private Collection)

before he could settle down for really serious work, events not of his making overtook him. In the summer months of 1940, Lithuania was overrun and annexed to the Soviet Union (as part of the Ribbentrop-Molotov pact a year earlier). This was swiftly followed by an order to all foreign diplomatic representatives to wind up operations by the end of August and leave. To all intents and purposes Sugihara's spy mission had come to a premature end, without achieving its principal objective – arriving at the approximate date of a German attack on the Soviet Union. At this juncture, while he was busy packing, he became involved in a new and totally unanticipated mission which was to leave an indelible imprint on him as well as on the lives of thousands of people.

As told by Sugihara many years later, "One August morning, I heard unusual noise on the street near the consulate. I looked out of the window of my home and saw a large crowd had gathered near the railing of the house." When he inquired through his staff what these people wanted, he learned that "with tears in their eyes, they were begging to be given Japanese transit visas in order to be able to get to other countries via Japan." Sugihara told the group of Polish-Jewish refugees that to grant visas to such a large group he needed clearance from his head office in Tokyo. After cabling Tokyo, Sugihara checked with the Soviet consulate to find out whether they would allow people passage through their territory if they possessed Japanese transit visas, and was given an affirmative reply, but on condition that the Japanese issue the visas beforehand to guarantee that the refugees did not remain stranded on Soviet soil. According to Sugihara's account, on August 10, 1940, he decided to wait no longer for a response from his superiors and instead take matters into his own hands and issue Japanese transit visas to all those asking for them.

Dr. Zerach Warhaftig gave a slightly different account of how Sugihara was swayed to undertake large-scale rescue operation. A Jewish refugee from war-torn Poland, and a Zionist leader, he was looking for ways to get as many Polish Jewish refugees out of the country. Before hearing of Sugihara, he had sounded out fellow Polish refugees, whose stay in Lithuania could be terminated at any moment, forcing them back into German-occupied Poland, to make sure to have with them valid personal papers should the occasion rise for a quick exit from Lithuania to a safe haven. As he told one rabbi, "We are sitting on a volcano, between Germany and the Soviet Union, and we must escape … At least we must make an effort to get them passports, to get them visas." At the time, travel possibilities were quite limited; visas were not available from the United States and other countries in the Western Hemisphere; France had just fallen to the Germans and England was fighting for its life. The only possible exit was through the Soviet Union, not yet embroiled in the war, and then movement farther east.

Consequently, when Warhaftig learned from others that Jan Zwartendijk, the Dutch consul-general in Kaunas, was prepared to issue visa-like declarations for travel to Curaçao, a distant Dutch-controlled island in the Caribbean Sea, as a final destination, he saw this as a unique opportunity to get out of war-torn Europe. As told by Warhafting, "We saw on the map that Curaçao was a small island; that to get there one had to cross the Soviet Union to Vladivostok; then to Japan; and from there go by boat via the Panama Canal. We needed two transit visas – from the Soviets and Japan." It was time to look up the Japanese diplomat. At the head of a delegation, Warhaftig was admitted into Sugihara's presence and explained to the startled diplomat how he could be of help get the refugees out of the country and on their way to that fabled island. Warhaftig pleaded with Sugihara for ten-day transit visas through Japan for the hundreds interested in traveling in that direction. He assured Sugihara that the refugees would bear all the costs of their voyage and that their temporary stay in Japan would not be a burden on the Japanese economy. Sugihara promised an answer within a short time.

According to Yukiko Sugihara, the diplomat's wife, after her husband's meeting with the refugees she noted a transformation in his demeanor. No longer was he the cool and dispassionate career diplomat, but a man deeply affected by the plight of others. As she describes it, her husband "came up to the second floor with a worried look. He sat at the table in silence and drank some coffee. He waited until it became quiet outside. Then he stood up and went to the window and looked out; so did I. We saw a little child standing behind his mother hiding himself in his mother's coat, and a girl with an expression of hunger and terror which made her look like an adult, and some others crouching in fatigue … It seemed that the many cares of the Jewish people occupied his mind … My husband and I are Christians of the Greek Church, so we desired earnestly to help the Jews."

Although, even before meeting the Jewish delegation, Sugihara had been issuing some transit visas to Jews, it was on an individual and limited basis, not on a massive scale. Now the question was of issuing visas to hundreds and perhaps more in quick succession and without the necessary formalities. Sugihara struggled with himself over this moral dilemma. In his 1967 memoir, Sugihara described the mental torments that afflicted him days before his fateful decision, and what led him to respond favorably. "I really had a difficult time, and for two whole nights was unable to sleep. I eventually decided to issue transit visas … I could not allow these people to die, people who had come to me for help with death staring them in the eyes. Whatever punishment might be imposed upon me, I knew I had to follow my conscience." He significantly added: "I did not pay any attention and just acted according to my sense of human justice, out of love for mankind." Having made that decision, Sugihara began to issue Japanese transit visas to anyone requesting them, to as many as several thousand people in an operation that continued right up to the moment of Sugihara's departure from Kaunas at the end of August. Some claim to have seen him stamping visas even at the train station.

With the small staff at his disposal, and faced with the August 31 deadline for leaving the country, Sugihara enlisted the help of Moshe Zupnik, a yeshiva student who had come to get a visa for himself. Sugihara asked him to help with the stamping of the Japanese visas on passports and other travel documents of the many people queuing up outside. Reflecting years later on this strange coincidence of working side by side with a Japanese diplomat, Zupnik was still full of amazement. "I still can't understand how Sugihara let me in, a boy. He didn't have any records or anything on me. He simply handed over the consular stamp and allowed me to make visas! He wanted to do good. He told me, 'I do it just because I have pity on the people. They want to get out so I let them have the visas.' He had a good heart and he was very outgoing and saved people … He did it wholeheartedly. And he was not formal. He listened to us and he knew that we were in danger and he did it."

While still in Lithuania, Sugihara began receiving alarmed telegrams from his Foreign Ministry in which concern was expressed about certain persons arriving in Japan on visas issued by Sugihara. These probably referred to the selective visas issued before the mass wave of Polish Jewish refugees. Refugees from Kaunas were reported to have arrived in the Japanese port city of Tsuruga with questionable documents. Evidently, Sugihara had neglected to apply customary procedures. For example, Lucille Camhi wrote that she and her sister were detained by the Japanese in Tsuruga, when they noticed that they did not have end-destination visas. "We told them that we expected to get a visas to the U.S. They said they would ask the U.S. Embassy to check." In the final account, the Jewish community in Kobe interceded in their behalf and the two sisters' stay was extended in Kobe for two months, until their American visas came through.

On August 16, Sugihara was told by his superiors: "Recently, we discovered Lithuanians who possess our transit visas which you issued. They were traveling to America and Canada. Among these there are several who do not possess enough money and who have not completed the procedure to receive their entry visas to the terminal countries. We cannot give them permission to land … There were several instances that left us confused and we do not know what to do.… You must make sure that they have completed the procedure for their entry visas and also they must posses the travel money or the money that they need during their stay in Japan. Otherwise, you should not give them the transit visa." While receiving these dispatches from Tokyo in which he was asked to use greater caution, Sugihara had already thrown caution to the wind as he issued, by his account, some 3,500 transit visas.

According to the estimate of Ernest Heppner, one of Sugihara's beneficiaries, 2,178 refugees had arrived in Japan with forged passports, illegal papers, and the Curaçao visas. Among them were about 70 rabbis and 350 yeshiva (talmudical) students. Dr. Warhaftig estimated the number of refugees who arrived in Japan at 2,800. Other beneficiaries of Sugihara's visas may have sidestepped Japan and, once past the Soviet Union, headed in other directions.

The visa recipients left the area in time, before the German attack on the Soviet Union on June 21, 1941, and were thus saved. They crossed Russia and most arrived in Japan, from where they continued to various destinations (Shanghai, the Philippines, Canada, the United States, and Palestine). Ironically, none of them ended up in Curaçao. Jack Friedman made it to Japan via Korea, where he was joined by his brother. They stayed in Japan for seven months before parting ways; Jack headed to Shanghai; his brother Bernard made it to Bombay, India. Irene Malowist recalled that American diplomats in Tokyo initially suspected him of being a Soviet spy because of his passage through Russia. His ten-day Japanese transit visa was also extended for many months, until his departure for America. As for Ludvik Salomon (later Lewis Salton), who sailed for Curaçao, when the boat docked in Panama he got off together with some other Jewish refugees and headed for Mexico. As for Zerach Warhaftig, he was able, in 1941, to continue from Japan to the United States.

By contrast to Sugihara's open-ended issuance visa, American diplomats stationed in Kaunas held back U.S. visas with a clenched fist – even below the allowable quota of refugees from Lithuania. On August 17, 1940, as the U.S. consulate was closing its doors, Vice-Consul Bernard Guffler smugly cabled Washington that "visas issued by American representatives at Kaunas are useless to 99% of the applicants despite the demand for them, since few can obtain proper travel documents and fewer can obtain exit visas or arrange transportation." Indeed "useless," because State Department policy and the U.S. diplomats on the spot had helped make them so. As aptly put by historian Hillel Levine, "What we do now know is that, unlike the American diplomats, Sugihara responded. He took initiative beyond his government's policies, beyond his responsibilities to carry those policies out, reacting as a human being first and an administrator second."

When Sugihara arrived in Berlin from Kaunas, the Japanese ambassador there asked him to open a consulate in Königsberg (today known as Kaliningrad and part of Russia); again a listening post on the German-Soviet Union border. He then moved to Bucharest, where he was taken captive by the Soviets in 1944 and allowed to return to a defeated Japan only in 1947. Soon after, Sugihara was summoned to the Japanese Foreign Ministry and asked to tender his resignation. According to one account, this was prompted by the retrenchment policy of the Foreign Ministry, since as an occupied country Japan had no need for an expert on Soviet affairs. Sugihara, however, claimed that his forced resignation was a punishment for the "Lithuanian incident;" for his stepping out of line in issuing so many visas contrary to instructions. The years that followed were difficult ones for Sugihara, as he moved from one job to another to support his family. In 1960, he was sent to Moscow as a trade representative for a Japanese firm, a job he held until his retirement in 1975.

Years later, asked about his motives, Sugihara had this to say:

"You want to know about my motives, don't you? Well, it is the kind of sentiments anyone would have when he actually sees the refugees face-to-face, begging with tears in their eyes. He just cannot help but sympathize with them. Among the refugees were the elderly and women. They were so desperate that they went so far as to kiss my shoes. Yes, I actually wit-

nessed such scenes with my own eyes ... People in Tokyo were not united [on a proper refugee policy]. I felt it kind of foolish to deal with them. So I made up my mind not to wait for their reply. I knew that somebody would surely complain in the future. But, I myself thought this would be the right thing to do. There is nothing wrong in saving many people's lives. If anybody sees anything wrong in the action, it is because something 'not pure' exists in their state of mind. The spirit of humanity, philanthropy ... neighborly friendship ... with this spirit, I ventured to do what I did, confronting this most difficult situation – and for this reason, I went ahead with redoubled courage."

In 1984, Yad Vashem declared Chiune-Sempo Sugihara a Righteous Among the Nations. In 1986, he passed away, aged 86. In Japan he is considered a national hero and a stamp bearing his photograph was issued in his memory.

Sukhinski, Anton
UKRAINE

*T*hey called him the village idiot. Anton, or Antosh, Sukhinski had great respect for all living creatures, and as a vegetarian would not only not eat meat but not even hurt a fly. He was seen talking to plants and animals and staring at a black circle on the wall in mystical meditation. Shelley Zeiger, whose family knew him from before the war, remembered how, when he was a boy, Sukhinski had cautioned him and his younger brother Michael not to swat flies. Instead, he showed them what to do; he would fill a bowl with sugar water to gather the flies in one place. Then, to the boys' delight, he made tiny straws so that the flies could have a drink. He was the butt of his neighbors' jokes, who usually avoided him. He was a loner and never married. Anton Sukhinski barely managed to eke out a living as a tinsmith, subsisting on the edge of poverty for the greater part of his life, living alone in a modest house in Zborov. Truly a very strange man and an oddball of sorts; to all intents and purposes, a person of no consequence. Or so his neighbors thought.

There was also something else about him. He would be heard repeating, "Do unto others what you would have them to do unto you. We have the choice to be good or evil," words taken from the New Testament. This sentiment was not at all foreign to his neighbors, but they interpreted it as applying to everyone except to Jews, though paradoxically the words had first been uttered by a Jew. During the Nazi period, he was the only one on his street, and perhaps in his section of Zborov, who displayed a truly humanitarian disposition. His respect for all living creatures made him decide to save Jews – while others either participated in the murderous orgy or turned their backs, and watching as bystanders.

On July 1, 1941, Zborov fell to the Germans, and this was followed by an open season on the town's Jews. Three days after their arrival, on July 4, 1941, they executed close to 1,000 Jewish men. The following year another thousand were deported to the Bełżec death camp. On April 9, 1943, 2,300 Jews (many of them brought in from surrounding towns) were rounded up, forced to dig their own graves behind the local sports stadium, and executed. In the final "action" in early July 1943, some 600 Jews were burned alive in their labor camp shacks. There were no more Jews in Zborov – except the very few in hiding.

In the first murderous raid, on July 4, 1941, Eva Halperin had lost her father and two brothers among the many others slaughtered. A year later, on August 28, 1942, her mother fell victim to another SS raid. Eva remained in the ghetto and watched helplessly as many died each day from typhus with no medicines to treat them. From the ghetto, she was dispatched to a labor camp where, on April 5, 1943, groups of workers were taken out to be shot. It was clear that the Germans intended to eliminate all remaining Jews – and quite soon. If one wished to stay alive, one had to find a place to hide.

Fortunately for Eva she was able to join the Zeiger family in their flight from the camp. Yitzhak Zeiger, originally from Ternopol, had moved his family to Zborov at the start of the war, where the family owned a summer home, and Eva Halperin had once tutored his two sons. Later, in the forced labor camp, he had obtained the position of work boss. When he finalized his plans to escape, he invited Eva to join his family, telling her that he knew from reliable sources of another Nazi raid on the labor camp, which could mean its final liquidation. Had she not accepted his offer, Eva admitted years later, she would not have been around to tell the story of her survival. The Zeiger family together with Eva fled the labor camp on June 23, 1943, and headed straight for the home of Anton Sukhinski, who had promised to shelter them in his ramshackle house. When he had earlier contacted the Zeigers and offered his help, the family was a bit reluctant to put their trust in the hands of this strange man. Yitzhak Zeiger's son, Michael, years later related that his mother, Sonya, had had a dream where her deceased mother told her to put her faith in Sukhinski. At any rate, for the Zeigers, it was either Sukhinski or no one. The group included Yitzhak and Sonya, their two sons, Shelley and Michael, aged six and eight, and well as a woman friend of the Zeigers. When they arrived at Sukhinski's house they met 16-year-old Ziporah Shtok, who had hidden elsewhere and was turned over to Sukhinski when the other party refused to keep her any longer. So together with Eva Halperin, there were now seven additional people in Sukhinski's house.

The 38-year-old Anton Sukhinski hid them in a cellar while he and Yitzhak Zeiger built an underground shelter, which also necessitated some digging on the outside. After two days, the place was ready and the people moved in. However, no sooner was this done than a group of "good" neighbors, alerted by the commotion, came over with weapons in hand to extort money from Mr. Zeiger – or else, they threatened, they would betray him to the Germans. At first, Yitzhak Zeiger gave in to the extortionists and paid them something, but they kept coming back. Zeiger realized that sooner or later, when the money ran out, they would probably betray them in any case, so it was better to put a stop to things right away. So when the armed men appeared again, Zeiger drew the pistol that he had stolen in the labor camp and a shootout commenced in which the woman friend in the Zeigler group was shot dead.

As the shots would certainly attract the Germans, the six fugitives fled in panic. Autumn was beginning, and in the Ukraine countryside this brought a sharp drop in the temperature as the cold weather began to set in. The fugitives were lightly dressed and some even barefoot as they fled in the middle of the night. They stopped at the house of a friend, who allowed them to sleep over and fed them. But as rumors spread in neighborhood about the presence of strangers, after several days their host told them that he regretted he could not keep them any longer.

Having no other place to go, they returned to Sukhinski's house in the dead of the night. They were not sure what kind of welcome they would get after the shootout, which may have compromised Sukhinski, thinking that perhaps he would no longer be inclined to take them in. As they moved closer to his house, "Our feet stumbled over stones and sank into the half-frozen puddles of muddy water," Eva related. "Our clothes were so wet that they stuck to our bodies." When he saw them standing before him, Anton could not suppress his joy; he was so relieved to see them still alive. "Opening his arms, and weeping from joy, he kissed us emotionally," Eva told. Whispering to make sure that none of the neighbors overheard, he said, "My precious ones, I am so happy you have come back to me. I'll make sure that they never torment you again. From now on, I'll fix it so that no one will be able to see you."

For the time being he hid them in the attic, and over the next three nights, with the help of the two Zeiger brothers, he dug a pit beneath the basement that he was sure could not be easily discovered. The pit was three meters deep, two meters in height, and about 1.20 meters in width. It had two entrances; one camouflaged with bundles of straw and the other from his bedroom through a trap door.

The six fugitives lived in that dismal hole, cramped together, for the next nine months, with virtually no room to move, and just barely able to stand up. A kerosene lamp afforded them some light. Sukhinski fed them whatever he could from vegetables that he would gather secretly; such as raw potatoes, raw beets, and some water. He would pass these to his charges by removing the trap door at night and lowering the food with a rope, then removing the bucket that served as a chamber pot for the six hidden persons below. The little food was distributed evenly among all, except for the two boys, who received an extra portion. Without Sukhinski they would have starved or suffocated. Michael Zeiger remembered sadly: "We were just like animals. All we had were the will to survive and a positive attitude that we would eventually get out. We were always sick, but there was nothing we could do. There were no doctors, no medicine. The will to survive was more critical than anything else."

Providing food for six hungry mouths was a major problem. Sukhinski did not dare to buy food beyond what was needed by just one person, for this would certainly have raised eyebrows, so he had his married brother, who lived nearby, get the extra food for him. His brother knew that Anton was up to, but did not inquire too much. "We were happy that 'Antos' was taking care of us," Eva recalled, "and he was only able to keep going because of his saintly patience and his tremendous love of life coupled with his determination to save us."

To pass the many hours in that dank hole, without being able to wash and constantly having to fight off the lice that sucked their blood, Yitzhak Zeiger told them story after story about what their lives would be like after the war. He described a world in which Jews were no longer the object of persecution. It was to them like daydreaming, but it kept their spirits up. Once, the kerosene light went out for lack of oxygen and the people in the hole began to feel dizzy and choke. They knocked on the trap door, and fortunately for them Anton was not out but there to open it and have them come up for some fresh air.

Ever since that October evening when the fugitives had returned to Sukhinski's home, Sukhinski's neighbors had been wondering what had happened to the six Jews, and in due course they began to suspect that Anton was still hiding them. He knew they were watching him; no longer the village idiot, he seemed to be outsmarting them with his innocent, captivating, but foxy smile. They reported their suspicions, and one day a party of German soldiers and Ukrainian militiamen descended on Sukhinski's house. The six people underneath the cellar were able to hear every word, and they listened fearfully as the soldiers searched the room above them and questioned Anton at gunpoint. As Michael Zeiger distinctly remembered years later, "We saw the light from their flashlights." They also poked the straw that covered the entrance with bayonets but did not discover it. Despite threats and abuse Anton revealed nothing, and eventually the soldiers left.

Another time, Sukhinski learned that the Germans were going to search the farm with dogs trained to find people. To make doubly sure that his people would not be discovered, in Shelley Zeiger's words, "He stayed up all night spreading waste from the outhouse and pungent herbs like pepper on the fields to throw them off their scent. They did come with the dogs, but they never found us." Shelley's brother Michael added that Anton went so far as to burn his mouth with sulfuric acid so that the soldiers could not elicit from him any words.

Days before the liberation, the Germans went down to the basement, right above the shelter, which they used for some military purpose, and the people down in the hole could distinctly hear their voices in German. This represented a great danger to the hidden people as well as to Sukhinski. The fugitives had to maintain absolute silence: no talking; no coughing; no sneezing and not the slightest sound. They stuffed their mouth with rags, just in case. For a few days they were alone, and with no food. Then the Germans left.

On July 24, 1944, the occupants of the hideout watched in terror as the trap door opened without the usual sign from Anton. "Our blood froze from fear, thinking the Germans had discovered us," Eva recalled. Instead it was good news. In a gentle voice Anton joyfully exclaimed: "My friends, you may leave. You are saved. The Russians have arrived." As it turned out, the liberation took place at the eleventh hour, for the roof of their hiding place collapsed just two days after they vacated it. As they crawled out of the hole, they were completely incapacitated. Michael relates: "We couldn't move. We were crippled. We were crawling on our knees. Being in a hole for such a long period and not moving – the dampness of the earth got into our bones." But they were free – among the very few from among the Jewish inhabitants of Zborov.

With the war finally over, the following year the survivors branched out. Eva Halperin left for Venezuela, where she married (Adler); Zipporah Shtok went to Israel; and the Zeigers headed for America, where Shelley Zeiger became a successful businessman who also imported Russian products. The dehumanizing experience of his early years had a profound effect on him. "It made me a stronger person. I fear nothing except God. When things get really rough, I think of how much worse it was. We never let our own children forget. And their children will know it too. It will be a good stabilizer."

In the early postwar years, the Zeigers regularly sent parcels of food and clothing to Anton Sukhinski, but in the late 1950s the acknowledgements stopped coming. It turned out that he had fallen ill and was hospitalized in Ternopol; therefore the silence. In 1988, Shelley Zeiger was able to locate Sukhinski again – at his old Zborov address. Overcome with excitement, he phoned his mother: "Antos is alive!" He then traveled to Zborov for an emotional reunion with his rescuer.

As Shelley and his wife approached Sukhinski's home, "Antos walked toward us carrying a loaf of bread covered with a traditionally decorated Ukrainian cloth. I knew the custom. I kissed the bread," Zeiger recalled. He remembered that Sukhinski once said to him, "Don't be taken in by people who are always saying prayers; the important thing is to give food and shelter when it is needed."

Over the years, the Zeigers offered to buy him, still alone and aging, an apartment either in Israel or America, but he declined, preferring to remain where he was, in the same ramshackle house where he performed what he considered the greatest act of his life – not merely protecting flies and other living creatures, big or small, but human beings – and overcoming all the concomitant dangers. Far from being a fool, he had fooled his neighbors for nine long months into believing there was no one in his home other than himself. In saving six lives, he had shown the true measure of his humanity. In 2002, at the age of 94, in Michael Zeiger's words, "Antosh" Sukhinski still has not given up his natural and so-to-speak innate flaw – "He still cares about others more than himself."

In 1974 Yad Vashem recognized Anton Sukhinski as Righteous Among the Nations.

Szumielewicz, Wiktoria & Stanislaw

POLAND

"*T*he summer of 1941 will forever remain the most traumatic and painful time of my life." So began the testimony of Eva Bergstein (born Nisenczwajg). She explained: "As the summer was slowly drawing to an end, so was my world. Life in the ghetto was becoming more difficult every day and the tension and desperation was clearly perceived through the eyes and intuition of a five year old. My parents, Moshe and Hena Nisencwajg, were influential people in Staszow, and were one of the last people to have their permits to leave the ghetto taken away from them. When my father, an eternal optimist, finally admitted to himself that the shadow of doom was evident, he acted quickly to get us out before the ghetto gates were shut to us forever."

This was easier said than done. Born in 1936 in Staszow, Poland, Eva was three years old when the war broke out in 1939. The events of the war left an indelible mark on her memory. "Although I was physically a child, my happy childhood was as abruptly and unmercifully taken from me as was my entire family." Of her extensive family of 18 members, only two survived – herself and her father's brother, Henryk Nisencwajg. One day, Eva's father told her she would have to leave and move in with a non-Jewish family, friends of her parents. It was only for a short time, she was assured as her father led her through the fields outside the Staszow ghetto. "After several hours of walking hand in hand and mostly in silence I knew that this was a very significant journey." The two hardly exchanged a word. "The journey, which was to be our last time together, was over much too soon as we came upon the Szumielewiczes in the open fields." Reflecting on that momentous journey many years after the war, Eva suddenly remembered the trauma experienced when she let go of her father's hand. "I was only five years old but I knew that I was letting go of my whole life; my family; my world. A metamorphosis took place within me. I ceased being a child and became an introspective and shrewd observer of life with an innate skill for survival."

As Eva felt Wiktoria's warm but unfamiliar hand on hers, she was overcome with the deepest grief; "perhaps I knew that I would never see my beloved father's face again; perhaps I knew that this was a farewell like no other before it; this was the final farewell of death." She walked silently between her new "parents," Stanislaw (or Stach) and Wiktoria Szumiele-wicz, the rest of the way to their farm in Ritviana. Her father, Moshe Nisencwajg, returned alone to the ghetto. Approaching her hosts' farm, Eva was instructed on her new cover story. She was henceforth to be known as Iwonka, an orphaned niece. "I was never to say anything about being Jewish and although they went on to explain all the consequences that this disclosure would bring, it was totally unnecessary … I wanted to live."

On the farm, Eva suffered from terrible nightmares almost every night. "I would awake trembling and screaming from these tormenting dreams about my family being tortured and killed in the ghetto." On each such occasion, Wiktoria was there to calm her by paint-ing a different picture for the frightened girl. "She would point out that the whole Jewish thing was a nightmare; that I was never really Jewish … If I were Jewish surely the Germans would have taken me away too. Since I am safe and with them I cannot be Jewish. I really am their niece, so how can I be Jewish if they are Christian. Next she asked me to call her Mother because, as she pointed out, my parents were dead and I was going to be their child anyway; it would be less confusing to others if I called her and Stach, Mother and Father. This I refused to do and we settled on Aunt and Uncle."

Eva decided to go along with the game. "I knew then that in order to survive I had to keep up the pretense of our game, even with Wiktoria, whom I was growing to love and trust." A while later, two of Eva's cousins joined her at her benefactor's home, Lucy and Janek Nisencwajgs, but Janek soon was moved elsewhere. Then suddenly, Eva and the three-year-old Lucy were huddled in a sleigh drawn by horses on a bitter cold night and quickly moved elsewhere. This happened after a neighbor had informed the Germans that the Szumielewiczes were sheltering Jewish children. Lucy and Eva were taken to a cloister in Klimatow. Later, Lucy too was removed, and Eva learned that Lucy and Janek were eventu-ally discovered and shot by the Germans.

Eva spent over a year in the cloister – not sure whether the nuns suspected her true iden-tity. She became very religious and took part in the confirmation ceremony. "My religious convictions were very sincere and not part of the facade that I had created. I was really beginning to believe in the Christian God, Jesus. He was protecting those who believed in him. Where was our God? Why were Jews being systematically destroyed? I was beginning to believe that there must be a reason and I was connecting this reason to religion." When the cloister was hit in a bombing raid, Eva was taken back by Wiktoria. "It was a joyous reunion." While she felt a little apprehensive regarding Stanislaw's disposition toward her, evidently erroneously, she had a wonderful rapport with his wife, Wiktoria. However, she could not agree to Wiktoria's request to call her "mother," though by this she would have conceded that her own mother was already lost to her. The Szumielewiczes moved from town to town, always avoiding places where relatives lived, for added security for little Eva. Only after liberation were they brought into the picture.

Eva was then enrolled at school for the first time. Walking home from school, Eva desperately searched the faces in the street in the hope of finding her father. "It was incomprehensible to me that anyone could kill him. I waited, expecting him to come for me." Aware of the child's predicament, Wiktoria, "always sensitive to my anxieties," one day told Eva that her parents had not survived the Holocaust. Eva's mother had fled into the forest in the hope of joining up with friendly partisans while pregnant with a child who was born in the forest. Betrayed by a Pole while she foraged for food in the city, she and the child were shot by the Germans. As for Eva's father, the Germans had sent him to Radom, where he worked in a munitions factory. Escaping with fellow prisoners in 1945, just a few months before the end of the war, they were eventually shot by the guards in a shootout in which some of the guards were also killed. The news of her parents' violent death created in Eva's mind a distancing from Judaism. "I did not want to be Jewish. I wanted to be a Catholic so that I could be protected by their God. I became very religious and a devout Catholic, never missing a Sunday service even if I had to go myself or with friends."

One day Wiktoria disclosed to Eva the existence of an aunt in Canada, and an uncle who had survived the conflagration, and that Eva was to be handed over to one of them – as earlier requested by Eva's mother in the event she did not survive. When she first saw uncle Henryk (the father of the martyred Janek and Lucy) on a visit at the Szumueliwic home, he looked to Eva like "an old, defeated man." He falsely assured her that her father had survived and was waiting for her in Kraków. Eva was torn between Wiktoria's account of her father's death and the uncle whom she felt could not be lying to her on such a crucial point. "I was nine years old and had to make a very important decision. Wiktoria insisted that she told me the truth and that Henryk was making up an outrageous story to get me away from her." She added that Henryk was moved by the loss of his two children, who had stayed for a while with the Szumielewiczes, a loss for which he was somehow blaming her. If, however, Eva wanted to return to the Jewish fold, it would be better to do so with the aunt in Canada, whom Wiktoria was prepared to contact.

Taking Henryk's at his word, Eva decided to follow him to Kraków, only to discover that he had not told her the truth. Henryk found it difficult to handle Eva, who longed for Wiktoria and went to church on Sundays, so he placed her in a Jewish-run orphanage. She was eventually moved to Prague, from where she continued to correspond with Wiktoria, longing to be reunited with her. The orphanage was a religious institute and Eva learned Hebrew and received a Zionist indoctrination. In August 1947, at the age of eleven, Eva left for Canada to live with her mother's sister. After her marriage, she resumed contact with Wiktoria, whom she invited to visit her in Canada in 1960, together with her newborn daughter, to meet Eva's own baby girl born six weeks prior to Wiktoria's arrival. "It was a very emotional reunion for us. I felt that I had my mother with me again." The next visit was following the death of her husband, Stanislaw. Eva hoped that Wiktoria and Basia, her seventeen-year-old daughter, would stay on in Canada to be near her, but Basia longed for Poland. Eva continued to be in close touch with her wartime benefactress.

As stated by Eva, "In the vortex of a world gone mad – my father carefully placed my hand in the hand of Wiktoria Szumielewicz – thus ensuring the continuity to his descendants and the survival of Judaism. My father chose wisely, he entrusted his most precious possession to a person worthy of his trust … a valiant lady and a very special human being." In 1980, when Eva Bergstein wrote to Yad Vashem, Wiktoria was close to 70 years old. "I am married to Sidney Bergstein and have three children, Heni, born May 14, 1960; Michelle, born June 4, 1963; and Joseph, born December 24, 1968 … Wiktoria Szumielewicz saved my life. From the summer of 1941 to the day we were liberated by the Russian army in 1945, she risked her life to save mine," and she asked that her rescuer be awarded the Righteous title.

Yad Vashem acceded to Eva's request and in 1981 conferred the title of Righteous Among the Nations on Wiktoria as well as her husband Stanislaw Szumielewicz.

Szwierszczak, Manko & Marynka Dukiewicz, Michal & Genowefa
POLAND

*F*or some Jews on the run, a hiding place in a tomb seemed the ideal place to escape the fury of the Nazi killing machine. This indeed was the case with the Rosen family in Buczacz, Poland, during the German occupation. In their deposition to Yad Vashem, Henry Rosen in Chicago and brothers Samuel and Yechiel in Israel gave a frightening and searing account of their survival for over a year hiding in a tomb and a nearby mortuary, the coffins therein having been removed to another location. Their survival depended on the goodwill and care of the cemetery's caretaker – Manko Szwierszczak.

Born in 1922, during the war, Henry Rosen lived in Buczacz with his family. As the Germans swept in on July 5, 1941, local Ukrainians staged a pogrom on the city's Jews. "I saw many families robbed and killed with knives. I helped to bury them in our Jewish cemetery." Soon thereafter, the Germans launched a killing raid, handpicking the most educated from a group of persons, who were marched to nearby Fedor Hill; were told to dig graves, undress and were shot. "I was hiding in the forest when I heard the shots," Henry recalled. Soon thereafter a ghetto was established, and the most physically strong were then conscripted into forced labor gangs and assigned to various construction details.

A year passed, when Henry was introduced by his brother Samuel to a Polish man by the name of Manko Szwierszczak – a janitor in the local Catholic cemetery, and both sides struck up a friendship. The two brothers occasionally listened to news from abroad from a hidden radio in the cemetery. Henry described Manko and wife, Marynka, as uneducated people but "very good Christians with hearts of angels" – and they were prepared to help the Rosens to stay alive. "We knew the end was coming. The Germans were going to massacre the Jews." So Henry and Samuel asked Manko to hide them in the Polish Catholic cemetery. He agreed and gave them a place under the roof of the chapel in the middle of the cemetery. There, in the still of the night, the two Rosens brought along a group of 40 Jews, including their mother and younger brother Yechiel. When all the people had squeezed inside, Henry got out and covered the entrance to the roof, then headed to an undisclosed location in the nearby forest. "The police were searching with dogs. They asked Manko if he had seen any Jews? When he said no, they beat him up but he still did not turn us in."

A few days after the Nazi raid, the group returned to the ghetto, only to discover to their horror that the Germans had taken over 2,000 Jews to the Bełżec death camp and a several hundred more to the dreadful Janowska camp in Lwow (today Lviv). Another massacre followed at the end of 1942 – with Jews again shot on Fedor Hill with the participation of Ukrainian collaborators. Then came a further "action" in Feb-

Manko Szwierszczak standing next to the grave where he hid five Jews

ruary 1943, at which time, Henry, running a fever, hid with his brothers under the stairs of their ghetto house, and luckily for them they were not discovered. Some 2,000 Jews were marched to Fedor Hill and shot. Little time was left for the remaining Jews, and to survive one had to quickly flee the ghetto. At this point, the Rosen brothers again contacted Manko and asked him whether he was prepared to hide them: 21-year-old Henry, Samuel, 18, Yechiel, 12, and their mother. Manko told them he would have to consult his wife. A week later he returned and said he would help them but he needed money to meet the additional expenses, such as food, since his was quite a poor family. The Rosens, too, had no money with them so they looked for a few other Jews to join them who could come up with some money – and found four men. The group, consisting of the three Rosen brothers and their mother, and the four other people got ready to move into a secluded place in the cemetery, inside a tomb! – as described by Henry Rosen:

"Manko knew the cemetery like he knew his own pocket. He was the third generation jani-tor of the cemetery. He showed us a few old tombs that had caved into the ground. We chose the largest one. We began to dig. We found three coffins... With his permission we moved

the coffins to another tomb. We cleaned out the tomb and then brought in blankets, pillows and dishes. At nighttime we all got into the tomb. Every day Manko would come and check to make sure the hole was not visible. We would cover it with a bush and he would put the statue of Mother Mary over it. We had a pipe to the outside for air. He would bring food for us."

In April 1943, a month after moving into the tomb, they heard shots outside. Samuel sneaked out to check what was happening. After a few hours he came back and told of hiding in the bushes and seeing the Germans kill two women and a small girl. He also saw the Ukrainian police searching Manko, on whom they found a watch, and beating him to find out who had given it to him. "The next day he came to us. He was black and blue from the beating. He said if they had killed me, he would not have said a word about hiding us. My mother kissed his hands and his wounds. We all hugged him." Only a few Jews were left in Buczacz, with many having committed suicide and others killed in the streets or on Fedor Hill. "We decided to stay in the cemetery. Summer was coming and we could go out at night and steal vegetables and water."

Life inside a tomb is not something that many people, even fugitives fleeing for their lives, are willing to put up with. So before the onset of the winter in late 1943, the four men brought with them by the Rosens said they had had enough, and since they still had enough money on them they wanted to go to the village to look for a better place. They left and were never heard from again. The four Rosens remained alone, but they too decided not to remain in the tomb, because of the telltale footprints left in the snow by Manko when he brought them food each evening. They found an alternative place in the cemetery's mortuary, where they dug a hole under the floor, passing the harsh winter of 1943–44 there.

Then something strange and unexpected happened, which almost spelled doom for the Rosen family. In March 1944, the fighting had reached the Buczacz area and the Germans placed anti-aircraft guns around the cemetery. One evening a group of German soldiers materialized above their hiding place. They appeared to the Rosens to be drunk by the way the moved around and their loud talk and laughter. It was terribly cold, so to keep warm the Germans began to jump up and down on the stone slab covering the hiding place. Suddenly the roof caved in and the Germans fell right on top of the fugitives. Seeing living people inside a tomb, the bewildered Germans at first took fright, and this gave the Rosens enough time to climb out and run for cover before the Germans realized what was going on. Henry and Samuel Rosen managed to reach the nearby forest and escape the bullets whizzing by, but their mother could not make it out of the tomb. She had swollen feet and was in poor health. From behind the bushes, the brothers watched as the Germans pulled her out and shot her in the back of the head. At night, the two brothers sneaked back to the cemetery to pick up the younger Yechiel, who had lost his way and was hiding in some ruins there. They also found the dead body of their mother.

The three brothers then ran to the nearby village of Podlesie and headed straight for the home of Michal Dukiewicz, whom they had known previously. He was a family friend and had hidden several family members who did not survive after they were discovered by Ukrainian collaborators in an incident whose details remained unclear. Before that, during the ghetto period, Michal had smuggled food to the Rosens inside the ghetto. He told the three brothers how he saw their grandparents being led away to a waiting train. He waved at them and they waved back to him. In Henry's words, "He said my grandfather had a prayer book under his arm and was holding my grandmother with his other hand. When he told us this, he was crying and very pale. I knew from that moment that I had a friend in him." On this occasion, Michal Dukiewicz gave the Rosen brothers a place to hide in his stable, on top of the hay, and supplied them with food and water. Before the final German retreat from the area, they swarmed into Michal's home looking not for fugitives but for concealed horses which the Germans had ordered the local farmers to hand over. German soldiers searched the barn, poking the hay with bayonets and barely missing the hidden Rosens. Finally, with the arrival of the Russians in April 1944, the three brothers could again breathe freely after a three-year period of crouching and running and keeping their heads close to the ground.

Henry Rosen's final words in his deposition are: "In my name, in the name of my brothers, and in the name of the whole family of more than 30 people who died in the Holocaust, I beg you to honor Manko Swierszczak and his wife, Marynka, and Michal Dukiewicz and his wife, Genowefa."

In 1983, Yad Vashem indeed conferred upon these four people the title of Righteous Among the Nations.

Taquet-Mertens, Marie

BELGIUM

*I*n 1985, Pierre-René Delvaux wrote to Yad Vashem asking for assistance in trying to locate some of the dozens of Jewish children who had been sheltered in a children's home in an isolated spot in the Ardennes region of Belgium, where Delvaux had served as a counselor. He explained what made him decide to look up the children over 40 years later:

> *"During the war, I was privileged to participate in the rescue of some sixty Jewish youth in the Queen Elizabeth Home in Jamoigne-sur-Semois in the Luxembourg province of Belgium ... I'd like to locate and renew contact with the Jewish children hidden in this home, but find myself faced with an almost insurmountable problem, due to the fact that on the one hand these children bore a false name (quite an unavoidable necessity!) and, on the other hand, being myself wanted by the Germans, I also carried a false name – Pierre Milet – and the children called me "Mr. Milet." You will therefore understand the difficulty facing me. Perhaps you can help me?... I am sixty-two years old; I am retired for reasons of health, and I would like very much to find them again. Since the end of the war, I think of them every day, for in a certain way they are my children.*

Together with this letter, Delvaux had also placed ads in the local press, and to his pleasant surprise, answers were not long in coming. In fact, 14 of the former children had a similar re-awakening and responded to Delvaux's quest. To Jacques Funkleder, one of these respondents, Delvaux reminisced about the many activities in that forest retreat, including the children's choir that practiced songs by Bach in four different musical tones. Fired by a sudden urge, Funkeleder set himself the task of helping to locate as many of the other children, after Delvaux expressed his deeply felt desire to create an association of these former residents of the Jamoigne children's home. He explained that this was required in order "to collect all our testimonies concerning these years, so as to transmit to our descendants what transpired among us – by having every one of us writing his personal testimony from memory." Delvaux's initiative inspired his former wards to nominate their former headmistress as well as the other counselors for the Yad Vashem

Reception in honor of Marie Taquet. David Inowlocki (left), one of the children she had saved

honorific of Righteous Among the Nations. Soon more material flowed to Yad Vashem on this episode and the curtain went up to reveal a rescue operation of considerable magnitude.

The Chateau du Faing (as the children's building was originally known) was located in the village of Jamoigne-sur-Semois, deep in the wooded Ardennes region of southeastern Belgium. The home was originally owned by a Catholic order and inhabited by nuns. In 1941 it was acquired by the Belgian Queen Mother Elizabeth and transformed into a home for retarded children, or those with parents in prison or the army – and no less important, also for Jewish children on the run. As confirmed by Delvaux: "When I arrived at the end of March 1943 as an instructor, there were 60 Jewish children. This number increased after November 15 with the addition of 12 more." Overall responsibility was in the hands of Princess Jean de Merode, in Brussels, who worked in close cooperation with Mrs. Yvonne Nevejean, head of the country's

Sleeping dormitory at Jamoigne children's home

national child welfare organization (Oeuvre National de l'Enfant, or ONE). Marie Taquet-Mertens was appointed headmistress, aided by her husband, Emile, as the home's director.[1]

Jacques Funkleder and his brother were brought to Jamoigne in May 1943 with other fleeing Jewish children through the intercession of the Jewish Defense Committee, a clandestine organization dedicated to the rescue of Jews. In Jamoigne, Funkleder's name became Van Humbeek. The first days were difficult as they tried to adjust to the new surroundings after being abruptly torn away from their parents. "However, the smile of Mrs. Taquet, as well as her husband," Jacques emphasized, "instilled confidence in us from the start, and we found there so much warmth that for us the chateau became a vacation camp." The home's staff also played a role in easing the pain of adjustment and the children soon became integrated into a boy scout-like regime, including communal singing, camaraderie, and sports. After returning from an outing, the children stood at attention in front of the chateau and sang in unison hymns in praise of Jamoigne, while Mrs. Taquet, standing on the top of the chateau's main staircase, acknowledged their hymns. Before dismissing them to their quarters, she verified to herself that all the children (including the Jewish ones, who were well known to her) were present and accounted for. What is more, before the lights were turned off at bedtime, Mrs. Taquet made it a habit of making the rounds of the bunks and giving every child a small kiss. "In this enclosure," Jacques noted, "we did not feel that we were persecuted; we felt safe in the midst of non-Jewish children."

Danger, however, lurked in the form of sudden German visits. On one that took place in September 1943, one of the staff had fortunately seen the Germans approaching through

---

1 Queen Mother Elizabeth as well as Yvonne Nevejean were also honored by Yad Vashem as Righteous Among the Nations.

the forest and sounded the alarm. All the children, Jewish and non-Jewish, were quickly assembled in the big ground floor hall. A German officer asked Mrs. Taquet point-blank: "Are there any Jewish children here?" She answered quietly: "Wouldn't that be very risky for us to do?" The officer bowed and left. The problem for the Jewish children was especially acute during the summer vacation months, when the non-Jewish children were sent home to their families, exposing the Jewish children to suspicious questions from inquisitive outsiders about their background. The solution was to take them to a nearby village for a month's stay, but there they lacked the feeling of warmth and security that they got at the Jamoigne home. "What a joy, what a holiday, when we returned to the chateau and saw the reassuring smile filled with warmth of Mrs. Taquet, her husband, Major Taquet (a reference to his military rank when he served in the Belgian army), as well as the instructors." Upon liberation, in September 1944, the children were returned to their families – to those who survived the Holocaust – or Jewish children's organizations.

In September 1987, Mrs. Taquet's former Jewish wards celebrated their first reunion with her. Pierre-René Delvaux greeted the assembled guests with a reading from Psalm 124: "Let Israel now say – if it had not been the Lord who was on our side, when men rose up against us, then they would have swallowed us alive, when their anger was kindled against us … Blessed be the Lord, who has not given us as prey to their teeth!"

A year later, on a visit to Yad Vashem, some of former hidden children reminisced about their stay in Jamoigne. "I think I was traumatized by the separation from my parents," David Inowlocki recalled, "so I tried not to think about anything, just to latch on to this hope of life which the place offered me." When he learned of Delvaux's efforts from a newspaper advertisement, "It was like a bolt. So I took the phone and called him … So we then started to organize the group." Dov Shaked, another former Jamoigne resident, arrived there under the name of Albert Mandier. In Jamoigne, Dov remembered sleeping in big dormitories housing several dozen children. Night pots were placed in the corners, which were frequently used by the children there. "I knew there had to be more Jewish children, but Mrs. Taquet cautioned me not to talk about it and not to develop close ties with them, with those kids I suspected of being Jewish," so that they would not stand out before the non-Jewish children. Akiva Kaminsky, born in 1936, remembered suddenly being told, in 1943, that he and his brother were soon to be moved from a Jewish children home to a new home. Before leaving, he was given a new name – Camée. "All my previous identity papers were burned." Arriving in Jamoigne, "I found there, for the first time since I could remember, a warm and loving home." Especially reassuring was Mrs. Taquet's habit of stopping at everyone's bedside each night and blessing them "with a good night wish and kiss." For this child, after a traumatic and inexplicable separation from his parents, such nocturnal smiles and kisses from the person who held the key to survival represented a significant psychological prop.

On May 15, 1998, the Jamoigne children held another reunion. On this solemn occasion, a commemorative plaque was placed on the facade of the Jamoigne home recalling the rescue of over 80 Jewish children behind the chateau's thick walls. In a special album presented to the 90-year-old Mrs. Taquet-Mertens, her former beneficiaries had assembled words of praise written during the war years for their headmistress on special occasions, such as the following paean by Gideon Glinoer (then Jules Kayser) and his brother Philippe:

"Oh, dear Madame Taquet, truly it is not you who raised me when I was hardly born. But now when I need to be saved, it is you with your great love who nourishes me and looks after me, to care for me as her own child ... Yes, all this, Madame Taquet, you have done it for me. On the occasion of Mother's Day, permit me to write a few sentences and wish you the best of happiness; so I wish you with all my heart."

Or, the following words by a still-unidentified child known only by his adopted name of Fernand Nivarlet:

"Long live, Maman ... You cannot believe how much we love you. You are for us the highest goodness. You exert yourself with all your heart for those who perhaps know much unhappiness. ... God has made you a tender mother for us ... so that every evening when we go to sleep, you come to place a kiss on our forehead. At such a moment, my heart stops. So, to be able to give you a charming lilac. The one who loves you so much. Fernand Nivarlet."

These words, inspired by feelings of love, thankfulness and hope, were composed in 1944 by Jewish children sheltered in a chateau in the dense Ardennes forest, while outside the chateau's protective walls Jewish children were being relentlessly hunted down and deported to concentration camps, to be delivered to the gas chambers and crematoria.

In 1987, Yad Vashem conferred on the 89-year-old former headmistress Marie Taquet-Mertens and her late husband, Emile, the title of Righteous Among the Nations. Also awarded this honorific were Pierre-René Delvaux, the initiator of the Jamoigne children's reunions, and six of his instructor colleagues. Two years later, Mrs. Taquet-Mertens died at the age of 91.

Tarasewicz, Hieronim & Bronislawa

POLAND

*E*liezer Livyatan, born in 1908, was already a grandfather (a married daughter had two children) when the war came to his home in Ignalino, a small town not far from Święciany in the Vilna district (now in Belarus), on June 22, 1941, with the German invasion of the Soviet Union. Ignalino had a population of 1,500, of which over half, some 800, were Jews. With the arrival of the Germans, large-scale executions took place with the participation of local inhabitants – especially the Lithuanian police. In Livyatan's words, "some of the farmers who knew us and were our friends were among the executioners." After the initial killing spree a ghetto was established in August 1941 for the remaining Jews, limited to one street and four or five families to each house. On the Jewish New Year holiday (Rosh Hashanah) in September of that year, Livyatan and six friends fled from his assigned work place and headed for Postawy, where Livyatan had a sister. While on route, they were apprehended by local people, who shot some of the fugitives. Livyatan was led into a forested area, where he was forced into a dilapidated former Polish army barracks together with other Jews. He decided to escape before the Lithuanians could carry out their murderous intent. With bullets being fired in his direction, Livyatan managed to run deeper into the woods. He was alone and decided to head back to his hometown, Ignalino, but found no more Jews. They had all been liquidated or removed elsewhere. A friendly Pole gave him something to eat, then asked him to leave. "He was afraid to keep me."

Hieronim Tarasewicz (center) with Eliezer Livyatan (right)

Livyatan wondered where he might go? He suddenly recalled a certain Lithuanian whom he knew well and who lived some three kilometers away. The man, named Michal Samukaniec, told Livyatan to hide in the hay next to the house. There, Livyatan lay hidden for a full day. Then Michal disclosed to Livyatan that he was hiding some Jews in the barn and led Livyatan there to join a woman and two children. Here too, the farmer took fright, and after an eight-day stay he asked the fugitive party to leave. Yet he took care to take the woman and her children in his horse-draw carriage to a different location. However, tragically for them, they were caught and shot. Livyatan decided to look up another Lithuanian farmer whom he knew, in the village of Petrowy, where he was allowed to stay for eight days. Livyatan continued to go deeper into the Belorussian countryside, and after aimlessly walking some 35 kilometers he arrived in Widz and found Jews still living in their homes. The Holocaust apparently had not yet reached that small locality. After a few days there, Livyatan decided to try again and look up his sister in Postawy, where he stayed for half a year.

Sensing the approaching danger, Eliezer Livyatan and cousin Tuvya decided to leave. They ran into an acquaintance, a farmer who agreed to supply them with food while they hid in the nearby woods. Thus, several weeks passed. Then the two were discovered by a group of farmers who wished to do them harm. "I had a bottle with me, which I claimed was a grenade that I was going to use against them. They took fright and left." At the same time, the friendly Lithuanian farmer (known as Rajza) also took fright and asked the two not to come to him any longer for food. For lack of any other alternative, Eliezer and his friend returned to Widz, for they had heard that the ghetto still existed there, but only stayed a short while. From there, Eliezer wandered to several other places, and March 1943 found him in the Swieciany ghetto. Some people were lured to return to the Vilna ghetto, but Eliezer and some of his friends decided not to fall for this ploy and instead try something else. Together with his cousin Tuvya, and the two Karsz brothers, Moshe and Leybele, he went to a farmer who had previously hidden Livyatan. However, this time he refused to take in any Jews. The four begged him and the farmer relented and agreed to only a one-night stay in the barn. The following morning the party split up; the two brothers went to check out a certain farmer while Eliezer and Tuvya headed farther out, deciding to go to the farmer Mudin in Petrawy who had hidden Eliezer earlier. This time, when he opened the door and saw the two, he told them to leave immediately. At a loss at to what to do next, the two decided to head for Nowe Święciany, a distance of 10 kilometers. On the way, they ran into a farmer who knew Livyatan's family, and he counseled them not to go to Nowe Swieciany since all Jews there had already been killed. "You're going straight toward death," he warned them. "What can we do?" they pleaded, "since no one is willing to take us in?" "Come to me," the man said, "where you can rest, then go into the forest." He then gave the two some whiskey to drink, indicated the direction of his home, and left.

At night, Eliezer and Tuvya headed in the direction of his home, some 20 kilometers away, and knocked at the door. An elderly woman answered. "Who are you?" Eliezer and Tuvya replied that the woman's son had invited them to come. However, since he was not home to be able to confirm this, she refused to let them in. The two panicked – where to go? A farmer known to Tuvya allowed them to stay for three days in his house. Afterwards, the two continued to Ignalino. As they passed the village of Balawiecki, another farmer known to Tuvya, allowed them to stay with him for two days. The two then headed toward the village of Pozwagina, where they stayed in the home of a farmer known to Eliezer for another two days.

On their way to Malbenowa, a farmer by the name of Satosz who happened to be a friend of Eliezer's father, recognized him and invited him and Tuvya to stay in the barn, hidden deep in the hay. It was the eve of Passover 1943, but what troubled Eliezer the most was the lice that infested his body. Satosz left and came back with an ointment. The two stayed there for two weeks. "I cannot keep you longer ... I am 60 years old," Satosz explained. "I cannot risk the life of my whole family [10 children]." Eliezer and Tuvya asked him where to go, and which farmers to avoid. He then mentioned a farmer known to him who lived not far away who would not betray them and would certainly keep them for a few weeks. Afterwards the two were welcome to return to Satosz, since in the man's opinion the war would anyway soon be over. So he and many others felt after the disastrous German defeat in the battle of Stalingrad, which had ended in February 1943. "We embraced and he wept. He also begged us not to disclose that we had been with him." This is how, after two long years of terrible travail, a hairsbreadth away from certain death, the two arrived at their final destination, the home of Hieronim Tarasewicz.

Eliezer and Tuvya knocked at the door and the following dialogue took place. "Who are you?" "We are Jews." "What do you want?" "Just to rest here." "I am afraid to let you in. I have strangers with me." "We could stay in the barn." "Stay in the barn." The two entered the barn and immediately fell asleep. At night, Hieronim Tarasewicz came to see them. He wept bitterly. "We also wept." He asked them from where they were. They answered – Ignalino, some 16 kilometers from his home. He said he knew both of the two men's families, and asked, "What do you want?" "We want to rest for a while." "How did you know to come here, since you don't know me?" At first they hesitated. Then something told them they could trust him, and they revealed the name of Satosz, where they had stayed for two weeks. "He embraced us. 'If my friend Satosz risked himself and kept you for two weeks, I can do the same for two weeks.' He told us to remain hidden in the hay in the loft. His wife brought us milk, straight from the cow. For the first time, we felt good. After two years of travail, we met a man like him. He is truly an angel."

Tarasewicz also told them that he had overheard his priest say that the Germans were breaking and the war would be over soon. It was simply a matter of weeks, he naively believed. "So you can stay for another two weeks." At the end of this period, his daughter Irka came to bring their food. "Father has decided that in the meantime you can stay on. The weather outside is bad. There's a heavy downpour." The following morning he himself brought breakfast and confirmed that they could stay for another two weeks. His wife would come to visit them; also his son Medek and sister Sonia in order to lighten the somber mood of the fugitives. The Germans are losing the war, they assured the two men. At the end of the second two weeks, Tarasewicz again came to see them. He was weeping. "Where will you go, poor Jews? Stay here for another two weeks. We will then see what to do. Perhaps during the next two weeks the Germans will be broken." Eliezer and Tuvya could not believe the man's heart-felt generosity. They also noted that on many occasions German soldiers stopped at his place and received from Tarasiewcz "shpek" (pork), eggs, butter, honey, and whisky.

Towards the end of this additional period of grace, he came and said. "Do you know what we've decided? If we're to hang, we'll hang together. Stay with us until the end." In Eliezer's words, "We thought we were dreaming, that we were asleep. No, he's standing next to us and saying: 'You will see deliverance here by me.' We embraced and wept." Eliezer hesitatingly queried: "We have nothing to pay you." "It's okay, you'll survive," was the reply, "and then we'll make up the account. You will still achieve great things. We will still see good days."

One day, as his daughter Irka was on her way with food for the men, she ran into some Germans. She was suddenly frightened and, in severe shock, became mentally unbalanced. She would sit in a chair and mumble to herself: "All because of the Jews, all because of the Jews." Her father took her to Vilnius for treatment in a hospital. Another potentially dangerous time was when the Germans ordered every farmer to choose someone from his family for labor in Germany. Hieronim decided to send his sister Sonia. From Germany, she would write home, adding in a coded language: "How are the bunnies [the two hidden men] doing?" A full year had passed since the two men's arrival. In July 1944, the Russians liberated the area. Eliezer and Tuvya left the loft after a 15-month stay – originally meant to be only two weeks.

Later, Eliezer and Tuvya learned that neighboring farmers who had collaborated with the Germans and had fled to the woods, and now returned, did not take kindly to the news that Hieronim had saved Jews. They broke into his house and vandalized it and took his horse and cow. They also wanted to harm him physically, but he fled and came to seek shelter with his former wards, who had in the meantime returned to Ignalino, staying with them for a few months. After leaving the area, they learned that some farmers had falsely reported him to the authorities for supplying the Germans every month with agricultural produce in return for tobacco. Hieronim Tarasewicz was thereupon arrested and exiled to Russia, where he was forced to remain for eight years. He then resettled in western Poland, in Ketczyn, Olsztyn province – very far from his original residence during the war years.

In 1966, Yad Vashem responded favorably to the request of Eliezer Livyatan and conferred the title of Righteous Among the Nations upon Hieronim and Bronislawa Tarasewicz.

Thomsen, Henry & Ellen and the Danish Underground

DENMARK

*T*he German occupation of Denmark was unique in many ways. The King and the Danish government remained in place and the Germans even maintained a diplomatic representative in the country. Germany granted Denmark a degree of autonomy that was unusual for a region under German occupation, including noninterference on the Jewish issue. This lasted until August 29, 1943, when the Germans imposed martial law in response to increased underground activity and disbanded the small Danish army. SS general Dr. Werner Best, the German envoy, assumed full powers as Reich plenipotentiary.

There were some 7,700 Jews in the country, whom the Germans decided to deport in one swoop on the night of October 1–2. On September 28, however, the commercial attaché in the German embassy, Georg Ferdinand Duckwitz, let out the secret to Danish friends, who in turn alerted the Jewish community as well as Danish underground operatives. On September 29, 1943, Rabbi Marcus Melchior broke the news to his community and advised them to stay away from their homes, with friends or elsewhere, and wait for further word from persons in the Danish Underground.

On October 2, 1943, the bishop of Copenhagen, Dr. H. Fuglsang-Damgaard

Ellen Thomsen (right) receiving the Righteous Among the Nations award by Israeli ambassador Esther Herlitz

issued a pastoral letter in which he condemned the deportation of the country's Jews. He gave the following reasons: "Because we shall never be able to forget that the Church's Lord, Jesus Christ, was born in Bethlehem of the Virgin Mary according to God's promise to His chosen people, Israel; because persecution of the Jews conflicts with the concept of man and of brotherly love; because it conflicts with the sense of justice which prevails in the Danish nation." He ended with the ringing words, "We will fight for our Jewish brothers and sisters to be able to retain the same liberty that we ourselves esteem higher than life itself… We must obey God rather than men."

The Germans had already launched their roundup of Jews before the bishop's message – on the night of October 1–2. They managed to find only 475 Jews; all the rest – slightly over 7,000 men, women, and children – were in hiding and speedily being spirited out of the country across the Sound, the narrow channel separating Denmark from Sweden. The organizers of the rescue operation, spearheaded by the Danish underground, enlisted the help of private persons who spontaneously made themselves available for the task at a moment's notice. They included doctors, schoolteachers, students, businessmen, taxi drivers, housewives and, of course, captains of fishing vessels. They lent a hand in ferrying some 7,220 Jews across to safety in Sweden, a neutral in the war, which had earlier indicated that they would be admitted.

Those caught and deported were sent to the Theresienstadt camp in Bohemia, where in contrast to Jewish inmates from other countries, they were treated less severely. This was due largely to the intervention of various public bodies in Denmark. The Germans allowed gift parcels from the Danish Red Cross to be received by Danish Jews in Theresienstadt. Of the 475 Jews who were deported there, most saw it through the war; only 53 died.

In the meantime, back in Denmark, at the Snekkersten Inn near the city of Elsinore in the north, where the Sound is at its narrowest point and on clear days the Swedish coast is visible, a group of people had gotten organized to help the Jews reach Swedish shores. The Snekkersten Inn became the hub of a network of clandestine routes along the coast. An estimated 1,000 people left for Sweden from this place. Fleeing Jews who could not immediately be taken over were hosted overnight at the Inn. However, when the Gestapo started raiding hotels, boarding houses, and inns, causing several Jews to be arrested, the rescuers switched to private lodgings, including beach houses not in use during the winter months.

Henry Thomsen was the man in charge at the Snekkersten Inn, the "captain" there, in much the same way as he had been a captain at sea for the past 20 years. Born in 1906, in Thisted, Northern Jutland, he was married to Ellen Margrethe Christensen and had christened his boat *Grethe*. He had built up his own organization at the Snekkersten Inn, where he now single-handedly led the Thomsen Group. He and many others in this large-scale rescue operation made a couple of trips a week to Sweden, taking fleeing Jews with them. Dr. Jørgen Gersfelt, who had developed his own organization, worked closely with Henry Thomsen. Among Thomsen's closest aides were Sven Seehusen and Leif Hendil. Many others joined them – some became deeply involved in various illegal work; others only in a single or a few trips across the waterway.

Erling Kiaer, captain of the Sewing Club's boat, made a total of 142 illegal crossings. He had originally been a farmer; then a bookbinder. As told by Birger Mikkelsen, "When it became difficult to get a hold of small boats, Kiaer talked about buying his own. He said he had very good knowledge of engines from his time as a farmer, but my wife said it would have been an advantage if he had been a sailor." As for Thormod Larsen, he was in charge of communication with the coast guard and the Danish State Railway ferries to Helsingborg. Dr. Halldor Finsen in Espergaerde and Dr. Jørgen Gersfelt in Snekkersten were active from the start, and as doctors they often had to administer sedatives to small children and very nervous people during the crossing to Sweden.

Dr. Gersfelt also acted as a chauffeur for the refugees within the area. It was difficult to get a hold of cars, and since the driving had to be synchronized, Gersfelt used his doctor's car and ran into many dramatic situations on the dark roads. "I had soon used the small amount of gasoline I had saved up from my rations; but luckily enough it proved not to be too difficult to arrange for more. I received ration cards from various people, including policemen, motor vehicle inspectors, and doctors. Gersfeld also remembered how his house was always full of Jews waiting for a ship. "All motorboats that were able to navigate maintained a regular service between Snekkersten and the Kobbervaerkshavnen harbor in Helsingborg [Sweden]. The Jews arrived by train and car, carrying heavy suitcases and small children in their arms, and piled onto the boats that were waiting for them with their engines running."

As Jonas Børgeson further related: "On Saturday morning a Jewish couple with two children asked me to take them to Sweden. I told them they had to be in the boat within 15 minutes, which, of course, they were. I sailed out and reached the middle of the Sound, where I met a Swedish patrol boat, which took them aboard. I made the trip in 40 minutes. When I reached land, I had the pleasure of seeing other fishermen getting ready to sail refugees across to freedom. On that Saturday, Sunday, and Monday, many refugees were taken across to peace and freedom."

Brothers Svend Åge and Viggo Andersen were fishermen. Svend Åge Andersen began by rowing across a family of five. Their colleague Erik Andersen (not related to the other Andersens) was once out at sea when suddenly there was a strong wind and the boat capsized and eight fleeing Jews began to drown. Svend Åge Andersen and a young man clung to the boat while an elderly woman hung on to one of the thwarts. After floating around for about an hour three exhausted people were found by a Swedish patrol vessel and taken to Helsingborg.

During the three days of the first weekend in October at least 1,000 people were moved across the Sound from Snekkersten. Børgesen estimated that every day until 9 p.m. all the harbor's nine fishing boats with engines were involved in this undertaking – his own *Astrid*, Axel Hansen's *Delphi*, and the other boats – *Hilbert, Margrethe, Brasholm, Poul, Duen, Håbet,* and *Karl*. They all ran the shuttle service to the Swedish harbors of Råå, Knähaken, and Helsingborg. On the night of Saturday October 9 the record set for a 24-hour period was reportedly 900 refugees moved to Sweden.

Fishing boats were naturally the most in demand and many fishermen could even manage several trips in a night. The worst danger was engine trouble out in the Sound, and in many instances boats drifted around for hours before the fault was repaired.

On the part of the Jewish fugitives, we have the story of Torben L. Meyer, who arrived in Snekkersten on September 3 and received a hearty welcome from a Mrs. Ingeborg: "There was no consideration or doubt. She and her brother gave their beds to us. Where they slept themselves, I have no idea. Loads of covers and pillows were taken out of cupboards and drawers and we organized ourselves once more. We were not allowed to go to sleep until we had had a cup of coffee, a cheese sandwich, and some cookies."

Rachel Posin, another fugitive person, was born 1920 in Lodz in Poland, and had arrived in Denmark in 1938. On October 2, 1943, she left Copenhagen by train, together with her aunt, Leah Rosenberg Kritter, cousin Jacob and wife Bertha, their three-year-old son, and two Jewish friends. "On the train, Bertha and I were sitting opposite a man reading the *Berlingske Tidende* newspaper. He was watching us over the paper and we became nervous: 'Bertha, Bertha – something is wrong. What are we going to do?' I said. But after the train had stopped at Springforbi station, he handed us a card. It said he was a Danish priest who had been traveling on the train all day. Every time he saw somebody looking Jewish he handed them a card with an address where they could get help." Arriving at Snekkersten, the party was met by Mrs. Gersfeld (her doctor husband happened to be away) and Bertha and the child were led upstairs and hidden in the attic. Rachel's uncle and aunt were sent to Røntofte, the home of Lau Lauritzen Junior. Jacob and Rachel were lodged for the night in rooms at Strandvejen. The next morning Jacob and Rachel walked to Snekkersten Inn, where they met Henry Thomsen. He said immediately, "Don't be afraid – you will get out."

While most embarkation points were in the north of Zeeland, for Leo Goldberger and his family their escape started a few kilometers south of Copenhagen. On the bitter cold night of October 3, 1943, Leo, his parents, and three brothers found themselves huddled in the bushes off the shores of Dragor, waiting for the prearranged signal of flashing lights. "My baby brother had been given sleeping pills; we were each carrying a suitcase with a few of our most treasured belonging.... We had to wade straight into the water, towards the light signals from the boat bobbing in three to four feet of city water. We were hauled aboard and covered with smelly canvasses in the cargo bay. I remember feeling a sense of absolute revulsion and outrage: What had we ever done to deserve this fate?" A Danish woman, Fanny Arnskov, a friend of the family, had arranged the flight.

One of the ordinary citizen rescuers, Elsebet Kieler, recounted how it worked. "The money we collected was quickly spent. We walked through the old city of Copenhagen looking for Jews. We would find them hiding in back yards and under stairs ... We would use empty flats, belonging to Jewish families who had already escaped, for these Jews, too, until we could get them away to Sweden ... A brother of my tutor was the director of the public baths in Copenhagen. His name was Hans Moller. He and his wife put their home at our disposal. We slept there when we didn't dare to sleep at home. We also used their flat as a reception area for Jews."

The monument to Henry Thomsen at one of the places of his boat crossing to Sweden (courtesy of the Friends of the Sound Elsinore, Denmark)

As for the attitude of the Danish police, it could not have been friendlier. The duty guards in the harbors and along the beaches were Danish coast guards consisting of young policemen who were prepared to support the Resistance movement. The policemen closed their eyes to the transports of Jews during the daytime. As reported by one rescuer, "It was a strange feeling that the last person you shook hands with was a policeman in uniform." Imagine escaping from Denmark saluted by the Danish police.

For example, during the first hectic days a pro-German Snekkersten resident informed the Danish police in Elsinore that he had seen a group of Jewish refugees getting into a rowboat. The police had to come out and arrest the refuges, but after the police vehicle had driven a short distance up the Strandvejen, the police let out the Jews and told them to call at Snekkersten Inn, where they could be helped to escape again.

In another incident, policemen had been called in to check a place where fleeing Jews were about to board a ship. The policemen signaled to the refugees with children to disappear in the dark and went through the motions of arresting eight refugees. They were taken to the police station in Elsinore and from there to Vestre Faengsel, a prison in Copenhagen. After one week's imprisonment they appeared before a judge and were imprisoned for attempted escape, but the detective constables collected them from the court and drove them in cars to Vedbaek and to an illegal transport leaving for Landskrona in Sweden.

Preben Munch-Nielsen, a 17-year-old who lived in Snekkersten related the following story. "In 1942 I went to school in Copenhagen by train every day. One day while I was cycling home in Snekkersten, I was stopped because I didn't have a light. A policeman told me off and asked what I had in my briefcase. He found a few illegal magazines but ignored them, closed the briefcase, and said: 'Next time, remember your bicycle light!' One year later at the beginning of October 1943, the same policeman was outside our house; I opened the door and he gave me some instructions: I was to pick up a number of Jews at the railroad station and take them to their night lodgings. The next day I was to escort them from Snekkersten through the woods to Espergaerde," from where they were to sail across to Sweden. These quite unlawful instructions had come from a policeman who a year earlier had stopped the young Preben for a traffic violation!

As for the occupying Germans, the movement of boats seemed to go on openly without any major hindrances on their part. The German patrol boats were large, clumsy, and with little motor power. The Germans were also undermined by their own rigid schedules, and one could always be sure that the Sound would be open every day at 12 noon. That was when the patrol boats were docked at Elsinore harbor while their crews ate lunch. At the same time, one had to be careful. One day the Germans arrived at Snekkersten Harbor and impounded the boats as they arrived back from transporting Jews to Scania. Seven boats were impounded and a total of 12 fishermen were arrested. They were imprisoned for some weeks. At the same time, not all Germans showed a particular eagerness to take part in the manhunt.

The Gestapo in Elsinore represented the most serious danger, and one of the most notorious of them was Hans Juhl. A major Gestapo raid in the fishing town of Gilleleje, on October 6, 1943, netted 80 Jews – arrested in the church loft by Juhl and his men. The fleeing Jews had come directly from Copenhagen; the children were deep in sleep after being injected by local doctors. More people were added, for a total of 80. Just the day before, seven fishing vessels had managed to get 102 men, 76 women, and 28 children to safety in Hoganas, Sweden. Inside the church, there was no light and no heat; outside it was bitterly cold. Pastor Kjeldgaard Jensen comforted the people and allayed their fears. At around midnight, German police set up machineguns and searchlights around the church. All 80 Jews were arrested and escorted to the nearby Mission House for further questioning. Only one person escaped. He hid in the clock tower between the bells. Thirty-eight were later released since they were only "half-Jewish." The rest were sent to the Theresienstadt camp. Reverend Jensen had a nervous breakdown the next morning when he learned of the arrest of these people for whom he had felt personal responsibility.

As for Henry Thomsen, the uncrowned "King" of Snekkersten, there are many stories of how he tricked the Gestapo. In Gersfeld's words: "Juhl sensed that it was among the guests at Snekkersten Inn that he would find the skippers who transported the Jewish refuges to Sweden. He often came to the inn, trying to make friends with Thomsen in order to obtain information. Thomsen pretended to go along with him, and promised Juhl to call him if any

Jews showed up. Thomsen had already informed all the Jews who arrived asking for a room that they should find private lodging instead, since there was a risk that the Gestapo might raid the inn at any time."

In 1944, as both Gersfelt and Thomsen moved to resistance activity, Gersfelt went underground for a time, then crossed into Sweden on May 10, 1940, while Thomsen remained where he was. He was arrested in August 1944, with six other Snekkersten residents. Ironically, he had been previously arrested twice, but released. This time the Gestapo knew they had caught the underground ringleader in the area and were not about to release him. Instead, on September 9, he was sent to the Neuengamme camp in northern Germany, where he died of maltreatment on December 4, 1944, and his body was cremated. He was 38 years old.

On September 4, 1946, a monument was unveiled, made of black granite, opposite the Snekkersten Inn – Henry Thomsen's favorite place, where he liked to sit and look over the Sound – which marked the day three years earlier when he had made his first illegal crossing to Sweden. The inscription read: *"Brave helper of refugees. H.C. Thomsen, born 18.9.1906, Thisted; died 4.12.44 in Neuengamme."*

In 1968, Henry's wife, Ellen Thomsen, planted a tree in the Avenue of the Righteous at Yad Vashem after she and her late husband were conferred the title of Righteous Among the Nations. Three additional trees adorn the Avenue of the Righteous: one for the Danish Resistance, another for the Danish people, many of whose sons and daughters spontaneously responded to the call to lend a hand in the rescue of Jews, and a third tree in the name of King Christian X, who threatened to wear the yellow star himself if it were imposed on the Jews of Denmark – making the Germans back down. A small Danish fishing boat is also on exhibit in the Yad Vashem historical museum – in honor of the many fishermen who made possible the rescue of 95% of their country's Jews – a feat unparalleled in any other German-occupied country.

"Why did we do it?" Preben Munch-Nielsen, one of Henry Thomsen's rescue couriers, was asked. His answer: "It was a matter of decency. It was simply the only decent thing to do."

Todorov, Aleksander & Blaga

MACEDONIA

*T*welve-year-old Kristina Todorova had had enough of the incomplete answers and unconvincing explanations given to her by her mother about her origins. She wanted to know for sure what lay behind the rumors and whispering alluding to her Jewish roots. She had to know who she really was. So one day, as she passed by the Jewish community offices in Skopje, Macedonia, she decided to stop in and ask some direct questions. She was shown to a certain person, whom she asked whether the name Aaron Behar, which she had found scribbled on a note at home, meant anything to the people there. The answer she received was to change her life forever. She was told that Aaron Behar was Jewish and her real father; that her name at birth had been Betty; that her "father" and "mother" Todorov were in truth foster parents; that they had saved her during the Holocaust, and that her true parents had been taken away and consumed in the flames of Holocaust. Betty stood still; she was speechless, overwhelmed and shocked by this revelation. A new dawn had broken over her still young life.

Betty was born in Skopje, Macedonia, then part of Yugoslavia, in April 1939 to Aaron and Rebecca Behar. Her father dealt in electrical goods. Soon after, Aaron Behar entered into partnership with Aleksander Todorov, and when Aleksander was married to Blaga, in 1941, the two families maintained friendly relations, to the extent that during the first years of her life Betty spent most of her time with the Todorovs, who loved and pampered her as though she was their own daughter. Occasionally, Betty even spent the night with them. Betty became so attached to them that once, "I asked mother to switch places with aunt Todorov, so she would be my mother and my mom would be my aunt."

Aleksander and Blaga Todorov with their son Sergei and Betty Bijenvenita Behar (right)

In the meantime, the Germans invaded Yugoslavia in April 1941 and dismembered the country, dividing it among its allies – Hungary, Italy, Bulgaria, and the independent Fascist state of Croatia. As for Bulgaria, she was given the coveted province of Macedonia, which she had always claimed as historically hers. The Jewish population there numbered 7,800 souls, of which 3,800 lived in the capital city of Skopje. With the Bulgarian occupation, restrictive measures against Jews were put into force, including the marking of Jewish stores with a special sign and the obligatory wearing of the yellow star for every Jew above the age of 10. On February 22, 1943, the Bulgarians agreed to hand over all Jews in Macedonia to the Germans for deportation to the death camps. On March 10, 1943, all Macedonian Jews were arrested; those in Skopje were taken to the Monopol tobacco factory in town, and two weeks later they were deported to the Treblinka death camp, where all were gassed upon arrival, including 2,000 children. Of the original 7,800 Jews in that province, only an estimated 200 survived the Holocaust.

In early 1943, when Jews began to be rounded up for forced labor, Aleksander Todorov obtained forged documents for the Behar family to enable them to flee to Albania, which was under Italian rule and considered a safe haven for Jews. The Behars set out in that direction. However, when Aaron learned that all papers were carefully scrutinized at the border, he evidently lost his nerve and decided to return to Skopje.

Soon after this came the order for all Jews in Skopje to report to the Monopol tobacco factory. They were told that the purpose of this was to send them off to perform labor. At the time, Betty happened to be staying with the Todorovs. Her father called them on the phone and asked them to bring their daughter so they could see her once more before setting out to that unknown labor facility – not suspecting the true nature of these "labor camps." Aleksander Todorov brought Betty home to her parents, but suddenly seized with an unexplainable fear she burst into tears and refused to accompany them to the Monopol factory assembly point. She asked to be taken back to the Todorov home. Her father agreed and before leaving wrapped up some values, including silverware, and handed it to Aleksander for safekeeping until the Behars returned from the unknown "labor camp."

By March 11, 1943, all of Skopje's 3,800 Jews were locked inside the Monopol factory compound, including the Behars, where they waited for two weeks before being deported. During that interval, Aleksander Todorov often went there to communicate with his friends, the Behars, and smuggle in food to them. He also wished to assure them that their daughter was healthy and in good care, and they should not worry about her. During these tense days, Bulgarian policemen searched Todorov's house, and mistook little Betty for Blaga Todorov's daughter, since she resembled her. To protect her further from the possible disclosure of her origin and arrest, Betty was often sent to relatives outside the city – to a different aunt each time. Little Betty had no idea at the time the reason for this constant travel, but she did not mind it at all. For as she said after the war, "During the two years that I stayed with the Todorovs, I was treated like a daughter by Blaga and had no idea that the Todorovs were not my real parents. I called Blaga 'mother' and Aleksander 'father' and for safety's sake they changed my name to Kristina Todorova, by which name the local children also addressed me."

With the war over, Macedonia reverted to Yugoslavia, and life resumed its previous tranquil course. But for Betty, disquieting rumors began to circulate around her about her true origins, and she heard people whispering that she was not really the child of the Todorovs but was in truth Jewish. Equally puzzling to Betty was the way her father sent her on several occasions to a certain Moshe Pijade, who worked in the office of the local Jewish community, with a package wrapped in newspaper and containing banknotes. Aleksander told Betty that this was merely a contribution to Jewish war orphans. But he also forbade her to tell the man who was sending the money or even her own name. The sums were reported in the local newspaper as contributions from an anonymous person for help to Holocaust victims.

So one day she asked her "mother" Blaga about all these rumors and innuendos concerning her true identity, but Blaga assured her that these rumors arose due to the fact that she was not born in Skopje but, supposedly, in Bulgaria. Blaga also went so far as to stain her name by hinting to people that Betty had been born to her as an out of wedlock child. She felt it was better to keep the truth from Betty so that she could continue to rear and educate the child. To reassure her further, Blaga took Betty to church and placed a religious medallion around her neck similar to those worn by other girls that she befriended. In 1946, Betty was enrolled at school, and Blaga made certain that Betty was taken directly there and back without stopping anywhere. Betty later learned that this was so she would not be accosted by people who might tell her whose daughter she really was. At times, when she was sent to pick up groceries, people in the store would hint to her that she was Jewish and that her "parents" were not who they said they were. Be that as it may, when in 1947 the Todorovs gave birth to a son, named Sergei, Betty felt even more at home and spent time playing and caring for her toddler brother.

In 1948, hard times came to the Todorov family when the Communist authorities arrested Aleksander on the charge being a capitalist. They confiscated all of the family's private property and took away the valuables left by Aaron Behar with Todorov, including the money and coins that Todorov diligently kept with him in remembrance of his old friend and business partner – Betty's father. Aleksander Todorov was tried and given a 14-year prison sentence.

Life at home took a turn for the worse, economically speaking, forcing Blaga to seek all kinds of work, mainly knitting and embroidery, the products of which she sold to bring in money. A few months after her husband's arrest, it was Blaga's turn to be taken in for questioning. She sat for three months in jail, during which time Betty stayed with a Todorov aunt from Belgrade

One day in 1951, when Betty was 12 years old, and with Aleksander in jail, she went through her father's belongings and found a note that said: "*Bienvenita [Betty] Behar will remain with Aleksander Todorov until we will return. Signed: Aaron Behar.*" At the time that name meant nothing to her. But when she started to connect this with the allusions and the whisperings that she heard around her, she began to wonder and dreaded the thought that perhaps she was not really the Todorovs' daughter.

She decided to take a closer look at the question of her birth and origin. Thus, one day as she passed by near the Jewish community center, she remembered having visited the place when her foster father would send her with the packages of money when she was six years old. As mentioned above, she went in and was told the truth about herself, her original name, her true Jewish parents, and their tragic fate. She was still trying to absorb this stunning news when the man asked her whether she wanted to go to Israel, for the Jewish community could arrange this. "I was in shock," she wrote later.

Hurrying home, she kept the staggering news to herself for about half a year. From time to time, she went back to visit the Jewish community center without her parents' knowledge, until one day she was spotted entering the community house by a friend of the Todorovs and he reported this to Blaga. When Betty came home, Blaga had her sit down and began to interrogate her, asking where she had been, what she was looking for, and so on. Before Betty had a chance to explain, Blaga burst into tears. She wept uncontrollably throughout that evening. Then she told Betty the whole truth – who she really was, what had happened to her parents, the meaning of the packages Aleksander had given her, and her father's valuables that they had kept with them. Blaga also told her of her husband's efforts after the war to discover the fate of Betty's parents through the Red Cross and the list of survivors at the Jewish community – all this, of course, without Betty's knowledge.

"When I heard all this, I felt a sudden urge to leave for Israel, made stronger when the community people told me that they had located relatives of mine living there." They later also tried to convince Betty's foster mother to let her leave. Blaga did not wish at all to part with Betty. "She loved me terribly, and the very thought of parting affected her health, but she said she would comply with my decision." Aleksander, who was still in prison, had evidently not been told yet of Betty's discovery. "Myself, I struggled with my feelings, and could not decide whether to leave my foster parents, and especially Sergey whom I loved very much. The thought of parting from him was impossible to bear. But, finally, I decided to leave for Israel."

Betty's "mother" prepared a new set of clothes for her and all sort of packages. "Father" received a furlough from prison for a few hours in order to accompany Betty to the train station. Moments before parting, all burst into tears and wept. Betty finally boarded the train, accompanied by a Jewish community chaperon, and arrived in Israel in 1952. She was then 13 years old, and going to a new and unknown country.

In Israel, she was sent to a kibbutz, where she remained until she was drafted into the army like other girls. In the army, she served as a nurse after taking a course. Throughout all this time, she maintained close contact with her beloved foster parents by mail. When she was released from the army, after a 22-month stint, she moved to Tel Aviv, where she met the man she was to marry – Menachem Ezoory. On their honeymoon, they went to visit the Todorovs in Yugoslavia, for Betty to introduce her husband to Blaga and Aleksander – finally released from prison after expiating his "capitalist sin." Upon their arrival, journalists came to the Todorov house to take pictures and write up the story – which appeared in the local press – of the exciting reunion after a lapse of many years.

"Today," Betty Ezoory wrote in 1979, I have two children, a son and daughter. Before each delivery, Blaga came to Israel to be with Betty and take care of her until after the birth. My brother, Sergey, is an architect, married with a child. He also visited me, and we are in close contact." Back in Skopje, Macedonia, Aleksander and Blaga Todorov were also honored by the Jewish community for rescuing little Betty Behar. Moreover, each year, on March 11, the Todorovs attend a commemoration ceremony at the local Jewish cemetery in honor of the Jews from Skopje arrested on that date and deported to the death camps – among whose victims are to be counted Betty's parents, Aaron and Rebecca Behar.

In 1980, Yad Vashem recognized Aleksander and Blaga Todorov as Righteous Among the Nations.

Tököly, Vincent & Anna

SLOVAKIA

*A*t the end of 1944, under the conditions prevailing in Slovakia, one of the pits that had once been used to store wine barrels in the fields of the village of Jarok, near Nitra, now served to hide two Jewish families numbering eight people, sheltering them from harm by the Germans and their Slovakian collaborators – with a local farming family caring for their needs for seven long months.

The Ressler family, father Moshe, mother Olga-Zipporah, and their three daughters, Aliza, 14, Rachel 11, and Miriam, 7, lived in the small town of Michalowce. When in 1942, the Fascist Slovak regime headed by a Catholic priest, Josef Tiso, began to hand over the Jews to the Germans for deportation to the camps, the Resslers arranged for the daughters to be smuggled over into Hungary, where Jews were still safe from deportation. When the Holocaust reached Hungary, after the German invasion there, on March 19, 1944, the children were returned to Slovakia and the family moved to the larger city of Nitra.

Anna Tököly, 1946

In late August 1944, the Slovak uprising was suppressed with the help of German troops, who from that moment became de facto rulers of the country and resumed the deportation of Jews, which had been halted by the Fascist regime in late 1942. On September 7, 1944, Moshe Ressler returned from synagogue and told his wife, Olga-Zipporah, and their three daughters that they must leave immediately. In Aliza's words, "We got up and left, taking with us the clothes on our backs and the shoes on our feet, nothing else. Father had some money. We ran without knowing where."

At night they slept in a cornfield. They then headed for the nearest forest. It was already fall, and the leaves were falling. They had run out of the little food they had brought with them. It was decided that the eldest daughter, Aliza, would enter the nearest village and buy some food. "I had no idea where to go." When she approached the village, she asked where the grocery was; to the villagers that was a sign that she was a stranger, but they did not bother her and she proceeded to buy some bread, jam, and a sausage. In the meantime, Aliza's mother was terribly worried about her daughter's absence and almost panicked.

The Resslers continued to hide in the forest for about 10 days, with Aliza going into the village to get food. On the tenth day, the family ran into another fleeing Jewish family in the forest, the Klugers, who told the Resslers that it was not safe to stay in the forest. Instead, he gave them the name of a farmer who would probably assist them in return for payment. The Resslers approached the farmer and he agreed to feed and shelter them in his house in return for money. They stayed with him for two weeks, until people in the village began to whisper about the presence of Jews, and the farmer, fearing for his safety, asked them to leave. He suggested that they try their luck in the nearby village of Jarok.

The Resslers left feeling downhearted and made their way to Jarok, but as they arrived at the edge of the village they noticed many open pits in the fields. The Resslers had already heard about these pits when they fled from Nitra. Many years ago theses big pits had served the farmers to store the barrels with the wine they produced from the village vineyards. The pits were no longer in use, so the Resslers decided to make use of one of them as a shelter. "It was a wonderful feeling, for it was warm inside compared with the cold weather that was already felt, especially in the evenings," Aliza related. This time, with no more money on them, the Resslers decided to send the two smaller girls into the village of Jarok to beg for food. The idea was that two little girls (aged 7 and 11) would arouse pity on the part of the villagers. It so happened that little Rachel and Miriam knocked on the door of Vincent and Anna Tököly, who immediately committed themselves to helping the Ressler family with food and other necessities.

In time, the Resslers ran into three young, fleeing Jews, the two Klein brothers and another person. They too joined them in the pit, and the fugitives now numbered eight persons, with the Tökölys caring for them. Vincent Tököly would visit them at least once a week, late at night, carrying a knapsack filled with food to last a full week. He would encourage them and raise their spirits, assuring them that the war would soon be over. In addition, he invited the people to drop into his home, one at a time, to wash up. On other occasions he would warn them of German search parties accompanied by Slovak collaborationist Hlinka Guards, looking for hidden Jews, and he would urge them to move farther away from the village until the search party left.

One day, Rachel went to get water from a stream and a policeman saw her and followed her. The Resslers were caught, taken to Nitra, and imprisoned, but somehow managed to make their escape and return to Jarok, on Christmas night, to "our pit," and reestablished contact with their benefactors. The Tökölys were glad to be able to continue to support them, without any demand for any sort of reward. Aliza tells of the many nights Vincent Tököly sat up with them in the pit, encouraging them with news of the approaching liberation.

After the war, the Resslers moved to Israel, and with Czechoslovakia turning communist, communications with outsiders was discouraged. Only after the downfall of the Communist regime in Czechoslovakia were the Resslers able to renew contact with the Tököly family in 1990. By then, Vincent and Anna had already died. The Ressler parents, Moshe and Zipporah, had also passed away, so the three daughters decided to invite the Tököly's daughter, Alžbeta Chudačikova, who in 1944 was seven years old and remembered well her parents aid to the Resslers, to visit Israel with her husband, Karol, in 1991.

Vincent and Anna Tököly were recognized by Yad Vashem as Righteous Among the Nations in 1993.

Toptani, Atif & Ganimet
ALBANIA

*I*n Albanian culture, when a person gives you his Besa, his word of honor to act in a certain way, then he is committed to abide by it whatever the circumstances. A common folktale is of a person fleeing the police after killing someone in a brawl and being hidden by a strange woman. When she learns that the victim is her own son, she still refuses to turn in the fugitive killer hiding with her, since she had given him her Besa – her word of honor – a pledge that no self-respecting Albanian would dare violate. So it was no wonder that when Mrs. Ganimet Toptani promised Mrs. Miriam Altaratz her family's help should it become necessary – as a self-respecting Albanian she felt committed and accountable for her pledge – for her Besa.

The Altaratz family originated in Belgrade, from where they fled during the German invasion of April 1941. Father Meir, wife Miriam, and seven-year-old son Yaakov ("Yasha") headed south, hoping to reach the Italian-controlled area of the dismembered country in the Kosovo region. Arriving in Prishtine, the region's capital, they were interned by the Italians for half a year in the city jail together with other fleeing Jews. In March 1942, to solve the problem of overcrowding, the Italians turned over to the Germans about 60 Jews, including Yaakov's aunt Frida Barta and husband Bandi and their ten-year-old daughter, Yehudith. Nothing was ever heard of them again – slaughtered by the Germans. Then, on July 8, 1942, the Italians expelled the rest of the Jews held by them to Albania proper, also under Italian control. The Altaratz family was directed to Kavaje, where they had to report every day at the local police station, but otherwise were free to lead their lives, work, and move around.

That somewhat idyllic situation changed abruptly on September 9, 1943, a day after Italy surrendered to the Allies and the Germans swept into Albania. The previous evening, the local Italian commander assembled the Jews and informed them of the order received to surrender to the Germans, expressing his regrets that he could no longer protect them. On this occasion, Albanian officials distributed to the assembled Jews original Albanian papers to help them conceal their Jewish origin and mingle with the local population. The following morning, the Altaratz family decided to head for Tirana, the capital city, where they felt they could more easily melt into the city's populace. On their way there they witnessed Italian military convoys surrendering to the Germans.

In Tirana, representing themselves as Moslem refugees from Bosnia, the Altaratzes rented a room with two women, one of whom was the widow of a policeman, which proved to serve as a protective cover for fugitives from the law. The three fleeing Altaratzes occupied a one-room apartment and were joined by Miriam's cousin, Sida Levi, and her son Michael. Sida's father had earlier been arrested by the Bulgarians in Skopje, Macedonia, and all traces of him were lost. In Tirana, under German occupation, the Altaratz family lived in constant fear of arrest. Father Meir did not dare leave the house and the children rarely ventured further than the courtyard. As the Altaratzes depleted their financial reserves, Miriam and aunt Sida decided to supplement their income by knitting sweaters and selling them to an expensive shop in the center of town.

Then one day, when Miriam and her son Yaakov had gone to the store with some of the sweaters and to take new orders and get more wool, Miriam was asked by the storekeeper to go to a certain house to take the measurements of an important client. The two arrived at a house that looked to them like a palace and were well received by a woman speaking an excellent German – Mrs. Ganimet Toptani. As she correctly discerned that the woman from the store was a fugitive Jew, Mrs. Toptani offered to help Miriam Altaratz and her family and even to hide them in her country estate should the need arise. As retold by Yaakov, "She also told us that we need not worry since she could easily ascertain if the Germans planned a raid or any other action against the Jews, since she and her husband were in the habit of entertaining senior German officers." So in case of danger she would send her husband with a car to get the Altaratz family and bring them to her estate. Before parting, Mrs. Toptani, who had a son Yaakov's age, gave Miriam some clothes for him. A bond had been created between the two women.

The Altaratzes later learned that Mrs. Toptani was a cousin of the deposed King Zog and that her father had served as the Albanian ambassador in Germany. Albania, with its three million people, 70 percent Muslim, and the rest Orthodox and Catholic Christians, had gained independence from Turkey in 1912. In April 1939, Fascist Italy had invaded Albania, occupying the country and deposing King Zog, who went into exile. When the Germans took over in September 1943 they allowed the country to be ruled by four regents. Political forces in the country were divided among nationalists, monarchists (clamoring for a return of King Zog), and the clandestine communists, who were supported by Tito's partisans in nearby Yugoslavia. Many of the educated class, including the Toptanis, had studied in Germany and Austria and therefore, while not espousing the Nazi philosophy, were more inclined to be sympathetic to them than the Italians who had invaded and occupied their country without reason. During the Italian period, some 2,000 Jews had sought shelter in the country, of which an estimated 1,200 had fled there from neighboring Yugoslavia and Greece. In spring 1944, the Germans asked the Albanian authorities for a list of all Jews and their addresses. Mehdi Frasheri, one of the four regents, not only refused the request, considering it a flagrant violation of the agreement and interference in the internal affairs of Albania, but also alerted two representatives of the Jewish community and informed them of the German demand. He assured them that as long as the current government was in power, the Jews would have nothing to fear.

Several weeks after the meeting between Miriam Altaratz and Ganimet Toptani, her husband, Atif Toptani, showed up in his car and told the Altaratz family to quickly gather their belongings and join him. For on the previous evening, at a dinner with high-ranking Germans, he had overheard them saying that a raid would soon take place in Tirana to seize all Jews who were hiding under false identities. Mr. Ganimet took the Altaratzes to his estate in Kamza, about an hour's drive from Tirana. The estate included several buildings, but the Altaratz family was accommodated in the main building, the same in which the Toptanis lived. The accommodation was free of charge. The estate was populated by field and household workers as well as some Italian soldiers who had deserted and were also in hiding.

Mr. Toptani was an agronomist and the farm on his estate served as an experimental station for various cultures. As told by Yaakov, "I remember well the peach orchard with its oversized and juicy fruit that we had not known before." There Yaakov's family remained sheltered for about half a year, between February and August 1944. This period ended suddenly when the Germans set up a military position very close to the estate and the daily contact with the Germans became dangerous. Mr. Toptani continued to calm his guests, saying, "You have nothing to worry about. Everyone knows that you are my relatives. No one will touch you." As for Sida Levi and her son Michael, Atif Toptani hid them in another place and moved them again to safe locations when the situation warranted it, also sheltering them in his house. Yaakov Altaratz related that one evening, as Mr. Toptani hosted senior German officers at a festive dinner in his house, he insisted that Mrs. Levi also attend. Frightened as she was, Mr. Toptani calmed her, saying, "You are family to me and need not worry." He introduced her as such to his guests, who on that merry occasion did not raise an eyebrow.

The Altaratz family stayed on the upper floor of the building. Near the upstairs staircase, a small foyer with a long, low table led to the Altaratz's apartment. The Toptanis had placed on the table various books, periodicals, and magazines, both in the German and Albanian languages, including Nazi literature, as a cover in any sudden raids. Such a raid indeed took place one evening in summer 1944, after everyone had returned to Tirana, leaving behind Yaakov and father Meir for a few more days. Firing was heard in vicinity and the estate was invaded by shouting German soldiers. They were intent on searching for hidden weapons after a German column, passing through the area had been fired upon by partisans, from the direction of Toptani's estate.

Meir Altaratz, who introduced himself under an assumed name as a relative of Toptani, who happened to be absent, spoke a good German and assured the officer in charge that he had no part in the shooting. Yaakov related, "I stood next to the German soldiers, who turned everything in the house upside down, searching for hidden weapons, and heard them speaking Serbo-Croatian but in a Bosnian dialect. They belonged to the Handjar division." It was a German unit set up by the Nazis within the ranks of the Waffen-SS, with the support and blessing of Haj Amin al Husseini, the exiled Mufti of Jerusalem and an ardent pro-Nazi. The officer noted the literature on the table and this persuaded him to allow Meir and his son to leave for Tirana, giving the two a signed pass allowing them through roadblocks on the way to the city. Arriving there, the Altaratzes rented a room with a distant relative of the Toptanis. There they hid for several more weeks until October 1944, when communist partisans liberated the city after street fighting that lasted 20 days, and instituted one of the most radical communist regimes of the time.

For many years thereafter, with Albania cut off from the rest of the world, even from other communist states, the Altaratzes, who had moved to Israel, had no contact with the Toptani family. They had learned that under communist rule, in addition to being one of the country's well-known and wealthy families, the Toptanis were also suspected of collaborating with the Germans and Italians, and consequently suffered persecution. When Albania reopened its doors to outsiders after the fall of the communist regime in 1991, Atif and Ganimet Toptani were no longer alive, and their only son, Edi, had resettled in Italy. It is well worth noting that with few exceptions the Jewish community in Albania survived the Nazi's one-year rule. The credit goes to the Albanian people who, with all their political and religious factions and views, rallied as one man to save the Jews in their midst.

In 1992 Atif and Ganimet Toptani were recognized by Yad Vashem as Righteous Among the Nations.

Totzke, Ilse Sonja

GERMANY

"*I* am opposed to the Nuremberg antisemitic laws. I no longer wish to live in a Germany headed by Adolf Hitler." Hardly the words that a sensible person facing imprisonment would say to one's Gestapo interrogators in Nazi Germany. But this is indeed what Ilse Sonja Totzke said, and her provocative words were dutifully noted in the Gestapo file on her.

Based on this file, we learn of the Gestapo's attempts to silence a German woman who challenged the Nazi philosophy of the primacy of race and, failing in that attempt, had her incarcerated in a concentration camp as an "incorrigible" person. The story takes place in Würzburg when, on September 27, 1939 (with Germany already at war), Miss Totzke's landlord informed the Gestapo of the "suspicious" behavior of Miss Totzke. For example, she claimed to be a music student but she did not show any particular interest in music studies. Moreover, her behavior revealed an attitude that conflicted with Nazi views. For example, in 1938 she had fraternized with two or three Jewish women. In short, she gave the impression of someone definitely not inclined to be part of the German *Volksgemeinschaft* (racial community), although she was not necessarily anti-German.

Half a year later, in March 1940, a certain Jakob Kraus, who lived across the street from Totzke, also reported her "unusual" behavior, such as going to great lengths to make sure no one knew her address, so that her mail box was always empty. She did not get up in the morning for work but slept until midday and spent most of her time at home, only stepping out at night. To continue with the informer's complaint, a year earlier a middle-aged man with a Jewish appearance had asked him concerning Miss Totzke. Also, she did not return the Hitler salute. Moreover, there was something definitely suspicious about her, seen also from the fact that she avoided her neighbors. Kraus was then told to keep an eye on Totzke's movements and report any further suspicious acts to the Gestapo.

Several months later, three more people enlisted by the Gestapo to spy on Totzke added their reports on Totzke's "suspicious" behavior, such as her anti-Nazi views, her "crazy" ideas, and according to Fritz Friedrich, who claimed to have known her for four years, her individualism and her opposition to being considered part of the German *Volksgemeinschaft* (racial community) – all these, grave offenses in Nazi Germany. In July 1940, a certain Theresia Kraus also reported that Miss Totzke did not always return the Hitler salute when seen speaking to people. Also, from conversations with her, one could detect her anti-German, pro-Jewish, and pro-French views (it was just after the end of the campaign in France). In addition, she kept to herself, left her apartment at night, and returned only at dawn ("our dog barks when she gets back"), and from time to time was visited by a Jewish-looking woman in her mid-thirties. Mrs. Kraus was asked by the Gestapo to keep tabs on Miss Totzke and report anything suspicious to them. At the time, the Gestapo concluded that Totzke's behavior was not yet to be considered hostile to the state. At the same time, to be able to make a better assessment, a closer watch on her movements was urged. This was followed by scrutiny of her mail for eight weeks.

Nearly a year later, on May 2, 1941, an informer reported to the Gestapo that Totzke was not obeying the anti-fraternization laws with regard to Jews, in that she had a very close friendship with a 15-year-old Jewish girl named Schwabacher. The latter had even told Totzke that under the circumstances she did not want Totzke to visit her. "Miss Totzke, nevertheless, comes to visit almost every day, staying for many hours, mostly from noon till evening, until Mrs. Schwabacher [probably the girl's mother] comes home."

The Gestapo finally decided to act and bring in Ilse Sonja Totzke for a preliminary interrogation while at the same time searching her house. According to Gestapo records, on September 5, 1941, in reply to questions, Miss Totzke gave the following information: Born in 1913 in Strasbourg to Protestant parents. Her father, Ernst Totzke, was an orchestra director. In 1919, the family moved back to Germany after Strasbourg reverted to France and settled in Mannheim, where her father got a musical post. Three years after her mother's death in 1921, and her father's remarriage, the family moved to Ludwigshafen, where two more girls were born. As for herself, Ilse began studying music in Würzburg. However, due to a traffic accident in 1935, she has since suffered from migraine. Medical costs, support of her stepsisters, and other expenses ate up the monies she had inherited when her father died in 1934.

"It is true that I have had contacts with Jews," Ilse Totzke admitted, but this was strictly for business purposes, not fraternization. She admitted to a special relationship with the Jewess Ottenberg since 1935. As for the so-called Schwabacher girl, she was actually not Jewish but a woman married to a Jewish man who had left for America. Totzke's parents had known Else's family when they all lived in Strasbourg, and therefore the special relationship. As for her purported French sympathies, it was limited to taking lessons in French with Professor Jeanne Camille Wolf-Donjen. Otherwise, she took no interest in politics. At the same time, she suddenly added, she wanted to make it clear that she did not agree with the State's treatment of Jews. "I cannot agree with the measures in this regard." She was not a communist, but simply held that every decent person was acceptable to her, without regard to his or her nationality. Finally, since 1941, she had been devoting her time strictly to art, especially wood carving.

While answering questions at Gestapo headquarters, Gestapo agents raided her home, and reported on the following "incriminating" literature found there – *The Mother* by the Jewish author Shalom Asch, and *Theodor Herzl – a Biography* by the equally Jewish Alex Bein. Other books considered suspect for not conforming to Nazi thinking included *Der Gezeichnete* by Jakob Picard; *Eine Zeit stirbt* by Georg Hermann; *Jewish History* by S. Müller; *Palestine Diary* by Manfred Sturmann; *The New Crusade* by Benjamin Disraeli, and *Um die Frau* women's brochures.

After analyzing her statement, the Gestapo summoned Totzke to another session, on October 28, 1941, and made her sign a statement. This included the biographical information already given and the following words. "To the charge that I have many contacts with Jews, that is true." This was due, she added, to conditions in the early 1930s and was related to renting suitable apartments that happened to be owned by Jews – not a matter of fraternizing with them. As for the Jewish Ottenberg family, she came to know her through her non-

Jewish tailor and a friendly relationship developed. This lasted for about two years, until the Ottenbergs left for England in 1935. "As for my contacts with Schwabacher, I don't know a 15-year-old Schwabacher, only a 35-year old who is married to a Jew who left for America two years ago. I admit I maintain contact with her, but she is an Aryan, née Else Klose, whom my parents knew well in Strasbourg. I have no contacts with Else's in-laws, who live on the ground floor whereas Else lives on the first floor.

"As for my attitude toward National Socialism [Nazism] – I don't mix in politics. At the same time, I find the measures against the Jews not right. I wish to emphasize I am not a communist. For me, every decent person is acceptable, irrespective of his nationality. I am not preoccupied with the Jewish question, and have not yet formed an opinion on this. Therefore, I did not think much about my contacts with Jews, and this also explains my non-committal attitude vis-à-vis the Volksgemeinschaft. I hereby declare that henceforth I will cease all contacts with Jews, including Schwabacher. I regret my behavior and admit that there definitely exists a difference between Aryans and Jews. I take into consideration that I have been warned by the Würzburg Gestapo about my continued contacts with Schwabacher. In addition, I am aware that in the event I shall again be found guilty of this, I will face the possibility of an immediate arrest and to be sent to a concentration camp."

A week later, on November 3, 1941, the Nuremberg Gestapo office informed all area affiliate offices (including Würzburg) of a new and stricter application of the non-fraternization prohibition concerning Jews, ordered by the government. It stated that in the event that an Aryan was arrested for maintaining friendly relations with Jews (who, incidentally, were beginning to the deported to camps in the east), then "for reeducation purposes," the Aryan party to the "offense" who has been found to violate this prohibition on three occasions was to be taken into custody and sent to a concentration camp for three months of confinement. As for the Jewish party, in all such instances the person involved was to be removed to a concentration camp.

Over a year later, Ilse Sonja Totzke was reported absent from her domicile, and had probably left for Berlin. Then, a month later – a shocking revelation. On March 4, 1943, the Mülhausen Gestapo (Mulhouse in the Alsace region, annexed to Germany) reported the arrest of Totzke in the company of the Jewess Eva Ruth Sara Basinsky (a Berlin kindergarten teacher) by the Swiss customs authorities, who turned the two women over to the German border police near St.-Ludwig. At her initial interrogation, Totzke had stated that in September 1942 she had been warned against continued contacts with Jews, and had been called in again in December 1942 for an interrogation on this charge. Fearing arrest and deportation to a concentration camp, she decided to flee the country. So as not go alone, she had gone to Berlin in order to persuade Mrs. Basinsky to join her.

In a further statement, Ilse Sonja Totzke gave a fuller account of her background and admitted that in 1941 she had signed a statement at the Würzburg Gestapo to the effect that she was aware that contact with Jews might lead to her incarceration in a concentration camp; that furthermore, fearing arrest, since he had continued to have contacts with Jews, she had decided to hide from the police and for that reason had gone to Berlin, where she was not known. While there, she confided to a certain Mrs. Strauss, an Aryan married to a Jew, of her decision and was referred to Ruth Sara Basinsky. This is how she got to know her, meeting her first in September 1942. At the time, she was looking for an apartment in Berlin, but was unsuccessful, so she took rooms in private homes and at times stayed over with Basinsky. She then returned for a time to Würzburg to resume her woodcarving work. However, when she received the December 1942 Gestapo summons, she returned to Berlin, but she could not find Basinsky. For six or seven days she stayed in various places, referred by people she had stopped in the zoo, then returned again to Würzbug; then left again on January 6, 1943, by train, via Heidelberg-Karlsruhe-Koehl, to Strasbourg. After a night's stay there she continued through Mülhausen to Sonnheim, where she stayed for two days, and continued to Münster, in Alsace, for a tree-day stay in various hotels. The purpose of all this was to check out the most feasible border crossing points into Switzerland.

Then, via Strasbourg, back to Würzburg, where she got some clothes, and brief stays in various cities; then back to Berlin on February 7, 1943, where she again tried to look up Basinsky. From her neighbors, Totzke learned that she been taken away to a Jewish camp at Auguststrasse. The next afternoon, or the day after, she waited for many hours outside the Jewish camp until she made contact with Basinsky, urging her to escape and cross into Switzerland with her. At first hesitant, Mrs. Basinsky finally agreed to join Totzke. Ilse Totzke added the following incriminating statement:

> *"I already thought for a long time of fleeing from Germany, since I did not feel comfortable under the regime of Adolf Hitler. Above all, I found the Nuremberg laws unacceptable, and for this reason I considered my relations with the Jews I have known to be right. In light of the renewed Gestapo summons, I decided to flee to Switzerland."*

As known, the Nuremberg Laws promulgated by the Nazi State in 1935 stripped all Jews of their German citizenship. The definition of who is a Jew was based on blood. Any person with at least three Jewish grandparents was to be considered Jewish irrespective of his or her current religious affiliation. Those with only two Jewish grandparents were classified as half-breeds, first class; with one Jewish grandparent – half-breeds, second class. They too would suffer from severe civic and economic restrictions. In addition, the law prohibited, under severe punishment, the marriage between Jews and Aryans, as well as sexual relations between the two. Jews were also forbidden to employ Aryan maids below the age of 45.

Returning to our story, Totzke then detailed to the Gestapo the trajectory of her voyage toward the Swiss border together with Basinsky. On February 12 or 13 – by train to Heidelberg for a seven-day stopover. "Every day we rented another room." Then, on to Strasbourg, "where again we changed rooms every day," always in small *Gasthauses* (inns). On February 26, 1943, by train via Mülhausen to Dürmenach. Arriving there at 7 in the evening, they immediately headed for the border. "I knew the way from summer 1942, from my vacation in Alsace. Already then, I had checked out the way to the border."

On the night of February 26–27, 1943, the two women successfully got across the barbed-wire fence at the German-Swiss border, near Neumühle, but were apprehended by Swiss customs officials. After declaring that they no longer wished to remain in Germany, they were forced to return late in the afternoon. That same evening they tried a second crossing at a point without barbed wire. After walking two to three hours on the Swiss side, they were again apprehended by Swiss custom officials. This time the Swiss decided to teach them a lesson, and on the morning February 28, 1943, they were handed over directly to the hands of German custom officials. As to how she came to the decision to take along Mrs. Basinsky, Ilse Totzke declared the following:

> *"I was not asked by anyone to take the Jewish woman along. I only felt compassionate for her and wished to save her from deportation. It is I who persuaded her to join me. For this, I did not receive from Basinsky or anyone else any payment. In addition, I was not helped by anyone to carry out my flight. I should like to repeat that I wished to flee Germany, since I am opposed to National Socialism. Above all, I cannot approve of the Nuremberg laws. I had decided to have myself interned in Switzerland. I did not wish to continue living in Germany, under any circumstances."*

The Mühlhausen police added the comment that with Totzke one was dealing with a stubborn individual who took nothing else into consideration. Returning her, handcuffed, to Würzburg, the Gestapo ordered her interned in a concentration camp. In a lengthy report on March 29, 1943, the Gestapo called Ilse Sonja Totzke a "lazy person" and asserted that one should not believe her declaration that she was not involved in other attempts to take Jews across the border; that she was an opponent of Nazism, of the Hitler regime, and of the Nuremberg laws; that her motive for assisting Basinsky was the sin of "compassion," so as to help her avoid deportation. Totzke, the Gestapo report continued, makes no secret of her opposition to Nazism. She is a "Jew-woman," and in light of her behavior she is beyond remedy. On May 23, 1943, Berlin Gestapo headquarters ordered her incarceration in the women's concentration camp of Ravensbrück. She reportedly survived, but has not been located. Likewise for Sara Ruth Basinsky, who reportedly was assigned to the women's "orchestra" in Auschwitz camp, and fortunately came out alive.

In 1995, Yad Vashem recognized Ilse Sonja Totzke as Righteous Among the Nations.

Trocmé, André & Magda

FRANCE

*I*n the summer of 1942, André Trocmé, the Protestant pastor in the hilly town of Chambon-sur-Lignon in southeastern France was asked by the regional prefect to welcome Georges Lamirand, the Youth Minister in the government of Marshal Pétain – better known as the Vichy regime – which maintained a policy of close collaboration with Nazi Germany, including the persecution and deportation of Jews. Lamirand would be arriving on an official visit on August 15, 1942, to boost support for the Vichy regime in the Protestant enclave known for its reserved attitude towards the powers that be. Lamirand was given a polite but cool reception – no flags in the windows and no one cheering him from the sidewalks. As he was leaving the Protestant temple, he was approached by a group of students of the Collège Cévénol who presented him with him with a petition, believed to have been drafted by Trocmé, and which read:

> *"Mr. Minister. We have learned of the terrible scenes that took place in Paris three weeks ago, when the French police under orders of the occupying power arrested in their homes all the Jewish families in Paris for their deportation. Fathers were torn from their families and deported to Germany; children were torn from their mothers, who shared the same fate as their fathers... We wish to let you know that we have among us a number of Jews. However, we make no distinction between Jews and non-Jews. This is contrary to the teaching of the Gospels. If our comrades receive an order to be deported or even to register, for the sole reason that they belong to another religion, they will disobey, and as for us, we will do our best to hide them among us."*

André and Magda Trocmé in Le Chambon-sur-Lignon (courtesy of Chambon Foundation, *Weapons of the Spirit*)

Lamirand was stunned at this direct challenge to government policy on the Jewish issue. At a loss for words, his face contorted in rage. Robert Bach, the regional prefect, who stood next to him, turned angrily to Trocmé: "Mr. Pastor, you have gone too far! We know you're behind this speech of theirs! On this day of national harmony, you sow discord." Trocmé snapped back: "There can be no question of national harmony when our brothers are threatened with deportation." To this Bach reportedly retorted: "It is true that I've already received orders, and I will carry them out. The Jews, who are strangers in this region, are not your brothers. They do not belong to your church or your homeland ... [The Fuehrer] has ordered the concentration of the Jews of Europe in Poland. There they will have their own lands and houses; they will lead a life that is suitable to them and will cease to corrupt the West. In a few days, my men will come to register the Jews in Chambon."

Unflinchingly, Trocmé replied: "We ignore what is a Jew. We only know what are human beings." Losing his composure, Bach warned: "Mr. Trocmé, you would do best to be prudent. Seven of your citizens write to me on a regular basis about your subversive activities. Up to now, I have taken no account of these letters, but I am keeping track. If you're not prudent, it is you whom I will be forced to deport. You've been warned. Goodbye!" Who was this man who, in the manner of the ancient Hebrew prophets, dared to confront the country's rulers on questions of morality?

Born in 1901 in northern France into an old Huguenot (Calvinist) family on his father's side and a German family on his mother's side, he witnessed the horrors of the World War I, which turned him into a sworn pacifist, abhorring all forms of violence. In 1926, while in New York studying at the Union Theological Seminary and tutoring David and Winthrop Rockefeller, he met and married the Italian-born Magda Grilli. When he accepted the post of pastor in Chambon-sur-Lignon in 1934 (which he held until 1948), he promised not to overtly propagate his pacifistic views. In his first sermon there, he nevertheless said: "No government can force us to kill; one has to find a way to resist Nazism without killing people," such as by following the biblical command of "Love thy neighbor as thyself," the Sermon on the Mount, the Parable of the Good Samaritan, and the religious principle of, "one should obey God rather than men."

Interestingly, in spite of his abhorrence of violence, in the 1930s he once toyed with the idea of assassinating Hitler. As he confidentially wrote in his private, unpublished memoirs, he wrestled with an inner conflict when he realized the danger posed by Hitler, who would certainly launch another devastating war. "Should I not take advantage of my knowledge of German to slip in among the entourage of Hitler and assassinate him before it's too late, before he brings a catastrophe to the world?" What stopped him was his determination not to deviate from his religious principles of non-violence as well as his increasing pastoral obligations in Le Chambon. A number of years passed, and in the summer of 1940 Trocmé witnessed the fall of France and the creation of a government modeled on other Fascist regimes, in his own land. He decided to take a stand.

On June 22, 1940, the day of France's surrender, Trocmé preached a sermon that was to guide his actions during the following four years of his country's occupation. "The duty of Christians is to respond to the violence that will be brought to bear on their consciences with the weapons of the spirit... We will resist whenever our adversaries demand of us compliance contrary to the injunctions of the

Le Chambon-sur-Lignon (in Carol Rittner & Sondra Myers, The Courage to Care: Rescuers of Jews during the Holocaust, New York University Press, 1986)

Gospels. We will do so without fear, as well as without pride and without hate." When news filtered in of the mass arrest of Jews in Paris on July 16, 1942, Trocmé declared from the pulpit, "This is a humiliation for Europe and for us French ... The Christian Church must get down on its knees and ask forgiveness from God for its impotence ... I can no longer keep silent." Earlier, with the news of the internment of thousands of Jews in French camps, Trocmé convened a church session at which he proposed to visit one of the camps as a goodwill ambassador, to distribute food. Arriving for this purpose in Marseilles, he met Burns Chalmers of the American Quakers, who told him of the difficulties in finding families willing to shelter people released from these camps. Turning to Trocmé, Chalmers asked: "Do you wish to be such a community?" Trocmé recalled at first hedging, wondering whether his town could bear the burden of sheltering so many people. Burns: "Find the homes and the staff. The Quakers and the Fellowship of Reconciliation will support you financially." Returning to Le Chambon, he asked his cousin, Daniel Trocmé, to open one such home. It was to be Les Grillons. Additional homes followed, and the rest is history. Le Chambon-sur-Lignon had been converted into a city of refuge for thousands of innocent people, consonant with the cities of refuge obligation commanded by laws of Moses.

The Vivarais–Le Chambon heights are situated in the southeast corner of the Haute-Loire department and include some 20 villages and hamlets, with Chambon-sur-Lignon and Mazet–St.Voy the main centers, and with a population of slightly above 6,000 souls, mostly Protestants – the descendants of the Huguenots. When the chase after Jews began, thousands flocked to this region and were welcomed with open arms and sheltered almost everywhere in this Protestant enclave. In Le Chambon itself, various Protestant organizations took in Jews in various hostels, such as the Coteau Fleuri by the Cimade organization and Les Grillons, Tante Soly, Les Roches, La Guespy, Faidoli, and Les Heures Claires by the Red Cross, the American Quakers, and the pacifist Fellowship of Reconciliation. In Tante Soly, for instance, 80% of the occupants were Jews according to its wartime owners, Solange and Emile Sèches. The Protestants of this area practiced a down-to-earth Christianity rooted in the Hebrew Bible and the New Testament. One Chambonnais gave the following explanation: "How can you call us 'good'? We were doing what had to be done. Who else could help them? And what has all this to do with goodness? Things had to be done, that's all, and we happened to be there to do them. You must understand that it was the most natural thing in the world to help these people." Simple and yet profound words. One Le Chambon rescuer reportedly was cautioned by a gendarme, "Be careful, Madame, you're being watched." To which, she replied, "But not by you! I am guarded by God above," and she pointed to the sky.

While many religious figures participated in this vast rescue operation, Pastor André Trocmé and wife Magda were undoubtedly the leading spirits in turning the Le Chambon area into towns and villages of refuge for fleeing Jews, who stayed there for various lengths of time before proceeding elsewhere – some to the Swiss border, which they hoped to cross one way or another, mostly illegally.

The young Jewish activist Denise Siekierski, who worked out of Marseilles, led many Jews into the Chambon area. "I had a room in Chambon where we hid hundreds of Jews," she recalled. Soon, people of all backgrounds, languages, and religions were seen circulating freely in Le Chambon, "believers and non-believers, Christians and Jews." Jewish teachers who had lost their jobs as a result of the regime's racial laws were hired in the town's private school, such as Daniel Isaac, who taught philosophy at the Collège Cévénol. His father, the famed historian Jules Isaac, and his mother, came to Le Chambon in 1942 in search of safety. It was there that Jules Isaac began to write about the origins of antisemitism within Christianity, later to appear in book form under the title *Jesus and Israel*. André Trocmé recalled the many conversations between the two, especially when in 1943 Isaac showed him the manuscript of his book, and in Trocmé's words "he beseeched me together with him to exonerate the Jews from the crime of deicide for which they had been accused for nineteen centuries. Of course, I did not have to be convinced."

Eli Ben Gal was another recipient of the help of the Le Chambon community. "It was one of the best times of my life," he said. "I spent the time looking for frogs, hunting snakes, chasing butterflies, and I shall never forget it." The Bible-toting people of the town and surrounding hamlets viewed the Jews as the People of God. As stated by Marie Brottes, a Le Chambon rescuer, in the film by Pierre Sauvage, *The Weapons of the Spirit*, "What? God has sent His people and we would not receive them?" To author Anny Latour, Trocmé revealed after the war that he had forbidden any form of proselytizing. "To the Jews who requested me to baptize them, as a way of escaping antisemitic laws, I always replied 'I cannot offer baptism unless it is asked for in complete honesty, and for religious conviction. There are other ways of saving you. During the occupation, not one Jewish child received an improper Christian upbringing. Not to respect the conscience of children who had been entrusted to us by parents who had disappeared – this would have been an abuse. What gave us such a right?"

Two weeks after Lamirand's visit, on August 25, 1942, the regional police chief came to see Trocmé, and asked him straight out to turn over to him the list of Jews in the region. Trocmé, no less defiant as before, responded: "I know nothing of these persons. But even if I possessed such a list, I would not furnish it to you. These people came to seek aid and refuge among the Protestants in this region. I am their pastor, in other words their shepherd. It is not the role of a shepherd to turn over the sheep placed in his care." At first flustered by this response, the police chief regained his composure and warned Trocmé that if he persisted in this refusal he would be arrested. Soon afterwards several police vans appeared on the scene and asked the Chambon inhabitants to lead them to where the Jews were staying. At the end of the day, only one Jew (of the hundreds, if not thousands, in the region at this particular point) was apprehended, a refugee from Austria who was released when it turned out that he was only a half-Jew. The gendarmes remained in town for three weeks, staging sudden raids on homes and isolated hamlets; then, discouraged and dispirited, they left empty-handed.

After his confrontation with Lamirand and Bach, Trocmé feared immediate arrest, but nothing happened until some six months later, when on February 13, 1943, Trocmé and two of his principal assistants, Pastor Edouard Théis and Roger Darcissac, were arrested and interned in camp St. Paul-D'Eyjeaux, near Limoges. During their five-week incarceration Pastor Boegner, head of the Protestant church in France, interceded with Vichy authorities for their release. Finally, as a condition of their liberation, Trocmé and his companions were asked to sign a statement committing themselves not to criticize Pétain nor disobey Vichy orders. Trocmé and Théis refused. A day later, the three were released. It was reported that the other prisoners in the camp were deported, and apparently there were no survivors.

On June 29, 1943, the Gestapo entered the fray, raiding the Maison des Roches, administered by André Trocmé's distant cousin, Daniel Trocmé, where some Jews were found among the 23 students. The Jewish students were taken away, with the exception of one who was very ill and another student who it was reported had saved a convalescing German soldier from drowning in the Lignon river. As for Daniel Trocmé, he was imprisoned and eventually deported to the Majdanek camp, where he perished on April 4, 1944. After this Gestapo raid, Trocmé and Théis were urged to disappear, and they remained in hiding until the spring of 1944. Historians differ as to the number of Jews who benefited from the aid of the Protestants of the *Plateau*, but most agree it was at least several thousand – in other words, every second inhabitant (the population numbered some 6,000 persons) probably participated in this giant rescue effort.

In, 1976, Yad Vashem conferred the title of Righteous Among the Nations on Pastor

André and Magda Trocmé. Also accorded the Righteous title were Daniel Trocmé (in 1976), and Pastor Edouard and Mildred Théis (in 1981). Many others in Le Chambon were honored with the Righteous title. In addition, in 1988, the inhabitants of Le Chambon-sur-Lignon and the entire Vivarais-Lignon plateau were collectively honored by Yad Vashem with a special citation, for their participation in the rescue of Jews.

Tsvileneva, Varvara
RUSSIA

*K*islovodsk is a spa city in the North Caucasus region, between the Black and Caspian seas (close to Georgia, Chechenia, and Azerbaijan), that due to the many mineral springs around the city, in earlier times, was home to many musicians, artists, and members of the Russian aristocracy. Its name means Sour Waters. It was, indeed paradoxically, a sour place for many Jews who had sought refuge in that city.

The tranquil atmosphere of the city was shattered with the start of the Battle of Caucasus, launched on August 3, 1942 by the German army, which was aimed at penetrating the oil fields of Azerbaijan. The Germans almost attained their goal, but were stopped, in September 1942, by the Red Army, near Mozok, on the Chechenian border, and also checked by the severe drain of German personnel to the ongoing Battle of Stalingrad. The Germans were evicted from that region in January 1943, but the Jews there paid the price of having fallen victims to the Nazis during their five-month occupation of that region.

Varvara Tsvileneva, born in 1915, had completed her studies of biology at the Leningrad University in 1937, and worked in the biology department of the Medical Institute in Leningrad (today renamed St. Petersburg), until the start of the war. With the city under siege by the Germans, in early April 1942, the medical institute was evacuated to Kislovodsk, a journey that lasted a full month over several thousand kilometers. The Jewish Vera Skoblo had worked as an assistant in the same

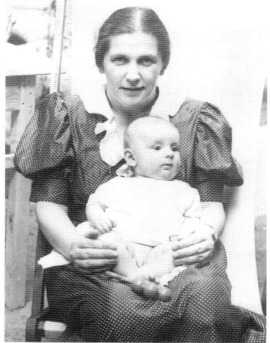

Varvara Tsvileneva and her baby son

biology department as Varvara Tsvileneva, and she and her family were on that same train journey, alongside Varvara and her mother. Joining Vera was her husband, Isaak, and their two children, Leonid (born 1935) and Inna (1937), as well as their niece Aleksandra (1928) and Vera's mother Hanna Lvova.

After the convoy arrived safely in Kislovodsk on May 3, 1942, Isaak Skoblo sought permission from the authorities to allow him to move further eastward, where he claimed he was offered work, but the request was denied. As the German army edged closer to the city, the population, which included many refugees from the war zone, began to be evacuated, and many left. Varvara decided to stay behind to be with her mother. The Skoblos too remained; Isaak was ill, and Vera's mother could not be moved. The Germans occupied Kislovodsk on August 11, 1942, and remained there until January 10, 1943.

The Germans immediately turned their attention to the Jews in the city, ordering them to don the yellow star on their outer clothes. At this point, Inna Skoblo remembered that some of the people, who had joined them on the trip from Leningrad, stopped greeting them, evidently for fear of the Germans.

Then came the order for the Jews to be "resettled," an innocent sounding codeword that actually stood for "murder." As stated by Varvara, "I suspected that it was meant to harm them. I suggested to Vera and Isaak to take their children and run into the hills." Vera was in good physical shape, but she did not want to leave her mother behind. The day after the "resettlement" order, the Skoblos left their home, telling their children, whom they left in the care of Varvara, that they were going to a certain collective farm for only a few days. Inna remembered her father's last departing words to Varvara, "The girls have lice, but please do not shave their hair, so they won't be taken for orphans [and taken away]." That was the last they were seen, for on September 9, 1942, all Jews in Kislovodsk were removed to nearby Minaralnyie Vody ("Mineral Waters") and murdered. The word of the killing soon spread among all inhabitants of the region.

Varvara Tsvileneva was left with the care of the Skoblo children, as well as Aleksandra, on top of her own mother. First she went to the Skoblo home to check on valuables they may have left behind, but was stopped and told to leave by the new occupants. "Thus began our existence, not knowing from day to day… Every time I sold something, with which to feed the children. Food consisted mainly of potatoes and cereals. I also picked up bricks left on the street to make a make-shift oven to keep warm." To outsiders, she presented the children as her nieces and nephews, whose father was in the Russian army. Naturally, many knew the truth, since many of the institute's workers were with the Skoblos during the month-long train ride, and saw the children with their parents. But no one betrayed them.

Then came the time of the inspection of identity cards. "I was afraid to show up and claim to have lost the children's credentials." Varvara fortunately met an attorney who in return for payment agreed to help, and forged new credentials for her.

Some of the institute people who had stayed behind tried to keep the institute in operation. A certain professor, named Wilhelm Schaak, an ethnic German, and head of the surgical department, agreed to head the institute. "Thanks to him," Varvara noted, "we survived, and were not taken for forced labor in Germany." The institute's management also knew the truth about the children, and offered Varvara a place in an abandoned rest home, outside the city, that served for some of the institute's lectures.

"How did we exist," Varvara asked in her deposition? The answer – odd and ends jobs. Varvara also took note of the children's education. Every now and then, an elderly person, an assistant at the chemistry department, came to give lessons to Aleksandra. "At the end of each lesson, we served him a warm meal. After all, we all suffered from hunger. Evenings, I read to the children, or quoted orally from books in my memory, also stories from Greek mythology."

After the Germans withdrew in January 1943, Varvara began to look up the children's relatives, from addresses left with her. Aleksandra's mother had, during the pre-war Stalinist wide-scale purges, been declared an "enemy of the people" – that is, not being a dyed in the wool communist, and deported to Siberia with her husband. In 1943, she was freed and assigned as a doctor in Tomsk, Siberia. Her husband, Isaak Skoblo's brother, did not survive the Siberian imprisonment. Varvara managed to contact Aleksandra's mother, and in April 1943, she journeyed to her with the children, and left the three children that she had saved with her. She later returned to Leningrad, and to her previous position in the biology department of the medical institute.

In 1996, Yad Vashem conferred on Varvara Tsvileneva the title of Righteous Among the Nations. Two years later, in April 1998, she joined a 50-person delegation of Righteous, invited by Yad Vashem to visit Israel and participate in the country's jubilee celebrations. It was just in time; she was already weak in health, and in December of that year, she died, in St. Petersburg.

Ülkümen, Selahattin
TURKEY

*I*n July 1944, with their troops in full retreat on all fronts, and the certainty of a lost war, Nazi Germany decided that it could not overlook the small and ancient Jewish community of faraway Rhodes in the Aegean Sea, off the shore of Turkey. The 1,700 Jews there, who were probably unaware of the Holocaust taking place on the European continent, were made to share their fate. The Germans set themselves the task of deporting these Jews by boat and train, over a distance of over a thousand kilometers, to the furnaces of Auschwitz, where most were immediately dispatched to the gas chambers. Only 160 survived the depredations of the camps. On the island itself, a small group of about 45 Jews escaped the bitter fate of their brethren through the intercession of the Turkish consul-general on the spot – Selahattin Ülkümen.

Rhodes is one of the oldest continuously existing Jewish communities. In the first century C.E., the Jewish historian Josephus Flavius mentioned King Herod the Great's earlier visit to the Jewish community there. Jews on the island underwent many vicissitudes as the island changed hands among Romans, Arabs, Crusaders, Turks, and Italians. Then in September 1943, when Italy capitulated to the Allies, the Germans took over. The Holocaust had reached this sun-drenched Mediterranean island.

Selahattin Ülkümen with Mathilde Turiel at Yad Vashem

Mathilde Turiel was among those who survived. Born in Izmir, Turkey, 1910, she had lived on Rhodes since 1933 and had kept her Turkish citizenship in addition to the Italian citizenship that she had received as a result of her marriage to an Italian Jew. Under Italian rule, life went on peacefully. In Turiel's words, "The Jews of Rhodes were unaware of what was happening to the Jewish population of the rest of Europe and did not know what was going to happen to them. We had no news because all communications were cut off; radios had been confiscated." The war on the continent was far away, very far away; North Africa had been liberated; and the Allies had landed in Italy. When the Germans arrived, life at first seemed to go on as usual. Then, on July 18, the Germans struck. Orders went out that all Jewish men were to present themselves at Gestapo headquarters on the following day, to be followed the next day by their wives and children. "We were warned that if we did not do so, our husbands would be killed," Mrs. Turiel emphasized in her deposition. As she was on her way with her two children and about to enter German headquarters, she ran into the Turkish consul-general at the door. "This was the first time I had ever seen him. He told me who he was and that I should not go in. He instructed me to wait a few blocks away while he went in to try to release my husband and save us from imprisonment. The other women and children had already entered headquarters. We were the last."

Her husband later related to her how, inside German headquarters, he overheard Ülkümen telling the Germans to release all the Turkish citizens and their families. To spread his protective wing over as many as possible, Ülkümen added 25 to 30 names to his list in addition to the 15 certified Turkish nationals. These others had allowed their Turkish citizenship to lapse, but Ülkümen considered them also worthy of his protection. The Gestapo officers at first objected, then bowed to Ülkümen's demand and allowed the 40 to 45 Jews on his list (including Turiel's family) to leave and go to the Turkish Consulate in order to obtain the documents that would confirm their Turkish nationality. However, since such documents could not be provided for everyone, Ülkümen argued before the Germans that under Turkish law spouses of Turkish citizens were also under the jurisdiction of Turkey, irrespective of their own citizenship, and he insisted that all the non-Turkish spouses be set free.

This somewhat heated debate took place as close to 1,700 Jews were being boarded on ships on their way to the Greek mainland, from where they were to continue on a long train trip to Auschwitz. The 40 to 50 Jews freed at Ülkümen's insistence were placed under house arrest for a while. A month later, due to the continuing deterioration of the military situation, German troops were withdrawn from Rhodes and Ülkümen's protected Jews breathed freely again.

Emilia Tarika was another person saved by Selahattin Ülkümen's timely intervention. Born in Turkey, she married a man of Italian nationality, which placed a question mark after her Turkish nationality. When the Germans ordered all Jews to present themselves, "in total despair, I decided to meet the consul. Although he resided quite far away, and there was no transportation due to the lack of fuel, I went on foot. Suddenly a car stopped near me, and the man (it was the consul) asked me why I was so upset. I explained the situation to him and he calmed me. I stressed that there were others like me, married to foreigners. He told me that all of us should come to the Albergo dell Termi hotel at 11 a.m., where he was scheduled to meet Nazi officials. Well, the person who told me all this was the man I was looking for so desperately, the Turkish consul, Mr. Ülkümen. I have always considered this chance meeting a miracle from heaven." After leaving the hotel, he told the terrified women assembled outside that he had managed to save the husbands. In Mrs. Tarika's words, "Only someone who has trembled in the presence of the SS is capable of appreciating the courage of Mr. Selahattin Ülkümen, who placed himself before the evil Nazi animals and snatched Jews from their fangs." Some time later, the men were released, while they watched the exodus of all the other Jews from the island; men, women, and children holding on to their satchels.

Albert and Renata Amato also have Ülkümen to thank for saving them from the dreaded deportation. The Amatos were Italians but, fortunately for them, Albert's mother had kept her Turkish passport and this miraculously saved the life of the rest of the family. By a stroke of good luck, Mrs. Amato ran into the Turkish consul in the street and told him what was happening. She then asked whether her husband's mother had to obey the German order to report. He told her categorically "no," and that any Turkish subject, irrespective of religion, was under his protection. The Amatos were then added to Ülkümen's list. Other people saved by Ülkümen were Moise and Victoria Soriano, their two children, and Moise Soriano's parents (not Turkish citizens), Isy and Batami Alhadeff, Joseph and Sara Alhadeff, Maurice Amato, Albert and Hartiye Franco and Enrico Franco, Leon Rosa, Maurice and Vittoria Soriano and Elio and Rita Soriano. These represent the few members of a once thriving Jewish community – the few saved through the initiative and generous intervention of Selahattin Ülkümen, Turkey's consul-general in Rhodes.

On September 1, 1944, Turkey severed relations with Germany before joining the Allied camp in the final military thrust against Nazi Germany, and thereby also to earn a seat in the future United Nations. According to one report, before the leaving the island Ülkümen's residence was bombed by the Germans and his wife was severely wounded. The reason for this has never been made clear. Whatever the explanation, Ülkümen hurriedly quit Rhodes on a Red Cross boat that took him and his wife to Athens, where he stayed in the Turkish embassy until February 1945. He then returned to Turkey.

In 1989, Yad Vashem bestowed on Selahattin Ülkümen the title of Righteous Among the Nations.

Valendovich, Elena

Belarus

"When [the Hebrew woman] could hide him no longer she got a papyrus basket for him, and plastered it with bitumen and pitch; she put the child in it and placed it among the reeds on the bank of the river. His sister stood at a distance, to see what would happen to him. The daughter of Pharaoh came down to bathe at the river … She saw the basket among the reeds and sent her maid to bring it. When she opened it, she saw the child. He was crying, and she took pity on him. 'This must be one of the Hebrew children,' she said.…She named him Moses, because she said, 'I drew him out of the water.'"

This passage, taken from the Bible (Exodus 2:1–10), tells of the rescue of the child Moses, the future great liberator and lawmaker of his people. The following story, taking place in Minsk, capital of Belarus, can be seen as a re-enactment of the earlier story, which took place several thousand years ago on the banks of the Nile River.

Desperate to save her infant daughter, Katia-Miriam Tokarski stole out of the Minsk ghetto with little Vala and set the child down on the pavement in front of a building with a bundle of clothing next to her while she hid at a safe distance to see what would happen. The child remained calm for a while as she played with a toy, then began to cry. Katia instinctively wanted to rush to her child, but as the child's weeping suddenly stopped she decided first to peek out of her hiding place to see what had caused the crying to stop. She saw a man holding the child in his hands. He had picked the child up, stood still, and was studying its face. Little Vala, as if instinctively, was touching the man's neck with her finger. From her hiding place, Katia could hardly control her feelings and wanted to run over to the stranger, but she held back and stayed where she was to see what would happen next. The man took the child firmly in his arms and walked away, with Katia following him at a safe distance and covering her face with a shawl. Eventually the man entered a house. Katia made a mental note of the address and left. She would later return to find out more about the man and about the woman to whom the child was handed inside the house. But for the moment, Katia sighed in relief – the child was apparently safe. It would not be destroyed, like Moses eluding Pharaoh's draconic order to kill all Hebrew males at birth.

When the German army entered Minsk on June 28, 1941, the city numbered close to 80,000 Jews. As the Germans emptied out nearby Jewish communities, the people there were forced into the Minsk ghetto, so that the Jewish population soon rose to 100,000. Then the killings began, with one murderous raid following another, and thousands falling on each such occasion – 30,000 in just one such raid during July 28–31, 1942. After this period, there were only 9,000 Jews left in the ghetto. These survivors were then moved to forced labor camps as the ghetto ceased formally to exist on October 21, 1943. On July 3, 1944, the Red Army liberated the city. There were hardly any Jewish survivors there to welcome the liberators; only those with partisans in the surrounding forests.

Katia Tokarski was one of the many persons herded into the ghetto in 1941, together with her mother and her then one-year-old daughter, Vala. Whenever a German raid seemed imminent, Katia managed to pass her daughter through the ghetto's barbed-wire fence into the hands of a friendly gentile woman outside. But this could not continue for too long, as the ghetto's population was being mercilessly decimated, with children not able to perform hard labor being first on the killer's list of victims. Some mothers had taken their children with them to hide in bunkers during German raids and then had to smother them to death, or allow others to do so, to stop crying that might give away the presence of the others hiding in these stifling underground lairs.

As it was obvious that the Germans would stop at nothing, until they had killed off the entire ghetto population, Katia urged her mother to flee with her to the non-Jewish side of the city and try to pass as non-Jews. After all, Katia's mother and her daughter had blond hair and fair complexions, so they would not be immediately noticed on the other side and could take their time to find some arrangement for themselves. "No, my daughter," Katia's mother replied, "I was born Jewish and want to die Jewish. Why go somewhere else only to meet death? I prefer to meet it here." Instead, she urged Katia to escape without her, but to take along her daughter, Vala. "Maybe the two of you will make it. A beautiful blond girl, and yourself speaking a good German! Who knows?"

However, Katia could not come to terms with the thought of leaving her mother alone, so she decided on another gambit – to leave her daughter someplace outside the ghetto and hope for the best. That is to say, hope that a compassionate person would pick up the child and take it home. In the early morning hours of September 1, 1942, Katia Kotarski reported as usually to her work detail, but this time with little Vala in her arms and completely covered up. The day had not yet dawned and in the semi-darkness the guards at the gate did not notice anything irregular. Once outside the ghetto, Katia slipped away as the work detail turned a corner and ran into the ruins of a bombed-out building. What followed was as described above: a man picked up the crying child and took it with him to a certain house. Katia noted its location and hurried back to her work detail.

That evening, back in the ghetto, Katia was restless; she had to find out into whose hands the child had been placed, especially when she was told by another woman, on another work detail, of having seen a little blond girl in the company of a woman in the neighborhood where Katia had dropped off little Vala. She had to see her, just one more time, to make sure that her girl was in good hands. Once day, about six weeks later, Katia again managed to slip away from her work group and rushed to the house which the man had entered with the child. She opened the first door she came to and pushing aside a curtain found herself face to face with her daughter.

"When she saw me, Vala stood up in her crib," Katia later related, and uttered a joyful shriek. Not a minute passed before a woman appeared, thinking that the child had been frightened by something, saw Katia, a total stranger to her, and immediately took the child in her arms. The woman instinctively felt that this was no mere stranger but someone closely linked to the child. So she placed little Vala back in the crib. Stepping close to the crib, Katia caressed Vala's leg. "She began to cry, and I cried too." Then the woman understood everything. The man who had picked up the child was there too, and the woman asked him to leave and lock the door on his way out. "That was the beginning of my friendship with Elena, my daughter's rescuer."

The man who had taken Vala home was Michael (Misha) Gromov, an escaped Russian prisoner of war, and his friend, Vala's caring "mother," was 42-year-old Elena Valendovich, who had found Misha wounded in the municipal park and had taken him to her home. She also had a six-year-old son, named Yevgeny. Gromov admitted that when he brought the abandoned child home from the street, Elena realized at once that the child was Jewish. To protect the child from inquisitive questions from neighbors, she told them that the girl was her niece from a distant village.

Elena offered to hide Katia as well, now or whenever she felt that the end was at hand for the Jews inside the ghetto. Katia thanked Elena for her generosity, but declined the offer; she had her own mother to look after. Dejected, she also told Elena that her own life meant little to her as long as her little girl was safe. "The safety of your home means more to me than my own life." Deeply moved by Katia's reply, Elena promised to take care of Vala no matter what. With this, the two women parted.

In the months that followed, Elena tended to the child's needs. Gromov's illegal earnings as a watchmaker helped bring in some money to defray everyday expenses. As for Vala, she quickly became accustomed to Elena and Misha, who for all intents and purposes she considered mother and father.

In the meantime, with Vala in safe hands, Katia was able to look out for herself. On March 30, 1943, she was able to make her escape from the doomed ghetto with her sister Dora Trebnik and a relatively large group of 25 people. They were helped by a German officer, Captain Willi Schultz, who had by then become disenchanted with his country's criminal misdeeds and had also fallen in love with one of the ghetto's young Jewish women. He decided to desert and take along some of the survivors of the ghetto who wished to join the partisans, stealing a military vehicle and taking them deep into the forest, where he surrendered to the partisans. Those helped by him, including Katia Kotarski, were able to join the Kutuzov partisan unit that was known to be operating in the vicinity. Unbeknownst to her, Elena had also left Minsk and moved to a village not too far from where Katia's unit was stationed, and had taken Vala along.

Over time, Katia heard rumors circulating of a woman with a little girl living in a village presently controlled by another partisan unit. Could this be her own Vala, and if so, was she still with Elena? A certain partisan once stopped by Katia and said, "Greetings from your daughter!" "How can you joke about this," she retorted. Soon afterwards, Katia was called to partisan headquarters and told that about 30 kilometers away, in a forest family camp under the control of the partisans, her daughter had been located and she was given permission to go and look her up. It indeed was little Vala, and she was there with Elena. This time, it was Katia who took the initiative, and with the assistance of her partisan unit arranged for Elena and the child to be housed in a village only a few kilometers from her base and controlled by her unit – close enough to enable Katia to visit her child every two or three days. This lasted until the liberation, which was close by, in July 1944. As for Misha Gromov, he too joined a partisan unit, but tragically, several days before the liberation of Minsk, he fell in battle.

In 1979 Yad Vashem recognized Elena Valendovich as Righteous Among the Nations.

Valu, Gizi

Hungary

"It is 1998, and I am writing this documentation to Yad Vashem, about the person who saved my life, my parents' and my uncle's life, risking her life day after day for months on end, only to keep us alive till we were liberated by the Russians in January 1945." So wrote Ági Shelly, born Bauer, in 1929 in Budapest, Hungary, and living in Australia. She wrote about Valu Gizi, a single woman during the Holocaust in Hungary, who prior to the war had worked as a secretary for the Shell Oil Company in Budapest.

As the story unfolded, Ági's family lived quite comfortably in prewar Budapest. Of her father's brothers, Ági's favorite was his youngest brother, Eugene, or as he was better known, Uncle Jenő. He was a bachelor and lived a happy-go-lucky life with few worries or cares. He was member of the stock exchange, and he lived in a spacious and luxurious apartment. Uncle Jenő's steady girl friend was a pretty and friendly woman called Gizi Valu. As Ági remembered her, "She was a small, petite young woman, who as I heard adored my uncle, but my uncle was not the marrying kind. I also heard that he occasionally had famous actresses coming to his apartment." On weekends, Uncle Jenő often spent time with his brother's family in their out-of-town estate, but Gizi was not invited. Ági did not find this unusual, as "I knew that my mother was very prim and proper and thought she could not like anything as bohemian as having my uncle's lover stay in our house." It was common knowledge that Gizi Valu had her own place; she met Jenő there, or at his bachelor's home.

In January 1944, Ági celebrated her 15th birthday. Two months later the situation for her and all the Jews in the country was to change dramatically, even tragically, as the Germans occupied the country. The Holocaust had come to Hungary. To add to the worries of the German presence, Ági's father, Dezső, was diagnosed with cancer in June 1944. He was operated on, but his surgeon, Professor Adam, told Ági's mother to expect the worse – that he could do nothing more for husband, as the cancer was spreading rapidly, and he would probably die within a few months. "My mother and I were devastated."

Under the new draconian antisemitic laws, all Jews in Budapest had to move into Jewish-designated homes. Luckily for the Bauers, their home on Andrassy Street 9 was classified as such a Jewish home, so no one had to move out. On the other hand, other Jews had to be allowed to move in, as they were forced out of their homes. Ági and her parents stayed together in one room, where she had to put up with her father's moans from the pain he was always in as well as her mother's muffled sobbing.

Somehow, Mr. Bauer still had the strength to arrange Swedish protective letters for his family. "I don't know how he got them but I know we were to move somewhere, to a house that had the Swedish protective emblem." The move into one of the Swedish protected houses was planned around September/October and the Bauer family started packing some belongings to be ready to leave at a moment's notice. Then, in a turn for the worse, on October 15, 1944, the fiercely antisemitic Arrow Cross movement seized power with the help of the Germans and instituted a reign of terror against the Jews in Budapest, including random killings on the streets or close to the Danube River, whose once "blue" waters were turning red with the blood of Jewish victims. One day, the Germans or Hungarian Arrow Cross invaded the Andrassy Street 9 building and took away every woman, man, and child to an unknown destination. "My father was so sick and so pale and thin that they did not bother to get him out of his bed; they thought he would die soon anyway."

Ági and her mother walked the streets of cold Budapest, feeling at times indifferent to their own fate, but were very worried about the seriously ill and weakened father left behind and alone. The Jewish column was led to the Óbuda brick factory that served as a way station to either deportation by train to a concentration camp or the start of a forced Death March toward the Austrian border. "We were there for about 3–4 days, when one cold sunny morning they gathered us in huge groups, and we were to walk guarded by German and Hungarian soldiers, and wild looking dogs." The column walked all day, not knowing what fate awaited them. Ági thought of only one thing, to escape. "I started to beg my mother to hold on to me and that we should try to walk away in the dark, away from the huge crowd. My mother was quite frightened that I had lost my sanity, and tried to quiet me down. I started to pull my mother, gently but firmly, and she followed, and we walked slowly away from the crowd, out towards the end of this bridge and some street." It was Pozsonyi Street, which Ági vaguely remembered was where one of the Swedish protected homes was located.

"I will never know how I maneuvered my mother up to this point. I will never know where I took the courage to do what I did, as I have never before or since done anything as courageous as this one thing. The most important step of my life, to escape towards survival." They managed to reach the Swedish home. As they walked in, they saw what seemed to Ági hundreds of people lying on the floor. But a pleasant surprise awaited Ági and her mother when they came across father Dezső, who had found his way there all by himself. "I heard him say how happy he was that we were together again, and this was all that mattered."

Ági does not remember how many days they were in the house. "I remember that we heard the name Wallenberg, but I did not know who he was." It was in this "safe house" that Agi started to hear about uncle Jenő and his wonderful Christian girlfriend Gizi, who was hiding him in an empty apartment on Alkotmany Street – "I think number 6 or 8." Ági heard her father and mother planning something for her, and only her – to be picked up by a policeman, known by Gizi, who together with her would come and take Ági along to Gizi's house, to be hidden there together with Uncle Jenő. There was not much for Ági to do but accede to her father's wishes. The day was set when the policeman and Gizi came to fetch Ági and take her out on the streets of Budapest, where danger lurked at every corner. "It was dark, it was cold, and I felt unmoved, maybe even a little bit happy to be together with my beloved uncle Jenő."

Gizi took Ági to a certain building, and to an apartment where uncle Jenő was sitting in a dark, cold room. He welcomed Ági with open arms:

"I remember Gizi talking very quietly, lovingly, and explaining to me that nobody must hear a sound from this room; we must ever be so quiet; we must not move, practically sit or lie all day on the floor. I remember there was one small sofa bed only. The rest was the bare

floor. I don't remember what we had to do about bathroom and toilet, but I remember that we were NOT to move out of this room, and everything else, like food, water, et cetera, she, Gizi, was to arrange to do for us."

And so it was. Days went by, and Gizi arrived every day, quietly letting herself in, bringing some hot soup or potatoes, and what was most important for uncle Jenő – cigarettes. She would stay with the two for a while. "I think she did something with the bucket that stood in the hallway, and had some water in it, and I think we used it also as our toilet." Gizi came and went, and Ági and Uncle Jenő stayed in the cold, dark room, either sitting or mainly lying on the floor.

Ági remembered the old newspapers that her uncle suggested that they use as mattresses. Days went by, while outside the Red Army closed its ring around the beleaguered city and shelled it constantly, more intensively with each passing day and while inside roaming armed Arrow Cross men vandalized and killed Jews whom they seized even from homes protected by diplomatic immunity. It was literally open season on the Jews and dangerous for Jews to be either indoors or outdoors, as well as risky for non-Jews to run the gauntlet of the Russian bombings. "Poor Gizi started to warn us that if by any chance she could not come one day, we must not worry, but she would have to be doubly careful of her life, and not chance the possible danger of being killed or even just wounded in a bombing attack. As I remember clearly, she said to the two of us, 'Nobody in the world knows about your whereabouts but me, so I must be doubly careful to stay alive, to keep you alive too.'"

Her father was constantly on Ági's mind, and she kept asking uncle Jenő and Gizi what would be their fate, and how long they could stay in the "safe house." There was one thing that kept Ági's and her uncle's spirit up, and this was the knowledge that Germans were losing on all fronts, and the Russians were advancing inside Hungary – actually outside of Budapest already. Gizi brought the news as well the meager food ration to keep the two in some kind of good spirits. Ági kept desperately begging Gizi to try to arrange for her parents to join them, and Gizi promised she would do her best to arrange something. Ági wondered – was it a mere empty promise, or something meant seriously? Then the dream became reality. In Ági's words:

"To me, a bit mystically oriented, and believing in something greater than can be explained in words, Gizi started to take the form of an Angel, an Angel who came, who went, who did nothing else, but overcame all horror and barriers, just to serve, to save her beloved Jenőkem, and as bonus his family as well. And one day, the door opened and I never knew how, but Angel has brought my parents to us."

What followed for still a good few weeks was close to a miracle as the winter settled in and it turned bitter cold, and in Ági's words, the people in that small room nearly froze to death. The shelling increased in intensity, often several times a day, so that sometimes for days Gizi could not come to see them, "and on those days we nearly died of hunger and thirst. Father was getting worse and worse, and again I don't know how and from where our guardian Angel got it, but she did bring father some morphine tablets to ease the pain. We lost count of dates, though we somehow guessed it must be near New Year, and thought it cannot be far for the Russians to come and liberate us. And so it was, one very cold January day, they arrived and we were saved from the Germans." The Bauers had been rescued – thanks to Uncle Jenő's compassionate lover, Gizi Valu.

Painfully, Ági Shelly readily admitted that with the war over, she does not remember her family's thanking Gizi, then or ever afterwards. "Gizi just stepped out of my life, and I never saw her again." With their home on Andrassy Street 9 seriously damaged from the bombing, the Bauers moved into the apartment of her mother's parents – together with her dying father, Dezső Bauer, who passed away on July 13, 1945.

As Ági resumed her studies, interrupted by the war, and finished high school privately – Gizi Valu was definitely out of her life. "My life was so upside down, how could I have thought of something like contacting the person who saved my life, the person that was Valu Gizi, the Angel." Adding to this, Uncle Jenő Bauer married his best friend's widow after he did not return from the camps, leaving her pregnant with his only child, whom he never lived to see. "I thought my uncle Jenő did the right thing that any good friend would do" by marrying beautiful Lilly, and a cousin was born to Ági, named Jutka. "Somehow the name Valu Gizi never came in to my mind again."

In 1949, Ági too married and together with her husband and her brother emigrated to Australia. Her mother joined her later. "We started to have our family, two children. We were successful and happy New Australians." Many years later, pangs of remorse began to resurface at having done nothing to acknowledge the kindness of her erstwhile rescuer, the lovely Gizi. "When I first realized this terrible negligence, I immediately wrote to my cousin Jutka, who lives with her family in Budapest. I explained to her why I would like her to find out for me what ever happened to Valu Gizi. She told me that she heard from her mother a few years before her mother's death that Valu Gizi had died."

Writing to Yad Vashem in 1998, Ági frankly admitted, "I am deeply ashamed, and find no excuse for the negligence and total lack of human concern, for not trying to find the person who saved our lives, to thank her and eventually honor her with the title of Righteous Christian that she really was. I would like to ask you with all sincerity that though unfortunately not in her life, but posthumously, that Valu Gizi be placed among the Righteous Ones, where she so very much belongs."

Ági Shelly's wish was granted, and in 1999 the name of Valu Gizi was added to the honorific list of Righteous Among the Nations and her name was etched in stone on the honor wall in the Yad Vashem Garden of the Righteous Among the Nations. Gizi Valu's self-sacrifice and courageous compassionate deed were not to be forgotten and swept away in history's dustbin, but with her elevation to the Righteous title she is destined to serve as a shining example of noble humanitarian behavior – thanks to the record left for posterity by one of her beneficiaries, Ági Shelly.

Vancourt, Raymond
Lombard, Raymonde
Pattyn, Alphonse & Jeanne
Siauve, Marie-Louise
France

*I*rene Johanna Elizabeth Kahn was born in Mannheim, Germany, in 1921, and with the Nazi rise to power she left for Lille, France, in 1934, where she joined relatives – Charles Ehrlich, wife Irma, and their two children, Claude and Eliane. There, Irene eventually learned office skills and found work with the Peugeot automobile company translating orders and invoices. She also tutored children in English and German. Her parents had managed to leave for safety in the United States before the onset of the Holocaust. In spring 1942, to avoid arrest as a foreign national Jew, it was arranged for her to become a governess with a family in the Loire valley region. In September of that year, she learned from a friend, Jeanne Pattyn, that the Gestapo had searched the Ehrlich home and had somehow forced them to disclose Irene's whereabouts. She had to leave immediately. Returning to Lille, she was met at the train station by Louise Siauve, Irene's former teacher, who took her in the darkness of curfew hours to a house that Alphonse Pattyn, husband of Jeanne, had already arranged for the fugitive Irene Kahn.

Entering a dimly lit hall, in Irene's words, "I found myself facing a tall man in priestly garb, and standing near him, a young woman." It was Monsieur l'Abbé Raymond Vancourt and his niece, Mademoiselle Raymonde Lombard." It happened to be the Jewish holiday and fast day of Yom Kippur, and feeling terribly exhausted from the tension of the day, Irene took ill and was a confined to bed for several days. A cardiologist was called and his prognosis was that Irene appeared to be suffering from a nervous breakdown. To recuperate, he suggested that Irene get up and find some interest in life "to keep my mind and body from going." Her benefactor, Father Vancourt, then suggested that Irene help him translate from German into French chapters of Nikolai Hartmann's *Grundzuge einer Metaphysik der Erkenntnis* ("Principles of a Metaphysics of Knowledge"). Irene's translation of the German philosopher appeared in French, in 1947 under the title *Principes d'une métaphysique de la connaissance,* with the following acknowledgment by Father Vancourt: "We find it necessary to thank Mademoiselle Irene Kahn, who during the years of hiding forced on her by the antisemitic persecutions helped us in this translation through her knowledge of German."

Born in 1902, Raymond Vancourt was ordained a priest in 1928. He then taught theology at the Greek Melchite Church of Sainte-Anne in Jerusalem. The year 1932 saw him studying ancient Oriental philosophy and theology in Rome, followed by his posting to Lille in 1934 to teach at the Jeanne d'Arc school. In 1941, in the midst of the war, he earned his doctorate and was appointed professor of theology. Other than his interest in Oriental religious thought, Vancourt was also known for his study of the thinking of Hegel and Kant, and he also tried to find similarities between certain aspects of Marxism and Christianity. He had also written on the Greek philosopher Aristotle. Other than his duties as the official chaplain of La Clinique St. Cathérine, Vancourt also served as professor of philosophy and theology at the Catholic University of Lille.

Irene stayed on in the Abbé's house for a long time, in fact until the area's liberation in late August 1944, together with Raymonde Lombard, the cleric's niece, who acted as housekeeper and was Irene's age. In her postwar account, Irene noted that during her stay there she did not go out. "I never opened the door to anyone ringing the bell; I never went to a window while the curtains were open." Irene was given the master bedroom and she circulated freely in the house. "All was open and accessible to me, as if I was already a member of the family." She helped out with household chores, with lots of woodwork to polish, floors to clean, cooking and washing to do. Through friends, Vancourt also got her false identity papers. When people dropped in to visit, they would be told that Irene was a friend of Raymonde's. Guests from the Sorbonne university who came to lecture in Lille would sometimes stay in Vancourt's home, and Irene's story had to be changed to fit changing circumstances. Irene recalled how at night she often lay in bed hearing the sound of boots coming nearer, stopping: "My heart would stop, and they would stomp on the sidewalk again, and my heart would race ahead of my breath while I was lying in a cold sweat ... However, a few times the bell would ring, Mr. L'Abbé would go to the door: it was sometimes German soldiers, and politely he would direct them away from the house, towering over them, determined, sure of himself, and probably praying with every fiber of his being ... but he would never let me know."

For a few weeks, Vancourt also provided shelter to two teenage Jewish girls who were eventually moved for their safety to a monastery. Irene's relatives, the Ehrlich family, also moved into the cleric's house and additional beds and cots were brought in to accommodate the additional people. The Ehrlich children, Claude and Eliane, aged 15 and 11, respectively, presented an additional problem, as they had to be kept busy and quiet, and kept indoors in spite of days of good weather. Mr. Ehrlich suffered from depression and Vancourt kept him busy rebinding his much worn books. In the summer of 1944, a new danger appeared in the form of the German V-1 and V-2 rockets aimed at England which sometimes misfired and fell into northern France, pretty close to Vancourt's home in Lille. French underground activists sometimes dropped in for short stays, such as Jean Lecanuet, who sought refuge after blowing up some bridges and other acts of sabotage. After the war, he served as mayor of Rouen. As the fighting kept getting nearer and the Allied armies approached, the Germans initiated house-to-house searches. The Abbé's wards would then spend nights at the St. Cathérine monastery.

Highly appreciative of her benefactor's generosity, Irene Kahn once asked Vancourt to have her converted. This would otherwise have been an opportune moment for the Catholic cleric, as Irene was years above and beyond the age where, according to Catholic teaching, baptism required the consent of a person's parents or legally appointed guardians. However, Vancourt's response to Irene's approach was of a different nature, which showed the true colors of the man's decency and humanity. In Irene's words, "His usually calm face became pained; I saw him upset for the first time. Then he took both my hands into his and in a firm voice, looking down at me, he said, 'Irene, I love you as a human being, and my respect for you as a Jew is deep and sincere; that's what you are. Don't ever ask me to do that. Even if you would ask me on bended knees, I would not do it and that's that.'" The cleric's great respect for the Jewish faith of his wards is similarly confirmed by Eliane Ehrlich, who married a rabbi after the war. She wrote: "I was then 11 years old. Not only did he not take advantage of the situation in order to convert us or turn us away from Judaism, but he insisted that we feel as though we were in our own homes, and for my father to lay his phylacteries as usual and to regularly celebrate the Sabbath and holidays."

After the war, Irene Kahn joined her parents in the United States. She was married to Nathan Diament, to whom she bore three children. After his tragic death in a car accident, Irene remarried and wrote her testimony in favor of Father Vancourt. In 1975, she joined her rescuer, Father Raymond Vancourt, in a tree planting ceremony in his honor at Yad Vashem. On this solemn occasion, he stated:

"It was already a great honor for us to be chosen by Providence to share, even in a very humble way, the immense suffering inflicted on the Jewish people during the last world war. As a man and a priest, it has always been my understanding that one aspect of my duty was to help relieve the suffering of those around me, to restore in them self-confidence and, as far as possible, to impart joy to them. Thus, when circumstances brought Mrs. [Irene] Diament [Kahn] into the stream of our lives (that of Mademoiselle Lombard and mine), a German Jewish woman who needed shelter; and later on, her uncle's family, and yet a whole cohort of Jewish children destined to be shipped to the crematorium ovens — we did not have the slightest shadow of doubt. Quite naturally, we did what any other person would have done in this situation, and we felt honored that God would want to use us as His humble servants to be instrumental in rescuing our fellow-man in his extreme suffering. Our fears — the risks we took — what were they in comparison to the immense tortures others had to endure? Once again, from that time on, it is we who owe you our gratitude. Today, you wish to thank us for the little we were able to do…. I repeat in all sincerity and from the depth of my heart — the honor we are receiving from you today, and by which we are touched, only reflects in our view the very great honor imparted to us when we were called upon to give shelter and joy to brethren crushed by doom."

In 1975, Yad Vashem conferred the title of Righteous Among the Nations upon Father Raymond Vancourt, as well as the other persons involved in the rescue of Irene Kahn and her relatives: Raymonde Lombard, Alphonse and Jeanne Pattyn, and Marie-Louise Siauve.

Van Damme, Alice & Emile & Léontine & Maria & Laura & Gaston & Adrienne

BELGIUM

*A*t the end of August 1942, 22-year-old Alice Van Damme was sitting quietly on a trolley car in Antwerp when suddenly it was stopped and Germans in uniform ordered everyone out. All the passengers were told to get up against a wall and hand over their identity cards for close inspection. What could all this be, Alice wondered? She decided to find out. In her words, "Realizing that something serious was happening, I slipped away and headed in the direction of the train station, where I saw many trucks parked. Amidst indescribable pandemonium, I saw soldiers, SS and/or Gestapo separating children from the parents who wished to cling to them. Men, women, and children were loaded onto the trucks as the crowd watched in bewilderment, feeling helpless in the face of such a horrific situation."

What Alice Van Damme was witnessing was a *razzia* – the term used for a forcible round-up of Jews in the city. "The suffering and the desperate mood of the Jews had upset me terribly, and it was then that I decided to ask my parents (for I was only 22 years old at the time) to be allowed to care for at least one Jewish child."

While this fleeting thought went through her mind in the uproar caused by the violent roundup of the Jews, Alice had heard someone shout the name of a Dr. Content and his address on Lange Leemstraat, where one could go to find out about helping Jews. This was a risky thing to have done, as the Gestapo could easily have taken down the name and address and gone to investigate. At any rate, Alice decided to act upon this information from an unknown person from among the deportees. As she said, "While still under the enormous impact of what I had seen, I begged my parents, when I returned to Belsele [where they lived], to allow me to look up this Dr. Content."

The following morning Alice headed for the address and met Dr. Content, who, it turned out, worked for the still existing but powerless Jewish community. Winning his trust, she was given the addresses of two places to look up immediately, one on the fashionable De Kaiserlei Boulevard. Hastening to the De Kaiserlei address, she arrived too late; the house was already locked up and under seal. The residents had apparently been rounded up. At the other address Alice met Mrs. Sobolsky, whose husband too had been picked up and deported, leaving his wife behind with his mother-in-law and the couple's two children, Marcel (aged four) and Johnny (18 months).

There was no time to lose, so on spur of the moment Alice decided to save Mrs. So-bolsky and her children. She took them to her parents, Emile and Léontine Van Damme, in Belsele, and readily agreed to shelter the two children in their home. As for Mrs. So-bolsky, she wished to return to Antwerp to look after her mother-in-law, and Alice ac-companied her back. With this act, Alice had already fulfilled her desire to save Jewish children from deportation. Would she be satisfied and stop at that? No at all; for her, this was but the initiation into an ever-expanding mission to save Jews threatened with deportation.

After safely settling the two children into her parents home, Alice decided to keep tabs on their mother and made it a point to visit the two Sobolsky women every week, bringing them much needed food, for they dared not leave their apartment for fear of being recognized and arrested. Barely a week later, during one of Alice's first visits, Mrs. Sobolsky asked her whether she would also help other Jews in danger, and she was given the address of Simonne Horowitz, who lived with her parents. So Alice Van Damme again embarked on a rescue mission. First she brought food to these people. The she checked out places where Simonne Horowitz could be hidden, which led Alice to turn to her sister Laura, who lived in Lokeren. Laura obliged, and another problem was solved.

Returning to Mrs. Sobolsky on her weekly visit, Alice met another woman there who had dropped in to visit, and she in turn asked Alice whether she would also take charge of two additional Jewish children, Henri and Sylvain Grunstein. Alice went to the Grunstein home with her sister-in-law Adrienne (married to Alice's brother Gaston), who agreed to shelter the two boys in her Belsele home for as long it took. During the first weeks of the children's stay there, they were given their benefactors' own bedroom as a psychological boost to minimize their pain at their traumatic separation from their parents. They remained there from September 12, 1942, to April 21, 1944, when they were betrayed and arrested by Flemish-speaking collaborators. Before that incident, Adrienne and Gaston also found a hiding place for the children's parents, Benzion and Henia Grunstein. Slowly but surely Alice Van Damme was involving and perhaps also entangling more members of her family in her ever-widening rescue net.

A few weeks after settling in the Grunstein children, Alice was asked to help two more women – Mrs. Karfiol and her mother-in-law, Mrs. Freifelt. Alice sent them to her parents, who were already keeping the Sobolsky children. Alice also accompanied the two women to Antwerp, where they sneaked back into their sealed houses to retrieve valuables with which to pay off the people who were keeping their children. Alice then took them back to her parents in Belsele. In the meantime, unfortunately for Mrs. Sobolsky and her mother-in-law, they were picked and deported, and did not survive.

Through all this, Alice managed to live her own life, and on February 26, 1943, she was married. Unbelievably, just a day before, she had again volunteered to accompany the Karfiol and Freifelt women to Antwerp for an additional break-in at their houses. As earlier, Alice was to rejoin them after two days at the place where they were staying after received from them a coded message in the mail with the words *Groeten uit Antwerpen* – "Hello from Antwerp." This time, something went wrong, and Alice waited in vain for the card that did not arrive. Instead she was called in for an interrogation by the Antwerp police, who informed her that the two women had been shot, or found shot, in their home. Though already under suspicion by the police, Alice was not bothered further. She was already married and living with her husband in Tronchiennes-lez-Gand, outside the city of Gand/Gent.

Three months later, little Johnny had to undergo an operation, but how was this to be done with his Jewish-sounding name of Grunstein, a name also appearing on the police wanted list? Again Alice stepped in to solve the problem. With her husband's consent, Alice declared Johnny to be her child, born out of wedlock, and with the help of reliable doctors, he was operated on in a Gand clinic under the name of Johnny Van Damme. Alice's mother, Léontine, sat at the boy's side at the clinic until he had sufficiently recovered to be taken back home with her.

Then someone betrayed Alice's parents to the authorities, who came to carry out a search. Alice's sister Maria was able to get out from her parents house in time, taking along the two children, Marcel and Johnny, and they remained with Alice for two weeks, after which they returned to her parents. Not finding the Jewish boys there, the police had left without arresting the Van Damme parents, but they were placed under police surveillance.

As for the Grunstein children, sheltered by Alice's married brother Gaston – the smaller Sylvain (born 1933) was allowed to go out, but not his elder brother Henri (born 1928), who was of school age, for it was feared that he would attract undue attention. To make it easier for the sequestered Henri, Alice and her husband invited him to stay with them for two months in their country home, where he could more easily be outside. This was done twice, at the end of 1943 and in the spring of 1944.

Then tragedy struck Alice's parents' home when the Gestapo raided the premises and this time found the two Sobolsky children, Marcel and Johnny. The Gestapo had Alice's sister Maria arrested on the spot. Alice's brother Gaston, who also happened to be in his parents' home, managed to escape with the Gestapo shooting at him. Gaston went into hiding on a farm and then in Alice's home for the two months preceding the country's liberation.

As for Maria's parents, the Gestapo forced them to lead the way to Gaston's home, where they expected he had gone to alert his wife, Adrienne. Not finding him there, the Gestapo arrested Adrienne and Henri Grunstein, one of the two boys sheltered there. Luckily his brother, Sylvain, was not at home at the time and escaped arrest. Maria was freed after ten days and Henri was placed in a Gestapo-supervised children's home. The following day, Alice's mother, Léontine, and Gaston's wife, Adrienne, were imprisoned. Léontine Van Damme remained in jail for several months until the country's liberation. She had also been involved with a clandestine organization that went by the name of the Socrates group. Léontime's daughter-in-law, Adrienne, was deported to the women's concentration camp of Ravensbrück and survived.

As for the three arrested children, they were snatched in time from the children's home with other Jewish children in a combined Jewish and non-Jewish clandestine operation on the eve of the German retreat from Belgium, and taken to safe places. Henri Grunstein was able to rejoin his brother Sylvain and parents, both of whom had been sheltered elsewhere.

Years later, in the United States, Henri Grunstein wrote, "I wish to add that the Van Dammes, a family of blacksmiths – father and son – did not seek to profit materially from our presence with them. My brother and myself, to this day, consider the Van Dammes our adoptive family." In 1993, on the 80th birthdays of Gaston and Adrienne Van Damme, rescuers of the Grunstein boys, the Jewish community of Belgium honored them with a special medallion and certificate. The two Grunstein brothers, Hirsch-Henri and Salomon-Sylvain, were present, having flown in from the United States.

This large-scale rescue operation had all begun on a simple streetcar ride in Antwerp when Alice Van Damme who was pretty much minding her own business, was catapulted into the drama of a raid on the city's Jews and heard someone call out a name. Then and there, literally on the spot, she decided to get involved, and carried along her entire family in an ever-expanding rescue operation – all this by a 22-year-old woman about to get married.

In 1996 Yad Vashem recognized as Righteous Among the Nations Alice Van Damme, her parents, Emile and Léontine Van Damme, her sisters, Maria and Laura, as well as her brother Gaston and wife Adrienne.

Vasileva, Nadejda
BULGARIA

On February 22, 1943, Germany and Bulgaria reached agreement on the start of the deportation of Bulgarian Jews. The first shipment would include 20,000 Jews, of which 14,000 would originate from the annexed Bulgarian territories of Macedonia and Thrace and 8,000 more from Bulgaria proper. On March 3, 1943, the Bulgarian cabinet approved the agreement. During the following days, over 4,000 Jews from towns in Thrace (a region formerly and now again part of Greece) on the Aegean Sea, were loaded into cattle cars and, bypassing Sofia, taken to Lom, Bulgaria, a city on the Danube River. There they were loaded onto boats which took them farther upstream, and then again taken by train on the final run – to Auschwitz, where most were gassed upon arrival. Some had already died on the way – from suffocation and lack of proper nourishment and medicine.

Nadejda Vasileva, a professional nurse living in Lom, happened to be visiting a friend, Penka Yivosheva, in mid-March of 1943. As her friend served coffee, she said, "I was unable to do any work in the house for three days, hearing the cries from the railroad station full of cars with Jews waiting to be sent to Germany." At this, Nadejda left her coffee on the table without finishing it and went into the next room, which had a view of the Danube River – and began to shake. In her words, "My heart almost broke when I saw heads and hands sticking out the cars and heard cries in three languages – Bulgarian, Turkish, and Ladino, voices screaming, 'Aren't there any human beings who will give us at least some water?' "

Nadejda Vasileva, born in 1891, had grown up among Jews in Nikopol, Bulgaria, and she remembered the kindness shown to her by a Jewish woman who gave her candies on the Sabbath, saying, "A pity, the girl has no father." Now, as she heard the cries coming from the cars, she remembered her unhappy childhood years. For a moment she fell into a faint, then came back to herself and began to act. In her words:

"I took a bucket, a big jar and a cup, filled them with water and went straight towards the cars. I was met by armed police and customs guards who shouted, 'Get Back! We'll shoot you like a dog!' One of them hit me with his rifle, shouting: 'Get Back!' I looked him straight in the eye and said, 'You, man, haven't you got a wife and children? You don't know what may

happen to them tomorrow, and don't you know me?' [He responded] 'I know that you are Vasileva's wife, but now I don't know you.' And he pushed me again. 'You may kill me, but let me give at least a drop of water to these poor people. Haven't you got any hearts – haven't you got any souls? How can you let people shout like animals for three days and three nights without giving them at least some water?' "

Disregarding the guard's threats, Vasileva went ahead, and surprisingly the other guards let her through, "because they saw that I was determined to go and was not afraid of being shot."

A big crowd had gathered near the port – Bulgarians, local Jews, and Turks – and all were crying at the horrifying sight. They started filling all kinds of utensils with water and passing them to Vasileva. "I went on distributing them, falling down, getting up, slipping on excrement, and a few gypsies sent by the crowd came nearer and helped me carry the water from car to car." All of a sudden, from the other side of the customs house, came a group of people in plainclothes and uniforms – in Bulgarian and what also appeared to be German uniforms. They came nearer and shouted at the guards, "Who gave permission to this woman to come and distribute water?" Nobody answered, fearing the armed men whose rifles were pointed towards them. Then a certain Slavi Pantov came forward and asked Vasileva, "Who asked you to do these crazy things? Get back! I'm going to have you arrested!"

He then turned to the policemen and ordered them: "Disperse the crowd, arrest all Jews; arrest this woman also!" He faced Vasileva again and asked, "Don't you know who I am?" Vasileva: "I know that you are Slavi Pantov and you are the President of the Merchants' Association and of the Red Cross. [He was also the local government-appointed Commissioner for Jewish Affairs.] Don't you know me? I am a nurse and I am doing my duty!" Pantov: "Who asked you to? Who gave you permission?" Vasileva: "I didn't ask permission from anybody – nobody asked me to do anything. On the contrary, the policemen were going to shoot me, but their hearts are not made of stone and they let me give water to these poor wretches." Pantov: "You go back home before it is too late." Everyone was watching to see the outcome of this confrontation. Pantov turned to the crowd and, pointing at Vasileva, exclaimed, "She's crazy."

Backing off, Nadejda Vasileva mingled with the crowd and recognized among them Rosa S. Yakova, the shoemaker's wife, a Jewess; also other Jewish women – Mrs. Vidas and Malka Alkan. She told them, "All Jews, please run away and hide yourselves. Slavi Pantov ordered that you should be arrested," and overcome with emotion she fainted again. When she regained consciousness, a policeman was staring at her. He said to her gently, "Now, madam, I beg you to go home; if not, I will have to take you to the police station."

As she started to leave the place, she ran into Dr. Alfandari, Bitu Beraha, and Miko B. Moshe – then president of the Jewish community in Lom. She asked the Jewish doctor what to do, and he dejectedly responded, "We too don't know; we are going home. They told us they would arrest us." At this point, Vasileva saw a large group of Bulgarian policemen in uniform coming from the other side of the town. She went over to them and said, "Would you tell me, gentlemen, was it a crime to give water to those poor people there in the cars who are being sent to Germany? I am a nurse, I didn't bring my card with me, but although he knows me, Mr. Pantov ordered that I should be arrested."

"Come with us, madam," was the response of these policemen, and gave her helpful advice. "Say that police chief Stambolov ordered that they let you back in." Using his name, she was allowed into the port, and was followed by a troupe of gypsies who came along carrying lemons, apples, matches, candles, sugar, cheese, yogurt, and other items. Vasileva began to hand out these provisions to the people inside the cars. "I was so happy that I could help there too." But then two custom guards came over and told her, "You had better go, Mrs. Vasileva; we have orders to arrest you; don't get us into trouble."

But instead Vasileva went to the government hospital to look up Dr. Tzikov, the man in charge there and under whose auspices she had earlier attended a nursing course. He sighed and said, "It is true, Mrs. Vasileva, that it is a great tragedy for these people, but what can we do? This is war. You see, there is a telegram that new transports are coming tonight and tomorrow. If you could start doing this work on your own initiative without thinking about the consequences, at least do it to the end, and don't say a word to anybody of what you have heard and seen, as there are strict and secret orders from a high place. I tell you in confidence that the local Jews propose to prepare some warm food and tea, but we shall say that it came from the Red Cross, if not they will not allow it." Vasileva answered that she was ready to distribute the food, and at the same time was going to ask for written permission by Pantov. As she left the hospital, three people were waiting for her, including the Jewish Miko Behar Moshe, whom she had earlier met, and Albert Beraha. "I told them to prepare warm food and take other necessary steps, but without the permission of Slavi Pantov I could not be of any use."

And indeed, they went over to Vasileva's house at 2 in the afternoon, getting a note from Pantov with permission to approach the next convoy of Jews from Thrace at the southern station, which was to arrive that afternoon. The food consisted of baked potatoes, cheese, sugar, yogurt, and fruit, as well as cigarettes.

Then at about 6:30 in the evening, Commissar for Jewish Affairs Pantov appeared on the scene, looked at everything and asked the policemen to disperse the crowd. He then started to inspect the food. Picking up a home-baked loaf of bread, he showed it to Vasileva and said, "Nothing can stop these Jews! You see, they made signs on the loaf!" He broke the loaf into pieces and contemptuously threw it on the ground. Disregarding Pantov's hostility, Vasileva started to distribute the food with the help of two or three gypsies and filled the utensils that were handed to her through openings in the cars or narrow windows. The smell from the cars was unbearable and the filth inside awful. "I did not have enough [water] to wash the dirty utensils." Vasileva also was helpless as she watched some of the gypsies stealing the food and stuffing it in their pockets. They also charged money for the water, cold or boiled, that they handed to the people inside the cars, filling their pockets with banknotes. Alone, Vasileva could do little to stop this thieving by some of the gypsies.

A kindhearted railway worker came over with a hose and let the water run so that the people could wash the utensils. He saw with tears in his eyes how the people inside the sealed cars were handing back the same utensils they had used for their excrement. Then Vasileva heard a woman from inside one of the cars shout, "Please, madam, give greetings to the local rabbi from his daughter, from Gumurdjina, and tell him that I don't know where I am going." Shouts were coming from another car – they did not have water or air. "Please," was the plea, "an old man died here three days ago. It stinks and last night a woman gave birth to a child and we haven't got any clothes to wrap it in!"

At ten o'clock, Slavi Pantov arrived on the scene again. He felt that enough had been done for the imprisoned Jews and ordered the distribution stopped, to be resumed the following morning. Suddenly a nurse in a foreign-looking uniform approached him. She had mistakenly taken him for a doctor and said to him, "Please, doctor, allow me to open this car," pointing to one of the cars, "so that I can take out my bag and medicines, and please tell them to allow me to go to the cars. There are many sick people, most of them suffering from dysentery." He looked at her, and turning red with rage he shouted, "Get out of my sight!" He then told the policemen who were on guard, "Take her – you know what to do!" – whatever that meant.

Next morning, Nadejda Vasileva waited until 10 o'clock for the new supplies to arrive. Nothing remained of the food from the previous day. She heard shouts from the cars. "Please, let us go outside to the toilets, we are dying, it stinks!" For this, permission was required. As she approached the cars, some of the filth fell from inside onto Vasileva's shoes and clothes. She decided on a drastic move.

"I climbed on one step and broke open the seals on the door of one of the cars and tried to open it, but this was impossible. A policeman came and asked me what I was doing. He said this was not allowed. There was no order! 'My friend,' I said, 'When you want to go to the toilet, do you wait for an order? Have a look! Even pigs could not breathe in that dirt.' One of them suffered a nervous breakdown. Kiril Georgiev Ghitzov, the railroad worker, looked at me and said, 'How dare you, madam, they will kill you like a dog!' "

Some local Jews succeeded in coming near the lines, among them Rosa, the wife of Meshulam Sabitaev, Malka Alkan, and Esther Copar. The three embraced Vasileva and said to her, weeping, "Your name will be written with golden letters in Jewish history!" One of the policemen came up and hit Rosa with the butt of his rifle.

At last, the guards started opening one of the cars and letting people go the toilets. Vasileva was shocked to see a policeman shouting to all the people from the car, "All who have rings, bracelets, and watches on their hands, hand them over." She thought to herself, "How dear the price these people had to pay in order to satisfy a physiological need!"

There was still the problem of the newborn baby, and Vasileva obtained a big package of diapers from Malka Alkan. However, the car had already been detached and sent to the port for embarkation. "I started going to the train station at the port, walking on the railroad line together with a gypsy boy who was carrying the package. In spite of the soldiers and police patrols that I met at every step, I kept going forward, answering their questions with, 'I have permission from the chief of police in Sofia, Stambolov,' and they would let me continue." When she reached the harbor, it was too late; the people had already been taken aboard the ship. Vasileva noted scraps of salted fish and empty cases of jam on the ground. "It was clear that the salted fish was for those who were going to their deaths – they should eat but not drink! Their only guilt was that they were born Jews!" "Oh!" Vasileva thought to herself in anguish, "What a pity that none of these poor wretches could ever come back and confirm what I have seen." After these dramatic events, Nadejda Vasileva received a carton of cigarettes on which a big yellow star had been drawn. On the back was a hate-filled message, "This is the reward from the Jews. You will go together with them where they are sent."

Immediately after Bulgaria's change of government and termination of its alliance with Nazi Germany, on October 20, 1944, Nadejda Vasileva received the following letter: "The Jewish community of Lom expresses its gratitude and the gratitude of all Jews of the town of Lom for your work at the port of Lom where you distributed food, medicine, water, etc., to the Jews of the Mediterranean coastal region who were expelled from Bulgaria at a time when the Fascist authorities forbade them even water. [Signed] Asher G. Levi – President and Moise H. Levi – Secretary."

In 2001 Yad Vashem recognized Nadejda Vasileva as Righteous Among the Nations.

Verduijn, Arie & Eeke and 22 additional rescuers
NETHERLANDS

*I*n April 1943, Karl and Bertha Winter in Eindhoven received the dreaded summons to report to the Westerbork camp in northern Netherlands for deportation. As Mrs. Winter lit the traditional Sabbath candles that Friday evening and the family sat down to ponder what to do next, there was a knock on the door. It was the 32-year-old Arie Verduijn from Helmond. Puffing away at his pipe, he said that he had heard from his brother-in-law, who knew the Winters, of their serious predicament, and had come to offer his family's help by taking their 14-year-old daughter Ruth with them. Ruth quickly packed some things, not forgetting her favorite doll, and left with Verduijn.

This story takes place in the southernmost part of the Netherlands, the provinces of North Brabant and Limburg, situated below the Rhine River, which flows into the country from nearby Germany and exits at the port city of Rotterdam. It was a region fiercely contested between British and German forces during the months from September to November 1944, entailing much suffering among the local population.

In 1936, Karl Winter and wife Bertha had left Nazi Germany for the Netherlands together with their two daughters, Ruth and Mirjam and settled in Eindhoven in the southern Netherlands, not far from the Belgian border. Then came the German invasion in May 1940, and three years later, in April 1943, came the dreaded deportation order. Forewarned of such an eventuality, the Winters had already arranged half a year earlier for their elder daughter, 20-year-old Mirjam, to be hidden and were in the process of arranging a hiding place for themselves and their second daughter, Ruth, when the feared summons arrived.

Arie Verduijn's sudden appearance had solved the problem for Ruth. The Verduijn household included Arie's 31-year-old wife Eeke, and their three daughters, aged six, five, and three, with Mrs. Verduijn expecting a fourth child. Ruth was warmly welcomed and treated like the other children. In her words, "Mrs. Verduijn, who before the war was a teacher, cared for me and comforted me when she noticed how hard it was for me not to be with my parents. As with her own children, she came to my bed at bedtime, tucked me in and gave me a good night kiss." While she was there, Ruth's parents and her sister, Mirjam, maintained contact with Verduijn, who carried letters from one to the other so that all knew how everyone was doing. From one of her father's coded letters, Ruth learned that Verduijn had helped falsify her parents' papers so that they went under the names Henricus Johannes Herps and Catharina Maria Wartenbergh. Sister Mirjam also dropped in on occasions, when she was between hiding places and had nowhere else to go.

A new danger made it necessary for Ruth to be moved elsewhere. This was due to the surprise daylight visit of Bertha Winter on June 11, 1943. She had left her previous hiding place for fear of German searches and had come to stay with her daughter at the Verduijn home. Arie Verduijn was stunned to see two girls walking beside Mrs. Winter as she made her way to the Verduijn house. Evidently Mrs. Winter had asked them for directions to the Verduijn home. Arie and Eeke were stricken with fear. The two girls were the daughters of a certain Klaassen, a known member of the NSB, the Dutch Nazi party, who lived just five houses down from the Verduijns. The two daughters, it was feared, would surely tell their family about the arrival of this Jewish-looking stranger. In desperation, Arie Verduijn checked with other people in his neighborhood if they were willing to shelter Mrs. Winter, even for a short while, but was turned down.

At home, over dinner, Arie prayed, "O God, what do you want us to do now. Don't let them pick us up and make orphans of our children." His wife approached him, put her hand on his and said softly. "Recall what you were reading yesterday at dinner time about Elisha, when the Syrians came to catch him? How he prayed, 'O Lord, strike these people with blindness?' He will strike His enemies again." Mrs. Winter, introduced as an "aunt," was allowed to stay for three weeks, time enough for other arrangements to be made for her. As for Ruth, after staying with the Verduijns from April to June 1943, she was taken by Arie Verduijn to Siege and Cornelia Postuma in Helenaveen, where she stayed for five months, until October 1943.

The Postumas were a large family with eight children, three of whom were still at home. Siege worked in a company harvesting the peat that grew in the nearby Peel marshland for use as fuel. "I was treated very well there, and knowing my problem with pork, they provided me with beef." As Mr. Postuma was in poor health, and could not bear the continuing mental strain of having a Jewish person in hiding with him, it was decided to move Ruth elsewhere, to the home of Hubert (Bert) and Louise Driessen, in Sevenum. "I cannot remember who brought me there," Ruth stated, and she is also not sure whether there were two or three children in the Driessen household. Be that as it may, for the two months that she was there, from November 1943 to January 1944, she was quite comfortable, even having a small room to herself, and during her free time (after helping out with household chores) she studied English through a correspondence course under her false name – Ria van der Veen. Hubert Driessen supported himself as a van driver and raised vegetables and potatoes in a private garden. Then an SS man was shot by the underground in the neighborhood and this led to a house-to-house search by the Germans. Mrs. Driessen quickly took Ruth to a Catholic prelate, who lived across the street.

Father Engelbert Gommans sheltered Ruth in his home for four days, until things had quieted down again. He also allowed her father to come over for a short stay. As someone connected with the underground, Gommans arranged new photos for the Winter parents for use with false identities and arranged a new hiding place for Ruth. It was to be with the Piet Verhaag family, still in Sevenum.

Ruth remembered Piet and Anna Verhaag's home as a cheerful place, and Ruth was given a room to herself. The family consisted of three small children, aged seven, six, and one. Piet Verhaag was quite well to do, owning a carpentry shop, a bar, and a bowling alley. So there was plenty of work to, but also much leisure time. Ruth arrived there in February 1944, and stayed until April, when for various reasons, including Anna's pregnancy, it was decided to take Ruth back to Helenaveen, but to a different family – the Ulens.

Victor and Wilhelmina Ulens, respectively 63 and 52 years of age, and with three grown daughters (26, 24, and 22), owned a little farm and some cattle. They lived near the Postuma family, where Ruth had stayed earlier. When she arrived there, she found three non-Jewish men already in hiding, one because of his underground activity; the other two to avoid being sent to Germany for forced labor. Ruth shared a room with two of the family's daughters, located in the granary. Of all the seven places that Ruth stayed during her 18 months of hiding, she felt the most comfortable with the Ulenses. "Mrs. Ulens told me to call her Aunt Mien and her husband Uncle Vic. She was like a mother to me; I shall not forget her goodness and love. She in particular was the soul of the family." Ruth stayed with them initially for three months, from April to the end of June 1944. "The time there was for me the best of all." As with the Gommans, Ruth's father came for a visit to see how his daughter was faring. Then, for reasons unexplained to Ruth, she was moved back to Verduijn's home in Helmond and learned that her parents had in the meantime also been taken in there for a while. This second time Ruth stayed with the Verduijns for two months, until the end of August 1944.

As the fighting moved closer to Helmond, she did what her father had told her in his coded letters to her – she return to the Ulenses in Helenaveen. When she arrived there, in September 1944, she found some more people – three relatives who had fled from Blerick, after the Germans had ordered the entire population to leave due to the fighting in the vicinity. The number of people in hiding had grown considerably. Then, on September 28, the Germans ordered the entire population to evacuate the place within two hours. After aimlessly searching for a place to stay, trudging on the road with a wheelbarrow on which they had loaded some belongings, they finally were taken in by a farmer and bedded down in an empty chicken coop. It took the British army two more months to break through the German line in an area known for its marshlands, making passage difficult. In the meantime, the Ulenses and their charges stayed indoors in the chicken coop, sleeping on straw provided by the farmer.

October 8, 1944, began with the early morning commotion of shouting and orders by the Germans. Soldiers came to look for men to send them for labor in Germany. The three hidden non-Jewish men, Victor Ulens, and the farmer's two sons were taken away. The women, children, and an old farmer were left alone as artillery fire grew stronger, with shells falling everywhere and forcing everyone to leave the chicken coop and stay in a cellar.

By early November, Ruth could not take it any longer. She was also anxious to know whether her father had also been taken away for labor in Germany. So during a pause in the bombing, she silently left and walked to the Verhaag home in Sevenum. There she met her sister, Mirjam, and her mother and was told that her father was hiding elsewhere, with Andries and Anna Willemssen (where Ruth's mother had else stayed before), also in Sevenum. She also learned that Verhaag had been seized by the Germans in church and conscripted for labor in Germany. Ruth decided to stay with her family at the Verhaag home until the soon-expected liberation. This took place on November 22, 1944. The preceding night, together with other people, 40 in all, the Winters and their benefactors had stayed in a shelter to avoid the terrible bombardment. The following morning, after several hours of eerie silence, two men ventured out of the cellar, and then came back shouting joyfully, "We are free, we are free; the Tommies are here."

As for Ruth's elder sister, Mirjam, her story is a similar epic of flight and survival among many families – some ready to help for only short periods, others for longer periods. As told by her, it was on a Friday evening when Bernadina (Diny) came to the Winters' home to turn the lights off, as the Orthodox Winters observed the religious prohibition against opening or closing lights on the Sabbath. Diny then sat with them for a little chat and after a while Mirjam asked her for a favor – to let her have her identity card. In Mirjam's words, "It was painful for me to ask her, but she did not hesitate for a moment to take it out of her handbag and give it to me with the simple statement, 'I shall find a way to handle the situation.'" Not another word was spoken about the matter.

Then came the day that Mirjam felt she had to go into hiding to avoid arrest and deportation. It was September 1942, and not knowing where to head, she dropped in at Diny's home, where she lived with her parents in Eindhoven. Mother Johanna Olofsen was busy ironing and engaged Mirjam in small talk. Finally Mirjam could not hold back any longer the purpose of her visit. "May I stay with you overnight," she blurted out? "I can't go home any more." Without hesitation, Mrs. Olofsen responded in a natural way while continuing her ironing, "Of course, Mirjam, you can stay here." It was more than just one night – it was two months. The Olofsen family consisted of Gerrit and Johanna, both 42, and their four children, aged 18 (Diny), 16, 13, and six. Gerrit eked out a living as a factory worker. The two months Mirjam stayed with them gave her time to find an alternative place for herself, with the Stavast family nearby.

Pieter and Cornelia Stavast and their three young children (aged, seven, four, and a six months) were neighbors of the Olofsons. Pieter was a blue collar worker and belonged to the same Protestant church as the Olofsens. When Mirjam's father offered to pay them ten guilders a week for his daughter's upkeep (without knowing where he would get the money), Pieter responded immediately (Mirjam: "Never shall I forget the reply"): "Mirjam can stay with us without paying; don't you worry, Mr. Winter." While there, during the evenings, Mirjam obliged her hosts by reading to their children from a children's Bible.

One evening Mirjam's parents and her sister, Ruth, appeared, asking to stay for just one night, as they were afraid to stay home that evening. The Stavasts turned their home over to them and took their children with them to sleep over at relatives. Winter passed and it was spring 1943, and danger came from the direction of a neighbor, a member of the NSB Dutch Nazi party, who hinted that he knew Mirjam's secret. It was time to move elsewhere, after a half a year's stay with her benefactors. The Stavasts gave Mirjam a small pocket Bible and reminded her she would always be welcome. She indeed took up the invitation and returned for short spells. But then a period of wandering began for Mirjam, stretching into months. She was helped by Piet Arts, a farmer and underground operative who found hiding places for many fleeing Jews in the Sevenum region. "I am not able to recall all the addresses where I was allowed to hide for one or two or sometimes even three weeks."

In one place where she stayed, the mother-in-law came over to visit and asked her son-in-law to get the 21-year-old woman out of the house. On a bus to a different location, she struck up a conversation with a 12-year old girl and this led to an invitation to stay over for a night at her family's home. "I was glad to have a full day ahead of me to go looking for a hiding-place." In another place, she shared a bed with a girl who had lice. "Thus my hair had to be shorn." In yet another place, she witnessed a brutal German roundup of people in the village and shooting at someone who tried to flee. At this, Mirjam panicked and threw into the toilet all her incriminating documents that could betray her Jewish origin.

Other places traversed by Mirjam included the Hubert and Maria Donders and Pieter and Maria Schreurs families. The Schreurses had three children, aged three, two, and two months. A farming family, they owned a few cows, pigs, chicken, rabbits, a meadow with fruit trees and a garden where they grew vegetables and potatoes. Mirjam was given a small room in the attic, which she shared with an owl and rats. "Living together with the owl was nice, but the rats were nasty." Pieter Schreurs worked in the cattle slaughterhouse in Sevenum. Mirjam stayed there from autumn 1943 until spring 1944 – over seven months. Then, Mirjam fell terribly ill and Mrs. Schreurs suddenly took fright and asked her to leave. As Mirjam left the house, she ran into Mr. Schreurs on his way home from work. "Where are you going so late," he asked her? When she told him what had caused her to leave, he responded angrily, but he could not overcome his wife's determined objections.

Mirjam's wandering resumed. For a few nights she stayed with a girl friend, other nights with her mother at the Willemssens; then with her father at his other hiding place, but just for one night, since the man who sheltered him told him he could not stay any longer, as his wife did not want them any longer. The man wept as he related the sad news to Mirjam's father. Mirjam then went to the Ulens family in Helenaveen, where she met her sister, Ruth. There she was allowed to stay in bed for a few weeks, until she had fully recuperated from her illness. It turned out that she had been sick with tuberculosis. From there she moved to the Verduijns, then back to the Willemssens, where she met her mother. Her father had moved in with a farmer's family, Johannes and Maria Hoeymakers, who lived elsewhere.

When the Willemssens were forced to abandon their home because of the intense shelling by British and Germans forces, Mirjam and her mother, Bertha, went to the Verhaag home. Bertha Winter remained there while Mirjam went to join her father in his hiding place, then she moved elsewhere, as chaos spread in this southern region of the country due to the intense fighting between the two opposing armies. She spent the last days before liberation with her parents and sister in a public shelter together with Mrs. Verhaag's family minus husband Piet, who had been recently taken away for forced labor in Germany.

After the liberation, when Mirjam mentioned to an English sergeant her and her family's life during the German occupation, he listened politely; then asked her scornfully from what propaganda she had picked up all these scandalous stories? She was taken aback. Already the horrors of the Holocaust were being denied.

The number of people who helped Karl and Bertha Winter, and their two daughters, Mirjam and Ruth, runs into over two dozen names. They include the following persons honored by Yad Vashem with the Righteous title: in 1977 – Piet Arts; in 1979 – Andries and Anna Willemssen; in 1982 – Victor and Wilhelmina Ulens; and in 1983 – Arie and Eeke Verduijn, Siege and Cornelia Postuma, Hubert and Louise Driessen, Father Engelbert Gommans, Piet and Anna Verhaag, Gerrit and Johanna Olofsen, Pieter and Cornelia Stavast, Hubert and Maria Donders, Pieter and Maria Schreurs, and Johannes and Maria Hoeymakers. These 24 rescuers endangered their lives to intermittently shelter and save the four Winter family members. In the words of Ruth Winter (later Steinman), "We came out alive out from this terrible time thanks to the help and self-sacrifice of all the people mentioned here and many more who risked their life to save us."

Veseli, Vesel & Fatima & Refik, Hamid & Xhemal

ALBANIA

*I*n 1990, Gavra Mandil, in Israel, addressed a letter to President Ramiz Alia, president of the communist state of Albania – a country with no diplomatic relations with Israel. He wrote:

> *"Your Excellency President Ramiz Alia. I was born in Yugoslavia in 1936 to a Jewish family. In 1941, we were imprisoned in a concentration camp in Prishtina [Kosovo] – and in 1942 we were deported, with many other Jewish-Yugoslav families to Albania and scattered there in different towns. Our family was at first located in Kavaja and later moved to Tirana. When Italy capitulated in the middle of the war in 1943, and the German troops occupied Albania, it became increasingly dangerous for all the Jewish refugees. Some of them were caught and deported to extermination camps in Germany from where nobody returned alive. But most of them were saved by the Albanian people. In those dark days, when danger and death were all around, the small and brave Albanian people proved their greatness! Without any fuss and without asking anything in return, the Albanian people performed the elementary human duty, and saved the lives of their Jewish refugees."*

Mandil then went on to detail the story of his family's rescue by an Albanian family, and asked to allow the family's representative, Refik Veseli, to be allowed to come to Israel to be officially honored for his and his family's courageous humanitarian help to Mandil's family.

Already three years earlier, in 1987, Gavra Mandil had written to Yad Vashem in great detail telling the story of his family's travails and miraculous rescue. Gavra was born in 1936, in Novi Sad, Yugoslavia, to Moshe and Ela. Gavra's father owned a flourishing photography shop. When the Germans invaded in April 1941, the family (including Gavra's younger sister, Irena) fled to Kosovo province, which was under Italian administration and was known not to persecute the Jews in the Nazi-German style. At first, the Mandils and other fugitive Jews were arrested and interned in a place from which, under the pressure of the Germans, groups of people were turned out and handed over to them for deportation to the camps. Towards end of summer 1942, a group of about 120 Jewish prisoners were able to persuade their Italian captors to move them farther into the interior of their administrative zone – to Albania proper – where they were dispersed to various locations and were only required to report daily at the local police station. Other than this small requirement, their movement was not restricted, under a policy known by its Italian appellation as *Confino Libero*. While

Liberation Day, Tirana, November 1944, Refik Veseli (second from left), Moshe Mandil (second from right) and his son Gavra holding a bottle

there, Moshe Mandil returned to his photography work and did some business snapping photos for local inhabitants from his home.

Small and mostly mountainous Albania, located on the eastern seaboard of the Adriatic Sea, wedged between Montenegro in the north and Greece in the south, numbered around two million people, mostly of the Islamic faith. Italy had invaded Albania in 1939 and remained there until September 8, 1943, when Italy capitulated to the Allies. The Germans immediately swept in and occupied the country until November 28, 1944, when they were forced out by a combination of Albanian partisan ac-

tivity and the German retreat from the Balkans. Some 2,000 Jews had found shelter in Albania under the lenient Italian administration, but this changed drastically when the Germans took over, and a veritable hunt for Jews began. At this point, in the words of Mandil, "there was not one Jewish family that did not find a hiding place among the local Albanian population, whether among the poor farmers or house or estate owners. Not one Jew remained without protection by one or another Albanian." Mandil added that the Albanians are plain folk people, but kindhearted and very humane. "Perhaps they were not educated on the heritage of Goethe and Schiller, but they attached the greatest importance to human life, in a most natural and understandable way."

As for Mandil's family, father Moshe felt that in the larger city of Tirana, the chances of survival, blending in with the local population, were better. Going there with his wife to make contact with total strangers, he decided to try out people who were in the same profession, so the two sought out stores dealing in photography. How surprised they were see a photo shop with a sign saying that it was owned and operated by a certain Neshed Prizerini – a former apprentice at Mandil's own photo shop in Yugoslava. "Our Neshad," in Gavra's words, welcomed his former employer, which led to Moshe's being invited to work in Neshed's lab, and to the Gavril family's being moved to Neshad's home. Moshe kept busy serving customers, including German officers who did not for a moment suspect that the man taking a picture of them was a fugitive Jew. In Neshad's shop, Moshe also met a 17-year-old apprentice, by the name of Refik Veseli, who had been sent by his parents from their village outpost of Kruja to learn the art of photography. The two became friends, with Moshe once telling Refik, "In today's conditions I cannot teach you more than the rudiments. But once the war over, and I will return to my studio in Novi Sad, came to us in Yugoslavia; there I will have the facilities and possibilities to teach you more." Little did Moshe realize at the time that this would indeed happen.

Soon it became too dangerous for the Mandils to remain in Tirana. At this point, Refik Veseli told them, "You are moving to my parents' home in Kruja." The Mandils later learned that Refik had previously consulted with his family and they had all agreed to welcome the four Mandils in their mountain home. Refik then took the Mandils on a long journey by mule over rocky terrain and via secondary roads to avoid military checkpoints – a journey lasting several days, with daylight hours spent in caves and forests and travel only by night. When they arrived in Kruja, Gavra's parents were hidden in a small room above the barn and cowshed, whereas the children were allowed to mingle with the host's own children. A little while later, Refik's younger brother, Xhemal, brought another Jewish family from Tirana – Yosef ben Yosef, his wife, Ruzhica, and his sister Finica. Ben Yosef, a Jewish fugitive from Yugoslavia like Mandil, had found employment in Tirana in a small clothing shop operated by Refik's elder brother, Hamid. Fearing arrest by the Germans, Ben Yosef turned to Hamid for help, and he decided to add them to the four Mandils already in his family's village home.

Both families remained hidden with the Vesselis for a full year, taking care not to mingle with the local villagers for added security. The adults tried to be of use by helping out with various household chores. During German bombings of the village to strike at partisan strongholds, the Veselis and their wards hid in a nearby rocky cave, one of many in this hilly terrain. The fall of 1944 saw an increase in military activity in the region and an intensification of German searches, and on one occasion they reoccupied Kruja after having been driven out by the partisans. Refik's father, Vesel, calmed the fears of his wards. "Only over our dead bodies would we allow them to come here and hurt us." Towards the end November 1944, Kruja was liberated, and with it the rest of the country.

Returning to Novi Sad, Yugoslavia, the Mandils reopened their prewar photography shop, and in 1946, Refik Veseli arrived there as an apprentice to improve his skills in the art of photography. After two years of training, Refik returned to his country, whereas the Mandils moved to Israel. Both sides maintained contact in spite of the difficult conditions in Albania, ruled by the fanatical communist regime of Enver Hoxha that discouraged communications between Albanians and foreigners.

In his 1987 letter to Yad Vashem, Gavra Mandil added that he felt an obligation, in the name of all those saved by the Albanian people, to acquit themselves of their debt to the Albanian people in general, and insofar as Mandil was concerned – to Refik Veseli in particular; he also wished the public in Israel to be made more aware of the contribution of the mostly Moslem Albanian population to the rescue of its Jewish population of some 2,000 souls.

Acknowledging Gavra Mandil's request in 1987, Yad Vashem conferred the title of Righteous Among the Nations on Refik Veseli and his parents, Vesel and Fatima. In 2004, upon receipt of additional information, Yad Vashem also awarded the Righteous title to Refik's brothers Hamid and Xhemal.

To get back to Gavra Mandil's 1990 letter to the president of Albania, there he emphasized that Refik Veseli and his late parents, Fatima and Vesel Veseli, were the first Albanians recognized as Righteous Among the Nations, and were invited to come to Israel to receive the honors accompanying such recognition as well as to plant a tree at Yad Vashem. "I am addressing you personally, Mr. President, the Albanian Government and your Foreign Ministry, to permit Refik and [wife] Drita Veseli to take this journey to Israel for this important occasion." Mandil enclosed an invitation from Yad Vashem as well photographs that Gavra's father, Moshe, had taken in Tirana on November 28, 1944, during the partisan victory parade, showing clearly President Enver Hoxha reviewing the liberation forces. That same year, in consequence of Mandil's letter to the Albanian president, Refik Veseli was allowed to travel to Israel and was honored in a public ceremony at Yad Vashem, on July 23, 1990.

In his 2004 Hebrew book, *Black and White Photos,* detailing his family's travails during the Holocaust, and their new lives in Israel, Gavra Mandil underscored the special and unique Albanian code of ethics that this people holds even more sacred than the Bible or the Koran. These state that: (1) everyone is equal before God; the beautiful as well as the ugly; (2) the home of an Albanian belongs to God and to one's guest; (3) a person has to protect a guest's honor, even at the risk of his own life; (4) at every moment, day and night, a person should be prepared to admit and welcome a guest with bread and salt and an open heart, and to offer him fire to warm him and a bed to sleep in. Whoever violated this code lost his self-respect and was to be ostracized by society, and even stood the risk of forfeiting his life. These are the guiding moral principles that accounted for the saving of the Jewish community in Albania.

Following the Veselis' recognition by Yad Vashem, dozens of other Albanians have also been awarded the honorific title of Righteous Among the Nations.

Vitus, Michal & Anna
and their daughter Viera (Vráblová)
Slovakia

*O*n January 15, 1944, Anna Vitus, a practicing midwife, had helped deliver Piroska-Pesel Ganz's son, Egon-Ezra – and the two women had formed a friendly relationship. Together with her husband, Michal, and daughter Viera (born 1914), the Vitus family lived in Nové Město nad Váhom, a town in western Slovakia. There were slightly over 2,000 Jews in Nové

Mĕsto in the early 1940s. In 1941, under the country's Fascist rule, Jewish children were expelled from public schools and Jewish businesses were forced to sell out. On March 30, 1942, the first contingent of 120 Jews was sent to the Majdanek concentration camp in Poland, to be followed by 55 women sent to Auschwitz on April 1. Hundreds more were deported in the following months, so that by the summer of that year there were hardly any Jews left in the city.

When in late August 1944 the Germans invaded the country to help suppress the Slovak uprising against the Fascist regime there, the hunt for Jews, halted in late 1942, was resumed with full German ferocity, aided by the Slovakian Hlinka Guard militia. Earlier, Anna Vitus had confided to Piroska Ganz that in the event of danger she and her family would be welcomed in the Vitus home. Now, alarmed by the German takeover, Anna Vitus renewed her invitation to Piroska Ganz. In the words of Piroska's brother-in-law, Ladislav Samuel Ganz, "We left at short notice, leaving everything behind." The Vituses warmly welcomed the fugitives into their home.

Anna's husband, Michal Vitus, was a builder by trade as well as a small farmer. He also did odd and ends jobs, like home repairs, tiling, and paving. He and his family lived in a large house on Hitlerova Ulica (Hitler Street), one of the main streets in Nové Mĕsto. In the backyard he had a barn, approximately 6 x 10 meters, where he stored hay and fodder for his cattle. In the haystack, Ladislav Ganz and his brother Menachem made a hiding place for their whole family that was well camouflaged. At first there were four people who took refuge there: Ladislav Ganz, his mother, Berya Ganz; his brother Menachem Ganz, and Menachem's wife, Piroska Ganz. At a later period, three more people were added: Ali Kraut and two women – Lili Waldmann and Aladar Kapusta. Piroska Ganz's two sons had been turned over the care of a non-Jewish widow in return for payment. The hidden people's only contact with the outside world was through the Vitus daughter, Viera, then a single woman, who brought them their daily food. As further explained by Ladislav, "To minimize her danger [of detection], we insisted on the minimum of food, just sufficient for survival, as the carrying of large amounts could have become conspicuous and dangerous."

Three times daily before the news, the radio announced that all those who were hiding Jews would share the fate of the Jews. Towards the end of October 1944, the Hlinka Guards, who in Slovakia were the equivalent of the German SS, raided the Vitus house in search of hidden Jews. First, they blocked all exits and then they began to search systematically every nook and cranny of the house and yard; finally they came to the barn. Twelve troopers entered and jabbed bayonets into the hay, but luckily did not discover the hidden people. During the raid Anna Vitus was forced to accompany the Guards, who constantly badgered her: "*Kde mate Zidov?*" – "Where have you got the Jews"? She kept giving the noncommittal answer, "*Co najdete je Vase*" – "What you find will be yours."

When the troopers left, the tension that had been building up in Anna Vitus brought on a mental breakdown and she told her charges to leave immediately. She could not longer take the tension; she was filled with fear. At this point, her daughter Viera interjected; "You can go to your brother, in Liptovský Svätý Mikuláš, but if they go outside and they are caught, that will be their end." She took her daughter's advice and left the house a day or two later. The hidden people remained but Michal Vitus suggested a more secure hiding place – the cellar under the house.

For this purpose, Michal Vitus and the hidden men put up a double brick wall that sealed off in the cellar an area of 2 1/2 by 3 1/2 meters. A glazed-in opening at ground level let in some light and was large enough to crawl out of at night. The entrance was well camouflaged behind stacks of corn that were also placed around the house in order not to attract attention to those in the cellar. A small aperture was used to bring food into the bunker and take out the pail every night. In that tiny place the people slept on the straw covered floor. Piroska Ganz's second son, two-year-old Moshe, had joined them. The hidden Ali Kraut, whose wife was non-Jewish, had managed to hide the little boy by shifting him from place to place among his friends, until the neighbors became suspicious and it was thought wise for both to disappear. With the help of Viera, Piroska's other baby son, Ezra, was placed in good hands.

Soon afterwards, when the search for Jews was intensified, and with so many people on hand, Michal Vitus' nerves gave out, and as had occurred with his wife, Anna, he felt he could no longer go on keeping the hidden people with him. Here, again, his daughter Viera came to the rescue. The exchange between father and daughter came when she heard him address the hidden people as follows:

> "**Father:** *You have to leave. I don't want them to kill me because of you. I have daughters that are not yet married, and I have to care for them.*
> **Viera:** *You cannot send them away now, for their life is in danger. You admitted them, and you have to keep them until the end of the war.*
> **Father:** *And if the Germans found them with us and they kill me?*
> **Viera:** *In the war many people die just like that. If you should die, at least you will know that you were killed because you tried to save people who committed no crime and no sin."*

These words of Viera left her father stunned, and he relented. Viera had saved the day for the hidden Jews in her home. Throughout all this time, Viera also acted as an intermediary between her charges and members of their family hidden elsewhere; she sold some of the fugitives' gold in order to pay for their expenses and kept them up to date with the news of the progress of the war, raising their spirits by telling them that liberation was on hand.

In the end of December 1944, when the fugitives ran out of money to help their rescuers with the added expenses, Father Michal and daughter Viera spoke to them in the following uplifting words, as remembered by Ladislav Ganz:

> "*Don't worry if you have no more money, we won't send you away. We are not doing this for money. You cannot pay us for the risks we are taking — we just want to help you, we want to save you. We have potatoes, carrots — some bread and milk to see us all through. Should it, God forbid, happen, that you will be discovered, we are fully aware that the penalty will be death for us too — but we shall die in the knowledge that we did the right thing in trying to save the lives of innocent people. If, God willing, we shall survive the war, you can give us something if you want to, if not there will be no hard feelings."*

Liberation came on April 5. All the hidden persons walked out of their hiding places free and unharmed, thanks to Viera Vitus' (later Vráblová) and her parents. In 1984, Yad Vashem recognized Michal and Anna Vitus and their daughter Viera as Righteous Among the Nations.

Vranetic, Ivan

CROATIA

*I*n 1943, many of the Jews from dismembered Yugoslavia, occupied two years earlier, had found a temporary safe haven in the Italian-controlled zone of the country, on the Dalmatian coast. To further protect them, the Italians moved many of the Jews either to the interior of Italy or to the island of Rab, off the Croatian coast, to the north of the Adriatic Sea. There, several thousand Jews lived in relative freedom, safe from the Germans and their Croatian allies, the notorious Ustaše (pronounced Ustashe) militia, who mercilessly pursued and killed Jews as well as Serbs living in Croatia – a fascist country during the war years, allied with Nazi Germany. When Italy, also an ally of Nazi Germany, but refraining from killing Jews, capitulated to the Allies on September 8, 1943, their forces withdrew from the island and a Jewish underground took control of the Jewish camp. Soon they were forced to evacuate it and crossed to the mainland, taking most of the Jews with them, the able-bodied among them made for the hills hoping to join up with Tito's partisans, leaving behind the elderly, the women, and the children, who set out for Topusko, an inland town located in an area infested with pro-German Ustaše militia.

Ivan Vranetic

The Jewish refugees received a cool welcome from the inhabitants of Topusko – many of whom were Ustaše sympathizers. Besides, the town suffered from a shortage of elementary necessities, mostly food, so the townspeople were not too happy to see refugees with their own special needs exacerbating their own plight. As Topusko was close to a partisan area, on many occasions Ustaše militiamen raided and sacked the town, wreaking vengeance on those suspected of pro-partisan sympathies and showing no mercy to Jews who fell into their hands.

Ivan Vranetic's parents had moved to Topusko in 1929 and opened a grocery. When the Jewish refugees began to stream into the town, 17-year-old Ivan took the desperate plight of the refugees to heart and decided to help them to the best of his ability, and even beyond that.

The first order of the day was to find accommodations for the refugees. There was a big shortage of suitable dwellings in Topusko, even for an overnight stay, but Ivan ran from place to place in search of houses or shacks that had been vacated due to the war. He would clean up these places in order to make them suitable for habitation. In addition, whenever an Ustaše attack was imminent, Vranetic warned the Jews to take to the woods, himself leading the way and arranging whatever transportation was available for those unable to walk.

Whenever necessary, he carried a child, an old or sick person on his back, and urged others to do likewise. He made it a special point to help the old and the sick and those burdened with children.

Erna Montiljo was among those helped by Vranetic. Born in 1919 in Sarajevo, Bosnia, into the Levi family, she had been among those moved by the Italians to Rab Island with her three-year-old daughter, a 12-year old sister, and an elderly mother. Erna's husband had been taken away by the Ustaše to Jasenovac, one of the most brutal concentration camps on the European landscape, where he perished. Arriving in Topusko, they were entirely without means, and few of the local population were willing to help. Then she met Ivan, affectionately known as Iviča (Ivitza). Seeing the haggard look on the faces of Erna and her family, their clothes unclean and unkempt from the hardships of wandering, he volunteered to help her out. He began by taking their belongings with him as he searched for a suitable place where they could spend the evenings; he brought bread to the children, and continued to care for them in the coming days. When Erna fell ill, as well as her daughter, he took the two to his parents' house, where they stayed until they felt better. Erna reported seeing Iviča helping others in a like manner, sheltering the sick in his parents' home – including scouring the surrounding villages for food (vegetables and fruit) and distributing it to the most needy people from among the refugees. As winter settled in, he got tree branches for heating or cooking.

Danger lurked from sudden Ustaše raids. Many sympathizers were also to be found in the town itself, as well as persons working for the Ustaše – spies and informers. Whenever news of an Ustaše incursion was received, Ivan urged the refugees to immediately flee in the opposite direction, into the forests, until the danger had passed. It was common knowledge that when the Ustaše caught someone helping Jews (or even suspected him of doing so) his fate was torture and death. In Erna's words, Ivan was always among the first to inform the refugees of the need to flee, showing the way. In those cases, as mentioned, he would take children, the old, and the sick on his back, such as Yehuda Cohen, who suffered from asthma and could not take much walking. Ivan (Iviča) Vranetic simply took him on his back during times of flight. Many times when Erna ran into the forest, Ivan carried her daughter, Ella, on his shoulders. "As I carried her," he said after the war, "I would rub her toes all the time because she didn't have shoes, but still two of her toes froze."

Erna recalled an incident that almost cost her life. It happened when a rumor spread that the Ustaše were about to come, in a particular offensive termed by the partisans the "seventh" one. Erna took her daughter, sister, and elderly mother and joined a group that fled from Topusko, but in the wrong direction – straight toward where the Ustaše were reported to be coming from. When Ivan learned of this, he ran towards them and, out of breath, caught up with them toward evening, and told them to immediately double back on their tracks before it was too late. He had saved them all. "I must point out," Erna emphasized in her statement to Yad Vashem, "that without his help, some of these people would not have survived. Also myself, I cannot imagine how I would have survived with two small children, and an old mother without his help."

In addition to Erna Montiljo's account, testimonies were also received from Michael Attias, Samuel Papo, Gina Deniti, Matilda Perera and daughter Gracia, and Avraham Altaratz – all testifying to Ivan Vranetic's superhuman efforts to help and save the stranded Jewish refugees in Topusko. In the words of Michael Attias, born in 1904 and originally from Sarajevo, "Vranetic was one of the few in town who stood at our side and helped us. He came to us each time there was danger as an angel from heaven. He found transportation for those not able to walk. He took children on his back, or an old man, and he would urge two or three other boys to do likewise. That was what he did with my old mother, who was not able to walk. Vranetic did it without any urging from us or other refugees; only from the goodness of his heart."

With the war over, the Jewish refugees left Topusko and returned to their former dwellings. As for Ivan Vranetic, he had in the meantime become closely attached to a group of refugees who originated in Sarajevo and especially to Erna Montilijo, with whom he had developed a more intimate attachment. Although she was six years his senior, he proposed marriage to her. At the time, after surviving the horrors of the Holocaust, where she had lost her husband, Erna was determined to move to the newly established state of Israel. Besides, her mother insisted that she marry a Jew and Ivan Vranetic was Catholic. In the end she married a Jewish man and bore him two children. As for Ivan, he had learned that his father was dying, so he rushed back to Topusko to help out and then stayed on to take care of his mother.

In 1963, Ivan Vranetic visited Israel to look up some of the people he had saved and met Erna again. She had since been divorced. The old love between the two was rekindled. He came back the following year – this time for good. The reason? Erna "was my first love," he said shyly, "and I cannot leave her." An additional reason, as he once confessed to Avraham Altaretz, one of the survivors, was out of a deep need to be with them.

Ivan Vranetic has since remained in Israel, doing various odd jobs to support Erna and her three children. He is currently the president of an association caring for the needs of non-Jewish rescuers of Jews who made Israel their home and were honored by Yad Vashem with the Righteous title – as he himself was – recognized in 1970. Ivan likes to say, "Everyone does what is best for himself. Everyone plans his own life. I did not come here to make money. I came here for love." Erna's daughter Ella stated to authors Gay Block and Malka Drucker, "He's the grandfather of my children. You know, he's not my father but he's not less than a father. I think maybe he's more."

Wallenberg, Raoul

SWEDEN

*I*t was an unforgettable sight. On a cold November 1944 day, not far from the Hungarian-Austrian border, a young-looking stranger who someone whispered was a Swedish diplomat named Wallenberg, walked past the SS officer supervising the deportation train, climbed up on the roof of the train, and began handing out safe-conduct passes through the doors, which had not yet been locked. In the words of one witness, Wallenberg "paid no attention when the Germans ordered him to get down, or when the Arrow Cross men began firing their guns and shouting at him to go away. Ignoring them, he calmly continued giving passes to the outstretched hands … After Wallenberg had distributed the last of the passes, he told everyone who had one to get off the train and walk over to a convoy of cars parked nearby … The Germans and Arrow Cross men were so dumbfounded that they let him get away with it." Who was this brazenly courageous diplomat who openly defied the Nazis in order to save as many Jews as possible?

Raoul Wallenberg

He was born into an aristocratic Swedish banking family in 1912. His father died when he was three months old. Raised by his mother and grandfather, he studied architecture; then joined the family banking business, gaining experience in a branch of the Holland Bank in Haifa, Palestine, where he first came in contact with Jewish refugees from Nazi Germany. Returning to Sweden, where he continued his banking and business career, in 1944 he learned that the Swedish government was looking for someone to work in its embassy in Budapest, Hungary, as a cover for the U.S.-based War Refugee Board. The purpose was to save the remnants of Hungarian Jewry, which at the time was being systematically decimated by the Germans, who had occupied Hungary on March 19, 1944, and their Hungarian collaborators.

Before agreeing to this dangerous mission, Wallenberg made several conditions – highly irregular for a diplomatic envoy – such as permission to provide asylum in the Swedish legation building; to use bribery, and to use the Allied intelligence services through the British and U.S. embassies in order to contact trustworthy people with links to the Hungarian government and the occupying Germans, and also a free hand to meet with high-level Hungarians as well as the country's leader, Miklos Horthy, without having to go through Swedish legation channels in Budapest. On June 23, 1944, the Swedish government agreed to these conditions, and Wallenberg made arrangements to leave for Hungary. He arrived in Budapest on July 9, 1944, carrying two rucksacks, a sleeping bag, a windbreaker, a revolver, and a list of 630 Hungarian Jewish applicants for Swedish visas, including 300 to 400 already approved by the Swedish legation in Budapest.

As a First Secretary in the Swedish embassy, Wallenberg learned that the Hungarian government, bowing to international pressure, had just ordered a halt to the deportation of Jews – after over 430,000 had already been sent to Auschwitz, where most were gassed upon arrival. However, fear remained that the Germans, whose army occupied the country, would force Hungary and its leader, Miklos Horthy, to renew the deportations in order to do away with the last major Jewish community in the country – the over 200,000 Jews still alive in the capital city of Budapest. Having learned from the Swiss diplomat Carl Lutz about the use of protective passes (*Schutzbrief*), whereby numerous Jews were awarded diplomatic protection on various dubious claims, Wallenberg decided to exploit this venue by issuing thousands of such documents, which at the time were honored by the Hungarian government. Many of these beneficiaries were housed in buildings purchased by Wallenberg and flying the Swedish flag, and thus granted extraterritorial privilege. In addition, with the assistance of a dedicated staff of mostly Jews, he set up an extensive network of hospitals, day-care centers, and soup kitchens for Jews under the protection of the Swedish government.

Elizabeth Kasser, who served as a personal interpreter for Raoul Wallenberg and accompanied him on his many meetings and confrontations with Fascist officials, described Wallenberg's unique personality and charm:

> *"I have never met such a devoted human being. He never cared about what could happen to himself. Probably he felt invulnerable. Entering a room with 15 men, Raoul Wallenberg would always be the center of attention. This 33-year-old had particular charisma … He was usually taciturn. He found it hard to tolerate talkative people. He was indifferent to what he ate. He never had time to eat. Probably he also never got an uninterrupted night's sleep. At dawn you could see him on his bicycle bringing food baskets to his wards."*

It looked like the Budapest Jews had gotten past the worst as the Russian armies closed in on Hungary when suddenly, on October 15, 1944, the Horthy regime was overthrown and replaced by an even more strident pro-Nazi and antisemitic one, headed by the Arrow Cross Party and its leader, Ferenc Szálasi. A new and unprecedented reign of terror descended on the Jews of Budapest as Arrow Cross gangs launched a killing spree against Jews in the streets, drowning many of them in the icy waters of the Danube River. At this crucial stage, Wallenberg again went into action, pleading with the new regime to recognize the protective passes and houses of the Swedish government, as well as of other neutral states, and using as a ploy the Hungarian hope that

Raoul Wallenberg (seated) with his Jewish assistants in his office in Budapest

the Swedish government would recognize of the new regime. When SS colonel Adolf Eichmann ordered what became a death march for tens of thousands of Jews toward the Austrian border, Wallenberg followed the straggling marchers in his car, many of whom were killed by Hungarian gendarmes for not keeping up with the rest, and succeeded in releasing many persons on the spurious claim that they had, or were on the process of obtaining, Swedish nationality. Those released were sent back to Budapest and to the International Ghetto set up by Wallenberg and other diplomats, where more than 30,000 Jews were sheltered as Budapest came under siege by the Soviet army. As told by Miriam Herzog, one of the marchers:

> *"The conditions were frightful. We walked thirty to forty kilometers a day in freezing rain, driven on all the time by the Hungarian gendarmes. We were all women and girls and I was 17 at the time. The gendarmes were brutal, beating those who could not keep up, leaving others to die in the ditches. It was terrible for the older women … Suddenly I heard a great commotion among the women. 'It's Wallenberg,' they said. I didn't think he could really help me, and anyway I was too weak now to move, so I lay there on the floor as dozens of women clustered around him, crying 'Save us, save us.' I remember being struck by how handsome he looked – and how clean – in his leather coat and fur hat, just like a being from another world, and I thought, 'Why does he bother with such wretched creatures as we?' As the women clustered around him, he said to them, 'Please you must forgive me but I cannot help all of you. I can only provide certificates for a hundred of you.' Then he said something which really surprised me. He said, 'I feel I have a mission to save the Jewish nation, and so I must rescue the young ones first.' I had never heard of the idea of a Jewish nation before. Jewish people, of course, but not a Jewish nation. He look around the room and began putting names down on a list and when he saw me lying on the floor he came over to me. He asked my name and added it to the list. After a day or two, the hundred of us whose names had been taken were moved out and put into a cattle car on a train bound for Budapest. There were a lot more danger and hardships for us, but we were alive – and it was thanks entirely to Wallenberg."*

Wallenberg was constantly running around – between the death marchers and those sheltered in Swedish homes in Budapest. As told by Joseph (Tommy) Lapid, currently chairman of the Yad Vashem Council:

> *"One morning, a group of these Hungarian Fascists came into the Swedish protected house and said that all the able-bodied women must go with them. We knew what this meant. My mother kissed me and I cried and she cried. We knew we were parting forever and she left me there, an orphan to all intents and purposes. Then, two or three hours later, to my amazement, my mother returned with the other women. It seemed like a mirage, a miracle. My mother was there – she was alive and she was hugging and kissing me, and she said one word: 'Wallenberg.' "*

Enraged at Wallenberg for hampering his work of eliminating the remnants of Hungarian Jewry, Adolf Eichmann, in a meeting with Wallenberg, hinted that his life could be in jeopardy. At this, coupled with threats from the Arrow Cross, Wallenberg took care to spend evenings and sleep in different locations. Finally, as the Red Army tightened its ring around Budapest, in January 1945, the Germans decided to withdraw from the Pest side of the city and simultaneously blow up the still-existing ghetto with its estimated 70,000 Jewish inhabitants. At this point, Wallenberg personally threatened the German commander that he would have him placed on trial for war crimes after the war if he went through with this criminal act. The German general relented and the ghetto was spared. Exact figures are hard to arrive at, but estimates credit Wallenberg with having saved tens of thousands of Jews.

With the Russians in control of Pest, on January 16, 1945, Wallenberg was apprehended on orders from Moscow and held in confinement, probably on the suspicion of being a spy for the Western Allies. Taken to Moscow, he was jailed in the infamous Lubyanka prison and held incommunicado. Efforts by the Swedish government to discover his whereabouts and obtain his release proved unsuccessful.

At first the Soviets denied having had a hand in arresting Raoul Wallenberg and incarcerating him in the Soviet Union. Then, suddenly, bowing to pressure from Sweden, on February 6, 1957, Deputy Foreign Minister Andrei Gromyko announced that the Soviet authorities had discovered a document signed by the head of the infirmary at Lubyanka prison, a certain A.L. Smoltsov, stating that Wallenberg had died on July 17, 1947, including the notation that Smoltsov was ordered to cremate the body and that this information had been reported to the head of the Soviet security service, Viktor Abakumov. The new Soviet version placed the blame squarely on the shoulders of the late Abakumov (already executed in 1953), who was charged with having given the Soviet Foreign Ministry incorrect information about Wallenberg for a number of years, and which explained the previous Soviet disclaimers that Wallenberg was in the Soviet Union.

The Swedish-Russian Working Group, in its exhaustive report in 2000, noted that a warrant for Wallenberg's arrest was signed by Bulganin, the Deputy Defense Minister, on January 17, 1945, probably with Stalin's consent. At Lubyanka prison, where Wallenberg arrived on February 6, 1945, he underwent several interrogations. The Working Group suggested the following possible explanations of the supposedly mysterious death of Wallenberg in July 1947. He had either succumbed to hardship and inhuman treatment; or to mental and physical strain. He may have been shot on the orders of Molotov and Abakumov, or Beria, with or without Stalin's knowledge, or died of a heart attack, which was induced by various forms of mental torture (including sound and light) and medical experimentation, and perhaps poison. As for Beria's role in this sordid affair, it has been suggested by a former KGB officer that his initial plan was to create the myth of a Jewish-Zionist anti-Soviet conspiracy, and for this purpose he needed Wallenberg in order to fabricate a case that he would later present to the paranoid Stalin. However, when Beria realized that he had made a mistake by pinpointing Wallenberg as one of the anti-Soviet conspiracy ringleaders, he not only feared for his life at the hands of an enraged Stalin, but also at the annoying consequences for the whole Soviet leadership. It would have been embarrassing, even dangerous, to suddenly inform Sweden that Wallenberg had been in a Soviet prison in Moscow all along on erroneous charges. What satisfactory explanation could one possibly give? His story would have created a scandal. It became essential, therefore, to remove the problem. Placing Wallenberg in another prison or camp was virtually the same as revealing his existence sooner or later. Anything Raoul Wallenberg himself might have said upon release would have been extremely embarrassing to the Soviets. Hence the likelihood of a decision to get rid of the man. However, to this day, the full Soviet documentation of the reasons for his arrest and incarceration are still missing, and his fate remains an unsolved mystery.

He was only 32 years old when last seen in Budapest. Before disappearing from sight, Raoul Wallenberg told his colleague in the rescue operation, Swedish diplomat Per Anger: "I'd never be able to go back to Stockholm without knowing deep down that I'd done all anyone could do to save as many Jews as possible." As he was led away by Soviet guards, Wallenberg reportedly said: "I don't know if they're protecting me or watching me. I'm not sure if I'm their guest or their prisoner." This is the last his colleagues saw of him.

In 1963, when the Yad Vashem-created Commission for the Designation of the Righteous decided to confer upon Raoul Wallenberg the Righteous honor, Commission Chairman, Justice Moshe Landau, noted that one should respect the wishes of Wallenberg's mother not to give up hope for the recovery of her still-living son. However, Mrs. Maj Von Dardel was not satisfied with this statement, and refused to receive the honor in her son's name, and instead asked that efforts be redoubled to find and free her son, who she believed was still alive. After her passing in 1979, a tree planting ceremony took place at Yad Vashem in the presence of her two children, Raoul's half-brother and-sister (from his mother's second marriage), Guy Von Dardel and Nina Lagergren. In January 1986, the State of Israel awarded its first honorary citizenship to Raoul Wallenberg in a ceremony held in the office of President Chaim Herzog and attended by the Swedish ambassador to Israel. The United States and Canada also awarded Wallenberg honorary citizenship.

To this day, the Wallenberg family and all people of good will still await a full explanation on the fate of this heroic and tragic figure who, through his benevolent acts in Budapest, exemplified the best and the most elevated form of humanitarian behavior.

Waszkinel, Piotr & Emilia

Poland

*F*ather Romuald Waszkinel had had enough of the unsatisfactory explanations of his origins. His father had already passed away and his mother had recovered from serious surgery. While she was still alive she was the only person who could tell him the truth about himself. But this had to be done now. Later it might be too late. One evening over dinner, when his mother was in a good mood, he decided, in his words, to go on the attack. Looking her straight in the eye, he asked her point blank to come out with it and tell him the truth. At this, his mother, Emilia, broke into a loud wail. Romuald said, "Mommy, let it go, let it out finally. After all, it concerns not only you but me as well! It's part of history. I have a right to know. You must tell me. After all, this is a beautiful chapter in your life. I will not love you any less." She recovered and told him to step into his room. "I remember the candle burning in the darkness. I was alone with my mother," Father Waszkinel later related. Romuald indeed was not her child, but the child of Jewish parents. One or two he asked? Two, she said. He had previously suspected that only one of his parents was Jewish, but not both. This was quite a revelation, and "I was not prepared for this." His mother then excused herself for having previously lied to him – she had only done it to protect him, she said. She then told him who he really was.

Romuald Waszkinel had been registered as born on February 28, 1943, although in truth it was on March 25, 1943 that his Jewish mother had placed him under the windowsill of his Polish foster mother, evidently eight days after his birth. "My Polish mother told me I was born on March 25; this was the day when she picked me up." Piotr and Emilia Waszkinel lived in a place near Święciany. Somehow, the mention of that place always produced fear in the heart of young Romuald, for reasons unknown to him. When after the war Święciany reverted to Lithuania, the Poles there were repatriated and the Waszkinels moved to Paleska, near Olsztyn. Nine years after Romuald's birth, in 1952, a sister was added to the family.

His parents loved him very much. His father, Piotr, who was a locksmith, sold a cow in order to buy an accordion for little Romuald. "I was not really spoiled, just loved, for at times father was capable of unbuckling his belt to give me a thrashing." Romuald always felt closer to his mother than to his father. "I always clung to her dress for fear that she would abandon me. I did not want to be alone. I was a crybaby who held on to her dress and followed her everywhere. I guess, subconsciously, I was afraid they would leave me." He did not know the reason why.

The atmosphere in Paleska was good. Romuald went to school and took an interest in his studies. Romuald remembered that when he was six, on his way home, he suddenly heard screams behind him: "Jew, Jew foundling," followed by loud laughter. "I took this very seriously. Coming home, I burst into tears. I told mother in a whimpering and stammer-

Romulad-Jakub Weksler-Waszkinel (left) with his Israeli uncle, in front of the Yad Vashem Honor Wall bearing the names of his rescuers

ing voice: 'They called me a *Żyd* [Jew] … I asked mother what was the meaning of *Żyd* ?'" His mother did not immediately answer; then asked if anyone else had ever called him this. "I said no." She then told Romuald not to pay attention to this stupid word. "This was my first confrontation with antisemitism. At the time, I did not know what Jew meant." At school, when people whispered among themselves that Romuald's father was not really his father, "I considered them fools and did not respond. In fact, high school was the happiest period of my life… I was a good student. I had a very active social life. I sang, played musical instruments, and danced. I was invited to many parties with my accordion."

Still, as he grew up, Romuald could not help but notice that he stood out because of his looks. "I had black hair and dark skin." But he reassured himself that he felt no different from the other children. "I wish to emphasize that I never had any problems; no one connected me with Jews." This was true, but not always. At times, during heated altercations between boys, they would taunt him, saying, "Do you know that your father is not really your father?" To which Romuald would snap, "You're stupid." At the time, he did not ask his parents about this. "They loved me so much that I was probably afraid to ask them." Maybe once or twice he did bring it up with his mother. She replied by shrugging her shoulders and saying it was a stupid question. Romuald was satisfied with this answer. At the age of 17 he graduated from high school.

At home, the atmosphere was very religious, and the Waszkinels attended church regularly. "Christianity was for my parents the breath of life. I prayed together with mother." Then, during his last year at high school, he picked up at school the fundamentals of the Christian faith from a priest. Romuald began to become more and more attracted to the religious life and told the priest that after graduation he wanted to study for the priesthood. Romuald was sure his parents would be happy about this, but it proved to be otherwise. "When I told this to father, he began to argue with me. I wondered why … He told me, 'Listen, you know that I go to church and pray, but one does not have to become a priest in order to believe in God. Think it over. Have your considered the significance of becoming a priest? Are you aware how hard it is?'" Romuald replied: "I don't know, and I'll go there to find out. Going there does not mean I must necessarily become a priest." To which his father said, "Going there, you will have to become a priest, or else it will be immoral." His father wanted Romuald to become a doctor; it was his dream. In addition, he emphasized to Romuald, "You will not have a family." Not wishing to upset his father, Romuald backed off and said, "Okay, I will become an actor."

As for his mother, she did not express an opinion; she just walked around the house crying. This was terribly upsetting to Romuald, and he could not understand their parents' attitude to something that in Polish society was considered a highly prestigious position. His mother told him in a carping voice, her mouth twisted, "Do what you want to do; this is your life, your fate. Do what you want to do. Only, be careful that you do not regret it. Do as you wish, do as you wish." Still puzzled by his parents' obdurate opposition, Romuald decided to follow through on his decision, and he was admitted to a Catholic seminary. It was September 1960, and Romuald was 17 years of age.

This turn of events caused a serious change in Romuald father's attitude. He began writing letters to Romuald that he had to see him urgently. When he came, he looked very sad, and was silent. He went into the chapel. He stood in front of the Madonna. Suddenly he fell to his knees and began to weep. "I did not understand why. I had never seen him weep before like this. At home he was always a stiff and inflexible person, and here he was crying." Taken aback, Romuald felt sorry that, for some inexplicable reason, he had caused his father such grief. But for what misdeed, he wondered? "After all," Romuald thought, "he loved me so much! He had never caused me harm!" His father, Piotr, then got up and left without saying a word. Romuald asked him, "Papa, are you sick?" "No," he replied, "I am quite healthy. Everything's fine. I have come to terms with it; do what you want to do." Romuald remained baffled by this incident. His father would not disclose to him the truth about his origin.

This was on a Sunday. The following Thursday, Romuald received an urgent phone call that his father was dead. He had slipped while walking down a staircase and fell hitting his head. The funeral was to be on Saturday. Romuald was filled with terrible pangs of guilt. "I had the feeling that I had caused his death; an inner feeling." He decided to discontinue his stay at the seminary. But his mother soothed his pain, "You did not kill anyone. You must return [to the seminary]. Go." But when he returned to the seminary, he told his supervisor Father that he could not stay on, for it had been against his father's wishes, and by disobeying his father he felt he had contributed to his accidental death. The supervisor told him to take time off to think things over seriously and not decide on the heels of his father's death. "If in another two to three months you still feel the same way, come back here and I will return your papers and you can leave. You are now in shock and you must not do something rash." Romuald's decision was to stay on, and on June 19, 1966, he took his priestly vows. It was for him a good omen, for the date coincided with celebrations of 1,000 years of Christianity in Poland.

However, just before that joyous occasion, another incident caused Romuald to further wonder what secret lay mysteriously hidden behind his origin and birth. It happened that before taking the vow Romuald was called in by his supervisor-bishop, the then rector, who suggested that he be baptized. "This greatly surprised me. Had I not been baptized at birth? With my own eyes, I saw the baptismal certificate." But the bishop pressed him on this point. "This raised doubts in my mind; something there is not right, not as it should be. I told the bishop: But my parents pray every day, and on Sundays, they attend church. How can one imagine that such parents would raise a child who had not undergone baptism, a thing so important for a Christian?" The bishop replied, without going into details, that he had it from reliable sources that there was something amiss in Romuald's baptism, adding, "There is no smoke without fire." Romuald countered that this was generally true, but that sometimes this was caused by human folly and in that case there would be smoke without fire. "I know for sure that I was baptized." The discussion turned unpleasant, at which point the bishop asked Romuald to leave. "I thought this is the end for me. I will be expelled. Upon leaving, I said to him: 'I will find the baptismal certificate,' to which he replied, 'One can falsify baptismals.'" To this, Romuald heard himself saying, "In the case of a Jew – yes. But why would it be necessary to falsify one for me?" The bishop did not reply.

It is not clear from the record whether Romuald was forced to go through a baptism ceremony. At any rate, after taking his vows, he was transferred to the Lublin Catholic University to continue his studies. He chose for his doctoral thesis the philosophy of the Frenchman Henri Bergson, the son of Jewish parents who had converted to Catholicism. Was this a mere coincidence? During his studies Romuald Waszkinel also began to take an interest in Jewish life in Poland during the war years. Through the following years, Romuald could not rid himself of the feeling that his family was hiding something from him. This instinctive feeling was strengthened by his appearance. "First of all, I did not look like anyone around me, not even my family. This seemed quite odd to me." Then he recalled the incident at the seminary with regard to his baptism. "I walked around with the feeling that there was something special about me, which even made me different from my family, from their way of thinking, from their genetic behavior … I was already a priest." Every time he questioned his mother, she would answer with her own question: "Don't I love you?"

Then in 1979, his mother took seriously ill and was admitted to a hospital for surgery. Romuald was told that the blood transfusion was not having its desired effect. They would make one last try, and if the results proved negative, then in consideration of her age Romuald was to expect the worst. Surprisingly, the second infusion proved successful and Emilia recovered. She was released, and lived for another ten years. But for Romuald, this was the last straw. He had to have her tell him about himself, while she was still among the living. A year later, over evening dinner, at his Lublin apartment, as related above, his mother finally disclosed to him all she knew about his real family and the circumstances of his childhood in her family. She began tell him who he really was.

Romuald's father was a tailor in Święciany, a mostly Polish town near Vilnius (Vilna), and during the German occupation he did some work for the Germans. Święciany had a small Jewish community of several thousand people. On April 5, 1943, all the town's Jews were told they were to be taken to the Vilna ghetto to join their brethren there. Instead, they were detoured to the nearby Ponary forest, where they were shot beside ditches. A month earlier, Emilia had been working in Romuald's father's workshop. When she told him that she had cared for a Russian girl, but her mother had taken her away and she felt bad about it, Romuald's father suggested that she take in another child – his newborn son. A meeting was arranged with the baby's mother. From her, Emilia learned that Romuald had a brother named Samuel, some four years older than he, who had been turned over for hiding to a Lithuanian family. But Samuel had been returned to his mother after the people refused to keep him any longer, perhaps out of fear, or because the money ran out. Romuald's parents wanted to make sure that at least their newborn baby would survive. But Emilia told the mother that they would kill her if they found a Jewish child in her home. Romuald's mother, whose name was Batya, used all her persuasive powers to try to get the hesitant Emilia to change her mind. "My dear lady, you constantly say you believe in Jesus, so take this child in the name of Jesus, in whom you believe so much. Perhaps, when he grows up, he will become a priest." Batya's frantic appeal had the desired effect, and Emilia agreed to take the month-old baby boy. The child's father knitted a special gown for the baby.

Towards evening, Batya stole out of the ghetto, which was not too well guarded, and placed the baby on Emilia's windowsill. Emilia was by then already married to Piotr Waszkinel. As agreed by both sides, Emilia watched closely from the window, then waited for 15 minutes to allow the child's mother to hasten away and opened the window and beheld the baby. She then came out of the house screaming for all to hear: "A child, a child!" People started to gather and stare. They unraveled the baby's clothing and noticed that he was not circumcised. So the baby was not Jewish – everything's O.K. Only one onlooker, a shoemaker, was not convinced. He ran around shouting, "It's a Jewish boy; I will catch his mother." And he began to run in the direction of the ghetto. But by then Batya was far away. Several days later, the Waszkinels had the baby registered as a foundling. The baby was named Romuald Waszkinel, the son of Piotr and Emilia. All the neighbors, of course, knew that Emilia had not given birth to the baby, but they were ignorant as to the identity of the baby's biological parents.

As for the baby's parents, a few weeks later they were probably among those murdered in the Ponary forest. Before that, Batya had secretly managed to visit Emilia on three occasions to have a last look at her baby. As for Romuald's brother, Samuel, he too disappeared during that deadly period of the Holocaust.

As Romuald listened to the story he felt both relief and pain. Relief that he was born Jewish, the religion of Jesus, and pain at the antisemitism that had brought about the Holocaust. "This feeling came to me as a volcanic eruption, with all its force. The fact that I was Jewish, this was something great for me. But this joy was mixed with pain. Why? Why did my father, a modest tailor, have to be killed? What was my little brother guilty of? He was not capable of harming anyone? What sin had my mother and the six million people committed?" After Emilia had finished speaking, Romuald embraced her and kissed her feelingly, "wishing to thank her in this way, in the name of my mother and my Jewish father." He then asked her, "Why did you not save my brother?" She said: "You don't understand a thing about those times. We feared for our lives. No one wants to be a hero by forfeiting one's life. Don't forget that the death penalty was imposed for saving a Jew. I was simply afraid."

That evening Romuald could not close his eyes. "I asked God that my parents would come to me in my sleep so that I could see them. This did not happen. So I felt more and more torn inside, for I wanted much to know my family's name." Soon after, luck was with him, as he happened to meet Sister Klara Jaroszynska, who had been honored by Yad Vashem for saving Jews and often traveled to Israel. He told her all he knew about himself and asked of her to help him locate relatives. She promised to help. On one of her trips to Israel she discovered that there was an association of Święciany survivors headed by a certain Mr. Kuversky. After hearing the details about Romuald's parents, they immediately told Sister Jaroszynska – surely, this must be none other than Jaakov Weksler. They even showed her a photo of his wife, Batya, taken in Poland. Jaroszynska returned from Israel in 1991 and brought the photo to Romuald Waszkinel. "I looked at these eyes, and saw my own eyes. All my life I searched for some resemblance. I immediately burst out crying. I had no doubt this was my mother."

He then visited Israel and met his father's brother, who took him to the Friday evening prayers at the synagogue. The next morning he returned to the synagogue and put on a *tallit*, the prayer shawl worn during services. He was called up to the Torah to give the traditional blessing. "I touched it like a real Jew. Everyone shook my hand. It was wonderful. I wept like a man unconscious."

He then returned to Poland and to his teaching at Lublin University. There he applied to have his name changed by adding his Jewish name to his Polish one. He now calls himself Romuald-Jakub Weksler-Waszkinel – Jakub being his father's name, as he does not know what he was named at birth.

For him Judaism and Christianity constitute one religion, and Poland remains his homeland. He puts this in the following words: "Poland is my Israel, but everything Polish to me includes my Judaism … I am a Jew, and no one has the right to chase me out of Poland, which is my homeland. For a people is first of all its language; culture is spirit, not flesh and blood." As to the prevalence of antisemitism among Christians, he had this to say,

"People often say that Hitler murdered Jews through Christian hands. There is a lot of truth in this, for in general Europe, so they say, was Christian. And Christian Europe did not behave properly, and still does not do so … It seems to me that if someone kills Jews, he

spits on Jesus, on the roots of Christianity. So the humiliation of Jews is the humiliation of Christianity; simply insulting one's own foundations, the insulting of one's own mother. So, antisemitism is ipso facto anti-Christian … When we mock Jews, we disparage the most precious value in Christianity."

In 1995, his foster parents and rescuers, Piotr and Emilia Waszkinel, were added to the Yad Vashem roster of Righteous Among the Nations.

Wegner, Armin Theophil
GERMANY

"*H*err Reichskanzler! In your proclamation of March 29, 1933, the German government outlawed commercial firms belonging to Jewish citizens." These were the first words of a long letter by Armin Wegner addressed directly to Hitler on April 11, 1933, two months after his accession to power in Germany, in protest and denunciation of the Nazi government's decision to launch a campaign of vilification and persecution against the country's Jews. Who was this courageous man who dared to challenge Hitler on an issue considered by him of the highest importance and brooking no interference?

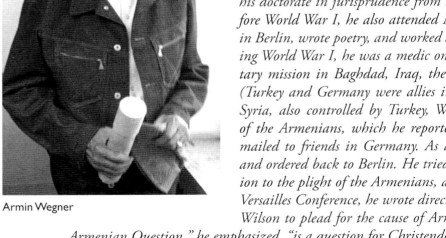

Armin Wegner

Armin Theophil Wegner, born in 1886, had studied law and political science in Zurich, Paris, and Berlin and in 1914 received his doctorate in jurisprudence from the University of Breslau. Before World War I, he also attended Max Reinhardt's acting school in Berlin, wrote poetry, and worked as a freelance journalist. During World War I, he was a medic on duty with the German military mission in Baghdad, Iraq, then part of the Turkish empire (Turkey and Germany were allies in the war). On his travels to Syria, also controlled by Turkey, Wegner witnessed the massacre of the Armenians, which he reported in letters and photographs mailed to friends in Germany. As a result, he was reprimanded and ordered back to Berlin. He tried in vain to alert public opinion to the plight of the Armenians, and in 1919, on the eve of the Versailles Conference, he wrote directly to U.S. president Woodrow Wilson to plead for the cause of Armenia at the conference. "The Armenian Question," he emphasized, "is a question for Christendom, for the whole human race … Mr. President, the wrong suffered by this people is immeasurable."

During the postwar years he wrote books on his travels through the Middle East and several European countries, as well as on other current topics, and his writings enjoyed wide circulation. While proud of his German heritage, he made no secret of his pacifistic views and his tolerance for other peoples and nations. It is no wonder that with the assumption of power by the Nazis, his books and articles were banned and were included with the writings of other authors that were burned, auto-da-fé style, in public ceremonies. Shocked by the strident antisemitism of the new regime, including the summary expulsion of Jews from various positions in the country's economy and academia – he drafted his personal April 11 letter to Adolf Hitler, which he mailed to Nazi Party headquarters in Munich. He was the sole German man of letters who dared to stick out his neck and take on the Nazi establishment on an issue considered by Hitler of greatest importance to his program for the regeneration of the German people. Wegner headed his letter of protest with the words *For Germany,* but it has since come to be better known under the title *The Warning.*

Every paragraph in this lengthy document opened with the words *Herr Reichskanzler!* (Mr. Chancellor, or Prime Minister). In his letter, Wegner protested the outlawing of commercial firms belonging to Jewish citizens, the April 1, 1933, boycott of Jewish-owned stores, the expulsion of Jewish lawyers, attorneys, surgeons, and stage directors from their positions, the dismissal of Jewish professors from the classroom, and other acts of aggression against the Jewish populace spurred by the new regime.

"Herr Reichskanzler," Wegner pleaded with Hitler, "justice has always been the pride of nations, and we should say in all candor that Jews contributed to Germany's becoming famous and held in esteem by the world … Remember Albert Einstein, a German Jew, who made the universe tremble, who, like Copernicus, penetrated space to give mankind a new vision of the universe! Remember Albert Ballin, a German Jew, creator of the great transatlantic line to the West, where the mightiest ship in the world sailed in the direction of the land of freedom. Ballin, who could not overcome the shame that his admired country visited on him, put an end to his life. Do you remember that Rathenau, a German Jew, made the *Allgemeine Gesellschaft zur Erzeugung von Strom von Kraft und Licht* [The Association for the Production of Electric Power and Light] a worldwide enterprise? It was Haber, a Jew, who, like a magician, drew nitrogen out of the air in his flask. It was Ehrlich, the wise doctor, who introduced a remedy to overcome syphilis among our people … Remember, I could fill many, many pages, if I only wanted to enumerate the names of those whose diligence and intelligence are registered for all times in our history. I ask you whether all these men and women have done all this as Jews or Germans?… We accepted the blood sacrifice of 12,000 Jewish men during the war. Are we permitted, even allowing the slightest trace of bitterness in our hearts, to deny their parents, sons, brothers, grandchildren, wives and sisters the right, gained through generations, to have a country, to be at home?"

Wegner went to on to dispute the claim that Jews cannot be truly German, since their roots are different. "What about Germany? Many tribes are mixed in the German people, Franks, Frieses, and Wends (a Slavic tribe). And Napoleon – wasn't he a Corsican? Didn't you come yourself to us from a neighboring country?" The Jews, Wegner reminded Hitler, even those who left Germany, are more attached to their home country than those who never left it. "'I love Germany,' I heard a son, a daughter, say during these days to their parents who planned to leave the country, troubled by being permanently threatened. 'Go alone, if you think you should!' they replied to their parents. 'Really, we should prefer to die here, I cannot be happy in a foreign country!'" I think so much emotional feeling is to be admired."

"*Herr Reichskanzler,*" Wegner continued to boldly lecture the new master of Germany, "not only the fate of our Jewish brothers is at stake – the fate of Germany is here at stake! In the name of the people for whom I not only have the right but feel obliged to speak, like every true German to whom the gift of speech has not been given to encourage guilt and silence when his heart is full of indignation – I address my words to you: Put an end to these events!" Then, in prophetic words,

"The Jews survived the Babylonian Exile, the years of slavery in Egypt, the Spanish Inquisition, the distress of the Crusades and sixteen hundred pogroms in Russia. With the same toughness that helped this people survive every hardship, the Jews will overcome this danger, too. The insult and misfortune, however, that Germany has burdened itself with will not be forgotten for a long time. The blow that Jews have to bear now must turn against ourselves … If you destroy their existence, you necessarily destroy German wealth. History teaches that nations who expelled Jews from their borders had to pay for it by poverty – no longer of any worth, they were reduced to misery … One hundred years after Goethe and Lessing, we return to the most cruel injuries of all times, the blind zeal of superstition … I say this not as a friend of the Jews, but as a friend of the Germans, being rooted in a family whose origins I can trace back to the days of the Crusaders. Out of love for my own people, I direct my words to you. While everyone remains silent during these days, I cannot be silent any longer, considering the dangers threatening Germany … No matter how much time may pass, one day the hour of redemption will come for the tortured, as well as punishment for the evildoers. The day will come when the first of April will only arouse a hideous shame in the memory of all Germans, when they will have to judge their deeds…

Herr Reichskanzler! A tormented heart speaks to you. The words are not only my words, they are the voice of fate warning you: Protect Germany by protecting the Jews … Restore to their position the outcasts, the doctors to their hospitals, the judges to their courts; don't exclude the children any longer from their schools, heal the afflicted hearts of the mothers, and the whole nation will be thankful to you. Think of it – Germany may be able to live without the Jews, but it cannot live without its honor and values … I ask you fervently: preserve the generosity, the pride, the conscience which are essential for our existence; preserve the honor of the German people!"

The letter was mailed to Hitler at the Nazi party chancellery in Munich and was forwarded from there to Berlin in May 1933 over the signature of Martin Bormann, Hitler's adjutant. The response was not too long in coming. Wegner was arrested on August 19, 1933, hauled to Gestapo headquarters on Prinz Albrecht Strasse in Berlin, for interrogation, and then moved to another building, where he was brutally beaten. He was subsequently incarcerated in prisons and three concentration camps, including Oranienburg. The British Quakers, at the request of Wegner's wife, Lola, who had in the meantime left for England, interceded on his behalf and he was released in the spring of 1934. In 1937, he moved to the fishing village of Positano, on the Gulf of Salerno in Italy, where after divorced from Lola, who moved to Palestine, he met his second wife, Irene Kowaliska, a Jewish convert to Protestantism, whom he married in 1945. There he eked out a living by teaching the German language. After the war, his income came from articles in German and Swiss newspapers on various topics, as well as radio programs for German and Swiss stations, including radio plays, travel reports, and reviews of modern German and Jewish literature.

In 1968, while on a visit to Israel, Yad Vashem conferred upon Armin T. Wegner the honorific Righteous Among the Nations title. As pointed out by Justice Moshe Landau, the chairman of the Commission for the Designation of the Righteous, when Wegner wrote to Hitler in 1933, people were already being arrested and sent to the camps. Wegner knew that he was risking his life, and he is one of the few Germans, perhaps the only one who suffered so greatly for daring to write directly to Hitler to prevent persecution on a larger scale. "Just as we should not differentiate between war criminals who bloodied their hands with murder from those who gave the order, in other words from an intellectual criminal – likewise Armin Wegner was an intellectual rescuer of Jews," Landau indicated. Wegner died in Italy in 1978, at the age of 92. In consideration for Wegner's earlier fight for the Armenian cause – in 1996, his body was re-interred in Yerevan, Armenia, at the request of the newly independent republic.

Weidt, Otto
and **some other Berliners**
GERMANY

*I*n the estimation of Inge Deutschkron, Holocaust survivor and journalist, the "Berliners" were the best of all the Germans during the Nazi reign of terror, if one may venture such a comparison. Although the capital of Nazi Germany, this metropolis, known for its big socialist and communist presence before the Nazi era, has the best record of any German city for Jews saved from perdition. Mrs. Deutschkron then went on to document the many Berlin residents who helped her and her mother survive the Nazi nightmare.

She was born in 1922, in Berlin, to Martin (a teacher by profession who was later dismissed by the Nazis) and Ella. In April 1939, her father left for England, promising to send for his wife and daughter. However, before he could finalize the necessary papers, the war intervened and they were stuck in Germany. Before the Nazi period, Inge was little, if at all, connected to her Jewish background. "We were socialists," she recalled. "I didn't know what a Jew was."

Already before the start of the war, Jews in Germany had undergone an escalating series of humiliating restrictions by the Nazi regime that assumed power in 1933, now intensified under the cover of the war. Jews had been dispossessed of all their belongings, their identity cards stamped with a big J (for "Jew"); their food input restricted – cream-rich milk, coffee, fruit and sweets were no longer available to them. Rations for Jews were eventually reduced to only potatoes, bread, small amounts of lard, turnips, sugar, and a little skimmed milk. Radio sets owned by Jews were confiscated and their telephones disconnected. Laundries were not allowed to accept washing from Jews and hairdressers were off-limits. Jews had to give up furs, cameras, binoculars, and electrical equipment of all kinds. Jews could not go to theaters, cinemas, and concert halls and had to do their shopping between four and five in the afternoon, and only in certain stores. Then they had to give up their apartments in houses owned by non-Jews and were crammed together in so-called Jewish houses. Inge and her mother were made to share a five-room flat with eleven other people.

Otto Weidt (seated left) with Alice Licht (standing)

With the start of the war in September 1939, Jews were conscripted for work, usually the hardest kind of manual labor and mostly very dirty work, too. Jewish men were put on garbage collection and street cleaning, or work in factories, where they were made to carry heavy loads, irrespective of the age of the men. Ella Deutschkron was assigned work in a munitions factory; her daughter, Inge, in an I.G. Farben-owned silk-spinning factory producing parachutes for the army. The working day was ten or twelve hours and the wages miserable. In the factories, any contact with non-Jewish workers, male or female, was strictly forbidden.

Then came the Jewish star decree of September 19, 1941, which stated that "Jews over six years of age are not allowed to appear in public without showing the Jewish star. This consists of a six-pointed star … It must be securely sewn on the left breast of the outer garment and must be visible;" visible to all for ridicule and harassment. This was followed with the start of deportations of Jews to camps and ghettos in the east – Poland and Lithuania – where most disappeared in the Holocaust.

At the factory, Inge could not take the difficult and humiliating conditions, including having to stand on her feet for long hours, and she managed to get a statement from a trusted doctor, to whom she was referred by Walter Rieck, a family friend (formerly dean of a school, who was dismissed by the Nazis and remained under Gestapo surveillance), that she could not work while standing. She was then referred to Otto Weidt's brush and broom workshop, which she had gone to before, but could not be hired then. At this plant, all but three persons were Jewish, who were blind and deaf mutes. This time too, Weidt (himself half-blind) did not have a vacancy for her, so he made an arrangement with a firm in the same brush manufacturing business that needed temporary help. However, the manager began to make indecent advances toward Inge, and when she related this to Weidt, he decided to take her back, and she was assigned secretarial work, in charge of shipping and the telephone.

Inge Deutschkron described Otto Weidt as a small man with a lined face in his early sixties; he was slim and fragile-looking but had a lion's heart. Over the years, he had employed in his workshop 165 physically handicapped Jews; he also supported over 50 Jews living underground and procured food and board and lodging for them. Twenty-seven of "his" Jews survived the war. Inge Deutschkron was one of them.

In Weidt's office, Inge met and befriended Alice Licht, who also did secretarial work and for whom Otto Weidt showed a special liking that gradually evolved into a romantic relationship – more so, it seems, on his part. Since Jews were only allowed by Nazi regulations to perform manual labor, Inge and Alice had to disappear immediately from the office into the workshop when a checkup was in the offing – no rare occurrence. Weidt became a kind of surrogate father for Inge. To keep up the charade of working his Jewish workers hard, he would occasionally call in the acting chief of the Jewish section of the Gestapo, Franz Prüfer, to show him how he was bearing down on his Jews, and the separate lavatory for the "Jewish swine." On these occasions, Weidt would put on a different face, yelling at a Jewish worker. "Is this supposed to be a broom?" After Prüfer left, Weidt would excuse himself for this kind of behavior.

He often went to the Gestapo to reclaim his workers listed for deportation whom he claimed were indispensable, and he usually got away with it. For this, he used bribery, such as liquor and cigarettes. In other plants employing Jews, conditions governing deportations varied constantly. One day a person would be spared because he did important war work; the next day the work of the firm concerned would no longer be regarded as vital to the war effort. Weidt was a bit more fortunate, appearing frequently at the Gestapo and removing his people from the deportation list on the pretext of filling army orders for brooms and brushes. Back in the workshop, he urged his workers not to work too fast so as to stretch the time needed to fill the orders and thus prolong their employment.

One day, in January 1943, the Gestapo picked up from their homes all the 50 Jewish workers, at the time in Weidt's workshop, and that morning none of the blind and deaf mutes appeared. Weidt took his white cane and went to Gestapo headquarters on Grosse Hamburgerstrasse to ask for their release. He later reported that he told them he would not settle for anything less than their release, right there and then – not promises that this would be done later. He miraculously succeeded, and to this day the full explanation of the Gestapo's agreement to this semi-blind man's demand is still a mystery. That same afternoon, his blind Jewish workers returned. He walked them back to his workshop at the head of a procession of people with yellow stars on their aprons and armbands, men with sticks helping each other walk. People watched this surreal and stirring scene as though it belonged to another time and another planet.

In the meantime, one deportation followed another in quick succession. Many if not most of Inge's relatives and friends were gone. At the time, Inge's mother, Ella Deutschkron, was working in a factory producing radio batteries and was therefore considered essential and not taken. February 27, 1943, was the black day for the remaining Jews of Berlin, when all Jews working in factories, about 9,000, were rounded up. Before that date 27,000 had lived in the Reich capital, 10,000 of them illegally. The remaining 8,000 were so-called "privileged" Jews in mixed marriages with non-Jewish partners and were spared for the moment. With the deportation of this last group, the Yellow Star disappeared from the Berlin street scene. Germans from all walks of life must surely have suspected that the Jews (men and women of all ages and conditions of health) had been sent to a bitter fate, but kept quiet, as did church leaders. Already a month earlier, 20-year-old Inge and mother Ella decided to go into hiding and began moving from place to place as the circumstances warranted. In Inge's words, "We certainly did not think that we would be living underground for nearly two years, moving from one place to another, never knowing peace, hunted and persecuted, always on the run, always in danger, always in fear of policemen."

At the broom and brushes workshop, Otto Weidt told Inge she could go on working for him. "But I'm registered here under my own name. They'll look for me here, surely," she protested. Weidt: "I reported a fortnight ago that you'd left. I've engaged a new girl in your place, someone called Gertrud Dereczewsky." This was to be Inge's new name. Weidt had paid off the Gertrud woman for the use her name and had received a work permit for her. Gertrud did not need to work in Weidt's workshop; she found a better-paying job – as a prostitute. As for Inge Deutschkron, she was now officially Weidt's secretary, "quite legally," he pointedly added. This charade came to an end when Madame Gertrud was picked up not in Berlin but in distant Budapest plying her trade, and the police traced her back to Weidt's plant. He replied that she had indeed worked for him for a time, but had left without a word and he was only too glad to be rid of her. That ended the problem for Weidt, but for Inge this also spelled the end of her stay in Weidt's workshop. Her semi-legal status was lost. In Weidt's workshop, the Jewish workers were by now gone, but Weidt was hiding Alice Licht and her parents in the workshop storage annex, as well as another Jewish family, the Horns and their two children.

During the deportation roundups, Inge and her mother found temporary refuge in the home of Emma Gumz, who had earlier helped out the two stricken women. Gumz operated a small laundry and had done the two women's washing without charge as well as providing food items not allowed to Jews, such as meat. Deutschkron's household belongings had been left with their friend, Walter Rieck.

Back in Weidt's workshop, tragedy struck the hidden Jews on October 15, 1943, when the Gestapo raided the premises on a tip from a Gestapo informer (unfortunately, in this case, a Jewish man married to a notorious Jewish Gestapo agent who had been promised that her parents would be spared if she pointed out other Jews in hiding) to whom Mr. Horn, on one of his outings, had inadvertently revealed the secret hiding place. Weidt himself was also arrested and taken to Gestapo headquarters, but he managed to talk himself out of detention and also persuade the Gestapo to send the Licht family not to Auschwitz but to the relatively less severe camp of Theresienstadt. From there, Alice Licht kept up a correspondence with Otto Weidt, who sent her food packages, which was then still permissible. Weidt was determined to save Alice, and when he found out that she had been moved to Auschwitz he took the highly unusual step of writing to the camp's administrative section offering his services as brush maker. In his letter, he pointed out that he was a supplier to various labor camps and the Berlin Gestapo of brooms for barracks and yards, scrubbing brushes, scouring brushes, street brooms, office brooms, dustpan brushes, and asked to be allowed to present a sample of these products on a visit to Auschwitz. On June 15, 1944, he received an acknowledgement and permission to present his assortment of brushes to the camp administration. Arriving there, he learned that in the meantime Licht had already been moved to another camp, in Christianstadt. While on the move from there to Bergen Belsen, she made her escape, in February 1945, and trudged her way back to Berlin, where she met Otto Weidt, who arranged a hiding place for her until the war's end. Her parents did not survive the depredations of the camps.

As for Inge Deutschkron, her stay in Gumz's place was short-lived, as the woman doing the ironing began to look suspiciously at Inge, who had no identity papers. Emma Gumz made her charges promise never to report for deportation, as she had learned from soldiers on leave of the bitter and deadly fate awaiting those sent out for so-called labor. Inge and Ella then got in touch with Dr. Ostrowski – a former socialist mayor of the village of Finsterwalde and later borough president in Berlin, who had been ousted by the Nazis and was married to a Jewish woman whom he refused to divorce, for that would have doomed her (and he was therefore under Gestapo surveillance). He was the father of a son and was having an affair with a certain Grete Sommer, with whom he had opened a stationery shop and rental library. Grete agreed to shelter Inge and her mother in the cubbyhole behind her shop during weekdays and on weekends on Ostrowski's houseboat outside the city.

Grete also invited Inge to work in her shop, selling stationery, pens, and toilet paper and helping with the lending library. After a while, Inge and Ella moved to several others places. In Inge's words, "My mother and I existed from one day to the next, and gradually became used to leading the lives of adventurers, tricksters, and dissemblers." Back at Grete's shop, one day Inge was approached by Käthe Schwartz, who was married to a professor of Roman law at Berlin university, who told her that her apartment had been destroyed in an air raid. Käthe was going to move to Ingolstadt, where she had relatives. She then confided to Inge and asked whether she could continue looking after a Jewish woman whom she was hiding. Inge laughed: "I'm Jewish myself." Käthe: "Why didn't you tell me before? I would have helped you." From that moment, Käthe helped out with food stamps. As for Käthe's hidden Jewish woman, named Lotte Eifert, she found a job as a governess in the home of a Nazi district leader in the Berlin suburb of Potsdam. Thanks to this, Inge and her mother received food ration cards regularly.

Lisa Holländer, a sister of Walter Rieck's wife, Jenny, was another Berliner who helped Inge. Her Jewish husband had been murdered in the Mauthausen concentration camp and she wanted to get even with the Nazis by helping out Jews. "You can stay as long as you wish," she told Inge and Ella; "I've got plenty of room." Her house had so many entrances and staircases that one could wander in and out without being seen. When Lisa's home took a direct hit in an air raid, on January 30, 1944, Inge and Ella had to move on. Throughout this period, Klara Grüger, who sheltered a Jewish man in her home, Hans Münzer, for over two years and married him after the war, owned a bakery and provided Inge and Ella with bread and other bakery products on a regular basis.

Making her way in a city under constant bombardment, Ella Deutschkron was accepted for work at Walter Rieck's textile printing shop under the name of Richter. Moving to Potsdam, Ella and Inge found an empty and uninhabitable cowshed and moved in there. Neighbors helped out with bedding, a table, and crockery, believing they had been "bombed out" in Berlin. Ella then moved on to another printer, Theodor Görner. He had been arrested, then released, but fined by the Nazis for keeping a half-Jewish girl whom he had adopted and whom he had tried to enroll in school.

In the meantime, in Potsdam, there was tension in the Rieck household. Rieck had taken up with Charlotte, a young film actress, while his wife and daughter were away in Bavaria. At one time, Inge and Ella had stayed temporarily with Rieck and had to move out suddenly when he told them the Gestapo was questioning him on the charge of harboring two Jewish women. It turned out that Walter's wife, Jenny, fuming with rage at her husband's infidelity, had decided to get back at him by reporting him to the Gestapo for sheltering two Jewish women. Rieck was able to assure the Gestapo that there was nothing behind this accusation, and disclosed to them the source of it all – his amorous relationship with the actress Charlotte. But Inge and Ella could not go back to the cowshed, since Jenny had disclosed the location to the Gestapo.

At this crucial moment, Theodor Görner came up with an idea for the two women to take the train to as close as possible to the front in the east. It was February 1945 and the Russian army was by then already on Germany's eastern border. Ella and Inge were to mix with the refugees fleeing the Russian advance, travel back with them to Berlin and legalize themselves that way. The two women followed this advice, traveled to Luebben, a railroad junction for refugees from the east; they then crossed over to another platform, and represented themselves as refugees who had lost all their papers. Back in Berlin, on a refugee train, they were sent to the Nazi Public Welfare Department, given new identity papers under the name of Ella Paula and Inge Richter, put up in a hostel, and given food and clothing coupons. Now they were legal.

When the siege of Berlin began, Ella and Inge moved back to the cowshed in Potsdam to await the arrival of the Russians, whose artillery could be heard in the distance. Liberation in Potsdam came on April 22, 1945, but they decided to remain hidden for several more days, for fear of maltreatment and rape by victory-drunk Russians.

After the war, the Deutschkrons were reunited with husband and father Martin, in London. Inge eventually worked in Germany as the correspondent of the Israeli newspaper *Maariv,* then settled in Israel and continued her journalistic work there. During her first postwar tour of Germany, she was shocked to see high-ranking Nazis still in power in the new government. She presently has two apartments, in Tel Aviv and Berlin. After petitioning Yad Vashem to have her rescuers acknowledged, she put down in writing the story of her life as a Jewess on the run in Berlin and the help received from her many benefactors – an account later dramatized on a Berlin stage. As for Otto Weidt's former workshop, on Rosenthalerstrasse 39, it has now been restored and turned into a museum dedicated to Weidt's rescue activity.

Despite all that she and her mother had gone through during the Nazi period, Inge Deutschkron retains a special affection for her "Berliners." As she wrote, "The overwhelming majority of Jews in Berlin had friends or neighbors who helped them get food beyond their official ration, grocers who gave their old customers a little something 'extra.'" She recalled that when the Jewish star promulgation came into effect, "an intangible and yet immediately perceptible wave of sympathy flowed towards us from our non-Jewish fellow citizens of Berlin, such as the middle-aged man on the subway who got up from his seat and insisted that we sit down." "The Berliners," she wrote – "so many Berliners helped us. The little people; the shopkeeper around the corner, the guard in the underground, the policeman in our district," and pointed out that about 10,000 Jews were estimated to be living underground in Berlin in the middle of 1943. Sure, Inge is careful to add, there is no denying the many, too many Nazis in this capital city of Nazi Germany, but at the same time, "without the aid of all those anonymous Berliners we would never have been able to stay underground for two years." Berlin was one of the most liberal cities in the world before the Nazis came, Inge reminds her readers. Of all her Berlin rescuers, Otto Weidt holds a special place in her heart. "Without him, I wouldn't be alive today."

As for Inge's friend Alice Licht, in 1946 she moved to America, from where she corresponded with Otto Weidt until his death a year later. Alice married, bore a son, and in 1973 moved to Israel, where she died in 1987. Traumatized by the Holocaust, especially her experiences in Theresienstadt and Auschwitz, and the loss of her parents, she kept that dark chapter in her life to herself, never speaking about it.

Whatever one's opinion on the debate about the help to Jews extended by the Berlin population, there is no doubt concerning the "Berliners" who risked their lives and freedom to help Inge Deutschkron, her mother, Ella, and Alice Licht.

Consequently, in 1971, Yad Vashem conferred the title of Righteous Among the Nations on Otto Weidt. The Righteous title was also awarded to the rescuers of the Deutschkrons and other Jews, mentioned in this story; in 1967 – to Theodor Görner; in 1971 – to Emma Gumz, Käthe Schwarz, Lisa Holländer, and Walter Rieck; and in 1986 – to Klara Grüger-Münzer.

Westerweel, Johan (Joop) & Wilhelmina
NETHERLANDS

*I*t was a memorable parting speech that his listeners would never forget. High up in the Pyrenees mountains separating France from Spain stood Joop Westerweel one freezing afternoon in early 1944, and bid his charges a safe passage and a new and meaningful beginning for them. They were members of a Zionist pioneering organization that had prepared themselves for a new life in Palestine, and Westerweel had led them all the way from occupied Netherlands through occupied Belgium and the whole length of occupied France – and here they stood, moments before finally quitting the part of Europe that was occupied by Hitler's forces. He told them:

"You are on the threshold of freedom. Soon you will arrive in the land of freedom and will fulfill your goal of building the land of Israel as a homeland for the world's Jews. I wish each of you happiness and good luck, but do not forget your comrades who fell along the road and by sacrificing their lives paved the way for your journey to freedom. Build up your land and erect a memorial for them, immortalizing their memory. Remember Shushu [arrested

by the Germans, he had committed suicide in prison] … and all the other comrades who gave their lives to rescue their comrades. Remember the world's suffering, and build your land in such a way that it justifies its existence by providing freedom for all its inhabitants and abandoning war."

"No more wars," were his final words. Not long afterward, on March 11, 1944, Joop Westerweel was betrayed and apprehended by the Nazis at a Dutch-Belgian border crossing point. He would never see freedom again. The Nazis had him executed. His wife, Wilhelmina, had been arrested earlier and was sent to the infamous Ravensbrück concentration camp. She was lucky to survive.

Johan (Joop) Westerweel with two of his children (Private Collection Mirjam Pinkhof-Waterman, Haifa)

From the preceding, one may gather that we are dealing with a nationalist firebrand, but this is very far from the truth. He was a sworn pacifist and opposed to any forms of nationalism, which he saw as the basic cause of all of the world's ills. He was born in Zutphen, in 1899, to parents who belonged to the Darbyite Church, also known as the Plymouth Brethren. His father ran a successful printing shop that he later devoted to publishing Christian religious material. At his home, his parents frowned at "immoral" acts, such as dancing and going to the cinema. At an early age, Joop was kept from participating in sports events (he happened to be a good athlete and full of physical energy throughout his life) and had to stay indoors all Sunday and study the Bible after attending church, while other children played outside. This strict upbringing caused Joop to rebel at an early age. At the same time, the religious fundamentalist atmosphere at home left a deep imprint on the young Joop – not in the sense of strict devotional practice of the Christian faith but of what he considered to be its underlying message of universal brotherhood. This led him to be attracted to the spiritual side of socialism and its secular-messianic message of universal solidarity, and so he became active in the Socialist movement. When he married at the age of 19, he set off with his wife for Indonesia, then a Dutch colony (Dutch East Indies), where he was offered a teaching position.

There he was soon in trouble for protesting the exploitation of the native population. He also felt uncomfortable with the other colonials and their way of thinking. These often met at drinking parties and spoke with disrespect about the native population. When he refused to report for compulsory military training, he was expelled from the colony and sent back home. His marriage was also turning sour.

Back in the Netherlands, he returned to his profession, which was also his favorite pastime – teaching. Together with Kees Boeke and his British-born wife, Betty, both Quakers, he opened a school called *De Werkplaats* (Workshop) in Bilthoven, where progressive and innovative educational methods were applied. Great emphasis was placed on handwork, such as carpentry and handicrafts. The educational purpose was to help each child be a person in his or her own right, what the child was capable of being; and to allow the children pedagogic freedom, with adults only in a supervisory position with as little interference as possible. At the *Workplaats* pupils and teachers called each other by their first names, something highly unusual in the country at the time. At first, Joop worked without salary; these were the years of the depression. It was there that Joop first met Mirjam Waterman, one of the teachers, and from her he learned about the plight of the Jews under Hitler.

Joop Westerweel had not changed a bit his almost anarchistic ideas and his opposition to any form of authority and militarism. This took him so far as even to be opposed to voting, which he never did in his life. He said that voting was a farce, since it would not really change anything. Things would remain the same whichever party attained power. Once he assembled a group in Bilthoven with their voting cards, which they placed in a makeshift ballot box, then burned it, in full public view. Also, at the time, every bike owner had to attach a license to his bike stating the year the tax was paid on it. This upset Joop, since he considered the bicycle a popular form of communication. Not only did he never acquire the license, but he would ride his bike through the city shouting, "I ride on the main street without a license." His refusal to pay taxes once led the government to seize all of his and his wife's scant household possessions, which were subsequently sold by public auction.

As a pacifist, he was opposed to military expenditures. In the process, he had formulated an idiosyncratic personal philosophy that combined elements of socialism and anarchism with his own version of evangelical Christianity. Though not a practicing Christian, he had a religious temperament and frequently cited passages from Psalms, Exodus, or the Gospel of Matthew. He looked upon freedom as the ultimate good and goal. He was steadfast to the point of being immovable, and throughout his life he made no distinction between theory and practice, between word and deed. People who met him

Wilhelmina (Willy) Westerweel

for the first time quickly got the impression that he was not an easy person to get along with, but at the same time he had captivating personality. He also knew how to inspire others.

In 1940, Joop Westerweel left the Werkplaats to take up a teaching position at the Montessori school in Rotterdam. Founded by Dr. Maria Montessori of Italy, the Montessori system appealed to Westerweel, since it was based on many of the same principles as the Werkplaats, such as encouraging young children to develop their unique talents and special needs as well as the emphasis on the uniqueness of each child and the recognition that children are different from adults in the way they develop and think.

By then Joop had already remarried – to Wilhelmina, or Willy (sometimes referred to simply as Wil). When she first met Joop, in 1927, she was immediately smitten by his personality, although he was nine years older and not yet divorced. Her middle-class parents were strongly opposed to their daughter's relationship to the non-conformist and idiosyncratic Joop, and this led to fiery altercations at home. At one point she decided to leave home as well as Joop, and took up a housekeeping position in another city. Several years later, she returned and again took up with Joop, who was by then divorced. This led to a final break with her family, as Willy and Joop moved into a rented apartment, and in 1933, their first child was born. Two more children were to follow in the coming years.

In Rotterdam, the Westerweels came face to face with the deportation of Jews when they witnessed Jews standing around and crying, consulting neighbors about what to take along, and with small children at their sides. Already, two years earlier, in October 1940, in a letter to a former student of the Werkplaats, Joop had written:

"Once again I said to Wil, 'How I wish I were a Jew … How delightful it must be not to be counted among those whom Hitler considers the elect … Oh, how I wish I had one real friend among the Jews … Someone who would truly accept me and receive me within the circle of those who are reviled, and where I would feel at home like a fish in water.'"

In August 1942, Joop and Willy returned to Rotterdam from a long outing in the Dutch countryside with their three children, and found their apartment occupied by a Jewish family. The Cohens, a 50-year old couple and their 19-year old daughter had been put there by a friend, for just a day, but in the meantime the friend was arrested before he could move them elsewhere. The Cohens, in panic, did not know what to do next. In the course of that evening the Westerweels decided to leave them in their apartment and go somewhere else with their children, until another arrangement could be made for the Cohens. It was the Westerweels' first act of help to Jews. They were soon to be involved in a rescue operation on a much broader scale.

Loosdrecht, near Utrecht, was a rural community in the west of the country, wedged between flat farmland, small woods, and a series of widely scattered lakes. There the Dutch branch of the *Hechalutz* movement, a Zionist youth organization, had a training farm, known as the *Loosdrechtsche Rade* (Loosdrecht Pavilion), for preparing a group of about 50 young people for a life of pioneering and agricultural work in Palestine. Joachim Simon (Shushu) and Menachem Pinkhof were the two leading counselors of the group. The farm also hosted a group of Jewish children who had been taken out of Germany under the *Kindertransport* operation in the late 1930s. On August 15, 1942, Menachem Pinkhof was told by a woman confidante working in the Jewish Council in Amsterdam of a planned raid on the farm, to take place in three days, on August 18, 1942, to arrest the first batch of youngsters there. Pinkhof and Simon desperately began seeking a means of escape for their charges. This is when Mirjam Waterman came into the picture.

She had taught at the *Werkplaats*, where she had known Joop Westerweel, and had left in 1940, when Jews were no longer allowed to teach in non-Jewish schools. She had returned home to Loosdrecht. One day, Mirjam received an urgent phone call from Menachem Pinkhof, to whom she was engaged. He had learned from her that a certain man named Westerweel was already hiding a Jewish couple in his home and might have useful underground contacts. Perhaps he could also be of help in this urgent matter? She immediately arranged for Joop to meet the counselors at the Loosdrecht farm.

The meeting between Joop Westerweel and the Loosdrecht group was a decisive turning point for him. He listened attentively as the youngsters told of their desire to help rebuild Palestine. Joop was impressed by the egalitarian flavor and communal spirit of the pioneers' everyday life, which accorded with his own deeply held principles of equality and solidarity in practical everyday matters. At the same time, because of his opposition to all forms of nationalism, he had reservations about the group's Zionist goals, but was persuaded by them that there was no other way, given the situation of the Jews in Europe. Eventually his doubts gave way to enthusiasm as he envisioned the construction of a new and just society in Palestine. He concluded that he had at last found a cause worthy of his fundamentalist piety and his faith in socialist goals. He had recognized in the group a sense of idealism and strong principles which he found attractive and worth helping.

Immediately swinging into action, Westerweel set in motion a far-ranging plan to temporarily hide the farm's staff and students with friendly non-Jewish families. He immediately started to organize his close friends to assist him to find hiding places for the several dozen youngsters of the Loosdrecht farm. Within four days all of them were spirited away and hidden. Of the original group of 50 youngsters, 33 are known to have survived; the rest were apprehended and deported. When the Germans arrived on the spot, they found an empty building, with only barking dogs to greet them.

This was Joop's initiation into what became much wider rescue activity in partnership with the *Hechalutz* leadership. From this moment he became a different person. He especially established a close relationship with Joachim Simon, better known as Shushu, in whom he found a soul mate. Shushu, originally from Berlin, had already tasted life in a concentration camp, that of Buchenwald, but had managed to leave Germany before the start of the war. In October 1942, he successfully smuggled his wife, Adina, across the border into Switzerland, but his contacts with underground circles in France made him believe that the safest route was Spain via the Pyrenees Mountains. Throughout the fall and early winter of 1942–43, Westerweel and Simon traveled back and forth into Belgium and France to make the necessary preparations. Returning to Brussels from France without Westerweel, Simon-Shushu was arrested on January 26 and imprisoned in Breda, where he committed suicide on January 27, 1943. Simon's arrest and suicide were a heavy personal blow to Westerweel. It was up to him now to take over the leadership of the group and plan the escape routes to the Spanish border. He was up to the task both in temperament and as a man of action.

Under wartime conditions the journey through Belgium and France, both fully occupied countries by 1943, was extremely dangerous, especially the border crossings. In France, it was made somewhat easier because the youngsters had managed to get papers identifying them as Dutch workers of the Todt Organization, the German construction firm that was building the coastal fortifications known as the Atlantic Wall, which as a bonus made it possible for them to stay in special hostels and eat in designated restaurants and cafeterias at reduced rates. Joop was opposed to the use of the false Todt documents of persons supposedly employed by the German army. His deeply ingrained anti-militarism did not allow him even to pretend to work for the German army. But he was overruled on this point. Westerweel and his colleagues were able to smuggle at least 70 youngsters across the Pyrenees into Spain between February 1943 and July 1944, from where they eventually proceeded by boat to Palestine.

As for those who stayed behind, hiding places had to be found for them. Joop turned to his former colleague Bouke Koning at the Werkplaats and another associate, Jan Smith (a bricklayer), as well as others known and trusted by him, and persuaded them to join him in the search for hiding places. He became the moving spirit of the group. Back at the Westerweel home, Willy also shared in her husband's clandestine activities. As she stated after the war, "There never was a day without problems. Always emergencies: 'Come pick up the boy, the address is not safe.' Or the identity card was on the police blacklist and one had to prepare another card. Joop was at his best, never tired. He worked at full speed, first as a teacher at the Montessori school, then after work in clandestine activity, which grew like a snowball."

One of Willy's tasks was to collect blank identity cards in Amsterdam, or from an illegal printing place in Weert, and bring them, with an inkpad, to Jews in order to take their fingerprints. "At the Rotterdam train station, baggage was inspected at both exits. When I saw this, I went to the shelter, where I stayed for a long while, until the inspectors had left the station. Then I started to tremble. It was not the first time that I noticed this post-traumatic effect. I also visited people in hiding to bring them money, ration cards, and books – as far as Limburg province, and Sevenum, a place where there were once more hidden people than residents." To avoid the slightest chance of detection and the discovery of the incriminating documents with them, the Westerweels constantly changed addresses.

A group of trustworthy helpers rallied around Westerweel and his colleagues which after the war came to be known as the Westerweel group. It consisted of both non-Jews and Jews who helped disperse throughout the country members of the pioneering organizations in sheltering homes. Members of the Westerweel group, besides Wilhelmina Westerweel, included some two dozen non-Jewish members (listed at end of article). On the Jewish side, the list is too long to mention more than just a few names beside the martyred Joachim Simon (Shushu): Menachem Pinkhof, Mirjam Waterman, Kurt Reilinger, and Letty Rüdelsheim. This large group and their affiliates were instrumental in rescuing 361 members of the various pioneer groups out of a prewar total of 821.

Tragedy struck both Joop and Wilhelmina Westerweel, but on different dates. Willy was arrested on December 15, 1943, when she participated in a plot to free Letty Rüdelsheim (later Ben Heled), who had been arrested earlier with seven Jews in her home. While the seven Jews were deported to Auschwitz, Letty passed as an Aryan and her papers were in order, so she was imprisoned as a non-Jewish accomplice. The rescue attempt was foiled because of the prison warden, who informed on the plotters to the Gestapo. Willy was taken to the notorious Vught concentration camp in The Netherlands and from there was later deported to the women's concentration camp of Ravensbrück in Germany. There she was assigned work for the German Siemens company, assembling various electronic components. She and the other prisoners suffered from a lack of warm clothing, malnutrition, and various infectious camp diseases. When she was injured in her work place, the wound became infected and she was moved to the camp's dispensary, from where women were dispatched to the gas chambers. Willy waited fearfully for her turn. Luckily for her, two weeks before the war's end, on April 22, 1945, she was permitted to join a group of freed prisoners under the auspices of the Swedish Red Cross making their way to Denmark, from where they continued by boat to Malmö in Sweden.

Three months after his wife's arrest, Joop also fell into the hands of the Germans. On March 11, 1944, he and his co-worker Bouke Koning were caught at the Dutch-Belgiun border with two Jewish women whom they were escorting. He was carrying with him a passport in the name of a certain Lelièvre, a border smuggler from Antwerp who had shot a German, and they were looking for him. After his arrest, he was brutally tortured, but he refused to divulge the names of his associates. In April 1944, an abortive attempt was made to rescue him, which resulted in the arrest of several more members of the Westerweel group, including Mirjam Waterman and Menachem Pinkhof, who were dispatched to the Bergen-Belsen concentration camp, which they luckily survived. The plan was to have Joop injected with dried blood, which would make it appear that he was bleeding and needed to be hospitalized. Then, once out of Vught camp, he was to suddenly get up and jump out of the van, where the plotters would be waiting for him. However, one of these plotters turned out to be a double agent and the plan was foiled. He was transferred to Vught camp and executed on August 11, 1944. He was 45 at the time of his death. His wife, Willy, who was then still in the Vught camp, was able to see him for the last time from a distance, through iron bars. She said, "We raised our hands in greeting to each other. In Vught, I learned that he had assembled other prisoners and lectured them on politics and read them poems."

In solitary confinement, awaiting execution, Joop Westerweel wrote a farewell message, under the title "Evening in the Cell." It read in part:

"There they are… all my comrades, standing side by side with me; together we have advanced along this road to confront the enemy … Whether I die or live is now all the same to me. A great light has dawned within me, enriching me. It is time for silent thoughts. The night is dark and long. But I am fully aglow from the splendor within me."

After the war, his many beneficiaries continued to remember and pay tribute to the man – known by his short stature, his large forehead, a pronounced nose, and a head covered with a great deal of wiry gray hair – who had inspired them so greatly as well as saving them. This iconoclast, who rebelled against his father's strict religious demeanor, is remembered as never having gone anywhere without a Bible in his knapsack. At tense moments he would read favorite passages from the Sermon on the Mount, especially the passage, "Blessed are those who are persecuted for righteousness' sake: for theirs is the kingdom of heaven. Blessed are you, when they revile you, and persecute you…."

Earlier, in August 1942, when the decision was taken to remove the *Hechalutz* pioneers from the Loosdrecht farm, some of the youngsters were tortured by the idea of leaving their relatives behind in Amsterdam, especially their parents, who might be put under German torture because of their children's actions. Should they not try something else, not leave but go underground, they asked? At this point, Westerweel would quote from Matthew, "Whoever loves father or mother more than me … is not worthy of me … And whoever does not take up the cross and follow me, is not worthy of me." As later stated by Menachem Pinkhof, "At that point, we realized there was no way we could go back on our plan. The die had been cast." On another occasion, he told them, "You're wrong in thinking I am helping you because you are Jewish. Even if you were blacks and Hottentots, no matter what, I would help you in the name of justice, for you are in need."

Long afterwards, one of *Hechalutz* members wrote: "He put the whole undertaking on an exclusively moral footing. He made it clear to us that we were setting off on a new road in underground activities that would give new sense and meaning to the values of the past." Those he saved have formed an organization to keep his memory alive and hold regular convocations in his honor. One of them has written: "The more the passage of time dims the darkness of the period which became the altar on which he gave his life, the stronger shines the nobility of his deeds."

In 1964 Yad Vashem recognized Johan (Joop) and Wilhelmina Westerweel as Righteous Among the Nations. Also awarded the Righteous honor were the following non-Jewish members of the Westerweel Group: Bouke Koning, Froukje Koning, Jan Smit, Michiel (Chiel) Salomé, Eugénie Boutet, Piet Arts, Frans Gerritsen, Henny de Haan, Tinus Schabbing, Tony Schabbing, Antje (Geerling) Roos, Katy Mulder, Piet Wildschut, Leni Oroszlan-de Jong, Philip Rümke, Gerda Ritman, Pim van Maanen, and Dirk van Schaik.

Wust, Elisabeth

GERMANY

*A*ugust 21, 1944, turned out to be an especially hot day in Berlin. Two women, clad in knickers, took the day off for a photo session in the park. The photos taken showed the two women kissing each other – more than innocently. The relationship between the two was obvious. When they got home, the Gestapo was waiting for them. Both were arrested – not for their lesbian relationship but because one of the women, a non-Jewish German, had been sheltering the other in her home – a Jewish woman named Felice Schragenheim. "She was the love of my life," Elisabeth Wust, better known as Lilly, said after the war. "I shall not forget the beautiful moments fifty years ago."

Born in 1913, Lilly was married to Gunther Wust and gave birth to four sons, for which she been decorated by the Nazi state. In gratitude for contributing four Aryan offspring, and also with respect to her husband's service in the German army, she was entitled to several bonuses, including a full-time maid. Gunther was not an ideal husband, as he was conducting several love affairs on the side. So was Lilly, as a result of which, according to her, one of her sons had been fathered by another man. Both husband and wife seemed to be satisfied with their loveless marital relationship, until Lilly met Felice and her life underwent a dramatic emotional change.

Felice Rachel Schragenheim was born in Berlin in 1922 to Albert and Erna – well-known dentists who also had another daughter, Irene. Albert, as a patriotic German, had dutifully served in the German army in World War I for the full four years of the war. At home, mother Erna lit the Sabbath candles every Friday. In 1930, Erna died in a car accident, and Albert remarried. He also purchased a house in Haifa, hoping to eventually settle in Palestine. However, in 1935, at the age of 48, he died of a heart attack. Felice's sister, Irene, managed to leave for England in 1938. Felice herself tried to leave for Palestine, or Australia, but came up against the bureaucracy. Then came the war, and the door was shut for travel overseas – Felice was stuck in Nazi Germany. When, in 1942, or 1943, she received an order for deportation, she decided not to appear and, instead, to go underground. Leaving a fake suicide note, she disappeared and was helped by her friends in the lesbian community of Berlin. This is how she met Ursula Schaaf, Elisabeth Wust's housemaid.

One day, in November 1942, Ursula took Lilly out of her self-imposed cloister of her home for a chat with Ursula's friends in the posh "Berlin" café next to one of the city's busiest subway (U-train) stations, near the city zoo. The café was known as a hangout for homosexuals and lesbians. There, Ursula introduced her landlady to Felice Schragenheim, who presented herself as Felice Schrader. "I was attracted to her from the first. It was the meeting that changed my life," Lilly wrote, not knowing at the time about Felice's Jewish origin. It was the start of an ever-closer relationship, with Felice often visiting Lilly at her home, dressed in tailor-made jackets and slacks. Lilly's children soon became accustomed to the new woman's visits, affectionately calling her Tante (Aunt) Felice.

Elisabeth Wust (Private Collection)

One evening, in early 1943, when Gunther was home on leave, Lilly caught him kissing the maid. Exasperated, Lilly rushed into the kitchen, where she ran into Felice, who started kissing her. Lilly slapped her in the face. "I was not yet prepared for this transformation – women's love." A bit later, on March 18, Lilly underwent surgery for a jaw infection, and Felice came often to visit her, always with a bouquet in her hands. On one of these visits, Felice attached a note to the flowers. Lilly read the following intimate message, "I yearn to give you everything, and to think only of one thing – you! I want to find the stars meant for you and me! Do you need explanations? I love you."

The day was March 25 and, as Lilly later wrote in her diary, "we declared March 25 our wedding day." In her diary, Lilly admitted that until then she had not known real love, only sexual encounters. With Felice it was different. "She only touched me, and I melted away. With Felice I understood who I am and what I want. With Felice I felt like walking on the clouds." Felice gave her lover a new name, "Aimée" (beloved), based on the heroine of a popular Berlin theater play in the 1930s. Felice chose for herself the name "Jaguar." The two referred to each other in their love letters by these two code names. They decided to keep their affair a secret, perhaps also in consideration of Lilly's sons. At the same time, Lilly decided to seek a divorce from Gunther, who was away with the army in Hungary. "I wanted only Felice," she wrote in her diary.

One day, Felice decided to lay her cards on the table. "Will you love me even if I tell you a secret" she asked her lover? Lilly responded by swearing that Felice was the only love of her life. Then Felice continued, "Lilly, I am Jewish and my name is Schragenheim, not Schrader." For a moment, Lilly did not move. "Then, suddenly, I realized the danger Felice was in … From the moment she disclosed to me her identity, it was as though she had placed her fate in my hands. All that night, we wept together, and swore to be faithful to one to another." The two led secret lives in the Berlin of the Nazi period. One – a Jew in the guise of a non-Jew, sought by the Nazi authorities and cohabiting with an "Aryan" woman. The other – a non-Jewish woman, mother of four children, whose husband was away with the German army, and in love with another woman – a Jew.

This secret love affair lasted from March 1943 to August 1944, when both women were arrested by the Gestapo, evidently on a tip by an informer. Lilly stated that she was well aware that in the event of discovery she risked being sent to a concentration camp, with her children removed to an orphanage.

Lilly was taken for interrogation. In consideration of her four sons, her decoration by the Nazi state, and her husband's service in the army, she was released and sent home. That evening, Lilly sadly noted in her diary, "Today the worst of all happened, which I feared all the time. They took away from me what I loved most. God almighty, bring back my love."

Lilly managed to see Felice just once more, visiting her in jail and bringing her fresh fruit and tomatoes. On September 8, 1944, Felice was deported to the Theresienstadt camp across the Czech border. Two weeks later, not able to still her yearning for Felice, Lilly decided on a bold step – to go to Theresienstadt and attempt to see her there. Entering the SS camp offices, she was met by one of the SS camp commanders. "Who are you and what do you want," he brusquely asked her? "I should appreciate if you will allow me to meet Felice Schragenheim and give her a small package." "Who do you think you are? How did you get here? And you have the insolence to bring food for a Jewish prisoner. I'll make sure to have you investigated…. Have you no racial pride?" He continued to threaten her with all sorts of punishments and promised to report her to the Berlin Gestapo, "and he threw me out. Fortunately for me, he did not have me arrested." Back in Berlin, Lilly was summoned by the Gestapo one day for a lengthy interrogation. "Only for the sake of your little children are we not sending you to a concentration camp." Instead, she was told to report to the police regularly.

As long as Felice was in Theresienstadt, she was able to correspond with Lilly, as was the policy in that camp for prisoners – a ploy to fool the world into believing that life in that camp was not at all too bad. In the meantime, Lilly initiated the annulment of her marriage from Gunther, who was listed as having disappeared on the eastern front. Perhaps to make up for the loss of Felice, Lilly decided to secretly shelter in her home several more Jewish women of the lesbian community. These included Lucie Sara Friedlaender (who committed suicide in August 1945), Dr. Rose Ollendorf (who returned to her teaching profession after the war, left for Denmark), and Kaethe Laserstein (who left for Sweden, where she died in 1950). This, however, proved no solace for Lilly, as these women could not compensate for the loss of Felice. As Elisabeth ("Lilly") wrote in her diary, on February 24, 1945: "The air raid alarm sounds twice every evening, and it is on a steady increase. There is much shooting. Felice, I love you so much. I am so lonely, although I am surrounded by people who deserve my love and care. Through them, I love you even more … I miss you so ardently. They correctly surmise the reason for my suffering… You understand, they love each other, and I painfully yearn for you. You – my only beloved person."

After the war, Lilly wrote to the Red Cross for news of Felice's fate, and was informed that she was no longer among the living. The date of her death was recorded as December 31, 1944, probably coinciding with the day she arrived either in Auschwitz or the Gross Rosen camp. As for Lilly's situation, since she had initiated the divorce, which went through while her husband was serving in the army, she had forfeited any benefits as a war widow. Only in 1981 did the West German government change its position and honor her (with the *Bundesverdienstkreuz*) for her help to Jews and opposition to the Nazi regime, an honor that came with a monthly stipend. She later went public with the story of her love for Felice, in a book as well as a movie. A final twist in Elisabeth Wust's life was to see one of her sons convert to Judaism and move to Israel.

In 1995, Elisabeth Wust was recognized by Yad Vashem as Righteous Among the Nations.

Xirouhakis, Stylianos & Damaskini & Antonis, Stratis, Marika & Manolis Païtakis, Manolis & Athena

GREECE

Crete is the largest of the Greek islands, and its history goes back to the dawn of civilization. Some historians speculate that the island is identical with the biblical Caphtor – the original home of the Philistines. The towns and cities there were often mentioned during the Hellenistic and Roman periods. The Jewish historian Philo and the New Testament testify to the existence of Jewish communities on the island. Much earlier, the island had produced two major civilizations, the Minoan and Mycenaean. Crete may best be known for the Minoan palace of King Minos at Knossos, built some 1,500 years before the current era, and the red-painted wooden columns of the temple, including the extensive frescoes portraying athletic feats that decorated the plastered walls. Most prominent among them are the bull riding, where young men man apparently leapt onto a charging bull's back, which was either a ritual or sport, or both. There is also the Myth of the Labyrinth, an elaborate mazelike structure constructed for King Minos to hold the Minotaur, a creature that was half-man and half-bull and was eventually killed by the Athenian hero Theseus. Ruled by various Greek dynasties, it passed through many hands – the Romans, Byzantines, Venetians, and Turks, and in 1912 was finally restored to Greece. There were some 300 Jews on the island when the Germans conquered it in May 1941, following their invasion of Greece on April 9, 1941.

At the time, the Avram family lived in Lárisa, to the north of Athens. The family head, Salvator Avram, had no illusions that the Greek army would be able to withstand the powerful German army and decided to flee with his family to Egypt to avoid living under Nazi occupation with all this implied for Jews. The government and royal family, except for the King, who was still in Crete, had already fled to Egypt. So Mr. Avram gathered his large family, which included his wife, Karolla (born Bensousan), his two children, two-year-old Moissis, and six-year-old Yolanda; Salvator's mother, Esther Avram (approaching 80), his sister Allegra Avraham (early forties), Karolla's youngest sister, Stella Bensousan (mid-twenties), and the family's 17-year-old non-Jewish maid – and they set out on the journey to Egypt via Crete.

Leaving Lárisa in a rented truck, the family headed for Gythion on the southern coast of Greece. There, Avram chartered a small fishing boat with its crew for the crossing to Crete. After a stormy trip, they arrived at Kastelli Kissamou on the northwestern coast of the island in mid- or late April 1941 and rented a furnished house, with rooms next door for Salvator's elderly mother and his sister Allegra. These dwellings were somewhat removed from the town proper and not far from a small British military installation.

No sooner had he arrived than Salvator Avram started making arrangements for the next phase of his voyage – across the Mediterranean Sea toward Egypt. That is how he met Stylianos Xirouhakis, who had several businesses in Kastelli Kissamou, including farming, fertilizers, wine making, and the production of hand-made shoes. Avram had changed his name to Sotirios, which is the Greek translation of Salvator. As he became friendly with Xirouhakis, Avram disclosed to him the true identity of his family, as Jewish. Xirouhakis put Avram in touch with the provincial authorities, and in mid-May 1941 Salvator "Sotirios" left Kastelli Kissamou for Hania, the administrative capital of Crete (where most of the island's Jews happened to live) in order to find a boat and the requisite documents for the voyage to Egypt.

It seemed that everything was proceeding smoothly when the Avram family went to sleep on the night of May 19, 1941 – only to awaken the next morning to the sound of bombing and strafing by the German air force. The invasion and battle of Crete had begun as the Germans landed gliders and paratroopers to combat the 40,000-odd Greek and British Empire troops. It was a bitterly contested campaign that ended on June 1, 1941, in a German victory after sustaining heavy losses.

When the bombing began on May 20, Salvator Avram hurried to Stylianos' farm in Pyrgos, just outside Kastelli, where the Xirouhakises had moved for greater safety and a sure supply of food. He found the family preparing to flee. "What will become of us, my friend," he asked Stylianos. The man had no answer. Then Salvator Avram looked him in the eye and said: "I now have only you and God." In Yolanda's words, "That is how the miracle happened that saved us from almost certain death." Xirouhakis said that the Avram family could join his family in their flight to Mount Tyliphos on the island, northwest of Kastelli.

Adding the Avram family meant more than doubling the group, with the concomitant risks and logistics problems. Movement was to be on foot or by mule and donkey. Xirouhakis had to borrow animals from relatives to accommodate the Avrams. A separate mule was required for Salvator's old and diabetic mother, and another mule for her son and granddaughter. A donkey was gotten for the two women and the maid, held on to little Moissis. Stylianos' daughter Marika also required a separate animal, as she suffered from a very severe case of children's diabetes and had a foot injury that would not heal. Salvator Avram, who had taken along an extensive first aid kit, ministered to her wound.

As for the Avrams' two-year-old, Moissis, he suffered from amoebic dysentery and cried a lot, and this created the danger of unwelcome attention, but there was nothing to be done. The Xirouhakis family brought along a goat to provide the Avram children with milk as well as some chickens for eggs. The Avrams were basically city folk, and adjusting to mountain living was something they would have to do quickly. Their escape was just in time. As Yolanda Avram (later Willis), wrote, "None of us knew that two days later, the first four Jews would be captured and executed by a German firing squad: a rabbi, his young Salonikan wife and two small children who, like us, were on their way to Egypt."

Stylianos Xirouhakis, on his horse, accompanied the Avrams on their mountain trek. The Xirouhakis women had left earlier with the supplies, escorted by the Xirouhakis sons, Stratis (aged 21), and Manolis (18) as guides. The two sons made "beds," from branches and leaves. The makeshift "mattresses" were covered with rough wool blankets and surrounded by thorny branches to shelter the people from roaming small animals. The two sons also gave their charges garlic, which was supposed to repel the snakes that were very prevalent in that region.

During their stay in mountainous Tyliphos, a wounded British soldier was brought in, and Avram spread a medicinal powder on his wound and changed his dressings before the man was moved to another location, where he could receive proper medical attention. Later, when the Xirouhakis sons, Stratis and Manolis, brought word that things were relatively quiet in the foothill villages of Messoghia, where the Xirouhakis couple had originally come from, they moved the Avrams there and dispersed them among relatives, who hid them in stables and caves – even in a unused king-size village oven.

By June 1, 1941, the Battle of Crete was over, but the Avrams stayed behind until they received word from the Xirouhakises that it was safe to return to Kastelli, where they remained in the care of the Xirouhakises. Marika Xirouhakis, who was a very religious woman, took Karola Avram (alias "Sotirios") along with her to church, to convince the other worshippers that the newcomers were of the same faith as themselves. Yolanda recalled that "Mother was used to pouring oil for the wick she lit when she visited the synagogue in peacetime. In the little church in Kastelli, she joined her friend in lighting candles and imitating her in the other rituals. This provided safety for our whole family."

Then suddenly Stylianos Xirouhakis was confidentially informed that he had better part from the Avrams, for the Germans suspected the "Sotirios" family of being Jewish. The Germans had already required the Jewish community in Hania to submit a list of all Jewish residents, to be signed by the rabbi and the mayor of Hania – a list submitted on August 24, 1941 – and the Avram-Sotirios family was not on it. Right away the Xirouhakis family mobilized to find a way to take the Avrams back to the Greek mainland, but to Athens, which was under Italian administration and where the Jews were not being harmed. Stratis went to make the arrangements with a captain from the mainland who could be trusted. In return for payment he agreed to take the Avrams back to Greece on his small boat. Stylianos Xirouhakis quickly arranged the necessary documents for the Avrams and also gave them several addresses on the Greek mainland in case they should need help. On the way there, they were flagged down by a German naval patrol and incarcerated, but their captors did not discover their captives' Jewish identity. Salvator Avram was able to talk his way out of the situation and the Germans were satisfied with the papers on him and allowed the family to continue to their destination. In Yolanda's words, "Neither the papers nor the crew, obtained via the Xirouhakis, gave us away. Once more, that family had saved our lives."

Life in Athens proved peaceful for the Avrams until the German takeover on September 9, 1943, when they replaced the Italians, who had surrendered to the Allies a day earlier – and the Jews there were again in danger. During the early phase of the German occupation, the Avram parents happened to be attending a theater performance and there they ran into Stratis Xirouhakis, who had also arrived in Athens. Stratis was with his oldest brother, Antonis, and the two were seated five rows in front of the Avrams. Stratis excitedly told his brother, who was an attorney, of his family's help to the Avrams on the island of Crete. For reasons of precaution, both sides decided to meet in the lobby, where they embraced. For Antonis this was the first time he had met the Avrams, as previously he had been in the Greek army fighting in the war against Italy on the Albanian front preceding the German invasion. His family, not having heard from his, had feared him lost in action.

From that moment, Stratis did not cease to help the Avram family again, under their assumed names. This chance meeting in particular saved the life of Stella Bensousan, the sister of Mrs. Avram, who had recently lost her husband, Isaac, in a German raid. Stratis took her to his sister Athena, who had recently married Manolis Païtakis, an attorney by profession. The young couple lived in a quiet neighborhood in the Athens suburb of Kallithea. Athena's youngest brother, also named Manolis, who was a university student at the School of Physics and Math, lived with them, and the three cared for Stella Bensousan. Manolis Xirouhakis became a messenger and courier between Stella and her family, who were hiding elsewhere.

As for little Yolanda, she first stayed with her parents in the Athens suburb of Kallithea, pretending to be their niece, because they had presented themselves as a childless couple in the neighborhood. For about six months, she was also hidden by a widow and her family in the suburb of Neos Kosmos who pretended that Yolanda was a niece from a different city; later, during the summer of 1944, two of the widow's sisters hid Yolanda in their summer residence of Rhea, near Athens; then she was returned to the widow, where she remained until the liberation in October 1944, and was able to rejoin her parents.

For years after the war, the Avram parents lived in Athens in a rent-controlled house, but for most of the time Salvator stayed at his work place in Lárisa. Every Easter, out of respect for Stylianos Xirouhakis, Salvator Avram would make a special trip to Athens and, together with his wife, Karolla, spend the day with the Xirouhakis family. As Yolanda explained, "And the old man marveled at the gratitude and respect of this Jewish man – this person whose beliefs were so completely different as to the meaning of Easter – who came to honor his rescuers on this, their most holy religious day."

Going back to school, Yolanda later earned a Fulbright scholarship and left for the United States to attend college. She had totally lost track of her family's rescuers, until May 18, 1996, when she addressed a convention of the Pan Cretan Association of America in commemoration of the 55th anniversary of the Battle of Crete. She was then helped to relocate the Xirouhakis family, with whom she had a momentous and moving reunion in Greece.

The "Battle of Crete" for the Avram family ended in victory for them – thanks to the symbolic "good forces" of the extensive Xirouhakis family who, like the legendary Athenian Theseus of old, defeated the "Minotaur," half-men and half-demons represented by the Nazi invaders.

In 1999, Yad Vashem recognized as Righteous Among the Nations, Stylianos and Damaskini Xirouhakis, and their children Antonis, Stratis, Marika & Manolis, as well as Manolis and Athena Païtakis.

Yatsyuk, Ivan & Serafina
Mironiuk, Savko & Okseniya
UKRAINE

*A*t nightfall, 21-year-old David Princental silently approached the Baptist village. He had been led to believe that he would find succor among these practitioners of a fundamentalist biblical faith. From one of the houses, out stepped a man in peasant garb walking directly towards David. Was he friend or foe? Would he do harm, as had many others in this part of the Ukraine, a region generally hostile to Jews, or extend a helping hand? As the two approached each other, the man stopped, looked David in the eye, and hesitated for a moment. He then took David by the hand and invited him into his house. "God has brought us an important guest," he joyfully exclaimed to his startled wife. "Come, let us thank the Lord for it." The man's name was Ivan Yatsyuk. He and his wife, Serafina, fell on their knees and murmured a silent prayer. David could hear them thanking God for the privilege of meeting a son of Israel and imploring Him to help save the surviving remnant. David could not believer his eyes and ears. So it was true! These people, of whom he had heard so much in the ghetto, truly existed, and they indeed went out of their way to help!

The story takes place in the Lutsk region, Volyn province, in northwest Ukraine. This region, historically contested between Poland and Russia, was of a mixed Polish-Ukrainian population with an admixture of Jews. Between the two world wars it was part of Poland; then, after the war, it reverted to Ukraine, itself within the Soviet Union. The Germans occupied Lutsk on June 27, 1941, and began to decimate the Jewish community. By November 1942, all of the 20,000 or so Jews of Lutsk had been murdered by the Germans; most of them shot in the nearby Polanka forest. David Princental was at the time in a German labor camp outside the city, with fellow Jews, and he knew it was merely a question of time that the bell would toll for these surviving Jews. Fleeing the camp, he decided to seek out the Polish Bron family, in the village of Osnitza, whom he had known before the war, and he stayed with them over the 1942–43 winter. He then decided to move on, and eventually join up with friendly partisans in the region – but how and in what direction? As he struggled within his mind, he recalled the business trips he had made with his grandfather in the Ukrainian countryside, and their visit to a peasant whom his grandfather had described as a "saint" and who belonged to one of the Baptists sects in the Volyn region. David's mind wandered back to what appeared to him as the strange prayers and ceremonies of these believers, held on the shores of the Styr river, where they had themselves baptized. At home, the family maidservant also belonged to the Baptists, and David fondly recalled her spirituality and her love of the Jewish people. It was at this point in his distress that he resolved to seek them out, and with their help reach areas controlled by partisans friendly to Jews.

Passing through Lutsk on his way to the Baptist area, David stopped off at Witold Fomienko's barbershop to catch up on news of surviving Jews. Fomienko, a Ukrainian, had helped

Jews inside the Lutsk ghetto and was presently hiding eight Jews in his home. Continuing on his way, he passed the home of a Polish peasant who was hiding several Jews in his home, and David was invited to stay over for a few days. He then continued on his way to search out a Baptist village, and was met by Yatsyuk, who was overwhelmed by the thought of having been chosen to be a savior of Jew. An unthinkable phenomenon in Ukraine!

That evening, after the Yatsyuks finished a short prayer of thanks to the Lord for having sent them a young Jew, they invited David to dine with them. Ivan's wife, Serafina, served milk with potatoes. Before eating, Ivan read from the Bible. Over dinner, he said to David, "Try to understand. I too am Jewish." To David's puzzlement, Ivan explained, "Spiritually I am a Jew, and this encounter with you gives me a lot to think about, because it verifies the prophet's word that a last remnant will be spared."

Ivan's house could only serve as a temporary haven because of a next-door-neighbor who was known to be a rabid Jew-hater, and it was feared that he would report David's presence to the police the moment he saw him. Late that night, Ivan took David to the home of another Baptist family, and in the weeks and months that followed he was rotated from one Baptist household to another – never staying with one family for too long, to avoid detection.

One evening Ivan called him aside to explain an additional reasons for David's constant moves from one Baptist to another. "We usually trust our fellow believers," Ivan said. "But in the final reckoning man is tested in adversity and difficult situations. Tonight we shall take you to someone who doesn't know you. His attitude and response will test the sincerity of his faith. There is no danger in this for you. At worst he will refuse you his hospitality, and in that case we'll take you somewhere else. But to us his response will be a serious indication of the strength and depth of his faith."

David was then led to a certain house and told to knock on the door. To the question who he was, he responded – a homeless person seeking shelter for a few nights. David could hear the man and his wife arguing whether to allow him in. Finally, the man behind the door said that the decision was not to allow a stranger in. At this David, blurted out, "What a world this is that refuses shelter to a Jew!" Hearing these words, the man behind the the door was overwhelmed by the revelation, and was heard saying to his wife, "But it's a Jew; how can we refuse?" The door swung open and David was given a hearty welcome.

On another occasion, the Baptist farmer with whom David was staying sat down beside him and said, "I see you are sad and depressed. Allow me to sing you a song that will strengthen your spirit." Then, in the original Hebrew, he began to chant Psalm 126, beginning with the words, "When Lord brought back those that returned to Zion."

On his stopover at the house of Savko and Okseniya Mironiuk, David was surprised to meet another Jewish youth already hiding there – in fact, a distant relative of his, named Ignatz Shatz. Yaslenski, another Baptist with whom David stayed for a few nights, saved his life when a group of ultra-nationalist partisans, known for their hatred of Jews, were tipped off by an informer and raided the farm. They dragged David out of the barn and were about to shoot him when Yaslenski began shouting, "You don't know what you are doing! This Jew is a wanderer – estranged and homeless. What has he done to you? If you kill this Jew, his blood will cry out for all eternity and will haunt you for the rest of your lives. Let him go!" Stunned by the threat of a divine curse, the partisans released David and drew away.

Eventually, David left the Baptist community and joined a partisan band in the forest. After the war, he moved to Israel and settled in a kibbutz, from where he continued to correspond with some of his rescuers. In one of Ivan Yatsyuk's letters to David Princental (now changed to Prital), he wrote the following:

"Many friends read with tears parts of your letter on the reclamation of the wilderness – barren for a thousand years. I see it as the fulfillment of God's promise to Israel, as we read in the Holy Scriptures that the desert shall bloom in the latter days and will be transformed into god's own garden (Isaiah 51:3; Ezekiel 36:33)… When we sing: 'When the Lord returned the captivity of Zion, we were as dreamers' – for us the dream has come true. 'The Lord has done greatly for us.' I am grateful that in spite of the many years since you left us, you have not forgotten me. I am told that a tree will be planted in my honor in the majestic city of Jerusalem, a city of all nations. But I am not worthy of that or any other honors, for they all pass away with death. A cloud fogs my conscience. Perhaps I could have done more for your people during those terrible days when I saw your starved brethren carrying heavy stones and begging for a crumb of bread from passers-by – so called Christians. Oh, how much I long to see you before leaving this woeful world!…I showed your letter to Savko and Oksenyia. They wept like small children as they remembered you. We constantly pray for you. May the Lord bless and keep you… I shall continue to pray for you. Ivan."

The Yatsyuks and Mironiuks were no exception in the Baptist communities spread over the Volyn region of the Ukraine. In saving Jews, they acted in a cohesive and collective way. They viewed it both as a religious imperative to save members of the Chosen People and as a God-sent gift and privilege. Saving Jews as a divine blessing – such thinking was radically different from the beliefs of many others in the Ukraine, who felt that their divine duty was to help the Germans do away with the Jews, and even actively participate in these heinous acts. At the other extreme, most Baptists in the Ukraine held fast to the belief that the Jews must be preserved – at all costs, and as a religious obligation.

In 1983, Yad Vashem conferred the title of Righteous Among the Nations on Ivan and Serafina Yatsyuk as well as Savko and Okseniya Mironiuk.

Zabinski, Jan & Antonina
POLAND

*R*egina Kenigswein was one of the many people who hid in the empty cages of the Warsaw Zoo. "It was like Noah's ark; people and animals mixed," she said. The people in Noah's ark, namely Noah's own family had to be saved from a divinely decreed deluge. Regina and the hundreds of other Jews, who hid in the Warsaw zoo, directed by Jan Zabinski, had to be saved from a man-made decree that denied them the right to live simply because they had been born.

Dr. Jan Zabinski was an agricultural engineer by training and a zoologist by profession. During his school days, he had had many Jewish friends. "I often quarreled with them; at times we even exchanged blows, but without any hard feelings. I considered them like everyone else." Before the war, Zabinski was director of the spacious Warsaw Zoological Garden, located on the right bank of the Vistula River, a post to which he had been appointed in 1929. The heavy German bombardment of Warsaw in September 1939 caused severe damage to the zoo. Many of the animals, especially the mammals, either died or were put to death after being injured. When the dust had settled, the remaining creatures were mostly birds, snakes, and amphibians. The Germans occupiers reconfirmed Zabinski's position as director of the zoo and also named him superintendent of the city's public parks. He lived with his wife, Antonina, and son Ryszard in a comfortable house on the zoo's grounds.

Jan Zabinski

When the Warsaw Jews were driven into a ghetto, Zabinski offered his home as a shelter for some of his Jewish academic colleagues, such as the famous Jewish entomologist Simon Tenenbaum, who had one of the biggest collection of large-size insects. Tenenbaum declined Zabinski's gracious offer, saying that at least in the ghetto his existence would have legal status, whereas with Zabinski he would be outside the pale of the law. He only had one request of Zabinski – to keep his large collection of insects, stored in 400 boxes, a request that Zabinski gladly obliged.

Zabinski decided to use the zoo's facilities as temporary hiding places for Jews on the run, especially those who had escaped from the ever-worsening conditions inside the Warsaw ghetto. He also hid a dozen Jews in his own two-story house on the zoo's grounds. Included among them were the wife of a Jewish attorney and her three daughters, one of whom suffered from mental instability and had to be constantly under watch. That family stayed with the Zabinskis for two whole years. Irena Meisel, one of Zabinski's Jewish associates, related that during one of her visits at the Zabinski house, this daughter suddenly had a serious mental attack and when her guardian's attention was distracted for a moment, she jumped out the window. She survived, and luckily for all concerned the incident went unnoticed by the visitors who happened to be there on that summer afternoon. Mrs. Meisel emphasizes the great danger this incident could have involved for everyone in the Zabinski household – rescuers and rescued alike. Interestingly, this mentally disturbed woman published a book of poems after the war. Jan Zabinski's wife, Antonina, was especially helpful to the people in her house, caring for all their needs. Zabinski's responsibility for the city's public gardens also gave him a pretext to enter the ghetto in order to examine the plants there, and this access served him well in trying to be of help to persons inside the ghetto.

Antonina Zabinski

Other than Zabinski's own home, the zoo's empty cages and other unused rooms and enclosures also served as sheltering places for Jews on the run; people who needed a temporary hiding place before finding something more permanent on the non-Jewish, or Aryan, side of the city. At night, when the place was closed to visitors, the hidden persons could step out of their lairs for a breath of fresh air. Among them was Regina Kenigswein with her three children. Zabinsky was especially fond of her family, remembering her father, Samuel Sobol, who before the war had supplied the zoo with fresh fruits and vegetables. After a two-month stay inside the zoo, Regina left for another shelter elsewhere in the sprawling city.

Whenever Zabinski had visitors and it was time to feed the hidden Jews, he would suddenly nod to his son and say in coded language, "Ryszard, it's time to feed the peacocks," or "Go feed the lizards." Jan Zabinski synchronized these rescue efforts with Jewish underground leaders, such as Dr. Adolf Berman and Rachel Auerbach, both of whom left records of Zabinski's help to them. No precise figures were kept of the Jewish people who passed through the zoo's grounds, but Zabinski estimated that the figure ran to well over a hundred, and perhaps to several hundred. "The largest group that ever stayed at one given time included 50 people," Zabinsky noted. As for Rachel Auerbach, Zabinski helped her get a job in a paper bag producing company, where she worked for a full year until the outbreak of the Polish rebellion. She kept her notes on the day's sad events buried in a secret place inside the zoo, notes that after the war served as the background for her book on the life and death of the Jewish community of Warsaw.

In August 1944, during the Polish uprising, Zabinski participated as an officer in the AK, the Polish underground. Wounded in the battle, he was taken prisoner and sent to a prisoner-of-war camp in Germany after the suppression of the uprising. As for his wife, Antonina, she fled the devastated city of Warsaw with her son and daughter, taking along the wife and children of the Jewish attorney that she had been sheltering in her home for two years. Together, they trekked over a distance of 120 kilometers to a safe place, where they waited out the war.

With the war over and Zabinski liberated from the German camp, he resumed his work in his previous profession and his studies of the animal kingdom. He is the author of many popular science books on biology and the psychology of animals. Mention of a few of his several dozen monographs gives an idea of the scope of his scientific interests: *Developmental States of the Beetles; First Birth of a Lycaor Pictus in Captivity; Anthology of the Deer; Psychology of Animals; How Insects Were Created;* and *Evolution.*

On a visit to Israel, in 1965, Jan Zabinski discounted his personal role in his unique rescue operation. "Sure I helped a bit. I hid Jews and provided them with food. Nothing more." He later pointed to his wife as his principal support. "My wife is the real hero … She was afraid of the possible consequences; she feared the likely revenge of the Nazis against us and our young son. She feared dying, but she kept silent and helped me. She never asked me to stop. She never said: 'Enough!' I knew how she felt, and I can therefore affirm that I was not the real hero, she was the true hero in our family." Concerning the risks to himself, Jan Zabinski had this to say: "The Germans had every reason to hang me, since I was involved in other illegal activities. Among others things, I gave lectures at illegal underground universities; I was active in the underground, and I allowed weapons to be stored on zoo grounds, so that hiding Jews did not add or diminish anything."

Finally, questioned about his motives in rescuing Jews, Zabinski replied modestly, "I risked my life and extended my hospitality not because they were Jews, but because they were persecuted people … They had been condemned to destruction for no offense on their part. This was shocking. I fulfilled a simple human obligation."

In 1965 Yad Vashem recognized Jan and Antonina Zabinski as Righteous Among the Nations.

Zefat, Albertus (Bertus) & Aaltje

NETHERLANDS

On a warm summer day, on August 15, 1942, Adolph From of the small Jewish community in Emmen, Drenthe province, had a discussion with Albertus Zefat, a business acquaintance of his who lived in the nearby farming village of Valthe. The conversation revolved around From's summons to report for deportation at the Westerbork transit camp, which he had just received. "I asked him what he thought about it, and he said: 'You must never do that, for then the Germans have got you in their claws. I shall take care of you as long as the war lasts.'" From decided to accept Zefat's invitation and went to his farm, where he was at first hidden in one of the sheds. Then Adolph's brother Bernard joined him there. As he recounted, in September 1942 he met Albertus Zefat in the home of his parents in Emmen, and Zefat told him that his brother Adolph was already hiding at his place and asked whether Bernard would like to join his brother. The second member of the From family accepted this generous offer and arrived at the Zefat farm on September 15, 1942.

Following this, other people gradually came over to be hidden, including several more of the From family – Adolph's parents, Samuel and Sara, and their daughter Rosa, as well as other fleeing Jews, including Mrs. Sitta Meiboom with daughter Bep, Mrs. G. de Jonge, Mrs. M. Jacobs, the Moos Gudema couple, Alfred van Dien, the Leo and Job Kropveld brothers, and Louis Bachrach. They did not all come at one time, but in stages. As for the From family and others from Emmen, it was just in time, for on October 3, 1942, 140 of the 180 Jews there were picked up in a sudden raid and deported.

Aaltje Zefat

The story of Leo Kropveld is a case in point. In July 1942 he and his parents had also fled in time – not directly to the Zefat farmhouse but to other accommodating homes. The 21-year-old Leo at first hid in a cornfield until sunset; then headed for a nearby farm, where he was allowed to hide in the barn for the night. A few hours later his father turned up at the same farm and was also taken in. Three days later Leo left the farm and found shelter successively in the homes of a farmer, a laborer, a butcher, and a railroad worker. "Most of them were religious and regarded the Jews as God's chosen people. That was why they helped." Finally, the railroad worker sent Leo to the chicken farm of Albertus and Aaltje Zefat, in the village of Valthe.

Arriving there on foot at the break of day, he was warmly received and hidden in one of the chicken coops. That evening he had dinner with the family and was introduced to the Zefats' three children – a boy and two handicapped girls who had polio and needed special care. This was already in 1943. Leo's older brother later joined him there. In the chicken coop, Leo and his brother were able to listen secretly to the Dutch radio broadcasts emanating from London. Evenings were spent in the Zefat household, "eating their bread and smoking his tobacco." It was a very scarce commodity, but Albertus Zefat graciously allowed his guests to have the tobacco, himself smoking tea leaves.

In Zefat's home, Leo Kropveld also met other of Zefat's clandestine associates in helping Jews and people otherwise sought by the Germans – such as the Warringa family, and especially Annechiena (Giena), daughter of Warrink and Aaltje. Giena had been sheltering Ab van Dien, a young Jewish man from Emmen who had been accused of subversive activities, but it was now impossible for him to stay any longer at her parents' house, and in August 1942 she had him moved to the Zefat farmstead.

At first, the Zefats hid 12 people in sheds as well as a chicken coop behind their house. The coop was camouflaged so as to appear abandoned but was fitted with a heating stove and electricity. In the meantime, the risks of detection had grown to a serious level and Albertus Zefat suggested that the group move to a neighboring wooded area, where he helped them build an underground hideout large enough to hold all of them and a shed in which to store food and other supplies. They built the shed with a slanted roof and iron poles. A telephone pole was placed in the center to help support it. The structure was then camouflaged with foliage. A well was dug in the corner for drinking water and a stove and furniture was brought to the hideout. Under cover of darkness, food, coal, and peat could be brought from the village by those involved in the rescue.

The addition of Leo Kropveld had raised the group's number to 12, and soon after his brother became the 13th member. The group spent all of their time in the forest but had dinner at the farm each night. Mrs. Aaltje Zefat cared for them, in Leo Kropveld's words, "as a mother-hen, baking her cakes and pastry. All 13 people felt happy, as far as one could feel happy."

Then it happened that Hendrik Westerink, son of a cottager, was on an illegal poaching trip in late 1942 and accidentally stumbled across the hiding place. In Leo Kropveld's words, "All of a sudden he stood in clear daylight in front of our cabin, afraid and completely stunned. Was he a German spy or a Dutch national in league with the enemy? Did we have to kill him?" They feared the worst. "The tension could be felt. We took the risk and let him go." It turned out that Hendrik and brother Andries were associated with Bertus Zefat and Gien Warringa in resistance activities. When they learned of Zefat's involvement in sheltering Jews, they also lent a hand in providing the hidden people with potatoes, bread, meat, butter, and milk.

When Albertus Zefat told them of rumors in the Valthe area about Jews in the forest area, making it necessary for them to move to another part of the woods, they needed no further prodding. In January 1943, the wooded hiding place was discovered by a group of the *Landwacht*, a special police force attached to the Dutch Nazi Party (NSB) whose duty it was to flush out resistance people as well as those sheltering Jews. The fugitive Jews were able to flee in time. This incident followed the accidental discovery of the hiding place by Hendrik Westerink, which had raised the prospect of further discovery by wanderers in that area. For their own security, the hidden persons had begun to seek an alternative hiding place. The old hideout was dismantled and a new one built at some distance.

In the new location they had to build another underground hideout and another shed. "That meant cutting down trees and digging out earth," Leo recalled. And all the time, Albertus Zefat was there, cutting and digging and warning them when they laughed too loudly. When the foundation was ready he brought the lumber and the roofing material. And when the hard day's work was done, he took everyone back to the farm for food and coffee. In the new dugout, the number of refugees rose to 20.

This time too Zefat's activities attracted too much attention, and he was arrested. Under interrogation, he refused to divulge any information about his charges' precise whereabouts. On July 27, 1944, at five in the morning, the *Grüne Polizei*, as the German security police in the Netherlands was known, drove to the Zefat's house. They searched the backyard and, not finding anyone, threatened to shoot Albertus Zefat if he did not speak. Zefat still refused to say anything and was indeed shot to death outside his own home. As the 13 people in the forest later learned from Mrs. Zefat, the police wanted to know where they were hiding.

Aaltje Zefat did not panic, nor lose heart. Instead, she cautioned them not to come to the house for dinner anymore but sent food to them through third parties and later persuaded several local families to take some of them in. The hidden people were then helped by Annechiena (Gien) Warringa and her parents, Warrink and Aaltje, where the people were moved for a few days' stay and then dispersed elsewhere, and she helped sustain the others who were hiding in the woods. Hendrik Westerink, who had earlier stumbled onto the hidden people in the woods, helped the widowed Mrs. Zefat look after those in hiding and used his experience as a farmer to help her cultivate her land until the end of the war.

When the village of Valthe was liberated about a year after this tragic incident, all 13 were alive and well. For Aaltje Zefat this was a moment of relief, for it meant the fulfillment of the mission she and her dead husband had undertaken. "Aaltje Zefat never uttered a single word of reproach," Leo Kropveld recalled. "She accepted the death, as did her children. They had one wish – that all of us would survive and thus their father would not have given his life in vain." As for motives, in the words of Louis Bachrach: "Both Zefat and Miss Warringa were brought up in a non-confessional working-class family and saw the suffocating hold on their Jewish compatriots as an onslaught of human rights." The killing of Albertus Zefat is so far the only recorded case of the execution of a rescuer on Dutch soil by the Germans not in a prison or camp (there were such others) but literally on the rescue site itself.

In 1972, Albertus and Aaltje Zefat were honored by Yad Vashem with the Righteous title. Also honored were the associates who assisted the Zefats and themselves also hid Jews in their homes or farms – including Aaltje Oldenburger (1979), Abeltje Hendriks-Aardema (1979), Constantijn Ter Veer (1979), Jan and Martha Niemeijer (1972), and Hendrik and Andries Westerink (1979). Earlier, in 1973, Warrink and Aaltje Warringa and their daughter Annechiena (Giena) were also added to the Righteous roster.

Zwonarz, Józef & Franciszka

POLAND

*I*n 1942, Dr. Natan Wallach and all other Jews in Sanok and the surrounding towns, between 20,000 and 25,000 people, were forcibly removed to a labor camp in Zaslaw, seven kilometers away. This place turned out to be a way station to another destination – the Bełzec death camp, a dreaded place where some 600,000 Jews would be put to death by gassing. During 1942, thousands of the Zaslaw camp detainees were rerouted to Bełzec. The Germans dispensed with thousands of others, by putting them out of the way in mass shootings on site. The camp was liquidated on January 15, 1943, when the remaining 2,500 Jews were either sent to Bełzec or shot on the spot.

During an earlier Nazi "action," on December 16, 1942, targeted were some 400 young women who worked in the camps' sewing factory, including Mrs. Jaffa Wallach. The Germans fired at the women, and luckily for Jaffa she accidentally fell into a haystack and the bullets missed her. She remained still until the mayhem ended, then crept back into the camp. The Wallachs decided it was high time to flee to their friend, Józef Zwonarz, in nearby Lesko – some seven kilometers away. Józef had been secretly bringing them food and provisions while they were in the Zaslaw labor camp and passed the word that they would be welcome in his home. After the recent execution, the Wallachs furtively made their way to his house. Józef Zwonarz had prepared a bunker underneath his workshop, where he did repair work for his clients. Professionally, he was a motor mechanic, and people brought their malfunctioning electrical equipment to his workshop for repair. Among his customers were Germans stationed in Sanok – even Gestapo agents, the dreaded Nazi secret police. Now a Jewish family of five would be hiding under the floor of the workshop.

At first only the Wallach couple arrived. That same month Jaffa's brother also joined them, having jumped from a train taking him to Bełzec. Later, Jaffa's other brother also was admitted. Finally, Jaffa's sister also joined them, after her previous hiding place had been discovered. Józef, an engineer by profession, was 45 years old at the time, married and the father of five children. Having already arranged for the Wallachs' young daughter to be sheltered by Jan and Magda Kąkol (pronounced Konkol), a forester, he now resolved to save her parents, Nathan Wallach and his wife.

The hiding place turned out to be quite cramped. "The tomb," as the occupants called it, measured 1.40 meter in length, 1.10 meters in width, and 90 centimeters in depth. In Natan Wallach's words, "For two years, we could not stand up, but had to sit or lie prone – two persons on one side and two on the other [initially there were four persons in the hideout], with our eight feet intertwined. For two years, we did not see the light of day. We never left the place." They also kept total silence during daylight hours, so as not to arouse any suspicions among the men who dropped into Zwonarz's workshop upstairs. Even when they slept, someone always stayed awake to silence anyone who snored. Someone could overhear them. Their reluctance to leave the "tomb" even at night was compounded by the precarious location of the Zwonarz house: to the right, Gestapo headquarters; to the left, the *Schutzpolizei* (Nazi security police); across the road, the Ukrainian police, "who were worse than the Gestapo," Wallach underlined.

Zwonarz laid out money from his meager income to keep his charges alive, for they had arrived at his place with nothing. As related by Nathan Wallach, "We had no money with which to buy food on the black market. We did not give him even one cent, for we had escaped from camp empty-handed." The fugitives were constantly hungry, for the food provided by Zwonarz was not enough. To help out, Zwonarz hired himself out as a farmhand in return for payment in kind, especially barley, and was absent for four to five days. During that period the fugitives, accustomed to his visits every other night, almost went mad with anxiety, fearing that he had been arrested by the Gestapo. Some in the bunker even considered committing suicide. "We had nothing to eat and drink. We could discern noises from outside, but not his voice. We thought the Gestapo had arrested him and we were desperate." Finally, Józef suddenly appeared. "There is no way to describe our joy. He said he had barley with him."

To provide for the cooking, Józef as a mechanic was able to fix up a small makeshift cooking stove. He also installed an electric light bulb in the bunker and brought them a radio so that they could secretly listen to the news. One of the Wallachs who had a knack with radios fixed up earphones. Józef Zwonarz also managed to connect the stove and other electrical appliances to a pole linked to the city's main circuit, so that the extra electrical consumption would not be traced back to his house. At the municipality they could not figure out the source of the additional 4,000 kilowatts. From the potatoes he brought them, they made chess pieces that helped alleviate their boredom and fear.

Zwonarz did not tell his family he was hiding Jews, and this greatly added to his difficulties, for he had to provide for his family of seven as well as for the five people hiding in his workshop. He did work for the Germans, but his income was meager. He sometimes stole leftover food from the Germans and brought it to the fugitives, especially butter. At times he brought them potatoes or bread from his own house, and sometimes he excused himself for not wanting to eat at the family table, asking instead that his meals be brought to him in the workshop, and these he then turned over to his charges. Wallach recalled, "He would visit us every evening. Removing the bunker cover, he would begin encouraging us." He tried to raise their spirits, sometimes with false news. "Oh, the Russians are already close," he would say. It turned out not to be true. Once Zwonarz bought them the biblical book of Daniel that he said he had found somewhere. The hiders went through the book hundreds, perhaps thousands of times. They were comforted by some of the miracles described there. Perhaps, they thought, a miracle will also take happen with them. Zwonarz used to joke with his charges, saying that he was a Jew like them; the only difference being that he was free and they were hidden. Otherwise – he was like them.

His constant comings and goings finally aroused the suspicions of his wife, Franciszka, and she concluded that he was having an affair. She also became aware that food was missing. When a precious ball of cotton yarn disappeared that she had prepared to knit cloth for her children, she gave free rein to her pent-up anger. Józef had taken the cotton and given it to Jaffa's sister, so that she could knit something for Jaffa's little girl, who was hiding elsewhere. Confronting Józef in the workshop, his wife accused him of dallying with another woman. Those hidden below could clearly overhear her angry shouting. "You ought to be ashamed, carrying on like this at such a late age … the father of five children." Not knowing know how to respond to her suspicions, he chose to remain silent. His wife even had people follow him to catch him with his girlfriend, but it came to nothing. In the words of Nathan Wallach, "He did not want his wife to know, reasoning that she might say the wrong thing in the wrong place."

As for the Wallachs' young daughter, Rena, born in 1938, Józef took her to his brother's daughter for hiding. When the neighbors began to suspect, Józef transferred her to an acquaintance of his, Jan Kąkol (pronounced Konkol), a forester near Lesko, who was prepared to shelter the child in his forest shack. The girl stayed there for a month, until there too people began to suspect. Kąkol then moved the child to a friend in Lwov, where she stayed for half a year; then she was returned to him, and Jan and wife Magda kept her until the liberation in July 1944. Through all this, Józef Zwonarz visited the young girl to find out how she was doing and assure her parents, hiding with him, that she was safe and sound.

As the Russians drew closer to Lesko in the spring of 1944, the city came under bombardment. A shell struck Józef's workshop and barely missed the place where the Wallachs were hiding. At this point, Józef decided to move his charges to the cellar of his house and he finally told his wife the truth. Her attitude changed for the better and she stood by her husband in helping the fugitive Jews for the six weeks that they hid in the cellar. To reach the cellar, the fugitives had to get from the bunker to the Zwonarz house, some 100 yards away. As they emerged, they discovered to their consternation that, after being immobilized for almost two years, they could not move their limbs. "I was the first one," Dr. Wallach testified. "I fell and could not get up. I could neither walk nor stand. I had to crawl to the house. We exited at nightfall, but the dim light was like the blazing sun to us, because we had not beheld light for almost two years." Reaching Zwonarz's cellar at last, they hid there for another six weeks until the Red Army moved in. While there, they learned from Zwonarz that a Polish farmer in the vicinity had been discovered hiding Jews. The Germans killed the Jews and the Polish family, and burned down his house.

After the liberation when they had regained enough strength, the Wallachs bade farewell to their benefactor and excused themselves for not being able to reward him. He, instead, responded by removing his wristwatch and handing it to them, together with a $10 bill, saying: "Take this, it's all I have. You'll need it to start a new life."

Zwonarz's neighbors, when they learned of his help to Jews, reacted quite negatively. He was ridiculed, abused, and reprimanded by many, who started to ostracize him and stopped placing orders with him for mechanical repairs. His response was: "I do not regret what I did. If I had to start again, I would do the same thing," and further: "I am not ashamed; I did what everyone should have done. They did not do it. They should be ashamed."

"Our Awakening Angel," Nathan Wallach called Józef Zwonarz, referring to the legendary angel who is to rouse the dead from their graves on Judgment Day. Wallach recalled that Zwonarz used to say, "I know that I am doing a good thing; I know that I am trying to save life, and the life of Jews is the same as the life of others, so I try to save Jews." The Wallachs still find it difficult to compass the boundless goodness of this man. "He took from his family and from his children's mouth." He was a dreamer with a heart of gold and great compassion for his fellow men, especially those unjustly threatened and persecuted.

In 1967, Yad Vashem conferred on Józef and Franciszka Zwonarz the title of Righteous Among the Nations. In 1984, Jan and Magda Kąkol were likewise accorded the Righteous title.

Index

Includes rescuers, rescued, and localities; rescuers honored as Righteous by Yad Vashem are highlighted.

B

LIST OF RIGHTEOUS ACCORDING TO COUNTRY

Names of entries are highlighted, and appear in book in alphabetical order. Consult Index for page numbers.

Selected Bibliography

Anger, Per. *With Raoul Wallenberg in Budapest.* New York: Holocaust Library, 1981.

Block, Gay & Drucker, Malka. *Rescuers.* New York: Holmes & Meier, 1992.

Braham, Randolph. *The Politics of Genocide: The Holocaust in Hungary.* New York: Columbia University, 1981.

Boom ten, Corrie. *The Hiding Place.* London: Hodder & Stoughton, 1971.

Chary, Frederick *The Bulgarian Jews and the Final Solution, 1940–1944.* Pittsburgh: University of Pittsburgh Press, 1972.

Dawidowicz, Lucy. *The War Against the Jews 1933–1945.* New York: Holt, Rinehart & Winston, 1975.

Donat, Alexander. *The Holocaust Kingdom: A Memoir.* London: Secker & Warburg, 1965.

Fogelman, Eva. *Conscience and Courage.* New York: Doubleday, 1994.

Friedman, Philip. *Their Brothers' Keepers.* New York: Holocaust Library, 1978.

Fry, Varian. *Surrender on Demand.* Boulder, Col.: Johnson Books, 1997.

Gilbert, Martin. *The Righteous.* London: Doubleday, 2002.

Gross, Leonard. *The Last Jews in Berlin.* New York: Simon & Schuster, 1982.

Gut-Opdyke, Irene. *In My Hands.* New York: Alfred A. Knopf, 1999.

Gutman, Israel (ed.). *Encyclopedia of the Holocaust.* New York: Macmillan, 1990.

Gutman, Israel. *The Encyclopedia of the Righteous Among the Nations.* Jerusalem: Yad Vashem, 2004-7.

Hackel, Sergei. *Pearl of Great Price: The Life of Mother Maria Skobtsova, 1891–1945.* London: Darton, Longman & Todd, 1981.

Hallie, Philip. *Lest Innocent Blood Be Shed.* New York: Harper & Row, 1979.

Hellman, Peter. *When Courage Was Stronger than Fear.* New York: Marlow, 1999.

Hilberg, Raul. *The Destruction of the European Jews.* New York: Holmes & Meier, 1985.

Land-Weber, Ellen. *To Save a Life.* Urbana & Chicago: University of Illinois, 2000.

Levi, Primo. *If This Is a Man.* London: Orion, 1959.

Lowrie, Donald. *The Hunted Children.* New York: Norton, 1963

Marrus, Michael & Paxon, Robert. *Vichy France and the Jews.* New York: Basic Books, 1981.

Michman, Dan (ed.), *Belgium and the Holocaust.* Jerusalem: Yad Vashem, 1988.

Moore, Bob. *Victims and Survivors: The Nazi Persecution of the Jews in the Netherlands, 1940–1945.* London: Arnold, 1997.

Oliner, Samuel, and Oliner, Pearl. *The Altruistic Personality.* New York: Free Press, 1988.

Paldiel, Mordecai. *Diplomat Heroes of the Holocaust.* Jersey City, N.J.: Ktav, 2006.

Paldiel, Mordecai. *Saving the Jews.* Rockville, Md.: Schreiber Publishing, 2000.

Paldiel, Mordecai. *Sheltering the Jews: Stories of Holocaust Rescuers.* Minneapolis: Fortress, 1996

Presser, Jacob. *The Destruction of the Dutch Jews.* New York: Dutton, 1969.

Rittner, Carol, and Myers, Sondra. *The Courage to Care: Rescuers of Jews during the Holocaust.* New York: New York University Press, 1986.

Silver, Eric. *The Book of the Just.* London: Weidenfeld & Nicolson, 1992.

Tec, Nechama. *When Light Pierced the Darkness.* New York: Oxford University,1986.

Yahil, Leni. *The Rescue of Danish Jewry.* Philadelphia: Jewish Publication Society, 1969.

Zuccotti, Susan. *The Holocaust, the French, and the Jews.* New York: Basic Books, 1993.

Zuccotti, Susan. *The Italians and the Holocaust.* New York: Basic Books, 1997.

Acknowledgements

With deep appreciation to the current members of the Commission for the Designation of the Righteous, for their dedicated work in the cause of the Righteous: Justice Jacob Türkel (Commission chairman), Avner Shalev (Yad Vashem Directorate chairman), and in alphabetical order by last name: Miriam Akavia, Benjamin Anolik, Jizhak Arnon, Chava Baruch, Dr. Chaim Basok, Natan Ben-Horin, Dr. Zipora Blecher, Dr. Eliezer Even, Dr. Gila Fatran, Dr. Daniel Fraenkel, Michael Gilad, Dr. Yosef Govrin, Prof. Joseph Katz, Anna Kopaev, Dr. Shmuel Krakowki, Dr. Lucien Lazare, Chaja Lifshitz, Dr. Ehud Loeb, Dov Matz, Batya Neuman, Dr. Iael Nidam-Orvieto, Justice Zvi Nussenblatt, Simha Rotem, Dr. Dov Schmorak, Liliane Seban-Winograd, Anna Shafran, Menachem Sharon, Baruch Shub, Miriam Steiner-Aviezer, Jael Sternberg-Tarshish, Lili Thau, Eliahu Valk, Joseph Winter.

Also, with special thanks to the work team in the Department for the Righteous, at Yad Vashem: Mina Yancu, Bozenna Rotman, Katya Gusarov, Nannie Braunstein-Beekman, Nona Agababian, Dvora Weis, Natalia Morozov, and Alla Kagalovsky.

Photo scanning: Amir Shauli; Yossi Ben-David.

Unless otherwise cited, all photographs were provided by the Yad Vashem Archives in Jerusalem.